The Treasury of David

of David

An Expository and Devotional Commentary on the Psalms

Volume VII   Psalms 125–150

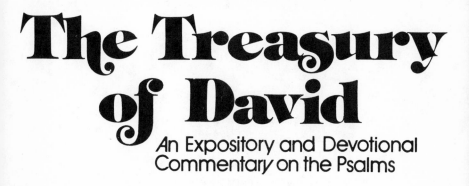

The Treasury of David

An Expository and Devotional Commentary on the Psalms

C. H. SPURGEON

Volume VII Psalms 125–150

BAKER BOOK HOUSE
Grand Rapids, Michigan

Reprinted from the original
seven-volume edition published
in London by Passmore & Alabaster

Third printing, January 1981

ISBN: 0-8010-8093-2 (seven-volume set)

Printed in the United States of America

PREFACE.

AT the end of all these years the last page of this Commentary is printed, and the seventh preface is requested. The demand sounds strangely in my ears. A preface when the work is done? It can be only nominally a preface, for it is really a farewell. I beg to introduce my closing volume, and then to retire with many apologies for having trespassed so much upon my reader's patience.

A tinge of sadness is on my spirit as I quit " The Treasury of David," never to find on this earth a richer storehouse, though the whole palace of revelation is open to me. Blessed have been the days spent in meditating, mourning, hoping, believing, and exulting with David! Can I hope to spend hours more joyous on this side of the golden gate? Perhaps not; for the seasons have been very choice in which the harp of the great poet of the sanctuary has charmed my ears. Yet the training which has come of these heavenly contemplations may haply go far to create and sustain a peaceful spirit which will never be without its own happy psalmody, and never without aspirations after something higher than it yet has known. The Book of Psalms instructs us in the use of wings as well as words: it sets us both mounting and singing. Often have I ceased my commenting upon the text, that I might rise with the psalm, and gaze upon visions of God. If I may only hope that these volumes will be as useful to other hearts in the reading as to mine in the writing, I shall be well rewarded by the prospect.

The former volumes have enjoyed a singular popularity. It may be questioned if in any age a commentary so large, upon a single book of the Bible, has enjoyed a circulation within measurable distance of that which has been obtained by this work. Among all orders of Christians " The Treasury " has found its way unrestrained by sectarian prejudice—another proof of the unity of the spiritual life, and the oneness of the food upon which it delights to feed.

The author may not dare to be proud of the generous acknowledg-
ments which he has received from men of all sections of the church ;
but, on the other hand, he cannot pass over them in ungrateful silence.   Conscious as he is of his many literary sins of omission and
of commission in these seven volumes, he is yet glad to have been
permitted to do his best, and to have received abundant encouragement in the doing of it.   Of all its good the glory is the Lord's ;
of all its weakness the unworthy author must bear the blame.

This last portion of the Psalms has not been the easiest part of
my gigantic task.   On the contrary, with the exception of *The Songs
of Degrees*, and one or two other Psalms, these later hymns and hallelujahs have not been largely expounded, nor frequently referred
to, by our great divines.   Failing the English, a larger use has been
made of the Latin authors ; and my esteemed friend, W. DURBAN,
B.A., has rendered me great service in their translation.   It would
astonish our readers if they could see what tomes have been read,
what folios have been covered with translations, and in the end
what tiny morsels have been culled from the vast mass for incorpo-
ration with this Treasury.   Heaps of earth have been sifted and
washed, and have yielded only here and there a little " dust of
gold."   No labour has been spared ; no difficulty has been shirked.
May the good Lord accept my service, and enrich his church by it
this day, and when I am gathered to my fathers !

My friend and amanuensis, Mr. J. L. KEYS, has continued to
search the British Museum and public Libraries for me ; and to
him and many other kind friends I owe many a quotation which
else might have been overlooked.   Of the extracts I am editor in
chief, and not much more ; for brethren such as Mr. HENSON,
of Kingsgate Street, have at sundry times, of their own accord, sent
me material more or less useful.   In the homiletical department my
obligations are exceedingly great, and are duly acknowledged under
initials.   My venerable friend the Rev. GEORGE ROGERS leads the
way ; but several other brethren, hailing from the Pastors' College,
follow with almost equal steps.   Thanks are hereby tendered to
them all, and to the multitude of authors from whom I have gathered flowers and fruits, fragrant and nourishing.

And now the colossal work is done !   To God be all glory.
More than twenty years have glided away while this pleasant labour
has been in the doing ; but the wealth of mercy which has been lav-
ished upon me during that time my grateful heart is unable to

measure. Surely goodness and mercy have followed me all those years, and made my heart to sing new psalms for new mercies. There is none like the God of Jeshurun. To him be all glory for ever and ever.

In these busy days, it would be greatly to the spiritual profit of Christian men if they were more familiar with the Book of Psalms, in which they would find a complete armoury for life's battles, and a perfect supply for life's needs. Here we have both delight and usefulness, consolation and instruction. For every condition there is a psalm, suitable and elevating. The Book supplies the babe in grace with penitent cries, and the perfected saint with triumphant songs. Its breadth of experience stretches from the jaws of hell to the gate of heaven. He who is acquainted with the marches of the Psalm-country knows that the land floweth with milk and honey, and he delights to travel therein. To such I have aspired to be a helpful companion.

Reader, I beseech David's God to bless thee ; and I pray thee, when it is well with thee, breathe a like prayer for

Thine heartily,

C. H. Spurgeon

Westwood,
   Upper Norwood,
     October, 1885.

INDEX

OF AUTHORS QUOTED OR REFERRED TO.

PSALM CXXV.

TITLE.—A Song of Degrees. *Another step is taken in the ascent, another station in the pilgrimage is reached : certainly a rise in the sense is here perceptible, since full assurance concerning years to come is a higher form of faith than the ascription of former escapes to the Lord. Faith has praised Jehovah for past deliverances, and here she rises to a confident joy in the present and future safety of believers. She asserts that they shall forever be secure who trust themselves with the Lord. We can imagine the pilgrims chanting this song when perambulating the city walls.*

We do not assert that David wrote this psalm, but we have as much ground for doing so as others have for declaring that it was written after the captivity. It would seem probable that all the Pilgrim Psalms were composed, or, at least, compiled by the same writer, and as some of them are certainly by David, there is no conclusive reason for taking away the rest from him.

DIVISION.—*First we have* a song *of holy confidence* (1, 2); *then* a promise, 3 ; *followed by* a prayer, 4 ; *and* a note of warning.

EXPOSITION.

THEY that trust in the LORD *shall be* as mount Zion, *which* cannot be removed, *but* abideth for ever.

2 *As* the mountains *are* round about Jerusalem, so the LORD *is* round about his people from henceforth even for ever.

3 For the rod of the wicked shall not rest upon the lot of the righteous ; lest the righteous put forth their hands unto iniquity.

4 Do good, O LORD, unto *those that be* good, and to *them that are* upright in their hearts.

5 As for such as turn aside unto their crooked ways, the LORD shall lead them forth with the workers of iniquity : *but* peace *shall be* upon Israel.

1. "*They that trust in the* LORD *shall be as mount Zion.*" The emphasis lies upon the object of their trust, namely, Jehovah the Lord. What a privilege to be allowed to repose in God ! How condescending is Jehovah to become the confidence of his people ! To trust elsewhere is vanity ; and the more implicit such misplaced trust becomes the more bitter will be the ensuing disappointment ; but to trust in the living God is sanctified common sense which needs no excuse, its result shall be its best vindication. There is no conceivable reason why we should not trust in Jehovah, and there is every possible argument for so doing ; but, apart from all argument, the end will prove the wisdom of the confidence. The result of faith is not occasional and accidental ; its blessing comes, not to some who trust, but to all who trust in the Lord. Trusters in Jehovah shall be as fixed, firm, and stable as the mount where David dwelt, and where the ark abode. To move mount Zion was impossible : the mere supposition was absurd. "*Which cannot be removed, but abideth for ever.*" Zion was the image of eternal steadfastness,—this hill which, according to the Hebrew, "sits to eternity," neither bowing down nor moving to and fro. Thus doth the trusting worshipper of Jehovah enjoy a restfulness which is the mirror of tranquillity ; and this not without cause, for his hope is sure, and of his confidence he can never be ashamed. As the Lord sitteth King for ever, so do his people sit enthroned in perfect peace when their trust in him is firm. This is, and is to be our portion ;

we are, we have been, we shall be as steadfast as the hill of God.   Zion cannot
be removed, and does not remove ; so the people of God can neither be moved
passively nor actively, by force from without or fickleness from within.   Faith in
God is a settling and establishing virtue ; he who by his strength setteth fast the
mountains, by that same power stays the hearts of them that trust in him.   This
steadfastness will endure " for ever," and we may be assured therefore that no
believer shall perish either in life or in death, in time or in eternity.   We trust in
an eternal God, and our safety shall be eternal.

2. "*As the mountains are round about Jerusalem, so the* LORD *is round about his
people from henceforth even for ever.*"   The hill of Zion is the type of the believer's
constancy, and the surrounding mountains are made emblems of the all-surrounding presence of the Lord.   The mountains around the holy city, though they do
not make a circular wall, are, nevertheless, set like sentinels to guard her gates.
God doth not enclose his people within ramparts and bulwarks, making their city
to be a prison ; but yet he so orders the arrangements of his providence that his
saints are as safe as if they dwelt behind the strongest fortifications.   What a
double security the two verses set before us !   First, we are established, and then
entrenched ; settled, and then sentinelled : made like a mount, and then protected as if by mountains.   This is no matter of poetry, it is so in fact ; and it is
no matter of temporary privilege, but it shall be so for ever.   Date when we
please, " from henceforth" Jehovah encircles his people : look on as far as we
please, the protection extends " even for ever."   Note, it is not said that Jehovah's power or wisdom defends believers, but he himself is round about them :
they have his personality for their protection, his Godhead for their guard.   We
are here taught that the Lord's people are those who trust him, for they are thus
described in the first verses : the line of faith is the line of grace, those who trust
in the Lord are chosen of the Lord.   The two verses together prove the eternal
safety of the saints : they must abide where God has placed them, and God must
for ever protect them from all evil.   It would be difficult to imagine greater
safety than is here set forth.

3. "*For the rod of the wicked shall not rest upon the lot of the righteous.*"   The
people of God are not to expect immunity from trial because the Lord surrounds
them, for they may feel the power and persecution of the ungodly.   Isaac, even
in Abraham's family, was mocked by Ishmael.   Assyria laid its sceptre even upon
Zion itself.   The graceless often bear rule and wield the rod ; and when they do
so they are pretty sure to make it fall heavily upon the Lord's believing people,
so that the godly cry out by reason of their oppressors.   Egypt's rod was exceeding heavy upon Israel, but the time came for it to be broken.   God has set a
limit to the woes of his chosen : the rod may light on their portion, but it shall
not *rest* upon it.   The righteous have a lot which none can take from them, for
God has appointed them heirs of it by gracious entail : on that lot the rod of the
wicked may fall, but over that lot it cannot have lasting sway.   The saints abide
for ever, but their troubles will not.   Here is a good argument in prayer for all
righteous ones who are in the hands of the wicked.

"*Lest the righteous put forth their hands unto iniquity.*"   The tendency of
oppression is to drive the best of men into some hasty deed for self-deliverance or
vengeance.   If the rack be too long used the patient sufferer may at last give
way ; and therefore the Lord puts a limit to the tyranny of the wicked.   He
ordained that an Israelite who deserved punishment should not be beaten without
measure : forty stripes save one was the appointed limit.   We may therefore expect that he will set a bound to the suffering of the innocent, and will not allow
them to be pushed to the uttermost extreme.   Especially in point of time he will
limit the domination of the persecutor, for length adds strength to oppression,
and makes it intolerable ; hence the Lord himself said of a certain tribulation,
" except those days should be shortened, there should no flesh be saved ; but for
the elect's sake those days shall be shortened."

It seems that even righteous men are in peril of sinning in evil days, and that
it is not the will of the Lord that they should yield to the stress of the times in

order to escape from suffering. The power and influence of wicked men when they are uppermost are used to lead or drive the righteous astray ; but the godly must not accept this as an excuse, and yield to the evil pressure ; far rather must they resist with all their might till it shall please God to stay the violence of the persecutor, and give his children rest. This the Lord here promises to do in due time.

4. "*Do good, O* Lord, *unto those that be good, and to them that are upright in their hearts.*" Men to be good at all must be good at heart. Those who trust in the Lord are good ; for faith is the root of righteousness, and the evidence of uprightness. Faith in God is a good and upright thing, and its influence makes the rest of the man good and upright. To such God will do good : the prayer of the text is but another form of promise, for that which the Lord prompts us to ask he virtually promises to give. Jehovah will take off evil from his people, and in the place thereof will enrich them with all manner of good. When the rod of the wicked is gone his own rod and staff shall comfort us. Meanwhile it is for us to pray that it may be well with all the upright who are now among men. God bless them, and do them good in every possible form. We wish well to those who do well. We are so plagued by the crooked that we would pour benedictions upon the upright.

5. "*As for such as turn aside unto their crooked ways, the* Lord *shall lead them forth with the workers of iniquity.*" Two kinds of men are always to be found, the upright and the men of crooked ways. Alas, there are some who pass from one class to another, not by a happy conversion, turning from the twisting lanes of deceit into the highway of truth, but by an unhappy declension leaving the main road of honesty and holiness for the bypaths of wickedness. Such apostates have been seen in all ages, and David knew enough of them ; he could never forget Saul, and Ahithophel, and others. How sad that men who once walked in the right way should turn aside from it ! Observe the course of the falsehearted : first, they look out for crooked ways ; next, they choose them and make them "*their* crooked ways" ; and then they turn aside into them. They never intend to go back unto perdition, but only to make a curve and drop into the right road again. The straight way becomes a little difficult, and so they make a circumbendibus, which all along aims at coming out right, though it may a little deviate from precision. These people are neither upright in heart, nor good, nor trusters in Jehovah, and therefore the Lord will deal otherwise with them than with his own people : when execution day comes these hypocrites and time-servers shall be led out to the same gallows as the openly wicked. All sin will one day be expelled the universe, even as criminals condemned to die are led out of the city ; then shall secret traitors find themselves ejected with open rebels. Divine truth will unveil their hidden pursuits, and lead them forth, and to the surprise of many they shall be set in the same rank with those who avowedly wrought iniquity.

"*But peace shall be upon Israel.*" In fact the execution of the deceivers shall tend to give the true Israel peace. When God is smiting the unfaithful not a blow shall fall upon the faithful. The chosen of the Lord shall not only be like Salem, but they shall have salem, or peace. Like a prince, Israel has prevailed with God, and therefore he need not fear the face of man ; his wrestlings are over, the blessing of peace has been pronounced upon him. He who has peace with God may enjoy peace concerning all things. Bind the first and last verses together : Israel trusts in the Lord (verse 1), and Israel has peace (verse 5).

EXPLANATORY NOTES.

Whole Psalm.—In the degrees of Christian virtue, this psalm represents the sixth step—the confidence which the Christian places in the Lord. "It teacheth us, while we ascend and raise our minds unto the Lord our God in loving charity and piety, not to fix our gaze upon men who are prosperous in the world with a false happiness."*—*H. T. Armfield, in "The Gradual Psalms,"* 1874.

Whole ,Psalm.—This short psalm may be summed up in those words of the prophet (Isaiah iii. 10, 11), "Say ye to the righteous, that it shall be well with him. Woe unto the wicked! it shall be ill with him." Thus are life and death, the blessing and the curse, set before us often in the psalms, as well as in the law and in the prophets.—*Matthew Henry, 1662—1714.*

Verse 1.—"*They that trust in the* LORD." Note how he commandeth no work here to be done, but only speaketh of trust. In popery in the time of trouble men were taught to enter into some kind of religion, to fast, to go on pilgrimage, and to do such other foolish works of devotion, which they devised as an high service unto God, and thereby thought to make condign satisfaction for sin and to merit eternal life. But here the Psalmist leadeth us the plain way unto God, pronouncing this to be the chiefest anchor of our salvation,—only to hope and trust in the Lord ; and declaring that the greatest service that we can do unto God is to trust him. For this is the nature of God—to create all things of nothing. Therefore he createth and bringeth forth in death, life ; in darkness, light. Now to believe this is the essential nature and most special property of faith. When God then seeth such a one as agreeth with his own nature, that is, which believeth to find in danger help, in poverty riches, in sin righteousness, and that for God's own mercy's sake in Christ alone, him can God neither hate nor forsake.—*Martin Luther* (1483—1546), *in "A Commentary on the Psalms of Degrees."*

Verse 1.—"*They that trust in the* LORD." All that deal with God must deal upon trust, and he will give comfort to those only that give credit to him, and make it appear they do so by quitting other confidences, and venturing to the utmost for God. The closer our expectations are confined to God, the higher our expectations may be raised.—*Matthew Henry.*

Verse 1.—"*They that trust,*" etc. Trust, therefore, in the Lord, *always, altogether, and for all things.*—*Robert Nisbet, in "The Songs of the Temple Pilgrims,"* 1863.

Verse 1.—" *Shall be as mount Zion.*" Some persons are like the sand—ever shifting and treacherous. See Matthew vii. 26. Some are like the sea—restless and unsettled. See Isaiah lvii. 20 ; James i. 6. Some are like the wind—uncertain and inconstant. See Ephesians iv. 14. Believers are like a mountain—strong, stable, and secure. To every soul that trusts him the Lord says, " Thou art Peter."—*W. H. J. Page, of Chelsea,* 1883.

Verse 1.—"*As mount Zion,*" etc. Great is the stability of a believer's felicity.—*John Trapp,* 1601—1669.

Verse 1.—"*Mount Zion, which cannot be removed,*" etc. Lieutenant Conder, reviewing Mr. Maudslay's important exploration, says, " It is especially valuable as showing that, however the masonry may have been destroyed and lost, we may yet hope to find indications of the ancient enceinte *in the rock scarps which are imperishable.*" This is very true ; for, while man can destroy what man' has made, the everlasting hills smile at his rage. Yet who can hear of it without perceiving the force and sublimity of that glorious description of the immobility of believers.

> " They that trust in Jehovah are as mount Zion,
> Which shall not be moved, it abideth for ever."
>
> —*James Neil, in "Palestine Explored,"* 1882.

Verse 1.—" *Cannot be removed,*" etc. They can never be removed from the Lord, though they may be removed from his house and ordinances, as sometimes David was ; and from his gracious presence, and sensible communion with him ; and out of the world by death : yet never from his heart's love, nor out of the covenant of his grace, which is sure and everlasting ; nor out of his family, into which they are taken ; nor from the Lord Jesus Christ, nor out of his hands and

---

* Augustine.

arms, nor from off his heart.; nor from off him, as the foundation on which they are laid ; nor out of a state of grace, either regeneration or justification ; but such abide in the love of God, in the covenant of his grace, in the hands of his Son, in the grace wherein they stand, and in the house of God for evermore.—*John Gill*, 1697—1771.

Verse 1.—*"Abideth for ever."* So surely as *"Mount Zion"* shall never be *" removed,"* so surely shall the church of God be preserved. Is it not strange that wicked and idolatrous powers have not joined together, dug down this mount, and carried it into the sea, that they might nullify a promise in which the people of God exult ! Till ye can carry Mount Zion into the Mediterranean Sea, the church of Christ shall grow and prevail. Hear this, yet murderous Mohammedans !—*Adam Clarke*, 1760—1832.

Verse 1.—*"Abideth."* Literally, *sitteth ;* as spoken of a mountain, " lieth" or " is situated " ; but here with the following *"for ever,"* used in a still stronger sense.—*J. J. Stewart Perowne*, 1868.

Verses 1, 2.—That which is here promised the saints is a perpetual preservation of them in that condition wherein they are ; both on the part of God, " he is round about them from henceforth even for ever" ; and on their parts, " *they shall not be removed,"*—that is, from the condition of acceptance with God wherein they are supposed to be,—but they shall abide for ever, and continue therein immovable unto the end. This is a plain promise of their continuance in that condition wherein they are, with their safety from thence, and not a promise of some other good' thing provided that they continue in that condition. Their being compared to mountains, and their stability, which consists in their being and continuing so, will admit no other sense. As mount Zion abides in its condition, so shall they ; and as the mountains about Jerusalem continue, so doth the Lord continue his presence unto them.

That expression which is used, verse 2, is weighty and full to this purpose, *"The* LORD *is round about his people from henceforth even for ever."* What can be spoken more fully, more pathetically ? Can any expression of men so set forth the safety of the saints ? The Lord is round about them, not to save them from this or that incursion, but from all ; not from one or two evils, but from every one whereby they are or may be assaulted. He is with them, and round about them on every side that no evil shall come nigh them. It is a most full expression of universal preservation, or of God's keeping his saints in his love and favour, upon all accounts whatsoever ; and that not for a season only, but it is " *henceforth,"* from his giving this promise unto their souls in particular, and their receiving of it, throughout all generations, " *even for ever."*—*John Owen*, 1616—1683.

Verse 2.—*"As the mountains are round about Jerusalem."* This image is not realised, as most persons familiar with our European scenery would wish and expect it to be realised. Jerusalem is not literally shut in by mountains, except on the eastern side, where it may be said to be enclosed by the arms of Olivet, with its outlying ridges on the north-east and south-west. Anyone facing Jerusalem westward, northward, or southward, will always see the city itself on an elevation higher than the hills in its immediate neighbourhood, its towers and walls standing out against the sky, and not against any high back-ground such as that which encloses the mountain towns and villages of our own Cumbrian or Westmoreland valleys. Nor, again, is the plain on which it stands enclosed by a continuous though distant circle of mountains, like that which gives its peculiar charm to Athens and Innspruck. The mountains in the neighbourhood of Jerusalem are of unequal height, and only in two or three instances—Neby-Samwil, Er-Rain, and Tuleil el-Ful—rising to any considerable elevation. Even Olivet is only a hundred and eighty feet above the top of Mount Zion. Still they act as a shelter : they must be surmounted before the traveller can see, or the invader attack, the Holy City ; and the distant line of Moab would always seem to rise as a wall against invaders from the remote east. It is these mountains, expressly including those beyond the Jordan, which are mentioned as "standing round about Jerusalem," in another and more terrible sense, when, on the night of the assault of Jerusalem by the Roman armies, they "echoed back" the screams of the inhabitants of the captured city, and the victorious shouts of the soldiers of Titus.*—*Arthur Penrhyn Stanley* (1815—1881), *in "Sinai and Palestine."*

Verse 2.—"*As the mountains are round about Jerusalem.*" Jerusalem is situated in the centre of a mountainous region, whose valleys have drawn around it in all directions a perfect net-work of deep ravines, the perpendicular walls of which constitute a very efficient system of defence.—*William M. Thomson, in "The Land and the Book,"* 1881.

Verse 2.—"*As the mountains are round about Jerusalem,*" etc. The mountains most emphatically stand "*round about Jerusalem,*" and in doing so must have greatly safeguarded it in ancient times. We are specially told that when Titus besieged the city, he found it impossible to invest it completely until he had built a wall round the entire sides of these mountains, nearly five miles long, with thirteen places at intervals in which he stationed garrisons, which added another mile and a quarter to these vast earthworks. "The whole was completed," says the Jewish historian, "in three days; so that what would naturally have required some months was done in so short an interval as is incredible." † Assaults upon the city, even then, could only be delivered effectively upon its level corner to the north-west, whence every hostile advance was necessarily directed in all its various sieges. To those familiar with these facts, beautifully bold, graphic, and forceful is the Psalmist's figure of the security of the Lord's people—

> "The mountains are round about Jerusalem;
> And Jehovah is round about his people,
> Henceforth, even for evermore."

These words must have been in Hebrew ears as sublime as they were comforting, and, when sung on the heights of Zion, inspiring in the last degree.—*James Neil.*

Verse 2.—"*The* LORD *is round about his people.*" It is not enough that we are compassed about with fiery walls, that is, with the sure custody, the continual watch and ward of the angels; but the Lord himself is our wall: so that every way we are defended by the Lord against all dangers. Above us is his heaven, on both sides he is as a wall, under us he is as a strong rock whereupon we stand · so are we everywhere sure and safe. Now if Satan through these munitions casts his darts at us, it must needs be that the Lord himself shall be hurt before we take harm. Great is our incredulity if we hear all these things in vain.—*Martin Luther.*

Verse 2.—"*From henceforth, even for ever.*" This amplification of the promise, taken from time or duration, should be carefully noted; for it shows that the promises made to the people of Israel pertain generally to the Church in every age, and are not to expire with that polity. Thus it expressly declares, that the Church will continuously endure in this life; which is most sweet consolation for pious minds, especially in great dangers and public calamities, when everything appears to threaten ruin and destruction.—*D. H. Mollerus,* 1639.

Verse 3.—"*The rod of the wicked.*" It is *their* rod, made for them; if God scourge his children a little with it, he doth but borrow it from the immediate and natural use for which it was ordained; their rod, their judgment. So it is called their cup: "This is the portion" and potion "of their cup." Ps. xi. 6.—*Thomas Adams, in "An Exposition of the Second Epistle of Peter,"* 1633.

Verse 3.—"*For the rod of the wicked,*" etc. According to Gussetius, this is to be understood of a measuring rod; laid not on persons, but on lands and estates; and best agrees with the lot, inheritance, and estate of the righteous; and may signify that though wicked men unjustly seize upon and retain the farms, possessions, and estates of good men, as if they were assigned to them by the measuring line; yet they shall not hold them long, or always.—*John Gill.*

---

* Josephus. Bell. Jud. vi. 5, 1.
† Josephus. Wars of the Jews. Book v. chap. xii. section 2.

Verse 3.—"*For the rod of the wicked shall not rest upon the lot of the righteous.*" No tyranny, although it appear firm and stable, is of long continuance : inasmuch as God does not relinquish the sceptre. This is manifest from the example of Pharaoh, of Saul, of Sennacherib, of Herod, and of others. Rightly, therefore, says Athanasius of Julian the Apostate, "That little cloud has quickly passed away." And how quickly beyond all human expectation the foundations of the ungodly are overthrown is fully declared in Psalm xxxvii.—*Solomon Gesner,* 1559—1605.

Verse 3.—"*Shall not rest,*" that is to say, "lie heavy," so as to oppress, as in Isa. xxv. 10, with a further sense of *continuance* of the oppression.—*J. J. Stewart Perowne.*

Verse 3.—"*Shall not rest,*" etc. The wrath of man, like water turned upon a mill, shall come on them with no more force than shall be sufficient for accomplishing God's gracious purposes on their souls : the rest, however menacing its power may be, shall be made to pass off by an opened sluice. Nevertheless the trouble shall be sufficient to try every man, and to prove the truth and measure of his integrity.—*Charles Simeon* (1759—1836), *in "Horæ Homileticæ."*

Verse 3.—"*The lot of the righteous.*" There is a fourfold lot belonging to the faithful. 1. The lot of the saints is the sufferings of the saints. "All that will live godly in Christ Jesus shall suffer persecution :" 2 Tim. iii. 12. 2. The lot of the saints is also that light and happiness they have in this world. The lot is "fallen unto me in pleasant places ; yea, I have a goodly heritage :" Ps. xvi. 6. When David sat at the sheepfold, which was his lot, he was thus prepared for the kingdom of Israel which was given him by lot from God. 3. But more specially faith, grace, and sanctification ; which give them just right and title to the inheritance of glory. Heaven is theirs now ; though not in possession, yet in succession. They have the earnest of it ; let them grow up to stature and perfection, and take it. 4. Lastly, they have the lot of heaven. Hell is the lot of the wicked : "Behold at evening-tide trouble ; and before the morning he is not. This is the portion of them that spoil us, and the lot of them that rob us" : Isa. xvii. 14. Therefore it is said of Judas, that he went "to his own place" : Acts i. 25. "Upon the wicked he shall rain snares, fire and brimstone, and an horrible tempest ; this shall be the portion of their cup" : Ps. xi. 6. But the lot of the righteous is faith, and the end of their faith the salvation of their souls. God gives them heaven, not for any foreseen worthiness in the receivers, for no worthiness of our own can make us our father's heirs ; but for his own mercy and favour in Christ, preparing heaven for us, and us for heaven. So that upon his decree it is alloted to us ; and unless heaven could lose God, we cannot lose heaven.

Here, then, consider how the lottery of Canaan may shadow out to us that blessed land of promise whereof the other was a type.—*Thomas Adams.*

Verse 3.—"*Lest the righteous put forth their hands unto iniquity.*" Lest overcome by impatiency, or drawn aside by the world's *allurements* or *affrightments,* they should yield and comply with the desires of the wicked, or seek to help themselves out of trouble by sinister practices. God (saith Chrysostom) acts like a lutanist, who will not let the strings of his lute be too slack, lest it mar the music, nor suffer them to be too hard stretched or screwed up, lest they break.—*John Trapp,* 1601—1669.

Verse 3.—"*Lest the righteous put forth their hands,*" etc. The trial is to prove faith, not to endanger it by too sharp a pressure : *lest,* overcome by this, even the faithful put forth a hand (as in Gen. iii. 22), to forbidden pleasure ; or (as in Exod. xxii. 8), to contamination : through force of custom gradually persuading to sinful compliance, or through despair of good, as the Psalmist (see Ps. xxxvii. and lxxiii.) describes some in his day who witnessed the prosperity of wicked men.—*The Speaker's Commentary,* 1871—1881.

Verse 4.—"*Do good, O Lord, unto those that be good.*" The Midrash here calls to mind a Talmudic riddle :—There came a good one (Moses Ex. ii. 2) and received a good thing (the Tôra, or Law, Prov. iv. 2) from the good One (God, Ps. cxlv. 9) for the good ones (Israel, Ps. cxxv. 4).—*Franz Delitzsch*, 1871.

Verse 4.—"*Do good, O* Lord, *unto those that be good.*" A favourite thought with Nehemiah. See Nehemiah ii. 8, 18 ; v. 19 ; xiii. 14, 31 : " Remember me, O my God, for *good*," the concluding words of his book.—*Christopher Wordsworth*, 1872.

Verse 4.—"*Do good, O* Lord, *unto those that be good.*" They consult their own good best, who do most good. I may say these three things of *those who do good* (and what is serving God but doing of good ? or what is doing good but serving God ?). First, they shall receive true good. Secondly, they shall for ever hold the best good, the chief good ; they shall not only spend their days and years in good ; but when their days and years are spent, they shall have good, and a greater good than any they had, in spending the days and years of this life. They shall have good in death, they shall come to a fuller enoyment of God, *the chief good*, when they have left and let fall the possession of all earthly goods. Thirdly, they that do good shall find all things working together for their good ; if they have a loss they shall receive good by it ; if they bear a cross, that cross shall bear good to them.—*Joseph Caryl*, 1602—1673.

Verse 4.—"*Do good, O* Lord, *unto those that be good,*" etc. Perhaps it may not prove unprofitable to enquire, with some minuteness, who are the persons for whom prayer is presented, and who have an interest in the Divine promises. They are brought before us under different denominations. In the first verse, they are described as trusting in the Lord : in the second verse, they are described as the Lord's people : in the third verse, they are called the righteous : in the fourth verse, they are called good and upright in heart : and in the fifth verse, they are called Israel. Let us collect these terms together, and endeavour to ascertain from them, what is their true condition and character, for whose security the Divine perfections are pledged. And while a rapid sketch is thus drawn, let each breathe the silent prayer, " Search me, O God, and know my heart ; try me, and know my thughts ; and see if there be any wicked way in me, and lead me in the way everlasting."—*N. M'Michael, in " The Pilgrim Psalms,"* 1860.

Verse 4.—"*Do good, O* Lord, *unto those that be good.*" Believers are described as " *good.*" The name is explained by the Spirit as implying the indwelling of the Holy Ghost and of faith. It is proof that no guile is harboured in their hearts. Prayer is made that God would visit them with goodness. This prayer indited by the Spirit amounts to a heavenly promise that they shall receive such honour.—*Henry Law, in "Family Devotion,"* 1878.

Verse 4.—"*Them that be good.*" Oh, brethren, the good in us is God in us. The inwardness makes the outwardness, the godliness the beauty. It is indisputable that it is Christ in us that makes all our Christianity. Oh, Christians who have no Christ in them—such Christians are poor, cheap imitations, and hollow shams—and Christ will, with infinite impatience, even infinite love, fling them away.—*Charles Stanford, in a Sermon preached before the Baptist Union,* 1876.

Verse 4.—"*Upright in their hearts.*" All true excellence has its seat here. It is not the good action which makes the good man : it is the good man who does the good action. The merit of an action depends entirely upon the motives which have prompted its performance ; and, tried by this simple test, how many deeds, which have wrung from the world its admiration and its glory, might well be described in old words, as nothing better than splendid sins. When the heart is wrong, all is wrong. When the heart is right, all is right.—*N. M'Michael.*

Verse 4.—"*Upright.*" Literally, *straight*, straightforward, as opposed to all moral obliquity whatever.—*Joseph Addison Alexander* (1809—1860), *in "The Psalms Translated and Explained."*

Verse 5.—"*Such as turn aside unto their crooked ways.*" This is the anxiety of the pastor in this pilgrim song. The shepherd would keep his sheep from straggling. His distress is that all in Israel are not true Israelites. Two sorts of people, described by the poet, have ever been in the church. The second class, instead of being at the trouble to "withstand in the evil day," will "put forth their hands unto iniquity." Rather than feel, they will follow the rod of the wicked. They will "turn aside unto their crooked ways," sooner than risk temporal and material interests.—*Edward Jewitt Robinson, in "The Caravan and the Temple,"* 1878.

Verse 5.—"*Such as turn aside unto their crooked ways.*" All the ways of sin are called "*crooked ways,*" and they are our own ways. The Psalmist calls them "*their* crooked ways"; that is, the ways of their own devising; whereas the way of holiness is the Lord's way. To exceed or do more; to be deficient or do less, than God requires, both these are "*crooked ways.*" The way of the Lord lies straight forward, right before us. "Whoso walketh uprightly shall be saved; but he that is perverse (or *crooked*) in his ways shall fall at once": Prov. xxviii. 18. The motion of a godly man is like that of the kine that carried the ark: "Who took the straight way to the way of Beth-shemesh, and went along the highway, lowing as they went, and turned not aside to the right hand or to the left": 1 Sam. vi. 12.—*Joseph Caryl.*

Verse 5.—"*Crooked ways.*" The ways of sinners are "*crooked*"; they shift from one pursuit to another, and turn hither and thither to deceive; they wind about a thousand ways to conceal their base intentions, to accomplish their iniquitous projects, or to escape the punishment of their crimes; yet disappointment, detection, confusion, and misery, are their inevitable portion.—*Thomas Scott,* 1747—1821.

Verse 5.—"*The* LORD *shall lead them forth with the workers of iniquity.*" They walked according to the prince of the air, and they shall go where the prince of the air is. God will bring forth men from their hiding-places. Though they walk among the drove of his children, in procession now, yet if they also walk in by-lanes of sin, God will rank them at the latter day, yea, often in this world, with the workers of iniquity. They walk after workers of iniquity here before God, and God will make manifest that it is so before he hath done with them. The reason, my brethren, why they are to be reckoned among workers of iniquity, and as walkers among them, though they sever themselves from them in respect of external conversation, is, because they agree in the same internal principle of sin. They walk in their lusts: every unregenerate man doth so. Refine him how you will, it is certain he doth in heart pursue "*crooked ways.*"—*Thomas Goodwin,* 1600—1679.

Verse 5.—Sometimes God takes away a barren professor by permitting him to fall into open profaneness. There is one that hath taken up a profession of the worthy name of the Lord Jesus Christ, but this profession is only a cloak; he secretly practiseth wickedness; he is a glutton, or a drunkard, or covetous, or unclean. Well, saith God, I will loose the reins of this professor, I will give him up to his vile affections. I will loose the reins of his sins before him, he shall be entangled with his filthy lusts, he shall be overcome of ungodly company. Thus they that turn aside to their own crooked ways, "*the Lord shall lead them forth with the workers of iniquity.*"—*John Bunyan,* 1628—1688.

Verse 5.—"*But peace shall be upon Israel.*" Do you ask, What is the peace upon Israel? I answer:—First, the peace of Israel, that is, of a believing and holy soul, is *from above,* and is higher than all the disturbances of the world; it rests upon him, and makes him calm and peaceful, and lifts him above the world: for upon him rests the Holy Spirit, who is the Comforter; who is essential love and uncreated peace. Secondly, the peace of a believing and holy soul is *internal;* for it is sent down from heaven upon his head, flows into his heart, and dwells there, and stills all agitations of mind. Thirdly, the peace of a believing and holy soul, is also *external.* It is a fountain of Paradise watering all the face of the earth: Gen. ii. 6: you see it in the man's face and life. Fourthly, the peace of a believing and holy soul is *divine:* for chiefly, it maintains peace with God. Fifthly, the peace of a believing and holy soul is *universal:* to wit, with neighbours, with God, with himself: in the body, in the eyes, in the ears, in tasting, smelling, feeling, in all the members, and in all the appetites. This peace is not disturbed by devils, the world, and the flesh, setting forth their honours, riches, pleasures. Sixthly, the peace of a believing and holy soul is peace *eternal* and never interrupted ; for it flows from an eternal and exhaustless fountain, even from God himself.—*Condensed from Le Blanc*, 1599—1669.

Verse 5.—"*Israel.*" The Israelites derived their joint names from the two chief parts of religion : Israelites, from Israel, whose prayer was his "strength" (Hosea xii. 3), and Jews, from Judah, whose name means "praise."—*George Seaton Bowes, in "Illustrative Gatherings,"* 1869.

HINTS TO THE VILLAGE PREACHER.

Whole Psalm.—I. The mark of the covenant : "They that trust." II. The security of the covenant (verses 1, 2). III. The rod of the covenant (verse 3). IV. The tenor of the covenant (verse 4). V. The spirit of the covenant,— "peace."

Verse 1.—See "Spurgeon's Sermons," No. 1,450 : "The Immortality of the Believer."

Verses 1, 2.—I. The believer's singularity : he trusts in Jehovah. II. The believer's stability : "abideth for ever." III. The believer's safety : "As the mountains," etc.

Verse 2.—The all-surrounding presence of Jehovah the glory, safety, and eternal blessedness of his people. Yet this to the wicked would be hell.

Verse 2.—See "Spurgeon's Sermons," Nos. 161–2 : "The Security of the Church."

Verse 2.—The endurance of mercy : "From henceforth even for ever."

Verse 2.—Saints hemmed-in by infinite love. I. *The City and the Girdle*, or *the symbols suparated*. 1. Jerusalem imaging God's people. Anciently chosen ; singularly honoured ; much beloved ; the shrine of Deity. 2. The Mountain Girdle setting forth Jehovah : Strength ; All-sidedness ; Sentinel through day and night. II. *The City within the Girdle*, or *the symbols related*. 1. Delightful Entanglement. The view from the windows ! (Jehovah "round about.") To be lost must *break through God !* Sound sleep and safe labour. 2. Omnipotent Circumvallation, suggesting—God's determination ; Satan's dismay. This mountain ring immutable.— *W. B. Haynes, of Stafford.*

Verse 3.—Observe, I. The Permission implied. The rod of the wicked may come upon the lot of the righteous. Why ? 1. That wickedness may be free to manifest itself. 2. That the righteous may be made to hate sin. 3. That the righteousness of God's retribution may be seen. 4. That the consolations of the righteous may abound. 2 Cor. i. 5. II. The Permanency denied : "The rod . . . shall *not rest*," etc. Illustrate by history of Job, Joseph, David, Daniel, Christ, martyrs, etc. III. The Probity tried and preserved : "Lest the righteous put forth," etc., by rebelling, sinful compromise, etc. 1. God will have it tried, to prove its worth, beauty, etc. 2. But no more than sufficiently tried.—*John Field, of Sevenoaks.*

Verses 3, 4.—I. The good defined : "The upright in heart ;" such as do not "turn aside," and are not "workers of iniquity." II. The good distressed : by "the rod of the wicked." III. The good delivered : "Do good " ; fulfil thy promise (verse 3).— *W. H. J. Page.*

Verse 4.—I. What it is to be good. II. What it is for God to do us good.

Verse 5.—Temporary Professors. I. The crucial test : "They turn aside." II. The crooked policy : they make crooked ways their own. III. The crushing doom : "led forth with workers of iniquity."

Verse 5.—Hypocrites. I. Their ways : "crooked." 1. Like the way of a winding stream, seeking out the fair level, or the easy descent. 2. Like the course of a tacking ship, which skilfully makes every wind to drive her forward. 3. Ways constructed upon no principle but that of pure selfishness. II. Their conduct under trial. They "turn aside." 1. From their religious profession. 2. From their former companions. 3. To become the worst scorners of spiritual things, and the most violent calumniators of spiritually-minded men. III. Their doom : "The Lord shall," etc. 1. In the judgment they shall be classed with the most flagrant of sinners ; " with the workers of iniquity." 2. They shall be exposed by an irresistible power : " The Lord shall lead them forth." 3. They shall meet with terrible execution with the wicked in hell.—*J. Field.*

Verse 5 (*last clause*).—To whom peace belongs. To " Israel " ; the chosen, the once wrestler, the now prevailing prince. Consider Jacob's life after he obtained the name of Israel ; note his trials, and his security under them as illustrating this text. Then take the text as a sure promise.

Verse 5 (*last clause*).—Enquire, I. Who are the Israel ? 1. Covenanted ones. 2. Circumcised in heart. 3. True worshippers. II. What is the peace ? 1. Peace of conscience. 2. Of friendship with God. 3. Of a settled and satisfied heart. 4. Of eternal glory, in reversion. III. Why the certainty (" shall be") ? 1. Christ has made peace for them. 2. The Holy Spirit brings peace to them. 3. They walk in the way of peace.—*J. Field.*

For list of Works upon the Psalms of Degrees, see "Treasury of David," Vol. VI., page 403.

PSALM CXXVI.

TITLE.—A Song of Degrees. *This is the seventh step, and we may therefore expect to meet with some special perfection of joy in it; nor shall we look in vain. We see here not only that Zion abides, but that her joy returns after sorrow. Abiding is not enough, fruitfulness is added. The pilgrims went'from blessing to blessing in their psalmody as they proceeded on their holy way. Happy people to whom every ascent was a song, every halt a hymn. Here the truster becomes a sower: faith works by love, obtains a present bliss, and secures a harvest of delight.*

There is nothing in this psalm by which we can decide its date, further than this,— that it is a song after a great deliverance from oppression. " Turning captivity" by no means requires an actual removal into banishment to fill out the idea ; rescue from any dire affliction or crushing tyranny would be fitly described as " captivity turned." Indeed, the passage is not applicable to captives in Babylon, for it is Zion itself which is in captivity, and not a part of her citizens: the holy city was in sorrow and distress ; though it could not be removed, the prosperity could be diminished. Some dark cloud lowered over the beloved capital, and its citizens prayed " Turn again our captivity, O Lord."

This psalm is in its right place and most fittingly follows its predecessor, for as in Psalm cxxv. we read that the rod of the wicked shall not rest upon the lot of the righteous, we here see it removed from them to their great joy. The word "turn" would seem to be the keynote of the song : it is a psalm of conversion—conversion from captivity ; and it may well be used to set forth the rapture of a pardoned soul when the anger of the Lord is turned away from it. We will call it, " Leading captivity captive."

The Psalm divides itself into a narrative (1, 2), a song (3), a prayer (4), and a promise (5 and 6).

EXPOSITION.

WHEN the LORD turned again the captivity of Zion, we were like them that dream.

2 Then was our mouth filled with laughter, and our tongue with singing : then said they among the heathen, The LORD hath done great things for them.

3 The LORD hath done great things for us ; *whereof* we are glad.

4 Turn again our captivity, O LORD, as the streams in the south.

5 They that sow in tears shall reap in joy.

6 He that goeth forth and weepeth, bearing precious seed, shall doubtless come again with rejoicing, bringing his sheaves *with him.*

1. "*When the* LORD *turned again the captivity of Zion, we were like them that dream.*" Being in trouble, the gracious pilgrims remember for their comfort times of national woe which were succeeded by remarkable deliverances Then sorrow was gone like a dream, and the joy which followed was so great that it seemed too good to be true, and they feared that it must be the vision of an idle brain. So sudden and so overwhelming was their joy that they felt like men out of themselves, ecstatic, or in a trance. The captivity had been great, and great was the deliverance ; for the great God himself had wrought it : it seemed too good to be actually true : each man said to himself,—

> " Is this a dream ? O if it be a dream,
> Let me sleep on, and do not wake me yet."

It was not the freedom of an individual which the Lord in mercy had wrought, but of all Zion, of the whole nation ; and this was reason enough for overflowing gladness. We need not instance the histories which illustrate this verse in connection with literal Israel ; but it is well to remember how often it has been true to ourselves. Let us look to the prison-houses from which we have been set free. Ah, me, what captives we have been ! At our first conversion what a turning again of captivity we experienced. Never shall that hour be forgotten. Joy ! Joy ! Joy ! Since then, from multiplied troubles, from depression of spirit, from miserable backsliding, from grievous doubt, we have been emancipated, and we are not able to describe the bliss which followed each emancipation.

> " When God reveal'd his gracious name
> And changed our mournful state,
> Our rapture seem'd a pleasing dream,
> The grace appeared so great."

This verse will have a higher fulfilment in the day of the final overthrow of the powers of darkness when the Lord shall come forth for the salvation and glorification of his redeemed. Then in a fuller sense than even at Pentecost our old men shall see visions, and our young men shall dream dreams : yea, all things shall be so wonderful, so far beyond all expectation, that those who behold them shall ask themselves whether it be not all a dream. The past is ever a sure prognostic of the future ; the thing which has been is the thing that shall be : we shall again and again find ourselves amazed at the wonderful goodness of the Lord. Let our hearts gratefully remember the former lovingkindnesses of the Lord : we were sadly low, sorely distressed, and completely past hope, but when Jehovah appeared he did not merely lift us out of despondency, he raised us into wondering happiness. The Lord who alone turns our captivity does nothing by halves : those whom he saves from hell he brings to heaven. He turns exile into ecstasy, and banishment into bliss.

2. "*Then was our mouth filled with laughter, and our tongue with singing.*" So full were they of joy that they could not contain themselves. They must express their joy and yet they could not find expression for it. Irrepressible mirth could do no other than laugh, for speech was far too dull a thing for it. The mercy was so unexpected, so amazing, so singular that they could not do less than laugh ; and they laughed much, so that their mouths were full of it, and that because their hearts were full too. When at last the tongue could move articulately, it could not be content simply to talk, but it must needs sing ; and sing heartily too, for it was full of singing. Doubtless the former pain added to the zest of the pleasure ; the captivity threw a brighter colour into the emancipation. The people remembered this joy-flood for years after, and here is the record of it turned into a song. Note the *then* and the *then.* God's *when* is our *then.* At the moment when he turns our captivity, the heart turns from its sorrow ; when he fills us with grace we are filled with gratitude. We were made to be as them that dream, but we both laughed and sang in our sleep. We are wide awake now, and though we can scarcely realize the blessing, yet we rejoice in it exceedingly.

"*Then said they among the heathen, the* LORD *hath done great things for them.*" The heathen heard the songs of Israel, and the better sort among them soon guessed the cause of their joy. Jehovah was known to be their God, and to him the other nations ascribed the emancipation of his people, reckoning it to be no small thing which the Lord had thus done ; for those who carried away the nations had never in any other instance restored a people to their ancient dwelling-place. These foreigners were no dreamers ; though they were only lookers-on, and not partakers in the surprising mercy, they plainly saw what had been done, and rightly ascribed it to the great Giver of all good. It is a blessed thing when saints set sinners talking about the lovingkindness of the Lord : and it is equally blessed when the saints who are hidden away in the world hear of what the Lord has done for his church, and themselves resolve to come out from their captivity and unite with the Lord's people. Ah, dear reader, Jehovah has indeed done marvellous things for his chosen, and these " great things" shall be themes for eternal praise among all intelligent creatures.

3. "*The* LORD *hath done great things for us; whereof we are glad.*" They did not deny the statement which reflected so much glory upon Jehovah : with exultation they admitted and repeated the statement of Jehovah's notable dealings with them. To themselves they appropriated the joyful assertion ; they said " The Lord hath done great things *for us*," and they declared their gladness at the fact. It is a poor modesty which is ashamed to own its joys in the Lord. Call it rather a robbery of God. There is so little of happiness abroad that if we possess a full share of it we ought not to hide our light under a bushel, but let it shine on all that are in the house. Let us avow our joy, and the reason of it, stating the " whereof " as well as the fact. None are so happy as those who are newly turned and returned from captivity ; none can more promptly and satisfactorily give a reason for the gladness that is in them. The Lord himself has blessed us, blessed us greatly, blessed us individually, blessed us assuredly ; and because of this we sing unto his name. I heard one say the other day in prayer " whereof we desire to be glad." Strange dilution and defilement of Scriptural language ! Surely if God has done great things for us we are glad, and cannot be otherwise. No doubt such language is meant to be lowly, but in truth it is loathsome.

4. "*Turn again our captivity, O* LORD." Remembering the former joy of a past rescue they cry to Jehovah for a repetition of it. When we pray for the turning of our captivity, it is wise to recall former instances thereof : nothing strengthens faith more effectually than the memory of a previous experience. " The Lord hath done" harmonizes well with the prayer, " Turn again." The text shows us how wise it is to resort anew to the Lord, who in former times has been so good to us. Where else should we go but to him who has done such great things for us ? Who can turn again our captivity but he who turned it before ?

"*As the streams in the south.*" Even as the Lord sends floods adown the dry beds of southern torrents after long droughts, so can he fill our wasted and wearied spirits with floods of holy delight. This the Lord can do for any of us, and he can do it at once, for nothing is too hard for the Lord. It is well for us thus to pray, and to bring our suit before him who is able to bless us exceeding abundantly. Do not let us forget the past, but in the presence of our present difficulty let us resort unto the Lord, and beseech him to do that for us which we cannot possibly do for ourselves,—that which no other power can perform on our behalf. Israel did return from the captivity in Babylon, and it was even as though a flood of people hastened to Zion. Suddenly and plenteously the people filled again the temple courts. In streams they shall also in the latter days return to their own land, and replenish it yet again. Like mighty torrents shall the nations flow unto the Lord in the day of his grace. May the Lord hasten it in his own time.

5. "*They that sow in tears shall reap in joy.*" Hence, present distress must not be viewed as if it would last for ever ; it is not the end, by any means, but only a means to the end. Sorrow is our sowing, rejoicing shall be our reaping. If there were no sowing in tears there would be no reaping in joy. If we were never captives we could never lead our captivity captive. Our mouth had never been filled with holy laughter if it had not been first filled with the bitterness of grief. We must sow : we may have to sow in the wet weather of sorrow ; but we shall reap, and reap in the bright summer season of joy. Let us keep to the work of this present sowing time, and find strength in the promise which is here so positively given us. Here is one of the Lord's shalls and wills ; it is freely given both to workers, waiters, and weepers, and they may rest assured that it will not fail : " in due season they *shall* reap."

This sentence may well pass current in the church as an inspired proverb. It is not every sowing which is thus insured against all danger, and guaranteed a harvest ; but the promise specially belongs to sowing *in tears*. When a man's heart is so stirred that he weeps over the sins of others, he is elect to usefulness. Winners of souls are first weepers for souls. As there is no birth without travail, so is there no spiritual harvest without painful tillage. When our own hearts are broken with grief at man's transgression we shall break other men's hearts : tears of earnestness beget tears of repentance : " deep calleth unto deep."

6. *"He."* The general assurance is applied to each one in particular. That which is spoken in the previous verse in the plural—" they," is here repeated in the singular—" he." *"He that goeth forth and weepeth, bearing precious seed, shall doubtless come again with rejoicing, bringing his sheaves with him."* He leaves his couch to go forth into the frosty air and tread the heavy soil ; and as he goes he weeps because of past failures, or because the ground is so sterile, or the weather so unseasonable, or his corn so scarce, and his enemies so plentiful and so eager to rob him of his reward. He drops a seed and a tear, a seed and a tear, and so goes on his way. In his basket he has seed which is precious to him, for he has little of it, and it is his hope for the next year. Each grain leaves his hand with anxious prayer that it may not be lost : he thinks little of himself, but much of his seed, and he eagerly asks, " Will it prosper ? shall I receive a reward for my labour ?" Yes, good husbandman, *doubtless* you will gather sheaves from your sowing. Because the Lord has written *doubtless*, take heed that you do not doubt. No reason for doubt can remain after the Lord has spoken. You will return to this field—not to sow, but to reap ; not to weep, but to rejoice ; and after awhile you will go home again with nimbler step than to-day, though with a heavier load, for you shall have sheaves to bear with you. Your handful shall be so greatly multiplied that many sheaves shall spring from it ; and you shall have the pleasure of reaping them and bringing them home to the place from which you went out weeping.

This is a figurative description of that which was literally described in the first three verses. It is the turning of the worker's captivity, when, instead of seed buried beneath black earth, he sees the waving crops inviting him to a golden harvest.

It is somewhat singular to find this promise of fruitfulness in close contact with return from captivity ; and yet it is so in our own experience, for when our own soul is revived the souls of others are blessed by our labours. If any of us, having been once lonesome and lingering captives, have now returned home, and have become longing and labouring sowers, may the Lord, who has already delivered us, soon transform us into glad-hearted reapers, and to him shall be praise for ever and ever. Amen.

EXPLANATORY NOTES.

Title.—Augustine interprets the title, " A Song of Degrees, i. e. a Song of drawing upwards," of the drawing (going) up to the heavenly Jerusalem. This is right, inasmuch as the deliverance from the captivity of sin and death should in an increased measure excite those feelings of gratitude which Israel must have felt on being delivered from their corporeal captivity ; in this respect again is the history of the outward theocracy a type of the history of the church.—*Augustus F. Tholuck,* 1856.

Whole Psalm.—In its Christian aspect the psalm represents the seventh of the " degrees" in our ascent to the Jerusalem that is above. The Christian's exultation at his deliverance from the spiritual captivity of sin.—*H. T. Armfield.*

Whole Psalm.—In mine opinion they go near to the sense and true meaning of the Psalm who do refer it to that great and general captivity of mankind under sin, death and the devil, and to the redemption purchased by the death and blood-shedding of Christ, and published in the Gospel. For this kind of speech which the Prophet useth here is of greater importance than that it may be applied only to Jewish particular captivities. For what great matter was it for these people of the Jews, being, as it were, a little handful, to be delivered out of temporal captivity, in comparison of the exceeding and incomparable deliverance whereby mankind was set at liberty from the power of their enemies, not tempo-

ral, but eternal, even from death, Satan and hell itself ?   Wherefore we take this
Psalm to be a prophecy of the redemption that should come by Jesus Christ, and
the publishing of the gospel, whereby the kingdom of Christ is advanced, and
death and the devil with all the powers of darkness are vanquished.—*Thomas
Stint, in An Exposition on Psalms cxxiv—cxxvi*, 1621.

Whole Psalm.—I believe this psalm is yet once more to be sung in still more
joyous strain ; once more will the glad tidings of Israel's restoration break upon
her scattered tribes, like the unreal shadow of a dream ; once more will the inhabitants of the various lands from among whom they come forth exclaim in
adoring wonder, "The Lord hath done great things for them," when they see
Israelite after Israelite and Jew after Jew, as on that wondrous night of Egypt,
with their loins girded, their shoes on their feet, and their staff in their hand,
hasting to obey the summons that recalls them to their own loved land !—*Barton
Bouchier* (1794—1865), *in "Manna in the Heart."*

Whole Psalm

> When, her sons from bonds redeeming,
>   God to Zion led the way,
> We were like to people dreaming
>   Thoughts of bliss too bright to stay.
>
> Fill'd with laughter, stood we gazing,
>   Loud our tongues in rapture sang ;
> Quickly with the news amazing
>   All the startled nations rang.
>
> "See Jehovah's works of glory !
>   Mark what love for them he had !"
> "Yes, FOR US ! Go tell the story.
>   This was done, and we are glad."
>
> Lord ! thy work of grace completing
>   All our exiled hosts restore,
> As in thirsty channels meeting
>   Southern streams refreshing pour.
>
> They that now in sorrow weeping
>   Tears and seed commingled sow,
> Soon, the fruitful harvest reaping,
>   Shall with joyful bosoms glow.
>
> Tho' the sower's heart is breaking,
>   Bearing forth the seed to shed,
> He shall come, the echoes waking,
>   Laden with his sheaves instead.

William Digby Seymour, in "The Hebrew Psalter. A New Metrical Translation,"
1882.

Verse 1.—"*When the Lord turned again the captivity.*"   As by the Lord's permission they were led into captivity, so only by his power they were set at liberty.
When the Israelites had served in a strange land four hundred years, it was not
Moses, but Jehovah, that brought them out of the land of Egypt, and out of the
house of bondage.   In like manner it was he and not Deborah that freed them for
Jabin after they had been vexed twenty years under the Canaanites.   It was he and
not Gideon that brought them out of the hands of the Midianites, after seven years'
servitude.   It was he and not Jephthah that delivered them from the Philistines
and Amorites after eighteen years' oppression.   Although in all these he did employ Moses and Deborah, Gideon and Jephthah, as instruments for their deliverance ; and so it was not Cyrus's valour, but the Lord's power ; not his policy, but
God's wisdom, that, overthrowing the enemies, gave to Cyrus the victory, and
put it into his heart to set his people at liberty ; for he upheld his hands to subdue nations.   He did weaken the loins of kings, and did open the doors before
him, he did go before him, and made the crooked places straight ; and he did
break the brazen doors, and burst the iron bars.   Isaiah xlv. 1, 2.—*John Hume,
in "The Jewes Deliverance,"* 1628.

Verse 1.—"*In Jehovah's turning (to) the turning of Zion.*"   Meaning to return to the return, or meet those returning, as it were, half way. The Hebrew noun dénotes *conversion*, in its spiritual sense, and the verb God's gracious condescension in accepting or responding to it.—*Joseph Addison Alexander.*

Verse 1.—"*The captivity of Zion.*" I ask, first, Why of *Zion ?* why not the captivity of Jerusalem, Judah, Israel ? Jerusalem, Judah, Israel, were led away captives, no less than Zion. They, the greater and more general ; why not *the captivity* of them, but of *Zion ?* It should seem there is more in Zion's captivity than in the rest, that choice is made of it before the rest. Why ? what was Zion ? We know it was but a hill in Jerusalem, on the north side. Why is that hill so honoured ? No reason in the world but this,—that upon it the Temple was built ; and so, that Zion is much spoken of, and much made of, it is only for the Temple's sake. For whose sake it is (even for his church), that "the Lord loveth the gates of Zion more than all the dwellings of Jacob" (Ps. lxxxvii. 2) ; loveth her more, and so her captivity goeth nearer him, and her deliverance better pleaseth him, than all Jacob besides. This maketh *Zion's captivity* to be mentioned chiefly, as chiefly regarded by God, and to be regarded by his people. As we see it was : when they sat by the waters of Babylon, that which made them weep was, "When we remembered thee, O Zion" ; that was their greatest grief. That their greatest grief, and this their greatest joy ; *Lætati sumus,* when news came (not, saith the Psalm, *in domos nostras,* We shall go everyone to his own house, but) in *domum Domini ibimus,* "We shall go to the house of the Lord, we shall appear before the God of gods in Zion."—*Lancelot Andrews,* 1555—1626.

Verse 1.—"*We were like them that dream.*" That is, they thought it was but mere fantasy and imagination.—*Sydrach Simpson,* 1658.

Verse 1.—"*We were like them that dream.*" Here you may observe that God doth often send succour and deliverance to the godly in the time of their affliction, distress, and adversity ; that many times they themselves do doubt of the truth thereof, and think that in very deed they are not delivered, but rather that they have dreamed. Peter, being imprisoned by Herod, when he was delivered by an angel, for all the light that did shine in the prison ; though the angel did smite him on the side and raised him up ; though he caused the chains to fall off his hands ; though he spake to him three several times, *Surge, cinge, circunda ;* "Arise quickly, gird thyself, and cast thy garment about thee" ; though he conducted him safely by the watches ; and though he caused the iron gates to open willingly ; yet for all this he was like unto them that dream. "For he wist not that it was true which was done by the angel ; but thought he saw a vision" : Acts xii. 9. When old Jacob was told by his sons that his son Joseph was alive, his heart failed, and he believed them not ; but when he had heard all that Joseph had said, and when he saw the chariots that Joseph had sent, then, as it were, raised from a sleep, and awakened from a dream, his spirit revived, and, rejoicing, he cried out, "I have enough ; Joseph my son is yet alive."

Lorinus seems to excuse this their distrust, because they were so over-ravished with joy, that they misdoubted the true cause of their joy : like the Apostles, who having Christ after his resurrection standing before them, they were so exceedingly joyed, that rejoicing they wondered and doubted ; and like the two Marys, when the angel told them of our Saviour Christ's resurrection, they returned from the sepulchre rejoicing, and yet withal fearing. It may be they feared the truth of so glad news, and doubted lest they were deceived by some apparition.—*John Hume.*

Verse 1.—"*We were like them that dream.*" We thought that we were dreaming ; we could hardly believe our eyes, when at the command of Cyrus, king of the Persians, we had returned to our own land. The same thing happened to the Greeks, when they heard that their country, being conquered by the Romans, had been made free by the Roman consul, P. Quinctius Flaminius. Livy says that when the herald had finished there was more good news than the people could receive all at once. They could scarcely believe that they had heard aright. They were looking on each other wonderingly, like sleepers on an empty dream.
—*John Le Clerc* [*Clericus*], 1657—1736.

Verse 1.—"*We were like them that dream,*" etc. In the lapse of seventy years the hope of restoration to their land, so long deferred, had mostly gone out in despair, save as it rested (in some minds) on their faith in God's promise. The policy of those great powers in the East had long been settled, viz., to break up the old tribes and kingdoms of Western Asia ; take the people into far eastern countries, and *never let them return.* No nation known to history, except the Jews, ever did return to rebuild their ancient cities and homes. Hence this joyous surprise.—*Henry Cowles, in " The Psalms ; with Notes,"* 1872.

Verse 1.—"*Like them that dream.*" It was no dream ; it was Jacob's dream become a reality. It was the promise, " I will bring thee back into this land " (Gen. xxviii. 15), fulfilled beyond all their hope.—*William Kay, in "The Psalms, with Notes, chiefly exegetical,"* 1871.

Verse 1.—"*We were like them that dream.*" The words should rather be translated, "*We are like unto those that are restored to health.*" The Hebrew word signifies to recover, or, to be restored to health. And so the same word is translated in Isai. xxxviii., when Hezekiah recovered, he made a psalm of praise, and said, " O Lord, by these things men live, and in all these things is the life of my spirit : so wilt thou recover me, and make me to live." It is the same word that is used here. Thus Cajetan, Shindler, and others would have it translated here ; and it suits best with the following words, " Then were our mouths filled with laughter, and our tongues with praise." When a man is in a good dream, his mouth is not filled with laughter, nor his tongue with praise : if a man be in a bad dream, his mouth is not filled with laughter, nor his tongue with praise ; but when a man is restored to health after a great sickness, it is so.—*William Bridge,* 1600—1670.

Verse 2.—"*Then was our mouth filled with laughter,*" etc. We must earnestly endeavour to learn this practice, or at the least to attain to some knowledge thereof ; and we must raise up ourselves with this consideration—that the gospel is nothing else but laughter and joy. This joy properly pertaineth to captives, that is, to those that feel the captivity of sin and death ; to the fleshy and tender hearts, terrified with the feeling of the wrath and judgment of God. These are the disciples in whose hearts should be planted laughter and joy, and that by the authority of the Holy Ghost, which this verse setteth forth. This people was in Zion, and, after the outward show of the kingdom and priesthood, did mightily flourish ; but if a man consider them according to the spirit, he shall see them to be in miserable captivity, and that their tongue is full of heaviness and mourning, because their heart is terrified with the sense of sin and death. This is Moses' tongue or Moses' mouth, full of wormwood and of the bitterness of death ; wherewith he designs to kill none but those which are too lively and full of security. But they who feel their captivity shall have their mouths filled with laughter and joy : that is, redemption and deliverance from sin and death shall be preached unto them. This is the sense and meaning of the Holy Ghost, that the mouth of such shall be filled with laughter, that is, their mouth shall show forth nothing else but great gladness through the inestimable consolations of the gospel, with voices of triumph and victory by Christ, overcoming Satan, destroying death, and taking away sins. This was first spoken unto the Jews ; for this laughter was first offered to that people, then having the promises. Now he turneth to the Gentiles, whom he calleth to the partaking of this laughter.—*Martin Luther.*

Verse 2.—"*Then was our mouth filled with laughter,*" etc. It was thus in the valley of Elah, where Goliath fell, and Philistia fled. It was thus at Baal-Perazim. It was thus when one morning, after many nights of gloom, Jerusalem arose at dawn of day, and found Sennacherib's thousands a camp of the dead. And it has all along been the manner of our God.

> " The Lord has wrought mightily
> In what he has done for us ;
> And we have been made glad."

Ever do this till conflict is over ! Just as thou dost with the streams of the south, year by year, so do with us—with all, with each. And we are confident thou wilt ; we are sure that we make no vain boast when we sing this psalm as descriptive of the experience of all thy pilgrims and worshippers.—*Andrew A. Bonar, in "Christ and his Church in the Book of Psalms,"* 1859.

Verse 2.—*"Then was our mouth filled with laughter."* They that were laughed at, now laugh, and a new song is put into their mouths. It was a laughter of joy in God, not scorn of their enemies.—*Matthew Henry.*

Verse 2.—*"Mouth"* ; *" tongue."* Lorinus, the Jesuit, hath observed that the Psalmist nominates the *mouth* and *tongue* in the singular, not *mouths* and *tongues* in the plural ; because all the faithful and the whole congregation of the Jews *univocè,* with one voice, with one consent, and, as it were, with one mouth, did praise and glorify the Lord.—*John Hume.*

Verse 2.—*"And our tongue with singing."* Out of the abundance of the heart the mouth speaks ; and if the heart be glad the tongue is glib. Joy cannot be suppressed in the heart, but it must be expressed with the tongue.—*John Hume.*

Verse 2.—*"Then said they among the heathen."* And what is it they said ? It is to the purpose. In this (as in many others) the heathens' saying cannot be mended. This they say : 1. That they were no quotidian, or common things ; but *" great."* 2. Then, these great things they ascribe not to *chance ;* that they *happened* not, but were *" done."* 3. Then, *"* done*" by God himself :* they see God in them. 4. Then, not done by God at random, without any particular aim ; but *purposely* done *for them.* 5. And yet, there is more in *magnificavit facere* (if we look well). For, *magna fecit* would have served all this ; but in saying *magnificavit facere,* they say *magnifecit illos, ut magna faceret pro illis.* He magnified them, or set greatly by them, for whom he would bring to pass so great a work. This said they among the " heathen."

And it is pity the " *heathen"* said it, and that the Jews themselves spake not these words first. But now, finding the " *heathen"* so saying ; and finding it was all true that they said, they must needs find themselves bound to say at least as much ; and more they could not say ; for more cannot be said. So much then, and no less than they. And this addeth a degree to the *dicebant,*—that the sound of it was so great among *the heathen* that it made an *echo* even in Jewry itself.—*Lancelot Andrews.*

Verse 2.—*"The* LORD *hath done great things."* *He multiplied to do great things ;* so the Chaldee, Syriac, and Arabic versions render it ; and the history of this deliverance makes it good.—*Thomas Hodges, in a Sermon entitled " Sion's Hallelujah,"* 1660.

Verses 2, 3.—There is this great difference between the praise which the heathen are forced to give to God, and that which the Lord's people heartily offer unto him : the one doth speak as having no interest nor share in the mercy ; the other do speak as they to whom the mercy is intended, and wherein they have their portion with others : *"He hath done great things for them,"* say the heathen : but, *" he hath done great things for us,"* say the Lord's people.—*David Dickson,* 1583—1662.

Verse 3.—*"The* LORD *hath done great things for us,"* etc. This verse is the marrow of the whole psalm, occasioned by the return of God's people out of Babel's captivity into their own country. Their deliverance was so great and incredible that when God brought it to pass they were *as men in a dream,* thinking it rather a dream, and a vain imagination, than a real truth. 1. Because it was so great a deliverance from so great and lasting a bondage, it seemed too good to be true. 2. It was sudden and unexpected, when they little thought or hoped for it. . . . . 3. All things seemed desperate, nothing more unlikely, or impossible rather. 4. The manner was so admirable (without the counsel, help, or strength of man : nay, it was beyond and against all human means) ; that they doubt whether these things be not the dreams of men that are awake.—*Thomas Taylor* (1576—1632), *in "A Mappe of Rome."*

Verse 3.—"*For us.*" What were we, might Sion say (who were glad to lick the dust of the feet of our enemies), that the Lord of heaven and earth should look so graciously upon us? The meanness of the receiver argueth the magnificence of the giver. " Who am I, that the mother of my Lord should visit me ?" this was a true and religious compliment of devout Elizabeth. The best of men are but the children of dust, and grand-children of nothing. And yet for the Lord to do " *great things*" for us ! this yet *greatens* those " *great things.*" Was it because *we were his church?* It was his superabounding grace to select us out of others, as it was our greater gracelessness, above all others, so to provoke him, as to force him to throw us into captivity. Or was it because *our humiliation,* in that disconsolate condition, did move him to so great compassion? Alas ! there was a choice of nations whom he might have taken in our room, that might have proved far more faithful than we have been for the one half of those favours we have enjoyed.

Or was it for *his covenant's sake* with our forefathers? Alas ! we had forfeited that long since, again and again, we know not how often. Wherefore, when we remember ourselves, we cannot but make this an aggravation of God's " *great things,*" that he should do them *for us,* FOR US, so very, very unworthy.—*Malachiah [or Matthew] Harris, in a Sermon entitled "Brittaines Hallelujah," 1639.*

Verse 4.—"*Turn again our captivity, O* LORD." A prayer for the perfecting of their deliverance. Let those that are returned to their own land be eased of their burdens which they are yet groaning under. Let those that remain in Babylon have their hearts stirred up, as ours were, to take the benefit of the liberty granted. The beginnings of mercy are encouragements to us to pray for the completing of it. While we are here in this world, there will still be matter for prayer, even when we are most furnished with matter for praise. When we are free, and in prosperity ourselves, we must not be unmindful of our brethren that are in trouble and under restraint.—*Matthew Henry.*

Verse 4.—"*Turn again our captivity.*" As Israel of old prayed that he would bring all their brethren scattered abroad in captivity back to their own land in one full stream, multitudinous, joyous, mighty, like the waters of Nile or Euphrates pouring over the parching fields of the south in the hot, dry summertide ; so now should the members of Christ's church ever pray " that all that profess and call themselves Christians may be led into the way of truth, and hold the faith in unity of spirit, in the bond of peace, and in righteousness of life."—*J. W. Burgon, in "A Plain Commentary," 1859.*

Verse 4.—The Psalmist cries—

> " Turn our captivity, O Jehovah,
> As aqueducts in the Negeb."

This Negeb, or South Country, the region stretching below Hebron, being comparatively dry and waterless, was doubtless irrigated by a system of small artificial channels. The words of the Psalmist imply that it is as easy for God to turn Israel back from Babylonian bondage to their own land, as for the horticulturist to direct the waters of the spring to any part of the land he chooses along the channels of the aqueducts.—*James Neil.*

Verse 4.—"*As the streams in the south.*" Then shall our captivity be perfectly changed, even as *the rivers* or *waters in the south,* which by the mighty work of God were dried up and utterly consumed. Whether ye understand here the Red Sea, or else the river of Jordan, it mattereth little. The similitude is this : Like as by thy mighty hand thou broughtest to pass miraculously that the waters were dried up and consumed, so dry up, O Lord, and bring to nothing all our captivity." Some do interpret this verse otherwise ; that is, Turn our captivity, O Lord, as the rivers in the south, which in the summer are dried up in the desert places by the heat of the sun, but in the winter are filled up again with plenty of water.—*Martin Luther.*

Verse 4.—"*Streams.*" The Hebrew word for " *streams*" means strictly a river's bed, the channel which holds water when water is there, but is often dry. Naturally there is joy for the husbandman when those valley-beds are filled again with flowing waters. So, the prayer is, let thy people return joyfully to their fatherland.—*Henry Cowles.*

Verse 4.—*"As the streams in the south."* Some render it, *As the mighty waters in the south.* Why would they have their captivity turned like those mighty floods in the south ? The reason is this, because the south is a dry country, where there are few springs, scarce a fountain to be found in a whole desert. What, then, are the waters they have in the south, in those parched countries ? They are these mighty strong torrents, which are caused by the showers of heaven : so the meaning of that prayer in the psalm is, that God would suddenly turn their captivity. Rivers come suddenly in the south : where no spring appears, nor any sign of a river, yet in an hour the water is up and the streams overflow. As when Elijah sent his servant toward the sea, in the time of Ahab, he went and looked, and said, "there is nothing" ; that is, no show of rain, not the least cloud to be seen ; yet presently the heavens grew black, and there was a great rain : 1 Kings xviii. 44. Thus let our captivity be turned thus speedily and suddenly, though there be no appearance of salvation, no more than there is of a fountain in the sandy desert, or of rain in the clearest of heavens, yet bring salvation for us. We use to say of things beyond our supply, Have we a spring of them ? or can we fetch them out of the clouds ? So though no ground appears whence such rivers should flow, yet let our salvation be as rivers in the south, as rivers fetched out of the clouds, and dropped in an instant immediately from the heavens.—*Joseph Caryl,* 1602—1673.

Verses 4, 5, 6.—The saints are oft feeding their hopes on the carcases of their slain fears. The time which God chose and the instrument he used to give the captive Jews their gaol delivery and liberty to return home were so incredible to them when it came to pass (like Peter whom the angel had carried out of prison, Acts xii.), it was some time before they could come to themselves and resolve whether it was a real truth, or but a pleasing dream. Now see, what effect this strange disappointment of their fears had upon their hope for afterward. It sends them to the throne of grace for the accomplishment of what was so marvellously begun. "The Lord hath done great things for us ; whereof we are glad. Turn again our captivity, O Lord " : verses 3, 4. They have got a hand-hold by this experiment of his power and mercy, and they will not now let him go till they have more ; yea, their hope is raised to such a pitch of confidence, that they draw a general conclusion from this particular experience for the comfort of themselves or others in any future distress : " They that sow in tears shall reap in joy," etc., verses 5, 6.—*William Gurnall,* 1617—1679.

Verse 5.—*" They that sow in tears."* I never saw people sowing in tears exactly, but have often known them to do it in fear and distress sufficient to draw them from any eye. In seasons of great scarcity, the poor peasants part in sorrow with every measure of precious seed cast into the ground. It is like taking bread out of the mouths of their children ; and in such times many bitter tears are actually shed over it. The distress is frequently so great that government is obliged to furnish seed, or none would be sown. Ibrahim Pasha did this more than once within my remembrance, copying the example, perhaps, of his great predecessor in Egypt when the seven years' famine was ended.

The thoughts of this psalm may likewise have been suggested by the extreme danger which frequently attends the farmer in his ploughing and sowing. The calamity which fell upon the husbandmen of Job when the oxen were ploughing, and the asses feeding beside them, and the Sabeans fell upon them and took them away, and slew the servants with the edge of the sword (Job i. 14, 15), is often repeated in our day. To understand this you must remember what I have just told you about the situation of the arable lands in the open country ; and here again we meet that verbal accuracy : the sower " *goes forth*"—that is, from the village. The people of Ibel and Khiem, in Merj' Aiyûn, for example, have their best grain-growing fields down in the 'Ard Hûleh, six or eight miles from their homes, and just that much nearer the lawless border of the desert. When the country is disturbed, or the government weak, they cannot sow these lands except at the risk of their lives. Indeed, they always *go forth* in large companies, and completely armed, ready to drop the plough and seize the musket at a moment's warning ; and yet, with all this care, many sad and fatal calamities overtake the men who must thus sow in tears. And still another origin may be found for the thoughts of the psalm in the extreme difficulty of the work itself in many places. The soil is rocky, impracticable, overgrown with sharp thorns ; and it costs much painful toil to break up and gather out the rock, cut and burn the briars, and to subdue the stubborn soil, especially with their feeble oxen and insignificant ploughs. Join all these together, and the sentiment is very forcibly brought out, that he who labors hard, in cold and rain, in fear and danger, in poverty and in want, casting his precious seed into the ground, will surely come again, at harvest-time, with rejoicing, and bearing his sheaves with him.—*W. M. Thomson.*

Verse 5.—"*They that sow in tears shall reap in joy,*" etc. This promise is conveyed under images borrowed from the instructive scenes of agriculture. In the sweat of his brow the husbandman tills his land, and casts the seed into the ground, where for a time it lies dead and buried. A dark and dreary winter succeeds, and all-seems to be lost ; but at the return of spring universal nature revives, and the once desolate fields are covered with corn which, when matured by the sun's heat, the cheerful reapers cut down, and it is brought home with triumphant shouts of joy. Here, O disciple of Jesus, behold an emblem of thy present labour and thy future reward ! Thou "sowest," perhaps, in "tears" ; thou doest thy duty amidst persecution, and affliction, sickness, pain, and sorrow ; thou labourest in the Church, and no account is made of thy labours, no profit seems likely to arise from them. Nay, thou must thyself drop into the dust of death, and all the storms of that winter must pass over thee, until thy form shall be perished, and thou shalt see corruption. Yet the day is coming when thou shalt "reap in joy," and plentiful shall be thy harvest. For thus thy blessed Master "went forth weeping," a man of sorrows and acquainted with grief, "bearing precious seed" and sowing it around him, till at length his own body was buried, like a grain of wheat, in the furrow of the grave. But he arose, and is now in heaven, from whence he shall "doubtless come again with rejoicing," with the voice of the archangel and the trump of God, "bringing his sheaves with him." Then shall every man receive the fruit of his works, and have praise of God.—*George Horne* (1730—1792), *in "A Commentary on the Psalms."*

Verse 5.—"*They that sow in tears shall reap in joy.*" They sow *in faith ;* and God will bless that seed : it shall grow up to heaven, for it is sown in the side of Jesus Christ who is in heaven. "He that believeth on God," this is the seed ; "shall have everlasting life" (John v. 24) ; this is the harvest. *Qui credit quod non videt, videbit quod credit,*—he that believes what he doth not see ; this is the seed : shall one day see what he hath believed ; this is the harvest.

They sow *in obedience :* this is also a blessed seed, that will not fail to prosper wheresoever it is cast. "If ye keep my commandments" ; this is the seed : "ye shall abide in my love" (John xv. 10) ; this is the harvest. (Rom. vi. 22), "Ye are become servants to God, and have your fruit unto holiness" ; this is the sowing : "and the end everlasting life" ; this is the reaping. *Obedientia in terris, regnabit in cœlis,*—he that serves God on earth, and sows the seed of obedience, shall in heaven reap the harvest of a kingdom.

They sow *in repentance;* and this seed must needs grow up to blessedness. . . Many saints have now reaped their crop in heaven, that sowed their seed in tears. David, Mary Magdalene, Peter ; as if they had made good the proverb, "No coming to heaven with dry eyes." Thus nature and God differ in their proceedings. To have a good crop on earth, we desire a fair seedtime ; but here a wet time of sowing shall bring the best harvest in the barn of heaven. "Blessed are they that mourn " ; this is the seeding : " for they shall be comfᵤrted " (Matt. v. 4) ; this is the harvest.

They sow *in renouncing the world*, and adherence to Christ ; and they reap a great harvest. " Behold," saith Peter to Christ, " we have forsaken all, and followed thee " (Matt. xix. 27) ; this is the seeding. " What shall we have therefore ?" What ? " You shall sit on twelve thrones, judging the twelve tribes of Israel " (verses 28, 29) ; all that you have lost shall be centupled to you : " and you shall inherit everlasting life" ; this is the harvest. " Sow to yourselves in righteousness, and reap in mercy" : Hos. x. 12.

They sow *in charity*. He that sows this seed shall be sure of a plentiful crop. " Whosoever shall give to drink to one of these little ones a cup of cold water only"—a little refreshing—" in the name of a disciple ; verily I say unto you, he shall in no wise lose his reward " : Matt. x. 42. But if he that giveth a little shall be thus recompensed, then " he that soweth bountifully shall reap bountifully " : 2 Cor. ix. 6. Therefore sparse abroad with a full hand, like a seedsman in a broad field, without fear. Doth any think he shall lose by his charity ? No worldling, when he sows his seed, thinks he shall lose his seed ; he hopes for increase at harvest. Darest thou trust the ground and not God ? Sure God is a better paymaster than the earth : grace doth give a larger recompense than nature. Below thou mayest receive forty grains for one ; but in heaven, (by the promise of Christ,) a hundred-fold : a " measure heapen, and shaken, and thrust together, and yet running over." " Blessed is he that considereth the poor " ; this is the seeding : " the Lord shall deliver him in the time of trouble" (Ps. xli. 1) ; this is the harvest.—*Thomas Adams.*

Verse 5.—"*They that sow in tears,*" etc. Observe two things here. I. That the afflictions of God's people are as sowing in tears. 1. In sowing ye know there is great pains. The land must be first tilled and dressed ; and there is pains in casting the seed into it ; and then it takes a great dressing all the year, before it be set in the barn-yard. 2. It requires great charges, too, and therefore it is called " precious seed." For ye know that seed corn is aye dearest. 3. There is also great hazard ; for corn, after it is sown, is subject to many dangers. And so it is with the children of God in a good cause. II. Then after the seed-time follows the harvest, and that comes with joy. There be three degrees of the happiness of God's children, in reaping of fruits. 1. In the first-fruits. Even when they are enduring anything for the Gospel of Christ, it carries contentment and fruit with it. 2. After the first-fruits, then come sheaves to refresh the husbandman, and to assure him that the full harvest is coming. The Lord now and then gives testimony of a full deliverance to his own people, especially of the deliverance of Sion, and lets them taste of the sheaves which they have reaped. 3. And lastly, they get the full harvest ; and that is gotten at the great and last day. Then we get peace without trouble, joy without grief, profit without loss, pleasure without pain ; and then we have a full sight of the face of God. —*Alexander Henderson.*

Verse 5.—"*They that sow in tears shall reap in joy.*" Gospel tears are not lost ; they are seeds of comfort : while the penitent doth pour out tears, God pours in joy. If thou wouldst be cheerful, saith Chrysostom, be sad. It was the end of Christ's anointing and coming into the world, that he might comfort them that mourn : Isaiah lxi, 3. Christ had the oil of gladness poured on him, as Chrysostom saith, that he might pour it on the mourner ; well then might the apostle call it " a repentance not to be repented of " : 2 Cor. vii. 10. . . . Here is sweet fruit from a bitter stock : Christ caused the earthen vessels to be filled with water, and then turned the water into wine : John ii. 9. So when the eye, that earthen vessel, hath been filled with water brim full, then Christ will turn the water of tears into the wine of joy. Holy mourning, saith St. Basil, is the seed out of which the flower of eternal joy doth grow.—*Thomas Watson* (—1690 ?), *in* "*The Beatitudes.*"

Verse 5.—"*They that sow in tears shall reap.*" We must take notice of the reapers : "*They* shall reap." Which *they ?* They that did sow : they shall, and none but they shall. They shall ; and good reason they should, because it was they that did sow. And though some that have sown in tears do complain of the lateness or thinness of the harvest, that they have not reaped in joy, as is here promised ; know that some grounds are later than others, and in some years the harvest falleth later than in others, and that God, who is the Lord of the harvest, in his good time will ripen thy joy, and thou shalt reap it : and in the meantime, if we try it narrowly, we shall find the cause in ourselves, both of the lateness of our joy, because we were too late in sowing our tears ; and of the thinness of our joy, because we did sow our tears too thin. And if after our sowing of tears we find no harvest of joy at all, we may be well assured that either our seed was not good, or else some of the mischances are come upon them, which came upon the seed that came to no good in the thirteenth of Matthew.— *Walter Balcanqual, in " a Sermon preached at St. Maries Spittle,"* 1623.

Verse 5.—*" They that sow in tears,"* etc. I saw in seedtime a husbandman at plough in a very rainy day. Asking him the reason why he would not rather leave off than labour in such foul weather, his answer was returned me in their country rhythm :—

> " Sow beans in the mud,
> And they'll come up like a wood."

This could not but remind me of David's expression, *" They that sow in tears shall reap in joy,"* etc.—*Thomas Fuller* (1608—1661), *in " Good Thoughts in Worse Times."*

Verse 5.—*"Sow in tears."* There are tears which are themselves the seed that we must sow ; tears of sorrow for sin, our own and others' ; tears of sympathy with the afflicted church ; and tears of tenderness in prayer and under the word. —*Matthew Henry.*

Verse 5.—*"Shall reap in joy."* This spiritual harvest comes not alike soon to all, no more than the other which is outward doth. But here's the comfort, whoever hath a seed-time of grace pass over his soul shall have his harvest-time also of joy : this law God hath bound himself to as strongly as to the other, which " is not to cease while the earth remaineth " (Gen. viii. 22) ; yea, more strongly ; for that was to the world in general, not to every country, town, or field in particular, for some of these may want a harvest, and yet God may keep his word : but God cannot perform his promise if any one particular saint should everlastingly go without his reaping time. And therefore you who think so basely of the gospel and the professors of it, because at present their peace and comfort are not come, should know that it is on the way to them, and comes to stay everlastingly with them ; whereas your peace is going from you every moment, and is sure to leave you without any hope of returning to you again. Look not how the Christian begins, but ends. The Spirit of God by his convictions comes into the soul with some terrors, but it closeth with peace and joy. As we say of the month of March, it enters like a lion, but goes out like a lamb. " Mark the perfect man, and behold the upright : for the end of that man is peace" : Psalm xxxvii. 37.—*William Gurnall.*

Verses 5, 6.—In my little reading and small experience, I have found that corn sown in dear years and times of scarcity hath yielded much more increase than at other times ; so that presently after much want, there hath followed great plenty of grain, even beyond expectation.—*Humphrey Hardwick, in a Sermon entitled "The Difficulty of Sion's Deliverance and Reformation,"* 1644.

Verses 5, 6.—Mind we the undoubted certainty of our harvest verified by divers absolute positive asseverations in the text : " *he shall reap* " ; " *he shall come again*" ; " *he shall bring his sheaves with him.*" Here's no item of contingency or possibility, but all absolute affirmations ; and you know heaven and earth shall pass away, but a jot of God's word shall not fail. Nothing shall prevent the harvest of a labourer in Sion's vineyard.—*Humphrey Hardwick.*

Verses 5, 6.—In a fuller, deeper sense, the sower in tears is the Man of sorrows himself. Believers know him thus. He has accomplished, in the sore travail of his soul, the seed time of affliction which is to bear its satisfying harvest when he shall again appear as the reaper of his own reward. He will fill his bosom with sheaves in that day of joy. The garner of his gladness will be filled to overflowing. By how much his affliction surpassed the natural measure of human grief, when he underwent for our sakes the dread realities of death and judgment; by so much shall the fulness of his pure delight as the eternal blesser of his people excel their joy (yet what a measure, too, is there!) whose sum of blessedness is to be for ever with the Lord.—*Arthur Pridham, in "Notes and Reflections on the Psalms,"* 1869.

Verse 6.—" *He that goeth forth and weepeth, bearing precious seed,*" etc. This is very expressive of a gospel minister's life; he goeth forth with the everlasting gospel which he preaches; he sows it as precious seed in the church of God; he waters it with tears and prayers; the Lord's blessing accompanies it; the Lord crowns his labours with success; he has seals to his ministry; and at the last day he shall doubtless come again with joy from the 'grave of death "*bringing his sheaves with him*"; and will, in the new Jerusalem state, be addressed by his Lord with, "Well done, good and faithful servant, enter thou into the joy of thy Lord."—*Samuel Eyles Pierce (1746—1829 ?), in "The Book of Psalms, an Epitome of the Old Testament Scripture."*

Verse 6.—"*He may go forth, he may go forth, and weep, bearing (his) load of seed. He shall come, he shall come with singing, bearing sheaves.*" The emphatic combination of the finite tense with the infinitive is altogether foreign from our idiom, and very imperfectly represented, in the ancient and some modern versions, by the active participle (*venientes venient*, coming they shall come), which conveys neither the peculiar form nor the precise sense of the Hebrew phrase. The best approximation to the force of the original is Luther's repetition of the finite tense, *he shall come, he shall come*, because in all such cases the infinitive is really defined or determined by the term which follows, and in sense, though not in form, assimilated to it.—*Joseph Addison Alexander.*

Verse 6.—

"Though he go, though he go, and be weeping,
    While bearing some handfuls of seed;
He shall come, he shall come with bright singing,
    While bearing his plentiful sheaves."

Ben-Tehillim, in "The Book of Psalms, in English Blank Verse," 1883.

Verse 6.—"*Goeth forth.*" The church must not only keep this seed in the store-house, for such as come to enquire for it; but must send her sowers forth to cast it among those who are ignorant of its value, or too indifferent to ask it at her hands. She must not sit weeping because men will not apply to her, but must go forth and bear the precious seed to the unwilling, the careless, the prejudiced, and the profligate.—*Edwin Sidney, in "The Pulpit,"* 1840.

Verse 6.—*Weeping* must not hinder sowing: when we suffer ill we must be doing well.—*Matthew Henry.*

Verse 6.—"*Precious seed.*" Seed-corn is always dearest; and when other corn is dear, then it is very dear; yet though never so dear, the husbandman resolves that he must have it; and he will deprive his own belly, and his wife and children of it, and will sow it, going out "*weeping*" with it. There is also great hazard; for corn, after it is sown, is subject to many dangers. And so is it, indeed, with the children of God in a good cause. Ye must resolve to undergo hazards also, in life, lands, moveables, or whatsoever else ye have in this world: rather hazard all these before either religion be in hazard, or your own souls.—*Alexander Henderson.*

Verse 6.—"*Precious seed.*" Aben Ezra, by the words rendered *precious seed*, or, as they may be, *a draught of seed*, understands the vessel in which the sower carries his seed, the seed basket, from whence he draws and takes out the seed, and scatters it; see Amos ix. 13: so the Targum, "bearing a tray of sowing corn."—*John Gill.*

Verse 6.—"*Precious seed.*" Faith is called "*precious seed*": *quod rarum est charum est.* Seed was accounted precious when all countries came unto Egypt to buy corn of Joseph, and truly faith must needs be precious, seeing that when Christ comes he shall hardly " find faith upon the earth" : Luke xviii. 8. The necessity of faith is such, that therefore it must need be precious ; for as the material seed is the only instrumental means to preserve the life of man ; for all the spices, honey, myrrh, nuts, and almonds, gold and silver, that were in Canaan, were not sufficient for Jacob and his children's sustenance ; but they were forced to repair unto Egypt for corn, that they might live and not die ; even so, without faith the soul is starved ; it is the food of it ; for, " the just man liveth by his faith" : Gal. iii. 11.—*John Hume.*

Verse 6.—"*Sheaves.*" The psalm which begins with " dream" and ends with " sheaves" invites us to think of Joseph ; Joseph, " in whom," according to S. Ambrose's beautiful application, " there was revealed the future resurrection of the Lord Jesus, to whom both his eleven disciples did obeisance when they saw him gone into Galilee, and to whom all the saints shall on their resurrection do obeisance, bringing forth the fruit of good works, as it is written, ' He shall doubtless come again with rejoicing, bringing his sheaves with him.' "—*H. T. Armfield.*

HINTS TO THE VILLAGE PREACHER.

Verse 1.—I. Sunny memories of what the Lord did, " he turned again the captivity," etc. II. Singular impressions,—we could not believe it to be true. III. Special discoveries—it was true, abiding, etc.

Verse 1.—A comparison and a contrast. I. The saved like them that dream. 1. In the strangeness of their experience. 2. In the ecstasy of their joy. II. The saved unlike them that dream. 1. In the reality of their experience. Dreams are unsubstantial things, but " the Lord turned "—an actual fact. 2. In their freedom from disappointment. No awakening to find it " but a dream" : see Isaiah xxix. 8. 3. In the endurance of their joy. The joy of dreams is soon forgotten, but this is " everlasting joy."—*W. H. J. P.*

Verse 2.—Saintly laughter. What creates it, and how it is justified.

Verse 2.—*Recipe for holy laughter.*—1. Lie in prison a few weeks. 2. Hear the Lord turning the key. 3. Follow him into the high-road. 4. Your sky will burst with sunshine, and your heart with song and laughter. 5. If this recipe is thought too expensive, try *keeping in the high-road.*—*W. B. H.*

Verses 2, 3.—I. Reports of God's doings. II. Experience of God's doings.

Verses 2, 3.—I. The Lord does great things for his people. II. These great things command the attention of the world. III. They inspire the joyful devotion of the saints.—*W. H. J. P.*

Verse 3.—" *The* LORD *hath done great things for us.*" In this acknowledgment and confession there are three noteworthy points of thankfulness. I. That they were " *great things*" which were done. II. Who it was who did them : " *the Lord.*" III. That they are done, not *against* us, but " *for* us."—*Alexander Henderson,* 1583—1646.

Verse 4.—Believers, rejoicing in their own deliverance, solicitous for a flood of prosperity to overflow the church. See the connection, verses 1—3. Remark, I. The doubting and despondent are too concerned about themselves, and too busy seeking comfort, to have either solicitude or energy to spare for the church's welfare ; but the joyful heart is free to be earnest for the church's good. II. Joyful believers, other things being equal, know more of the constraining power of Christ's love, which makes them anxious for his glory and the success of his cause. III. The joyful can appreciate more fully the contrast of their condition to that of the undelivered, and for their sake cannot fail to be anxious for the church through whose ministry their deliverance comes. IV. The joyful are, in general, the most believing and the most hopeful ; their expectation of success leads them to prayer, and impels them to effort.—*J. F.*

Verse 4.—I. The dried-up Christian. II. His unhappy condition. III. His one hope. IV. Result when realized.

Verse 5.—*The Christian Husbandman.* I. Illustrate the metaphor. The husbandman has a great variety of work before him ; every season and every day brings its proper business. So the Christian has duties in the closet, in the family, in the church, in the world, etc., etc. II. Whence it is that many Christians sow in tears. 1. It may be owing to the badness of the soil. 2. The inclemency of the season. 3. The malice and opposition of enemies. 4. Past disappointments. III. What connection there is between sowing in tears and reaping in joy. 1. A joyful harvest, by God's blessing, is the natural consequence of a dripping seed-time. 2. God, who cannot lie, hath promised it. IV. When this joyful harvest may be expected. It must not be expected in our wintry world, for there is not sun enough to ripen it. Heaven is the Christian's summer. When you come to reap the fruits of your present trials, you will bless God, who made you sow in tears. *Improvement.* 1. How greatly are they to blame who in this busy time stand all the day idle ! 2. How greatly have Christians the advantage of the rest of the world ! 3. Let the hope and prospect of this joyful harvest support us under all the glooms and distresses of this vale of tears.—*Outline of a Sermon by Samuel Lavington,* 1726—1807.

Verse 5.—Two pictures. The connecting " *shall.*"

Verse 5.—I. There must be sowing before reaping. II. What men sow they will reap. If they sow precious seed, they will reap precious seed. III. In proportion as they sow they will reap. " He that soweth sparingly," etc. IV. The sowing may be with sorrow, but the reaping will be with joy. V. In proportion to the sorrow of sowing will be the joy of reaping.—*G. R.*

Verse 6.—In the two parts of this verse we may behold a threefold antithesis or opposition ; in the *progress,* 1. A sojourning : " He that now goeth on his way." 2. A sorrowing : " weeping." 3. A sowing : " and beareth forth good seed." In the *regress* there are three opposites unto these. 1. Returning : " He shall doubtless come again." 2. A Rejoicing : " with joy." 3. A Reaping : " and bring his sheaves with him."—*John Hume.*

Verse 6.—"*Doubtless.*" Or the reasons why our labour cannot be in vain in the Lord.

Verse 6.—"*Bringing his sheaves with him.*" The faithful sower's return to his Lord. Successful, knowing it, personally honoured, abundantly recompensed.

Verse 6.—See " Spurgeon's Sermon," No. 867 : " Tearful Sowing and Joyful Reaping."

Verse 6.—I. The sorrowful sower. 1. His activity—"'he goeth forth." 2. His humility—" and weepeth." 3. His fidelity—" bearing precious seed." II. The joyful reaper. 1. His certain harvest-time—" shall doubtless come again." 2. His abundant joy—" with rejoicing." 3. His rich rewards—" bringing his sheaves with him."—*W. H. J. P.*

WORK UPON THE HUNDRED AND TWENTY-SIXTH PSALM.

THE JEWES DELIVERANCE Out of Babylon, and the MSYTERY OF OUR Redemption : *Plainely demonstrated in ten Sermons* upon the 126. Psalme. . . . . Preached in Yorkshire, By IOHN HVME, *Minister of the Word.* . . . . London. . . . . 1628 [4to].

PSALM CXXVII.

TITLE.—**A Song of Degrees for Solomon.** *It was meet that the builder of the holy house should be remembered by the pilgrims to its sacred shrine. The title probably indicates that David wrote it for his wise son, in whom he so greatly rejoiced, and whose name Jedidiah, or "beloved of the Lord," is introduced into the second verse. The spirit of his name, "Solomon, or peaceable," breathes through the whole of this most charming song. If Solomon himself was the author, it comes fitly from him who reared the house of the Lord. Observe how in each of these songs the heart is fixed upon Jehovah only. Read the first verses of these Psalms, from Psalm cxx. to the present song, and they run thus : " I cried unto the Lord," " I will lift up mine eyes to the hills," " Let us go unto the house of the Lord," " Unto thee will I lift up mine eyes," " If it had not been the Lord," "They that trust in the Lord," " When the Lord turned again the captivity." The Lord and the Lord alone is thus lauded at each step of these songs of the ascents. O for a life whose every halting-place shall suggest a new song unto the Lord !*

SUBJECT.—*God's blessing on his people as their one great necessity and privilege is here spoken of. We are here taught that builders of houses and cities, systems and fortunes, empires and churches all labour in vain without the Lord; but under the divine favour they enjoy perfect rest. Sons, who are in the Hebrew called "builders," are set forth as building up families under the same divine blessing, to the great honour and happiness of their parents. It is* THE BUILDER'S PSALM. *" Every house is builded by some man, but he that built all things is God," and unto God be praise.*

EXPOSITION.

EXCEPT the LORD build the house, they labour in vain that build it : except the LORD keep the city, the watchman waketh *but* in vain.

2 *It is* vain for you to rise up early, to sit up late, to eat the bread of sorrows : *for* so he giveth his beloved sleep.

3 Lo, the children *are* an heritage of the LORD : *and* the fruit of the womb *is his* reward.

4 As arrows *are* in the hand of a mighty man ; so *are* children of the youth.

5 Happy *is* the man that hath his quiver full of them : they shall not be ashamed, but they shall speak with the enemies in the gate.

1. "*Except the* LORD *build the house, they labour in vain that build it.*" The word *vain* is the key-note here, and we hear it ring out clearly three times. Men desiring to build know that they must labour, and accordingly they put forth all their skill and strength ; but let them remember that if Jehovah is not with them their designs will prove failures. So was it with the Babel builders ; they said, " Go to, let us build us a city and a tower" ; and the Lord returned their words into their own bosoms, saying, " Go to, let us go down and there confound their language." In vain they toiled, for the Lord's face was against them. When Solomon resolved to build a house for the Lord, matters were very different, for all things united under God to aid him in his great undertaking : even the heathen were at his beck and call that he might erect a temple for the Lord his God. In the same manner God blessed him in the erection of his own palace ; for this verse evidently refers to all sorts of house-building. Without God we are nothing. Great houses have been erected by ambitious men ; but like the base-

less fabric of a vision they have passed away, and scarce a stone remains to tell where once they stood. The wealthy builder of a Non-such Palace, could he revisit the glimpses of the moon, would be perplexed to find a relic of his former pride : he laboured in vain, for the place of his travail knows not a trace of his handiwork. The like may be said of the builders of castles and abbeys : when the mode of life indicated by these piles ceased to be endurable by the Lord, the massive walls of ancient architects crumbled into ruins, and their toil melted like the froth of vanity. Not only do we now spend our strength for nought without Jehovah, but all who have ever laboured apart from him come under the same sentence. Trowel and hammer, saw and plane are instruments of vanity unless the Lord be the Master-builder.

"*Except the* LORD *keep the city, the watchman waketh but in vain.*" Around the wall the sentinels pace with constant step ; but yet the city is betrayed unless the unsleeping Watcher is with them. We are not safe because of watchmen if Jehovah refuses to watch over us. Even if the guards are wakeful, and do their duty, still the place may be surprised if God be not there. " I, the Lord, do keep it," is better than an army of sleepless guards. Note that the Psalmist does not bid the builder cease from labouring, nor suggest that watchmen should neglect their duty, nor that men should show their trust in God by doing nothing : nay, he supposes that they will do all that they can do, and then he forbids their fixing their trust in what they have done, and assures them that all creature effort will be in vain unless the Creator puts forth his power, to render second causes effectual. Holy Scripture indorses the order of Cromwell—" Trust in God, and keep your powder dry" : only here the sense is varied, and we are told that the dried powder will not win the victory unless we trust in God. Happy is the man who hits the golden mean by so working as to believe in God, and so believing in God as to work without fear.

In Scriptural phrase a dispensation or system is called a house. Moses was faithful as a servant over all his house ; and as long as the Lord was with that house it stood and prospered ; but when he left it, the builders of it became foolish and their labour was lost. They sought to maintain the walls of Judaism, but sought in vain : they watched around every ceremony and tradition, but their care was idle. Of every church, and every system of religious thought, this is equally true : unless the Lord is in it, and is honoured by it, the whole structure must sooner or later fall in hopeless ruin. Much can be done by man ; he can both labour and watch ; but without the Lord he has accomplished nothing, and his wakefulness has not warded off evil.

2. "*It is vain for you to rise up early, to sit up late, to eat the bread of sorrows.*" Because the Lord is mainly to be rested in, all carking care is mere vanity and vexation of spirit. We are bound to be diligent, for this the Lord blesses ; we ought not to be anxious, for that dishonours the Lord, and can never secure his favour. Some deny themselves needful rest ; the morning sees them rise before they are rested, the evening sees them toiling long after the curfew has tolled the knell of parting day. They threaten to bring themselves into the sleep of death by neglect of the sleep which refreshes life. Nor is their sleeplessness the only index of their daily fret ; they stint themselves in their meals, they eat the commonest food, and the smallest possible quantity of it, and what they do swallow is washed down with the salt tears of grief, for they fear that daily bread will fail them. Hard earned is their food, scantily rationed, and scarcely ever sweetened, but perpetually smeared with sorrow ; and all because they have no faith in God, and find no joy except in hoarding up the gold which is their only trust. Not thus, not thus, would the Lord have his children live. He would have them, as princes of the blood, lead a happy and restful life. Let them take a fair measure of rest and a due portion of food, for it is for their health. Of course the true believer will never be lazy or extravagant ; if he should be he will have to suffer for it ; but he will not think it needful or right to be worried and miserly. Faith brings calm with it, and banishes the disturbers who both by day and by night murder peace.

"*For so he giveth his beloved sleep.*" Through faith the Lord makes his chosen ones to rest in him in happy freedom from care. The text may mean that God gives blessings to his beloved in sleep, even as he gave Solomon the desire of his heart while he slept. The meaning is much the same : those whom the Lord loves are delivered from the fret and fume of life, and take a sweet repose upon the bosom of their Lord. He rests them ; blesses them while resting ; blesses them more in resting than others in their moiling and toiling. God is sure to give the best thing to his beloved, and we here see that he gives them sleep—that is a laying aside of care, a forgetfulness of need, a quiet leaving of matters with God : this kind of sleep is better than riches and honour. Note how Jesus slept amid the hurly-burly of a storm at sea. He knew that he was in his Father's hands, and therefore he was so quiet in spirit that the billows rocked him to sleep : it would be much oftener the same with us if we were more like HIM.

It is to be hoped that those who built Solomon's temple were allowed to work at it steadily and joyfully. Surely such a house was not built by unwilling labourers. One would hope that the workmen were not called upon to hurry up in the morning nor to protract their labours far into the night ; but we would fain believe that they went on steadily, resting duly, and eating their bread with joy. So, at least, should the spiritual temple be erected ; though, truth to tell, the workers upon its walls are all too apt to grow cumbered with much serving, all too ready to forget their Lord, and to dream that the building is to be done by themselves alone. How much happier might we be if we would but trust the Lord's house to the Lord of the house ! What is far more important, how much better would our building and watching be done if we would but confide in the Lord who both builds and keeps his own church !

3. "*Lo, children are an heritage of the* LORD." This points to another mode of building up a house, namely, by leaving descendants to keep our name and family alive upon the earth. Without this what is a man's purpose in accumulating wealth ! To what purpose does he build a house if he has none in his household to hold the house after him ? What boots it that he is the possessor of broad acres if he has no heir ? Yet in this matter a man is powerless without the Lord. The great Napoleon, with all his sinful care on this point, could not create a dynasty. Hundreds of wealthy persons would give half their estates if they could hear the cry of a babe born of their own bodies. Children are a heritage which Jehovah himself must give, or a man will die childless, and thus his house will be unbuilt.

"*And the fruit of the womb is his reward,*" or a reward from God. He gives children, not as a penalty nor as a burden, but as a favour. They are a token for good if men know how to receive them, and educate them. They are " doubtful blessings" only because we are doubtful persons. Where society is rightly ordered children are regarded, not as an incumbrance, but as an inheritance ; and they are received, not with regret, but as a reward. If we are over-crowded in England, and so seem to be embarrassed with too large an increase, we must remember that the Lord does not order us to remain in this narrow island, but would have us fill those boundless regions which wait for the axe and the plough. Yet even here, with all the straits of limited incomes, our best possessions are our own dear offspring, for whom we bless God every day.

4. "*As arrows are in the hand of a mighty man ; so are children of the youth.*" Children born to men in their early days, by God's blessing become the comfort of their riper years. A man of war is glad of weapons which may fly where he cannot : good sons are their father's arrows speeding to hit the mark which their sires aim at. What wonders a good man can accomplish if he has affectionate children to second his desires, and lend themselves to his designs ! To this end we must have our children in hand while they are yet children, or they are never likely to be so when they are grown up ; and we must try to point them and straighten them, so as to make arrows of them in their youth, lest they should prove crooked and unserviceable in after life. Let the Lord favour us with loyal, obedient, affectionate offspring, and we shall find in them our best helpers. We

shall see them shot forth into life to our comfort and delight, if we take care from the very beginning that they are directed to the right point.

5. *"Happy is the man that hath his quiver full of them."* Those who have no children bewail the fact ; those who have few children see them soon gone, and the house is silent, and their life has lost a charm ; those who have many gracious children are upon the whole the happiest. Of course a large number of children means a large number of trials ; but when these are met by faith in the Lord it also means a mass of love, and a multitude of joys. The writer of this comment gives it as his own observation, that he has seen the most frequent unhappiness in marriages which are unfruitful ; that he has himself been most grateful for two of the best of sons ; but as they have both grown up, and he has no child at home, he has without a tinge of murmuring, or even wishing that he were otherwise circumstanced, felt that it might have been a blessing to have had a more numerous family : he therefore heartily agrees with the Psalmist's verdict herein expressed. He has known a family in which there were some twelve daughters and three sons, and he never expects to witness upon earth greater domestic felicity than fell to the lot of their parents, who rejoiced in all their children, as the children also rejoiced in their parents and in one another. When sons and daughters are arrows, it is well to have a quiver full of them ; but if they are only sticks, knotty and useless, the fewer of them the better. While those are blessed whose quiver is full, there is no reason to doubt that many are blessed who have no quiver at all ; for a quiet life may not need such a warlike weapon. Moreover, a quiver may be small and yet full ; and then the blessing is obtained. In any case we may be sure that a man's life consisteth not in the abundance of children that he possesseth.

"They shall not be ashamed, but they shall speak with the enemies in the gate." They can meet foes both in law and in fight. Nobody cares to meddle with a man who can gather a clan of brave sons about him. He speaks to purpose whose own sons make his words emphatic by the resolve to carry out their father's wishes. This is the blessing of Abraham, the old covenant benediction, " Thy seed shall possess the gate of his enemies" ; and it is sure to all the beloved of the Lord in some sense or other. Doth not the Lord Jesus thus triumph in his seed ? Looked at literally, this favour cometh of the Lord : without his will there would be no children to build up the house, and without his grace there would be no good children to be their parent's strength. If this must be left with the Lord, let us leave every other thing in the same hands. He will undertake for us and prosper our trustful endeavours, and we shall enjoy a tranquil life, and prove ourselves to be our Lord's beloved by the calm and quiet of our spirit. We need not doubt that if God gives us children as a reward he will also send us the food and raiment which he knows they need.

He who is the father of a host of spiritual children is unquestionably happy. He can answer all opponents by pointing to souls who have been saved by his means. Converts are emphatically the heritage of the Lord, and the reward of the preacher's soul travail. By these, under the power of the Holy Ghost, the city of the church is both built up and watched, and the Lord has the glory of it.

EXPLANATORY NOTES.

Title.—*"A Song of Degrees for Solomon."* This psalm has Solomon's name prefixed to the title, for the purpose that the very builder of the Temple may teach us that he availed nothing to build it without the help of the Lord.—*The Venerable Bede* (672–3—735), *in Neale and Littledale.*

Whole Psalm.—Viewed as one of the " Degrees" in Christian virtue, the ninth, the psalm is directed against self-reliance.—*H. T. Armfield.*

Whole Psalm.—The steps or degrees in this psalm, though distinctly marked, are not so regular as in some others.

The twice repeated " *in vain*" of verse 1 may be regarded as the motto or " degree" for verse 2. The correspondence between the two clauses in verse 1 is also very striking. It is as if, on entering on some spiritual undertaking, or even in referring to the present state of matters, the Psalmist emphatically disclaimed as *vain* every other interposition or help than that of Jehovah. And of this " *in vain*" it is well constantly to remind ourselves, especially in seasons of activity and in times of peace ; for then we are most liable to fall into the snare of this *vanity.*

The next " degree" is that of success and prosperity (verses 3, 4), which is ascribed to the same Jehovah whose help and protection constituted the commencement and continuance, as now the completion of our well-being. Hence also verse 5 goes not beyond this, but contemplates the highest symbol of full security, influence, and power, in the figurative language of the Old Testament, which St. Augustine refers to " spiritual children, shot forth like arrows into all the world."—*Alfred Edersheim, in " The Golden Diary of Heart Converse with Jesus in the Book of Psalms,"* 1877.

Whole Psalm.—Solomon, the wisest and richest of kings, after having proved, both from experience and careful observation, that there was nothing but vanity in the life and labours of man, comes to this conclusion, that there is nothing better for a man in this life than that he should moderate his cares and labours, enjoy what he has, and fear God and keep his commandments : to this end he directs all that is debated in the Book of Ecclesiastes. Very similar are the argument and intention of the Psalm ; the authorship of which is ascribed to Solomon in the Inscription, and which there is no reason to doubt. Nor would it be safe, either to call in doubt any inscription without an urgent reason, or to give any other sense to the letter ל than that of *authorship,* unless it be meant that all the inscriptions are uncertain. Again, if the collectors of the psalms added *titles* according to their own opinion and judgment, there would be no reason why they should have left so many psalms without any title. This psalm, therefore, is *Solomon's,* with whose genius and condition it well agrees, as is clear from *Ecclesiastes,* with which it may be compared, and from many *proverbs* on the same subject. . . . The design is, to draw men away from excessive labours and anxious cares ; and to excite godliness and faith in Jehovah. To this the psalm manifestly tends : for since men, desirous of the happiness and stability of their houses, are unable to secure this by their own endeavours, but need the blessing of God, who gives prosperity with even lighter labours to those that fear him ; it is their duty to put a limit to their labours and cares, and to seek the favour of God, by conforming their life and conduct to his will, and confiding in him.—*Herman Venema,* 1697—1787.

Verse 1.—"*Except the* LORD *build.*" It is a fact that בן, *ben, a son,* and בת, *bath, a daughter,* and בית, *beith, a house,* come from the same root, בנה, *banah, to build ;* because sons and daughters build up a household, or constitute a *family,* as much and as really as stones and timber constitute a *building.* Now it is true that unless the good hand of God be upon us we cannot prosperously build a place of worship for his name. Unless we have his blessing, a dwelling-house cannot be comfortably erected. And if his blessing be not on our children, the house (the family) may be built up ; but instead of its being the house of God, it will be the synagogue of Satan. All marriages that are not under God's blessing will be a private and public curse.—*Adam Clarke.*

Verse 1.—"*Except the* LORD *build the house,*" etc. He does not say, Unless the Lord consents and is willing that the house should be built and the city kept : but, " Unless the Lord *build ;* unless he *keep.*" Hence, in order that the building and keeping may be prosperous and successful, there is necessary, not only the consent of God, but also his working is required : and that working without which nothing can be accomplished, that may be attempted by man. He does not say, Unless the Lord help ; but unless the Lord build, unless he keep ; *i.e.*, Unless he do all himself. He does not say, To little purpose he labours and watches ; but to no purpose he labours, both the builder and the keeper. Therefore, all the efficacy of labours and cares is dependent on the operation and providence of God ; and all human strength, care, and industry is in itself vain.

It should be noticed, that he does not say, Because the Lord builds the house he labours in vain who builds it, and, because the Lord keeps the city the watchman waketh in vain : but, If the Lord do not build the house, if he do not keep the city ; he labours in vain who builds the house ; he waketh in vain who keeps the city. He is far from thinking that the care and human labour, which is employed in the building of houses and keeping of cities, is to be regarded as useless, because the Lord builds and keeps ; since it is then the more especially useful and effectual when the Lord himself is the builder and keeper. The Holy Spirit is not the patron of lazy and inert men ; but he directs the minds of those who labour to the providence and power of God.— *Wolfgang Musculus*, 1497—1563.

Verse 1.—"*Except the* LORD *build the house.*" On the lintel of the door in many an old English house, we may still read the words, *Nisi Dominus frustra*—the Latin version of the opening words of the psalm. Let us also trust in him, and inscribe these words over the portal of " the house of our pilgrimage" ; and beyond a doubt all *will* be well with us, both in this world and in that which is to come.—*Samuel Cox, in "The Pilgrim Psalms,"* 1874.

Verse 1.—"*Except the* LORD *build the house,*" etc. In the beginning of the contest with Britain, when we were sensible of danger, we had daily prayers in this room for the Divine protection. Our prayers, sir, were heard, and they were graciously answered. All of us who were engaged in the struggle must have observed frequent instances of a superintending Providence in our favour. To that kind Providence we owe this happy opportunity of consulting in peace on the means of establishing our future national felicity. And have we now forgotten this powerful Friend ? or do we imagine we no longer need his assistance ? I have lived for a long time [81 years] ; and the longer I live the more convincing proofs I see of this truth, that God governs in the affairs of man. And if a sparrow cannot fall to the ground without his notice, is it probable that an empire can rise without his aid ? We have been assured, sir, in the sacred writings, that " Except the LORD build the house, they labour in vain that build it." I firmly believe this ; and I also believe that without his concurring aid we shall proceed in this political building no better than the builders of Babel : we shall be divided by our little, partial, local interests ; our prospects will be confounded ; and we ourselves shall become a reproach and a by-word down to future ages. And what is worse, mankind may hereafter, from this unfortunate instance, despair of establishing government by human wisdom, and leave it to chance, war, or conquest. I therefore beg leave to move that henceforth prayers, imploring the assistance of Heaven and its blessing on our deliberations, be held in this assembly every morning before we proceed to business ; and that one or more of the clergy of this city be requested to officiate in that service.—*Benjamin Franklin : Speech in Convention for forming a Constitution for the United States,* 1787.

Verse 1.—Note, how he puts first the building of the house, and then subjoins the keeping of the city. He advances from the part to the whole ; for the city consists of houses.— *Wolfgang Musculus.*

Verse 1.—"*Except the* LORD *keep the city,*" etc. Fires may break out in spite of the watchmen ; a tempest may sweep over it ; bands of armed men may assail it ; or the pestilence may suddenly come into it, and spread desolation through its dwellings.—*Albert Barnes* (1798—1870), *in "Notes on the Psalms."*

Verse 1.—One important lesson which Madame Guyon learned from her temptations and follies was that of her entire dependence on Divine grace. " I became," she says, " deeply assured of what the prophet hath said, ' *Except the* LORD *keep the city, the watchman waketh but in vain.*' When I looked to thee, O my Lord ! thou wast my faithful keeper ; thou didst continually defend my heart against all kinds of enemies. But, alas ! when left to myself, I was all weakness. How easily did my enemies prevail over me ! Let others ascribe their victories to their own fidelity : as for myself, I shall never attribute them to anything else than thy paternal care. I have too often experienced, to my cost, what I should be without thee, to presume in the least on any wisdom or efforts of my own. It is to thee, O God, my Deliverer, that I owe everything ! And it is a source of infinite satisfaction, that I am thus indebted to thee."—*From the Life of Jeanne Bouvier de la Mothe Guyon,* 1648—1717.

Verse 1.—

> If God build not the house, and lay
>   The groundwork sure—whoever build,
> It cannot stand one stormy day.
>   If God be not the city's shield,
> If he be not their bars and wall,
> In vain is watch-tower, men, and all.
>
> Though then thou wak'st when others rest,
>   Though rising thou prevent'st the sun,
> Though with lean care thou daily feast,
>   Thy labour's lost, and thou undone;
> But God his child will feed and keep,
> And draw the curtains to his sleep.

> —*Phineas Fletcher,* 1584—1650.

Verse 2.—"*It is vain for you to rise up early, to sit up late,*" etc. The Psalmist is exhorting to give over undue and anxious labour to accomplish our designs. The phrases in the Hebrew are " making early to rise" and " making late to sit" —not " up," but *down.* This means an artificial lengthening of the day. The law of work is in our nature. The limitations of effort are set forth in nature. In order that all may be accomplished by the human race which is necessary to be done for human progress, all men must work. But no man should work beyond his physical and intellectual ability, nor beyond the hours which nature allots. No net result of good to the individual or to the race comes of any artificial prolonging of the day at either end. Early rising, eating one's breakfast by candlelight, and prolonged vigils, the scholar's " midnight oil," are a delusion and a snare. Work while it is day. When the night comes, rest. The other animals do this, and, as races, fare as well as this anxious human race.

"*The bread of sorrows*" means the bread of toil, of wearisome effort. Do what you ought to do, and the Lord will take care of that which you cannot do. Compare Prov. x. 22 : " The blessing of the Lord, it maketh rich, and he addeth no sorrow with it," which means, " The blessing of Jehovah maketh rich, and toil can add nothing thereto." Compare also Matt. vi. 25 : " Take no thought [be not anxious] for your life," etc.

"*For so he giveth his beloved sleep.*" The "*for*" is not in the original. "*So*" means " with just the same result" or " all the same," or " without more trouble." That is the signification of the Hebrew word as it occurs. "*His beloved*" may work and sleep ; and what is needed will be provided just as certainly as if they laboured unduly, with anxiety. It has been suggested that the translation should be " *in sleep.*" While they are sleeping, the Heavenly Father is carrying forward his work for them. Or, while they wake and work, the Lord giveth to them, and so he does when they rest and sleep.—*Charles F. Deems, in* "*The Study,*" 1879.

Verse 2.—The Lord's Temple was built without any looking unto or dependence on man ; all human wisdom and confidence was rejected on the whole ; the plan was given by the Lord God himself ; the model of it was in Solomon's possession ; nothing was left to the wit or wisdom of men ; there was no reason to rise up early, to sit up late, to eat the bread of sorrows, whilst engaged in this good work ; no, I should conceive it was a season of grace to such as were employed in the building ; somewhat like what it was with you and me when engaged in God's holy ordinances. I should conceive the minds of the workmen at perfect peace, their conversation together much on the grand subject of the Temple, and its intention as referring to the glorious Messiah, its grand and glorious antitype.

I should conceive their minds were wholly disencumbered from all carking cares. They did not rise early without being refreshed in body and mind ; they did not sit up late as though they wanted ; they were not careful how they should provide for their families ; they were, as the beloved of the Lord, perfectly contented ; they enjoyed sweet sleep and refreshment by it, this was from the Lord ; he giveth his beloved ones sleep.—*Samuel Eyles Pierce.*

Verse 2.—"*It is vain,*" etc. Some take this place in a more particular and restrained sense ; as if David would intimate that all their agitations to oppose the reign of Solomon, though backed with much care and industry, should be fruitless ; though Absalom and Adonijah were tortured with the care of their own ambitious designs, yet God would give Jedidiah, or his beloved, rest ; that is, the kingdom should safely be devolved upon Solomon, who took no such pains to court the people, and to raise himself up into their esteem as Absalom and Adonijah did. The meaning is, that though worldly men fare never so hardly, beat their brains, tire their spirits, rack their consciences, yet many times all is for nothing ; either God doth not give them an estate, or not the comfort of it. But his beloved, without any of these racking cares, enjoy contentment ; if they have not the world, they have sleep and rest ; with silence submitting to the will of God, and with quietness waiting for the blessing of God. Well, then, acknowledge the providence that you may come under the blessing of it : labour *without God* cannot prosper ; *against God* and against his will in his word, will surely miscarry.—*Thomas Manton,* 1620—1677.

Verse 2.—"*It is vain for you to rise up early, to sit up late, to eat the bread of sorrows : for so he giveth his beloved sleep.*" No prayer without work, no work without prayer.—

> By caring and fretting,
> By agony and fear,
> There is of God no getting,
> But prayer he will hear.

—From J. P. Lange's Commentary on James, 1862.

Verse 2.—"*Eat the bread of sorrows.*" Living a life of misery and labours, fretting at their own disappointments, eaten up with envy at the advancement of others, afflicted overmuch with losses and wrongs. There is no end of all their labours. Some have died of it, others been distracted and put out of their wits ; so that you are never like to see good days as long as you cherish the love of the world, but will still lie under self-tormenting care and trouble of mind, by which a man grateth on his own flesh.—*Thomas Manton.*

Verse 2.—"*So he giveth his beloved sleep.*" כֵּן יִתֵּן לִידִידוֹ שֵׁנָה. These latter words are variously rendered, and sufficiently obscurely, because all take this כֵּן as a particle of comparison, which does not seem to be in place here : some even omit it altogether. But כֵּן also signifies "*well,*" "*rightly*" : 2 Kings vii. 9 ; Num. xxvii. 7. Why should we not render it here, "*He giveth to His beloved to sleep well* " : i.e., While those who, mistrusting God, attribute all things to their own labour, do not sleep well ; for truly they "*rise early and sit up late*" ; he gives to his beloved this grace, that reposing in his fatherly care and goodness, they fully enjoy their sleep, as those who know that such anxious labour is not necessary for them : or, "*Truly, he giveth to his beloved sleep ;*" *as* כֵּן may be the same as אָכֵן. But שֵׁנָה may betaken for בְּשֵׁנָה, and rendered, "*Truly, he giveth to his beloved in sleep ;*" viz., that he should be refreshed by this means.—*Louis De Dieu,* 1590—1642.

Verse 2 (last clause).—The sentence may be read either, *he will give sleep to his beloved,* or, *he will give in sleeping ;* that is, he will give them those things which unbelievers labour to acquire by their own industry. The particle כֵּן, *ken, thus,* is put to express certainty ; for with the view of producing a more undoubted persuasion of the truth—that God gives food to his people without any great care on their part—which seems incredible and a fiction, Solomon points to the thing as it were with the finger. He indeed speaks as if God nourished the slothfulness of his servants by his gentle treatment ; but as we know that men are created with the design of their being occupied, and as in the subsequent Psalm we shall find that the servants of God are accounted happy when they eat the labour of their hands, it is certain that the word *sleep* is not to be understood as implying slothfulness, but a placid labour, to which true believers subject themselves by the obedience of faith. Whence proceeds this so great ardour in the unbelieving, that they move not a finger without a tumult or bustle, in other words, without tormenting themselves with superfluous cares, but because they attribute nothing to the providence of God ! The faithful, on the other hand, although they lead a laborious life, yet follow their vocations with composed and tranquil minds. Thus their hands are not idle, but their minds repose in the stillness of faith, as if they were asleep.—*John Calvin*, 1509—1564.

Verse 2.—"*He giveth his beloved sleep.*" It is *a peculiar rest*, it is a rest peculiar to sons, to saints, to heirs, to beloved ones. "So he gives *his beloved* rest," or as the Hebrew hath it, dearling, or dear beloved, quiet rest, without care or sorrow. The Hebrew word שׁנא, *shena*, is written with א, a quiet dumb letter, which is not usual, to denote the more quietness and rest. This rest is a crown that God sets only upon the head of saints ; it is a gold chain that he only puts about his children's necks ; it is a jewel that he only hangs between his beloved's breasts : it is a flower that he only sticks in his darlings' bosoms. This rest is a tree of life that is proper and peculiar to the inhabitants of that heavenly country ; it is children's bread, and shall never be given to dogs.—*Thomas Brooks*, 1608—1680.

Verse 2 (last clause).—As the Lord *gave* a precious gift to his *beloved*, the first Adam, while he *slept*, by taking a rib from his side, and by *building* therefrom a woman, Eve, his bride, the Mother of all living ; so, while Christ, the Second Adam, the true Jedidiah, the Well-beloved Son of God, was sleeping in death on the cross, God formed for him, in his death, and by his death,—even by the life-giving streams flowing from his own precious side,—the Church, the spiritual Eve, the Mother of all living ; and gave her to him as his bride. Thus he *built* for him in his *sleep* the spiritual Temple of his Church.—*Christopher Wordsworth*.

Verse 2.—Quiet sleep is the gift of God, and it is the love of God to give quiet sleep.

1. '*Tis God's gift* when we have it : quiet sleep does revive nature as the dew or small rain does refresh the grass. Now, as the prophet speaks (Jer. xiv. 22), "Are there any of the gods of the heathen can cause rain, or can the heavens give showers ?" so it may be said : Are there any of the creatures in earth or heaven that can give sleep ? That God which gives showers of rain must give hours of rest : peaceable repose is God's peculiar *gift*.

2. '*Tis God's love* when he gives it, "*for so he giveth his beloved sleep*" ; that is, sleep with quietness : yea, the Hebrew word, *shena*, for *sleep*, being with *aleph*, a quiet or resting letter, otherwise than is usual, it signifies the greater quietness in time of sleep. And whereas some apply the peace only to Solomon, who was called Jedidiah, the beloved of the Lord, to whom God gave sleep ; the Septuagint turns the Hebrew word plurally, "*so God giveth his beloved ones sleep*" ; to his saints in general God gives quiet sleep as a token of his love ; yea, in the times of their greatest peril. Thus Peter in prison when he was bound with chains, beset with soldiers, and to die the next day, yet see how fast he was found asleep (Acts xii. 6, 7) : "The same night Peter was sleeping, and behold the angel of the Lord came upon him, and a light shined in the prison," yet Peter slept till the angel smote him on the side and raised him up : so God "gives his beloved sleep," and let his beloved give him the honour ; and the rather because *herein God answers our prayer, herein God fulfils his promise.*

Is it not *our prayer* that God would prevent affrighting, and afford refreshing sleep ? and is it not God's answer when in sleep he doth sustain us ? "I cried (says David) unto the Lord with my voice, and he heard me out of his holy hill. I laid me down and slept, for the Lord sustained me" : Ps. iii. 4, 5.

Is it not *God's promise* to vouchsafe sleep free from frights ? "When thou liest down, thou shalt not be afraid : yea, thou shalt lie down, and thy sleep shall be sweet" : Prov. iii. 24. Hence God's servants while they are in the wilderness and woods of this world, they sleep safely, and devils as wild beasts can do them no harm. Ezek. xxxiv. 25. Have we through God's blessing this benefit, let us abundantly give praise and live praise unto God hereupon. Yea, large praise belongs to the Lord for quiet sleep from men of all sorts.—*Philip Goodwin, in "The Mystery of Dreams,"* 1658.

Verse 2.—*"So he giveth his beloved sleep."* The world would give its favourites power, wealth, distinction ; God gives " *sleep*." Could he give anything better ? To give sleep when the storm is raging ; to give sleep when conscience is arraying a long catalogue of sins ; to give sleep when evil angels are trying to overturn our confidence in Christ ; to give sleep when death is approaching, when judgment is at hand—oh ! what gift could be more suitable ? what more worthy of God ? or what more precious to the soul ?

But we do not mean to enlarge upon the various senses which might thus be assigned to the gift. You will see for yourselves that sleep, as denoting repose and refreshment, may be regarded as symbolising " the rest which remaineth for the righteous," which is the gift of God to his chosen. " Surely he giveth his beloved sleep," may be taken as parallel to what is promised in Isaiah—" Thou wilt keep him in perfect peace whose mind is stayed on thee." Whatever you can understand by the " peace" in the one case, you may also understand by the " *sleep*" in the other. But throughout the Old and New Testaments, and especially the latter, sleep, as you know, is often put for death. " He slept with his fathers" is a common expression in the Jewish Scriptures. To " sleep in Jesus" is a common way of speaking of those who die in the faith of the Redeemer.

Suppose, then, we take the " *sleep*" in our text as denoting death, and confine our discourse to an illustration of the passage under this one point-of view. "*Surely he giveth his beloved sleep.*" What an aspect will this confer on death—to regard it as God's gift—a gift which he vouchsafes to those whom he loves !

It is not " he *sendeth* his beloved sleep," which might be true whilst God himself remained at a distance ; it is " he *giveth* his beloved sleep" ; as though God himself brought the sleep, and laid it on the eyes of the weary Christian warrior. And if God himself have to do with the dissolution, can we not trust him that he will loosen gently the silver cord, and use all kindness and tenderness in " taking down the earthly house of this tabernacle" ? I know not more comforting words than those of our text, whether for the being uttered in the sick-room of the righteous, or breathed over their graves. They might almost take the pain from disease, as they certainly do the dishonour from death. What is bestowed by God as a " gift on his beloved " will assuredly occupy his care, his watchfulness, his solicitude ; and I conclude, therefore, that he is present, in some special and extraordinary sense when the righteous lie dying ; ay, and that he sets his seal, and plants his guardianship where the righteous lie dead. " O death, where is thy sting ? O grave, where is thy victory ?" Let the saint be but constant in the profession of godliness, and his last hours shall be those in which Deity himself shall stand almost visibly at his side, and his last resting-place that which he shall shadow with his wings. Sickness may be protracted and distressing ; " earth to earth, ashes to ashes, dust to dust," may be plaintively breathed over the unconscious dead ; but nothing in all this lengthened struggle, nothing in all this apparent defeat, can harm the righteous man—nay, nothing can be other than for his present good and his eternal glory, seeing that death with all its accompaniments is but joy—God's gift to his beloved. Dry your tears, ye that stand around the bed of the dying believer, the parting moment is almost at hand —a cold damp is on the forehead—the eye is fixed—the pulse too feeble to be felt —are you staggered at such a spectacle ? Nay ! let faith do its part ! The chamber is crowded with glorious forms ; angels are waiting there to take charge of the disembodied soul ; a hand gentler than any human is closing those eyes ; and a voice sweeter than any human is whispering—"*Surely the Lord giveth his beloved sleep.*"—*Henry Melvill (1798—1871), in a Sermon entitled "Death the Gift of God."*

Verse 2. —*"For so he giveth his beloved sleep."* One night I could not rest, and in the wild wanderings of my thoughts I met this text, and communed with it : "*So he giveth his beloved sleep.*" In my reverie, as I was on the border of the land of dreams, methought I was in a castle. Around its massive walls there ran a deep moat. Watchmen paced the walls both day and night. It was a fine old fortress, bidding defiance to the foe ; but I was not happy in it. I thought I lay upon a couch ; but scarcely had I closed my eyes, ere a trumpet blew, " To arms ! To arms !" and when the danger was overpast, I lay me down again. " To arms ! To arms !" once more resounded, and again I started up. Never could I rest. I thought I had my armour on, and moved about perpetually clad in mail, rushing each hour to the castle top, aroused by some fresh alarm. At one time a foe was coming from the west ; at another from the east. I thought I had a treasure somewhere down in some deep part of the castle, and all my care was to guard it. I dreaded, I feared, I trembled lest it should be taken from me. I awoke, and I thought I would not live in such a tower as that for all its grandeur. It was the castle of discontent, the castle of ambition, in which man never rests. It is ever, " To arms ! To arms !" There is a foe here, or a foe there. His dear-loved treasure must be guarded. Sleep never crossed the drawbridge of the castle of discontent. Then I thought I would supplement it by another reverie. I was in a cottage. It was in what poets call a beautiful and pleasant place, but I cared not for that. I had no treasure in the world, save one sparkling jewel on my breast : and I thought I put my hand on that and went to sleep, nor did I wake till morning light. That treasure was a quiet conscience and the love of God—" the peace that passeth all understanding." I slept, because I slept in the house of content, satisfied with what I had. Go, ye overreaching misers ! Go, ye grasping, ambitious men ! I envy not your life of inquietude. The sleep of statesmen is often broken ; the dream of the miser is always evil ; the sleep of the man who loves gain is never hearty ; but God " *giveth,*" by contentment, " *his beloved sleep.*"—*C. H. S.*

Verse 2.—"*He giveth his beloved sleep.*"

> Of all the thoughts of God that are
> Borne inward unto souls afar,
>   Along the Psalmist's music deep,
> Now tell me if that any is,
> For gift or grace surpassing this—
> " *He giveth his beloved sleep.*"
>
>   —*Elizabeth Barrett Browning,* 1809—1861.

Verse 3.—"*Lo, children are an heritage of the* LORD." There is no reason, therefore, why you should be apprehensive for your families and country ; there is no reason why you should weary yourselves with such great and such restless labour. God will be with you and your children, since they are his heritage.—*Thomas Le Blanc.*

Verse 3.—"*Lo, children are an heritage of the* LORD." That is, to many God gives children in place of temporal good. To many others he gives houses, lands, and thousands of gold and silver, and with them the womb that beareth not ; and these are their inheritance. The poor man has from God a number of children, without lands or money ; these are his inheritance ; and God shows himself their father, feeding and supporting them by a chain of miraculous providences. Where is the *poor man* who would give up his *six children* with the prospect of having *more,* for the *thousands* or *millions* of him who is the *centre* of his *own existence,* and has neither *root* nor *branch* but his forlorn solitary self upon the face of the earth ? Let the fruitful family, however poor, lay this to heart : "*Children are an heritage of the* LORD : *and the fruit of the womb is his reward.*" And he who gave them will feed them ; for it is a fact, and the *maxim* formed on it has never failed, " Wherever God sends mouths, he sends meat." " Murmur not," said an Arab to his friend, " because thy family is large ; know that it is for *their sakes* that God feeds *thee.*"—*Adam Clarke.*

Verse 3.—"*Children are an heritage of the* LORD." The Hebrew seems to imply that children are an heritage belonging to the Lord, and not an heritage given by the Lord, as most English readers appear to take it. The Targum likewise bears this out.—*H. T. Armfield.*

Verse 3.—"*Children are an heritage of the* LORD," etc. The Psalmist speaks of what children are unto godly and holy parents, for unto such only is any blessing given by God as a reward, and the Psalmist expressly speaks of blessings which God gives his beloved ones, and this blessing of children he makes to be the last and greatest. It is also as certain that he speaks of children as supposed to be holy and godly ; for otherwise they are not a reward, but a curse, and a sorrow to him that begat them. The psalm was made, as appears by the title of it, " *of* or *for Solomon*," and therefore, as it is more than probable, was penned, as that other psalm, the 72nd, which bears the same title, by David the father, of and for Solomon his son, who was, for his father's sake, "the beloved of God" (2 Sam. xii. 24, 25), and upon whom the sure covenant and mercies of David were entailed, together with his kingdom. And what is said in this psalm, in the verses before, fitly agrees to him, for he it was who was to build God's house, to keep and preserve Jerusalem the city, and the kingdom in peace, and to have rest, or as the Psalmist calls it (verse 3), quiet sleep given him by God, from all his enemies round about him. And for this, compare the prophecy of him (1 Chron. xxii. 9, 10) with the instructions here given him in the three first verses of this psalm, and ye will see how fitly this psalm concerns him.—*Thomas Goodwin.*

Verse 3.—"*Children are an heritage of the* LORD." Hence note, 'tis one of the greatest outward blessings to have a family full of dutiful children. To have many children is the next blessing to much grace. To have many children about us is better than to have much wealth about us. To have store of these olive plants (as the Psalmist calls them) round about our table is better than to have store of oil and wine upon our table. We know the worth of dead, or rather life-less treasures, but who knows the worth of living treasures ? Every man who hath children hath not a blessing in them, yet children are a blessing, and some have many blessings in one child. Children are chiefly a blessing to the children of God. "*Lo, children are an heritage of the* LORD : *and the fruit of the womb is his reward.*" But are not houses and lands, gold and silver, an heritage bestowed by the Lord upon his people ? Doubtless they are, for the earth is his, and the ful-ness of it, and he gives it to the children of men. But though all things are of God, yet all things are not alike of him : children are more of God than houses and lands.—*Joseph Caryl.*

Verse 3.—Children !—might one say as the word was uttered—I left mine in my distant home, in poverty, their wants and numbers increasing, with the means of providing for their comfort daily narrowing. Even should my life be pro-longed, they will be children of want, but with sickness and warnings of death upon me, they will soon be helpless and friendless orphans. Yes ! but will God be neglectful of his own heritage ? will he turn a gift into a sorrow ? Poor as thou art, repine not at the number of thy children. Though lions lack thou shalt not, if thou seekest him ; and know that it may be even for their sakes that he feedeth thee. If even thou wouldst not part with one of them for thousands of gold and silver, believe that he who is the fountain of all tenderness regards them with yet deeper love, and will make them now, in thy hour of trial, a means of increasing thy dependence on him, and soon thy support and pride.

Children !—might another say, as the psalm referred to them—on their open-ing promise the breath of the destroyer has been poured. They are ripening vis-ibly for the grave, and their very smile and caress cause my wounded heart to bleed anew. Yes, mourner ; but *God's heritage !* may he not claim his own ? They are in safe keeping when in his, and will soon be restored to thee in the better land, where death will make them ministering angels at his throne ; nay, they will be the first to welcome thee to its glories, to love and worship with thee throughout eternity.

Children ! this word to a third, of an even sadder and more anxious spirit, might seem like the planting of a dagger in his heart. His children have forsaken their father's God. Their associates were the vain and vicious ; their pleasures were the pleasures of folly and shame ; their lives barren of all promise, their souls destitute of all purpose, and steeled against all reproof. True, but *the heritage of the Lord still.* Hast thou, sorrowing parent, asked him for wisdom to keep it for him ? Have due thought, prayer, watchful and holy living been expended on that heritage of God ? No culture, no harvest in the soil ; no prayer, no blessing from the soul. "Train up a child in the way he should go, and when he is old he will not depart from it," is a promise that though sometimes, yet but seldom has missed fulfilment. Bring them to Jesus, and, unchanged in his tenderness, he will still lay his hands upon them and bless them.—*Robert Nisbet.*

Verse 3.—"*The fruit of the womb is his reward.*" John Howard Hinton's daughter said to him as she knelt by his death bed :—" There is no greater blessing than for children to have godly parents." "And the next," said the dying father, with a beam of gratitude, " for parents to have godly children."—*Memoir in Baptist Handbook,* 1875.

Verse 4.—"*As arrows.*" Well doth David call children " *arrows*" ; for if they be well bred, they shoot at their parents' enemies ; and if they be evil bred, they shoot at their parents.—*Henry Smith,* 1560—1591.

Verse 4.—"*As arrows.*" Children are compared to " *arrows.*" Now, we know that sticks are not by nature arrows ; they do not grow so, but they are made so ; by nature they are knotty and rugged, but by art they are made smooth and handsome. So children by nature are rugged and untoward, but by education are refined and reformed, made pliable to the divine will and pleasure.—*George Swinnock,* 1627—1673.

Verse 4.—"*As arrows.*" " Our children are what we make them. They are represented '*As arrows in the hand of a mighty man,*' and *arrows* go the way we aim them."

Verse 4.—"*As arrows.*" In a collection of *Chinese Proverbs and Apophthegms,* subjoined to *Hau Kiou Choaan,* or, *The Pleasing History,* I find a proverb cited from *Du Halde,* which seems full to our purpose. It is this :—" When a son is born into a family, a bow and arrow are hung before the gate." To which the following note is added : " As no such custom appears to be literally observed, this should seem to be a metaphorical expression, signifying that a new protector is added to the family," equivalent to that of the Psalms,—" *as arrows,*" etc.— *James Merrick* (1720—1769), *in "Annotations on the Psalms."*

Verse 4.—"*Children of the youth*" are " *arrows in the hand,*" which, with prudence, may be directed aright to the mark, God's glory, and the service of their generation ; but afterwards, when they are gone abroad in the world, they are arrows out of the hand ; it is too late to bend them then. But these " *arrows in the hand* " too often prove arrows in the heart, a constant grief to their godly parents, whose grey hairs they bring with sorrow to the grave.—*Matthew Henry.*

Verse 4.—"*Children of the youth.*" *Sons of youth, i.e.,* born while their parents are still young. See Gen. xxxvii. 2 ; Isa. liv. 6. The allusion is not only to their vigour (Gen. xlix. 3), but the value of their aid to the parent in declining age.—*Joseph Addison Alexander.*

Verse 4.—"*Children of the youth.*" If the right interpretation is commonly given to this phrase, this psalm greatly encourages early marriages. It is a growing evil of modern times that marriages are so often deferred till it is highly improbable that in the course of nature the father can live to mould his offspring to habits of honour and virtue.—*William Swan Plumer* (1802—1880), *in "Studies in the Book of Psalms."*

Verse 5.—"*Happy is the man that hath his quiver full of them.*" Dr. Guthrie used to say, " I am rich in nothing but children." They were eleven in number.

Verse 5.—"*Quiver full.*" Many children make many prayers, and many prayers bring much blessing.—*German Proverb.*

Verse 5.—The Rev. Moses Browne had twelve children. On one remarking to him, "Sir, you have just as many children as Jacob," he replied, "Yes, and I have Jacob's God to provide for them."—*G. S. Bowes.*

Verse 5.—I remember a great man coming into my house, at Waltham, and seeing all my children standing in the order of their age and stature, said, "These are they that make rich men poor." But he straight received this answer, "Nay, my lord, these are they that make a poor man rich ; for there is not one of these whom we would part with for all your wealth." It is easy to observe that none are so gripple and hardfisted as the childless ; whereas those, who, for the maintenance of large families, are inured to frequent disbursements, find such experience of Divine providence in the faithful management of their affairs, as that they lay out with more cheerfulness what they receive. Wherein their care must be abated when God takes it off from them to himself ; and, if they be not wanting to themselves, their faith gives them ease in casting their burden upon him, who hath more power and more right to it, since our children are more his than our own. He that feedeth the young ravens, can he fail the best of his creatures ?— *Joseph Hall,* 1574—1656.

Verse 5.—"*They shall not be ashamed,*" etc. Able enough he shall be to defend himself, and keep off all injuries, being fortified by his children ; and if it happen that he hath a cause depending in the gate, and to be tried before the judges, he shall have the patronage of his children, and not suffer in his plea for want of advocates ; his sons will stand up in a just cause for him.— *William Nicholson* (—— 1671), *in "David's Harp Strung and Tuned."*

Verse 5.—"*But they shall speak.*" "*But destroy*" is the marginal version, and is here much more emphatical than the rendering "*speak.*" For this sense see 2 Chron. xxii. 10. Others refer it to litigation, when they shall successfully defend the cause of their parents. But as I do not see how their number or vigour could add weight to their evidence in a judicial cause, I prefer the sense given.— *Benjamin Boothroyd,* 1768—1836.

Verse 5.—" *With the enemies in the gate.*" Probably the Psalmist alludes here to the defence of a besieged city ; the gate was very commonly the point of attack, and the taking of it rendered the conquest of the place easy : compare Gen. xxii. 17 ; xxiv. 60.—*Daniel Cresswell* (1776—1844), *in "The Psalms . . . . with Critical and Explanatory Notes,"* 1843.

Verse 5.—

> This is the pride, the glory of a man,
> To train obedient children in his house,
> Prompt on his enemies t' avenge his wrongs,
> And with the father's zeal in honour high
> To hold his friends.
> —*Sophocles' "Antigone." R. Potter's Translation.*

HINTS TO THE VILLAGE PREACHER.

Verse 1.—I. The human hand without the hand of God is in vain. II. The human eye without the eye of God is in vain. Or, I. God is to be acknowledged in all our works. 1. By seeking his direction before them. 2. By depending upon his help in them. 3. By giving him the glory of them. II. In all our cares. 1. By owning our short sight. 2. By trusting to his foresight.— *G. R.*

Verse 1 (*first part*).—Illustrate the principles : I. In building up character. II. In constructing plans of life and of work. III. In framing schemes of happiness. IV. In rearing a hope of eternal life. V. In raising and enlarging the church.—*J. F.*

Verses 1, 2.—I. What we may not expect : namely, God to work without our building, watching, etc. II. What we may expect : Failure if we are without God. III. What we should not do : Fret, worry, etc. IV. What we may do : So trust as to rest in peace.

Verse 2 (*with Psalm* cxxvi. 2).   The labour of the law contrasted with the laughter of the gospel.

Verse 2.—"*The bread of sorrows.*"   I. When God sends it, it is good to eat it. II. When we bake it ourselves, it is vain to eat it.   III. When the devil brings it, it is deadly meat.

Verse 2 (*last clause*).—Blessings that come to us in sleep. 1. Renewed health and vigour of body. 2. Mental repose and refreshment. 3. Sweeter thoughts and holier purposes. 4. Providential gifts. The rains fall, the fruits of the earth grow and ripen, the mill wheel goes round, the ship pursues her voyage, etc., while we slumber. Often when we are doing nothing for ourselves God is doing most.—*W. H. J. P.*

Verse 2 (*last clause*).—See "Spurgeon's Sermons," No. 12 : "The Peculiar Sleep of the Beloved."

Verse 3.—Sermon by Thomas Manton. Works : vol. xviii. pp. 84—95. [Nichol's Edition.]

Verses 3—5.—Children. Consider : I. The effects of receiving them as a heritage from the Lord. 1. Parents will trust in the Lord for their provision and safety. 2. Will regard them as a sacred trust from the Lord, of whose care they must render an account. 3. Will train them up in the fear of the Lord. 4. Will often consult God concerning them. 5. Will render them up uncomplainingly when the Lord calls them to himself by death. II. The effects of their right training. 1. They become the parents' joy. 2. The permanent record of the parents' wisdom. 3. The support and solace of the parents' old age. 4. The transmitters of their parents' virtues to another generation ; for well-trained children become, in their turn, wise parents.—*J. F.*

Verse 4.—The spiritual uses of children. I. When they die in infancy, awakening parents. II. When they go home from Sunday-school carrying holy influences. III. When they become converted. IV. When they grow up and become useful men and women.

Verses 4, 5.—I. The dependence of children upon parents. 1. For safety. They are in their quiver. 2. For direction. They are sent forth by them. 3. For support. They are in the hands of the mighty. II. The dependence of parents upon children. 1. For defence. Who will hear a parent spoken against ? 2. For happiness. "A wise son maketh," etc. Children elicit some of the noblest and tenderest emotions of human nature. Happy is the Christian minister who with a full quiver can say, "Here am I, and the children which thou hast given me."—*G. R.*

Verse 6.—"The Reward of Well-doing Sure." Sermon by Henry Melvill, in "The Pulpit," 1856.

PSALM CXXVIII.

EXPOSITION.

B LESSED *is* every one that feareth the LORD ; that walketh in his ways.

2 For thou shalt eat the labour of thine hands : happy *shalt* thou *be,* and *it shall be* well with thee.

3 Thy wife *shall be* as a fruitful vine by the sides of thine house : thy children like olive plants round about thy table.

4 Behold, that thus shall the man be blessed that feareth the LORD.

5 The LORD shall bless thee out of Zion : and thou shalt see the good of Jerusalem all the days of thy life.

6 Yea, thou shalt 'see thy children's children, *and* peace upon Israel.

1. "*Blessed is every one that feareth the* LORD." The last psalm ended with a blessing,—for the word there translated "happy" is the same as that which is here rendered "blessed" : thus the two songs are joined by a catch-word. There is also in them a close community of subject. The fear of God is the corner-stone of all blessedness. We must reverence the ever-blessed God before we can be blessed ourselves. Some think that this life is an evil, an infliction, a thing upon which rests a curse ; but it is not so ; the God-fearing man has a present blessing resting upon him. It is not true that it would be to him "something better not to be." He is happy now, for he is the child of the happy God, the ever-living Jehovah ; and he is even here a joint-heir with Jesus Christ, whose heritage is not misery, but joy. This is true of every one of the God-fearing, of all conditions, in all ages : each one and every one is blessed. Their blessedness may not always be seen by carnal reason, but it is always a fact, for God himself declares that it is so ; and we know that those whom he blesses are blessed indeed. Let us cultivate that holy filial fear of Jehovah which is the essence of all true religion ;—the fear of reverence, of dread to offend, of anxiety to please, and of entire submission and obedience. This fear of the Lord is the fit fountain of holy living : we look in vain for holiness apart from it : none but those who fear the Lord will ever walk in his ways.

"*That walketh in his ways.*" The religious life, which God declares to be blessed, must be practical as well as emotional. It is idle to talk of fearing the

Lord if we act like those who have no care whether there be a God or no. God's ways will be our ways if we have a sincere reverence for him : if the heart is joined unto God, the feet will follow hard after him. A man's heart will be seen in his walk, and the blessing will come where heart and walk are both with God. Note that the first psalm links the benediction with the walk in a negative way, " Blessed is the man that walketh *not*," etc. ; but here we find it in connection with the positive form of our conversation. To enjoy the divine blessing we must be active, and walk ; we must be methodical, and walk in certain ways ; and we must be godly, and walk in the Lord's ways. God's ways are blessed ways ; they were cast up by the Blessed One, they were trodden by him in whom we are blessed, they are frequented by the blessed, they are provided with means of blessing, they are paved with present blessings, and they lead to eternal blessedness : who would not desire to walk in them ?

2. "*For thou shalt eat the labour of thine hands.*" The general doctrine of the first verse here receives a personal application : note the change to the second person : "*thou* shalt eat," etc. This is the portion of. God's saints,—to work, and to find a reward in so doing. God is the God of labourers. We are not to leave our worldly callings because the Lord has called us by grace : we are not promised a blessing upon romantic idleness or unreasonable dreaming, but upon hard work and honest industry. Though we are in God's hands we are to be supported by our own hands. He will give us daily bread, but it must be made our own by labour. All kinds of labour are here included ; for if one toils by the sweat of his brow, and another does so by the sweat of his brain, there is no difference in the blessing ; save that it is generally more healthy to work with the body than with the mind only. Without God it would be vain to labour ; but when we are labourers together with God a promise is set before us. The promise is that labour shall be fruitful, and that he who performs it shall himself enjoy the recompense of it. It is a grievous ill for a man to slave his life away and receive no fair remuneration for his toil : as a rule, God's servants rise out of such bondage and claim their own, and receive it : at any rate, this verse may encourage them to do so. "The labourer is worthy of his hire." Under the Theocracy the chosen people could see this promise literally fulfilled ; but when evil rulers oppressed them their earnings were withheld by churls, and their harvests were snatched away from them by marauders. Had they walked in the fear of the Lord they would never have known such great evils. Some men never enjoy their labour, for they give themselves no time for rest. Eagerness to get takes from them the ability to enjoy. Surely, if it is worth while to labour, it is worth while to eat of that labour. "*Happy shalt thou be*," or, *Oh, thy happinesses.* Heaped up happinesses in the plural belong to that man who fears the Lord. He is happy, and he shall be happy in a thousand ways. The context leads us to expect family happiness. Our God is our household God. The Romans had their Lares and Penates, but we have far more than they in the one only living and true God. "*And it shall be well with thee,*" or, *good for thee.* Yes, good is for the good ; and it shall be well with those who do well.

> " What cheering words are these !
> Their sweetness who can tell ?
> In time, and to eternal days,
> 'Tis with the righteous well."

If we fear God we may dismiss all other fear. In walking in God's ways we shall be under his protection, provision, and approval ; danger and destruction shall be far from us : all things shall work our good. In God's view it would not be a blessed thing for us to live without exertion, nor to eat the unearned bread of dependence : the happiest state on earth is one in which we have something to do, strength to do it with, and a fair return for what we have done. This, with the divine blessing, is all that we ought to desire, and it is sufficient for any man who fears the Lord and abhors covetousness. Having food and raiment, let us be therewith content.

3. "*Thy wife.*" To reach the full of earthly felicity a man must not be alone. A helpmeet was needed in Paradise, and assuredly she is not less necessary out of it. He that findeth a wife findeth a good thing. It is not every man that feareth the Lord who has a wife ; but if he has, she shall share in his blessedness and increase it.

"*Shall be as a fruitful vine.*" To complete domestic bliss children are sent. They come as the lawful fruit of marriage, even as clusters appear upon the vine. For the grapes the vine was planted ; for children was the wife provided. It is generally well with any creature when it fulfils its purpose, and it is so far well with married people when the great design of their union is brought about. They must not look upon fruitfulness as a burden, but as a blessing. Good wives are also fruitful in kindness, thrift, helpfulness, and affection : if they bear no children, they are by no means barren if they yield us the wine of consolation and the clusters of comfort. Truly blessed is the man whose wife is fruitful in those good works which are suitable to her near and dear position.

"*By the sides of thine house.*" She keeps to the house : she is a home bird. Some imagine that she is like a vine which is nailed up to the house-wall ; but they have no such custom in Palestine, neither is it pleasant to think of a wife as growing up by a wall, and as bound to the very bricks and mortar of her husband's dwelling. No, she is a fruitful vine, and a faithful housekeeper ; if you wish to find her, she is within the house : she is to be found both inside and outside the home, but her chief usefulness is in the inner side of the dwelling, which she adorns. Eastern houses usually have an open square in the centre, and the various rooms are ranged around the sides,—there shall the wife be found, busy in one room or another, as the hour of the day demands. She keeps at home, and so keeps the home. It is her husband's house, and she is her husband's ; as the text puts it—"thy wife," and "thy house" ; but by her loving care her husband is made so happy that he is glad to own her as an equal proprietor with himself, for he is hers, and the house is hers too.

"*Thy children like olive plants round about thy table.*" Hundreds of times have I seen the young olive plants springing up around the parent stem, and it has always made me think of this verse. The Psalmist never intended to suggest the idea of olive plants round a table, but of young people springing up around their parents, even as olive plants surround the fine, well-rooted tree. The figure is very striking, and would be sure to present itself to the mind of every observer in the olive country. How beautiful to see the gnarled olive, still bearing abundant fruit, surrounded with a little band of sturdy successors, any one of which would be able to take its place should the central olive be blown down, or removed in any other way. The notion of a table in a bower may suit a cockney in a tea-garden, but would never occur to an oriental poet ; it is not the olive plants, but the children, that are round about the table. Moreover, note that it is not olive *branches*, but *plants*,—a very different thing. Our children gather around our table to be fed, and this involves expenses : how much better is this than to see them pining upon beds of sickness, unable to come for their meals ! What a blessing to have sufficient to put upon the table ! Let us for this benefit praise the bounty of the Lord. The wife is busy all over the house, but the youngsters are busiest at meal-times ; and if the blessing of the Lord rest upon the family, no sight can be more delightful. Here we have the vine and the olive blended—joy from the fruitful wife, and solid comfort from the growing family ; these are the choicest products earth can yield : our families are gardens of the Lord. It may help us to value the privileges of our home if we consider where we should be if they were withdrawn. What if the dear partner of our life were removed from the sides of our house to the recesses of the sepulchre ? What is the trouble of children compared with the sorrow of their loss ? Think, dear father, what would be your grief if you had to cry with Job, "Oh that I were as in months past, as in the days when God preserved me ; when my children were about me."

4. "*Behold, that thus shall the man be blessed that feareth the* LORD." Mark this.

Put a *Nota Bene* against it, for it is worthy of observation. It is not to be inferred that all blessed men are married, and are fathers ; but that this is the way in which the Lord favours godly people who are placed in domestic life. He makes their relationships happy and profitable. In this fashion does Jehovah bless God-fearing households, for he is the God of all the families of Israel. We have seen this blessing scores of times, and we have never ceased to admire in domestic peace the sweetest of human felicity. Family blessedness comes from the Lord, and is a part of his plan for the preservation of a godly race, and for the maintenance of his worship in the land. To the Lord alone we must look for it. The possession of riches will not ensure it ; the choice of a healthy and beautiful bride will not ensure it ; the birth of numerous comely children will not ensure it : there must be the blessing of God, the influence of piety, the result of holy living.

5. "*The* Lord *shall bless thee out of Zion.*" A spiritual blessing shall be received by the gracious man, and this shall crown all his temporal mercies. He is one among the many who make up God's inheritance ; his tent is part and parcel of the encampment around the tabernacle ; and therefore, when the benediction is pronounced at the centre it shall radiate to him in his place. The blessing of the house of God shall be upon his house. The priestly benediction which is recorded in Numbers vi. 24—26, runs thus : "The Lord bless thee, and keep thee : the Lord make his face shine upon thee, and be gracious unto thee : the Lord lift up his countenance upon thee, and give thee peace." This is it which shall come upon the head of the God-fearing man. Zion was the centre of blessing, and to it the people looked when they sought for mercy : from the altar of sacrifice, from the mercy-seat, from the Shekinah-light, yea, from Jehovah himself, the blessing shall come to each one of his holy people. "*And thou shalt see the good of Jerusalem all the days of thy life.*" He shall have a patriot's joy as well as a patriarch's peace. God shall give him to see his country prosper, and its metropolitan city flourish. When tent-mercies are followed by temple-mercies, and these are attended by national mercies,—the man, the worshipper, the patriot is trebly favoured of the Lord. This favour is to be permanent throughout the good man's life, and that life is to be a long one, for he is to see his sons' sons. Many a time does true religion bring such blessings to men ; and when these good things are denied them, they have a greater reward as a compensation.

6. "*Yea, thou shalt see thy children's children.*" This is a great pleasure. Men live their young lives over again in their grandchildren. Does not Solomon say that "children's children are the crown of old men" ? So they are. The good man is glad that a pious stock is likely to be continued ; he rejoices in the belief that other homes as happy as his own will be built up wherein altars to the glory of God shall smoke with the morning and evening sacrifice. This promise implies long life, and that life rendered happy by its being continued in our offspring. It is one token of the immortality of man that he derives joy from extending his life in the lives of his descendants.

"*And peace upon Israel.*" With this sweet word Psalm cxxv. was closed. It is a favourite formula. Let God's own heritage be at peace, and we are all glad of it. We count it our own prosperity for the chosen of the Lord to find rest and quiet. Jacob was sorely tossed about ; his life knew little of peace ; but yet the Lord delivered him out of all his tribulations, and brought him to a place of rest in Goshen for a while, and afterwards to sleep with his fathers in the cave of Machpelah. His glorious Seed was grievously afflicted and at last crucified ; but he has risen to eternal peace, and in his peace we dwell. Israel's spiritual descendants still share his chequered conditions, but there remains a rest for them also, and they shall have peace from the God of peace. Israel was a praying petitioner in the days of his wrestling, but he became a prevailing prince, and therein his soul found peace. Yes, all around it is true—"Peace upon Israel ! Peace upon Israel."

EXPLANATORY NOTES.

Whole Psalm.—Psalm cxxviii. follows Psalm cxxvii. for the same reason as Psalm ii. follows Psalm i. In both instances they are Psalms placed together, of which one begins with *ashré* (happy, very happy), and the other ends with *ashré*. In other respects Psalm cxxviii. and cxxvii. supplement one another. They are related to one another much as the New Testament parables of the treasure in the field and the one pearl are related. That which makes man happy is represented in Psalm cxxvii. as a gift coming as a blessing, and in Psalm cxxviii. as a reward coming as a blessing, that which is briefly indicated in the word שָׂכָר, *sakar*, *reward*, in cxxvii. 3 being here expanded and unfolded. There it appears as a gift of grace in contrast to the God-estranged self-activity of man ; here as a fruit of the *ora et labora.*—*Franz Delitzsch.*

Whole Psalm.—It is to be observed, that here all men are spoken to as wedded ; because this is the ordinary estate of most people. See I. Cor. vii. 1, 2. At this day every Jew is bound to marry at about eighteen years of age, or before twenty ; else he is accounted as one that liveth in sin.—*John Trapp.*

Whole Psalm.—This Psalm is an ἐπιθαλαμιος λογος, written for the commendation, instruction, and consolation of those who are either already married or are about to enter on that kind of life. It enumerates, therefore, at the commencement, as is usual in songs of this kind, all those things which are regarded as burdens in the married life, such as the labours in seeking to provide for the whole family ; the spouse, and that marriage bond, which, as it were, binds a man and seems to make him a slave, just as that character says in the comedy, "I have taken a wife ; I have sold my liberty :" lastly, the education of the children, which certainly is most laborious, and requires the largest expenditure. To lighten the burden of all these things, there is added to each a blessing or a promise, so that they might appear slight. And at the close, it subjoins in general, a spiritual promise, which easily makes light of all the labours and disquiets of the married life ; even if they should be the very heaviest. The blessing comes from Zion or the Church : for there is nothing so burdensome and difficult, but what it can be easily borne by those who are the members of the true Church, and know the sources of true consolation.—*D. H. Mollerus.*

Verse 1.—"*Blessed is every one that feareth the* LORD," etc. Here we have the living fountain of the blessing which rests upon the conjugal and domestic state. When worldly prudence attempts to choose a wife and form a household, it can apply its hand only to so much of the work as has its seat upon earth, and is visible to the eye of sense. It builds, so to speak, the first and the second story, adds cornice and pediment, and the fabric presents a fair appearance—but it has no foundation. Whenever you see the household of a married pair continuing to defy every storm, you may be sure that it rests upon a sure foundation, lying beyond the reach of human sense, and that that foundation is *the fear of the Lord.* To the fear of the Lord, therefore, the holy Psalmist has wisely given a place in front of this beautiful psalm, which celebrates the blessing that descends upon conjugal and domestic life.—*Augustus F. Tholuck, in "Hours of Christian Devotion,"* 1870.

Verse 1.—"*Blessed is every one that feareth the* LORD." There is a fear of the Lord which hath terror in it and not blessedness. The apprehension with which a warring rebel regards his triumphant and offended sovereign, or the feelings of a fraudulent bankrupt towards a stern creditor, or, a conscience-stricken criminal to a righteous judge, are frequently types of men's feelings in regard to God. This evidently cannot be the *fear* which the "*blessed*" of this psalm feel. Nor can theirs, on the other hand, be the tormenting fear of self-reproach.

Their fear is that which the believed revelations given of him in his Word produce. It is the fear which a child feels towards an honoured parent,—a fear to offend : it is that which they who have been rescued from destruction feel to the benefactor who nobly and at the vastest sacrifice interposed for their safety,—a fear to act unworthily of his kindness : it is that which fills the breast of a pardoned and grateful rebel in the presence of a venerated sovereign at whose throne he is permitted to stand in honour,—a fear lest he should ever forget his goodness, and give him cause to regret it. Such is the fear of the Christian now : a fear which reverence for majesty, gratitude for mercies, dread of displeasure, desire of approval, and longing for the fellowship of heaven, inspire ; the fear of angels and the blessed Son ; the fear not of sorrow but of love, which shrinks with instinctive recoil from doing aught that would tend to grieve, or from denying aught that would tend to honour. Religion is the grand and the only wisdom ; and since the beginning, the middle, and the end of it, is the fear of the Lord, blessed is every man that is swayed by it.—*Robert Nisbet, in "The Songs of the Temple Pilgrims,"* 1863.

Verse 1.—*"Blessed is every one that feareth the* Lord." Let us take a little of the character of the blessed man. Who is it that is undaunted ? *"The man that feareth God."* Fear sounds rather contrary to blessedness ; hath an air of misery ; but add whom. He that " feareth *the* Lord " ; that touch turns it into gold. He that so fears, fears not : he shall not be afraid ; all petty fears are swallowed up in this great fear ; and this great fear is as sweet and pleasing as little fears are anxious and vexing. Secure of other things, he can say—" If my God be pleased, no matter who is displeased : no matter who despise me, if he account me his. Though all forsake me, though my dearest friends grow estranged, if he reject me not, that is my only fear ; and for that I am not perplexed, I know he will not." A believer hath no fear but of the displeasure of heaven, the anger of God to fall upon him ; he accounts that only terrible ; but yet he doth not fear it ; doth not apprehend it will fall on him, is better persuaded of the goodness of God. So this fear is still joined with trust :—" Behold the eye of the Lord is upon them that fear him, upon them that hope in his mercy" : Ps. xxxiii. 18.—*Robert Leighton,* 1611—1684.

Verse 1.—*"Blessed is every one,"* etc. There is a stress on *all* (*" every one"*), teaching that no disparity of sex or condition, of rank or wealth, affects the degree of happiness granted by God to every one of his true servants in their several stations. It is to be observed, further, that whenever the fear of the Lord is mentioned in Holy Writ, it is never set by itself, as though sufficient for the consummation of our faith, but always has something added or prefixed, by which to estimate its due proportion of peerfction, according as it is stated by Solomon in the Proverbs (ii. 3—5).—*J. M. Neale and R. F. Littledale, in "A Commentary on the Psalms from Primitive and Mediæval Writers,"* 1860.

Verse 1.—*"Blessed is every one,"* etc. It is a precious promise, but perhaps thou art tempted to say in thy heart, not meant for every one. Wilt thou answer against the Lord ? Hear him speak in the song. He says, " *every one.*" *"Blessed is every one that feareth the* Lord." None are excluded but those who will not walk in his ways.—*Edward Jewett Robinson.*

Verse 1.—*"Blessed,"* etc. The adage, " That it is best not to be born at all, or to die as soon as possible," has certainly been long since received by the common consent of almost all men. Carnal reason judges either that all mankind without exception are miserable, or that fortune is more favourable to ungodly and wicked men than to the good. To the sentiment that those are blessed who fear the Lord, it has an entire aversion. So much the more requisite, then, is it to dwell upon the consideration of this truth. Farther, as this blessedness is not apparent to the eye, it is of importance, in order to our being able to apprehend it, first to attend to the definition which will be given of it by-and-bye ; and secondly, to know that it depends chiefly upon the protection of God. Although we collect together all the circumstances which seem to contribute to a happy life, surely nothing will be found more desirable than to be kept hidden under the guardianship of God. If this blessing is, in our estimation, to be preferred, as it deserves, to all other good things, whoever is persuaded that the care of God is exercised about the world and human affairs, will at the same time unquestionably acknowledge that what is here laid down is the chief point of happiness. —*John Calvin.*

Verse 1.—"*That feareth the* LORD ; *that walketh in his ways.*" The fear of the Lord is the internal principle ; but unless there be a corresponding expression in the outward life, what reason is there to suppose that it has any existence at all ? Observe also, that there is no walking in the ways of the Lord, until his fear be established in the heart. There can be no genuine morality apart from the fear of God. How can a man obey God while his affections are alienated from him ? —*N. M'Michael.*

Verse 1.—"*That walketh in his ways.*" God makes blessed those that walk in his ways, because he himself walks with them. This is said concerning David, and it is explained how that companionship blessed him, 2 Sam. v. 10 : "And David went on, and grew great, and the Lord God of hosts was with him" : where the "and" may be taken as the causal particle "because." That God does indeed join himself to those who walk in his ways as companion and leader we have in 2 Chron. xvii. 3, 4 : "And the Lord was with Jehoshaphat, because he walked in the first ways of his father David, and sought not unto Baalim ; but sought to the Lord God of his father."—*Thomas Le Blanc.*

Verse 2.—"*For thou shalt eat the labour of thine hands,*" etc. There is a four-fold literal sense here : Thou shalt live by honest, peaceful labour, not by rapine and violence on that produced by the toil of others, nor yet indolently and luxuriously ; thou shalt "*eat,*" and not penuriously stint thyself and others ; thy crops shall not be blighted, but shall bring forth abundantly ; and no enemy shall destroy or carry off thy harvest. And these two latter interpretations accord best with the converse punishments threatened to the disobedient by Moses. "*Thou shalt eat the labour of thine hands.*" But he who hates labour does not eat of it, nor can he say, "My meat is to do the will of him that sent me, and to finish his work" : John iv. 34. On the other hand, he to whom such labour is a delight, does not merely look forward in hope to the future fruits or rewards of labour, but even here and now finds sustenance and pleasure in toiling for God ; so that it is "*well*" with him in the world, even amidst all its cares and troubles, and he "*shall be happy*" in that which is to come, whence sorrow is banished for ever, as it is written in the gospel : "Blessed is he that shall eat bread in the kingdom of God" : Luke xiv. 15.—*Neale and Littledale.*

Verse 2.—"*Thou shalt eat the labour of thine hands,*" etc. This must they learn also which are married, that they must labour. For the law of nature requireth that the husband should sustain and nourish his wife and his children. For after that man and wife do know that they ought to fear God their Creator, who not only made them, but gave his blessing also unto his creature ; this secondly must they know, that something they must do that they consume not their days in ease and idleness. Hesiod, the poet, giveth his counsel, that first thou shouldst get thee a house, then a wife, and also an ox to till the ground. . . . For albeit that our diligence, care, and travail is not able to maintain our family, yet God useth such as a means by the which he will bless us.—*Martin Luther.*

Verse 2.—"*Thou shalt eat the labour of thine hands.*" Men have dreamed fascinating dreams of removing the disabilities and limitations of the world and the evils of life, without sorrow. Poets have pictured earthly paradises, where life would be one long festival,—

"Summer isles of Eden lying in dark purple spheres of sea."

But vain are all such dreams and longings. They are of human, not of Divine origin, and spring from a root of selfishness and not of holiness. They cannot be realized in a fallen world, full of sorrow because full of sin. All blessings in man's economy are got from pains. Happiness is the flower that grows from a thorn of sorrow transformed by man's cultivation. The beautiful myth which placed the golden apples of the Hesperides in a garden guarded by dragons, is an allegory illustrative of the great human fact, that not till we have slain the dragons of selfishness and sloth can we obtain any of the golden successes of life. Supposing it were possible that we could obtain the objects of our desire without any toil or trouble, we should not enjoy them.   To benefit us really, they must be the growths of our own self-denial and labour.   And this is the great lesson which the miracles of our Lord, wrought in the manner in which they were, unfolded.   They teach us that, in both temporal and spiritual things, we should not so throw ourselves upon the providence or grace of God as to neglect the part we have ourselves to act,—that God crowns every honest and faithful effort of man with success :   "*Blessed is every one that feareth the* LORD ; *that walketh in his ways. For thou shalt eat the labour of thine hands : happy shalt thou be, and it shall be well with thee.*"—*Hugh Macmillan, in "The Ministry of Nature,"* 1871.

Verse 2 (*first clause*).—

> Labour, the symbol of man's punishment ;
> Labour, the secret of man's happiness.
> —*James Montgomery,* 1771—1854.

Verse 2.—"*Happy shalt thou be.*"   Oh trust in the Lord for happiness as well as for help !   All the springs of happiness are in him.   Trust " in him who giveth us all things richly to enjoy" ; who, of his own rich and free mercy, holds them out to us, as in his own hand, that, receiving them as his gifts, and as pledges of his love, we may enjoy all that we possess.   It is his love gives a relish to all we taste, puts life and sweetness into all ; while every creature leads us up to the great Creator, and all earth is a scale to heaven.   He transfuses the joys that are at his own right hand into all that he bestows on his thankful children, who, having fellowship with the Father and his Son Jesus Christ, enjoy him in all and above all.—*John Wesley,* 1703—1791.

Verse 2.—"*Happy shalt thou be.*"   Mr. Disraeli puts these remarkable words into the mouth of one of his characters :—" Youth is a blunder ; manhood a struggle ; old age a regret."   A sad and cheerless view of life's progress that ! It may be true, in measure, of a life separated from godliness ; it certainly is not true of a life allied with godliness.   Let there be " life and godliness," and then youth is not a blunder, but a wise purpose and a glowing hope ; manhood is not a struggle only, but a conquest and a joy ; old age is not a regret, but a rich memory and a glorious prospect.— *R. P. Macmaster, in "The Baptist Magazine,"* 1878.

Verse 3.—"*Thy wife shall be as a fruitful vine,*" etc.   The comparison would perhaps be brought out more clearly by arranging the verse as follows :—

> " Thy wife shall be in the inner part of thy house
> Like a fruitful vine ;
> Thy children round about thy table
> Like the shoots of the olive."

In the inner part, literally, " *the sides of thy house,*" as in Amos vi. 10, *i.e.,* the women's apartments, as marking the proper sphere of the wife engaged in her domestic duties, and also to some extent her seclusion, though this was far less amongst the Jews than amongst other Orientals.

The " *vine*" is an emblem chiefly of *fruitfulness,* but perhaps also of dependence, as needing support ; the " *olive,*" of vigorous, healthy, joyous life.   The same figure is employed by Euripides, *Herc. Fur.,* 839. *Med.* 1098.—*J. J. Stewart Perowne.*

Verse 3.—"*Thy wife shall be as a fruitful vine,*" etc.   We do not remember to have met with a single instance, in the East, of vines trained *against the walls of a house,* or of olives near or about a house.   Neither have we read of such instances.   The passage doubtless derives its figures from the fertility of the vine, and from the appearance of the olive, or the order in which olive trees are planted. The construction would then be : " Thy wife, in the sides (interior apartments) of thy house, shall be as the fruitful vine, and thy children round about thy table, like olive plants."—*John Kitto* (1804—1854), *in "The Pictorial Bible."*

Verse 3.—"*Thy wife shall be as a fruitful vine by the sides of thine house.*" The wife is likened not to thorns or briers, nor even to oaks or to other fruits and trees, but to the vine ; and also to a vine neither in a vineyard nor in a garden, but set by the walls of the house ; also not barren, but fertile and fruit-bearing. This admonishes husbands as well as wives of their duties. For as the walls support the vine, and defend it against the force of winds and tempests, so ought husbands, as far as is in their power, to defend their wives by their godly conversation and wholesome teachings and institutions against the pestilential wind of the old serpent ; also against the injuries of evil-disposed men. " He that loveth his wife loveth himself. For no man ever yet hated his own flesh ; but nourisheth and cherisheth it, even as the Lord the Church" : Ephes. v. 28, 29.

Further, the vine is exceedingly fragile wood, and not meet for any work, Ezek. xv. 4. Husbands, therefore, should remember that they ought to behave towards their wives patiently and prudently, as with the weaker vessel ; not keeping in mind the fragility of the wood, but the abundance and sweetness of the fruit. If husbands observe this, that will happen to them which Scripture says concerning the peaceful time of Solomon, " And Judah and Israel dwelt safely, every man under his vine and under his fig tree" : 1 Kings iv. 25. Such was the married life of Abraham with Sarah, Isaac with Rebecca, Jacob with Leah and Rachel.—*Solomon Gesner.*

Verse 3.—"*A fruitful vine by the sides of thine house.*" It does not say *on* the sides of the house, but *by* the sides. The passage probably refers to the trellissed, bowers which often lead up to the houses, and are covered with vines, the grapes hanging over head. Sitting in these bowers is sitting under our own vines : Micah iv. 4. I have seen in Constantinople grapes hanging over the people's heads in the principal streets, the vines being trained from one side of the street to the other.—*John Gadsby, in "My Wanderings,"* 1860.

Verse 3.—"*By the sides of thine house.*" Not on the roof, nor on the floor ; the one is too high, she is no ruler ; the other too low, she is no slave : but in the sides, an equal place between both.—*Thomas Adams.*

Verse 3.—"*By the sides of thine house.*" The house is her proper place ; for she is " the beauty of the house" ; there her business lies, there she is safe. The ancients painting them with a snail under their feet, and the Egyptians denying their women shoes, and the Scythians burning the bride's chariot axle-tree at her door, when she was brought to her husband's house, and the angel's asking Abraham where Sarah was (though he knew well enough), that it might be observed, she was " in the tent," do all intimate, that, by the law of nature, and by the rules of religion, the wife ought to keep at home, unless urgent necessity do call her abroad.—*Richard Steele* (—1692), *in "The Morning Exercises."*

Verse 3.—As it is visible that the good man's sons being " *like olive plants round about his table,*" means not that they should be like the olive plants which grew round his table, it being, I presume, a thought in Bishop Patrick that will not be defended, that the Psalmist refers to a table spread in an arbour composed of young olive trees, for we find no such arbours in the Levant, nor is the tree very proper for such a purpose ; so in like manner the first clause must signify, thy wife *shall be in the sides,* or private apartments, *of thy house, fruitful as a thriving vine :* the place here mentioned (the sides of the house) referring to the wife, not to the vine ; as the other (the table) refers to the children, not to the olives. Nor is this a new thought, it is a remark that Musculus and other interpreters have made. The Hebrew word, translated *sides,* is very well known to signify the more *private apartments* of a house, as they have also remarked ; and he that reads Dr. Shaw's description of an Eastern house, must immediately see the propriety of calling the private apartments *its sides.* Such a house consists of a square court, which the doctor observes, is called *the midst* of the house : and private apartments round it, which may as properly be called *its sides* in consequence : into this middle of the house, or this quadrangle, company, he tells us, are sometimes received, in which *other authors* tell us their *wives* remain concealed at such times. —*Thomas Harmer,* 1719—1788.

Verse 3.--"*Thy children like olive plants,*" etc. Follow me into the grove, and I will show you what may have suggested the comparison. Here we have hit upon a beautiful illustration. This aged and decayed tree is surrounded, as you see, by several young and thrifty shoots, which spring from the root of the venerable parent. They seem to uphold, protect, and embrace it, we may even fancy that they now bear that load of fruit which would otherwise be demanded of the feeble parent. Thus do good and affectionate children gather round the table of the righteous. Each contributes something to the common wealth and welfare of the whole—a beautiful sight, with which may God refresh the eyes of every friend of mine.—*W. M. Thomson.*

Verse 3.—Man by nature, uninfluenced by grace, is " a wild olive tree" ; and the object of most parents is merely to cultivate this wild olive tree. What anxiety is there about accomplishments which, how attractive soever, are but the dying blossoms of this wild olive tree !—*Richard Cecil,* 1748—1810.

Verse 3.—Although the world is carried away by irregular desires after various objects, between which it is perpetually fluctuating in its choice, God gives us in this psalm a description of what he considers to be a blessing beyond all riches, and therefore we ought to hold it in high estimation. If a man has a wife of amiable manners as the companion of his life, let him set no less value upon this blessing than Solomon did, who, in Prov. xix. 14, affirms that it is God alone who gives a good wife. In like manner, if a man be a father of a numerous offspring, let him receive that goodly boon with a thankful heart.—*John Calvin.*

Verse 3.—Before the fall Paradise was man's home ; since the fall home has been his Paradise.—*Augustus William Hare* (1792–1834), *and Julius Charles Hare* (1795–1855), *in " Guesses at Truth."*

Verse 4.—As Haman caused it to be proclaimed (Esther vi. 9), " Thus shall it be done to the man whom the king delighteth to honour" ; so here, " *Behold, that thus shall the man be blessed that feareth the Lord.*" He shall be blessed in his wife, and blessed in his children ; so blessed in both that the Psalmist calls all to behold it, as a rare, beautiful, yea, wonderful sight : " *Behold, thus shall the man be blessed.*" And yet the man fearing God shall be blessed more than *thus :* his blessing shall come in the best way (verse 5) : " *The Lord shall bless thee out of Zion*" *;* his temporal mercies shall come in a spiritual way, yea, he shall have spiritual blessings : " *He shall bless thee out of Zion*" *;* and he shall have blessings beyond his own walls : " *Thou shalt see the good of Jerusalem all the days of thy life. Yea, thou shalt see thy children's children, and peace upon Israel.*" Sometimes a good man can take no content in his family mercies because of the church's afflictions ; he " prefers Jerusalem above his chief joy" (Ps. cxxxvii. 6), and while that is mourning he cannot but be sorrowing, though his own house be full of joy. Sometimes a man's own family is so afflicted, and his house so full of sorrow, that he cannot but mourn, even when Jerusalem rejoiceth and Zion is glad. But when a good man looks home to his own house and sees good there ; when also he looks abroad to Jerusalem and sees good there too, how full is his joy ! how complete is his blessedness ! and, " *Behold, thus the man is blessed that feareth the Lord.*"—*Joseph Caryl.*

Verse 4.—"*Behold, that thus shall the man be blessed,*" etc. It is asserted with a note commanding attention : *behold* it by faith in the promise ; *behold* it by observation in the performance of the promise ; *behold* it with assurance that it shall be so, for God is faithful ; and with admiration that it should be so ; for we merit no favour, no blessing from him.—*Matthew Henry.*

Verse 5.—" *Thou shalt see the good of Jerusalem,*" etc. What is added concerning " *the good of Jerusalem*" is to be regarded as enjoining upon the godly the duty not only of seeking their own individual welfare, or of being devoted to their own peculiar interests ; but rather of having it as their chief desire to see the Church of God in a flourishing condition. It would be a very unreasonable thing for each member to desire what may be profitable for itself, while in the meantime the body was neglected. From our extreme proneness to err in this respect, the prophet, with good reason, recommends solicitude about the public welfare ; and he mingles together domestic blessings and the common benefits of the church in such a way as to show us that they are things joined together, and which it is unlawful to put asunder.—*John Calvin.*

Verse 6.—Lord, let thy blessing so accompany my endeavours in their breedings, that all my sons may be Benaiahs, the Lord's building, and then they will all be Abners, their father's light ; and that all my daughters may be Bethias, the Lord's daughters, and then they will all be Abigails, their father's joy.— *George Swinnock.*

Verse 6.—Religion is as favourable for long life as for happiness. She promotes long life by destroying those evils, the tendency of which is to limit the duration of human existence. War sweeps millions into a premature grave. Men live longer in Christian than in heathen countries. They live longer in Protestant than in Roman Catholic countries. The direct effect of true religion is to increase the period of human life. " Length of days is in her right hand."—*N. M'Michael.*

Verse 6.—Connecting this with the next Psalm we find the following in a famous Scotch divine :—" ' *Peace upon Israel.*' The great blessing of peace, which the Lord hath promised to his people even in this life, (for where the Lord gives mercy to any, he gives them peace also, peace and grace are inseparably joined together,) this peace, I say, does not consist in this, that the people of God shall have no enemies ; no, for there is an immortal and endless enmity against them. Neither does their peace consist in this, that their enemies shall not assault them ; neither does it consist in this, that their enemies shall not molest or afflict them. We do but deceive ourselves if so be that we imagine, so long as we are in this our pilgrimage, and in our warfare here, if we promise to ourselves a peace of this kind ; for while we live in this world, we shall still have enemies, and these enemies shall assault us, and persecute and afflict us."—*Alexander Henderson.*

HINTS TO THE VILLAGE PREACHER.

Verse 1.—The universality of the blessedness of God-fearing men. Circum: stances, personal or relative, cannot alter the blessing ; nor age, nor public opinion, nor even their own sense of unworthiness.

Verse 1.—Consider : I. The union of a right fear with a right walk. 1. There is a wrong fear, because slavish ; this never can lead to genuine obedience, which must be willingly and cheerfully rendered. 2. But the fear of reverence and filial love will surely turn the feet to God's ways, keep them steadfast therein, and wing them with speed. II. The blessedness of him in whom they are united. 1. It is blessedness of life ; for that is prospered. 2. It is blessedness of domestic happiness ; for where the head of a family is holy, the family is the home of peace. 3. It is the blessedness of a holy influence in every sphere of his activity. 4. It is deep-felt heart-blessedness in walking with God. 5. And all is but a prelude to the everlasting blessedness of heaven.—*J. F.*

Verse 2.—The blessedness of the righteous are first generalized, then particularized. Here they are divided into three particulars. I. The fruit of past labours. II. Present enjoyment. III. Future welfare : "It shall be well with thee." Well in time ; well in death ; well at the last judgment ; well for ever.—*G. R.*

Verse 2.—I. Labour a blessing to him who fears God. II. The fruits of labour the result of God's blessing. III. The enjoyment of the fruits of labour a further blessing from God.—*W. H. J. P.*

Verse 2 (*first clause*).—Success in life. I. Its source—God's blessing. II. Its channel—our own labour. III. The measure in which it is promised—as much as we can eat. More is above the promise. IV. The enjoyment. We are permitted to eat or enjoy our labour.

Verse 2 (*second clause*).—Godly happiness.   I. Follows upon God's blessing.
II. Grows out of character : "feareth the Lord."   III. Follows labour : see preceding sentence.   IV. It is supported by well-being : see following sentence.

Verse 2 (*last clause*).—I. It shall be well with thee while thou livest.   II. It
shall be better with thee when thou diest.   III. It shall be best of all with thee in
eternity.—*Adapted from Matthew Henry.*

Verse 3.—The blessing of children.   I. They are round our table—expense,
anxiety, responsibility, pleasure.   II. They are like olive plants—strong, planted
in order, coming on to succeed us, fruitful for God—as the olive provided oil for
the lamp.

Verse 3.—A complete family picture.   Here are the husband, the wife, the
children, the house, the rooms in the side, the table.   We should ask a blessing
upon each, bless God for each, and use each in a blessed manner.

Verse 4.—Domestic happiness the peculiar blessing of piety.   Show how it produces and maintains it.

Verse 5.—The blessing out of Zion.   See Numbers vi. 24—26.

Verse 5.—Two priceless mercies.   I. The house of God a blessing to our house.
It is connected with our own salvation, edification, consolation, etc.   It is our
hope for the conversion of our children and servants, etc.   It is the place of their
education, and for the formation of helpful friendship, etc.   II. Our house a
blessing to God's house.   Personal interest in the church, hospitality, generosity,
service, etc.   Children aiding holy work.   Wife useful, etc.

Verse 6.—Old age blessed when—I. Life has been spent in the fear of God.
II. When it is surrounded to its close by human affection.   III. When it maintains its interest in the cause of God.—*W. H. J. P.*

Verse 6 (*last clause*).—Church peace—its excellence, its enemies, its friends, its
fruits.

PSALM CXXIX.

TITLE.—A Song of Degrees. *I fail to see how this is a step beyond the previous psalm; and yet it is clearly the song of an older and more tried individual, who looks back upon a life of affliction in which he suffered all along, even from his youth. Inasmuch as patience is a higher, or at least more difficult, grace than domestic love, the ascent or progress may perhaps be seen in that direction. Probably if we knew more of the stations on the road to the Temple we should see a reason for the order of these psalms; but as that information cannot be obtained, we must take the songs as we find them, and remember that, as we do not now go on pilgrimages to Zion, it is our curiosity and not our necessity which is a loser by our not knowing the cause of the arrangement of the songs in this Pilgrim Psalter.*

AUTHOR, ETC.—*It does not seem to us at all needful to ascribe this psalm to a period subsequent to the captivity: indeed, it is more suitable to a time when as yet the enemy had not so far prevailed as to have carried the people into a distant land. It is a mingled hymn of sorrow and of strong resolve. Though sorely smitten, the afflicted one is heart-whole, and scorns to yield in the least degree to the enemy. The poet sings the trials of Israel, verses 1—3; the interposition of the Lord, verse 4; and the unblessed condition of Israel's foes, verses 5—8. It is a rustic song, full of allusions to husbandry. It reminds us of the books of Ruth and Amos.*

EXPOSITION.

MANY a time have they afflicted me from my youth, may Israel now say:

2 Many a time have they afflicted me from my youth: yet they have not prevailed against me.

3 The plowers plowed upon my back: they made long their furrows.

4 The LORD is righteous: he hath cut asunder the cords of the wicked.

5 Let them all be confounded and turned back that hate Zion.

6 Let them be as the grass *upon* the housetops, which withereth afore it groweth up:

7 Wherewith the mower filleth not his hand; nor he that bindeth sheaves his bosom.

8 Neither do they which go by say, The blessing of the LORD *be* upon you: we bless you in the name of the LORD.

1. "*Many a time have they afflicted me from my youth, may Israel now say.*" In her present hour of trial she may remember her former afflictions and speak of them for her comfort, drawing from them the assurance that he who has been with her for so long will not desert her in the end. The song begins abruptly. The poet has been musing, and the fire burns, therefore speaks he with his tongue; he cannot help it, he feels that he must speak, and therefore "may now say" what he has to say. The trials of the church have been repeated again and again, times beyond all count: the same afflictions are fulfilled in us as in our fathers. Jacob of old found his days full of trouble; each Israelite is often harassed; and Israel as a whole has proceeded from tribulation to tribulation. "Many a time," Israel says, because she could not say how many times. She speaks of her assailants as "they," because it would be impossible to write or even to know all their names. They had straitened, harassed, and fought against her from the earliest days of her history—from her youth; and they had contin-

ued their assaults right on without ceasing. Persecution is the heirloom of the church, and the ensign of the elect. Israel among the nations was peculiar, and this peculiarity brought against her many restless foes, who could never be easy unless they were warring against the people of God. When in Canaan, at the first, the chosen household was often severely tried ; in Egypt it was heavily oppressed ; in the wilderness it was fiercely assailed ; and in the promised land it was often surrounded by deadly enemies. It was something for the afflicted nation that it survived to *say*, " Many a time have they afflicted me." The affliction began early—" from my youth" ; and it continued late. The earliest years of Israel and of the Church of God are spent in trial. Babes in grace are cradled in opposition. No sooner is the man-child born than the dragon is after it. " It is," however, " good for a man that he bear the yoke in his youth," and he shall see it to be so when in after days he tells the tale.

2. "*Many a time have they afflicted me from my youth.*" Israel repeats her statement of her repeated afflictions. The fact was uppermost in her thoughts, and she could not help soliloquizing upon it again and again. These repetitions are after the manner of poetry : thus she makes a sonnet out of her sorrows, music out of her miseries. "*Yet they have not prevailed against me.*" We seem to hear the beat of timbrels and the clash of cymbals here : the foe is derided ; his malice has failed. That "*yet*" breaks in like the blast of trumpets, or the roll of kettledrums. "Cast down, but not destroyed," is the shout of a victor. Israel has wrestled, and has overcome in the struggle. Who wonders ? If Israel overcame the angel of the covenant, what man or devil shall vanquish him ? The fight was oft renewed and long protracted : the champion severely felt the conflict, and was at times fearful of the issue ; but at length he takes breath, and cries, " Yet they have not prevailed against me." " Many a time ;" yes, " many a time," the enemy has had his opportunity and his vantage, but not so much as once has he gained the victory.

3. "*The plowers plowed up on my back.*" The scourgers tore the flesh as ploughmen furrow a field. The people were maltreated like a criminal given over to the lictors with their cruel whips ; the back of the nation was scored and furrowed by oppression. It is a grand piece of imagery condensed into few words. A writer says the metaphor is muddled, but he is mistaken : there are several figures, like wheel within wheel, but there is no confusion. The afflicted nation was, as it were, lashed by her adversaries so cruelly that each blow left a long red mark, or perhaps a bleeding wound, upon her back and shoulders, comparable to a furrow which tears up the ground from one end of the field to the other. Many a heart has been in like case ; smitten and sore wounded by them that use the scourge of the tongue ; so smitten that their whole character has been cut up and scored by calumny. The true church has in every age had fellowship with her Lord under his cruel flagellations : his sufferings were a prophecy of what she would be called hereafter to endure, and the foreshadowing has been fulfilled. Zion has in this sense been ploughed as a field.

"*They made long their furrows :*"—as if delighting in their cruel labour. They missed not an inch, but went from end to end of the field, meaning to make thorough work of their congenial engagement. Those who laid on the scourge did it with a thoroughness which showed how hearty was their hate. Assuredly the enemies of Christ's church never spare pains to inflict the utmost injury : they never do the work of the devil deceitfully, or hold back their hand from blood. They smite so as to plough into the man ; they plough the quivering flesh as if it were clods of clay ; they plough deep and long with countless furrows ; until they leave no portion of the church unfurrowed or unassailed. Ah me ! Well did Latimer say that there was no busier ploughman in all the world than the devil : whoever makes short furrows, he does not. Whoever baulks and shirks, he is thorough in all that he does. Whoever stops work at sundown, he never does. He and his children plough like practised ploughmen ; but they prefer to carry on their pernicious work upon the saints behind their backs, for they are as cowardly as they are cruel.

4. "*The* LORD *is righteous.*" Whatever men may be, Jehovah remains just, and will therefore keep covenant with his people and deal out justice to their oppressors. Here is the hinge of the condition : this makes the turning point of Israel's distress. The Lord bears with the long furrows of the wicked, but he will surely make them cease from their ploughing before he has done with them. "*He hath cut asunder the cords of the wicked.*" The rope which binds the oxen to the plough is cut ; the cord which bound the victim is broken ; the bond which held the enemies in cruel unity has snapped. As in Psalm cxxiv. 7 we read, " the snare is broken ; we are escaped," so here the breaking of the enemies' instrument of oppression is Israel's release. Sooner or later a righteous God will interpose, and when he does so, his action will be most effectual ; he does not unfasten, but cuts asunder, the harness which the ungodly use in their labour of hate. Never has God used a nation to chastise his Israel without destroying that nation when the chastisement has come to a close : he hates those who hurt his people even though he permits their hate to triumph for a while for his own purpose. If any man would have his harness cut, let him begin to plough one of the Lord's fields with the plough of persecution. The shortest way to ruin is to meddle with a saint : the divine warning is, " He that toucheth you toucheth the apple of his eye."

5. "*Let them all be confounded and turned back that hate Zion.*" And so say we right heartily : and in this case *vox populi* is *vox Dei*, for so it shall be. If this be an imprecation, let it stand ; for our heart says " Amen" to it. It is but justice that those who hate, harass, and hurt the good should be brought to naught. Those who confound right and wrong ought to be confounded, and those who turn back from God ought to be turned back. Loyal subjects wish ill to those who plot against their king.

> " Confound their politics,
> Frustrate their knavish tricks,"

is but a proper wish, and contains within it no trace of personal ill-will. We desire their welfare as men, their downfall as traitors. Let their conspiracies be confounded, their policies be turned back. How can we wish prosperity to those who would destroy that which is dearest to our hearts ? This present age is so flippant that if a man loves the Saviour he is styled a fanatic, and if he hates the powers of evil he is named a bigot. As for ourselves, despite all objectors, we join heartily in this commination ; and would revive in our heart the old practice of Ebal and Gerizim, where those were blessed who bless God, and those were cursed who make themselves a curse to the righteous. We have heard men desire a thousand times that the gallows might be the reward of the assassins who murdered two inoffensive men in Dublin, and we could never 'censure the wish ; for justice ought to be rendered to the evil as well as to the good. Besides, the church of God is so useful, so beautiful, so innocent of harm, so fraught with good, that those who do her wrong are wronging all mankind and deserve to be treated as the enemies of the human race. Study a chapter from the " Book of Martyrs," and see if you do not feel inclined to read an imprecatory psalm over Bishop Bonner and Bloody Mary. It may be that some wretched nineteenth century sentimentalist will blame you : if so, read another *over him*.

6. "*Let them be as the grass upon the housetops, which withereth afore it groweth up.*" Grass on the housetop is soon up and soon down. It sprouts in the heat, finds enough nutriment to send up a green blade, and then it dies away before it reaches maturity, because it has neither earth nor moisture sufficient for its proper development. Before it grows up it dies ; it needs not to be plucked up, for it hastens to decay of itself. Such is and such ought to be the lot of the enemies of God's people. Transient is their prosperity ; speedy is their destruction. The height of their position, as it hastens their progress, so it hurries their doom. Had they been lower in station they had perhaps been longer in being. " Soon ripe, soon rotten," is an old proverb. Soon plotting and soon rotting, is a version of the old adage which will suit in this place. We have seen grass on the rustic

thatch of our own country cottages which will serve for an illustration almost as well as that which comes up so readily on the flat roofs and domes of eastern habitations. The idea is—they make speed to success, and equal speed to failure. Persecutors are all sound and fury, flash and flame ; but they speedily vanish—more speedily than is common to men. Grass in the field withers, but not so speedily as grass on the housetops. Without a mower the tufts of verdure perish from the roofs, and so do opposers pass away by other deaths than fall to the common lot of men ; they are gone, and none is the worse. If they are missed at all, their absence is never regretted. Grass on the housetop is a nonentity in the world : the house is not impoverished when the last blade is dried up : and, even so, the opposers of Christ pass away, and none lament them. One of the fathers said of the apostate emperor Julian, "That little cloud will soon be gone" ; and so it was. Every sceptical system of philosophy has much the same history ; and the like may be said of each heresy. Poor, rootless things, they are and are not : they come and go, even though no one rises against them. Evil carries the seeds of dissolution within itself. So let it be.

7. "*Wherewith the mower filleth not his hand ; nor he that bindeth sheaves his bosom.*" When with his sickle the husbandman would cut down the tufts, he found nothing to lay hold upon : the grass promised fairly enough, but there was no fulfilment, there was nothing to cut or to carry, nothing for the hand to grasp, nothing for the lap to gather. Easterns carry their corn in their bosoms, but in this case there was nothing to bear home. Thus do the wicked come to nothing. By God's just appointment they prove a disappointment. Their fire ends in smoke ; their verdure turns to vanity ; their flourishing is but a form of withering. No one profits by them, least of all are they profitable to themselves. Their aim is bad, their work is worse, their end is worst of all.

8. "*Neither do they which go by say, The blessing of the* LORD *be upon you: we bless you in the name of the* LORD." In harvest times men bless each other in the name of the Lord ; but there is nothing in the course and conduct of the ungodly man to suggest the giving or receiving of a benediction. Upon a survey of the sinner's life from beginning to end, we feel more inclined to weep than to rejoice, and we feel bound rather to wish him failure than success. We dare not use pious expressions as mere compliments, and hence we dare not wish God-speed to evil men lest we be partakers of their evil deeds. When persecutors are worrying the saints, we cannot say, " The blessing of the Lord be upon you." When they slander the godly and oppose the doctrine of the cross, we dare not bless them in the name of the Lord. It would be infamous to compromise the name of the righteous Jehovah by pronouncing his blessing upon unrighteous deeds.

See how godly men are roughly ploughed by their adversaries, and yet a harvest comes of it which endures and produces blessing ; while the ungodly, though they flourish for a while and enjoy a complete immunity, dwelling, as they think, quite above the reach of harm, are found in a short time to have gone their way and to have left no trace behind. Lord, number me with thy saints. Let me share their grief if I may also partake of their glory. Thus would I make this psalm my own, and magnify thy name, because thine afflicted ones are not destroyed, and thy persecuted ones are not forsaken.

EXPLANATORY NOTES.

Whole Psalm.—In the " degrees" of Christian virtue the psalm corresponds to the tenth step, which is patience in adversity.—*H. T. Armfield.*

Whole Psalm.—The following incident in connection with the glorious return of the Vaudois under Henri Arnaud is related in Muston's " Israel of the Alps " :—
" After these successes the gallant patriots took an oath of fidelity to each other, and celebrated divine service in one of their own churches, for the first time since

their banishment. The enthusiasm of the moment was irrepressible; they chanted the seventy-fourth psalm to the clash of arms; and Henri Arnaud, mounting the pulpit with a sword in one hand and a Bible in the other, preached from the Hundred and twenty-ninth psalm, and once more declared, in the face of heaven, that he would never resume his pastoral office in patience and peace, until he should witness the restoration of his brethren to their ancient and rightful settlements."

Verse 1.—"*Many a time have they afflicted me from my youth.*" 1. How *old* these afflictions are: "*From my youth.*" Ay, from my infancy, birth and conception. 2. There is the *frequency* and *iteration* of these afflictions. They were *oft* and *many:* "*many a time.*" 3. There is the *greivousness* of these afflictions, expressed by a comparison. "The plowers plowed upon my back: they made long their furrows." So these were *old* afflictions—*from her youth.* They were *many a time:* more times than can be numbered. And then they were *grievous*, even like iron ploughs, drawing deep and long furrows on their back.—*Alexander Henderson.*

Verse 1.—"*Many a time have they afflicted me,*" etc. God had one Son, and but one Son, without sin; but never any without sorrow. We may be God's children, and yet still under persecution; his Israel, and afflicted from our youth up. We may feel God's hand as a Father upon us when he strikes us as well as when he strokes us. When he strokes us, it is lest we faint under his hand; and when he strikes us, it is that we should know his hand.—*Abraham Wright* (1611—1690), *in "A Practical Commentary upon the Psalms."*

Verse 1.—"*They.*" The persecutors deserve not a name. The rich man is not named (as Lazarus is) because not worthy: Luke xvi. "They shall be written in the earth": Jeremiah xvii. 13.—*John Trapp.*

Verse 1.—"*They.*" In speaking of the enemies of Israel simply by the pronoun "*they,*" without being more specific, the Psalmist aggravates the greatness of the evil more than if he had expressly named the Assyrians or the Egyptians. By not specifying any particular class of foes, he tacitly intimates that the world is filled with innumerable bands of enemies, whom Satan easily arms for the destruction of good men, his object being that new wars may arise continually on every side. History certainly bears ample testimony that the people of God had not to deal with a few enemies, but that they were assaulted by almost the whole world; and further, that they were molested not only by external foes, but also by those of an internal kind, by such as professed to belong to the Church.—*John Calvin.*

Verse 1.—"*They afflicted me.*" Why are these afflictions of the righteous? Whence is it that he who has given up his Son to death for them, should deny them earthly blessings? Why is faith a mourner so frequently here below, and with all that heroic firmness in her aspect, and hope of glory in her eye, why needs she to be painted with so deep a sorrow on her countenance, and the trace of continual tears on her cheek? First, we reply, *for her own safety.* Place religion out of the reach of sorrow, and soon she would pine and perish. God is said to choose his people in the furnace, because they oftenest choose him there.

It is ever from the cross that the most earnest "My God" proceeds, and never is the cry heard but he speeds forth at its utterance, who once hung there, to support, to comfort, and to save.

As it is only in affliction God is *sought*, so by many it is only in affliction God is *known.* This, one of the kings of these worshippers of the Temple found. "When Manasseh was brought to affliction, *then* he knew that the Lord he was God": 2 Chronicles xxxiii. 12, 13.

But, further, it is only by affliction *we ourselves are known.* What is the source of that profound and obstinate indifference to divine truth which prevails among men of the world, except the proud conviction that they may dispense with it? It is only when they are crushed as the worm they are made to feel that the dust is their source; only when earthly props are withdrawn will they take hold of that arm of omnipotence which Jesus offers, and which he has offered so long in vain.

While men know themselves, they *know their sin* also in affliction. What is the natural course and experience of the unbelieving of mankind ? Transgression, remorse, and then forgetfulness ; new transgression, new sorrow, and again forgetfulness. How shall this carelessness be broken? How convince them that they stand in need of a Saviour as the first and deepest want of their being, and that they can only secure deliverance from wrath eternal by a prompt and urgent application to him ? By nothing so effectually as by affliction. God's children, who had forgotten him, arise and go to their Father when thus smitten by the scourge of sorrow ; and no sooner is the penitent *"Father, I have sinned "* spoken, than they are clasped in his arms, and safe and happy in his love.

It is, further, by affliction that the *world* is known to God's children. God's great rival is the world. The lust of the flesh, pleasure ; the lust of the eye, desire ; the pride of life, the longing to be deemed superior to those about us,— comprise everything man naturally covets. Give us ease, honour, distinction, and all life's good will seem obtained. *But what wilt thou do, when he shall judge thee ?* This is a question fitted to alarm the happiest of the children of prosperity.

What so frequently and effectually shows the necessity of piety as the sharp teachings of affliction ? They show what moralists and preachers never could, that riches profit not in the day of death, that pleasures most fully enjoyed bring no soothing to the terrors which nearness to eternity presents, and that friends, however affectionate, cannot plead for and save us at the bar of God. " Miserable comforters are they all," and it is for the very purpose of inspiring this conviction, along with a belief that it is Jesus alone who can comfort in the hour of need, that affliction is sent to God's children.—*Robert Nisbet.*

Verse 1.—*"From my youth."* The first that ever died, died for religion ; so early came martyrdom into the world.—*John Trapp.*

Verses 1, 2.—1. The visible Church from the beginning of the world is one body, and, as it were, one man, growing up from infancy to riper age ; for so speaketh the church here : *"Many a time have they afflicted me from my youth."* 2. The wicked enemies of the church, they also are one body, one adverse army, from the beginning of the world continuing war against the church : *"Many a time have they afflicted me from my youth."* 3. As the former injuries done to the church are owned by the church, in after-ages, as done against the same body, so also the persecution of former enemies is imputed and put upon the score of present persecutors : *"Many a time have they afflicted me from my youth, may Israel now say."* 4. New experience of persecution, when they call to mind the exercise of the church in former ages, serves much for encouragement and consolation in troubles : *"Many a time have they afflicted me from my youth, may Israel now say."* 5. Albeit this hath been the endeavour of the wicked in all ages to destroy the church, yet God hath still preserved her from age to age : *" Yet they have not prevailed."*—*David Dickson.*

Verses 1, 2.—When the prophet says twice, *"They have afflicted me," " they have afflicted me,"* the repetition is not superfluous, it being intended to teach us that the people of God had not merely once or twice to enter the conflict, but that their patience had been tried by continual exercises.—*John Calvin.*

Verse 2.—*"Many a time,"* etc. The Christian Church may adopt the language of the Hebrew Church : " Many a time have they afflicted me from my youth : yet they have not prevailed against me." What afflictions were endured by the Christian Church from her youth up ! How feeble was that youth! How small the number of the apostles to whom our Lord gave his gospel in charge ! How destitute were they of human learning, of worldly influence, of secular power ! To effect their destruction, and to frustrate their object—the glory of God and the salvation of men—the dungeon and the mine, the rack and the gibbet, were all successively employed. The ploughers ploughed their back, and made long their furrows. Their property was confiscated ; their persons were imprisoned ;

their civil rights were taken from them ; their heads rolled on the scaffold ; their bodies were consumed at the burning pile ; they were thrown, amidst the ringing shouts of the multitude, to the wild beasts of the amphitheatre. Despite, however, of every opposition, our holy religion took root and grew upward. Not all the fury of ten persecutions could exterminate it from the earth. The teeth of wild beasts could not grind it to powder ; the fire could not burn it ; the waters could not drown it ; the dungeon could not confine it. Truth is eternal, like the great God from whose bosom it springs, and therefore it cannot be destroyed. And because Christianity is the truth, and no lie, her enemies have never prevailed against her.—*M. M'Michael.*

Verse 2.—" *Yet they have not prevailed against me.*" The words are the same as in Gen. xxxii. 28. The blessing won by Jacob, when he wrestled with the angel, remained in his descendants. During the long night of the Captivity the faithful had wrestled in faithful prayer ; now the morning had appeared, and Israel was raised to a higher stage of privilege.—*W. Kay.*

Verse 2.—" *Yet they have not prevailed against me.*" Israel prevailed with God in wrestling with him, and therefore it is that he prevails with men also. If so be that we will wrestle with God for a blesssing, and prevail with him, then we need not to fear but we shall wrestle the enemies out of it also. If we be the people of God, and persist in wrestling against his enemies, we need not fear but that we shall be victorious.—*Alexander Henderson.*

Verse 3.—" *The plowers plowed,*" etc. There does not seem to be any need to look for an interpretation of this in scourging, or any other bodily infliction of pain ; it seems to be " a figurative mode of expressing severe oppression." Roberts informs us that when, in the East, a man is in much trouble through oppressors, he says, " How they plough me and turn me up."—*Ingram Cobbin,* 1839.

Verse 3.—" *The plowers plowed,*" etc. The great Husbandman who owns this plough (at least by whose permission this plough goes), is God. Not only is it God who makes your common ploughs to gang, and sends the gospel into a land, but it is God also who disposes and overrules this same plough of persecution. For without his license the plough cannot be yoked ; and being yoked, cannot enter to gang till he direct ; and he tempers the irons, so that they cannot go one inch deeper than he thinks meet. When he thinks it time to quit work, then presently he cuts their cords, so that they cannot go once about after he thinks it time to quit work. Albeit when they yoke, they resolve to have all the land upside down, yet he will let them plough no more of it than he sees meet. Now for the ploughmen of this plough, they are Satan and the evil angels ; they hold the plough, and are goad-men to it ; and they yoke in the oxen into the plough, and drive them up with their goads. And they have a sort of music also, which they whistle into their ears, to make them go the faster ; and that is the allurements and provocations of the world. And for the oxen who draw into this plough, it may be princes when they turn persecutors of the kirk ; it may be prelates ; it may be politicians in the world : these are the oxen, Satan and the ill spirits inciting them, and stirring them up to go forward in their intended course. Then consider here that the plough and the ploughmen and oxen go about as God thinks meet ; but what is it that they are doing in the meantime ? Nothing else but preparing the ground for seed, and so the Lord employs them to prepare his people better to receive the seed of his word and of his Spirit.—*Alexander Henderson.*

Verse 3.—God fails not to sow blessings in the furrows, which the plowers plow upon the back of the church.—*Jeremy Taylor,* 1613—1667.

Verse 3.—" *The plowers plowed upon my back : they made long their furrows.*" When the Lord Jesus Christ was in his suffering state, and during his passion, these words here predicted of him were most expressly realized. Whilst he remained in the hands of the Roman soldiers they stript him of his raiment ; they bound him with cords to a pillar ; they flogged him. This was so performed by them, that they made ridges in his back and sides : they tore skin and flesh, and made him bare even to the bone, so that his body was like a ploughed field ; the gashes made in it were like ridges made in a ploughed field ; these were on his back. " *The plowers plowed upon my back : they made long their furrows.*" Whilst every part of our Lord's sorrows and sufferings is most minutely set forth in the sacred hymns, psalms, and songs, contained in what we style the Book of Psalms, yet we shall never comprehend what our most blessed Lord, in every part of his life, and in his passion and death, underwent for us : may the Lord the Spirit imprint this fresh expression used on this subject effectually upon us. Our Lord's words here are very expressive of the violence of his tormentors and their rage against him, and of the wounds and torments they had inflicted on him.

What must the feelings of our Lord have been when they made such furrows on his back, that it was all furrowed and welted with such long wounds, that it was more like a ploughed field than anything else. Blessings on him for his grace and patience, it is " with his stripes we are healed."—*Samuel Eyles Pierce.*

Verse 3.—" *They made long their furrows.*" The apparent harshness of this figure will disappear if it be considered to refer to severe public scourgings. To those who have been so unhappy as to witness such scourgings this allusion will then appear most expressive. The long wales or wounds which the scourge leaves at each stroke may most aptly be compared either to *furrows* or (as the original admits) to the *ridges between the furrows.* The *furrows* made by the plough in the East are very superficial, and (although straight) are usually carried to a great length, the fields not being enclosed as in this country.—*John Kitto, in* "*The Pictorial Bible.*"

Verse 4.—" *The* LORD *is righteous : he hath cut asunder the cords of the wicked ;*" *i.e.*, he has put an end to their domination and tyranny over us. In the Hebrew word which is rendered " *cords*" there is a reference to the *harness* with which the oxen were fastened to the plough ; and so to the *involved machinations* and *cruelties* of the enemy. The Hebrew word properly denotes thick *twisted cords ;* figuratively, intertwined wickedness ; Micah vii. 3. "*The cords of the wicked,*" therefore, signify their *power, dominion, tyranny,* wickedness, and violence. These cords God is said "*to have cut,*" so that *he should have made an end ;* and, therefore " *to have cut*" *for ever,* so that they should never be reunited.—*Hermann Venema.*

Verse 4.—" *He hath cut asunder the cords of the wicked.*" The enemies' power has been broken ; *God has cut asunder the cords of the wicked,* has cut their gears, their traces, and so spoiled their ploughing ; has cut their scourges, and so spoiled their lashing ; has cut the bands of union, by which they were combined together ; he has cut the bands of captivity, in which they held God's people. God has many ways of disabling wicked men to do the mischief they design against his church, and shaming their counsels.—*Matthew Henry.*

Verse 4.—" *He hath cut asunder the cords of the wicked.*" He repeateth the same praise of God in delivering his church from oppression of the enemy, under the similitude of cutting the cords of the plough, which tilleth up another man's field. Whence learn, 1. The enemies of the church do no more regard her than they do the earth under their feet, and do seek to make their own advantage of her, as usurpers use to do in possessing and labouring of another man's field. "*The plowers plowed upon my back.*" 2. The Lord useth to suffer his enemies to break up the fallow ground of his people's proud and stiff hearts with the plough of persecution, and to draw deep and long furrows on them : "*They made long their furrows.*" 3. What the enemies do against the church the Lord maketh use of for manuring the church, which is his field, albeit they intend no good to God's church, yet they serve in God's wisdom to prepare the Lord's people for receiving the seed of God's word ; for the similitude speaketh of their tilling of the church, but nothing of their sowing, for that is reserved for the Lord himself, who is owner of the field. 4. When the wicked have performed so much of God's husbandry as he thinketh good to suffer them, then he stoppeth their design, and looseth their plough. "*He hath cut asunder the cords of the wicked.*"— *David Dickson.*

Verse 5.—If any one be desirous to accept these words, "*Let them be confounded and turned backward*," as they sound, he will devoutly explain the imprecation : that is to say, it may be an imprecation of good confusion, which leads to repentance, and of turning to God from sin : thus Bellarmine.   There is a confounding by bringing grace, glory, and turning from the evil way.   Thus some enemies and persecutors of the Christians have been holily confounded and turned to the faith of Christ ; as St. Paul, who full of wrath and slaughter was going to Damascus that he might afflict the believers, but was graciously confounded on the road.—*Thomas Le Blanc.*

Verse 5.—"*Let them all be confounded*."   Mr. Emerson told a convention of rationalists once, in this city, that the morality of the New Testament is scientific and perfect.   But the morality of the New Testament is that of the Old.   "Yes," you say ; "but what of the imprecatory psalms ?"   A renowned professor, who, as Germany thinks, has done more for New England theology than any man since Jonathan Edwards, was once walking in this city with a clergyman of a radical faith, who objected to the doctrine that the Bible is inspired, and did so on the ground of the imprecatory psalms.   The replies of the usual kind were made ; and it was presumed that David expressed the Divine purpose in praying that his enemies might be destroyed, and that he gave utterance only to the natural righteous indignation of conscience against unspeakable iniquity.   But the doubter would not be satisfied.   The two came at last to a newspaper bulletin, on which the words were written,—"Baltimore to be shelled at twelve o'clock."   "I am glad of it," said the radical preacher ; "I am glad of it."   "And so am I," said his companion, "but I hardly dare say so, for fear you should say that I am uttering an imprecatory psalm."—*Joseph Cook, in Boston Monday Lectures.* "*Transcendentalism.*"

Verse 5.—"*And turned back ;*" from pursuing their designs and accomplishing them ; as the Assyrian monarch was, who had a hook put into his nose, and a bridle in his lips, and was turned back by the way he came : Isaiah xxxvii. 29.— *John Gill.*

Verse 5.—"*All those who hate Zion.*"   Note that he does not say, All who hate *me ;* but " *all who hate Zion.*"   Thus the saints are not led to this from the desire of revenge, but from zeal for the people of God, so that they pray for the confusion and repression of the ungodly.— *Wolfgang Musculus.*

Verse 6.—" *Let them be as the grass upon the housetops.*"   They are rightly compared to " *grass on the housetops ;*" for more contemptuously the Holy Ghost could not speak of them.   For this grass is such, that it soon withereth away before the sickle be put into it.   Yea, no man thinketh it worthy to be cut down, no man regardeth it, every man suffereth it to brag for a while, and to show itself unto men from the housetops as though it were something when it is nothing. So the wicked persecutors in the world, which are taken to be mighty and terrible according to the outward show, are of all men most contemptible.   For Christians do not once think of plucking them up or cutting them down ; they persecute them not, they revenge not their own injuries, but suffer them to increase, to brag and glory as much as they list.   For they know that they cannot abide the violence of a vehement wind.   Yea, though all things be in quietness, yet as grass upon the housetops, by little and little, withereth away through the heat of the sun, so tyrannies upon small occasions do perish and soon vanish away.   The faithful, therefore, in suffering do prevail, and overcome ; but the wicked in doing are overthrown, and miserably perish, as all the histories of all times and ages do plainly witness.—*Martin Luther.*

Verse 6.—" *Like grass upon the housetops.*"   The flat roofs of the Eastern houses " are plastered with a composition of mortar, tar, ashes, and sand," in the crevices of which grass often springs.   The houses of the poor in the country were formed of a plaster of mud and straw, where the grass would grow still more freely : as all the images are taken from country life, it is doubtless to country dwellings that the poet refers.—*J. J. Stewart Perowne.*

Verse 6.—"*Like grass upon the housetops.*" The enemies of Zion may have an elevated position in the nation, they may seem to promise growth, but having no root in themselves, like the hearers on the stony ground, give no promise of fruit. Their profession dies away and leaves no benefit to the church, as it claims no blessing from others.— *William Wilson* (1783—1873), *in "The Book of Psalms, with an Exposition."*

Verse 6.—"*Grass upon the housetops.*" In the morning the master of the house laid in a stock of earth, which was carried up, and spread evenly on the top of the house, which is flat. The whole roof is thus formed of mere earth, laid on and rolled hard and flat. On the top of every house is a large stone roller, for the purpose of hardening and flattening this layer of rude soil, so that the rain may not penetrate ; but upon this surface, as may be supposed, grass and weeds grow freely, but never come to maturity. It is to such grass the Psalmist alludes as useless and bad.— *William Jowett, in "Christian Researches in Syria and the Holy Land,"* 1825.

Verse 7.—"*The mower filleth not his hand,*" etc. The grain was rather pulled than cut, and as each handful was taken the reaper gave it a flourishing swing up into his bosom.— *Mrs Finn, in " Home in the Holy Land,"* 1866.

Verse 7.—"*He that bindeth sheaves his bosom.*" A practice prevails in hot climates of sending out persons into the woods and other wild places to collect the grass, which would otherwise be wasted ; and it is no uncommon thing in the evening to see groups of grass-cutters in the market, waiting to dispose of their bundles or sheaves, which are often so large that one is disposed to wonder how they could have been conveyed from the woods upon one man's shoulders.— *Maria Calcott, in "A Scripture Herbal,"* 1842.

Verse 8.—The latter expressions are most refreshingly Arabic. Nothing is more natural than for them, when passing by a fruit-tree or corn-field loaded with a rich crop to exclaim, "*Barak Allah !*" God bless you ! We bless you in the name of the *Lord !— W. M. Thomson.*

HINTS TO THE VILLAGE PREACHER.

Verse 1.—Affliction as it comes to saints from men of the world. I. Reason for it—enmity of the serpent's seed. II. Modes of its display—persecution, ridicule, slander, disdain, etc. III. Comfort under it. So persecuted they the prophets : so the Master. It is their nature. They cannot kill the soul. It is but for a time, etc.

Verses 1 and 2.—I. How far persecution for righteousness' sake may go. 1. It may be great : "afflicted," "afflicted." 2. It may be frequent : "Many a time." 3. It may be early : "From my youth." II. How far it cannot go. 1. It may seem to prevail. 2. It may prevail in some degree. 3. It cannot ultimately prevail. 4. It shall cause that to which it is opposed increasingly to prevail. — *G. R.*

Verses 1—4.—Israel persecuted but not forsaken. Persecution. I. Whence it came : "they." II. How it came : " Many a time," " from my youth," severely : " afflicted," " ploughed." III. Why it came. Human and Satanic hatred, and Divine permission. IV. What came of it : "not prevailed "—to destroy, to drive to despair, to lead to sin. God's righteousness manifested in upholding his people, baffling their foes, etc.

Verses 1—4.—The enemies of God's church. I. Their violence : " The plowers plowed," etc. II. Their persistency : "Many a time . . . . from my youth." III. Their failure : " Yet they have not prevailed." IV. Their great opponent : " The Lord . . . . hath cut asunder."— *J. F.*

Verse 3.—I. Literally fulfilled. 1. In Christ. Matt. xxvii. 26 ; xx. 19 ; Mark xv. 15 ; Luke xviii. 33 ; John xix. 1. 2. In his followers. Matt. x. 17 ; Acts xvi. 23 ; 2 Cor. vi. 5 ; xi. 23, 24 ; Heb. xi. 36. And frequently in subsequent persecutions. II. Figuratively. In secret calumnies both in Christ and his followers.— *G. R.*

Verse 4.—Israel's song of triumph. I. The Lord is righteous in permitting these afflictions to come upon his people. II. He is righteous in keeping his promise of deliverance to his people. III. He is righteous in visiting the enemies of his people with judgment.— *W. H. J. P.*

Verse 5.—I. An inexcusable hatred described : " hate Zion," God's church and cause. For, 1. Her people are righteous. 2. Her faith is a gospel. 3. Her mission is peace. 4. Her very existence is the world's preservation. II. An inveterate sinfulness indicated : " Them that hate Zion." For, whatever moral virtues they may boast of, they must be, 1. Enemies to the human race. 2. In defiant opposition to God. 3. Perversely blind, as Saul, or radically vile. 4. Devil-like. III. An instinctive feeling of a good man expressed : " Let them all be," etc. Prompted by, 1. His love to God. 2. Love to man. 3. Love to righteousness. Hence, its existence is in itself a pledge that the righteous God will respect and comply with it.— *J. F.*

Verses 5—8.—I. The characters described. 1. They do not love Zion. They say not, " Lord, I have loved the habitation of thine house," etc. 2. They hate Zion— both its King and its subjects. II. Their prosperity : " As the grass," etc. III. Their end. 1. Shame : " Let them be confounded." 2. Loss : " Turned back." 3. Disappointment. No mowing ; no reaping. 4. Dishonour. Unblessed by others as well as in themselves.— *G. R.*

Verses 6—9.—The wicked flourishing and perishing. I. Eminent in position. II. Envied in prosperity. III. Evanescent in duration. IV. Empty as to solidity. V. Excepted from blessing.

PSALM CXXX.

TITLE.—A Song of Degrees. *It would be hard to see any upward step from the preceding to the present psalm, and therefore it is possible that the steps or ascents are in the song itself : certainly it does rise rapidly out of the depths of anguish to the heights of assurance. It follows well upon cxxix.: when we have overcome the trials which arise from man we are the better prepared to meet those sharper sorrows which arise out of our matters towards God. He who has borne the scourges of the wicked is trained in all patience to wait the dealings of the Holy Lord. We name this the* DE PROFUNDIS PSALM : *" Out of the depths" is the leading word of it : out of those depths we cry, wait, watch, and hope. In this psalm we hear of the pearl of redemption, verses 7 and 8 : perhaps the sweet singer would never have found that precious thing had he not been cast into the depths. " Pearls lie deep."*

DIVISION.—*The first two verses reveal an intense desire ; and the next two are a humble confession of repentance and faith, verses 3 and 4. In verses 5 and 6 waiting watchfulness is declared and resolved upon ; and in the last two verses joyful expectation, both for himself and all Israel, finds expression.*

EXPOSITION.

OUT of the depths have I cried unto thee, O LORD.

2 Lord, hear my voice : let thine ears be attentive to the voice of my supplications.

3 If thou, LORD, shouldest mark iniquities, O Lord, who shall stand ?

4 But *there is* forgiveness with thee, that that thou mayest be feared.

5 I wait for the LORD, my soul doth wait, and in his word do I hope.

6 My soul *waiteth* for the Lord more than they that watch for the morning : *I say, more than* they that watch for the morning.

7 Let Israel hope in the LORD : for with the LORD *there is* mercy, and with him *is* plenteous redemption.

7 And he shall redeem Israel from all his iniquities.

1. "*Out of the depths have I cried unto thee, O* LORD." This is the Psalmist's statement and plea : he had never ceased to pray even when brought into the lowest state. The depths usually silence all they engulf, but they could not close the mouth of this servant of the Lord ; on the contrary, it was in the abyss itself that he cried unto Jehovah. Beneath the floods prayer lived and struggled ; yea, above the roar of the billows rose the cry of faith. It little matters where we are if we can pray ; but prayer is never more real and acceptable than when it rises out of the worst places. Deep places beget deep devotion. Depths of earnestness are stirred by depths of tribulation. Diamonds sparkle most amid the darkness. Prayer *de profundis* gives to God *gloria in excelsis*. The more distressed we are, the more excellent is the faith which trusts bravely in the Lord, and therefore appeals to him, and to him alone. Good men may be in the depths of temporal and spiritual trouble ; but good men in such cases look only to their God, and they stir themselves up to be more instant and earnest in prayer than at other times. The depth of their distress moves the depths of their being ; and from the bottom of their hearts an exceeding great and bitter cry rises unto the one living and true God. David had often been in the deep, and as often had he

pleaded with Jehovah, his God, in whose hand are all deep places. He prayed, and remembered that he had prayed, and pleaded that he had prayed ; hoping ere long to receive an answer. It would be dreadful to look back on trouble and feel forced to own that we did not cry unto the Lord in it ; but it is most comforting to know that whatever we did not do, or could not do, yet we did pray, even in our worst times. He that prays in the depth will not sink out of his depth. He that cries out of the depths shall soon sing in the heights.

2. "*Lord, hear my voice.*" It is all we ask ; but nothing less will content us. If the Lord will but hear us we will leave it to his superior wisdom to decide whether he will answer us or no. It is better for our prayer to be heard than answered. If the Lord were to make an absolute promise to answer all our requests it might be rather a curse than a blessing, for it would be casting the responsibility of our lives upon ourselves, and we should be placed in a very anxious position : but now the Lord hears our desires, and that is enough ; we only wish him to grant them if his infinite wisdom sees that it would be for our good and for his glory. Note that the Psalmist spoke audibly in prayer : this is not at all needful, but it is exceedingly helpful ; for the use of the voice assists the thoughts. Still, there is a voice in silent supplication, a voice in our weeping, a voice in that sorrow which cannot find a tongue : that voice the Lord will hear if its cry is meant for his ear. "*Let thine ears be attentive to the voice of my supplication.*" The Psalmist's cry is a beggar's petition ; he begs the great King and Lord to lend an ear to it. He has supplicated many times, but always with one voice, or for one purpose ; and he begs to be noticed in the one matter which he has pressed with so much importunity. He would have the King hearken, consider, remember, and weigh his request. He is confused, and his prayer may therefore be broken, and difficult to understand ; he begs therefore that his Lord will give the more earnest and compassionate heed to the voice of his many and painful pleadings. When we have already prayed over our troubles it is well to pray over our prayers. If we can find no more words, let us entreat the Lord to hear those petitions which we have already presented. If we have faithfully obeyed the precept by praying without ceasing, we may be confident that the Lord will faithfully fulfil the promise by helping us without fail. Though the Psalmist was under a painful sense of sin, and so was in the depth, his faith pleaded in the teeth of conscious unworthiness ; for well he knew that the Lord's keeping his promise depends upon his own character and not upon that of his erring creatures.

3. "*If thou, LORD, shouldest mark iniquities, O Lord, who shall stand ?*" If JAH, the all-seeing, should in strict justice call every man to account for every want of conformity to righteousness, where would any one of us be ? Truly, he does record all our transgressions ; but as yet he does not act upon the record, but lays it aside till another day. If men were to be judged upon no system but that of works, who among us could answer for himself at the Lord's bar, and hope to stand clear and accepted ? This verse shows that the Psalmist was under a sense of sin, and felt it imperative upon him not only to cry as a suppliant but to confess as a sinner. Here he owns that he cannot stand before the great King in his own righteousness, and he is so struck with a sense of the holiness of God, and the rectitude of the law that he is convinced that no man of mortal race can answer for himself before a Judge so perfect, concerning a law so divine. Well does he cry, "O Lord, who shall stand ?" None can do so : there is none that doeth good ; no, not one. Iniquities are matters which are not according to equity : what a multitude we have of these ! Jehovah, who sees all, and is also our *Adonai*, or Lord, will assuredly bring us into judgment concerning those thoughts, and words, and works which are not in exact conformity to his law. Were it not for the Lord Jesus, could we hope to stand ? Dare we meet him in the dread day of account on the footing of law and equity ? What a mercy it is that we need not do so, for the next verse sets forth another way of acceptance to which we flee.

4. "*But there is forgiveness with thee.*" Blessed *but*. Free, full, sovereign par-

don is in the hand of the great King : it is his prerogative to forgive, and he delights to exercise it.   Because his nature is mercy, and because he has provided a sacrifice for sin, therefore forgiveness is with him for all that come to him confessing their sins.   The power of pardon is permanently resident with God : he has forgiveness ready to his hand at this instant.   *"That thou mayest be feared."* This is the fruitful root of piety.   None fear the Lord like those who have experienced his forgiving love.   Gratitude for pardon produces far more fear and reverence of God than all the dread which is inspired by punishment.   If the Lord were to execute justice upon all, there would be none left to fear him ; if all were under apprehension of his deserved wrath, despair would harden them against fearing him : it is grace which leads the way to a holy regard of God, and a fear of grieving him.

5. *" I wait for the* LORD, *my soul doth wait."*   Expecting him to come to me in love, I quietly wait for his appearing ; I wait *upon* him in service, and *for* him in faith.   For God I wait and for him only : if he will manifest himself I shall have nothing more to wait for ; but until he shall appear for my help I must wait on, hoping even in the depths.   This waiting of mine is no mere formal act, my very soul is in it,—" my soul doth wait."   I wait and I wait—mark the repetition ! " My soul waits," and then again, " My soul waits" ; to make sure work of the waiting.   It is well to deal with the Lord intensely.   Such repetitions are the reverse of vain repetitions.   If the Lord Jehovah makes us wait, let us do so with our whole hearts ; for blessed are all they that wait for him.   He is worth waiting for.   The waiting itself is beneficial to us : it tries faith, exercises patience, trains submission, and endears the blessing when it comes.   The Lord's people have always been a waiting people : they waited for the First Advent, and now they wait for the Second.   They waited for a sense of pardon, and now they wait for perfect sanctification.   They waited in the depths, and they are not now wearied with waiting in a happier condition.   They have cried and they do wait ; probably their past prayer sustains their present patience.

"And in his word do I hope."   This is the source, strength, and sweetness of waiting.   Those who do not hope cannot wait ; but if we hope for that we see not, then do we with patience wait for it.   God's word is a true word, but at times it tarries ; if ours is true faith it will wait the Lord's time.   A word from the Lord is as bread to the soul of the believer ; and, refreshed thereby, it holds out through the night of sorrow expecting the dawn of deliverance and delight. Waiting, we study the word, believe the word, hope in the word, and live on the word ; and all because it is *" his* word,"—the word of him who never speaks in vain.   Jehovah's word is a firm ground for a waiting soul to rest upon.

6. *" My soul waiteth for the Lord more than they that watch for the morning."* Men who guard a city, and women who wait by the sick, long for daylight. Worshippers tarrying for the morning sacrifice, the kindling of the incense and the lighting of the lamps, mingle fervent prayers with their holy vigils, and pine for the hour when the lamb shall smoke upon the altar.   David, however, waited more than these, waited longer, waited more longingly, waited more expectantly. He was not afraid of the great Adonai before whom none can stand in their own righteousness, for he had put on the righteousness of faith, and therefore longed for gracious audience with the Holy One.   God was no more dreaded by him than light is dreaded by those engaged in a lawful calling.   He pined and yearned after his God.   *"I say, more than they that watch for the morning."*   The figure was not strong enough, though one can hardly think of anything more vigorous : he felt that his own eagerness was unique and unrivalled.   Oh to be thus hungry and thirsty after God !   Our version spoils the abruptness of the language ; the original runs thus—" My soul for the Lord more than those watching for the morning—watching for the morning."   This is a fine poetical repeat. We long for the favour of the Lord more than weary sentinels long for the morning light which will release them from their tedious watch.   Indeed this is true. He that has once rejoiced in communion with God is sore tried by the hidings of his face, and grows faint with strong desire for the Lord's appearing,

> "When wilt thou come unto me, Lord?
> Until thou dost appear,
> I count each moment for a day,
> Each minute for a year."

7. "*Let Israel hope in the* LORD." Or, "Hope thou, Israel, in Jehovah." Jehovah is Israel's God; therefore, let Israel hope in him. What one Israelite does he wishes all Israel to do. That man has a just right to exhort others who is himself setting the example. Israel of old waited upon Jehovah and wrestled all the night long, and at last he went his way succoured by the Hope of Israel : the like shall happen to all his seed. God has great things in store for his people ; they ought to have large expectations. "*For with the* LORD *there is mercy.*" This is in his very nature, and by the light of nature it may be seen. But we have also the light of grace, and therefore we see still more of his mercy. With us there is sin ; but hope is ours, because " with the Lord there is mercy." Our comfort lies not in that which is with us, but in that which is with our God. Let us look out of self and its poverty to Jehovah and his riches of mercy. "*And with him is plenteous redemption.*" He can and will redeem all his people out of their many and great troubles ; nay, their redemption is already wrought out and laid up with him, so that he can at any time give his waiting ones the full benefit thereof. The attribute of mercy, and the fact of redemption, are two most sufficient reasons for hoping in Jehovah ; and the fact that there is no mercy or deliverance elsewhere should effectually wean the soul from all idolatry. Are not these deep things of God a grand comfort for those who are crying out of the depths ? Is it not better to be in the deeps with David, hoping in God's mercy, than up on the mountain-tops, boasting in our own fancied righteousness ?

8. "*And he shall redeem Israel from all his iniquities.*" Our iniquities are our worst dangers : if saved from these, we are saved altogether ; but there is no salvation from them except by redemption. What a blessing that this is here promised in terms which remove it out of the region of question : the Lord shall certainly redeem his believing people from all their sins. Well may the redemption be plenteous since it concerns all Israel and all iniquities ! Truly, our psalm has ascended to a great height in this verse : this is no cry out of the depths, but a chorale in the heights. Redemption is the top of covenant blessings. When it shall be experienced by all Israel, the latter-day glory shall have come, and the Lord's people shall say, " Now, Lord, what wait we for ?" Is not this a clear prophecy of the coming of our Lord Jesus the first time ? and may we not now regard it as the promise of his second and more glorious coming for the redemption of the body ? For this our soul doth wait : yea, our heart and our flesh cry out for it with joyful expectation.

EXPLANATORY NOTES.

Whole Psalm.—The psalm is the eleventh in the order of the gradual psalms, and treats of the eleventh step in the spiritual ascent, viz., penitential prayer.—*H. T. Armfield.*

Whole Psalm.—Of the psalms which are called Penitential this is the chiefest. But, as it is the most excellent, so it has been perverted to the most disgraceful abuse in the Popedom : *e.g.*, that it should be mumbled in the lowest voice by slow bellies, in the sepulchral vigils for their liberation of souls from purgatory : as if David were here treating of the dead, when he has not even spoken a word about them ; but says that he himself, a living man, was calling upon God ; and exhorts the Israelites, living men also, to do the same. But leaving the buffooneries of the Papists we will rather consider the true meaning and use of the psalm. It contains the most ardent prayer of a man grievously distressed by a sense of the Divine anger against sin : by earnest turning to God and penitence, he is seeking the forgiveness of his iniquities.—*Solomon Gesner.*

Whole Psalm.—The Holy Ghost layeth out here two opposite passions most plainly—*fear*, in respect of evil-deserving sins, and *hope*, in regard of undeserved mercies.—*Alexander Roberts.* 1610.

Whole Psalm.—The passionate earnestness of the psalm is enhanced by the repetition eight times in it of the Divine Name.—*The Speaker's Commentary*, 1873.

Whole Psalm.—This psalm, perhaps more than any other, is marked by its mountains : depth ; prayer ; conviction ; light ; hope ; waiting ; watching ; longing ; confidence ; assurance ; universal happiness and joy. . . . . Just as the barometer marks the rising of the weather, so does this psalm, sentence by sentence, record the progress of the soul. And you may test yourself by it, as by a rule or measure, and ask yourself at each line, " Have I reached to this ? Have I reached to this ?" and so take your spiritual gauge.—*James Vaughan, in "Steps to Heaven,"* 1878.

Whole Psalm.—Whosoever he was that wrote this psalm, he maketh mention and rehearsal of that prayer that he made to his God in the time of his great danger, and this he doth to the fifth verse ; then finding in experience a comfortable answer, and how good a thing it was to pray to God, and to wait on him, he professeth, that, as before, he had awaited on him, so still in time coming he would await on him, and this he doeth to the seventh verse. In the third and last part, he turneth him to Israel, to the church, and exhorteth them to await on God, as he had done, promising them mercy and redemption from all their iniquities if they would await on him.—*Robert Rollock*, 1555—1599.

Whole Psalm.—Luther being once asked which were the best psalms, replied, *Psalmi Paulini ;* and when his companions at table pressed him to say which these were, he answered : Psalms xxxii., li., cxxx., and cxliii.—*Franz Delitzsch.*

Whole Psalm.—Luther, when he was buffeted by the devil at Coburg, and in great affliction, said to those about him, *Venite, in contemptum Diaboli, Psalmum, De Profundis, quatuor vocibus cantemus ;* " Come, let us sing that Psalm, ' Out of the depths,' etc., in derision of the devil."—*John Trapp.*

Whole Psalm.—The circumstances in which Dr. John Owen's Exposition of Psalm cxxx. originated are peculiarly interesting. Dr. Owen himself, in a statement made to Mr. Richard Davis, who ultimately became pastor of a church in Rowel, Northamptonshire, explains the occasion which led him to a very careful examination of the fourth verse in the psalm. Mr. Davis, being under religious impressions, had sought a conference with Owen. In the course of the conversation, Dr. Owen put the question, " Young man, pray in what manner do you think to go to God ?" " Through the Mediator, sir," answered Mr. Davis. " That is easily said," replied the doctor, " but I assure you it is another thing to go to God through the Mediator than many who make use of the expression are aware of. I myself preached Christ," he continued, " some years, when I had but very little, if any, experimental acquaintance with access to God through Christ ; until the Lord was pleased to visit me with sore affliction, whereby I was brought to the mouth of the grave, and under which my soul was oppressed with horror and darkness ; but God graciously relieved my spirit by a powerful application of Psalm cxxx. 4, ' *But there is forgiveness with thee, that thou mayest be feared,*' from whence I received special instruction, peace and comfort, in drawing near to God through the Mediator, and preached thereupon immediately after my recovery."—*William H. Goold, editor of Owen's Collected Works*, 1851.

Verse 1.—" *Out of the depths have I cried unto thee, O* LORD." Is there not a depth of sin, and a depth of misery by reason of sin, and a depth of sorrow by reason of misery ? In all which, both David was, and I, God help me, am deeply plunged ; and are not these depths enough out of which to cry ? And yet, perhaps, none of these depths is that which David means ; but there are depths of danger—a danger of body and a danger of soul, and out of these it seems that David cried ; for the danger of his body was so deep that it had brought him to death's door, and the danger of his soul so deep that it had almost brought him to the gates of despair ; and had he not just cause then to say, " *Out of the depths have I cried to thee, O God*"? And yet there is a depth besides these that must help to lift us out of these—a depth of devotion, without which depth our crying out of other depths will never be heard. For devotion is a fire that puts a heat into our crying, and carries it up into *cœlum empyræum*—the heaven of fire, where God himself is. And now join all these depths together--the depth of sin, of misery, of sorrow, the depth of danger, and the depth of devotion,—and then tell me if David had not, if I have not, as just cause as ever Jonah had to say, " Out of the depths have I cried to thee, O God." Indeed, to cry out of the depths hath many considerable circumstances to move God to hear : it acknowledgeth his infinite power when no distance can hinder his assistance ; it presents our own faith when no extremity can weaken our hope ; it magnifies God's goodness when he, the Most High, regards the most low ; it expresseth our own earnestness, seeing crying out of depths must needs be a deep cry ; and if each of these singly, and by itself, be motive sufficient to move God to hear, how strong must the motive needs be when they are all united ? and united they are all in crying out of the depths ; and therefore now that I cry to thee out of the depths, be moved, O God, in thy great mercy to " *hear my voice.*"

It is cause enough for God not to hear some because they do not cry—cause enough not to hear some that cry because not out of the depths ; but when crying and out of the depths are joined together, it was never known that God refused to hear ; and therefore now that I cry to thee out of the depths, be pleased, O God, in thy great mercy to hear my voice.—*Sir Richard Baker, in* "*Meditations and Disquisitions upon the Three last Psalmes of David,*" 1639.

Verse 1.—"Out of the depths." By the deep places (as all the ancients consent) is meant the deep places of afflictions, and the deep places of the heart troubled for sin. Afflictions are compared to deep waters. Ps. xviii. 16 : " He drew me out of many waters." " Save me, O God, for the waters are come in unto my soul." And surely God's children are often cast into very desperate cases, and plunged into deep miseries, to the end that they may send out of a contrite and feeling heart such prayers as may mount aloft and pierce the heavens. When we are in prosperity our prayers come from our lips ; and therefore the Lord is forced to cast us down, that our prayers may come from our hearts, and that our senses may be wakened from the security in which they are lying. Albeit the throne of God be most high, yet he delighteth to hear the petition of hearts that are most low, that are most cast down by the sight of sin. There is no affliction, neither any place so low (yea, if as low as the belly of the whale wherein Jonah lay) which can separate us from the love of the Lord, or stay our prayers from coming before him. Those that are farthest cast down are not farthest from God, but are nearest unto him. God is near to a contrite heart, and it is the proper seat where his Spirit dwelleth : Isa. lxvi. 2. And thus God dealeth with us, as men do with such houses that they are minded to build sumptuously and on high ; for then they dig deep grounds for the foundation. Thus God purposing to make a fair show of Daniel, and the three children in Babel ; of Joseph in Egypt ; of David in Israel ; he first threw them into the deep waters of affliction. Daniel is cast into the den of lions ; the three children are thrown into the fiery furnace ; Joseph is imprisoned ; David exiled. Yet all those he exalted and made glorious temples to himself. Mark hereby the dulness of our nature, that is such, that God is forced to use sharp remedies to awaken us. Jonah lay sleeping in the ship, when the tempest of God's wrath was pursuing him : God therefore threw him into the belly of the whale, and the bottom of the deep, that from those deep places he might cry to him.

When, therefore, we are troubled by heavy sickness, or poverty, or oppressed by the tyranny of men, let us make profit and use thereof, considering that God hath cast his best children into such dangers for their profit ; and that it is better to be in deep dangers praying, than on the high mountains of vanity playing.—*Archibald Symson, in "A Sacred Septenarie,"* 1638.

Verse 1.—"Out of the depths." " Depths !" oh ! into what " *depths*" men can sink ! How far from happiness, glory, and goodness men can fall.

There is the depth of *poverty.* A man can become utterly stripped of all earthly possessions and worldly friends! Sometimes we come upon a man, still living, but in such abject circumstances, that it strikes us as a marvel that a human being can sink lower than the beasts of the field.

Then there is the depth of *sorrow.* Billow after billow breaks over the man, friend after friend departs, lover and friend are put into darkness. All the fountains of his nature are broken up. He is like a water-logged ship, from the top waves plunging down as if into the bottom of the sea. So often in such depths, sometimes like Jonah in the whale's belly, the monster carrying him down, down, down, into darkness.

There are depths after depths of *mental darkness,* when the soul becomes more and more sorrowful, down to that very depth which is just this side of *despair.* Earth hollow, heaven empty, the air heavy, every form a deformity, all sounds discord, the past a gloom, the present a puzzle, the future a horror. One more step down, and the man will stand in the chamber of despair, the floor of which is blisteringly hot, while the air is biting cold as the polar atmosphere. To what depths the spirit of a man may fall!

But the most horrible depth into which a man's soul can descend is *sin.* Sometimes we begin on gradual slopes, and slide so swiftly that we soon reach great depths; depths in which there are horrors that are neither in poverty, nor sorrow, nor mental depression. It is sin, it is an outrage against God and ourselves. We feel that there is no bottom. Each opening depth reveals a greater deep. This is really the bottomless pit, with everlasting accumulations of speed, and perpetual lacerations as we descend. Oh, depths below depths! Oh, falls from light to gloom, from gloom to darkness! Oh, the hell of sin!

What can we do? We can simply *cry,* CRY, CRY! But, let us cry to God. Useless, injurious are other cries. They are mere expressions of impotency, or protests against imaginary fate. But the cry of the spirit to the Most High is a manful cry. Out of the depths of all poverty, all sorrow, all mental depression, all sin, *cry unto God!—From "The Study and the Pulpit,"* 1877.

Verse 1.—*"Out of the depths have I cried."*

> Up from the deeps, O God, I cry to thee!
> Hear my soul's prayer, hear thou her litany,
> O thou who sayest, "Come, wanderer, home to me."
>
> Up from the deeps of sorrow, wherein lie
> Dark secrets veil'd from earth's unpitying eye,
> My prayers, like star-crown'd angels, Godward fly.
>
> From the calm bosom when in quiet hour
> God's Holy Spirit reigns with largest power,
> Then shall each thought in prayer's white blossom flower.
>
> Not from life's shallows, where the waters sleep,
> A dull, low marsh where stagnant vapours creep,
> But ocean-voiced, deep calling unto deep.
>
> As he of old, King David, call'd to thee,
> As cries the heart of poor humanity,
> "Clamavi, Domine, exaudi me!"
>
> *—C. S. Fenner.*

Verse 1.—But when he crieth from the deep, he riseth from the deep, and his very cry suffereth him not to be long at the bottom.—*Augustine.*

Verse 1.—It has been well said that the verse puts before us six conditions of true prayer: it is lowly, "*out of the deep*"; fervent, "*have I called*"; direct to God himself, "*unto thee*"; reverent, "O Lord"; awed, "Lord," a solemn title, is again used; one's very own, "hear *my voice.*"—*Neale and Littledale.*

Verse 1.—*"Have I cried."* There are many kinds and degrees of prayer in the world; from the coldest form to the intensest agony. Every one prays; but very few "cry." But of those who do "cry to God," the majority would say, —"*I owe it to the depths.* I learnt it there. I often prayed before; but never—till I was carried down very deep—did I *cry.*" "Out of the depths have I *cried* unto thee, O Lord." It is well worth while to go down into any "depth" to be taught to "cry."

It is not too much to say that we do not know what prayer may be till we have "*cried.*" And we seldom rise till we have gone very deep. "I die! I perish! I am lost! Help, Lord! Help me! Save me now! Do it *now*, Lord, or I am lost. O Lord, hear! O Lord, forgive! O Lord, hearken and do; defer not, for thine own sake, O my God!"

In mid-day, if you are taken from the bright and sunny scenes of light, and go down into the bottom of a pit. you may see the stars, which were invisible to you in the upper air. And how many could say that things they knew not in life's noon, they have found in life's midnight, and that they owe their glimpses of glory, and their best avenues of thought, and thè importunacy of prayer, and the victories of faith, to seasons when they walked in very dark places. "*Out of the depths* have I cried unto thee, O Lord."—*James Vaughan.*

Verse 1.—"*Have I cried unto thee, Jehovah.*" God gave out that name Jehovah to his people to confirm their faith in the stability of his promises: Exod. iii. He who is Being himself will assuredly give being and subsistence to his promises. Being to deal with God about the promises of grace, he makes his application to him under this name: "*I call upon thee, Jehovah.*"—*John Owen, in "A Practical Exposition upon Psalm cxxx."*

Verse 2.—"*Lord, hear my voice,*" etc. Every prayer should have its reverent invocation, as every temple its porch. The two greatest prayers in the Old Testament—Solomon's prayer and Daniel's prayer—both have it very emphatically. And it is a very distinct part of our own perfect model: "Our Father, which art in heaven, hallowed bè thy name." On our part it is deferential, and puts the mind into its proper form; while it places the great God, whom it addresses, where he ought to be,—in the awe of his glory; in the magnitude of his power; in the infinitude of his wisdom and love.

Never think little of that part of your prayer: never omit, never hurry over the opening address. Do not go into his presence without a pause, or some devout ascription. "*Lord, hear my voice: let thine ears be attentive to the voice of my supplications.*" True, he is always listening and waiting for his children's "cry,"—far more prepared to answer, than we are to ask. And the very fact that we are praying is a proof of his attention,—for who but he put it into our hearts to make that prayer? Nevertheless. it becomes us, and honours him, to establish, at the outset, the right relationship between a creature and his Creator; between a child and his Father: "Lord, hear my voice: let thine ears be attentive to the voice of my supplication."—*James Vaughan.*

Verse 2.—"*Lord.*" Hebrew, *Adonai.* As *Jehovah* marks his unchangeable faithfulness to his promises of delivering his people, so *Adonai* his *Lordship* over all hindrances in the way of his delivering them.—*Andrew Robert Fausset, in "A Commentary, Critical, Experimental and Practical,"* 1866.

Verse 2.—"*Lord, hear my voice,*" etc. The expressions are metaphorical, and borrowed from the carriage of a parent to a child, and upon the matter his suit is this,—Lord, notice me when I pray, as a parent will notice his distressed child's cry when he is like to ruin. "*Let thine ears be attentive to the voice of my supplications;*" that goes a little further; that as a parent knowing a child to be in hazard, he will listen and hearken attentively if he can hear him cry, and notice and ponder that cry, and what he cries for; so he pleaded with God, that he would be waiting on and attentive, to see and hear if a cry should come from him, and that he would affectionately ponder and notice it when he hears it.—*George Hutcheson,* —1678.

Verse 3.—"*If thou,* Lord, *shouldest mark iniquities,*" etc. But doth not the Lord mark iniquity? Doth not he take notice of every sin acted by any of the children of men, especially by his own children? Why, then, doth the Psalmist put it upon an *if?* "*If thou,* Lord, *shouldest mark iniquity.*" 'Tis true, the Lord marks all iniquity to know it, but he doth not mark any iniquity in his children to condemn them for it : so the meaning of the psalm is, that if the Lord should mark sin with a strict and severe eye, as a judge, to charge it upon the person sinning, no man could bear it.

The word rendered *to mark* notes, first, to watch, or to observe with strictest diligence, and is therefore in the noun rendered *a watch-tower*, upon which a man is placed to take observation of all things that are done, and of all persons that pass by, or approach and come near. A watchman placed upon a high tower is bound industriously and critically to observe all passengers and passages, all that his eye can reach. So saith the text,—If thou shouldst mark as a watchman, and eye with rigour everything that passeth from us, " *who shall stand ?*" that is, make good his cause in the day of his judgment and trial before thee ?

Secondly, the word signifieth to keep in mind, to lay up, to have, as it were, a store and stock, a memorial or record, of such and such things by us. In that sense it is said (Gen. xxxvii. 11), " Joseph's brethren envied him ; but his father observed the saying" : he marked what Joseph spake about his dreams, he laid it up, and did not let it pass away as a dream, or as a vision of the night. Thus, by "*If the Lord should mark iniquity,*" we understand—if he should treasure up our sins in his memory, and keep them by him, " *who were able to stand when accounted with ?*" The Lord, in a way of grace, seeth as if he saw, not, and winks at us oftentimes when we do amiss.—*Joseph Caryl.*

Verse 3.—Let thine ears be attentive to the voice of my supplication, but let not thine eyes be intentive to the stains of my sin ; for "*If thou,* LORD, *shouldest mark iniquities, O Lord, who shall stand ?*" or who shall be able to abide it ? Did not the angels fall when thou markedst their follies ? Can flesh, which is but dust, be clean before thee, when the stars, which are of a far purer substance, are not ? Can anything be clean in thy sight which is not as clean as thy sight ? and can any cleanness be equal to thine ! Alas ! O Lord, we are neither angels nor stars, and how then can we stand when those fell ? how can we be clean when these be impure ? If thou shouldest mark what is done amiss, there would be marking-work enough for thee as long as the world lasts ; for what action of man is free from stain of sin, or from defect of righteousness ? Therefore, mark not anything in me, O God, that I have done, but mark that only in me which thou hast done thyself. Mark in me thine own image ; and then thou mayest look upn me, and yet say still, as once thou saidst, *Et erant omnia valde bona* [" And all things were very good "].—*Sir Richard Baker.*

Verse 3 (whole verse).—We are introduced at once into all the solemnities of a criminal court. The judge is seated on the bench : the culprit is standing at the bar, charged with a capital offence : the witnesses are giving their evidence against him. The judge is listening attentively to everything which is said ; and in order to assist his memory, he takes notes of the more important parts. If the Lord were to try us after this fashion, what would be the result ? Suppose him seated on his throne of inflexible righteousness, taking notes, with a pen in his hand, of the transgressions which are proven against us. Nothing is omitted. Every sin is marked down with its peculiar aggravations. There is no possibility of escape from the deserved condemnation. The evidence against us is clear, and copious, and overwhelming. A thousandth part of it is sufficient to determine our doom. The Judge has no alternative but to pronounce the awful sentence. We must die a felon's death. " *If thou,* LORD, *shouldest mark iniquities, O Lord, who shall stand ?*"—*N. M'Michael.*

Verse 3.—"*If thou,* LORD, *shouldest mark.*" If thou shouldst inquire and scrutinize, and then shouldst retain and impute : (for the Hebrew word imports both :) if thou shouldst inquire, thou wouldst find something of iniquity in the most righteous of mankind ; and when thou hast found it, if thou shouldst retain it, and call him to an account for it, he could by no means free himself of the charge, or expiate the crime. Inquiring, thou wouldst easily find iniquity ; but the sinner by the most diligent inquiry will not be able to discover a ransom, and therefore will be unable to stand, will have no place on which to rest his foot, but will fall by the irresistible judgments of thy law, and the sentence of thy justice.—*Robert Leighton.*

Verse 3.—"*If thou,* LORD." He here fixes on another name of God, which is Jah : a name, though from the same root as the former, yet seldom used but to intimate and express the terrible majesty of God . " He rideth on the heavens, and is extolled by his name JAH :" Ps. lxviii. 4. He is to deal now with God about the guilt of sin : and God is represented to the soul as great and terrible, that he may know what to expect and look for, if the matter must be tried out according to the demerit of sin.—*John Owen.*

Verse 3.—"*If thou,* LORD . . . *O Lord.*" Mark here that in this third verse he two times nameth God by *the Lord* (as he doth also in the ninth verse), showing to us hereby his earnest desire to take hold of God with both his hands. He nameth him not only *Adonai,* but also *Jah* (which two signify his nature and power) ; all the qualities of God must be conjoined and concur together for us : although he be *Adonai,* yet if he be not also *Jah* we are undone.—*Archibald Symson.*

Verse 3.—" LORD . . . *Lord.*" If God should show himself as JAH, no creature would be able to stand before him, who is *Adonai,* and can therefore carry out his judicial will or purpose.—*Franz Delitzsch.*

Verse 3.—" *Iniquities.*" The literal meaning of the word "*iniquity*" is "a thing which is not equal," or "not fair." Whatever breaks a command of God is " not equal." It does not match with what man is, nor with what God is. It does not keep the high level of the law. It is altogether out of proportion to all that God has done. It destroys the harmony of creation. It does not rise even to the height of conscience. Still more, it mars and makes a flaw in the divine government. Therefore sin is an unequal thing, fitting nothing, disarranging everything. And it is *not fair.* It is not fair to that God upon whose empire it is a trespass. It is not fair to your fellow-creatures, to whom it may be a very great injury. It is not fair to yourself, for your happiness lies in obedience. Therefore we call sin "*iniquity.*" Or, as the Prayer-Book Version expresses the same idea, "a thing amiss," missing its proper mark. " If thou shouldest be extreme to mark what is done amiss."—*James Vaughan.*

Verse 3.—" *O Lord, who shall stand ?*" As soon as God manifests signs of anger, even those who appear to be the most holy adopt this language. If God should determine to deal with them according to justice, and call them to his tribunal, not one would be able to stand ; but would be compelled to fly for refuge to the mercy of God. See the confessions of Moses, Job, David, Nehemiah, Isaiah, Daniel, Paul, and others of the apostles. Hear Christ teaching his disciples to cry to the Father who is in heaven, "*Forgive us our trespasses !* " If before God the Patriarchs, Prophets, and Apostles, although possessing unusual holiness, nevertheless fell down, and as suppliants prayed for forgiveness, what shall be done with those who add sin to sin ?—*D. H. Mollerus.*

Verses 3, 4.—These two verses contain the sum of all the Scriptures. In the third is the form of repentance, and in the fourth the mercies of the Lord. These are the two mountains, Gerizim and Ebal, mentioned in Deut. xxvii. 12, 13. These are the pillars in Solomon's temple (1 Kings vii. 21), called Jachin and Boaz. We must, with Paul, persuade ourselves that we are come from Mount Sinai to Mount Zion, where mercy is, although some sour grapes must be eaten by the way. Jeremy tasted in his vision first a bitter fig out of one basket, then a sweet fig out of the other. In the days of Moses the waters were first bitter, then sweetened by the sweet wood. And Elisha cast in salt into the pottage of the sons of the prophets, then it became wholesome.—*Archibald Symson.*

Verses 3, 4.—As I was thus in musing and in my studies, considering how to love the the LORD, and to express my love to him, that saying came in upon me : " *If thou,* LORD, *shouldest mark iniquities, O Lord, who shall stand ? But there is forgiveness with thee, that thou mayest be feared.*" These were good words to me, especially the latter part thereof ; to wit, that there is forgiveness with thee that thou mayest be feared ; that is, as then I understood it, that he might be loved

and had in reverence ; for it was thus made out to me, that the great God did set
so high an esteem upon the love of his poor creatures, that rather than he would
go without their love he would pardon their transgressions.—*John Bunyan.*

Verse 4.—"*But there is forgiveness with thee, that thou mayest be feared.*"   One
would think that punishment should procure fear, and forgiveness love ; but *nemo
majus diligit, quam qui maxime veretur offendere*—no man more truly loves God
than he that is most fearful to offend him.   " Thy mercy reacheth to the heavens,
and thy faithfulness to the clouds"—that is, above all sublimities.   God is glorious in all his works, but most glorious in his works of mercy ; and this may be
one reason why St. Paul calls the gospel of Christ a " glorious gospel" : 1 Tim.
i. 11.   Solomon tells us, " It is the glory of a man to pass by an offence."   Herein
is God most glorious, in that he passeth by all the offences of his children.   Lord,
who can know thee and not love thee, know thee and not fear thee ?   We fear
thee for thy justice, and love thee for thy mercy ; yea, fear thee for thy mercy, and
love thee for thy justice ; for thou art infinitely good in both —*Thomas Adams.*

Verse 4.—"*But there is forgiveness with thee, that thou mayest be feared.*"   But is
this not a mistaking in David to say, There is mercy with God, that he may be
feared ; all as one to say, There is severity with him, that he may be loved ?
for if we cannot love one for being severe, how should we fear him for being
merciful ?   Should it not, therefore, have been rather said, There is justice with
thee, that thou mayest be feared ?   seeing it is justice that strikes a terror and
keeps in awe ; mercy breeds a boldness, and boldness cannot stand with fear, and
therefore not fear with mercy.   But is there not, I may say, an active fear, not
to offend God, as well as a passive fear for having offended him ?   and with
God's mercy may well stand the active fear, though not so well, perhaps, the
passive fear which is incident properly to his justice.

There is a common error in the world, to think we may be the bolder to sin
because God is merciful ; but, O my soul, take heed of this error, for God's mercy
is to no such purpose ; it is not to make us bold, but to make us fear : the
greater his mercy is, the greater ought our fear to be, for there is mercy with him
that he may be feared.   Unless we fear, he may choose whether he will be merciful or no ; or rather, we may be sure he will not be merciful, seeing he hath mercy
for none but for them that fear him ; and there is great reason for this, for to
whom should mercy show itself but to them that need it ?   and if we think we need
it we will certainly fear.   Oh, therefore, most gracious God, make me to fear thee ;
for as thou wilt not be merciful to me unless I fear thee, so I cannot fear thee
unless thou first be merciful unto me.—*Sir Richard Baker.*

Verse 4.— "*But there is forgiveness with thee, that thou mayest be feared.*"   Even
Saul himself will lift up his voice and weep when he seeth a clear testimony of
the love and undeserved kindness of David.   Hast thou never beheld a condemned
prisoner dissolved in tears upon the unexpected and unmerited receipt of a pardon,
who all the time before was as hard as a flint ?   The hammer of the law may
break the icy heart of man with terrors and horrors, and yet it may remain ice
still, unchanged ; but when the fire of love kindly thaweth its ice, it is changed
and dissolved into water—it is no longer ice, but of another nature.—*George
Swinnock.*

Verse 4.—"*But there is forgiveness with thee, that thou mayest be feared.*"   The
Evangelical doctrine of the gratuitous forgiveness of sins does not of itself beget
carelessness, as the Papists falsely allege ; but rather a true and genuine fear of
God ; like as the Psalmist here shows that this is the final cause and effect of the
doctrine.—*Solomon Gesner.*

Verse 4.—"*But there is forgiveness with thee,*" etc.   His judgments and his wrath
may make us astonished and stupefied ; but, if there be no more, they will never
make us to come to God.   Then if this be not sufficient, what more is requisite ?
Even a sight of the Lord's mercy, for that is most forcible to allure, as the prophet
saith here, and as the church of God sayeth (Cant. i. 3), " Because of the savour
of thy good ointments, therefore the virgins love thee."   This only is forcible to

allure the sinner : for all the judgments of God, and curses of the law, will never allure him. What was the chief thing that moved the prodigal son to return home to his father ? Was it chiefly the distress, the disgrace and poverty where-with he was burdened, or the famine that almost caused him to starve ? No, but the chief thing was this, he remembered that he had a loving father. That maketh him to resolve with an humble confession to go home. Luke xv. Even so is it with the sinner ; it is not terrors and threatenings that chiefly will move him to come to God, but the consideration of his manifold and great mercies.— *Robert Rollock.*

Verse 4.—"*But.*" How significant is that word "*but!*" As if you heard justice clamouring, "Let the sinner die," and the fiends in hell howling, "Cast him down into the fires," and conscience shrieking, "Let him perish," and nature itself groaning beneath his weight, the earth weary with carrying him, and the sun tired with shining upon the traitor, the very air sick with finding breath for one who only spends it in disobedience to God. The man is about to be destroyed, to be swallowed up quick, when suddenly there comes this thrice-blessed "*but,*" which stops the reckless course of ruin, puts forth its strong arm bearing a golden shield between the sinner and destruction, and pronounces these words, "*But there is forgiveness with God, that he may be feared.*"—*C. H. S.*

Verse 4.—"*There is a propitiation with thee,*" so some read it : Jesus Christ is the great propitiation, the ransom which God has found ; he is ever with him, as advocate for us, and through him we hope to obtain forgiveness.—*Matthew Henry.*

Verse 4.—"*Forgiveness.*" Hebrew, *selichah,* a word used only here and by Daniel once (ix. 9), and by Nehemiah (ix. 17).—*Christopher Wordsworth.*

Verse 4.—"*That thou mayest be feared.*" This forgiveness, this smile of God, binds the soul to God with a beautiful fear. Fear to lose one glance of love. Fear to lose one work of kindness. Fear to be carried away from the heaven of his presence by an insidious current of worldliness. Fear of slumber. Fear of error. Fear of not enough pleasing him. Our duty, then, is to drink deep of God's forgiving love. To be filled with it is to be filled with purity, fervency, and faith. Our sins have to hide their diminished heads, and slink away through crevices, when forgiveness—when Christ—enters the soul.—*George Bowen, in* "*Daily Meditations,*" 1873.

Verses 4, 5, 7, 8.—David puts his soul out of all fear of God's taking this course [reckoning strictly] with poor penitent souls, by laying down this comfortable conclusion, as an indubitable truth : "*But there is forgiveness with thee, that thou mayest be feared.*" That is, there is forgiveness in thy nature, thou carriest a par-doning heart in thy bosom ; yea, there is forgiveness in thy promise ; thy merciful heart doth not only incline thee to thoughts of forgiving ; but thy faithful prom-ise binds thee to draw forth the same unto all that humbly and seasonably lay claim thereunto. Now, this foundation laid, see what superstructure this holy man raiseth (verse 5) : "*I wait for the* Lord, *my soul doth wait, and in his word do I hope.*" As if he had said, Lord, I take thee at thy word, and am resolved by thy grace to wait at the door of thy promise, never to stir thence till I have my promised dole (forgiveness of my sins) sent out unto me. And this is so sweet a morsel, that he is loth to eat it alone, and therefore he sends down the dish, even to the lower end of the table, that every godly person may taste with him of it (verses 7, 8) : "*Let Israel hope in the* Lord : *for with the* Lord *there is mercy, and with him is plenteous redemption. And he shall redeem Israel from all his iniquities.*" As if he had said, That which is a ground of hope to me, notwithstanding the clamour of my sins, affords as solid and firm a bottom to any true Israelite or sin-cere soul in the world, did he but rightly understand himself, and the mind of God in his promise. Yea, I have as strong a faith for such as [for] my own soul, and I durst pawn the eternity of my happiness upon this principle,—that God should redeem every sincere Israelite from all his iniquities.—*William Gurnall.*

Verse 5.—"*I wait for the* Lord," etc. We pronounce this a most blessed post-ure of the believer. It runs counter to everything that is natural, and, therefore, it is all the more a supernatural grace of the gracious soul. In the first place it is *the posture of faith.* Here is the gracious soul hanging in faith upon God in Christ Jesus ; upon the veracity of God to fulfil his promise, upon the power of God to help him in difficulty, upon the wisdom of God to counsel him in perplexity, upon the love of God to shield him in danger, upon the omniscience of God to guide him with his eye, and upon the omnipresence of God to cheer him with his presence, at all times and in all places, his sun and shield. Oh, have faith in God.

It is also a *prayerful posture.* The soul waiting *for* God, is the soul waiting *upon* God. The Lord often shuts us up to this waiting for his interposition on our behalf, that he may keep us waiting and watching at the foot of his cross, in earnest, believing, importunate prayer. Oh, it is the waiting *for* the Lord that keeps the soul waiting *upon* the Lord !

It is also *the posture of a patient waiting* for the Lord. There is not a more God-honouring grace of the Christian character than *patience*—a patient waiting on and for the Lord. It is that Christian grace, the fruit of the Spirit, which will enable you to bear with dignity, calmness, and submission the afflictive dealings of your Heavenly Father, the rebuke of the world, and the wounding of the saints.

It is *the posture of rest.* A soul-waiting for the Lord is a soul-resting in the Lord. Waiting and resting ! Wearied with traversing in vain the wide circle of human expedients ; coming to the end of all your own wisdom, strength, and resources ; your uneasy, jaded spirit is brought into this resting posture of waiting on, and waiting for, the Lord ; and thus folds its drooping wings upon the very bosom of God. Oh, how real and instant is the rest found in Jesus ! Reposing in him, however profound the depth of the soul, however dark the clouds that drape it, or surging the waters that overwhelm it, all is sunshine and serenity within.—*Condensed from "Soul-Depths and Soul-Heights," by Octavius Winslow,* 1874.

Verse 5.—"I wait for the Lord." *Waiting* is a great part of life's discipline, and therefore God often exercises the grace of waiting. *Waiting* has four purposes. It practises the patience of faith. It gives time for preparation for the coming gift. It makes the blessing the sweeter when it arrives. And it shows the sovereignty of God,—to give just *when* and just *as* he pleases. It may be difficult to define exactly what the Psalmist had in his mind when he said, " I wait *for the Lord,* my soul doth wait, and in his word do I hope. My soul waiteth *for the Lord* more than they that watch for the morning." It may have been the Messiah, whose coming was a thing close at hand to the mind of the ancient Jews, just as the Second Advent is to us.

It may have been some special interposition of Divine Providence. But more probably, looking at the place which it occupies, and at the whole tenor of the psalm, and its line of thought, " The Lord " he waited for so intently was that full sense of safety, peace, and love which God's felt presence gives, and which is, indeed, nothing else but the coming of the Lord most sensibly and palpably into an anxious and longing heart.

The picture of *the waiting man* is a striking one. It is as of one on the ridge of a journey, looking onward on his way, standing on tiptoe, and therefore needing something to lean on, and to support him. "*I wait for the Lord,*"—spiritually, with my deepest thoughts—in the very centre of my being—"*I wait for the Lord, my soul doth wait.*" And I rest, I stay myself on what thou, O Lord, hast said. " My soul doth wait, and *in his word* do I hope."

In all your *waitings* remember two things : Let it not be so much the event which you wait for, as the Lord *of* the event ; the Lord *in* the event. And take care that you have a promise underneath you,—" In his word do I hope,"—else " waiting" will be too much for you, and after all it may be in vain.—*James Vaughan.*

Verse 5.—"I wait . . . I hope." Waiting and hoping ever attend the same thing. No man will wait at all for that which he hath no hope of, and he who hath hope will wait always. He gives not over waiting, till he gives over hoping. The object of hope is some future good, but the act of hoping is at present good, and that is present pay to bear our charges in waiting. The word implies both a patient waiting and a hopeful trusting. So Christ expounds it (Matt. xii. 21), rendering that of the prophet (Isa. i. xlii. 4), "The isles shall wait for his law," thus, "In his name shall the Gentiles trust."—*Joseph Caryl.*

Verses 5, 6.—In these two verses he doth four times make mention of his hope, and attendance upon God and his word, to let us see how sure a hold we should take on God, and with how many temptations our faith is assaulted, when we can see no reason thereof. Nothing will bear us up but hope. *Spero meliora.* What encourageth husbandmen and mariners against the surges and waves of the sea, and evil weather, but hope of better times? What comforteth a sick man in time of sickness, but hope of health? or a poor man in his distress, but hope of riches? or a prisoner, but hope of liberty? or a banished man, but hope to come home? All these hopes may fail, as oftentimes wanting a warrant. Albeit a physician may encourage a sick man by his fair words, yet he cannot give him an assurance of his recovery, for his health dependeth on God: friends and courtiers may promise poor men relief, but all men are liars; only God is faithful who hath promised. Therefore let us fix our faith on God, and our hope in God; for he will stand by his promise. No man hath hoped in him in vain, neither was ever any disappointed of his hope.—*Archibald Symson.*

Verses 5, 7.—Faith doth ultimately centre in the Deity. God himself in his glorious nature, is the ultimate object whereunto our faith is resolved. The promise, simply considered, is not the object of trust, but God in the promise; and from the consideration of that we ascend to the Deity, and cast our anchor there. "Hope in the word" is the first act, but succeeded by hoping in the Lord: "*In his word do I hope*": that is not all; but, "*Let Israel hope in the Lord.*" That is the ultimate object of faith, wherein the essence of our happiness consists, and that is God. God himself is the true and full portion of the soul.—*Stephen Charnock, 1628—1680.*

Verse 6.—"*My soul waiteth for the* Lord." And now, my soul, what do I live for but only to wait upon God, and to wait for God? To wait upon him, to do him service, to wait for him, to be enabled to do him better service; to wait upon him, as being Lord of all; and to wait for him, as being the rewarder of all; to wait upon him whose service is better than any other command, and to wait for him whose expectation is better than any other possession. Let others, therefore, wait upon the world, wait for the world; I, O God, will wait upon thee, for thee, seeing I find more true contentment in this waiting than all the world can give me in enjoying; for how can I doubt of receiving reward by my waiting for thee when my waiting for thee is itself the reward of my waiting upon thee? And therefore my soul waiteth; for if my soul did not wait, what were my waiting worth? no more than I were worth myself, if I had not a soul; but my soul puts a life into my waiting, and makes it become a living sacrifice. Alas, my frail body is very unfit to make a waiter: it rather needs to be waited upon itself: it must have so much resting, so often leave to be excused from waiting, that if God should have no other waiters than bodies, he would be left oftentimes to wait upon himself; but my soul is *Divinæ particula auræ* [a portion of the Divine breath], endued with all qualities fit for a waiter; and hath it not received its abilities, O God, from thee? And therefore my soul waiteth, and is so intentive in the service that it waits "*more than they that watch for the morning.*"—*Sir Richard Baker.*

Verse 6.—*Hammond* thus renders the verse:—"My soul hasteneth to the Lord from the guards in the morning, the guards in the morning."

Verse 6.—"*More than they that watch for the morning.*" Look, as the weary sentinel that is wet and stiff with cold and the dews of the night, or as the porters that watched in the Temple, the Levites, were waiting for the daylight, so "more than they that watch for the morning" was he waiting for some glimpse of God's favour. Though he do not presently ease us of our smart or gratify our desires, yet we are to wait upon God. In time we shall have a good answer. God's delays are not denials. Day will come at length, though the weary sentinel or watchman counts it long first ; so God will come at length ; he will not be at our beck. We have deserved nothing, but must wait for him in the diligent use of means ; as Benhadad's servants watched for the word "brother," or anything of kindness to drop from the king of Israel.—*Thomas Manton.*

Verse 6.—"*More than they that watch for the morning.*" How many in the hallowed precincts of the Temple turned with anxious eye to the east, for the first red streak over Moab's mountains that gave intimation of approaching day ; yet it was not for deliverance they waited, but for the accustomed hour when the morning sacrifice could be offered, and the soul be relieved of its gratitude in the hymn of thanksgiving, and of the burden of its sorrows and sins by prayer, and could draw that strength from renewed intercourse with heaven, that would enable it in this world to breathe the spirit and engage in the beneficent and holy deeds of a better.—*Robert Nisbet.*

Verse 6.—"*I say, more than they that watch for the morning,*" for must there not be a proportion between the cause and effect? If my cause of watching be more than theirs, should not my watching be more than theirs? They that watch for the morning have good cause, no doubt, to watch for it, that it may bring them the light of day ; but have not I more cause to watch, who wait for the light that lighteth every one that comes into the world? They that watch for the morning wait but for the rising of the sun to free them from darkness, that hinders their sight ; but I wait for the rising of the Sun of righteousness to dispel the horrors of darkness that affright my soul. They watch for the morning that they may have light to walk by ; but I wait for the Dayspring from on High to give light to them that sit in darkness and in the shadow of death, and to guide our feet into the way of peace. But though there may be question made of the intentiveness of our watching, yet of the extensiveness there can be none, for they that watch for the morning watch at most but a piece of the night ; but I have watched whole days and whole nights, and may I not then justly say, I wait *more* than they that watch for the morning?—*Sir Richard Baker.*

Verse 6.—Holy men like Simeon, and devout priests like Zacharias, there were, amidst this seething people, who, brooding, longing, waiting, chanted to themselves day by day the words of the Psalmist, "*My soul waiteth for the Lord more than they that watch for the morning.*" As lovers that watch for the appointed coming, and start at the quivering of a leaf, the flight of a bird, or the humming of a bee, and grow weary of the tense strain, so did the Jews watch for their Deliverer. It is one of the most piteous sights of history, especially when we reflect that he came,—and they knew him not.—*Henry Ward Beecher, in his "Life of Jesus the Christ."*

Verse 6.—"*Watch.*" We do injustice to that good and happy word, "*watch*," when we take it as watching against ; against a danger ; against a coming evil. It will bear that interpretation ; but it is a far higher, and better, and more filial thing to watch *for* a coming good than to watch *against* an approaching evil.

So, "*watching for,*" we send up our arrows of prayer, and then look trustingly to see where they are coming down again. So, "*watching for,*" we listen, in silence, for the familiar voice we love. So, "*watching for,*" we expect the Bridegroom !

Take care, that as one always standing on the eve,—not of danger, but of happiness,—your "*watch*" be the "*watch*" of love, and confidence, and cheerful hope.—*James Vaughan.*

Verse 6.—In the year 1830, on the night preceding the 1st of August, the day the slaves in our West Indian Colonies were to come into possession of the freedom promised them, many of them, we are told, never went to bed at all. Thousands, and tens of thousands of them, assembled in their places of worship, engaging in devotional duties, and singing praises to God, waiting for the first streak of the light of the morning of that day on which they were to be made free. Some of their number were sent to the hills, from which they might obtain the first view of the coming day, and, by a signal, intimate to their brethren down in the valley the dawn of the day that was to make them men, and no longer, as they had hitherto been, mere goods and chattels,—men with souls that God had created to live forever. How eagerly must these men have watched for the morning! —*T. W. Aveling, in " The Biblical Museum,"* 1872.

Verse 7.—"Let Israel hope in the LORD.*"* This title is applied to all the Lord's people ; it sets forth *their dignity*—they are PRINCES ; it refers to *their experience* —they wrestle with God in prayer, and they prevail. Despondency does not become a prince, much less a Christian. Our God is " THE GOD OF HOPE " ; and we should hope in him. Israel should hope in his mercy, in his patience, in his provision, in his plenteous redemption. They should hope for light in darkness ; for strength in weakness ; for direction in perplexity ; for deliverance in danger ; for victory in conflict ; and for triumph in death.

They should hope in God confidently, because he hath promised ; prayerfully, for he loves to hear from us ; obediently, for his precepts are to be observed by us ; and constantly, for he is always the same.—*James Smith* (1802—1862), *in "The Believer's Daily Remembrancer."*

Verse 7.—"Let Israel hope in the LORD.*"* Whereas, in all preceding verses of the psalm, the thoughts, the sorrows, the prayer, the penitence, the awe, the waiting, the watching, were all personal and confined to himself ; here a great change has taken place, and it is no longer "*I*," but "*Israel*" ; all Israel. " Let *Israel* hope in the Lord : for with the Lord there is mercy, and with him is plenteous redemption. And he shall redeem *Israel* from all his iniquities." This is as it always ought to be. . . . It is the genius of our religion to go forth to multitudes.—*James Vaughan.*

Verse 7.—"For with the LORD *there is mercy."* Mercy has been shown to us, but it dwells in God. It is one of his perfections. The exercise of it is his delight. There is mercy with the Lord in all its *fulness ;* he never was more merciful than now, neither will he ever be. There is mercy with the Lord in all its *tenderness,* he is full of compassion, his bowels are troubled for us, his tender mercies are over us. There is mercy with him in all its *variety,* it suits every case. Here is mercy that receives sinners, mercy that restores backsliders, mercy that keeps believers. Here is the mercy that pardons sin, that introduces to the enjoyment of all gospel privileges, and that blesses the praying soul far beyond its expectations. With the Lord there is mercy, and he loves to display it, he is ready to impart it, he has determined to exalt and glorify it.

There is mercy with the Lord ; this should encourage the miserable to approach him ; this informs the fearful that they need bring nothing to induce him to bless them ; this calls upon backsliders to return to him ; and this is calculated to cheer the tried Christian, under all his troubles and distresses. Remember, mercy is like God, it is infinite and eternal. Mercy is always on the throne. Mercy may be obtained by any sinner.—*James Smith.*

Verse 7.—" With him is plenteous redemption." This plenteous redemption leaves behind it no more relics of sin than Moses left hoofs of beasts behind him in Egypt. It redeems not only from the fault, but from the punishment ; not only *a tanto,* but *a toto* [not only from such, but also from all sin and penalty] ; not only from the sense but from the fear of pain ; and in the fault, not only from the guilt, but from the stain ; not only from being censured, but from being questioned. Or is it meant by a plenteous redemption that not only he leads captivity captive, but gives gifts unto men ? For what good is it to a prisoner to have his pardon, if he be kept in prison still for not paying his fees ? but if the prince, together with the pardon, sends also a largess that may maintain him when he is set at liberty, this, indeed, is a plenteous redemption ; and such is the redemption that God's mercy procures unto us. It not only delivers us from a dungeon, but puts us in possession of a palace ; it not only frees us from eating bread in the sweat of our brows, but it restores us to Paradise, where all fruits are growing of their own accord ; it not only clears us from being captives, but endears us to be children ; and not only children, but heirs ; and not only heirs, but co-heirs with Christ ; and who can deny this to be a plenteous redemption ? Or is it said a plenteous redemption in regard of the price that was paid to redeem us ? for we are redeemed with a price, not of gold or precious stones, but with the precious blood of the Lamb slain before the foundation of the world. For God so loved the world that he gave his only Son to be a ransom for us ; and this I am sure is a plenteous redemption.—*Sir Richard Baker.*

Verse 7.—"*Plenteous redemption,*" or more literally, "redemption plenteously." He calls it plenteous, as Luther says, because such is the straitness of our heart, the slenderness of our hopes, the weakness of our faith, that it far exceeds all our capacity, all our petitions and all our desires.—*J. J. Stewart Perowne.*

Verses 7, 8.—This psalm containeth an evident prophecy of the Messias ; in setting forth his plentiful redemption, and that he should redeem Israel, that is, the Church, from all their sins. Which words in their full sense were used by an angel to Joseph, in telling him that the child's name should be JESUS, "because he should save his people from their sins" : Matt. i. 21.—*Sir John Hayward* (1560—1627), *in "David's Tears,"* 1623.

Verse 8.—"*He will redeem.*" HE emphatic, He alone, for none other can.— *J. J. Stewart Perowne.*

Verse 8.—"*From his iniquities.*" Not only from the punishment (as Ewald and Hupfeld). The redemption includes the forgiveness of sins, the breaking of the power and dominion of sin, and the setting free from all the consequences of sin. —*J. J. Stewart Perowne.*

Verse 8.—"*Iniquities.*" Iniquities of *eye*—has conscience no voice there ? Is no iniquity ever practised by your eye ? Let conscience speak. Iniquity of *ear*— is there no iniquity that enters into your heart through the ear ? You cannot listen to a conversation in the street without iniquity entering into your heart through what Bunyan calls "Ear-gate." Iniquity of *lip*—do you always keep your tongue as with a bridle ? Do your lips never drop anything unbecoming the gospel ? Is there no carnal conversation, no angry word at home, no expression that you would not like the saints of God to hear ? What ! your lips always kept so strictly that there is never a single expression dropped from them which you would be ashamed to utter before an assembly of God's people ? Iniquity of *thought*—if your eyes, ears, and lips are clean, is there no iniquity of thought ? What ! in that workshop within, no iniquitous suggestions, no evil workings ? Oh, how ignorant must we be of ourselves, if we feel that we have no iniquity of thought ! Iniquity of *imagination*—does not fancy sometimes bring before you scenes of sensuality in which your carnal nature is vile enough to revel ? Iniquity of *memory*—does not memory sometimes bring back sins you formerly committed, and your evil nature is perhaps base enough to desire they had been greater ? Iniquity of *feeling*—no enmity against God's people ever working ? no pride of heart ? no covetousness ? no hypocrisy ? no self-righteousness ? no sensuality ? no base thought that you cannot disclose even to your bosom friend ? But here is the blessed promise—a promise only suited to Israel : for all but Israel lose sight of their iniquities, and justify themselves in self-righteousness. None but Israel feel and confess their iniquities, and therefore to Israel is the promise of redemption limited : "He shall redeem *Israel* from all his iniquities." What ! *all ?* Yes. Not *one* left ? No, not a trace, not a shade, not the shadow of a shade ; all buried, all gone, all swallowed up, all blotted out, all freely pardoned, all cast behind God's back.—*Joseph C. Philpot,* 1802—1869.

Verse 8.—What a graceful and appropriate conclusion of this comprehensive and instructive psalm ! Like the sun, it dawns veiled in cloud, it sets bathed in splendour ; it opens with soul-depth, it closes with soul-height. Redemption from all iniquity ! It baffles the most descriptive language, and distances the highest measurement. The most vivid imagination faints in conceiving it, the most glowing image fails in portraying it, and faith droops her wing in the bold attempt to scale its summit. *"He shall redeem Israel from all his iniquities."* The verse is a word-painting of man restored, and of Paradise regained.—*Octavius Winslow.*

HINTS TO THE VILLAGE PREACHER.

Verse 1.—The assertion of an experienced believer. I. I have cried—that is, I have earnestly, constantly, truthfully prayed. II. I have cried only unto thee. Nothing could draw me to other confidences, or make me despair of thee. III. I have cried in distress. At my worst, temporally or spiritually, I have cried out of the depths. IV. I therefore infer—that I am thy child, no hypocrite, no apostate ; and that thou hast heard and wilt hear me evermore.

Verse 1.—I. What we are to understand by "the depths." Great misery and distress. II. How men get into "the depths." By sin and unbelief. III. What gracious souls do when in "the depths." Cry unto the Lord. IV. How the Lord lifts praying souls out of "the depths" ; "He shall redeem," etc., verse 8. — *W. H. J. P.*

Verse 1.—I. In the pit. II. The morning-star seen : "Thee, O Lord." III. Prayer flutters up "out of the depths."—*W. B. H.*

Verses 1, 2.—I. The depths from which prayer may rise. 1. Of affliction. 2. Of conviction. 3. Of desertion. II. The height to which it may ascend. 1. To the hearing of God. 2. To a patient hearing. "Hear my voice." 3. To an attentive hearing.

Or, I. We should pray at all times. II. We should pray that our prayers may be heard. III. We should pray until we know we are heard. IV. We should pray in faith that when heard we have the thing we have asked. "That which thou hast prayed to me against the King of Assyria I have heard." God had heard. That was enough. It was the death of Sennacherib and the overthrow of his host.—*G. R.*

Verses 1, 2.—Consider, I. The psalmist's condition in the light of a warning. Evidently, through sin, he came into the depths ; see verses 3 and 4. Learn, 1. The need of watchfulness on the part of all. 2. That backsliding will, sooner or later, bring great trouble of soul. II. His sometime continuance in that condition, in the light of a Divine judgment : "I *have* cried." Certainly his first cry had not brought deliverance. 1. The realization of pardon is a Divine work, dependent upon God's pleasure. Ps. lxxxv. 8. 2. But he will not always nor often speak pardon at the first asking ; for He will make His people reverence his holiness, feel the bitterness of sinning, learn caution, etc. III. His conduct while in that condition in the light of a direction. He, 1, Seeks deliverance only of God. 2. Is intensely earnest in his application : "I cried." 3. Is importunate in his pleading : "Hear my voice," etc.—*J. F.*

Verse 2.—Attention from God to us—how to gain it. I. Let us plead the name which commands attention. II. Let us ourselves pay attention to God's word. III. Let us give earnest attention to what we ask, and how we ask. IV. Let us attentively watch for a reply.

Verse 2.—"*Lord, hear my voice.*" I. Though it be faint by reason of distance —hear it. II. Though it be broken because of my distress—hear it. III. Though it be unworthy on account of my iniquities—hear it.— *W. H. J. P.*

Verse 3.—I. The supposition : "If thou, Lord, shouldst mark iniquities." 1. It is scriptural. 2. It is reasonable. If God is not indifferent towards men, he must observe their sins. If he is holy, he must manifest indignation against sin. If he is the Creator of conscience, he must certainly uphold its verdict against sin. If he is not wholly on the side of sin, how can he fail to avenge the mischiefs and miseries sin has caused ? II. The question it suggests : "Who shall stand ?" A question, 1. Not difficult to answer. 2. Of solemn import to all. 3. Which ought to be seriously pondered without delay. II.. The possibility it hints at. "If thou, Lord." The "if" hints at the possibility that God may not mark sin. The possibility, 1. Is reasonable, providing it can be without damage to God's righteousness ; for the Creator and Preserver of men cannot delight in condemning and punishing. 2. Is a God-honouring reality, through the blood of Christ, Rom. iii. 21—26. 3. Becomes a glorious certainty in the experience of penitent and believing souls.—*J. F.*

Verses 3, 4.—I. The Confession. He could not stand. II. The Confidence. "There is forgiveness." III. The Consequence. "That thou mayest be feared."

Verses 3, 4. —I. The fearful supposition. II. The solemn interrogation. III. The Divine consolation.— *W. J.*

Verse 4.—*Forgiveness with God.* I. The proofs of it. 1. Divine declarations. 2. Invitations and promises, Is. i. 18. 3. The bestowment of pardon so effectually as to give assurance and joy. 2 Sam. xii. 13. Ps. xxxii. 5. Luke vii. 47–8. 1 John ii. 12. II. The reason of it. 1. In God's nature there is the desire to forgive ; the gift of Christ is sufficient evidence for it. 2. But, the text speaks not so much of a desire as it asserts the existence of a forgiveness being "with" God, therefore ready to be dispensed. The blood of Christ is the reason (Col. i. 14) ; by it the disposition to forgive righteously manifests itself in the forgiving act : Rom. iii. 25, 26. 3. Hence, forgiveness for all who believe is sure : Rom. iii. 25 ; 1 John ii. 1, 2. III. The result of its realization : "That thou mayest be feared " : with a reverential fear, and spiritual worship. 1. The possibility of forgiveness begets in an anxious soul true penitence, as opposed to terror and despair. 2. The hope of receiving it begets earnest seeking and prayerfulness. 3. A believing reception of it gives peace and rest, and, exciting grateful love, leads to spiritual worship and filial service.—*J. F.*

Verse 4.—*"There is forgiveness."* I. It is needed. II. God alone can give it. III. It may be had. IV. We may know that we have it.

Verse 4.—I. A most cheering announcement : "There is forgiveness with thee." 1. A fact certain. 2. A fact in the present tense. 3. A fact which arises out of God himself. 4. A fact stated in general terms. 5. A fact to be meditated upon with delight. II. A most admirable design : "That thou mayest be feared." 1. Very contrary to the abuse made of it by rebels, triflers, and procrastinators. 2. Very different from the pretended fears of legalists. 3. No pardon, no fear of God—devils, reprobates. 4. No pardon, none survive to fear him. 5. But the means of pardon encourage faith, repentance, prayer ; and the receipt of pardon creates love, suggests obedience, inflames zeal.

Verse 4.— See " Spurgeon's Sermons," No. 351 : " Plenteous Redemption."

Verse 4.—Tender Light. I. The Angel by the Throne : "Forgiveness with Thee." II. The shadow that enhances his sweet majesty : "If," "But." III. The homage resultant from his ministry ; universal from highest to least.— *W. B. H.*

Verses 5, 6.—Three postures : Waiting, Hoping, Watching.

Verses 5, 6.—1. The seeking sinner. 2. The Christian mourner, 3. The loving intercessor. 4. The spiritual labourer. 5. The dying believer.-— *W. J.*

Verses 5, 6.—I. We are to wait on God. 1. By faith : " In his word do I hope." 2. By prayer. Prayer can wait when it has a promise to rest upon. II. We are to wait for God : " I wait for the Lord." " My soul waiteth for the Lord more," etc. 1. Because he has his own time for giving. 2. Because what he gives is worth waiting for.— *G. R.*

Verse 6.— *"More than they."* I. For the darker sorrow his absence causes. II. For the richer splendour his coming must bring. III. For the greater might of our indwelling love.— *W. B. H.*

Verse 6.—I. A long, dark night : The Lord absent. II. An eager, hopeful watcher : Waiting the Lord's return. III. A bright, blessed morning : The time of the Lord's appearing.— *W. H. J. P.*

Verse 7.—Redeeming grace the sole hope of the holiest.— *W. B. H.*

Verse 7.—I. A divine exhortation : " Let Israel hope in the LORD." II. A spiritual reason : " For with the LORD there is mercy," etc. III. A gracious promise : " He shall redeem Israel from all his iniquities."—*J. C. Philpot.*

Verses 7, 8.—It is our wisdom to have personal dealings with God. I. The first exercise of faith must be upon the Lord himself. This is the natural order, the necessary order, easiest, wisest, and most profitable order. Begin where all begins. II. Exercises of faith about other things must still be in connection with the Lord. Mercy—" with the Lord." Plenteous redemption " with him." III. Exercises of faith, whatever their object, must *all* settle on him. " HE shall redeem," etc.

Verse 8.—I. The Redemption : " From all iniquities." II. The Redeemer : " The Lord." See Titus ii. 14. III. The Redeemed : " Israel."—*W. H. J. P.*

WORKS UPON THE HUNDRED AND THIRTIETH PSALM.

A TREATISE concerning the fruitful Sayings of David, THE King and Prophet, IN THE *Seven Penitential Psalms*. . . . By the Right Reverend Father in God IOHN FISHER, DD. and Bp. of *Rochester*. Printed in the Year MDCCXIV. [This is a reprint in 12mo. of the Black Letter 4to. described on page 114 of Vol. II. of " The Treasury of David." The work is more curious than useful.]

" AN EXPOSITION upon some select Psalms of David. . . . Written by that faithful servant of God M. Robert Rollok. . . . And translated out of Latine into English by C[harles] L[umisden] . . . Edinborgh . . . 1600," [8vo.] contains a short exposition on Psalm CXXX.

In " Select Works of Robert Rollock," edited for the Wodrow Society by William M. Gunn, Esq., Vol. I. pp. 451—481, there are two expository Sermons on Psalm CXXX.

AN EXPOSITION UPON THE HUNDRED AND THIRTIETH PSALM. Gathered out of some of the Ancient Fathers and later writers by ALEXANDER ROBERTS. Bachelor of Divinity and Preacher of the Word of God at Kings Linn in Norfolk. London . . . 1610. [4to.]

David's Tears. By SIR JOHN HAYWARD, Knight, Doctor of Lawe. London. Printed by John Bell, 1623. [4to.] On Psalms VI., XXXII., and CXXX.

THE SAINTS' COMFORTS. Being the substance of diverse Sermons. Preached on *Psalm* 130, the beginning [verses 1—5]. . . . By a Reverend Divine now with God. [Richard Sibbes.] London. . . . 1638. [18mo.] Reprinted in Vol. VI. of Sibbes' Works, Nichol's edition, 1863.

A Godly and Fruitful Exposition on the CXXX. PSALME, the sixt of the *Penitentials*, in A SACRED SEPTENARIE, OR, A GODLY AND FRUITFULL EXPOSITION ON THE SEVEN PSALMS OF REPENTANCE. . . . By Mr. ARCHIBALD SYMSON, late Pastor of the church at *Dalkeeth* in *Scotland*. *LONDON*. . . . 1638. [4to.]

In " MEDITATIONS AND DISQUISITIONS upon The Three last Psalmes of DAVID. *By* SIR RICHARD BAKER, *Knight*" [4to. 1639], there is an Exposition of Psalm CXXX. It will be found in Higham's reprint [1882] of Sir R. Baker's Expositions of the Psalms, pp. 257—271.

A Practical Exposition upon Psalm CXXX. ; wherein the Nature of the Forgiveness of Sin is declared ; the Truth and Reality of it asserted ; and the case of a Soul Distressed with the Guilt of Sin, and Relieved by a Discovery of Forgiveness with God, is at large Discoursed [By John Owen, D.D., 4to.], 1668, 1669, 1680. There are modern reprints of this Exposition ; and it is in Vol. VI. of Owen's Works, edited by W. H. Goold, 1881.

In " The Whole Works of Robert Leighton, D.D., Archbishop of Glasgow, 4 vols., 8vo., 1725," there are " Meditations on Psalm CXXX." Vol. II. pp. 510 – 540.

FORTY-FIVE SERMONS upon THE CXXX. PSALME. Preached at *IRWIN.* By that Eminent Servant of *Jesus Christ*, Mr. *George Hutcheson* [—1678], Minister of the Gospel. *Edinburgh* . . . 1691. [8vo.]

In " Sermons preached in Christ Church, Brighton, from October, 1877, to July, 1878, by the Rev. James Vaughan, M.A. [London, 1878]," there is a Course of Lenten Sermons on the 130th Psalm, entitled " Steps to Heaven."

PSALM CXXXI.

Title.—A Song of Degrees of David. *It is both by David and of David : he is the author and the subject of it, and many incidents of his life may be employed to illustrate it. Comparing all the psalms to gems, we should liken this to a pearl : how beautifully it will adorn the neck of patience. It is one of the shortest psalms to read, but one of the longest to learn. It speaks of a young child, but it contains the experience of a man in Christ. Lowliness and humility are here seen in connection with a sanctified heart, a will subdued to the mind of God, and a hope looking to the Lord alone. Happy is the man who can without falsehood use these words as his own ; for he wears about him the likeness of his Lord, who said, " I am meek and lowly in heart." The psalm is in advance of all the Songs of Degrees which have preceded it ; for lowliness is one of the highest attainments in the divine life. There are also steps in this Song of Degrees : it is a short ladder, if we count the words ; but yet it rises to a great height, reaching from deep humility to fixed confidence. Le Blanc thinks that this is a song of the Israelites who returned from Babylon with humble hearts, weaned from their idols. At any rate, after any spiritual captivity let it be the expression of our hearts.*

EXPOSITION.

LORD, my heart is not haughty, nor mine eyes lofty : neither do I exercise myself in great matters, or in things too high for me.

2 Surely I have behaved and quieted myself, as a child that is weaned of his mother : my soul *is* even as a weaned child.

3 Let Israel hope in the LORD from henceforth and for ever.

1. "LORD, *my heart is not haughty.*" The psalm deals with the Lord, and is a solitary colloquy with him, not a discourse before men. We have a sufficient audience when we speak with the Lord, and we may say to him many things which were not proper for the ears of men. The holy man makes his appeal to Jehovah, who alone knows the heart : a man should be slow to do this upon any matter, for the Lord is not to be trifled with ; and when anyone ventures on such an appeal he should be sure of his case. He begins with his heart, for that is the centre of our nature, and if pride be there it defiles everything ; just as mire in the spring causes mud in all the streams. It is a grand thing for a man to know his own heart so as to be able to speak before the Lord about it. It is beyond all things deceitful and desperately wicked, who can know it ? Who can know it unless taught by the Spirit of God ? It is a still greater thing if, upon searching himself thoroughly, a man can solemnly protest unto the Omniscient One that his heart is not haughty : that is to say, neither proud in his opinion of himself, contemptuous to others, nor self-righteous before the Lord ; neither boastful of the past, proud of the present, nor ambitious for the future. "*Nor mine eyes lofty.*" What the heart desires the eyes look for. Where the desires run the glances usually follow. This holy man felt that he did not seek after elevated places as being he might gratify his self-esteem, neither did he look down upon others as being his inferiors. A proud look the Lord hates ; and in this all men are agreed with him ; yea, even the proud themselves hate haughtiness in the gestures of others. Lofty eyes are so generally hateful that haughty men have been known to avoid the manners natural to the proud in order to escape the ill-will of their fellows. The pride which apes humility always takes care to cast its eyes downward, since every man's consciousness tells him that contemptuous glances are the sure ensigns of a boastful spirit. In Psalm cxxi. David lifted up his eyes to the hills ; but here he declares that they were not lifted up in any other sense. When the heart is right, and the eyes are right, the whole man is on the road to a healthy

and happy condition. Let us take care that we do not use the language of this psalm unless, indeed, it be true as to ourselves ; for there is no worse pride than that which claims humility when it does not possess it.

"Neither do I exercise myself in great matters." As a private man he did not usurp the power of the king or devise plots against him : he minded his own business, and left others to mind theirs. As a thoughtful man he did not pry into things unrevealed ; he was not speculative, self-conceited or opinionated. As a secular person he did not thrust himself into the priesthood as Saul had done before him, and as Uzziah did after him. It is well so to exercise ourselves unto godliness that we know our true sphere, and diligently keep to it. Many through wishing to be great have failed to be good : they were not content to adorn the lowly stations which the Lord appointed them, and so they have rushed at grandeur and power, and found destruction where they looked for honour. *"Or in things too high for me."* High things may suit others who are of greater stature, and yet they may be quite unfit for us. A man does well to know his own size. Ascertaining his own capacity, he will be foolish if he aims at that which is beyond his reach, straining himself, and thus injuring himself. Such is the vanity of many men that if a work be within their range they despise it, and think it beneath them : the only service which they are willing to undertake is that to which they have never been called, and for which they are by no means qualified. What a haughty heart must he have who will not serve God at all unless he may be trusted with five talents at the least ! His looks are indeed lofty who disdains to be a light among his poor friends and neighbours here below, but demands to be created a star of the first magnitude to shine among the upper ranks, and to be admired by gazing crowds. It is just on God's part that those who wish to be everything should end in being nothing. It is a righteous retribution from God when every matter turns out to be too great for the man who would only handle great matters, and everything proves to be too high for the man who exercised himself in things too high for him. Lord, make us lowly, keep us lowly, fix us for ever in lowliness. Help us to be in such a case that the confession of this verse may come from our lips as a truthful utterance which we dare make before the Judge of all the earth.

2. *"Surely I have behaved and quieted myself."* The original bears somewhat of the form of an oath, and therefore our translators exhibited great judgment in introducing the word " surely" ; it is not a literal version, but it correctly gives the meaning. The Psalmist had been upon his best behaviour, and had smoothed down the roughnesses of his self-will ; by holy effort he had mastered his own spirit, so that towards God he was not rebellious, even as towards man he was not haughty. It is no easy thing to quiet yourself : sooner may a man calm the sea, or rule the wind, or tame a tiger, than quiet himself. We are clamorous, uneasy, petulant ; and nothing but grace can make us quiet under afflictions, irritations, and disappointments. *"As a child that is weaned of his mother."* He had become as subdued and content as a child whose weaning is fully accomplished. The Easterns put off the time of weaning far later than we do, and we may conclude that the process grows none the easier by being postponed. At last there must be an end to the suckling period, and then a battle begins : the child is denied his comfort, and therefore frets and worries, flies into pets, or sinks into sulks. It is facing its first great sorrow, and it is in sore distress. Yet time brings not only alleviations, but the ending of the conflict ; the boy ere long is quite content to find his nourishment at the table with his brothers, and he feels no lingering wish to return to those dear fountains from which he once sustained his life. He is no longer angry with his mother, but buries his head in that very bosom after which he pined so grievously : he is weaned *on* his mother rather than *from* her.

> " My soul doth like a weanling rest,
>   I cease to weep ;
> So mother's lap, though dried her breast,
>   Can lull to sleep."

To the weaned child his mother is his comfort though she has denied him comfort. It is a blessed mark of growth out of spiritual infancy when we can forego the joys which once appeared to be essential, and can find our solace in him who denies them to us : then we behave manfully, and every childish complaint is hushed. If the Lord removes our dearest delight we bow to his will without a murmuring thought ; in fact, we find a delight in giving up our delight. This is no spontaneous fruit of nature, but a well-tended product of divine grace : it grows out of humility and lowliness, and it is the stem upon which peace blooms as a fair flower. *"My soul is even as a weaned child"*; or it may be read, " as a weaned child on me my soul," as if his soul leaned upon him in mute submission, neither boasting nor complaining. It is not every child of God who arrives at this weanedness speedily. Some are sucklings when they ought to be fathers ; others are hard to wean, and cry, and fight, and rage against their heavenly parent's discipline. When we think ourselves safely through the weaning, we sadly discover that the old appetites are rather wounded than slain, and we begin crying again for the breasts which we had given up. It is easy to begin shouting before we are out of the wood, and no doubt hundreds have sung this psalm long before they have understood it. Blessed are those afflictions which subdue our affections, which wean us from self-sufficiency, which educate us into Christian manliness, which teach us to love God not merely when he comforts us, but even when he tries us. Well might the sacred poet repeat his figure of the weaned child ; it is worthy of admiration and imitation ; it is doubly desirable and difficult of attainment. Such weanedness from self springs from the gentle humility declared in the former verse, and partly accounts for its existence. If pride is gone, submission will be sure to follow ; and, on the other hand, if pride is to be driven out, self must also be vanquished.

3. *"Let Israel hope in the* LORD *from henceforth and for ever."* See how lovingly a man who is weaned from self thinks of others ! David thinks of his people, and loses himself in his care for Israel. How he prizes the grace of hope ! He has given up the things which are seen, and therefore he values the treasures which are not seen except by the eyes of hope. There is room for the largest hope when self is gone, ground for eternal hope when transient things no longer hold the mastery of our spirits. This verse is the lesson of experience : a man of God who had been taught to renounce the world and live upon the Lord alone, here exhorts all his friends and companions to do the same. He found it a blessed thing to live by hope, and therefore he would have all his kinsmen do the same. Let all the nation hope, let all their hope be in Jehovah, let them at once begin hoping " from henceforth," and let them continue hoping " for ever." Weaning takes the child out of a temporary condition into a state in which he will continue for the rest of his life : to rise above the world is to enter upon a heavenly existence which can never end. When we cease to hanker for the world we begin hoping in the Lord. O Lord, as a parent weans a child, so do thou wean me, and then shall I fix all my hope on thee alone.

EXPLANATORY NOTES.

Whole Psalm.—This little song is inscribed לְדָוִד because it is like an echo of the answer (2 Sam. vi. 21 sq.) with which David repelled the mocking observation of Michal when he danced before the Ark in a linen ephod, and therefore not in kingly attire, but in the common raiment of the priests : *I esteem myself still less than I now show it, and I appear base in mine own eyes.* In general David is the model of the state of mind which the poet expresses here. He did not push himself forward, but suffered himself to be drawn forth out of seclusion. He did not take possession of the throne violently ; but after Samuel has anointed him, he willingly and patiently traverses the long, thorny, circuitous way of deep abasement, until he receives from God's hand that which God's promise had assured to him. The persecution by Saul lasted about ten years, and his kingship in Hebron, at first only incipient, seven years and a half. He left it entirely to God to remove Saul and Ishbosheth. He let Shimei curse. He left Jerusalem before Absalom. Submission to God's guidance, resignation to his dispensations, contentment with that which was allotted to him, are the distinguishing traits of his noble character.—*Franz Delitzsch.*

Whole Psalm.—Psalm cxxx. is a Song of Forgiveness ; Psalm cxxxi. is a Song of Humility : the former celebrates the blessedness of the man whose transgressions are pardoned ; the latter celebrates the blessedness of the man who is of a meek and lowly spirit. Forgiveness *should* humble us. Forgiveness implies sin ; and should not the sinner clothe himself with humility ? and when not for any desert of his, but simply by the free grace of Heaven, his sins have been pardoned, should he not bind the garments of humility still more closely about him ? The man who is of a nature at once sincere and sweet, will be even more humbled by the sense of an undeserved forgiveness than by the memory of the sins from which it has cleansed him. Very fitly, therefore, does the psalm of humility follow the psalm which sings of the Divine loving-kindness and tender mercy.— *Samuel Cox.*

Whole Psalm.—This psalm, which records the meek and humble spirit of those who are the true worshippers of the Temple, doubtless belongs, as its title announces, to the time of David. It is exactly in the spirit of that humble thanksgiving made by him, after the divine revelation by Nathan of the future blessings of his posterity (1 Chron. xxii. 9—11) ; and forms a most appropriate introduction to the following psalm, the theme of which is evidently the dedication of the Temple.—*John Jebb.*

Verse 1.—" LORD, *my heart is not haughty.*" For the truth of his plea he appealeth to God ; and from all those who are affected like David, God will accept of the appeal.

Firstly. He could in truth of heart appeal to God : " LORD, *my heart is not haughty.*" He appealeth to him who knoweth all things. " Lord, from whom nothing is hid, thou knowest that this is the very disposition of my soul. If I have anything, it is from thee ; it is thy providence which brought me from following the ewes great with young to feed and govern thy people." Such a holy man would not rashly invoke God, and take his holy name in vain ; but knowing his integrity, durst call God to witness. The saints are wont to do so upon like occasions ; as Peter (John xxi. 17) ; " Lord, thou knowest all things ; thou knowest that I love thee." They know they have a God that will not be deceived with any shows, and that he knoweth and approveth them for such as he findeth them to be.

Secondly. From those that are affected like David, God will accept the appeal ; for in the account of God we are that which we sincerely desire and endeavour to be, and that which is the general course and tenor of our lives, though there be some intermixture of failing. David saith, " LORD, *my heart is not haughty*" *;* and yet he was not altogether free from pride. His profession respecteth his sincere purpose and constant endeavour, and the predominant disposition of his soul. God himself confirmeth such appeals by his own testimony : 1 Kings xv. 5, " My servant David did that which was right in the eyes of the Lord, neither departed from all that which he had commanded him, save only in the matter of Uriah." . . . . By all this it is shown that the plea of sincerity is allowed by God, though there be some mixture of failings and weaknesses.

Thirdly. Is not this boasting like the Pharisee ? Luke xviii. 9, " God, I thank thee, I am not like other men." If David were thus humble, why doth he speak of it ? Is he not guilty of pride while he seemeth to speak against pride ?

This is spoken either as, (1.) A necessary vindication ; or (2.) A necessary instruction. 1. As a necessary vindication against the censures and calumnies of his adversaries. Saul's courtiers accused him as aspiring after the kingdom ; yea, his own brother taxed him with pride when he came first abroad : 1 Sam. xvii.

28, " I know thy pride, and the naughtiness of thine heart ; for thou art come down that thou mightest see the battle." If his brother would calumniate his actions, much more might others. Now it is for the honour of God that his children, as they would not commit a fault, so they should not be under the suspicion of it ; therefore he appealeth to God. 2. A necessary instruction ; for whatsoever David said or wrote here, he said or wrote by the inspiration of the Holy Ghost, that Israel may learn how to hope in God. Herein David is a notable pattern of duty both to superiors and inferiors.—*Thomas Manton.*

Verse 1.—*"My heart is not haughty."* Albeit pride is a common vice, which attendeth vain man in every degree of excellency and supposed worth in him, yet the grace of God is able to keep humble a wise, rich, and potent man, yea, to keep humble a king and conqueror ; for it is no less a person than David who saith here, *"Lord, my heart is not haughty.—David Dickson.*

Verse 1.—*"Nor mine eyes lofty."* Pride has its seat in the heart ; but its principal expression is in the eye. The eye is the mirror of the soul ; and from it mental and moral characteristics may be ascertained, with no small degree of precision. What a world of meaning is sometimes concentrated in a single glance ! But of all the passions, pride is most clearly revealed in the eyes. There can scarcely be a mistake here. We are all familiar with a class of phrases, which run in pairs. We speak of sin and misery ; holiness and happiness ; peace and prosperity ; war and desolation. Among these may be numbered, the proud heart and the haughty look. " There is a generation, Oh, how lofty are their eyes ! and their eyelids are lifted up." " Him that hath an high look and a proud heart I will not suffer." . . . A proud look is one of the seven things which are an abomination unto the Lord. It is said of him, " Thou wilt save the afflicted people ; but wilt bring down high looks." And hence David makes the acknowledgment : Lord, thou knowest all things ; thou knowest that pride has no existence in my heart. Thou knowest that no pride flashes forth from mine eyes.—*N. M'Michael.*

Verse 1.—*"Nor mine eyes lofty."* He had neither a scornful nor an aspiring look. *"My eyes are not lofty,"* either to look with envy upon those that are above me, or to look with disdain upon those that are below me. Where there is a proud heart, there is commonly a proud look (Prov. vi. 17) ; but the humble publican will not so much as lift up his eyes.—*Matthew Henry.*

Verse 1.—*"Neither have I occupied myself,"* etc. One cannot admire enough the prayer of Anselm, a profound divine of our own country, in the eleventh century. " I do not seek, O Lord, to penetrate thy depths. I by no means think my intellect equal to them : but I long to understand in some degree thy truth, which my heart believes and loves. For I do not seek to understand that I may believe ; but I believe, that I may understand."—*N. M'Michael.*

Verse 1.—*"Great matters . . . things too high for me."* The great and wonderful things meant are God's secret purposes, and sovereign means for their accomplishment, in which man is not called to co-operate, but to acquiesce. As David practised this forbearance by the patient expectation of the kingdom, both before and after the death of Saul, so he here describes it as a characteristic of the chosen people.—*Joseph Addison Alexander.*

Verses 1, 2.—Our Father is our superior ; it is fit therefore that we be resigned to his will. " Honour thy father and thy mother" (Exod. xx. 12) ; how much more our heavenly Father ! (Heb. xii. 9). See David's spirit in the case : " Lord, *my heart is not haughty,"* etc.: Ps. cxxxi. 1, 2. As if he had said, " I will keep within my own sphere ; I will not stretch beyond my line, in prescribing to God ; but submit to his will, ' *as a weaned child,*' taken from its dear breasts" : intimating that he would wean himself from whatever God removed from him. How patiently did Isaac permit himself to be bound and sacrificed by Abraham ! Gen. xxii. 9. And yet he was of age and strength sufficient to have struggled for his life, being twenty-five years old ; but that holy young man abhorred the thought of striving with his father. And shall not we resign ourselves to our God and Father in Christ Jesus ?—*John Singleton* (—1706), *in "The Morning Exercises."*

Verses 1, 2.—It has always been my aim, and it is my prayer, to have no plan as regards myself ; well assured as I am that the place where the Saviour sees meet to place me must ever be the best place for me.—*Robert Murray M'Cheyne*, 1813—1843.

Verse 2.—"*Surely I have behaved and quieted myself*," etc. Oh, how sapless and insipid doth the world grow to the soul that is making meet for heaven ! " I am crucified to the world, and this world to me." Gal. vi. 14. In vain doth this harlot think to allure me by her attractions of profit and pleasure. " Surely I have behaved and quieted myself, as a child that is weaned of his mother : my soul is even as a weaned child." There is no more relish in these gaudy things to my palate, than in the white of an egg ; everything grows a burden to me, were it not my duty to follow my calling, and be thankful for my enjoyments. Methinks I have my wife, husband, and dearest relations, as if I had none ; I weep for outward losses, as if I wept not ; rejoice in comforts below as if I rejoiced not (1 Cor. vii. 29, 30) ; my thoughts are taken up with other objects. The men of the world slight me, many seem to be weary of me, and I am as weary of them. It is none of these earthly things that my heart is set upon ; my soul is set on things above, my treasure is in heaven, and I would have my heart there also : I have sent before me all my goods into another country, and am shortly for removing ; and when I look about me, I see a bare, empty house, and am ready to say with Monica, What do I here ? my father, husband, mother (Jerusalem above), my brethren, sisters, best friends are above. Methinks, I grudge the world any portion of my heart, and think not these temporal visible things worth a cast of my eye compared with things invisible and eternal : 2 Cor. iv. 18.—*Oliver Heywood*, 1629—1702.

Verse 2 (*first clause*).—"*If I have not restrained*," or quieted, and compelled to silence, " *my soul*." It is a Hebrew phrase of asseveration and of swearing : as if he would say, I have thoroughly imposed silence on my soul, that it should be tranquil, and should bear patiently the divinely imposed cross. Just as in the following Psalm we hear a like form of asseveration : " If I will come into the tabernacle of my house," meaning " I will not come," etc.—*Solomon Gesner*.

Verse 2.—"*I have behaved and quieted myself, as a child that is weaned*." Weaned from what ? Self-sufficiency, self-will, self-seeking. From creatures and the things of the world—not, indeed, as to their use, but as to any dependence upon them for his happiness and portion. . . . Yet this experience is no easy attainment. The very form of expression—" I have behaved and *quieted* myself," reminds us of some risings which were with difficulty subdued. There is a difference here between Christ and Christians. In him the exercise of grace encountered no adverse principles ; but in them it meets with constant opposition. The flesh lusteth against the spirit ; and when we would do good evil is present with us ; hence the warfare within. So it is with " the child that is weaned." The task to the mother is trying and troublesome. The infant cries, and seems to sob out his heart. He thinks it very hard in her, and knows not what she means by her seeming cruelty, and the mother's fondness renders all her firmness necessary to keep her at the process ; and sometimes she also weeps at the importunity of his dear looks, and big tears, and stretched-out hands. But it must be done, and therefore, though she pities, she perseveres ; and after a while he is soothed and satisfied, forgets the breast, and no longer feels even a hankering after his former pleasure. But how is the weaning of the child accomplished ? By embittering the member to his lips ; by the removal of the object in the absence and concealment of the mother ; by the substitution of other food ; by the influence of time. So it is with us. We love the world, and it deceives us. We depend on creatures, and they fail us, and pierce us through with many sorrows. We enter forbidden paths, and follow after our lovers ; and our way is hedged up with thorns ; and we then say, " Return unto thy rest, O my soul ; and now, Lord, what wait I for ? My hope is in thee." The enjoyment of a greater good subdues the relish of a less. What are the indulgences of sin, or the dissipations of the world to one who is abundantly satisfied with the goodness of God's house, and is made to drink of the river of his pleasures ?— *William Jay* (1769—1853), *in "Evening Exercises for the Closet."*

Verse 2.—*"As a child that is weaned of his mother."* Though the weaned child has not what it would have, or what it naturally most desireth, the milk of the breast—yet it is contented with what the mother giveth—it rests upon her love and provision. So are we to be content with what providence alloweth us : Heb. xiii. 5, " Let your conversation be without covetousness, and be content with such things as ye have" ; and Phil. iv. 11, " I have learned, in whatsoever state I am, therewith to be content." Whatever pleaseth our heavenly Father should please us. The child that is put from the breast to a harder diet is yet contented at last. The child doth not prescribe what it will eat, drink, or put on. Children are in no care for enlarging possessions, heaping up riches, aspiring after dignities and honours ; but meekly take what is provided for them. The child, when it has lost the food which nature provideth for it, is not solicitous, but wholly referreth itself to the mother, hangeth upon the mother. So for everything whatsoever should we depend upon God, refer ourselves to God, and expect all things from him : Ps. lxii. 5, " My soul, wait thou only upon God ; for my expectation is from him." With such a simplicity of submission should we rest and depend upon God. Let us take heed of being over wise and provident for ourselves, but let us trust our Father which is in heaven, and refer ourselves to his wise and holy government.—*Thomas Manton.*

Verse 2.—*"As a child that is weaned of his mother."* Weaned from the world, the riches, honours, pleasures, and profits of it ; as well as from nature, from self, from his own righteousness, and all dependence upon it ; and as a child that is weaned from the breast wholly depends on its nurse for sustenance, so did he wholly depend upon God, his providence, grace, and strength ; and as to the kingdom, he had no more covetous desires after it than a weaned child has to the breast, and was very willing to wait the due time for the enjoyment of it. The Targum has it, " as one weaned on the breasts of its mother, I am strengthened in the law." This is to be understood not of a child whilst weaning, when it is usually peevish, fretful, and froward, but when it is weaned, and is quiet and easy in its mother's arms without the breast.—*John Gill.*

Verse 2.—*"My soul is even as a weaned child."* In its *nature,* weanedness of soul differs essentially from that disgust with the world, to which its ill-usage and meanness sometimes give rise. It is one thing to be angry with the world, or ashamed of it, and another to be weaned from it. Alter the world, ennoble it, and many a proud mind that now despises, would court it. It is different also from that weariness of spirit which generally follows a free indulgence in earthly enjoyments. There is such a thing as wearing out the affections. Solomon appears to have done this at one period of his life. " I have not a wish left," said a well-known sensualist of our own country, who had drunk as deeply as he could drink of the world's cup. " Were all the earth contains spread out before me, I do not know a thing I would take the trouble of putting out my hand to reach."

This weanedness of soul presupposes a power left in the soul of loving and desiring. It is not the destruction of its appetite, but the controlling and changing of it. A weaned child still hungers, but it hungers no more after the food that once delighted it ; it is quiet without it ; it can feed on other things : so a soul weaned from the world, still pants as much as ever for food and happiness, but it no longer seeks them in worldly things, or desires to do so. There is nothing in the world that it feels necessary for its happiness. This thing in it it loves, and that thing it values ; but it knows that it can do without them, and it is ready to do without them whenever God pleases.

Let us inquire now into *the sources of this frame of mind*—how we get it. One thing is certain—it is not our work. We do not bring ourselves to it. No infant weans itself. The truth is, it is God that must wean us from the world. We shall never leave it of our own accord. It is God's own right hand that must draw us from it.   And how ?   The figure in the text will partly tell us.   1. *By embittering the world to us.*   2. At other times *the Lord removes from us the thing we love.*   3. But he weans us most from the earth *by giving us better food.* — *Condensed from a Sermon by Charles Bradley, entitled "Weanedness of Soul,"* 1836.

Verse 2.—*"As a weaned child."*   That is, meek, modest, humble, submissive, simple, etc.   See Matt. xviii. 1, 2, 3, 4.—*Henry Ainsworth.*—1622.

Verse 2.—Here is David's picture of himself. . . . Observe, the *" child "*— which is drawn for us to copy—is *" weaned " :* the process is complete ; it has been truly disciplined ; the lesson is learned ; and now it rests in its " weaning." The whole image expresses a repose which follows a struggle.   *"Surely I have behaved and quieted myself, as a child that is weaned of his mother" ;* or, more literally, *" on* his mother" : now content to lie still on the very place of its privation,—" as a child that is weaned on his mother."

That obedience would be a tame and valueless thing, which was not the consequence of quiet control.   A mere apathetic state is the very opposite of obedience that may be truly so called.   But this is the point of the similitude,—there has been a distress, and a battle, and a self-victory ; and now the stilled will is hushed into submission and contentment ; ready to forego what is most liked, and to take just whatever is given it—" *a weaned child.*"

I do not believe that it was ever the intention of God that any man should so merge and lose his will in the Divine, that he should have no distinct will of his own.   There have been many who have tried to attain this annihilation of will ; and they have made it the great aim and end of life.   But the character of the dispensation does not allow it.   I do not believe it to be a possible thing ; and if it were possible, I do not believe that it would be after the mind of God.   It is not man's present relation to his Maker.   None of the saints in the Bible did more than submit a strong existing will.   The Lord Jesus Christ himself did no more.   " What shall I say ?   Father, save me from this hour ; but for this cause came I unto this hour.   Father, glorify thy name.   Not my will, but thine be done."   Evidently two things—" My will," " Thy will."   It was an instantly and perfectly subjugated will,—nevertheless, a will.

And this is what is required of us ; and what the nature of our manhood, and the provisions of our religion have to assume.   A will, decidedly a will : the more decided the will, the stronger the character, and the greater the man.   But a will that is always being given up, separated, conformed, constantly, increasingly conformed.   The unity of the two wills is heaven.— *Condensed from a Sermon by James Vaughan.*

Verse 3.—*"Let Israel hope in the* Lord."   After the example, therefore, of the King of Israel, who thus demeaned himself in his afflictions, lowly, contented, and resigned, casting all his care upon the Father who cared for him, and patiently waiting his time for deliverance and salvation ; after this their example and pattern, let his faithful people hope and trust, not in themselves, their wisdom, or their power, but in Jehovah alone, who will not fail to exalt them, as he hath already exalted their Redeemer, if they do but follow his steps.—*George Horne.*

Verse 3.—*"Let Israel hope in the* Lord."   Though David could himself wait patiently and quietly for the crown designed him, yet perhaps Israel, the people whose darling he was, would be ready to attempt something in favour of him before the time ; he therefore endeavours to quiet them too, and bids them '• *hope in the* Lord " that *they* should see a happy change of the face of affairs in due time.   Thus " it is good to hope, and quietly to wait for the salvation of the Lord."—*Matthew Henry.*

Verse 3.—*"Let Israel hope in the* Lord," etc.   Remember that he is *Jehovah.* 1. Wise to plan.   2. Good to purpose.   3. Strong to execute, and that he will withhold no good thing from them that walk uprightly.   4. Trust *" from henceforth."*   If you have not begun before, begin now.   5. And do not be weary ; trust *" for ever."*   Your case can never be out of the reach of God's power and mercy.—*Adam Clarke.*

HINTS TO THE VILLAGE PREACHER.

Verse 1.—*Humility.* I. A profession which ought to befit every child of God. II. A profession which nevertheless many children of God cannot truthfully make. Point out the prevalence of pride and ambition even in the church. III. A profession which can only be justified through the possession of the spirit of Christ (Matt. xi. 29, 30 ; xviii. 1—5).—*C. A. D.*

Verse 2.—The soul is as a weaned child : I. In conversion. II. In sanctification, which is a continual weaning from the world and sin. III. In bereavement. IV. In affliction of every kind. V. In death.—*G. R.*

Verse 2.—I. The soul has to be weaned as well as the body. 1. It is first nourished by others. 2. It is afterward thrown upon its own resources. II. The soul is weaned from one thing by giving its attention to another. 1. From worldly things by heavenly. 2. From self-righteousness by the righteousness of another. 3. From sin to holiness. 4. From the world to Christ. 5. From self to God.—*G. R.*

Verse 2.—I. A desirable condition : " As a weaned child." II. A difficult task—to subdue and quiet self. III. A delightful result : " Surely . . . . my soul is as a weaned child."—*W. H. J. P.*

Verse 2.—I. Soul-fretfulness : weak, dishonourable, rebellious. II. Soul-government ; throne often abdicated ; God gives each the sceptre of self-rule ; necessary to successful life. III. Soul-quiet : its sweetness ; its power. Come, Holy Spirit, breathe it upon us !—*W. B. H.*

Verse 2.—See " Spurgeon's Sermons," No. 1210 : " The Weaned Child."

Verses 2, 3.—The weaned child hoping in the Lord : I. The first weaning of the soul, the grand event of a man's history. II. The joy in the Lord that springs up in every weaned soul : " My soul is even as a weaned child ; let Israel hope in the Lord from henceforth and for ever." III. The daily weaning of the soul through life. IV. The earnest desires and the fruitful work of every weaned soul.—*A. Moody Stuart.*

Verse 3.—I. The encouragement to hope in God. 1. As a covenant God, " the God of Israel." 2. As a covenant-keeping God : " From henceforth," etc. II. The effect of this hope. 1. The humility and dependence in the first verse. 2. The contentment and weaning in the second verse. Would Israel be thus humble and obedient as a little child ? " Let Israel hope," etc.—*G. R.*

Verse 3.—*The Voice of Hope heard in the Calm.* I. Calmed souls appreciate God. Quiet favours contemplation. God's majesty, perfection, and praise so discovered. II. Calmed souls confide in God ; seen to be so worthy of trust. III. Calmed souls look fearlessly into eternity ; " from henceforth and for ever." —*W. B. H.*

Verse 3.—*Hope on, hope ever.* I. For the past warrants such confidence. II. For the present demands such confidence. III. For the future will justify such confidence.—*W. H. J. P.*

WORK UPON THE HUNDRED AND THIRTY-FIRST PSALM.

" SEVERAL [FIVE] SERMONS UPON PSALM CXXXI," in the Works of Thomas Manton, D.D. Vol. v., folio, pp. 961—1007 ; they may also be found in Vol. xxi. pp. 406—462 of the new edition of Manton's Works, published by James Nisbet and Co., 1874.

PSALM CXXXII.

TITLE.—A Song of Degrees. *A joyful song indeed: let all pilgrims to the New Jerusalem sing it often. The degrees or ascents are very visible; the theme ascends step by step from "afflictions" to a "crown," from "remember David," to "I will make the horn of David to bud." The latter half is like the over-arching sky bending above "the fields of the wood" which are found in the resolves and prayers of the former portion.*

DIVISION.—*Our translators have rightly divided this psalm. It contains a statement of David's anxious care to build a house for the Lord (verses 1 to 7); a prayer at the removal of the Ark (verses 8 to 10); and a pleading of the divine covenant and its promises (verses 11 to 18).*

EXPOSITION.

LORD, remember David, *and* all his afflictions:

2 How he sware unto the LORD, *and* vowed unto the mighty *God* of Jacob;

3 Surely I will not come into the tabernacle of my house, nor go up into my bed;

4 I will not give sleep to mine eyes, *or* slumber to mine eyelids,

5 Until I find out a place for the LORD, an habitation for the mighty *God* of Jacob.

6 Lo, we heard of it at Ephratah: we found it in the fields of the wood.

7 We will go into his tabernacles: we will worship at his footstool.

1. "LORD, *remember David, and all his afflictions.*" With David the covenant was made, and therefore his name is pleaded on behalf of his descendants, and the people who would be blessed by his dynasty. Jehovah, who changes not, will never forget one of his servants, or fail to keep his covenant; yet for this thing he is to be entreated. That which we are assured the Lord will do must, nevertheless, be made a matter of prayer. The request is that the Lord would *remember*, and this is a word full of meaning. We know that the Lord remembered Noah, and assuaged the flood; he remembered Abraham, and sent Lot out of Sodom; he remembered Rachel, and Hannah, and gave them children; he remembered his mercy to the house of Israel, and delivered his people. That is a choice song wherein we sing, "He *remembered us* in our low estate: for his mercy endureth for ever"; and this is a notable prayer, "Lord, remember me." The plea is urged with God that he would bless the family of David for the sake of their progenitor; how much stronger is our master-argument in prayer that God would deal well with us for Jesus' sake! David had no personal merit; the plea is based upon the covenant graciously made with him: but Jesus has deserts which are his own, and of boundless merit—these we may urge without hesitation. When the Lord was angry with the reigning prince, the people cried, "Lord, remember David"; and when they needed any special blessing, again they sang, "Lord, remember David." This was good pleading, but it was not so good as ours, which runs on this wise, "Lord, remember *Jesus,* and all his afflictions."

The *afflictions* of David here meant were those which came upon him as a godly man in his endeavours to maintain the worship of Jehovah, and to provide for its decent and suitable celebration. There was always an ungodly party in the nation, and these persons were never slow to slander, hinder, and molest the servant of the Lord. Whatever were David's faults, he kept true to the one, only, living, and true God ; and for this he was a speckled bird among monarchs. Since he zealously delighted in the worship of Jehovah, his God, he was despised and ridiculed by those who could not understand his enthusiasm. God will never forget what his people suffer for his sake. No doubt innumerable blessings descend upon families and nations through the godly lives and patient sufferings of the saints. We cannot be saved by the merits of others, but beyond all question we are benefited by their virtues. Paul saith, " God is not unrighteous to forget your work and labour of love, which ye have showed toward his name." Under the New Testament dispensation, as well as under the Old, there is a full reward for the righteous. That reward frequently comes upon their descendants rather than upon themselves : they sow, and their successors reap. We may at this day pray—Lord, remember the martyrs and confessors of our race, who suffered for thy name's sake, and bless our people and nation with gospel grace for our fathers' sakes.

2. *"How he sware unto the* Lord, *and vowed unto the mighty God of Jacob."* Moved by intense devotion, David expressed his resolve in the form of a solemn vow, which was sealed with an oath. The fewer of such vows the better under a dispensation whose great Representative has said, " swear not at all." Perhaps even in this case it had been wiser to have left the pious resolve in the hands of God in the form of a prayer ; for the vow was not actually fulfilled as intended, since the Lord forbade David to build him a temple. We had better not swear to do anything before we know the Lord's mind about it, and then we shall not need to swear. The instance of David's vows shows that vows are allowable, but it does not prove that they are desirable. Probably David went too far in his words, and it is well that the Lord did not hold him to the letter of his bond, but accepted the will for the deed, and the meaning of his promise instead of the literal sense of it. David imitated Jacob, that great maker of vows at Bethel, and upon him rested the blessing pronounced on Jacob by Isaac, " God Almighty bless thee" (Gen. xxviii. 3), which was remembered by the patriarch on his death-bed, when he spoke of " the mighty God of Jacob." God is mighty to hear us, and to help us in performing our vow. We should be full of awe at the idea of making any promise to the Mighty God : to dare to trifle with him would be grievous indeed. It is observable that affliction led both David and Jacob into covenant dealings with the Lord : many vows are made in anguish of soul. We may also remark that, if the votive obligations of David are to be remembered of the Lord, much more are the suretyship engagements of the Lord Jesus before the mind of the great Lord, to whom our soul turns in the hour of our distress.

Note, upon this verse, that Jehovah was the God of Jacob, the same God evermore ; that he had this for his attribute, that he is mighty—mighty to succour his Jacobs who put their trust in him, though their afflictions be many. He is, moreover, specially *the Mighty One* of his people ; he is the God of Jacob in a sense in which he is not the God of unbelievers. So here we have three points concerning our God : —*name,* Jehovah ; *attribute,* mighty ; *special relationship,* " mighty God of Jacob." He it is who is asked to remember David and his trials, and there is a plea for that blessing in each one of the three points.

3. *"Surely I will not come into the tabernacle of my house, nor go up into my bed."* Our translators give the meaning, though not the literal form, of David's vow, which ran thus, " If I go"—" If I go up," etc. This was an elliptical form of imprecation, implying more than it expressed, and having therefore about it a mystery which made it all the more solemn. David would not take his ease in his house, nor his rest in his bed, till he had determined upon a place for the worship of Jehovah. The ark had been neglected, the Tabernacle had fallen into disrespect ; he would find the ark, and build for it a suitable house ; he felt that he could not take pleasure in his own palace till this was done. David meant well, but he spake more than he could carry out. His language was hyperboli-

cal, and the Lord knew what he meant : zeal does not always measure its terms, for it is not thoughtful of the criticisms of men, but is carried away with love to the Lord, who reads the hearts of his people. David would not think himself housed till he had built a house for the Lord, nor would he reckon himself rested till he had said, "Arise, O Lord, into thy rest." Alas, we have many around us who will never carry their care for the Lord's worship too far ! No fear of their being indiscreet ! They are housed and bedded, and as for the Lord, his people may meet in a barn, or never meet at all, it will be all the same to them. Observe that Jacob in his vow spoke of the stone being God's house, and David's vow also deals with a house for God.

4. "*I will not give sleep to mine eyes, or slumber to mine eyelids.*" He could not enjoy sleep till he had done his best to provide a place for the ark. It is a strong expression, and it is not to be coolly discussed by us. Remember that the man was all on fire, and he was writing poetry also, and therefore his language is not that which we should employ in cold blood. Everybody can see what he means, and how intensely he means it. Oh, that many more were seized with sleeplessness because the house of the Lord lies waste ! They can slumber fast enough, and not even disturb themselves with a dream, though the cause of God should be brought to the lowest ebb by their covetousness. What is to become of those who have no care about divine things, and never give a thought to the claims of their God ?

5. "*Until I find out a place for the* LORD, *an habitation for the mighty God of Jacob.*" He resolved to find a place where Jehovah would allow his worship to be celebrated, a house where God would fix the symbol of his presence, and commune with his people. At that time, in all David's land, there was no proper place for that ark whereon the Lord had placed the mercy-seat, where prayer could be offered, and where the manifested glory shone forth. All things had fallen into decay, and the outward forms of public worship were too much disregarded ; hence the King resolves to be first and foremost in establishing a better order of things.

Yet one cannot help remembering that the holy resolve of David gave to a place and a house much more importance than the Lord himself ever attached to such matters. This is indicated in Nathan's message from the Lord to the king—" Go and tell my servant David, Thus saith the Lord, Shalt thou build me an house for me to dwell in ? Whereas I have not dwelt in any house since the time that I brought up the children of Israel out of Egypt, even to this day, but have walked in a tent and in a tabernacle. In all the places wherein I have walked with all the children of Israel spake I a word with any of the tribes of Israel, whom I commanded to feed my people Israel, saying, Why build ye not me an house of cedar ?" Stephen in his inspired speech puts the matter plainly : " Solomon built him an house. Howbeit the Most High dwelleth not in temples made with hands." It is a striking fact that true religion never flourished more in Israel than before the temple was built, and that from the day of the erection of that magnificent house the spirit of godliness declined. Good men may have on their hearts matters which seem to them of chief importance, and it may be acceptable with God that they should seek to carry them out ; and yet in his infinite wisdom he may judge it best to prevent their executing their designs. God does not measure his people's actions by their wisdom, or want of wisdom, but by the sincere desire for his glory which has led up to them. David's resolution, though he was not allowed to fulfil it, brought a blessing upon him : the Lord promised to build the house of David, because he had desired to build the house of the Lord. Moreover, the King was allowed to prepare the treasure for the erection of the glorious edifice which was built by his son and successor. The Lord shows the acceptance of what we desire to do by permitting us to do something else which his infinite mind judges to be fitter for us, and more honourable to himself.

6. Meanwhile, where was the habitation of God among men ? He was wont to shine forth from between the cherubim, but where was the ark ? It was like a hidden thing, a stranger in its own land. "*Lo, we heard of it at Ephratah.*"

Rumours came that it was somewhere in the land of Ephraim, in a. temporary lodging ; rather an object of dread than of delight. Is it not wonderful that so renowned a symbol of the presence of the Lord should be lingering in neglect—a neglect so great that it was remarkable that we should have heard of its whereabouts at all ? When a man begins to think upon God and his service it is comforting that the gospel is heard of. Considering the opposition which it has encountered it is marvellous that it should be heard of, and heard of in a place remote from the central city ; but yet we are sorrowful that it is only in connection with some poor despised place that we do hear of it. What is Ephratah ? Who at this time knows where it was ? How could the ark have remained there so long ?

David instituted a search for the ark. It had to be hunted for high and low ; and at last at Kirjath-jearim, the forest-city, he came upon it. How often do souls find Christ and his salvation in out-of-the-way places ! What matters where we meet with him so long as we do behold him, and find life in him ? That is a blessed Eureka which is embedded in our text—" *we found it.*" The matter began with hearing, led on to a search, and concluded in a joyful find. "*We found it in the fields of the wood.*" Alas that there should be no room for the Lord in the palaces of kings, so that he must needs take to the woods. If Christ be in a wood he will yet be found of those who seek for him. He is as near in the rustic home, embowered among the trees, as in the open streets of the city ; yea, he will answer prayer offered from the heart of the black forest where the lone traveller seems out of all hope of hearing. The text presents us with an instance of one whose heart was set upon finding the place where God would meet with him ; this made him quick of hearing, and so the cheering news soon reached him. The tidings renewed his ardour, and led him to stick at no difficulties in his search ; and so it came to pass that, where he could hardly have expected it, he lighted upon the treasure which he so much prized.

7. "*We will go into his tabernacles.*" Having found the place where he dwells we will hasten thereto. He has many dwellings in one in the various courts of his house, and each of these shall receive the reverence due : in each the priest shall offer for us the appointed service ; and our hearts shall go where our bodies may not enter. David is not alone, he is represented as having sought for the ark with others, for so the word " *we*" implies ; and now they are glad to attend him in his pilgrimage to the chosen shrine, saying, "*We* found it, *we* will go." Because these are the Lord's courts we will resort to them. "*We will worship at his footstool.*" The best ordered earthly house can be no more than the footstool of so great a King. His ark can only reveal the glories of his feet, according to his promise that he will make the place of his feet glorious : yet thither will we hasten with joy, in glad companionship, and there will we adorn him. Where Jehovah is, there shall he be worshipped. It is well not only to go to the Lord's house, but to *worship* there : we do but profane his tabernacles.if we enter them for any other purpose.

Before leaving this verse let us note the ascent of this psalm of degrees—" We heard . . . we found . . . we will go . . . we will worship."

8 Arise, O LORD, into thy rest ; thou, and the ark of thy strength.

9 Let thy priests be clothed with righteousness ; and let thy saints shout for joy.

10 For thy servant David's sake turn not away the face of thine anointed.

8. In these three verses we see the finders of the ark removing it to its appointed place, using a formula somewhat like to that used by Moses when he said, " Rise up, Lord," and again, " Return, O Lord, unto the many thousands of Israel." The ark had been long upon the move, and no fit place had been found for it in

Canaan, but now devout men have prepared a temple, and they sing, "*Arise, O Lord, into thy rest ; thou, and the ark of thy strength.*" They hoped that now the covenant symbol had found a permanent abode—a rest, and they trusted that Jehovah would now abide with it for ever. Vain would it be for the ark to be settled if the Lord did not continue with it, and perpetually shine forth from between the cherubim. Unless the Lord shall rest with us there is no rest for us ; unless the ark of his strength abide with us we are ourselves without strength. The ark of the covenant is here mentioned by a name which it well deserved ; for in its captivity it smote its captors, and broke their gods, and when it was brought back it guarded its own honour by the death of those who dared to treat it with disrespect. The power of God was thus connected with the sacred chest. Reverently, therefore, did Solomon pray concerning it as he besought the living God to consecrate the temple by his presence. It is the Lord and the covenant, or rather say the covenant Jehovah whose presence we desire in our assemblies, and this presence is the strength of his people. Oh that the Lord would indeed abide in all the churches, and cause his power to be revealed in Zion.

9. "*Let thy priests be clothed with righteousness.*" No garment is so resplendent as that of a holy character. In this glorious robe our great High-priest is evermore arrayed, and he would have all his people adorned in the same manner. Then only are priests fit to appear before the Lord, and to minister for the profit of the people, when their lives are dignified with goodness. They must ever remember that they are God's priests, and should therefore wear the livery of their Lord, which is holiness : they are not only to have righteousness, but to be clothed with it, so that upon every part of them righteousness shall be conspicuous. Whoever looks upon God's servants should see holiness if they see nothing else. Now, this righteousness of the ministers of the temple is prayed for in connection with the presence of the Lord ; and this instructs us that holiness is only to be found among those who commune with God, and only comes to them through his visitation of their spirits. God will dwell among a holy people ; and on the other hand, where God is the people become holy.

"*And let thy saints shout for joy.*" Holiness and happiness go together ; where the one is found, the other ought never to be far away. Holy persons have a right to great and demonstrative joy : they may shout because of it. Since they are saints, and thy saints, and thou hast come to dwell with them, O Lord, thou hast made it their duty to rejoice, and to let others know of their joy. The sentence, while it may read as a permit, is also a precept : saints are commanded to rejoice in the Lord. Happy religion which makes it a duty to be glad ! Where righteousness is the clothing, joy may well be the occupation.

10. "*For thy servant David's sake turn not away the face of thine anointed.*" King Solomon was praying, and here the people pray for him that his face may not be turned away, or that he may not be refused an audience. It is a dreadful thing to have our face turned away from God, or to have his face turned away from us. If we are anointed of the Spirit the Lord will look upon us with favour. Specially is this true of HIM who represents us, and is on our behalf the *Christ*—the truly anointed of the Lord. Jesus is both our David and God's anointed ; in him is found in fulness that which David received in measure. For his sake all those who are anointed in him are accepted. God blessed Solomon and succeeding kings, for David's sake ; and he will bless us for Jesus' sake. How condescending was the Son of the Highest to take upon himself the form of a *servant*, to be anointed for us, and to go in before the mercy-seat to plead on our behalf ! The psalm sings of the ark, and it may well remind us of the going in of the anointed priest within the veil : all depended upon his acceptance, and therefore well do the people pray, " Turn not away the face of thine anointed."

Thus, in these three verses, we have a prayer for the temple, the ark, the priests, the Levites, the people, and the king : in each petition there is a fulness of meaning well worthy of careful thought. We cannot plead too much in detail ; the fault of most prayers is their indefiniteness. In God's house and worship everything needs a blessing, and every person connected therewith needs it continually. As David vowed and prayed when he was minded to house the ark, so now the prayer is continued when the temple is consecrated, and the Lord deigns to fill it with his glory. We shall never have done praying till we have done needing.

11 The LORD hath sworn *in* truth unto David ; he will not turn from it ; Of the fruit of thy body will I set upon thy throne.

12 If thy children will keep my covenant and my testimony that I shall teach them, their children shall also sit upon thy throne for evermore.

13 For the LORD hath chosen Zion ; he hath desired *it* for his habitation.

14 This *is* my rest for ever : here will I dwell ; for I have desired it.

15 I will abundantly bless her provision : I will satisfy her poor with bread.

16 I will also clothe her priests with salvation : and her saints shall shout aloud for joy.

17 There will I make the horn of David to bud : I have ordained a lamp for mine anointed.

18 His enemies will I clothe with shame : but upon himself shall his crown flourish.

11. Here we come to a grand covenant pleading of the kind which is always prevalent with the Lord. "*The LORD hath sworn in truth unto David.*" We cannot urge anything with God which is equal to his own word and oath. Jehovah swears that our faith may have strong confidence in it : he cannot forswear himself. He swears *in truth*, for he means every word that he utters ; men may be perjured, but none will be so profane as to imagine this of the God of truth. By Nathan this covenant of Jehovah was conveyed to David, and there was no delusion in it. "*He will not turn from it.*" Jehovah is not a changeable being. He never turns from his purpose, much less from his promise solemnly ratified by oath. He turneth never. He is not a man that he should lie, nor the son of man that he should repent. What a rock they stand upon who have an immutable oath of God for their foundation ! We know that this covenant was really made with Christ, the spiritual seed of David, for Peter quotes it at Pentecost, saying, "Men and brethren, let me freely speak unto you of the patriarch David, that he is both dead and buried, and his sepulchre is with us unto this day. Therefore being a prophet, and knowing that God had sworn with an oath to him, that of the fruit of his loins, according to the flesh, he would raise up Christ to sit on his throne ; he seeing this before spake of the resurrection of Christ." Christ therefore sits on a sure throne for ever and ever, seeing that he has kept the covenant, and through him the blessing comes upon Zion, whose poor are blessed in him. "*Of the fruit of thy body will I set upon thy throne.*" Jesus sprang from the race of David, as the evangelists are careful to record ; he was " of the house and lineage of David " : at this day he is the King of the Jews, and the Lord has also given him the heathen for his inheritance. He must reign, and of his kingdom there shall be no end. God himself has set him on the throne, and no rebellion of men or devils can shake his dominion. The honour of Jehovah is concerned in his reign, and therefore it is never in danger ; for the Lord will not suffer his oath to be dishonoured.

12. "*If thy children will keep my covenant and my testimony that I shall teach them.*" There is a condition to the covenant so far as it concerned kings of David's line before the coming of the true Seed ; but *he* has fulfilled that condition, and made the covenant indefeasible henceforth and for ever as to himself and the

spiritual seed in him. Considered as it related to temporal things it was no small blessing for David's dynasty to be secured the throne upon good behaviour. These monarchs held their crowns from God upon the terms of loyalty to their superior Sovereign, the Lord who had elevated them to their high position. They were to be faithful to the covenant by obedience to the divine law, and by belief of divine truth. They were to accept Jehovah as their Lord and their Teacher, regarding him in both relations as in covenant with them. What a condesension on God's part to be their teacher ! How gladly ought they to render intelligent obedience ! What a proper, righteous, and needful stipulation for God to make that they should be true to him when the reward was the promise, *"Their children shall also sit upon thy throne for evermore."* If they will sit at his feet God will make them sit on a throne ; if they will keep the covenant they shall keep the crown from generation to generation.

The kingdom of Judah might have stood to this day had its kings been faithful to the Lord. No internal revolt or external attack could have overthrown the royal house of David : it fell by its own sin, and by nothing else. The Lord was continually provoked, but he was amazingly long-suffering, for long after seceding Israel had gone into captivity, Judah still remained. Miracles of mercy were shown to her. Divine patience exceeded all limits, for the Lord's regard for David was exceeding great. The princes of David's house seemed set on ruining themselves, and nothing could save them ; justice waited long, but it was bound at last to unsheathe the sword and strike. Still, if in the letter man's breach of promise caused the covenant to fail, yet in spirit and essence the Lord has been true to it, for Jesus reigns, and holds the throne for ever. David's seed is still royal, for he was the progenitor according to the flesh of him who is King of kings and Lord of lords.

This verse shows us the need of family piety. Parents must see to it that their children know the fear of the Lord, and they must beg the Lord himself to teach them his truth. We have no hereditary right to the divine favour : the Lord keeps up his friendship to families from generation to generation, for he is loth to leave the descendants of his servants, and never does so except under grievous and long-continued provocation. As believers, we are all in a measure under some such covenant as that of David : certain of us can look backward for four generations of saintly ancestors, and we are now glad to look forward and to see our children, and our children's children, walking in the truth. Yet we know that grace does not run in the blood, and we are filled with holy fear lest in any of our seed there should be an evil heart of unbelief in departing from the living God.

13. *"For the* LORD *hath chosen Zion."* It was no more than any other Canaanite town till God chose it, David captured it, Solomon built it, and the Lord dwelt in it. So was the church a mere Jebusite stronghold till grace chose it, conquered it, rebuilt it, and dwelt in it. Jehovah has chosen his people, and hence they are his people. He has chosen the church, and hence it is what it is. Thus in the covenant David and Zion, Christ and his people, go together. David is for Zion, and Zion for David : the interests of Christ and his people are mutual. *"He hath desired it for his habitation."* David's question is answered. The Lord has spoken : the site of the temple is fixed : the place of the divine manifestation is determined. Indwelling follows upon election, and arises out of it : Zion is chosen, chosen for a habitation of God. The desire of God to dwell among the people whom he has chosen for himself is very gracious and yet very natural : his love will not rest apart from those upon whom he has placed it. God desires to abide with those whom he has loved with an everlasting love ; and we do not wonder that it should be so, for we also desire the company of our beloved ones. It is a double marvel, that the Lord should choose and desire such poor creatures as we are : the indwelling of the Holy Ghost in believers is a wonder of grace parallel to the incarnation of the Son of God. God in the church is the wonder of heaven, the miracle of eternity, the glory of infinite love.

14. *"This is my rest for ever."* Oh, glorious words ! It is God himself who

here speaks. Think of rest for God ! A Sabbath for the Eternal and a place of abiding for the Infinite. He calls Zion *my rest.* Here his love remains and displays itself with delight. " He shall rest in his love." And this *for ever.* He will not seek another place of repose, nor grow weary of his saints. In Christ the heart of Deity is filled with content, and for his sake he is satisfied with his people, and will be so world without end. These august words declare a distinctive choice—*this* and no other ; a certain choice—*this* which is well known to me ; a present choice—*this* which is here at this moment. God has made his election of old, he has not changed it, and he never will repent of it : his church was his rest and *is* his rest still. As he will not turn from his oath, so he will never turn from his choice. Oh, that we may enter into *his* rest, may be part and parcel of his church, and yield by our loving faith a delight to the mind of him who taketh pleasure in them that fear him, in them that hope in his mercy. "*Here will I dwell ; for I have desired it.*" Again are we filled with wonder that he who fills all things should dwell in Zion—should dwell in his church. God does not unwillingly visit his chosen ; he desires to dwell with them ; he desires them. He is already in Zion, for he says *here,* as one upon the spot. Not only will he occasionally come to his church, but he will dwell in it, as his fixed abode. He cared not for the magnificence of Solomon's temple, but he determined that at the mercy-seat he would be found by suppliants, and that thence he would shine forth in brightness of grace among the favoured nation. All this, however, was but a type of the spiritual house, of which Jesus is foundation and cornerstone, upon which all the living stones are builded together for an habitation of God through the Spirit. Oh, the sweetness of the thought that God *desires* to dwell in his people and rest among them ! Surely if it be his desire he will cause it to be so. If the desire of the righteous shall be granted much more shall the desire of the righteous God be accomplished. This is the joy of our souls, for surely we shall rest in God, and certainly our desire is to dwell in him. This also is the end of our fears for the church of God ; for if the Lord dwell in her, she shall not be moved ; if the Lord desire her, the devil cannot destroy her.

15. "*I will abundantly bless her provision.*" It must be so. How can we be without a blessing when the Lord is among us ? We live upon his word, we are clothed by his charity, we are armed by his power : all sorts of provision are in him, and how can they be otherwise than blessed ? The provision is to be *abundantly blessed ;* then it will be abundant and blessed. Daily provision, royal provision, satisfying provision, overflowingly joyful provision the church shall receive ; and the divine benediction shall cause us to receive it with faith, to feed upon it by experience, to grow upon it by sanctification, to be strengthened by it to labour, cheered by it to patience, and built up by it to perfection. "*I will satisfy her poor with bread.*" The citizens of Zion are poor in themselves, poor in spirit, and often poor in pocket, but their hearts and souls shall dwell in such abundance that they shall neither need more nor desire more. Satisfaction is the crown of experience. Where God rests his people shall be satisfied. They are to be satisfied with what the Lord himself calls " *bread,*" and we may be sure that he knows what is really bread for souls. He will not give us a stone. The Lord's poor shall " have food convenient for them" : that which will suit their palate, remove their hunger, fill their desire, build up their frame, and perfect their growth. The breadth of earth is " the bread that perisheth," but the bread of God endureth to life eternal. In the church where God rests his people shall not starve ; the Lord would never rest if they did. He did not take rest for six days till he had prepared the world for the first man to live in ; he would not stay his hand till all things were ready ; therefore, we may be sure if the Lord rests it is because " it is finished," and the Lord hath prepared of his goodness for the poor. Where God finds his desire his people shall find theirs ; if he is satisfied, they shall be.

Taking the two clauses together, we see that nothing but an abundant blessing in the church will satisfy the Lord's poor people : they are naked and miserable till that comes. All the provision that Solomon himself could make would not have satisfied the saints of his day : they looked higher, and longed for the Lord's own boundless blessing, and hungered for the bread which came down from heaven. Blessed be the Lord, they had in this verse two of the "I wills" of God to rest upon, and nothing could be a better support to their faith.

16. More is promised than was prayed for. See how the ninth verse asks for the priests to be clad in righteousness, and the answer is, "*I will also clothe her priests with salvation.*" God is wont to do exceeding abundantly, above all that we ask or even think. Righteousness is but one feature of blessing, salvation is the whole of it. What cloth of gold is this ! What more than regal array ! Garments of salvation ! we know who has woven them, who has dyed them, and who has given them to his people. These are the best robes for priests and preachers, for princes and people ; there is none like them ; give them me. Not every priest shall be thus clothed, but only *her* priests, those who truly belong to Zion, by faith which is in Christ Jesus, who hath made them priests unto God. These are clothed by the Lord himself, and none can clothe as he does. If even the grass of the field is so clothed by the Creator as to outvie Solomon in all his glory, how must his own children be clad ? Truly he shall be admired in his saints ; the liveries of his servants shall be the wonder of heaven. "*And her saints shall shout aloud for joy.*" Again we have a golden answer to a silver prayer. The Psalmist would have the "saints shout for joy." "That they shall do," saith the Lord, "and *aloud* too" ; they shall be exceedingly full of delight ; their songs and shouts shall be so hearty that they shall sound as the noise of many waters, and as great thunders. These joyful ones are not, however, the mimic saints of superstition, but *her* saints, saints of the Most High, "sanctified in Christ Jesus." These shall be so abundantly blessed and so satisfied, and so apparelled that they can do no otherwise than shout to show their astonishment, their triumph, their gratitude, their exultation, their enthusiasm, their joy in the Lord. Zion has no dumb saints. The sight of God at rest among his chosen is enough to make the most silent shout. If the morning stars sang together when the earth and heavens were made, much more will all the sons of God shout for joy when the new heavens and the new earth are finished, and the New Jerusalem comes down out of heaven from God, prepared as a bride for her husband. Meanwhile, even now the dwelling of the Lord among us is a perennial fountain of sparkling delight to all holy minds. This shouting for joy is guaranteed to Zion's holy ones : God says they *shall* shout aloud, and depend upon it they will : who shall stop them of this glorying ? The Lord hath said by his Spirit, "let them shout," and then he has promised that "they shall shout aloud " : who is he that shall make them hold their peace ? The Bridegroom is with them, and shall the children of the bride-chamber fast ? Nay, verily, we rejoice, yea and will rejoice.

17. "*There will I make the horn of David to bud.*" In Zion David's dynasty shall develop power and glory. In our notes from other authors we have included a description of the growth of the horns of stags, which is the natural fact from which we conceive the expression in the text to be borrowed. As the stag is made noble and strong by the development of his horns, so the house of David shall advance from strength to strength. This was to be by the work of the Lord— "there will I make," and therefore it would be sure and solid growth. When God makes us to bud none can cause us to fade. When David's descendants left the Lord and the worship of his house, they declined in all respects, for it was only through the Lord, and in connection with his worship that their horn would bud.

"*I have ordained a lamp for mine anointed.*" David's name was to be illustrious, and brilliant as a lamp ; it was to continue shining like a lamp in the sanctuary ; it was thus to be a comfort to the people, and an enlightenment to the nations. God would not suffer the light of David to go out by the extinction of his race : his holy ordinances had decreed that the house of his servant should remain in the midst of Israel. What a lamp is our Lord Jesus ! A light to lighten the Gentiles, and the glory of his people Israel. As the anointed—the true Christ, he shall be the light of heaven itself. Oh for grace to receive our illumination and our consolation from Jesus Christ alone.

18. *"His enemies will I clothe with shame."* They shall be utterly defeated, they shall loathe their evil design, they shall be despised for having hated the Ever Blessed One. Their shame they will be unable to hide, it shall cover them : God will array them in it for ever, and it shall be their convict dress to all eternity. *"But upon himself shall his crown flourish."* Green shall be his laurels of victory. He shall win and wear the crown of honour, and his inherited diadem shall increase in splendour. Is it not so to this hour with Jesus ? His kingdom cannot fail, his imperial glories cannot fade. It is *himself* that we delight to honour ; it is to himself that the honour comes, and upon himself that it flourishes. If others snatch at his crown their traitorous aims are defeated ; but he in his own person reigns with ever growing splendour.

> " Crown him, crown him,
> Crowns become the victor's brow."

EXPLANATORY NOTES.

Whole Psalm.—Lightfoot ascribes this psalm to David, and supposes it to have been composed on the second removal of the ark from the house of Obed-edom : 1 Chron. xv. 4, etc. But the mention of David's name in the tenth verse in the third person, and the terms there employed, militate against his being the author. Others ascribe it to Solomon, who, they think, wrote it about the time of the removing of the ark into the Temple which he had built for it : 2 Chron. v. 2, etc. Others are of opinion, that it was composed by Solomon for the solemn services that were celebrated at the dedication of the Temple.—*James Anderson's note to Calvin in loc.*

Whole Psalm.—The psalm is divided into four stanzas of ten lines, each of which contains the name of David. The first part begins with speaking of David's vow to the Lord ; the third with the Lord's promise to David.—*William Kay.*

Whole Psalm.—The parallelisms need to be traced with some care. Verses 1, 2, 3, 4, 5, 6 are answered by verse 12 ; verse 7 by verse 13 ; verse 8 by verse 14 ; verse 9 by verses 15, 16 ; verse 10 by verses 17, 18.

An attention to these parallelisms is often necessary to bring out the meaning of Scripture.—*Joseph Angus, in "The Bible Handbook,"* 1862.

Verse 1.—" LORD, *remember."* It is a gracious privilege to be permitted to be God's remembrancers. Faith is encouraged to remind him of his covenant, and of his precious promises. There is, indeed, no forgetfulness with him. The past, as also the future, is a present page before his eye. But by this exercise we impress on our own minds invaluable lessons.—*Henry Law.*

Verse 1.—*"Remember David, and all his afflictions."* Solomon was a wise man, yet pleads not any merit of his own ;—I am not worthy, for whom thou shouldst do this, but, " LORD, *remember David,"* with whom thou madest the covenant ; as Moses prayed (Exod. xxxii. 13), *"Remember Abraham,"* the first trustee of the covenant ; remember " *all his afflictions;"* all the troubles of his life, which his being anointed was the occasion of ; or his care and concern about the ark, and what an uneasiness it was to him that the ark was in curtains (2 Sam. vii. 2). *Remember all his humility and weakness,* so some read it ; all that pious and devout affection with which he had made the following vow.—*Matthew Henry.*

Verse 1.—*"Remember . . . all his afflictions."* The sufferings of believers for the cause of truth are not meritorious, but neither are they in vain ; they are not forgotten by God. Matt. v. 11, 12.—*Christopher Starke,* 1740.

Verse 1.—*"Afflictions."* The Hebrew word for " *afflictions"* is akin to the word for " trouble" in 1 Chron. xxii. 14 : " Now, behold, in my *trouble* I have prepared for the house of the Lord an hundred thousand talents of gold."—*H. T. Armfield.*

Verses 1, 2.—If the Jew could rightly appeal to God to show mercy to his church and nation for the sake of that shepherd youth whom he had advanced to the kingdom, much more shall we justly plead our cause in the name of David's son (called *David* four times in the prophets), and of *all his trouble*, all the sorrows of his birth and infancy, his ministry and passion and death, which he bore as a consequence of his self-dedication to his father's will, when his priesthood, fore-ordained from all eternity, was confirmed with an oath, "for those [Levitical] priests were made without [swearing] an oath ; but this with an oath by him that said unto him, The Lord sware and will not repent, Thou art a priest for ever after the order of Melchizedek" : Heb. vii. 21 ; Ps. cx. 4.—*Theodoret and Cassiodorus, in Neale and Littledale.*

Verse 2.—"*And vowed.*" The history does not record the time nor the occasion of this vow ; but history does record how it was ever in David's thoughts and on David's heart. David, indeed, in the first verse, asks of God to remember his afflictions, and then records his vow ; and you may, perhaps, think that the vow was the consequence of his afflictions, and that he made it contingent on his deliverance. . . . It is far more consistent with the character of David to look upon the affliction to which he alludes as resulting from the Lord's not permitting him to carry out his purpose of erecting an earthly habitation for the God of heaven, inasmuch as he had shed blood abundantly. And if, as is more than probable, amid that blood which he had shed, David's conscience recalled the blood of Uriah as swelling the measure, he could not but be deeply afflicted, even while he acknowledged the righteousness of the sentence.

But though not permitted of God to execute his purpose, we cannot but feel and own that it was a noble resolution which David here makes ; and though recorded in all the amplification of Oriental imagery, it expresses the holy determination of the Psalmist to forego every occupation and pursuit, and not to allow a single day to elapse till he had at least fixed on the site of the future temple.—*Barton Bouchier.*

Verse 2.—"*He vowed.*" He who is ready to vow on every occasion will break his vow on every occasion. It is a necessary rule, that "we be as sparing in making our vows as may be" ; there being many great inconveniences attending frequent and multiplied vows. It is very observable, that the Scripture mentioneth very few examples of vows, compared with the many instances of very great and wonderful providences ; as if it would give us some instances, that we might know what we have to do, and yet would give us but few, that we might know we are not to do it often. You read Jacob lived seven score and seven years (Gen. xlvii. 28) ; but you read, I think, but of one vow that he made. Our extraordinary exigencies are not many; and, I say, our vows should not be more. Let this, then, be the first necessary ingredient of a well-ordered vow. Let it be no oftener made than the pressing greatness of an evil to be removed, or the alluring excellency of a blessing extraordinary to be obtained, will well warrant. Jephthah's vow was so far right ; he had just occasion ; there was a great and pressing danger to be removed ; there was an excellent blessing to be obtained : the danger was, lest Israel should be enslaved ; the blessing was victory over their enemies. This warranted his vow, though his rashness marred it. It was in David's troubles that David sware, and vowed a vow to the Most High ; and Jacob forbare to vow until his more than ordinary case bade his vow, and warranted him in so doing : Gen. xxviii. 20. Let us do as he did,—spare to vow, until such case puts us on it.—*Henry Hurst* (1629 ?—1690), *in "The Morning Exercises."*

Verse 2.—"*Vowed unto the mighty God of Jacob.*" The first holy votary that ever we read of was Jacob here mentioned in this text, who is therefore called the father of vows : and upon this account some think David mentions God here under the title of "*the mighty God of Jacob*," rather than any other, because of his vow.—*Abraham Wright.*

Verse 2.—"*The mighty God of Jacob.*" The title *strong one of Jacob*, by which God is here designated, first used by Jacob himself, Gen. xlix. 24, and thence more generally used as is clear from Isaiah i. 24, xlix. 26, and other places, here sets forth God both as the *most mighty* who is able most severely to punish perjury, and with whom no one may dare to contend, and also as the *defender* and most mighty vindicator of Israel, such as Jacob had proved him, and all his descendants, in particular David, who frequently rejoiced and gloried in this mighty one and defender. Such a mighty one of Jacob was worthy to have a temple built for him, and was so great that he would not suffer perjury.—*Hermann Venema.*

Verse 2.—Where the interpreters have translated, "*the God of Jacob,*" it is in the Hebrew, "*the mighty* in Jacob." Which name is sometimes attributed unto the angels, and sometimes it is also applied to other things wherein are great strength and fortitude ; as to a lion, an ox, and such like. But here it is a singular word of faith, signifying that God is the power and strength of his people ; for only faith ascribeth this unto God. Reason and the flesh do attribute more to riches, and such other worldly helps as man seeth and knoweth. All such carnal helps are very idols, which deceive men, and draw them to perdition ; but this is the strength and fortitude of the people, to have God present with them. . . . So the Scripture saith in another place : "Some trust in chariots, and some in horses, but we will remember the name of the Lord." Likewise Paul saith : "Be strong in the Lord, and in the power of his might." For this power is eternal, and deceiveth not. All other powers are not only deceitful, but they are transitory, and continue but for a moment.—*Martin Luther.*

Verse 3.—"*Surely I will not come into the tabernacle of my house,*" etc. To avoid the absurdity of thinking that David should make such a rash and unwarrantable vow as this might seem to be, that till he had his desire satisfied in that which is afterwards expressed he would abide in the open air, and never go within his doors, nor ever take any rest, either by day or by night, some say that David spake this with reference to his purpose of taking the fort of Zion from the Jebusites (2 Sam. v. 6), where by revelation he knew that God meant to have the ark settled, and which he might probably think would be accomplished within some short time. And then others again say, that he meant it only of that stately cedar house, which he had lately built for himself at Jerusalem (2 Sam. vii. 1, 2), to wit, that he would not go into that house ; and so also that he would not go up unto his bed, nor (verse 4) give any sleep to his eyes, nor slumber to his eyelids, to wit, in that house. But neither of these expositions gives me any satisfaction. I rather take these to be hyperbolical expressions of the continual, exceeding great care wherewith he was perplexed about providing a settled place for the ark to rest in, like that in Prov. vi. 4, 5 : "Give not sleep to thine eyes, nor slumber to thine eyelids ; deliver thyself as a roe from the hand of the hunter," etc. Neither is it any more in effect than if he had said, I will never lay by this care to mind myself in anything whatsoever : I shall never with any content abide in mine own house, nor with any quiet rest in my bed, until, etc.—*Arthur Jackson,* 1593—1666.

Verse 3.—"*Surely I will not come into the tabernacle of my house,*" etc. When he had built himself a palace (1 Chron. xv. 1), it appears by the context, that he did not *bless* it (ch. xvi. 43), nor consequently live in it (for that he might not do till it were blest) until he had first prepared a place, and brought up the ark to it.—*Henry Hammond.*

Verse 3.—"*Surely I will not come,*" etc. Our translation of the verse is justified by Aben Ezra, who remarks that אם is here to be translated not in its usual sense of "if,"—"if I shall come"—but as introducing a vow, "I will not come." This idiom, it may be observed, is more or less missed by our existing translation of Hebrews iv. 5 : "And in this place again, If they shall enter into my rest"—a translation which is the more curious from the fact that the idiom in the present psalm is hit off exactly in the preceding chapter, Hebrews iii. 11 : "So I sware in my wrath, They shall not enter into my rest."—*H. T. Armfield.*

Verse 3.—"*I will not come into the tent which is my house.*" What does this singular form of expression denote ? Is it " an instance of the way in which the associations of the old patriarchal tent life fixed themselves in the language of the people," as Perowne suggests ? or does David deliberately select it to imply that even his palace is but a tent as compared with the House that he will rear for God ?—*Samuel Cox.*

Verse 3.—"*Nor go up into my bed.*" From the expression of the Psalmist it would seem that a lofty bed was not only a necessary luxury, but a sign of superior rank. This idea was very prevalent in the period of the revival of the arts on the Continent, where the state bed, often six feet high, always stood on a dais in an alcove, richly curtained off from the saloon. In the East the same custom still continues, and a verse in the Koran declares it to be one of the delights of the faithful in paradise that " they shall repose themselves on lofty beds" (Cap. 56, " The Inevitable"). Frequently these state beds were composed of the most costly and magnificent materials. The prophet Amos speaks of ivory beds (Amos vi. 4) ; Nero had a golden one ; that of the Mogul Aurungzeebe was jewelled ; and, lastly, in the privy purse expenses of our own profligate Charles II., we read of a " silver bedstead for Mrs. Gwynn." And to this day the state bedsteads in the viceregal palace at Cairo are executed in the same metal, and are supposed to have cost upwards of £3,000 each.—*From " The Biblical Museum,"* 1879.

Verses 3—5.—"*Surely I will not come,*" etc. These were all types and figures of Christ, the true David, who, in his desire of raising a living temple, and an everlasting tabernacle to God, spent whole nights in prayer, and truly, neither entered his house, nor went up into his bed, nor gave slumber to his eyelids, nor rest to his temples, and presented to himself " a glorious church, not having spot, nor wrinkle, nor any such thing," nor built " with corruptible gold or silver," but with his own precious sweat and more precious blood ; it was with them he built that city in heaven that was seen by St. John in the Apocalypse, and " was ornamented with all manner of precious stones." Hecen, we can all understand the amount of care, cost, and labour we need to erect a becoming temple in our hearts to God.—*Robert Bellarmine* (1542—1621), *in "A Commentary on the Book of Psalms."*

Verses 3—5.—This admirable zeal of this pious king condemns the indifference of those who leave the sacred places which are dependent upon their care in a condition of shameful neglect, while they lavish all their care to make for themselves sumptuous houses.—*Pasquier Quesnel* (1634—1719), *dans "Les Pseaumes, avec des Reflexions,"* 1700.

Verse 5.—"*An habitation for the mighty God of Jacob.*" Jacob " vowed a vow," when he declared, " this . . . shall be God's house" : Gen. xxviii. 20—22. David accordingly preserved a reminiscence of the fact, when he vowed a vow in connection with a similar object.—*H. T. Armfield.*

Verse 6.—" *We heard of it at Ephratah.*" This is commonly understood of Bethlehem, as that place had this name. But the ark never was at Bethlehem, at least we read of no such thing. There was a district called by this name, or one closely resembling it, where Elkanah, Samuel's father, lived, and whence Jeroboam came, both of whom are called Ephrathites. 1 Sam. i. 1 ; 1 Kings xi. 26. This was in the tribe of Ephraim, and is probably the place meant by the Psalmist. Now the ark had been for a long series of years at Shiloh, which is in Ephraim, when it was taken to be present at the battle with the Philistines, in which Hophni and Phinehas, the sons of Eli, were slain, and when thirty thousand of the Israelites lost their lives, together with the capture of the ark. The frightful report of this calamity was brought to Eli, and occasioned his instant death. This appears to be the event referred to in the words, " *We heard of it at Ephratah*" ; and a grievous report it was, not likely to be soon forgotten.

" *We found it in the fields of Jaar.*" After the ark had been for some time in the land of the Philistines, they sent it away, and it came to Bethshemesh, in the tribe of Judah. 1 Sam. vi. 12. In the immediate vicinity of this place was also

Kirjath-jearim, i.e. the city of Jaar, to which the ark was removed ; for the Bethshemites were afraid to retain it, as many thousands of them had lost their lives, for the violation of the sanctity of the ark, by looking into it. As this slaughter took place close by, if not in the fields of Jaar, the Psalmist, with reference to it, says, " *We found it in the fields of Jaar.*" Having glanced at these two afflictive and memorable events, he goes on with his direct design, of encouraging the people to perform due honour to the ark, and to the temple, by contrasting with the sad occurrences to which he had adverted their present joy and prosperity.— *William Walford, in " The Book of Psalms. A New Translation, with Notes."* 1837.

Verse 6.—"*We heard of it at Ephratah,*" etc. Either of the ark which David and others had heard of, that it formerly was at Shiloh (Josh. xviii. 1), here called Ephratah, as some think ; so the Ephraimites are called Ephrathites (Jud. xii. 5) ; and Elkanah of Ramathaim-zophim, of Mount Ephraim, is said to be an Ephrathite (1 Sam. i. 1) ; but this tribe the Lord chose not, but the tribe of Judah, for his habitation ; and rejected the tabernacle of Shiloh, and removed it from thence (Ps. lxxviii. 60, 67, 68). "*We found it in the fields of the wood ;*" at Kirjath-jearim, which signifies *the city of woods ;* being built among woods, and surrounded with them : here the ark was twenty years, and here David found it ; and from hence he brought it to the house of Obed-edom, and from thence to Zion.

Christ has been *found in the fields of the wood ;* in a low, mean, abject state, as this phrase signifies : Ezek. xvi. 5. The shepherds found him rejected from being in the inn, there being no room for him, and lying in a manger (Luke ii. 7, 16) ; the angels found him in the wilderness, among the wild beasts of the field (Mark i. 13) ; nor had he the convenience even of foxes and birds of the air ; he had no habitation or place where to lay his head : Matt. viii. 20. And he is to be found in the field of the Scriptures, where this rich treasure and pearl of great price lies hid : Matt. xiii. 44.—*John Gill.*

Verse 6.—"*We heard of it at Ephratah.*" The only explanation, equally agreeable to usage and the context, is that which makes Ephratah the ancient name of Bethlehem (Gen. xlviii. 7), here mentioned as the place where David spent his youth, and where he used to hear of the ark, although he never saw it till long afterwards, when he found it in the fields of the wood, in the neighbourhood of *Kirjath-jearim,* which name means Forest-town, or City of the Woods. Compare 1 Sam. vii. 1 with 2 Sam. vi. 3, 4.—*Joseph Addison Alexander.*

Verse 6.—"*We heard of it at Ephratah,*" etc. Having prepared a sumptuous tabernacle, or tent, for the ark on Mount Zion, in the " City of David," a great national assembly was summoned, at which all the tribes were invited to attend its removal to this new sanctuary. The excitement spread over all Israel. " We heard men say at Ephratah [Bethlehem], in the south of the land, and we found them repeat it in the woody Lebanon," sings the writer of the 132nd Psalm, according to Ewald's rendering. " Let us go into his tabernacle ; let us worship at his footstool." The very words of the summons were fitted to rouse the deepest feelings of the nation, for they were to gather at Baalah, of Judah, another name for Kirjath-jearim, to " bring up thence" to the mountain capital " the Ark of God, called by the name, the name of Jehovah of Hosts that dwelleth between the cherubim " : 2 Sam. vi. 2. It " had not been enquired at in the days of Saul " ; but, when restored, the nation would have their great palladium once more in their midst, and could " appear before God in Zion," and be instructed and taught in the way they should go.—*Cunningham Geikie, in "Hours with the Bible."* 1881.

Verse 6.—"*Ephratah.*" The Psalmist says, that David himself, even when a youth in Bethlehem-Ephratah, heard of the sojourn of the ark in Kirjath-jearim, and that it was a fond dream of David's boyhood to be permitted to bring up the ark to some settled habitation, which he desired *to find* (verse 5).—*Christopher Wordsworth.*

Verse 6.—" *We found it.*" The Church can never long be hid. The sun reappears after a short eclipse.—*Henry Law.*

Verse 6.—It is not always where we first seek God that he is to be found. " We *heard* of it at Ephratah : we *found* it in the fields of the wood." We must not be governed by hearsay in seeking for God in Christ ; but seek for ourselves until we find.   It is not in every house of prayer that God in Christ can be found : after seeking him in gorgeous temples we may find him " in the fields of the wood." " If any man shall say unto you, Lo, here is Christ, or lo, there ; believe it not" upon his own testimony, but seek him for yourselves.—*George Rogers*, 1883.

Verse 7.—" *We will go . . . we will worship.*"   Note their agreement and joint consent, which is visible in the pronoun " *we*" : " *We will go.*" " *We*" taketh in a whole nation, a whole people, the whole world, and maketh them one.   " *We*" maketh a commonwealth ; and " *we*" maketh a church.   We go up to the house of the Lord together, and we hope to go to heaven together.   Note their alacrity and cheerfulness in going.   Their long absence rendered the object more glorious.   For, what we love and want, we love the more and desire the more earnestly.   When Hezekiah, having been " sick unto death," had a longer lease of life granted him, he asketh the question, " What is the sign" (not, *that I shall live*, but) " that I shall go up to the house of the Lord ?"   Isaiah xxxviii. 1—22.   Love is on the wing, cheerful to meet its object ; yea, it reacheth it at a distance, and is united to it while it is afar off. . . . " *We will go.*"   We long to be there.   We will hasten our pace.   We will break through all difficulties in the way.— *Condensed from Anthony Farindon.*

Verse 7 (*first clause*).—" *Tabernacles*" are spoken of in the plural number, and this it may be (though we may doubt whether the Psalmist had such minute distinctions in his eye) because there was in the Temple an inner sanctuary, a middle apartment, and then the court.   It is of more importance to attend to the epithet which follows, where the Psalmist calls the Ark of the Covenant *God's footstool*, to intimate that the sanctuary could never contain the immensity of God's essence, as men were apt absurdly to imagine.   The mere outward Temple with all its majesty being no more than his footstool, his people were called upon to look upwards to the heavens, and fix their contemplations with due reverence upon God himself.—*John Calvin.*

Verse 7.—The Lord's "*footstool*" here mentioned was either *the Ark of the Testimony* itself, or the place at least where it stood, called *Debir*, or the *Holy of Holies*, towards which the Jews in their temple used to worship.   The very next words argue so much : "*Arise, O* LORD, *into thy rest ; thou, and the ark of thy strength*" ; and it is plain out of 1 Chron. xxviii. 2, where David saith concerning his purpose to have built God an house, " I had in mine heart to build an house of rest for the ark of the covenant of the Lord, and for the *footstool* of our God," where the conjunction *and* is exegetical, and the same with *that is.* According to this expression the prophet Jeremy also, in the beginning of the second of his Lamentations, bewaileth that " the Lord had cast down the beauty of Israel " (that is, his glorious Temple), " and remembered not his *footstool* " (that is, the Ark of the Covenant), " in the day of his wrath" ; as Isaiah lx. 7, and lxiv. 11 ; Ps. xcvi. 6.

That this is the true and genuine meaning of this phrase of *worshipping the Lord towards his footstool*, besides the confessed custom of the time, is evidently confirmed by a parallel expression of this worshipping posture (Ps. xxviii. 2) : " Hear the voice of my supplications when I cry unto thee, when I lift up mine hands אֶל־דְּבִיר קָדְשֶׁךָ towards thy *holy oracle*" ; that is, towards the Most Holy place where the ark stood, and from whence God gave his answers.   For that דביר *Debir*, which is here translated " *oracle*" was the *Sanctum Sanctorum* or Most Holy place, is clear out of the sixth and eighth chapters of the First Book of Kings ; where in the former we read (verse 19) that " Solomon prepared the *oracle* or *Debir*, to set the ark of the covenant of the Lord there" : in the latter (verse 6), that " the priests brought in the ark of the covenant of the Lord unto his place, into the oracle of the house, to the most holy place, even under the wings of the cherubims."   Wherefore the authors of the translation used in our Liturgy rendered this passage of the psalm, " When I hold up my hands toward the mercy seat of thy holy temple" ; namely, having respect to the meaning thereof. Thus you see that one of the two must needs be this *scabellum pedum*, or "*footstool*" of God, either *the ark* or *mercy-seat* itself, or the *adytum Templi*, the Most Holy place, where it stood. For that it is not the whole Temple at large (though it might be so called), but some thing or part of those that are within it, the first words of my text ("*We will go into his tabernacles*") do argue. If, then, it be *the ark* (whose *cover* was that which we call the *mercy-seat*), it seems to have been so called in respect of God's sitting upon the cherubims, under which the ark lay, as it were his footstool : whence sometimes it is described, " The ark of the covenant of the Lord of Hosts, which sitteth upon the cherubims" : 1 Sam. iv. 4. If the *ark*, with the *cover* thereof (*the mercy-seat*), be considered as God's *throne*, then the place thereof, the *Debir*, may not unfitly be termed his "*footstool*." Or, lastly, if we consider heaven to be the throne of God, as indeed it is, then whatsoever place or monument of presence he hath here on earth is in true esteem no more than his "*footstool*."—*Joseph Mede*, 1586—1638.

Verse 8.—"*Arise, O* LORD, *into thy rest ; thou, and the ark of thy strength.*" Whenever the camp was about to move, Moses used the language found in the first part of this verse. "*Arise* (or rise up), *O Jehovah.*"—*William Swan Plumer.*

Verse 8.—"*Thou, and the ark of thy strength.*" " Both he that sanctifieth and they who are sanctified are all of one" : Heb. ii. 11. Now Christ, our Great High Priest, is gone up into the holy resting-place. Of him it is said, " Arise" : for he arose from the dead, and ascended into heaven. And to his "*ark,*" the church, it is said, " Arise" : because he lives, all in him shall live also.—*Edward Simms, in "A Spiritual Commentary on the Book of Psalms,*" 1882.

Verse 8.—"*The ark of thy strength.*" The historical records of the ark are numerous, and deeply interesting. Miracles were often wrought at its presence. At the passage of the Jordan, no sooner were the feet of the priests which bare this holy vessel dipped in the brim of the river, than the waters rose up upon an heap, and the people of God passed over on dry ground—" clean over Jordan" : Joshua iii. 14—17. At the siege of Jericho, the ark occupied a most prominent position in the daily procession of the tribes around the doomed city. . . . It was, however, captured by the Philistines, and Hophni and Phineas, Eli's wicked sons, in whose care it was placed, slain. Thus the Lord " delivered his strength into captivity and his glory into the enemy's hand " : Ps. lxxviii. 61.—*Frank H. White, in " Christ in the Tabernacle,*" 1877.

Verse 9 (first clause).—The chief badge and cognizance of the Lord's minister is the true doctrine of justification and obedience of faith in a holy conversation : "*Let thy priests be clothed with righteousness.*"—*David Dickson.*

Verse 9.—"*Let thy priests be clothed with righteousness.*"

> Holiness on the head,
> Light and perfections on the breast,
> Harmonious bells below, raising the dead
> To lead them unto life and rest.
> Thus are true *Aarons* drest, etc.
>
> *George Herbert*, 1593—1633.

Verse 9.—"*Saints.*" If the very names given by God's prophets to his people are such as *saints, gracious ones, merciful ones,* surely his professed people ought to see to it that they are not cruel, untender, or *unholy.*—*William Swan Plumer.*

Verses 9, 16.—Let us notice the prayer, verse 9, with the answer, verse 16. The prayer asks in behalf of the priests " *righteousness*" *:* the answer is, " I will clothe her priests with *salvation,*" *i.e.,* with what shows forth God's *gracious character.* Caring for the interest of God, the worshipper finds his own interest fully cared for. And now, after spreading the Lord's pledged word (verses 11, 12) before him, the worshipper hears the Lord himself utter the reply, *q.d.,* " I will do all that has been sought."—*A. A. Bonar.*

Verse 10.—*"For thy servant David's sake."* Solomon's plea for the divine blessing to rest upon him as king, *"For thy servant David's sake,"* was justified in its use by God : Is. xxxvii. 35. It gives no countenance to the idea of intercession on the part of deceased saints ; for it is not a prayer to David, but a pleading with God for the sake of David. Nor does it support the idea of works of supererogation on the part of David ; it only implies a special divine delight in David, on account of which God was pleased to honour David's name during succeeding generations ; and if the delight itself is pure grace, the expression of it, in any way, must be grace. Nor does it even give countenance to the idea that God's converting and saving grace may be expected by any man because his parents or ancestors were delighted in by God ; for a plea of this character is in Scripture strictly confined to two instances, Abraham and David, with both of whom a special covenant was made, including their descendants, and it was just this covenant that authorised the use of the plea by those who by promise were specially interested, and by none others, and for the ends contemplated by the covenant. But it did prefigure the great Christian plea, " For Christ Jesus' sake" ; just as God's selection of individual men and making them centres of revelation and religion, in the old time, prefigured " The man Christ Jesus" as the centre and basis of religion for all time. Hence in the plea, " For Christ's sake," the old pleas referred to are abolished, as the Jewish ritual is abolished. Christ bids us use His name : John xiv. 13, 14 ; xvi. 26, etc. To believe the false notions mentioned above, or to trust in any other name for divine, gracious favour, is to dishonour the name of Christ. " For Christ's sake" is effective on account of the great covenant, the merits of Christ, and his session in heaven.— *John Field (of Sevenoaks),* 1883.

Verse 10.—*"For thy servant David's sake."* The frequency with which God is urged to hear and answer prayer *for David's sake* (1 Kings xi. 12, 13 ; xv. 4 ; 2 Kings viii. 19, etc.), is not to be explained by making *David* mean the promise to David, nor from the personal favour of which he was the object, but for his historical position as the great theocratical model, in whom it pleased God that the old economy should reach its culminating point, and who is always held up as the type and representative of the Messiah, so that all the intervening kings are mere connecting links, and their reigns mere repetitions and continuations of the reign of David, with more or less resemblance as they happened to be good or bad. Hence the frequency with which his name appears in the later Scriptures, compared with even the last of his successors, and the otherwise inexplicable transfer of that name to the Messiah himself.—*Joseph Addison Alexander.*

Verse 10.—*"For thy servant David's sake."* When Sennacherib's army lay around Jerusalem besieging it, God brought deliverance for Israel partly out of regard to the prayer of the devout Hezekiah, but partly also out of respect for the pious memory of David, the hero-king, the man after God's own heart. The message sent through Isaiah to the king concluded thus : " Therefore thus saith the Lord concerning the king of Assyria, he shall not come into this city, nor shoot an arrow there, nor come before it with shield, nor cast a bank against it. By the way that he came, by the same shall he return, and shall not come into this city, saith the Lord. For I will defend this city, to save it, for mine own sake, and for my servant David's sake" : 2 Kings xix. 32—4. What a respect is shown to David's name by its being thus put on a level with God ! *Mine own sake, and David's sake.—Alexander Balmain Bruce, in* " *The Galilean Gospel,*" 1882.

Verse 10.—*"Turn not away the face,"* etc. As if in displeasure, or in forgetfulness.—*Albert Barnes.*

Verse 10.—*"Thine anointed."* What is meant by *" thine anointed "?* Is it David himself ; or some definite king among his merely human descendants ; or does it apply to each or any of them as they come into office to bear the responsibilities of this line of anointed kings? I incline to the latter construction, under which the petition is applicable to any one or to all the anointed successors of David. For David's sake let every one of them be admitted to free audience before thee, and his prayer be evermore availing. The context contemplates a long line of kings descended from David. It was pertinent to make them all the subjects of this prayer.—*Henry Cowles.*

Verse 11.—"*The* LORD *hath sworn.*" The most potent weapon with God is his own word. They remind him, therefore, as did Ethan in Psalm lxxxix. 20, etc., of the solemn words which he had spoken by Nathan, and which must at that time have been still fresh in the memory of all. Solomon, too, made mention of those glorious words of comfort in his prayer at the dedication of the temple.—*Augustus F. Tholuck.*

Verse 11, 12.—This psalm is one of those fifteen which are called Psalms of Degrees ; of which title whatsoever reason can be given fitting the rest, surely if we consider the argument of this, it may well import the excellency thereof, and why ? It is nothing else but a sacred emulation, wherein God and a king contend ; the king in piety, God in bounty. The king declares himself to be a most eminent pattern of zeal, and God himself to be a most magnificent rewarder of his servants. The king debarreth himself of all worldly content, while he is busily providing to entertain God ; and God, who filleth heaven and earth, vouchsafeth to lodge in that place which was provided by the king. The king presents his supplication not only for himself, but also for his charge, the priests, the people ; and God restraineth not his blessing to the king, but also at his suit enlargeth it to church and commonweal. Finally, the king bindeth himself to make good his duty with a votive oath, and God restipulateth with an oath that which he promised both to king and kingdom : to the kingdom in the words that follow ; but to the king in those that I have now read to you.

This speech, then, is directed unto the king ; but it containeth a blessing which redounds unto his issue, "*the fruit of his body.*" This blessing is no less than a royal succession in the throne of David : David's sons shall inherit it, but it is God that states them in it. They shall sit, but *I will set* them, yea, so set them that they shall never fall ; they shall sit for ever ; the succession shall be perpetual. And hitherto the promise runs absolute : it is qualified in that which followeth.

The king was busy to build God's house ; and see how God answers him, promising the building of the king's house ! God requites a building with a building. There is a very apt illusion in the word, upon which the son of Syrach also plays, when he saith, that children and the building of a city make a perpetual name ; how much more if they be a royal offspring, that are destined to sit upon a throne ? And God promiseth David sons for this honourable end—" *to sit upon his throne.*"—*Arthur Lake,* —1626.

Verse 12.—"*If thy children will keep my covenant,*" etc. Lest David's sons, if they be left without law, should live without care, they must know that the succession shall be perpetual ; but the promise is conditional ; if David's sons conform themselves to God, " *if they keep my covenant,*" whereof they cannot pretend ignorance. And they have an authentical record : the record, " *my testimonies*" ; authentical, "*I myself will teach them.*" You see the king's blessing, it is very great ; but lest the promise thereof be thought too good to be true, God secures the king with a most unchangeable warrant. The warrant is his oath, "*The Lord sware*" ; and this warrant is, 1. Unchangeable, because sincere ; he swore in truth. 2. Stable, *he will not turn from it.* And what could king David desire more for his own house than a promise of such a blessing, and such a warrant of that promise ? Yes he might, and no doubt he did desire [more] ; and God also intended to him more than the letter of this promise doth express, even the accomplishment of the truth whereof this was but a type. And what is that ? The establishment of the kingdom of Jesus Christ.—*Arthur Lake.*

Verse 12.—"*That I shall teach them.*" Here is to be noted that he addeth, " *which I will teach them*" ; for he will be the teacher and will be heard. He wills not that church councils should be heard, or such as teach that which he hath not taught. . . . God giveth no authority unto man above the word. So should he set man, that is to say, dust and dung, above himself ; for what is the word, but God himself ? This word they that honour, obey, and keep, are the true church indeed, be they never so contemptible in the world ; but they which do not, are the church of Satan, and accursed of God. And this is the cause why it is expressly set down in the text, "*The testimonies which I will teach them.*" For so will God use the ministry of teachers and pastors in the church, that he notwithstanding will be their chief Pastor, and all other ministers and pastors whatsoever, yea, the church itself, shall be ruled and governed by the word.—*Martin Luther.*

Verse 12.—"*Their children shall also sit upon thy throne for evermore.*" As if he had said, this promise as touching Christ will I accomplish, and will undoubtedly establish the throne unto my servant David ; but do not ye, which in the meantime sit on this throne, and govern this kingdom, presume upon the promise, and think that you cannot err, or that I will wink at your errors, and not rather condemn and severely punish them. Therefore either govern your kingdom according to my word, or else I will root you out and destroy you for ever. This promise he now amplifieth, and setteth forth more at large.—*Martin Luther.*

Verse 13.—"*For the* LORD *hath chosen Zion,*" etc. The Lord's pitching upon any place to dwell there cometh not of the worthiness of the place, or persons, but from God's good pleasure alone. The Lord having chosen his church, resteth in his love to her : he smelleth a sweet savour of Christ, and this maketh his seat among his people steadfast.—*David Dickson.*

Verse 13.—"*For the* LORD *hath chosen Zion.*" Here, of a singular purpose, he useth the same word which Moses used (Deut. xvi. 6) : " As the place which the Lord thy God *shall choose* to place his name in." For at the beginning there was no certain place appointed wherein the tabernacle should remain ; but it wandered, not only from place to place, but also from tribe to tribe, as Ephraim, Manasseh, Dan, etc.

Moreover, by the word, " *hath chosen,*" he overthroweth all kinds of worship and religion of men's own devising and choosing, whereof there was an infinite number among the Jews. Election or choice belongeth not unto us ; but we must yield obedience to the voice of the Lord. Else shall that happen unto us which Jeremiah threateneth : " That they have chosen that I will reject." These things destroy and confound the inventions, the devices and devotions, the false and counterfeit religions, which we have seen in the papacy. . . . God is not served but when that is done which he hath commanded. Wherefore election or choice pertaineth not to us, so that what God hath commanded, that we must do.—*Martin Luther.*

Verse 14.—"*This is my rest for ever.*" Of the Christian church we may affirm with undoubted certainty, that it is *God's rest for ever:* after this dispensation of his will, there will never succeed another ; Christianity closes and completes the Divine communication from God to man ; nothing greater, nothing better can or will be imparted to him on this side eternity ; and even in heaven itself we shall, through an everlasting duration, be employed in contemplating and adoring the riches of that grace, the brightest glories of which have been realized in the consummations of Calvary, the ascension of the Messiah, the breaking down of all national peculiarity, and the gift and mission of the Divine Spirit. Let the argument of the apostle to the Hebrews be fully weighed, and the conclusion of every mind must be, that God has " removed those things that are shaken, as of things that are made, that those things which cannot be shaken may remain :" Heb. xii. 27.—*John Morison, in "An Exposition of the Book of Psalms,"* 1829.

Verse 14.—"*This is my rest for ever.*" The heart of the saints is the dwelling-place of God. He rests in those who rest in him. He rests when he causes us to rest.—*Pasquier Quesnel.*

Verse 14.—"*Dwell.*" The word translated " *dwell* " means originally to *sit,* and especially to sit enthroned, so that this idea would be necessarily suggested with the other to a Hebrew reader.—*Joseph Addison Alexander.*

Verses 14—18.—Now that he might apparently see how near the Lord is to all them that call upon him in faithfulness and truth, he waiteth not long for an answer, but carries it away with him before he departs. For to David's petition, "*Return, O* Lord, *unto thy resting-place, thou, and the ark of thy strength*"; God's answer is this,—" This shall be my resting-place, here will I dwell, for I have a delight therein. I will bless her victuals with increase, and will satisfy her poor with bread." To David's petition, "*Let thy priests be clothed with righteousness, and let thy saints sing with joyfulness,*" God's answer is this : " I will clothe her priests with salvation : and her saints shall rejoice and sing." Lastly, to David's petition, "*For thy servant David's sake turn not away the face of thine anointed,*" God's answer is this : " There will I make the horn of David to flourish : I have ordained a light for mine anointed. As for his enemies, I will clothe them with shame ; but upon himself shall his crown flourish." As if he should have said, —Turn away the face of mine anointed ? Nay, that will I never do ; I will indeed turn away the face of the enemies of mine anointed ; their face shall be covered with confusion, and clothed with shame. But contrariwise, I have ordained a light for mine anointed. He shall even have a light in his face and a crown upon his head. " As for his enemies, I will clothe them with shame ; but upon himself shall his crown flourish."—*Thomas Playfere*, 1633.

Verse 15.—"*I will abundantly bless her provision,*" etc. The *provision* of Zion, the church of God, the word and ordinances, of which Christ is the sum and substance ; the gospel is milk for babes, and meat for strong men ; the ordinances are a feast of fat things ; Christ's flesh is meat indeed, and his blood drink indeed ; the whole provision is spiritual, savoury, salutary, strengthening, satisfying, and nourishing, when the Lord blesses it ; as he does to those who hunger and thirst after it, and feed upon it by faith ; so that their souls grow thereby, and they become fat and flourishing ; grace increases in them, and they are fruitful in every good work ; and this the Lord promises to do *abundantly,* in a very large way and manner ; or *certainly,* for it is, in the original text, " in blessing I will bless," that is, will surely bless, as this phrase is sometimes rendered.
"*I will satisfy her poor with bread.*" Zion has her poor ; persons may be poor and yet belong to Zion, belong to Zion and yet be poor ; there are poor in all the churches of Christ : our Lord told his disciples that they had the poor, and might expect to have them, always with them ; and particular directions are given to take care of Zion's poor under the gospel dispensation, that they may not want bread in a literal sense : though by the *poor* are chiefly designed the Lord's afflicted and distressed ones ; or those who in a spiritual sense are poor, sensible of their spiritual poverty, and seeking after the true riches ; or are poor in spirit, to whom the kingdom of heaven belongs ; these the Lord promises to satisfy, to fill them to the full with the bread of the gospel, made of the finest of the wheat, of which there is enough and to spare in his house ; and with Christ the bread of life, of which those that eat shall never die, but live for ever.—*John Gill.*
Verse 15.—"*Her provision I will bless, I will bless.*" The repetition of the verb may express either certainty or fulness. *I will surely bless,* or *I will bless abundantly.—Joseph Addison Alexander.*
Verse 15.—"*I will abundantly bless her provision.*" Believe it, a saint hath rare fare, gallant cheer, and rich diet, and all at free cost. He is feasted all the day long ; he is brought oft into the banqueting-house, and hath the rarest, the costliest, the wholesomest diet, that which is most hearty and strengthening, that which is most dainty and pleasant, and the greatest variety, and nothing is wanting that may make his state happy, except a full enjoyment of glory itself. The Lord gives him all the experiences of his power and goodness to his Church in former ages to feed his hopes upon ; nay, many choice providences, many answers of prayer, many foretastes of glory, many ordinances, especially that great one of the Lord's Supper, at which Christ and all his benefits are served up in a royal dish to refresh and feast the faith, hope, and love of the saints. And that which

sweetens all this—he knows that all this is but a little to what he shall shortly live upon when he comes to the marriage-supper; then he shall always be feasted and never surfeited. And beside all this, he hath the sweet and refreshing incomes of the Spirit, filling him with such true pleasure, that he can easily spare the most sumptuous banquet, the noblest feast, and highest worldly delights, as infinitely short of one hour's treatment in his Friend's chamber. And, if this be his entertainment in the inn, what shall he have at the court? If this heavenly manna be his food in the wilderness, at what rate is he like to live when he comes into Canaan? If this be the provision of the way, what is that of the country?—*John Janeway, about* 1670.

Verse 15.—*"I will satisfy her poor with bread."* Christ is a satisfying good. A wooden loaf, a silver loaf, a golden loaf will not satisfy a hungry man; the man must have bread. The dainties and dignities of the world, the grandeur and glory of the world, the plenty and prosperity of the world, the puff and popularity of the world, will not satisfy a soul sailing by the gates of hell, and crying out of the depths; it must be a Christ. "Children, or I die," was the cry of the woman; a Christ, or I die—a Christ, or I am damned, is the doleful ditty and doleful dialect of a despairing or desponding soul. "He that loveth silver shall not be satisfied therewith; nor he that loveth abundance with increase:" Eccles. v. 10. It is a good observation, that the world is round, but the heart of man is triangular. Now, all the globe of the world will not fill the triangular heart of man. What of the world and in the world can give quietness, when Christ, the Sun of Righteousness, goes down upon the soul? The heart is a three-square, and nothing but a trinity in unity and a unity in trinity will satisfy this. Not riches, nor relations, nor barns, nor bags, will satisfy a convinced and deserted soul. This person can say concerning his bags as a great person upon a sick, if not a dying, bed, did concerning his bags,—Away, and away for ever. Though there be bag upon bag, yet they are altogether insignificant in a dying hour; these bags, they are but as so many ciphers before a figure. This is the cry of despairing and desponding souls: "O satisfy us early with thy mercy; that we may rejoice and be glad all our days:" Ps. xc. 14.—*Richard Mayhew,* 1679.

Verse 15.—*"I will satisfy her poor with bread."* Dainties I will not promise them; a *sufficiency,* but not a *superfluity :* poor they may be, but not destitute; bread they shall have, and of that *God's plenty,* as they say; enough to bring them to their Father's house, "where there is bread enough." Let not, therefore, the poor Israelite fear to bring his offerings, or to disfurnish himself for God's worship, etc.—*John Trapp.*

Verse 16.—*"I will clothe her priests with salvation."* Their salvation shall be evident and conspicuous, just as a garment is.—*Aben-Ezra.*

Verse 16.—God's presence is an earnest of all good; for all this follows upon "here will I dwell." By it he giveth meat to the hungry, and comfort to the poor, even the Bread of Life to the believing and repenting soul; by it he himself is the sanctification of his priests, and his righteousness and salvation is their most glorious vesture; and by his presence he maketh his elect ever glad, filling their hearts with joy and their mouths with songs.—*J. W. Burgon.*

Verse 16.—*"Her saints shall shout aloud for joy."* It would astonish and amuse a European stranger to hear these natives sing. They have not the least idea either of harmony or melody; noise is what they best understand, and he that sings the loudest is considered to sing the best. I have occasionally remonstrated with them on the subject; but the reply I once received silenced me for ever after. "Sing softly, brother," I said to one of the principal members. "Sing softly!" he replied, "is it you, our father, who tells us to sing softly? Did you ever hear us sing the praises of our Hindoo gods? how we threw our heads backward, and with all our might shouted out the praises of those who are no gods! And now do you tell us to *whisper* the praises of Jesus? No, sir, we cannot— we must express in loud tones our gratitude to him who loved us, and died for us!" And so they continued to sing with all their might, and without further remonstrance.—*G. Gogerly, in "The Pioneers: a Narrative of the Bengal Mission,"* 1870.

Verse 17.—*"There will I make the horn of David to bud,"* etc. A metaphor taken from those goodly creatures, as stags, and such like ; whose chiefest beauty and strength consisteth in their horns, especially when they bud and branch abroad. —*Thomas Playfere.*

Verse 17.—*"The horn of David."* This image of *a horn* is frequent in the Old Testament. . . . The explanation must be found neither in the horns of the altar on which criminals sought to lay hold, nor in the horns with which they ornamented their helmets ; the figure is taken from the horns of the bull, in which the power of this animal resides. It is a natural image among an agricultural people. . . . Just as the strength of the animal is concentrated in its horn, so all the delivering power granted to the family of David for the advantage of the people will be concentrated in the Messiah.—*F. Godet, in " A Commentary on the Gospel of St. Luke."* 1875.

Verse 17.—*"Make the horn to bud."* In the beginning of the month of March the common stag, or red deer, is lurking in the sequestered spots of his forest home, harmless as his mate, and as timorous. Soon a pair of prominences make their appearance on his forehead, covered with a velvety skin. In a few days these little prominences have attained some length, and give the first indication of their true form. Grasp one of these in the hand and it will be found burning hot to the touch, for the blood runs fiercely through the velvety skin, depositing at every touch a minute portion of bony matter. More and more rapidly grow the horns, the carotid arteries enlarging in order to supply a sufficiency of nourishment, and in the short period of ten weeks the enormous mass of bony matter has been completed. Such a process is almost, if not entirely, without parallel in the history of the animal kingdom.—*J. G. Wood, in "The Illustrated Natural History,"* 1861.

Verse 17.—*"The horn."* My friend, Mr. Graham, of Damascus, says, concerning the horns worn by eastern women, " This head-dress is of dough, tin, silver, or gold, according to the wealth of the different classes. The rank is also indicated by the length of it. The nobler the lady, the longer the horn. Some of them are more than an English yard." I procured at Damascus an ancient gem, representing a *man* wearing the horn. In the present day, its use is confined to the women.—*John Wilson, in "The Lands of the Bible,"* 1847.

Verse 17.—*"I have ordained a lamp for mine anointed."* This clause contains an allusion to the law, which cannot be preserved in any version. The word translated " *lamp*" is used to designate the several burners of the golden candlestick (Ex. xxv. 37 ; xxxv. 14 ; xxxvii. 23 ; xxxix. 37), and the verb here joined with it is the one applied to the ordering or tending of the sacred lights by the priests (Ex. xxvii. 21 ; Lev. xxvii. 3). The meaning of the whole verse is, that the promise of old made to David and to Zion should be yet fulfilled, however dark and inauspicious present appearances.—*Joseph Addison Alexander.*

Verse 17.—*"I have ordained a lamp for mine anointed."* We here remark, 1. The designation given unto Christ by God his Father ; he is *" mine anointed."* Though he be despised and rejected of men ; though an unbelieving world see no form or comeliness in him, why he should be desired, yet I own him, and challenge him as mine Anointed, the Prophet, Priest, and King of my church. " I have found David my servant : with my holy oil have I anointed him : with whom my hand shall be established : mine arm also shall strengthen him" : Ps. lxxxix. 20, 21.

2. The great means of God's appointment for manifesting the glory of Christ to a lost world ; he has provided " *a lamp*" for his Anointed. The use of a lamp is to give light to people in the darkness of the night ; so the word of God, particularly the gospel, is a light shining in a dark place, until the day of glory dawn, when the Lord God and the Lamb will be the light of the ransomed for endless evermore.

3. The authority by which this lamp is lighted and carried through this dark world ; it is " *ordained* " of God ; and by his commandment it is that we preach and spread the light of the gospel (Mark xvi. 15, 20).—*Ebenezer Erskine*, 1680—.

Verse 17.—"*I have ordained a lamp for mine anointed.*" That is, I have ordained prosperity and blessings for him ; blessings upon his person, and especially the blessing of posterity. Children are as a *lamp* or *candle* in their father's house, making the name of their ancestors conspicuous ; hence in Scripture a child given to succeed his father is called a *lamp*. When God by Ahijah the prophet told Jeroboam that God would take the kingdom out of the hand of Solomon's son, and give it unto him, even ten tribes ; he yet adds (1 Kings xi. 36), " And unto his son will I give one tribe, that David my servant may have a light (*lamp* or *candle*) alway before me in Jerusalem, the city which I have chosen me to put my name there." And again (1 Kings xv. 4), when Abijam the son of Rehoboam proved wicked, the text saith, " Nevertheless for David's sake did the Lord his God give him a *lamp* (or *candle*) in Jerusalem, to set up his son after him."—*Joseph Caryl.*

Verses 17, 18.—God having chosen David's family, he here promiseth to bless that also with suitable blessings.

1. Growing power : "*There* (in Zion) *will I make the horn of David to bud.*" The royal dignity should increase more and more, and constant additions be made to the lustre of it. Christ is the " horn of salvation," noting a plentiful and powerful salvation, which God hath raised up and made to bud " in the house of his servant David." David had promised to use his power for God's glory, to cut off the horns of the wicked, and to exalt the horns of the righteous (Ps. lxxv. 10) ; and in recompense for it, God here promises to make his horn to bud ; for to them that have power and use it well, more shall be given.

2. Lasting honour : "*I have ordained a lamp for mine anointed.*" Thou wilt " light my candle" (Ps. xviii. 28) : that lamp is likely to burn brightly which God ordains. A lamp is a successor ; for when a lamp is almost out, another may be lighted by it : it is a succession ; for by this means David shall not want a man to stand before God. Christ is the lamp and the light of the world.

3. Complete victory. "*His enemies,*" that have formed designs against him, " *will I clothe with shame,*" when they shall see their designs baffled. Let the enemies of all good governors expect to be clothed with shame, and especially the enemies of the Lord Jesus and his government, who shall rise in the last great day " to everlasting shame and contempt."

4. Universal prosperity : "*Upon himself shall his crown flourish,*" *i.e.*, his government shall be more and more his honour. This was to have its full accomplishment in Christ Jesus, whose crown of honour and power shall never fade, nor the flowers of it wither. The crowns of earthly princes " endure not to all generations" (Prov. xxvii. 24) ; but Christ's crown shall endure to all eternity, and the crowns reserved for his faithful subjects are such as " fade not away."—*Matthew Henry.*

Verse 18.—"*His enemies will I clothe with shame.*" That is, *shame* shall so inseparably cover them, that as wheresoever a man goeth, he carrieth his clothes with him ; so wheresoever they go they shall carry their *shame* with them. And that which is strangest of all, they which are ashamed use to clothe or cover their shame, and then think themselves well enough ; but David's enemies shall be so ashamed, that even the very covering of their shame shall be a discovering of it ; and the clothing or cloaking of their ignominy shall be nothing else but a girding of it more closely and more inseparably unto them.—*Thomas Playfere.*

Verse 18.—"*Upon himself shall the crown flourish.*" This idea seems to be taken from the nature of the ancient crowns bestowed upon conquerors. From the earliest periods of history, the laurel, olive, ivy, etc., furnished crowns to adorn the heads of heroes, who had conquered in the field of battle, gained the prize in the race, or performed some other important service to the public. These were the dear-bought rewards of the most heroic exploits of antiquity. This sets the propriety of the phrase in full view. The idea of a crown of gold and jewels flourishing, is at least unnatural ; whereas, flourishing is natural to laurels, oaks, etc. These were put upon the heads of the victors in full verdure, and their merit seemed to make them flourish on their heads, in fresher green. The literal crown which Jesus wore was also of the vegetable kind, and the thorn of sorrow never flourished in such vigour as on his head. Now he has got the crown of life, which shall not fade away, like the perishing verdure of the crowns of other heroes. It shall flourish for ever, with all the vigour of immortality, and bring forth all the olive-fruits of peace for his people. Its branches shall spread, and furnish crowns for all the victors in the spiritual warfare.—*Alexander Pirie*, —1804.

HINTS TO THE VILLAGE PREACHER.

Verse 1.—I. The Lord remembers Jesus, our David : he loves him, he delights in him, he is with him. II. In that memory his griefs have a prominent place— " all his afflictions." III. Yet the Lord would be put in remembrance by his people.

Verses 1, 2.—Concerning his people, I. The Lord remembers, 1. Their persons. 2. Their afflictions. 3. Their vows. II. The Lord remembers them, 1. To accept them. 2. To sympathize with them. 3. To assist them.

Verses 1, 2.—I. God remembers his people, each one : " Remember David." The Spirit maketh intercession within us according to the will of God. II. He remembers their afflictions : " David and all his afflictions." " I know thy works and thy tribulation." III. He remembers their vows, especially, 1. Those which relate to his service. 2. Those which are solemnly made. 3. Those which are faithfully performed.—*G. R.*

Verses 1—5.—Notice, I. How painfully David felt what he conceived to be a dishonouring of God, which he thought he might be able to remedy. Consider " his afflictions,"—because the ark dwelt within curtains, while he himself dwelt in a house of cedar : 2 Sam. vii. 2. Consider, 1. Its singularity. Most find affliction in personal losses ; very few suffer from a cause like this. 2. The little sympathy such a feeling meets with from the most of men. " If God means to convert the heathen, he can do it without you, young man," was said to Dr., then Mr. Carey, when heathenism was an affliction to him. 3. Its fittingness to a really God-fearing man. 4. Its pleasingness to God : 1 Sam. ii. 30. II. How earnestly he set himself to remedy the evil he deplored : " He sware," etc. There cannot be the least doubt that he would have foregone the enjoyment of temporal luxuries until he had accomplished the work dear to his heart, if he had been permitted of God. Remark, 1. There is little zeal for God's honour when self-denial is not exercised for the sake of his cause. 2. Were a like zeal generally shown by God's people, there would be more givers and more liberal gifts ; more workers, and the work more heartily and better done. 3. It would be well to astonish the world, and deserve the commendations of the righteous by becoming enthusiasts for the honour of God.—*J. F.*

Verses 3—5.—I. We should desire a habitation for God more than for ourselves. God should have the best of everything. " See, now, I dwell in a house of cedar, but the ark of God dwelleth within curtains." II. We should be guided by the house of God in seeking a house for ourselves : " Surely I will not come," etc. III. We should labour for the prosperity of God's house even more than of our own. Nothing should make sleep more sweet to us than when the church of God prospers ; nothing keep us more awake than when it declines : " I will not give sleep," etc. (verse 4) ; " Is it time for you, O ye, to dwell in your ceiled houses, and this house lie waste ?"—*G. R.*

Verse 5.—Something to live for—to find fresh habitations for God. I. The Condescension implied : God *with us*. II. The Districts explored : hearts, homes, " dark places of the earth." III. The Royalty of the Work. It makes King David busy, and is labour worthy of a king.—*W. B. H.*

Verse 5.—"*A place for the* LORD." In the heart, the home, the assembly, the life. Everywhere we must find or make a place for the Lord.

Verse 5.—"*The mighty God of Jacob.*" I. Mighty, and therefore he joined heaven and earth at Bethel. II. Mighty, and therefore brought Jacob back from Mesopotamia. III. Mighty, and yet wrestled with him at Jabbok. IV. Mighty, and yet allowed him to be afflicted. V. Mighty, and therefore gave him full deliverance.

Verses 6, 7.—We shall use this for practical purposes. A soul longing to meet with God. God has appointed a meeting place. I. *We know what it is.* A mercy-seat, a throne of grace, a place of revealed glory. Within it the law preserved. Heavenly food—pot of manna. Holy rule—Aaron's rod. II. *We desire to find it.* Intensely. Immediately. Reverently. Longing to receive it. III. *We heard of it.* In our young days. We almost forget where. From ministers, from holy men, from those who loved us. IV. *We found it.* Where we least expected it. In a despised place. In a lonely place. Where we lost ourselves. Very near us—where we hid like Adam among the trees. V. *We will go.* To God in Christ. For all he gives. To dwell with him. To learn of him. VI. *We will worship.* Humbly. Solemnly. Gratefully. Preparing for heaven.

Verse 7.—I. The Place : " His tabernacles." 1. Built for God. 2. Accepted by God : present everywhere, he is especially present here. II. The Attendance : " We will go," etc. There God is present to meet us, and there we should be present to meet him. III. The Design : 1. For adoration. 2. For self-consecration : " We will worship at his footstool."—*G. R.*

Verses 8, 9.—I. The Presence of God desired—1. That it may be signally manifested : " Arise" and enter. 2. That it may be gracious : " Thou and the ark" —that he may be present on the mercy-seat. 3. That it may be felt : accompanied with power : " The ark of thy strength." 4. That it may be abiding : " Arise into thy rest." II. The reasons for this desire. 1. With respect to the priests or ministers : " Let thy priests," etc. : not their own righteousness, but as a clothing : let them speak of " garments of salvation" and " robes of righteousness." 2. With respect to the worshippers : " And let thy saints," etc. Let ministers preach the gift of righteousness ; not that which grows out of man's nature, but that which is " unto all and upon all them that believe," and saints will shout for joy.—*G. R.*

Verse 9.—Consider, I. The importance of a righteous ministry in the church. II. The connection between such a ministry and a joyous people. III. The dependence of both on the gracious working of God.—*J. F.*

Verse 9 (second clause).—I. Saints. II. Shouting. III. Explaining—" for joy." IV. Encouraging—" Let thy saints shout."

Verse 9 (second clause).—The connection between holiness and joy.

Verses 9, 16.—*The Spiritual Vestry.* I. The Vestments : 1. Righteousness ; for which the costliest stole is a poor substitute. 2. Salvation : learning, oratory, etc., of small account in comparison. II. The Procuring of the vestments : 1. Must be from God. 2. Earnest prayer should constantly arise from all saints. III. The Robing : 1. By God's own hand ! 2. Their beauty and power who are so invested. 3. The persons are " thy priests."—*W. B. H.*

Verses 9, 16.—I. Priests and Saints. II. Vestments. III. " Hymns Ancient and Modern." IV. The Real Presence : God giving the garments and the joy.

Verse 10.—I. An evil to be deprecated : " Turn not away the face"—so that he cannot see thee, or be seen of thee, or accepted, or allowed to hope. II. A plea to be employed, " for thy servant David's sake"—thy covenant with him, his zeal, his consecration, his afflictions, his service. Good gospel pleading, such as may be used on many occasions.

Verse 11.—I. The divine oath. II. Its eternal stability. III. The everlasting Kingship.

Verse 11 (middle clause).—Our confidence : " He will not turn from it." He is not a changing God. He foreknew everything. He is able to carry out his purpose. His honour is bound up in it. His oath can never be broken.

Verse 12.—Family favour may be perpetual, but the conditions must be observed.

Verse 13.—I. Sovereign choice. II. Condescending indwelling. III. Eternal rest. IV. Gracious reason—" I have desired it."

Verse 14.—I. *God finding rest in his church.* 1. The three persons honoured. 2. The divine nature exercised. 3. Eternal purposes fulfilled. 4. Almighty energies rewarded. 5. Tremendous sacrifices remembered. 6. Glorious attributes extolled. 7. Dearest relationships indulged. II. *This rest enduring for ever.* 1. There will always be a church. 2. That church will always be such as God can rest in. 3. That church will therefore be secure on earth. 4. That church will be glorified eternally in heaven.

Verse 15.—I. Blessed provision. II. Satisfied people—" satisfy her poor." III. Glorified God—" I will." IV. Happy place—Zion.

Verses 16, 18.—Two forms of clothing : salvation and shame, prepared for his priests and his enemies. Which will you wear ?

Verse 17.—A Lamp ordained for God's Anointed. Being the Substance of Two Sermons, by Ebenezer Erskine. [Works, Vol. 3, pp. 3—41.]

Verses 17, 18.—I. The budding horn of growing power. II. The perpetual lamp of constant brightness. III. The sordid array of defeated foes. IV. The unfading wreath of glorious sovereignty.

Verse 18.—I. *His enemies clothed.* 1. Who are they ? The openly profane. The moral but irreligious. The self-righteous. The hypocritical. 2. How clothed with shame ? In repentance, in disappointment, in remorse, in destruction. Sin detected. Self defeated. Hopes scattered. 3. Who clothes them ? The Lord. He will shame them thoroughly. II. *Himself crowned.* 1. His crown : his dominion and glory. 2. Its flourishing. Glory extending. Subjects increasing. Wealth growing. Foes fearing, etc.

Verse 18 (*last clause*).—The Lord Jesus himself the source, sustenance, and centre of the prosperity of his kingdom.

WORK UPON THE HUNDRED AND THIRTY-SECOND PSALM.

In "*The Works* of JOHN BOYS," 1626, folio, pp. 821—5, there is an Exposition of Psalm cxxxii. [This is a poor and lean performance.]

PSALM CXXXIII.

TITLE.—A Song of Degrees of David. *We see no reason for depriving David of the authorship of this sparkling sonnet. He knew by experience the bitterness occasioned by divisions in families, and was well prepared to celebrate in choicest psalmody the blessing of unity for which he sighed. Among the "songs of degrees," this hymn has certainly attained unto a good degree, and even in common literature it is frequently quoted for its perfume and dew. In this psalm there is no wry word, all is "sweetness and light,"—a notable ascent from Psalm cxx. with which the Pilgrims set out. That is full of war and lamentation, but this sings of peace and pleasantness. The visitors to Zion were about to return, and this may have been their hymn of joy because they had seen such union among the tribes who had gathered at the common altar. The previous psalm, which sings of the covenant, had also revealed the centre of Israel's unity in the Lord's anointed and the promises made to him. No wonder that brethren dwell in unity when God dwells among them, and finds his rest in them. Our translators have given to this psalm an admirable explanatory heading, "The benefit of the communion of saints." These good men often hit off the meaning of a passage in a few words.*

EXPOSITION.

BEHOLD, how good and how pleasant *it is* for brethren to dwell together in unity!

2 *It is* like the precious ointment upon the head, that ran down upon the beard, *even* Aaron's beard : that went down to the skirts of his garments ;

3 As the dew of Hermon, *and as the dew* that descended upon the mountains of Zion : for there the LORD commanded the blessing, *even* life for evermore.

1. *"Behold."* It is a wonder seldom seen, therefore behold it ! It may be seen, for it is the characteristic of real saints,—therefore fail not to inspect it ! It is well worthy of admiration ; pause and gaze upon it ! It will charm you into imitation, therefore note it well ! God looks on with approval, therefore consider it with attention. *"How good and how pleasant it is for brethren to dwell together in unity !"* No one can tell the exceeding excellence of such a condition ; and so the Psalmist uses the word "how" twice ;—Behold how good ! and how pleasant ! He does not attempt to measure either the good or the pleasure, but invites us to behold for ourselves. The combination of the two adjectives " good " and " pleasant," is more remarkable than the conjunction of two stars of the first magnitude : for a thing to be " good " is good, but for it also to be pleasant is better. All men love pleasant things, and yet it frequently happens that the pleasure is evil ; but here the condition is as good as it is pleasant, as pleasant as it is good, for the same " how" is set before each qualifying word.

For *brethren* according to the flesh to dwell together is not always wise ; for experience teaches that they are better a little apart, and it is shameful for them to dwell together in disunion. They had much better part in peace like Abraham and Lot, than dwell together in envy like Joseph's brothers. When brethren can and do dwell together *in unity*, then is their communion worthy to be gazed upon and sung of in holy psalmody. Such sights ought often to be seen among those who are near of kin, for they are brethren, and therefore should be united in heart and aim ; they dwell together, and it is for their mutual comfort that there should be no strife ; and yet how many families are rent by fierce feuds, and exhibit a spectacle which is neither good nor pleasant !

As to brethren in spirit, they ought to dwell together in church fellowship, and in that fellowship one essential matter is unity. We can dispense with uniformity if we possess unity : oneness of life, truth, and way ; oneness in Christ Jesus ; oneness of object and spirit—these we must have, or our assemblies will be synagogues of contention rather than churches of Christ. The closer the unity the better ; for the more of the good and the pleasant there will be. Since we are imperfect beings, somewhat of the evil and the unpleasant is sure to intrude ; but this will readily be neutralized and easily ejected by the true love of the saints, if it really exists. Christian unity is good in itself, good for ourselves, good for the brethren, good for our converts, good for the outside world ; and for certain it is pleasant ; for a loving heart must have pleasure and give pleasure in associating with others of like nature. A church united for years in earnest service of the Lord is a well of goodness and joy to all those who dwell round about it.

2. *"It is like the precious ointment upon the head."* In order that we may the better behold brotherly unity David gives us a resemblance, so that as in a glass we may perceive its blessedness. It has *a sweet perfume* about it, comparable to that precious ointment with which the first High Priest was anointed at his ordination. It is *a holy thing,* and so again is like the oil of consecration which was to be used only in the Lord's service. What a sacred thing must brotherly love be when it can be likened to an oil which must never be poured on any man but on the Lord's high-priest alone ! It is a *diffusive* thing : being poured on his head the fragrant oil flowed down upon Aaron's head, and thence dropped upon his garments till the utmost hem was anointed therewith ; and even so doth brotherly love extend its benign power and bless all who are beneath its influence. Hearty concord brings a benediction upon all concerned ; its goodness and pleasure are shared in by the lowliest members of the household ; even the servants are the better and the happier because of the lovely unity among the members of the family. *It has a special use* about it ; for as by the anointing oil Aaron was set apart for the special service of Jehovah, even so those who dwell in love are the better fitted to glorify God in his church. The Lord is not likely to use for his glory those who are devoid of love ; they lack the anointing needful to make them priests unto the Lord. *"That ran down upon the beard, even Aaron's beard."* This is a chief point of comparison, that as the oil did not remain confined to the place where it first fell, but flowed adown the High Priest's hair and bedewed his beard, even so brotherly love descending from the head distils and descends, anointing as it runs, and perfuming all it lights upon. *"That went down to the skirts of his garments."* Once set in motion it would not cease from flowing. It might seem as if it were better not to smear his garments with oil, but the sacred unguent could not be restrained, it flowed over his holy robes ; even thus does brotherly love not only flow over the hearts upon which it was first poured out, and descend to those who are an inferior part of the mystical body of Christ, but it runs where it is not sought for, asking neither leave nor license to make its way. Christian affection knows no limits of parish, nation, sect, or age. Is the man a believer in Christ ? Then he is in the one body, and I must yield him an abiding love. Is he one of the poorest, one of the least spiritual, one of the least lovable ? Then he is as the skirts of the garment, and my heart's love must fall even upon him. Brotherly love comes from the head, but falls to the feet. Its way is downward. It " ran down," and it " went down" : love for the brethren condescends to men of low estate, it is not puffed up, but is lowly and meek. This is no small part of its excellence : oil would not anoint if it did not flow down, neither would brotherly love diffuse its blessing if it did not descend.

3. *"As the dew of Hermon, and as the dew that descended upon the mountains of Zion."* From the loftier mountains the moisture appears to be wafted to the lesser hills : the dews of Hermon fall on Zion. The Alpine Lebanon ministers to the minor elevation of the city of David ; and so does brotherly love descend from the higher to the lower, refreshing and enlivening in its course. Holy concord is as dew, mysteriously blessed, full of life and growth for all plants of grace. It brings with it so much benediction that it is as no common dew, but

as that of Hermon which is specially copious, and far-reaching. The proper rendering is, " As the dew of Hermon that descended upon the mountains of Zion," and this tallies with the figure which has been already used ; and sets forth by a second simile the sweet descending diffusiveness of brotherly unity. *"For there the* LORD *commanded the blessing, even life for evermore."* That is, in Zion, or better still, in the place where brotherly love abounds. Where love reigns God reigns. Where love wishes blessing, there God commands the blessing. God has but to command, and it is done. He is so pleased to see his dear children happy in one another that he fails not to make them happy in himself. He gives especially his best blessing of eternal life, for love is life·; dwelling together in love we have begun the enjoyments of eternity, and these shall not be taken from us. Let us love for evermore, and we shall live for evermore. This makes Christian brotherhood so good and pleasant ; it has Jehovah's blessing resting upon it, and it cannot be otherwise than sacred like " the precious ointment," and heavenly like " the dew of Hermon."

O for more of this rare virtue ! Not the love which comes and goes, but that which dwells ; not that spirit which separates and secludes, but that which dwells together ; not that mind which is all for debate and difference, but that which dwells together in unity. Never shall we know the full power of the anointing till we are of one heart and of one spirit ; never will the sacred dew of the Spirit descend in all its fulness till we are perfectly joined together in the same mind ; never will the covenanted and commanded blessing come forth from the Lord our God till once again we shall have " one Lord, one faith, one baptism." Lord, lead us into this most precious spiritual unity, for thy Son's sake. Amen.

EXPLANATORY NOTES.

Whole Psalm.—This psalm is an effusion of holy joy occasioned by the sight of the gathering of Israel as one great household at the yearly feasts. . . . There might likewise be an allusion to the previous jealousies and alienations in the family of Israel, which seemed to be exchanged for mutual concord and affection, on David's accession to the throne of the whole nation.—*Joseph Addison Alexander.*

Verse 1.—*" Behold how good and how pleasant it is,"* etc. There are three things wherein it is very pleasant to behold the people of God joining in one.

1. When they join or are *one in opinion* and judgment, when they all think the same thing, and are of one mind in the truth.

2. When they join together and are *one in affection,* when they are all of one heart, though possibly they are not all of one mind ; or, when they meet in affection, though not in opinion. When David had spoken admiringly of this goodly sight, he spoke declaratively concerning the goodness of it (verse 2) : *"It is like the precious ointment upon the head."* 'Tis so, first, for the sweetness of it ; 'tis so, secondly, for the diffusiveness of it (as followeth), *" that ran down upon the beard, even Aaron's beard : that went down to the skirts of his garments."*

3. It is a blessed thing to see them joining *together in duty,* either as duty is considered—First, *in doing that which is good ;* or, when, as the apostle's word is (2 Cor. vi. 1), they are, among themselves, " workers together" in any good work : we say (to fill up the text), " workers together with God." That's a blessed sight indeed, when we join with God, and God joineth with us in his work. It is also a blessed sight when all the ministers of Jesus Christ, and many as members of Jesus Christ, join in any good work, in this especially, to beseech all we have to do with " that they receive not the grace of God in vain." Secondly, *in turning from evil,* and putting iniquity far from them ; in praying for the pardon of sin, and making their peace with God. 'Tis a good work to turn away from evil, especially when all who are concerned in it join in it. . . . As to join in sin, and to be brethren in iniquity, is the worst of unions, indeed, a com-

bination against God ; so to join as brethren in mourning for sin and repenting of our iniquities is a blessed union, and highly pleasing to God.—*Joseph Caryl.*

Verse 1.—"*How good and how pleasant it is,*" etc.   The terms of this praise and commendation, or the particulars whereof it consists, is taken from a twofold qualification.

1. Brotherly concord and the improvement of it in all occasional expressions is a very great good.   This is, and will appear to be so in sundry considerations.

As, *First*, in regard of the *Author* and *owner* of it, which is *God himself*, who lays special claim hereunto.   Therefore in Scripture we find him to be from hence denominated and intitled.   1 Cor. xiv. 33.   "God is not the author of confusion (or of unquietness), but the author of peace.   2 Cor. xiii. 11.   "The God of peace and love."   Peace is called "the peace of God :" Phil. iv. 7.   And God is called the "God of peace ;" each of which expressions does refer it and reduce it to him, and does thereby advance it.   Look, then, how far forth God himself is said to be good, so far forth is this dwelling in unity good also, as it is commanded and owned by him, as it appears thus to be.

Secondly. It is good in the *nature* of it ; it is good, as any grace is good.   It is good morally.   Love is a fruit of the Spirit : Gal. v. 22.   And so to dwell in love and unity one with another is a goodness reducible thereunto.   It is good spiritually ; it is not only such a good as is taught by moral philosophy, and practised by the students thereof, but it is taught by the *Holy Ghost himself*, and is a part of the work of regeneration and of the new creature in us, especially if we take it in the full latitude and extent of it, as it becomes us to do.

Thirdly. It is good in the *effects* and *consequences* and *concomitants* of it : it has much good.   It is *bonum utile*.   A great deal of advantage comes by brethren's dwelling together in unity, especially *spiritual advantage*, and for the doing and receiving of good.

2. The second qualification is, the sweetness of it, because it is "*pleasant :*" it is not only *bonum utile*, and *bonum honestum*, but it is also *bonum jucundum ;* it has a great deal of pleasure in it.   Pleasure is such a kind of goodness, especially to some kind of persons, as that they care not almost what they do or part with to obtain it, and all other good besides is nothing to them, if it be devoid of this.   Therefore for the further commendation of this fraternal unity to us, there is this also to be considered, that it is "*pleasant.*"   Thus it is with respect to all sorts of persons whatsoever, that are made sensible of it.

First. It is *pleasant to God*, it is such as is very acceptable to him ; it is that which he much delights in, wheresoever he observes it ; being himself a God of peace, he does therefore so much the more delight in peaceable Christians, and such as do relate to himself.   How much do natural parents rejoice in the agreement of their children, to see them loving and friendly and kind and courteous to one another, oh, it pleases them and joys them at their very heart ! and so it is likewise with God to those who are truly his.

Secondly. This brotherly unity is also *pleasant to ourselves*, who accordingly shall have so much the greater pleasure in it and from it.

Thirdly. It is also *pleasing to others*, indeed to all men else besides, that are standers-by and spectators of it.   "*Behold, how pleasant it is,*" etc.   It is pleasant to all beholders : "He that in these things serveth Christ is acceptable to God, and approved of men," says the apostle : Rom. xiv. 18.—*Thomas Horton,* —1673.

Verse 1.—"*Pleasant.*"   It is a pleasant thing for the saints and people of God to agree together ; for the same word which is used here for "*pleasant,*" is used also in the Hebrew for a harmony of music, such as when they rise to the highest strains of the viol, when the strings are all put in order to make up a harmony ; so pleasant is it, such pleasantness is there in the saints' agreement.   The same word is used also in the Hebrew for the pleasantness of a corn field.   When a field is clothed with corn, though it be cut down, yet it is very pleasant, oh, how pleasant is it ; and such is the saints' agreement.   The same word in the Psalmist is used also for the sweetness of honey, and of sweet things in opposition to bitter things.   And thus you see the pleasantness of it, by its being compared to

the harmony of music, to the corn field, to the sweetness of honey, to the precious
ointment that ran down Aaron's beard, and to the dew that fell upon Hermon
and the hills of Zion : and all this to discover the pleasantness, profitableness,
and sweetness of the saints' agreement.   It is a pleasant thing to behold the sun,
but it is much more pleasant to behold the saints' agreement and unity among
themselves.— *William Bridge.*

Verse 1.—*"Brethren."*   Abraham made this name, " *brethren,*" a mediator to
keep peace between Lot and him : " Are we not brethren ?" saith Abraham.   As
if he should say, Shall brethren fall out for trifles, like infidels ?   This was
enough to pacify Lot, for Abraham to put him in mind that they were brethren ;
when he heard the name of brethren, straight his heart yielded, and the strife
was ended.   So this should be the lawyer to end quarrels between Christians, to
call to mind that they are brethren.   And they which have spent all at law have
wished that they had taken this lawyer, to think, with Lot, whether it were meet
for brethren to strive like enemies.—*Henry Smith.*

Verse 1.—*"Brethren."*   Some critics observe that the Hebrew word for a *brother*
is of near brotherhood or alliance with two other words, whereof the first signifies
one, and the other *alike* or *together*, to show that " *brethren*" ought to be as *one*,
and *alike*, or *together ;* which latter is by an elegant *paranomasia* joined with it :
" Behold, how good and how pleasant it is for *brethren to dwell together in unity*,"
or, as we put it in the margin, " *to dwell even together.*"   So then, the very word
whereby " *brethren*" are expressed notes that there ought to be a *nearness*, a *similitude*, yea, a *oneness* (if I may so speak) between them in their affections and
actions.—*Joseph Caryl.*

Verse 1.— *To dwell* is a word of residence, and abode, and continuation.   There
is also pertaining to the love and concord of brethren a perseverance and persistency in it ; not only to be together, or to come together, or to meet together for
some certain time ; but *to dwell* together in unity, this is which is here so extolled
and commended unto us.   It seems to be no such great matter, nor to carry
any such great difficulty in it, for men to command themselves to some expressions of peace and friendship for some short space of time (though there are many
now and then who are hardly able to do that) ; but to hold out in it, and to continue so long, this endurance is almost impossible to them.   Yet this is that
which is required of them as *Christians* and as " *brethren*" one to another, even
to " *dwell together in unity ;*" to follow peace, and love, and concord, and
mutual agreement, not only upon some occasional meetings, but all along the
whole course of their lives, while they converse and live together.—*Thomas
Horton.*

Verse 1.—*"Together in unity."*   If there be but one God, as God is one, so let
them that serve him be one.   This is what Christ prayed so heartily for.   " That
they may be one :" John xvii. 21.   Christians should be one, 1. *In judgment.*
The apostle exhorts to be all of one mind.   1 Cor. i. 10.   How sad is it to see
religion wearing a coat of divers colours ; to see Christians of so many opinions,
and going so many different ways !   It is Satan that has sown these tares of
division.   Matt. xiii. 39.   He first divided men from God, and then one man
from another.   2. One *in affection.*   They should have one heart.   " The multitude of them that believed were of one heart and of one soul " : Acts iv. 32.   As
in music, though there be several strings of a viol, yet all make one sweet harmony ; so, though there are several Christians, yet there should be one sweet
harmony of affection among them.   There is but one God, and they that serve
him should be one.   There is nothing that would render the true religion more
lovely, or make more proselytes to it, than to see the professors of it tied together
with the heart-strings of love.   If God be one, let all that profess him be of one
mind, and one heart, and thus fulfil Christ's prayer, " that they all may be one."
—*Thomas Watson.*

Verse 2.—*"Precious ointment upon the head."*   Though every priest was
anointed, yet only the high priest was anointed on the *head*, and there is a tradi-

tion that this rite was omitted after the Captivity, so that there is a special stress on the name of Aaron.—*Neale and Littledale.*

Verse 2.—"*The precious ointment . . . that ran down upon the beard . . . that went down to the skirts of his garments.*" Magnificence, misnamed by churls extravagance and waste, is the invariable attribute of all true love. David recognized this truth when he selected the profuse anointing of Aaron with the oil of consecration at his installation into the office of High Priest as a fit emblem of brotherly love. There was waste in that anointing, too, as well as in the one which took place at Bethany. For the oil was not *sprinkled* on the head of Aaron, though that might have been sufficient for the purpose of a mere ceremony. The vessel was emptied on the High Priest's person, so that its contents flowed down from the head upon the beard, and even to the skirts of the sacerdotal robes. In that very waste lay the point of the resemblance for David. It was a feature that was very likely to strike his mind, for he, too, was a wasteful man in his way. He had loved God in a manner which exposed him to the charge of extravagance. He had danced before the Lord, for example, when the ark was brought up from the house of Obed-edom to Jerusalem, forgetful of his dignity, exceeding the bounds of decorum, and, as it might seem, without excuse, as a much less hearty demonstration would have served the purpose of a religious solemnity.—*Alexander Balmain Bruce, in "The Training of the Twelve,"* 1877.

Verse 2.—' *The precious ointment . . . that ran down.*" Of the Hebrew perfumes an immense quantity was annually manufactured and consumed, of which we have a very significant indication in the fact that the holy anointing oil of the tabernacle and temple was never made in smaller quantities than 750 ounces of solids compounded with five quarts of oil, and was so profusely employed that when applied to Aaron's head it flowed down over his beard and breast, to the very skirts of his garments.—*Hugh Macmillan, in "The Ministry of Nature,"* 1871.

Verse 2.—"*That ran down . . . that went down,*" etc. Christ's grace is so diffusive of itself, that it conveys holiness to us, "running down from the head to the skirts," to all his members. He was not only anointed himself, but he is our anointer. Therefore it is called "the oil of gladness," because it rejoiceth our hearts, by giving us spiritual gladness, and peace of conscience.—*Thomas Adams.*

Verse 2.—"*Down upon the beard, even Aaron's beard : that went down to the skirts of his garments.*" Not the extremity of them, as our version inclines to ; for not so great a quantity of oil was poured upon him ; nor would it have been decent to have his clothes thus greased from top to bottom ; but the upper part of his garment, the top of his coat, on which the beard lay, as Zarchi ; the neck or collar of it, as Kimchi and Ben Melech ; the hole in which the head went through when it was put on, about which there was a band, that it might not be rent : Exod. xxviii. 32, and xxxix. 23 ; where the Septuagint use the same word as here.—*John Gill.*

Verses 2, 3.—In this prayer and song of the unity of the church, it is noteworthy how, commencing with the fundamental idea of "*brethren,*" we rise to the realization of the Elder Brother, who is our common anointed High Priest. It is the bond of his priesthood which joins us together as brethren. It is the common anointing which flows down even to the skirts of the garment of our High Priest which marks our being brethren. Whether we dwell north or south, meeting in Zion, and sharing in the blessings of that eternal Priesthood of Christ, we form in reality, and before our Father, but one family—"the whole family in earth and heaven." Our real bond of union consists in the "flowing down," the "running down," or "descending" of the common blsssing, which marks the steps in this Psalm of Degrees (verses 2, 3). And if "the dew of Hermon" has descended upon "the mountains of Zion," long after the sun has risen shall gladsome fruit appear—in some twenty, in some thirty, and in some a hundred-fold.—*Alfred Edersheim.*

Verse 3.—"*As the dew of Hermon,*" etc. "What we read in the 133rd Psalm of the dew of Hermon descending upon the mountains of Zion," says Van de Velde in his "Travels" (Bd. i. S. 97), "is now become quite clear to me. Here as I sat at the foot of Hermon, I understood how the water-drops which rose from its forest-mantled heights, and out of the highest ravines, which are filled the whole year round with snow, after the sun's rays have attenuated them and moistened the atmosphere with them, descend at evening-time as a heavy dew upon the lower mountains which lie round about as its spurs. One ought to have seen Hermon with its white-golden crown glistening aloft in the blue sky, in order to be able rightly to understand the figure. Nowhere in the whole country is so heavy a dew perceptible as in the districts near to Hermon." To this dew the poet likens brotherly love. This is "*as the dew of Hermon*" : of such pristine freshness and thus refreshing, possessing such pristine power and thus quickening, thus born from above (cx. 3), and in fact like the dew of Hermon which comes down upon the mountains of Zion—a feature in the picture which is taken from the natural reality ; for an abundant dew, when warm days have preceded, might very well be diverted to Jerusalem by the operation of the cold current of air sweeping down from the north over Hermon. We know, indeed, from our own experience how far off a cold air coming from the Alps is perceptible, and produces its effects. The figure of the poet is therefore as true to nature as it is beautiful. When brethren bound together in love also meet together in one place, and, in fact, when brethren of the north unite with brethren in the south in Jerusalem, the city which is the mother of all, at the great Feasts, it is as when the dew of Mount Hermon, which is covered with deep, almost eternal snow, descends upon the bare, unfruitful—and therefore longing for such quickening—mountains round about Zion. In Jerusalem must love and all that is good meet. —*Franz Delitzsch.*

Verse 3.—"*As the dew of Hermon,*" etc. As touching this similitude, I think the prophet useth the common manner of speaking. For whereas the mountains oftentimes seem to those that behold them afar off, to reach up even unto heaven, the dew which cometh from heaven seemeth to fall from the high mountains unto the hills which are under them. Therefore he saith that the dew descendeth from Hermon unto the mount Sion, because it so seemeth unto those that do behold it afar off.—*Martin Luther.*

Verse 3.—"*As the dew of Hermon.*" The dews of the mists that rose from the watery ravines, or of the clouds that rested on the summit of Hermon, were perpetual witnesses of freshness and coolness—the sources, as it seemed, of all the moisture, which was to the land of Palestine what the fragrant oil was to the garments of the High Priest ; what the influence of brotherly love was to the whole community.—*Arthur Penrhyn Stanley* (1815—1881), *in "Sinai and Palestine."*

Verse 3.—"*Dew of Hermon.*" We had sensible proof at Rasheiya of the copiousness of the "*dew of Hermon,*" spoken of in Ps. cxxxiii. 3, where "Zion" is only another name for the same mountain. Unlike most other mountains which gradually rise from lofty table-lands and often at a distance from the sea, Hermon starts at once to the height of nearly ten thousand feet, from a platform scarcely above the sea level. This platform, too—the upper Jordan valley, and marshes of Merom—is for the most part an impenetrable swamp of unknown depth, whence the seething vapour, under the rays of an almost tropical sun, is constantly ascending into the upper atmosphere during the day. The vapour, coming in contact with the snowy sides of the mountain, is rapidly congealed, and is precipitated in the evening in the form of a dew, the most copious we ever experienced. It penetrated everywhere, and saturated everything. The floor of our tent was soaked, our bed was covered with it, our guns were dripping, and dewdrops hung about everywhere. No wonder that the foot of Hermon is clad with orchards and gardens of such marvellous fertility in this land of droughts. —*Henry Baker Tristram*, 1867.

Verse 3.—"*As the dew of Hermon that descended upon the mountains of Zion.*"—

So the dews on Hermon's hill
Which the summer clouds distill,
Floating southward in the night,
Pearly gems on Zion light.

— *William Digby Seymour.*

Verse 3.—"*There the* LORD *commanded the blessing.*" God commands his blessing where peace is cultivated ; by which is meant, that he testifies how much he is pleased with concord amongst men, by showering down blessings upon them. The same sentiment is expressed by Paul in other words (2 Cor. xiii. 11 ; Phil. iv. 9), "Live in peace, and the God of peace shall be with you."—*John Calvin.*

Verse 3.—"*The* LORD *commanded the blessing.*" By a bare word of command he blesseth : "*there he commands the blessing,*" that blessing of blessings, "*even life for evermore*" ; like as it is said, "he commanded, and they were created" : Ps. cxlviii. 5. So he commands and we are blessed."—*Thomas Goodwin.*

Verse 3.—"*The* LORD *commanded the blessing.*" It is an allusion possibly to great persons, to a general, or an emperor : "Where the word of a king is, there is power." The centurion said, "I say to one soldier, Go, and he goeth ; to another, Come, and he cometh ; to a third, Do this, and he doth it." So God commandeth one ordinance, "Go and build up such a saint," and it goeth ; he saith to another ordinance, "Come, and call home such a sinner," and it doth it ; God's words and work go together. Men cannot enable others, or give them power to obey them ; they may bid a lame man walk, or a blind man see ; but they cannot enable them to walk or see : God with his word giveth strength to do the thing commanded ; as in the old, so in the new creation, "He spake, and it was done ; he commanded, and it stood fast :" Ps. xxxiii. 9. But there the Lord commands his blessing, "*even life for evermore.*" The stream of regeneration, or a spiritual life, which shall never cease, but still go forward and increase, till it swell to, and be swallowed up in the ocean of eternal life, "*even life for evermore.*"—*George Swinnock.*

HINTS TO THE VILLAGE PREACHER.

Verse 1.—Christian unity. I. Its admirable excellences. II. The signs of its existence. III. The causes of its decay. IV. The means of its renewal.

Verse 1.—The saints are here contemplated, I. In their brotherhood. II. In their concord. III. In their felicity.— *W. J.*

Verses 1—3.—Six blessings which dwell with unity. 1. Goodness. 2. Pleasure. 3. Anointing. 4. Dew. 5. God's blessing. 6. Eternal life.

Verses 1—3.—I. The contemplation : brethren dwelling together in unity. 1. In a family. 2. In a Christian church. 3. Brethren of the same denomination. 4. Of different denominations. II. Its commendation. 1. Literally : "good and pleasant." 2. Figuratively : fragrant as the priestly anointing ; fruitful as the dew on Hermon. 3. Spiritually, it has a blessing from God, that gives life, and continues for evermore !— *G. R.*

Verses 1—3.—On Christians dwelling together in unity as a church. I. *Its propriety,* on account of fraternal relationship : "*For brethren.*" The Christian brotherhood is so unique, sacred and lasting, that a lack of unity is a disgrace. They are brethren, 1. Because born of God, who is "the God of peace." Their claim to the brotherhood is dependent upon likeness to Him : Mat. v. 9. 2. Because united to Christ, who as elder brother desires unity : John xvii. 20, 21. Not to seek it is virtually to disown Him. 3. Because "by one Spirit are we all baptized into one body" (1 Cor. xii. 13), wherein unity must be kept : Eph. iv. 3. 4. Because destined to "dwell together in unity," for ever in heaven ; therefore we should aim at it here. II. *Its peculiar excellency :* both "good and pleasant." 1. Good, in respect of church work and influence ; of mutual edification and growth in grace (2 Cor. xiii. 11) ; of the success of prayer (Mat. xviii. 19) ; of recommending the gospel to others.   2. Pleasant, as productive of happiness : as pleasing to God.   III. *Its promotion* and maintenance.   1. Seeking the glory of God unites ; in opposition to self-honour which divides.   2. Love to Christ as a constraining power unites each to the other as it binds all closely to Christ.   3. Activity in ministering to others, rather than desiring to be ministered unto, binds heart to heart.—*J. F.*

Verse 2.—There must have been special reasons why a priestly anointing should be selected for the comparison, and why that of Aaron, rather than of any other of the high priests.   They are these—I. *The ointment was "holy,"* prepared in accordance with the Divine prescription : Ex. xxx. 23—25.   Church union is sacred.   It must spring from the love commanded by God ; be based on the principles laid down by God ; and exist for the ends appointed of God.   II. *The anointing was from God through Moses,* who acted on behalf of God in the matter. Church unity is of the Holy Spirit (1 Cor. xiii. 13), through Jesus as mediator. Therefore it should be prayed for, and thankfully acknowledged.   III. *By the anointing, Aaron became consecrated,* and officially qualified to act as priest.   By unity the Church, as a whole, lives its life of consecration, and effectively ministers in the priesthood assigned it.   IV. *The oil was diffusive ;* it rested not on Aaron's head, but flowed down to the skirts of his garments.   Unity will, in time, make its way from a few to the whole, especially from the leaders in a church to the rest of its members.   Hence, it is a personal matter.   Each should realize it, and by love and wise conduct diffuse it.—*J. F.*

Verses 2, 3.—Christian love scatters blessing by the way of down-coming : " ran down," " went down," " descended."   I. God to his saints.   II. Saint to saint.   III. Saint to sinner.

Verse 3.—The chosen place for blessing.   A church ; a church united, a church bedewed of the Spirit.   What a blessing for the world that there is a commanded place of blessing !

Verse 3 (*first clause*).—This should be rendered, " As the dew of Hermon, that cometh down on the mountains of Zion."   From the snows upon the lofty Hermon, the moisture raised by the sun is carried in the form of vapour, by the wind towards the lesser elevations of Zion, upon which it falls as a copious dew. Thus, Christian concord in church-fellowship—I. Despises not the little ones, *i.e.* the mean, poor, and less gifted.   It, 1. Recognises that God is the Father, and Christ is the Redeemer of all believers alike.   2. Acknowledges oneness of faith as the true basis of fellowship ; not wealth, social position or talent.   3. Believes that the least member is essential to the completeness of Christ's body.   4. Realises that everything which renders one in any way superior to another is the gift of God.   II. Distributes of its abundance to the needy : Acts iv. 32—37.   1. The wealthy to the poor : 1 John iii. 17.   2. The learned to the ignorant.   3. The joyful to the sorrowing.   4. The steadfast to the erring : Jas. v. 19.   III. Displays its value more by loving generosity, than by a conspicuous appearance before the world.   As Hermon was more valuable to Zion for its dew than for its adornment of the landscape.   1. A generous activity exhibits and requires more real grace than showy architecture or ornate worship does.   2. Through it, godliness flourishes more than by a vaunted respectability.   Zion was fertilized by the dew, not by the grandeur of Hermon.   3. By it the heart of Christ is touched and his reward secured : Mark ix. 40, 42.—*J. F.*

Verse 3.—*Commanded Mercy.*   Elsewhere goodness is bestowed, but in Zion it is commanded.   I. Commanded mercy implies that it must necessarily be given. II. Commanded mercy attends commanded unity.   III. Commanded mercy secures life more abundantly, " life for evermore."—*W. B. H.*

PSALM CXXXIV.

TITLE.—A Song of Degrees. *We have now reached the last of the Gradual Psalms. The Pilgrims are going home, and are singing the last song in their psalter. They leave early in the morning, before the day has fully commenced, for the journey is long for many of them. While yet the night lingers they are on the move. As soon as they are outside the gates they see the guards upon the temple wall, and the lamps shining from the windows of the chambers which surround the sanctuary ; therefore, moved by the sight, they chant a farewell to the perpetual attendants upon the holy shrine. Their parting exhortation arouses the priests to pronounce upon them a blessing out of the holy place : this benediction is contained in the third verse. The priests as good as say, " You have desired us to bless the Lord, and now we pray the Lord to bless you."*
The psalm teaches us to pray for those who are continually ministering before the Lord, and it invites all ministers to pronounce benedictions upon their loving and prayerful people

EXPOSITION.

BEHOLD, bless ye the LORD, all *ye* servants of the LORD, which by night stand in the house of the LORD.

2 Lift up your hands *in* the sanctuary, and bless the LORD.

3 The LORD that made heaven and earth bless thee out of Zion.

1. "*Behold.*" By this call the pilgrims bespeak the attention of the night-watch. They shout to them—Behold ! The retiring pilgrims stir up the holy brotherhood of those who are appointed to keep the watch of the house of the Lord. Let them look around them upon the holy place, and everywhere " behold " reasons for sacred praise. Let them look above them at night and magnify him that made heaven and earth, and lighted the one with stars and the other with his love. Let them see to it that their hallelujahs never come to an end. Their departing brethren arouse them with the shrill cry of " Behold !" Behold !—see, take care, be on the watch, diligently mind your work, and incessantly adore and bless Jehovah's name.

"*Bless ye the* LORD." Think well of Jehovah, and speak well of him. Adore him with reverence, draw near to him with love, delight in him with exultation. Be not content with praise, such as all his works render to him ; but, as his saints, see that ye " bless" him. He blesses you ; therefore, be zealous to bless him. The word " bless" is the characteristic word of the psalm. The first two verses stir us up to bless Jehovah, and in the last verse Jehovah's blessing is invoked upon the people. Oh to abound in blessing ! May *blessed* and *blessing* be the two words which describe our lives. Let others flatter their fellows, or bless their stars, or praise themselves ; as for us, we will bless Jehovah, from whom all blessings flow. "*All ye servants of the* LORD." It is your office to bless him ; take care that you lead the way therein. Servants should speak well of their masters. Not one of you should serve him as of compulsion, but all should bless him while you serve him ; yea, bless him for permitting you to serve him, fitting you to serve him, and accepting your service. To be a servant of Jehovah is an incalculable honour, a blessing beyond all estimate. To be a servant in his temple, a domestic in his house, is even more a delight and a glory : if those who are ever with the Lord, and dwell in his own temple, do not bless the Lord, who will ? "*Which by night stand in the house of the* LORD." We can well understand how the holy pilgrims half envied those consecrated ones who guarded the temple, and attended to the necessary offices thereof through the hours of night. To the silence and solemnity of night there was added the awful glory of the place where Jehovah had ordained that his worship should be celebrated ; blessed were the priests and Levites who were ordained to a service so sublime. That these should bless the Lord throughout their nightly vigils was most fitting : the people would have them mark this, and never fail in the duty. They were not to move about like so many machines, but to put their hearts into all their duties, and worship spiritually in the whole course of their duty. It would be well to watch, but better still to be " watching unto prayer" and praise.

When night settles down on a church the Lord has his watchers and holy ones still guarding his truth, and these must not be discouraged, but must bless the Lord even when the darkest hours draw on. Be it ours to cheer them, and lay upon them this charge—to bless the Lord at all times, and let his praise be continually in their mouths.

2. "*Lift up your hands in the sanctuary.*" In the holy place they must be busy, full of strength, wide-awake, energetic, and moved with holy ardour. Hands, heart, and every other part of their manhood must be upraised, elevated, and consecrated to the adoring service of the Lord. As the angels praise God day without night, so must the angels of the churches be instant in season and out of season. "*And bless the* LORD." This is their main business. They are to bless men by their teaching, but they must yet more bless Jehovah with their worship. Too often men look at public worship only from the side of its usefulness to the people ; but the other matter is of even higher importance : we must see to it that the Lord God is adored, extolled, and had in reverence. For a second time the word " bless" is used, and applied to Jehovah. Bless the Lord, O my soul, and let every other soul bless him. There will be no drowsiness about even midnight devotion if the heart is set upon blessing God in Christ Jesus, which is the gospel translation of God in the sanctuary.

3. This last verse is the answer from the temple to the pilgrims preparing to depart as the day breaks. It is the ancient blessing of the high-priest condensed, and poured forth upon each individual pilgrim. "*The* LORD *that made heaven and earth bless thee out of Zion.*" Ye are scattering and going to your homes one by one ; may the benediction come upon you one by one. You have been up to Jehovah's city and temple at his bidding ; return each one with such a benediction as only he can give—divine, infinite, effectual, eternal. You are not going away from Jehovah's works or glories, for he made the heaven above you and the earth on which you dwell. He is your Creator, and he can bless you with untold mercies ; he can create joy and peace in your hearts, and make for you a new heaven and a new earth. May the Maker of all things make you to abound in blessings.

The benediction comes from the City of the Great King, from his appointed ministers, by virtue of his covenant, and so it is said to be " out of Zion." To this day the Lord blesses each one of his people through his church, his gospel, and the ordinances of his house. It is in communion with the saints that we receive untold benisons. May each one of us obtain yet more of the blessing which cometh from the Lord alone. Zion cannot bless us ; the holiest ministers can only wish us a blessing ; but Jehovah can and will bless each one of his waiting people. So may it be at this good hour. Do we desire it ? Let us then bless the Lord ourselves. Let us do it a second time. Then we may confidently hope that the third time we think of blessing we shall find ourselves conscious receivers of it from the Ever-blessed One. Amen.

EXPLANATORY NOTES.

Whole Psalm.—It is a beautiful little ode, equally full of sublimity and simplicity. It is commonly supposed to be the work of David. With what admiration should we contemplate the man whose zeal in the cause of religion thus urged him to embrace every opportunity that could occur to him, among the lowest as well as the highest ranks of life, of promoting the praise and glory of his Creator ; now composing penitential hymns for his own closet ; now leading the temple service in national eulogies of the sublimest pitch to which human language can reach ; and now descending to the class of the watchmen and patrol of the temple and the city, and tuning their lips to a reverential utterance of the name and the service of God !—*John Mason Good* (1764—1827), *in "An Historical Outline of the Book of Psalms."*

Whole Psalm.—This psalm consists of a greeting, verses 1, 2, and the reply thereto. The greeting is addressed to those priests and Levites who have the night-watch in the Temple ; and this antiphon is purposely placed at the end of the collection of Songs of Degrees in order to take the place of a final beracha* In this sense Luther styles the psalm *epiphonema superiorum.†* It is also in other respects an appropriate finale.—*Franz Delitzsch.*

Whole Psalm.—The last cloud of smoke from the evening sacrifice has mixed with the blue sky, the last note of the evening hymn has died away on the ear. The watch is being set for the night. The twenty-four Levites, the three priests, and the captain of the guard, whose duty it was to keep ward from sunset to sunrise over the hallowed precincts, are already at their several posts, and the multitude are retiring through the gates, which will soon be shut, to many of them to open no more. But they cannot depart without one last expression of the piety that fills their hearts ; and turning to the watchers on tower and battlement, they address them in holy song, in what was at once a brotherly admonition and a touching prayer : "*Behold, bless ye the* LORD, *all ye servants of the* LORD, *which by night stand in the house of the* LORD. *Lift up your hands in the sanctuary, and bless the* LORD." The pious guard are not unprepared for the appeal, and from their lofty heights, in words that float over the peopled city and down into the quiet valley of the Kedron, like the melody of angels, they respond to each worshipper who thus addressed them with a benedictory farewell : "*The* LORD *bless thee out of Zion, even he who made heaven and earth.*"—*Robert Nisbet.*

Whole Psalm.—The tabernacle and temple were served by priests during the *night* as well as the day. Those priests renewed the altar fire, fed the lamps, and guarded the sacred structure from intrusion and from plunder. The psalm before us was prepared for the priests who served the sacred place by night. They were in danger of slumbering ; and they were in danger of idle reverie. Oh, how much time is wasted in mere reverie—in letting thought wander, and wander, and wander ! The priests were in danger, we say, of slumbering, of idle reverie, of vain thoughts, of useless meditation, and of profitless talk : and therefore it is written,—"*Behold, bless ye the* LORD, *all ye servants of the* LORD, *which by night stand in the house of the* LORD." Is it your duty to spend the night in watching ? then spend the night in worship. Do not let the time of watching be idle, wasted time ; but when others are slumbering and sleeping, and you are necessarily watchful, sustain the praises of God's house ; let there be praise in Zion—still praise by night as well as by day ! "*Lift up your hands in the sanctuary, and bless the* LORD."

We may suppose these words to be addressed to the sacred sentinels, by the head of their course, or by the captain of the guard, or even by the high priest. We can imagine the captain of the guard coming in during the night watches, and saying to the priests who were guarding the temple, "*Behold, bless ye the* LORD, *all ye servants of the* LORD, *which by night stand in the house of the* LORD." Or we could imagine the high priest, when the watch was set for the first part of the night, going to the priests who were under his control, and addressing to them these same soul-stirring words. Now our text is the response of these sacred sentinels. As they listened to the captain of the guard, or to the high priest, telling them to worship by night in the courts of the Lord—to lift up their hands

---

* Blessing.
† "I take this psalm to be a conclusion of those things which were spoken of before."—*Luther.*

in the sanctuary, and bless the Lord—they answered him, "*The* LORD *that made heaven and earth bless thee out of Zion.*" So that here you have brought before you the interesting and instructive subject of mutual benediction—the saints blessing each other.—*Samuel Martin,* 1817—1878.

Verse 1.—The Targum explains the first verse of the Temple watch. " The cus-¹ tom in the Second Temple appears to have been this. After midnight the chief of the door-keepers took the key of the inner Temple, and went with some of the priests through the small postern of the Fire Gate. In the inner court this watch divided itself into two companies, each carrying a burning torch ; one company turned west, the other east, and so they compassed the court to see whether all were in readiness for the Temple service on the following morning. In the bake-house, where the *Mincha* (" meat-offering") of the High Priest was baked, they met with the cry, ' All well.' Meanwhile the rest of the priests arose, bathed themselves, and put on their garments. They then went into the stone chamber (one half of which was the hall of session of the Sanhedrim), and there, under the superintendence of the officer who gave the watchword, and one of the Sanhe-drim, surrounded by the priests clad in their robes of office, their several duties for the coming day were assigned to each of the priests by lot. Luke i. 9."— *J. J. Stewart Perowne.*

Verse 1.—"*Behold.*" The psalm begins with the demonstrative adverb *Behold !* setting the matter of their duty before their eyes, for they were to be stimulated to devotion by looking constantly to the Temple. We are to notice the psalmist's design in urging the duty of praise so earnestly upon them. Many of the Levites, through the tendency which there is in all men to abuse ceremonies, considered that nothing more was necessary than standing idly in the Temple, and thus overlooked the principal part of their duty. The psalmist would show that merely to keep nightly watch over the Temple, kindle the lamps, and superintend the sacrifices, was of no importance, unless they served God spiritually, and re-ferred all outward ceremonies to that which must be considered the main sacri-fice,—the celebration of God's praises. You may think it a very laborious service, as if he had said, to stand at watch in the Temple, while others sleep in their own houses ; but the worship which God requires is something more excellent than this, and demands of you to sing his praises before all the people.—*John Calvin.*

Verse 1.—"*Behold.*" The first word in this verse, "*Behold,*" seemeth to point at the reasons which the priests in the Temple had to bless Jehovah ; as if it had been said, Behold, the house of God is built, the holy services are appointed, and the Lord hath given you rest from your enemies, that you may serve him accept-ably ; set about it, therefore, with gratitude and alacrity. We read (1 Chron. ix. 33) that the Levitical singers were " employed in their work day and night" ; to the end, doubtless, that the earthly sanctuary might bear some resemblance to that above, where St. John tells us, the redeemed " are before the throne of God, and serve him day and night in his temple" : Rev. vii. 15.— *George Horne.*

Verse 1.—"*Behold, bless ye the* LORD, *all ye servants of the* LORD." From the exhortation to the Lord's ministers, learn, that the public worship of God is to be carefully looked unto ; and all men, but especially ministers, had need to be stirred up to take heed to themselves, and to the work of God's public worship, when they go about it ; for so much doth " *behold* " in this place import.—*David Dickson.*

Verse 1. —"*By night.*" Even by night the Lord is to be remembered, and his praises are to be rehearsed.—*Martin Geier,* 1614—1681.

Verse 1.—"*Stand in the house of the* LORD." The Rabbins say, that the high priest only sat in the sanctuary (as did Eli, 1 Sam. i. 9) ; the rest stood, as ready pressed to do their office.—*John Trapp.*

Verse 1.—" *Which stand in the house of the* LORD." You who have now a per-manent house, and no longer, like pilgrims, have to dwell in tents.—*Robert Bellarmine.*

Verse 1.—" *Which stand in the house of the* LORD." Let not this your frequent
being in his presence breed in you contempt ; as the saying is, ' Too much famil-
iarity breedeth contempt ; ' but bless him always, acknowledge, and with reverence praise his excellency.—*John Mayer*, 1653.

Verse 2.—"*Lift up your hands*," etc. The lifting up of the hands was a gesture
in prayer, it was an intimation of their expectation of receiving blessings from the
Lord, and it was also an acknowledgment of their having received the same.—
Samuel Eyles Pierce.

Verse 2.—"*In the sanctuary.*" The Hebrew work signifying *holiness* as well as
the *holy place* may here be taken in the former sense, the latter having been sufficiently expressed (verse 1) by " the house of the Lord." . . . The priests (which
are here spoken to) before their officiating, which is here expressed by *lifting up*
their *hands,* were obliged to wash their hands.—*Henry Hammond.*

Verse 3.—"*The* LORD *that made heaven and earth bless thee out of Zion.*" He
doth not say, the Lord that made the earth bless thee out of heaven ; nor, the
Lord that made heaven bless thee out of heaven ; but " *bless thee out of Zion.*"
As if he would teach us that all blessings come as immediately and primarily
from heaven, so mediately and secondarily from *Zion,* where the Temple stood.
If ever, therefore, we would have blessings outward, inward, private, public,
secular, spiritual ; if ever we would have blessing in our estate, blessing in our
land, blessing in our souls, we must pray for it, and pray for it here, in *Zion,* in
God's house : for from the piety there exercised all blessings flow, as from a
fountain that can never be drawn dry.—*Abraham Wright.*

Verse 3.—"*The* LORD *that made heaven and earth,*" etc. The priestly benediction brings God before us in a twofold character. He is described first as the
Creator of the universe. He is described, in the second place, as dwelling " in
Zion." In the first aspect, he is represented as the God of nature ; in the second,
as the God of grace. When I contemplate him as the Creator of the universe,
there is abundant proof that he *can* bless me. When I contemplate him as dwelling in the Church, there is abundant proof that he *will* bless me. Both of these
elements are essential to our faith.—*N. M'Michael.*

Verse 3.—"*The* LORD *that made heaven and earth,*" etc. As the priests were
called upon to bless God in behalf of the people, so here they bless the people in
behalf of God. Between the verses we may suppose the previous request to be
complied with. The priests, having blessed God, turn and bless the people.
The obvious allusion to the sacerdotal blessing (Num. vi. 23—27), favours the
optative construction of this verse, which really includes a prediction—the Lord
will bless thee.—*Joseph Addison Alexander.*

Verse 3.—"*The* LORD *bless thee.*" All men lie under the curse, till God brings
them into the fellowship of his church, and pronounce them blessed by his word,
as "*The* LORD *bless thee*" doth import.—*David Dickson.*

Verse 3.—"*The* LORD *bless thee out of Zion.*" The Church is the conservator of
Divine revelation ; the Church is the offerer on earth of true worship ; it consists
of a company of priests, a royal priesthood, part of whose mission is " to offer up
spiritual sacrifices acceptable to God by Jesus Christ." The Church is the heritor
of the covenants. God's covenants are made with his Church, and his promises
are addressed chiefly to his Church. The Church is the scene of special Divine
ministrations, God shows himself to his Church as he does not to that which is
called the world. It is also the scene of special heavenly influences : and in a
sense next to that in which God is said to reside in heaven, the Church is the
dwelling-place of the Most High. Now, what is it to be *blessed out of Zion ?* It
is surely to be blessed with Zion's blessings, and to have Zion's endowments and
gifts rendered sources of advantage and profit to us.—*Samuel Martin.*

Verse 3.—"*Bless thee.*" The singular instead of the plural " bless *you,*" because the words are taken from the form used by the High Priest in blessing the
people. Num. vi. 24.—*J. J. Stewart Perowne.*

Verse 3.—*"Bless thee."* It is addressed to the church as one person, and to each individual in this united, unit-like church.—*Franz Delitzsch.*

HINTS TO THE VILLAGE PREACHER.

Whole Psalm.—There are two things in this psalm. I. Our blessing God : verses 1, 2. 1. How ? By gratitude, by love, by obedience, by prayer, by praise. 2. Where ? " in the house of the Lord," " in the sanctuary." 3. When ? Not in the day merely, but at night. Some of old spent the whole night, others part of the night, in the temple, praising God. As Christ spent whole nights in prayer for his people, they should not think it too much occasionally to spend whole nights in praise of him. Evening services should not be neglected on the Sabbath, nor on other days of the week.

II. God blessing us : verse 3. 1. The persons blessed : " bless thee"—every one who blesses him. 2. The condition : " out of Zion." In the fulfilment of religious duties, not in the neglect of them. 3. The blessing itself : of the Lord. They are blessed whom he blesses.—*G. R.*

Whole Psalm.—I. God—Jehovah—the fountain of blessing. II. The heavens and the earth, evidence of divine capacity to bless. III. The church, a channel of blessing. IV. The saints, the means of spreading blessing, through the spirit of blessing. V. The riches involved in the divine benediction.—*Samuel Martin.*

Whole Psalm.—I. Unique service : temple watching, night-sentinelship. II. Sublime society : the awful things of the sanctuary. III. Holy uplifting : hands, hearts, eyes. IV. Praise in the darkness heard far up in the light. V. Response from the stars fulfilling the prayer : " The Creator Lord bless *thee.*"—*W. B. H.*

Verse 1.—I. Night settles on the holy place : dark periods of church story. II. But God has his guards : Wycliffe and his band watching for the Reformation ; Waldenses, etc. Never a night so dark but God is praised and served. III. Be it night or day, let the Levites fulfil their courses.—*W. B. H.*

Verse 1.—The Lord's servants exhorted to be, 1. Devout and joyful in their service. Sing at your work, though it be in the dark. 2. Zealous to employ every season of service aright. " By night," as by day, " bless the Lord." 3. Careful to avoid all hindrances to devotion in their service. When tempted to indolence and drowsiness, say—

> " Wake, and lift up thyself, my heart,
> And with the angels bear thy part,
> Who all night long, unwearied, sing
> High praise to the Eternal King."

W. H. J. P.

Verse 1.—Directions for worship. I. It should be with great care : " Behold." II. With grateful joy : " Bless ye the Lord." III. Unanimously : " all ye." IV. With holy reverence, as by " servants of the Lord." V. With unflagging constancy : " stand by night."

Verse 1.—" Ye that stand by night." The night-watchmen of the Lord's house, their value, their obscurity, their danger-slumber, their consolation, their dignity, their reward.

Verse 2.—Ingredients of worship. I. Uplifted hands. Energy, courage, prayer, aspiration. II. Uplifted hearts. Thank, praise, adore, and love the Lord.

Verse 3.—The Divine Benediction. I. From the Creator : ample, new, varied, boundless, enduring—all illustrated by his making heaven and earth. II. From the Redeemer : blessings most needful, rich, effectual, abiding,—all illustrated and guaranteed by his dwelling among men, purchasing a church, building an abode, revealing his glory, reigning on his throne.

PSALM CXXXV.

GENERAL REMARKS.—*This Psalm has no title. It is mainly made up of selections from other Scriptures. It has been called a mosaic, and compared to a tesselated pavement. At the outset, its first two verses are taken from Ps. cxxxiv.; while the latter part of verse 2 and the commencement of verse 3 put us in mind of Ps. cxvi. 19; and verse 4 suggests Deut. vii. 6. Does not verse 5 remind us of Ps. xcv. 3? As for verse 7, it is almost identical with Jer. x. 13, which may have been taken from it. The passage contained in verse 13 is to be found in Ex. iii. 15, and verse 14 in Deut. xxxii. 36. The closing verses, 8 to 12, are in Ps. cxxxvi. From verse 15 to the end the strain is a repetition of Ps. cxv. This process of tracing the expressions to other sources might be pushed further without straining the quotations; the whole psalm is a compound of many choice extracts, and yet it has all the continuity and freshness of an original poem. The Holy Spirit occasionally repeats himself; not because he has any lack of thoughts or words, but because it is expedient for us that we hear the same things in the same form. Yet, when our great Teacher uses repetition, it is usually with instructive variations, which deserve our careful attention.*

DIVISION.—*The first fourteen verses contain an exhortation to praise Jehovah for his goodness (verse 3), for his electing love (verse 4), his greatness (5—7), his judgments (8—12), his unchanging character (13), and his love towards his people. This is followed by a denunciation of idols (verses 15 to 18), and a further exhortation to bless the name of the Lord. It is a song full of life, vigour, variety, and devotion.*

EXPOSITION.

PRAISE ye the LORD. Praise ye the name of the LORD; praise *him*, O ye servants of the LORD.

2 Ye that stand in the house of the LORD, in the courts of the house of our God,

3 Praise the LORD; for the LORD *is* good : sing praises unto his name; for *it is* pleasant.

4 For the LORD hath chosen Jacob unto himself, *and* Israel for his peculiar treasure.

5 For I know that the LORD *is* great, and *that* our Lord *is* above all gods.

6 Whatsoever the LORD pleased, *that* did he in heaven, and in earth, in the seas, and all deep places.

7 He causeth the vapours to ascend from the ends of the earth; he maketh lightnings for the rain; he bringeth the wind out of his treasuries.

8 Who smote the firstborn of Egypt, both of man and beast.

9 *Who* sent tokens and wonders into the midst of thee, O Egypt, upon Pharaoh, and upon all his servants.

10 Who smote great nations, and slew mighty kings;

11 Sihon king of the Amorites, and Og king of Bashan, and all the kingdoms of Canaan;

12 And gave their land *for* an heritage, an heritage unto Israel his people.

13 Thy name, O LORD, *endureth* for ever; *and* thy memorial, O LORD, throughout all generations.

14 For the LORD will judge his people, and he will repent himself concerning his servants.

1. "*Praise ye the* LORD," or, *Hallelujah.* Let those who are themselves full of holy praise labour to excite the like spirit in others. It is not enough for us to praise God ourselves, we are quite unequal to such a work ; let us call in all our friends and neighbours, and if they have been slack in such service, let us stir them up to it with loving exhortations. "*Praise ye the name of the* LORD." Let his character be extolled by you, and let all that he has revealed concerning himself be the subject of your song ; for this is truly his *name.* Specially let his holy and incommunicable name of " Jehovah" be the object of your adoration. By that name he sets forth his self-existence, and his immutability; let these arouse your praises of his Godhead. Think of him with love, admire him with heartiness, and then extol him with ardour. Do not only magnify the Lord because he is God ; but study his character and his doings, and thus render intelligent, appreciative praise. "*Praise him, O ye servants of the* LORD." If others are silent, you must not be ; you must be the first to celebrate his praises. You are " servants," and this is part of your service ; his " name" is named upon you, therefore celebrate his name with praises ; you know what a blessed Master he is, therefore speak well of him. Those who shun his service are sure to neglect his praise ; but as grace has made you his own personal servants, let your hearts make you his court-musicians. Here we see the servant of the Lord arousing his fellow-servants by three times calling upon them to praise. Are we, then, so slow in such a sweet employ ? Or is it that when we do our utmost it is all too little for such a Lord ? Both are true. We do not praise enough ; we cannot praise too much. We ought to be always at it ; answering to the command here given—Praise, Praise, Praise. Let the Three-in-one have the praises of our spirit, soul, and body. For the past, the present, and the future, let us render three-fold hallelujahs.

2. "*Ye that stand in the house of the* LORD, *in the courts of the house of our God.*" You are highly favoured ; you are the domestics of the palace, nearest to the Father of the heavenly family, privileged to find your home in his house ; therefore you must, beyond all others, abound in thanksgiving. You " stand;" or abide in the temple ; you are constant occupants of its various courts ; and therefore from you we expect unceasing praise. Should not ministers be celebrated for celebrating the praises of Jehovah ? Should not church officers and church-members excel all others in the excellent duty of adoration ? Should not all of every degree who wait even in his outer courts unite in his worship ? Ought not the least and feeblest of his people to proclaim his praises, in company with those who live nearest to him ? Is it not a proper thing to remind them of their obligations ? Is not the Psalmist wise when he does so in this case and in many others ? Those who can call Jehovah " *our* God " are highly blessed, and therefore should abound in the work of blessing him. Perhaps this is the sweetest word in these two verses. " This God is our God for ever and ever." " Our God " signifies possession, communion in possession, assurance of possession, delight in possession. Oh the unutterable joy of calling God our own !

3. "*Praise the* LORD." Do it again ; continue to do it ; do it better and more heartily ; do it in growing numbers ; do it at once. There are good reasons for praising the Lord, and among the first is this—"*for the* LORD *is good.*" He is so good that there is none good in the same sense or degree. He is so good that all good is found in him, flows from him, and is rewarded by him. The word God is brief for good ; and truly God is the essence of goodness. Should not his goodness be well spoken of ? Yea, with our best thoughts, and words, and hymns let us glorify his name. "*Sing praises unto his name ; for it is pleasant.*" The adjective may apply to the singing and to the name—they are both pleasant. The vocal expression of praise by sacred song is one of our greatest delights. We were created for this purpose, and hence it is a joy to us. It is a charming duty to praise the lovely name of our God. All pleasure is to be found in the joyful

worship of Jehovah ; all joys are in his sacred name as perfumes lie slumbering
in a garden of flowers. The mind expands, the soul is lifted up, the heart
warms, the whole being is filled with delight when we are engaged in singing
the high praises of our Father, Redeemer, Comforter. When in any occupation
goodness and pleasure unite, we do well to follow it up without stint : yet it is to
be feared that few of us sing to the Lord at all in proportion as we talk to men.

4. "*For the* LORD *hath chosen Jacob unto himself.*" Jehovah hath chosen Jacob.
Should not the sons of Jacob praise' him who has so singularly favoured them ?
Election is one of the most forcible arguments for adoring love. Chosen ! chosen
unto himself !—who can be grateful enough for being concerned in this privilege ?
" Jacob have I loved," said Jehovah, 'and he gave no reason for his love except
that he chose to love. Jacob had then done neither good nor evil, yet thus the
Lord determined, and thus he spake. If it be said that the choice was made
upon foresight of Jacob's character, it is, perhaps, even more remarkable ; for
there was little enough about Jacob that could deserve special choice. By nature
Jacob was by no means the most lovable of men. No, it was sovereign grace
which dictated the choice. But, mark, it was not a choice whose main result was
the personal welfare of Jacob's seed : the nation was chosen by God *unto himself*,
to answer the divine ends and purposes in blessing all mankind. Jacob's race
was chosen to be the Lord's own, to be the trustees of his truth, the maintainers
of his worship, the mirrors of his mercy. Chosen they were ; but mainly for this
end, that they might be a peculiar people, set apart unto the service of the true
God.

"*And Israel for his peculiar treasure.*" God's choice exalts ; for here the name
is changed from Jacob, the supplanter, to Israel, the prince. The love of God
gives a new name and imparts a new value ; for the comparison to a royal treasure is a most honourable one. As kings have a special regalia, and a selection of
the rarest jewels, so the Lord deigns to reckon his chosen nation as his wealth,
his delight, his glory. What an honour to the spiritual Israel that they are all
this to the Lord their God ! We are a people near and dear unto him ; precious
and honourable in his sight. How can we refuse our loudest, heartiest, sweetest
music ? If *we* did not extol him, the stones in the street would cry out against us.

5. "*For I know that the* LORD *is great, and that our Lord is above all gods.*" The
greatness of God is as much a reason for adoration as his goodness, when we are
once reconciled to him. God is great positively, great comparatively, and great
superlatively—" above all gods." Of this the Psalmist had an assured personal
persuasion. He says positively, " I know." It is knowledge worth possessing.
He knew by observation, inspiration, and realization ; he was no agnostic, he was
certain and clear upon the matter. He not only knows the greatness of Jehovah,
but that as the Adonai, or Ruler, " our Lord " is infinitely superior to all the
imaginary deities of the heathen, and to all great ones besides.

> " Let princes hear, let angels know,
>   How mean their natures seem ;
> Those gods on high, and gods below,
>   When once compared with him."

Many have thought to worship Jehovah, and other gods with him ; but this holy
man tolerated no such notion. Others have thought to combine their religion
with obedience to the unrighteous laws of tyrannical princes ; this, also, the
sweet singer of Israel denounced ; for he regarded the living God as altogether
above all men, who as magistrates and princes have been called gods. Observe
here the fourth of the five " fors." Verses 3, 4, 5, and 14 contain reasons for
praise, each set forth with " for." A fruitful meditation might be suggested by
this.

6. "*Whatsoever the* LORD *pleased, that did he in heaven, and in earth, in the seas,
and all deep places.*" His will is carried out throughout all space. The king's
warrant runs in every portion of the universe. The heathen divided the great
domain ; but Jupiter does not rule in heaven, nor Neptune on the sea, nor Pluto
in the lower regions ; Jehovah rules over all. His decree is not defeated, his

purpose is not frustrated : in no one point is his good pleasure set aside.   The word " whatsoever" is of the widest range and includes all things, and the four words of place which are mentioned comprehend all space ; therefore the declaration of the text knows neither limit nor exception.   Jehovah works his will : he pleases to do, and he performs the deed.   None can stay his hand.   How different this from the gods whom the heathen fabled to be subject to all the disappointments, failures, and passions of men !   How contrary even to those so-called Christian conceptions of God which subordinate him to the will of man, and make his eternal purposes the football of human caprice.   Our theology teaches us no such degrading notions of the Eternal as that he can be baffled by man. " His purpose shall stand, and he will do all his pleasure."   No region is too high, no abyss too deep, no land too distant, no sea too wide for his omnipotence : his divine pleasure travels post over all the realm of nature, and his behests are obeyed.

7.   *"He causeth the vapours to ascend from the ends of the earth."*   Here we are taught the power of God in creation.   The process of evaporation is passed by unnoticed by the many, because they see it going on all around them ; the usual ceases to be wonderful to the thoughtless, but it remains a marvel to the instructed.   When we consider upon what an immense scale evaporation is continually going on, and how needful it is for the existence of all life, we may well admire the wisdom and the power which are displayed therein.   All around us from every point of the horizon the vapour rises, condenses into clouds, and ultimately descends as rain.   Whence the vapours originally ascended from which our showers are formed it would be impossible to tell ; most probably the main part of them comes from the tropical regions, and other remote places at " the ends of the earth."   It is the Lord who causes them to rise, and not a mere law.   What is law without a force at the back of it ?   *"He maketh lightnings for the rain."*   There is an intimate connection between lightning and rain, and this would seem to be more apparent in Palestine than even with ourselves ; for we constantly read of thunderstorms in that country as attending heavy down-pours of rain.   Lightning is not to be regarded as a lawless force, but as a part of that wonderful machinery by which the earth is kept in a fit condition : a force as much under the control of God as any other, a force most essential to our existence.   The ever-changing waters, rains, winds, and electric currents circulate as if they were the life-blood and vital spirits of the universe.   *"He bringeth the wind out of his treasuries."*   This great force which seems left to its own wild will is really under the supreme and careful government of the Lord.   As a monarch is specially master of the contents of his own treasure, so is our God the Lord of the tempest and hurricane ; and as princes do not spend their treasure without taking note and count of it, so the Lord does not permit the wind to be wasted, or squandered without purpose.   Everything in the material world is under the immediate direction and control of the Lord of all.   Observe how the Psalmist brings before us the personal action of Jehovah : " he causeth," " he maketh," " he bringeth."   Everywhere the Lord worketh all things, and there is no power which escapes his supremacy.   It is well for us that it is so : one bandit force wandering through the Lord's domains defying his control would cast fear and trembling over all the provinces of providence.   Let us praise Jehovah for the power and wisdom with which he rules clouds, and lightnings, and winds, and all other mighty and mysterious agencies.

8.   *" Who smote the firstborn of Egypt, both of man and beast."*   Herein the Lord is to be praised ; for this deadly smiting was an act of justice against Egypt, and of love to Israel.   But what a blow it was !   All the firstborn slain in a moment ! How it must have horrified the nation, and cowed the boldest enemies of Israel ! Beasts because of their relationship to man as domestic animals are in many ways made to suffer with him.   The firstborn of beasts must die as well as the firstborn of their owners, for the blow was meant to astound and overwhelm, and it accomplished its purpose.   The firstborn of God had been sorely smitten, and they were set free by the Lord's meting out to their oppressors the like treatment.

9. "*Who sent tokens and wonders into the midst of thee, O Egypt, upon Pharaoh, and upon all his servants.*" The Lord is still seen by the Psalmist as sending judgments upon rebellious men ; he keeps before us the personal action of God, "who sent tokens," etc. The more distinctly God is seen the better. Even in plagues he is to be seen, as truly as in mercies. The plagues were not only terrible wonders which astounded men, but forcible tokens or signs by which they were instructed. No doubt the plagues were aimed at the various deities of the Egyptians, and were a grand exposure of their impotence ; each one had its own special significance. The judgments of the Lord were no side blows, they struck the nation at the heart ; he sent his bolts "into the midst of thee, O Egypt !" These marvels happened in the centre of the proud and exclusive nation of Egypt, which thought itself far superior to other lands ; and many of these plagues touched the nation in points upon which it prided itself. The Psalmist addresses that haughty nation, saying, "O Egypt," as though reminding it of the lessons which it had been taught by the Lord's right hand. Imperious Pharaoh had been the ringleader in defying Jehovah, and he was made personally to smart for it ; nor did his flattering courtiers escape, upon each one of them the scourge fell heavily. God's servants are far better off than Pharaoh's servants : those who stand in the courts of Jehovah are delivered, but the courtiers of Pharaoh are smitten all of them, for they were all partakers in his evil deeds. The Lord is to be praised for thus rescuing his own people, and causing their cruel adversaries to bite the dust. Let no true Israelite forget the song of the Red Sea, but anew let us hear a voice summoning us to exulting praise : "Sing unto the Lord, for he hath triumphed gloriously."

10. "*Who smote great nations, and slew mighty kings.*" The nations of Canaan joined in the desperate resistance offered by their monarchs, and so they were smitten ; while their kings, the ringleaders of the fight, were slain. Those who resist the divine purpose will find it hard to kick against the pricks. The greatness of the nations and the might of the kings availed nothing against the Lord. He is prepared to mete out vengeance to those who oppose his designs : those who dream of him as too tender to come to blows have mistaken the God of Israel. He intended to bless the world through his chosen people, and he would not be turned from his purpose : cost what it might, he would preserve the candle of truth which he had lighted, even though the blood of nations should be spilt in its defence. The wars against the Canaanite races were a price paid for the setting up of a nation which was to preserve for the whole world the lively oracles of God.

11. "*Sihon king of the Amorites, and Og king of Bashan.*" These two kings were the first to oppose, and they were amongst the most notable of the adversaries : their being smitten is therefore a special object of song for loyal Israelites. The enmity of these two kings was wanton and unprovoked, and hence their overthrow was the more welcome to Israel. Sihon had been victorious in his war with Moab, and thought to make short work with Israel, but he was speedily overthrown : Og was of the race of the giants, and by his huge size inspired the tribes with dread; but they were encouraged by the previous overthrow of Sihon, and soon the giant king fell beneath their sword. "*And all the kingdoms of Canaan.*" Many were these petty principalities, and some of them were populous and valiant ; but they all fell beneath the conquering hand of Joshua, for the Lord was with him. Even so shall all the foes of the Lord's believing people in these days be put to the rout : Satan and the world shall be overthrown, and all the hosts of sin shall be destroyed, for our greater Joshua leads forth our armies, conquering and to conquer.

Note that in this verse we have the details of matters which were mentioned in the bulk in the previous stanza : it is well when we have sung of mercies in the gross to consider them one by one, and give to each individual blessing a share in our song. It is well to preserve abundant memorials of the Lord's deliverance, so that we not only sing of mighty kings as a class, but also of "Sihon king of the Amorites, and Og king of Bashan" as distinct persons."

12. *"And gave their land for an heritage, an heritage unto Israel his people."* Jehovah is Lord Paramount, and permits men to hold their lands upon lease, terminable at his pleasure. The nations of Canaan had become loathsome with abominable vices, and they were condemned by the great Judge of all the earth to be cut off from the face of the country which they defiled. The twelve tribes were charged to act as their executioners, and as their fee they were to receive Canaan as a possession. Of old the Lord had given this land to Abraham and his seed by a covenant of salt, but he allowed the Amorites and other tribes to sojourn in it till their iniquity was full, and then he bade his people come and take their own out of the holders' hands. Canaan was their heritage because they were the Lord's heritage, and he gave it to them actually because he had long before given it to them by promise.

The Lord's chosen still have a heritage from which none can keep them back. Covenant blessings of inestimable value are secured to them ; and, as surely as God has a people, his people shall have a heritage. To them it comes by gift, though they have to fight for it. Often does it happen when they slay a sin or conquer a difficulty that they are enriched by the spoil : to them even evils work for good, and trials ensure triumphs. No enemy shall prevail so as to really injure them, for they shall find a heritage where once they were opposed by " all the kingdoms of Canaan."

13. *"Thy name, O* Lord, *endureth for ever."* God's name is eternal, and will never be changed. His character is immutable ; his fame and honour also shall remain to all eternity. There shall always be life in the name of Jesus, and sweetness and consolation. Those upon whom the Lord's name is named in verity and truth shall be preserved by it, and kept from all evil, world without end. Jehovah is a name which shall outlive the ages, and retain the fulness of its glory and might for ever. *"And thy memorial, O* Lord, *throughout all generations."* Never shall men forget thee, O Lord. The ordinances of thine house shall keep thee in men's memories, and thine everlasting gospel and the grace which goes therewith shall be abiding remembrancers of thee. Grateful hearts will for ever beat to thy praise, and enlightened minds shall continue to marvel at all thy wondrous works. Men's memorials decay, but the memorial of the Lord abideth evermore. What a comfort to desponding minds, trembling for the ark of the Lord ! No, precious Name, thou shalt never perish ! Fame of the Eternal, thou shalt never grow dim !

This verse must be construed in its connection, and it teaches us that the honour and glory gained by the Lord in the overthrow of the mighty kings would never die out. Israel for long ages reaped the benefit of the *prestige* which the divine victories had brought to the nation. Moreover, the Lord in thus keeping his covenant which he made with Abraham, when he promised to give the land to his seed, was making it clear that his memorial contained in promises and covenant would never be out of his sight. His name endures in all its truthfulness, for those who occupied Israel's land were driven out that the true heirs might dwell therein in peace.

14. *"For the* Lord *will judge his people."* He will exercise personal discipline over them, and not leave it to their foes to maltreat them at pleasure. When the correction is ended he will arise and avenge them of their oppressors, who for a while were used by him as his rod. He may seem to forget his people, but it is not so ; he will undertake their cause and deliver them. The judges of Israel were also her deliverers, and such is the Lord of hosts : in this sense—as ruling, preserving, and delivering his chosen—Jehovah will judge his people. *"And he will repent himself concerning his servants."* When he has smitten them, and they lie low before him, he will pity them as a father pitieth his children, for he doth not afflict willingly. The psalm speaks after the manner of men : the nearest description that words can give of the Lord's feeling towards his suffering servants is that he repents the evil which he inflicted upon them. He acts as if he had changed his mind and regretted smiting them. It goes to the heart of God to see his beloved ones oppressed by their enemies : though they deserve all they

suffer, and more than all, yet the Lord cannot see them smart without a pang. It is remarkable that the nations by which God has afflicted Israel have all been destroyed as if the tender Father hated the instruments of his children's correction. The chosen nation is here called, first, " his people," and then " his servants :" as his people he judges them, as his servants he finds comfort in them, for so the word may be read. He is most tender to them when he sees their service ; hence the Scripture saith, ' I will spare them, as a man spareth his own son that serveth him.' Should not the " servants" of God praise him ? He plagued Pharaoh's servants ; but as for his own he has mercy upon them, and returns to them in love after he has in the truest affection smitten them for their iniquities. " Praise him, O ye servants of the Lord."

Now we come to the Psalmist's denunciation of idols, which follows most naturally upon his celebration of the one only living and true God.

15 The idols of the heathen *are* silver and gold, the work of men's hands.

16 They have mouths, but they speak not ; eyes have they, but they see not ;

17 They have ears, but they hear not ; neither is there *any* breath in their mouths.

18 They that make them are like unto them : *so is* every one that trusteth in them.

15. "*The idols of the heathen are silver and gold, the work of men's hands.*" Their essential material is dead metal, their attributes are but the qualities of senseless substances, and what of form and fashion they exhibit they derive from the skill and labour of those who worship them. It is the height of insanity to worship metallic manufactures. Though silver and gold are useful to us when we rightly employ them, there is nothing about them which can entitle them to reverence and worship. If we did not know the sorrowful fact to be indisputable, it would seem to be impossible that intelligent beings could bow down before substances which they must themselves refine from the ore, and fashion into form. One would think it less absurd to worship one's own hands than to adore that which those hands have made. What great works can these mock deities perform for man when they are themselves the works of man ? Idols are fitter to be played with, like dolls by babes, than to be adored by grown-up men. Hands are better used in breaking than in making objects which can be put to such an idiotic use. Yet the heathen love their abominable deities better than silver and gold : it were well if we could say that some professed believers in the Lord had as much love for *him*.

16. "*They have mouths.*" For their makers fashioned them like themselves. An opening is made where the mouth should be, and yet it is no mouth, for they eat not, *they speak not*. They cannot communicate with their worshippers ; they are dumb as death. If they cannot even speak, they are not even so worthy of worship as our children at school. Jehovah speaks, and it is done : but these images utter never a word. Surely, if they could speak, they would rebuke their votaries. Is not their silence a still more powerful rebuke ? When our philosophical teachers deny that God has made any verbal revelation of himself they also confess that their god is dumb.

"*Eyes have they, but they see not.*" Who would adore a blind man—how can the heathen be so mad as to bow themselves before a blind image ? The eyes of idols have frequently been very costly ; diamonds have been used for that purpose ; but of what avail is the expense, since they see nothing ? If they cannot even see us, how can they know our wants, appreciate our sacrifices, or spy out for us the means of help ? What a wretched thing, that a man who can see should bow down before an image which is blind ! The worshipper is certainly physically in advance of his god, and yet mentally he is on a level with it ; for assuredly his foolish heart is darkened, or he would not so absurdly play the fool.

17. "*They have ears*," and very large ones, too, if we remember certain of the Hindoo idols. "*But they hear not.*" Useless are their ears ; in fact, they are mere counterfeits and deceits. Ears which men make are always deaf : the secret of hearing is wrapped up with the mystery of life, and both are in the unsearchable mind of the Lord. It seems that these heathen gods are dumb, and blind, and deaf—a pretty bundle of infirmities to be found in a deity ! "*Neither is there any breath in their mouths ;*" they are dead, no sign of life is perceptible ; and breathing, which is of the essence of animal life, they never knew. Shall a man waste his breath in crying to an idol which has no breath ? Shall life offer up petitions to death ? Verily, this is a turning of things upside down.

18. "*They that make them are like unto them.*" they are as blockish, as senseless, as stupid as the gods they have made, and, like them they are the objects of divine abhorrence, and shall be broken in pieces in due time. "*So is every one that trusteth in them.*" The idol-worshippers are as bad as the idol-makers ; for if there were none to worship, there would be no market for the degrading manufacture. Idolaters are spiritually dead, they are the mere images of men, their best being is gone, they are not what they seem. Their mouths do not really pray, their eyes see not the truth, their ears hear not the voice of the Lord, and the life of God is not in them. Those who believe in their own inventions in religion betray great folly, and an utter absence of the quickening Spirit. Gracious men can see the absurdity of forsaking the true God and setting up rivals in his place ; but those who perpetrate this crime think not so : on the contrary, they pride themselves upon their great wisdom, and boast of " advanced thought" and " modern culture." Others there are who believe in a baptismal regeneration which does not renew the nature, and they make members of Christ and children of God who have none of the spirit of Christ, or the signs of adoption. May we be saved from such mimicry of divine work lest we also become like our idols.

19 Bless the LORD, O house of Israel : bless the LORD, O house of Aaron :

20 Bless the LORD, O house of Levi : ye that fear the LORD, bless the LORD.

21 Blessed be the the LORD out of Zion, which dwelleth at Jerusalem. Praise ye the LORD.

19. "*Bless the* LORD, *O house of Israel.*" All of you, in all your tribes, praise the one Jehovah. Each tribe, from Reuben to Benjamin, has its own special cause for blessing the Lord, and the nation as a whole has substantial reasons for pouring out benedictions upon his name. Those whom God has named " the house of Israel," a family of prevailing princes, ought to show their loyalty by thankfully bowing before their sovereign Lord. "*Bless the* LORD, *O house of Aaron.*" These were elected to high office and permitted to draw very near to the divine presence ; therefore they beyond all others were bound to bless the Lord. Those who are favoured to be leaders in the church should be foremost in adoration. In God's house the house of Aaron should feel bound to speak well of his name before all the house of Israel.

20. "*Bless the* LORD, *O house of Levi.*" These helped the priests in other things, let them aid them in this also. The house of Israel comprehends all the chosen seed ; then we come down to the smaller but more central ring of the house of Aaron, and now we widen out to the whole tribe of Levi. Let reverence and adoration spread from man to man until the whole lump of humanity shall be leavened. The house of Levi had choice reasons for blessing God : read the Levite story and see. Remember that the whole of the Levites were set apart for holy service, and supported by the tribes allotted to them ; therefore they were in honour bound above all others to worship Jehovah with cheerfulness.

"*Ye that fear the* LORD, *bless the* LORD." These are the choicer spirits, the truly spiritual : they are not the Lord's in name only, but in heart and spirit. The Father seeketh such to worship him. If Aaron and Levi both forget and fail, these will not. It may be that this verse is intended to bring in God-fearing men who were not included under Israel, Aaron, and Levi. They were Gentile prose-lytes, and this verse opens the door and bids them enter. Those who fear God need not wait for any other qualification for sacred service : godly fear proves us to be in the covenant with Israel, in the priesthood with Aaron, and in the ser-vice of the Lord with Levi. Filial fear, such as saints feel towards the Lord, does not hinder their praise ; nay, it is the main source and fountain of their adoration.

21. "*Blessed be the* LORD *out of Zion, which dwelleth at Jerusalem.*" Let him be most praised at home. Where he blesses most, let him be blessed most. Let the beloved mount of Zion and the chosen city of Jerusalem echo his praises. He remains among his people : he is their dwelling-place, and they are his dwelling-place : let this intimate communion ensure intense gratitude on the part of his chosen. The temple of holy solemnities which is Christ, and the city of the Great King, which is the church, may fitly be regarded as the head-quarters of the praises of Jehovah, the God of Israel. "*Praise ye the* LORD." Hallelujah. Amen, and Amen.

EXPLANATORY NOTES.

Whole Psalm.—This glorious psalm of universal praise, placed at the end of the "Songs of Up-goings," which flow into it, and find their response in it, may be likened to a large and beautiful lake, into which rivers discharge their waters, and lose themselves in its calm expanse.—*Chr. Wordsworth.*

Whole Psalm.—This psalm differs from that which went before. Its drift is not only to stir up the priests and Levites, as it was in the former, to this duty of praising God, but *the people* also : and that, 1. Because the arguments which here he brings to press this duty, did in common concern both priests and people ; and, 2. Because that clause, which is here added, " *in the courts of the house of our God,*" may be extended to the people, as well as to the priests, seeing there were some courts in the Temple which were for the people to worship God in.—*Arthur Jackson.*

Whole Psalm.—This is a song of praise to the Lord for his goodness as the Lord of creation, in seven verses ; for his grace as the deliverer of his people, in seven more : and for his unity as the only true and living God, in seven more.—*James C. Murphy.*

Whole Psalm.—This seems to have been the morning hymn which the Levites were called upon to sing at the opening of the gates of the Temple ; and, as some think, the one before was used at shutting them in the evening.—*John Kitto, in* "*The Pictorial Bible.*"

Verse 1.—This verse and the following are word for word with the first verse of the last psalm, and are now repeated, with the view of keeping up the praise then and there commenced.—*Robert Bellarmine.*

Verse 1.—"*Praise ye the* LORD." *Hallelujah* is the Hebrew word, It signifies " *Praise ye the* LORD." By this the faithful do provoke one another to give thanks unto God, and they cheer up their hearts and tune their spirits to perform this duty in the best manner, by making this preface as it were thereunto. True joy of the Holy Ghost will not endure to be kept and cooped up in any one man's breast and bosom, but it striveth to get companions both for the pouring out and imparting of itself unto them, that they may be filled and refreshed out of this spring of joy ; as also that itself may be the more increased and inflamed by the united rejoicing of many good hearts together, that are all baptized in one spirit, and are thereby made able to inflame and to edify one another.—*Thomas Bright-man* (1557—1607), *in "The Revelation of St. John Illustrated."*

Verse 1.—"*Praise ye* the name *of the* LORD." That is, the Lord himself, and the perfections of his nature ; his greatness, goodness, grace, and mercy ; his holiness, justice, power, truth, and faithfulness. Also his word, by which he makes known himself : this is a distinguishing blessing to his people, for which he is to be praised : see Ps. xlviii. 1, and Ps. cxlvii. 19, 20.—*John Gill.*

Verse 1.—"*The name of* the LORD." The first discovery of the name I AM, which signifies the Divine eternity, as well as immutability, was for the comfort of the oppressed Israelites in Egypt : Exodus iii. 14, 15. It was then published from the secret place of the Almighty, as the only strong cordial to refresh them. It hath not yet, it shall not ever, lose its virtue in any of the miseries that have or shall successively befall the church. 'Tis as durable as the God whose name it is : he is still I AM and the same to the church as he was then to his Israel. His spiritual Israel have a greater right to the glories of it than the carnal Israel could have. No oppression can be greater than theirs ; what was a comfort suited to that distress hath the same suitableness to every other oppression. It was not a temporary name, but a name for ever, his " memorial to all genera-tions" (verse 15), and reacheth to the church of the Gentiles, with whom he treats as the God of Abraham, ratifying that covenant by the Messiah, which he made with Abraham the father of the faithful.—*Stephen Charnock.*

Verse 1.—"*The name of* the LORD." Jehovah is called " *the name*" as far ex-ceeding all other names, and as being proper and peculiar only to the true God. Other things are sometimes called gods, but nothing is or can be called Jehovah but only the Almighty Creator of the world. . "That men may know," saith David, " that thou, whose name alone is Jehovah, art the Most High over all the earth" : Ps. lxxxiii. 18. From his calling himself JEHOVAH the LORD, we may easily gather what kind of thoughts he would have us, his creatures, entertain in our minds concerning him. When we think of him, we must raise our thoughts above all things else, and think of him as the Universal Being of the world, that gives essence and existence to all things in it : as Jehovah, the Being in whom we particularly, as well as other things, live and move, and have our being : as Jehovah, the Lord paramount over the whole world, to whom all angels and arch-angels in heaven, with all the kings and kingdoms upon earth, are entirely sub-ject : as Jehovah, in whom all perfections are so perfectly united that they are all but one infinite perfection : as Jehovah, knowledge itself, always actually know-ing all things that ever were, or are, or will be, or can be known : as Jehovah, wisdom itself, always contriving, ordering, and disposing of all, and everything, in the best order, after the best manner, and to the best possible end : as Jeho-vah, power, omnipotence itself, continually doing what he wills, only by willing it should be done, and always working either with means or without means, as he himself sees good : as Jehovah, light and glory itself, shining forth in and by and through everything that is made or done in the whole world : as Jehovah, holi-ness, purity, simplicity, greatness, majesty, eminency, super-eminency itself, in-finitely exalted above all things else, existing in, and of himself, and having all things else continually subsisting in him : as Jehovah, goodness itself, doing and making all things good, and so communicating his goodness to all his creatures as to be the only fountain of all the goodness that is in any of them : as Jehovah, justice and righteousness itself, giving to all their due, and exacting no more of any man than what is absolutely due to him : as Jehovah, mercy itself, pardoning and forgiving all the sins that mankind commit against him, so soon as they repent and turn to him : as Jehovah, patience and longsuffering itself, bearing a long time, even with those who continue in their rebellions against him, waiting for their coming to a due sense of their folly and madness, that he may be gra-cious and merciful to them ; as Jehovah, love and kindness, and bounty itself, freely distributing his blessings among all his creatures, both good and bad, just and unjust, those that love him, and those that love him not : as Jehovah, truth and faithfulness itself, always performing what he promiseth to his people : as

Jehovah, infinitude, immensity itself, in all things, to all things, beyond all things, everywhere, wholly, essentially, continually present : as Jehovah, constancy, immutability, eternity itself, without any variableness, or shadow of change ; yesterday, to-day, and for ever the same. In a word, when we think of the Most High God, Father, Son, and Holy Ghost, we should think of him as Jehovah, Unity in Trinity, Trinity in Unity, Three Persons, One Being, One Essence, One Lord, One Jehovah, blessed for ever. This is that glorious, that Almighty Being, which the Psalmist here means when he saith, *"Praise ye the name of the* LORD.*"—William Beveridge,* 1636—1708.

Verse 1.—*"Praise him, O ye servants of the* LORD.*"* For ye will do nothing out of place by praising your Lord *as servants.* And if ye were to be for ever only servants, ye ought to praise the Lord ; how much more ought those servants to praise the Lord who have obtained the privilege of sons ?--*Augustine.*

Verse 1.—*"Praise,"* *"praise,"* *"praise."* When duties are thus inculcated, it noteth the necessity and excellency thereof ; together with our dulness and backwardness thereunto.—*John Trapp.*

Verses 1, 2, 21.—*"Praise."* To prevent any feeling of weariness which might arise from the very frequent repetition of this exhortation to praise God, it is only necessary to remember that there is no sacrifice in which he takes greater delight than in the expression of praise. Thus (Ps. l. 14), " Sacrifice unto the Lord thanksgiving, and pay thy vows unto the Most High ;" and (Ps. cxvi. 12, 13), " What shall I render unto the LORD for all his benefits toward me ? I will take the cup of salvation, and call upon the name of the LORD." Particular attention is to be paid to those passages of Scripture which speak in such high terms of that worship of God which is spiritual ; otherwise we may be led, in the exercise of a misguided zeal, to spend our labour upon trifles, and in this respect imitate the example of too many who have wearied themselves with ridiculous attempts to invent additions to the service of God, while they have neglected what is of all other things most important. That is the reason why the Holy Spirit so repeatedly inculcates the duty of praise. It is that we may not undervalue, or grow careless in this devotional exercise. It implies, too, an indirect censure of our tardiness in proceeding to the duty; for he would not reiterate the admonition were we ready and active in the discharge of it.—*John Calvin.*

Verses 1, 2, 3.—As *Gotthold* was one day passing a tradesman's house, he heard the notes of a psalm, with which the family were concluding their morning meal. He was deeply affected, and, with a full heart, said to himself : O my God, how pleasing to my ears is the sound of thy praise, and how comforting to my soul the thought that there are still a few who bless thee for thy goodness. Alas, the great bulk of mankind have become brutalized, and resemble the swine, which in harvest gather and fatten upon the acorns beneath the oak, but show to the tree, which bore them, no other thanks than rubbing off its bark, and tearing up the sod around it. In former times, it was the law in certain monasteries, that the chanting of the praise of God should know no interruption, and that one choir of monks should, at stated intervals, relieve another in the holy employment. To the superstition and trust in human works, of which there may have been here a mixture, we justly assign a place among the wood, hay, and stubble (1 Cor. iii. 12). At the same time it is undeniably right that thy praise should never cease ; and were men to be silent, the very stones would cry out. We must begin eternal life here below, not only in our conscience, but also with our praise. Our soul ought to be like a flower, not merely receiving the gentle influence of heaven, but, in its turn, and as if in gratitude, exhaling also a sweet and pleasant perfume. It should be our desire, as it once was that of a pious man, that our hearts should melt and dissolve like incense in the fire of love, and yield the sweet fragrance of praise : or we should be like the holy martyr who professed himself willing to be consumed, if from his ashes a little flower might spring and blossom to the glory of God. We should be ready to give our very blood to fertilize the garden of the church, and render it more productive of the fruit of praise.

Well then, my God, I will praise and extol thee with heart and mouth to the utmost of my power. Oh, that without the interruptions which eating, and drinking, and sleep require, I could apply myself to this heavenly calling ! Every mouthful of air which I inhale is mixed with the goodness which preserves my life ; let every breath which I exhale be mingled at least with a hearty desire for thy honour and praise.

Hallelujah ! Ye holy angels, ye children of men, and all ye creatures, praise the Lord with me, and let us exalt his name together.—*Christian Scriver* [*Gotthold*], 1629—1693.

Verse 3.—"*Praise the* LORD." *Hallelujah* (praise to Jah !) *for good* (*is*) *Jehovah. Make music to his name, for it is lovely.* The last words may also be translated, *he is lovely*, i.e. an object worthy of supreme attachment.—*Joseph Addison Alexander.*

Verse 3.—"*Praise the* LORD ; *for the* LORD *is good.*" That is, originally, transcendently, effectively ; he is good, and doeth good (Ps. cxix. 68), and is therefore to be praised with mind, mouth, and practice.—*John Trapp.*

Verse 3.—"*Sing praises unto his name ; for it is pleasant.*" The work of praising God hath a sort of reward joined with it. When we praise God most we get much benefit by so doing : it is so comely in itself, so pleasant unto God, and profitable to the person that offereth praises, so fit to cheer up his spirit, and strengthen his faith in God, whose praises are the pillars of the believer's confidence and comfort, that a man should be allured thereunto : "*Sing praises unto his name ; for it is pleasant ;*" and this is the second motive or reason to praise God [the first being that "the Lord is good "].—*David Dickson.*

Verse 4.—"*For the* LORD *hath chosen,*" etc. God's distinguishing grace should make his elect lift up many a humble, joyful, and thankful heart to him.—*John Trapp.*

Verse 4.—"*Jacob,*" "*Israel.*" Praise the Lord for enrolling you in this company. To quicken you in this work of praise, consider what you were ; you were not a people, God raised you up from the very dunghill to this preferment ; remember your past estate. Look, as old Jacob considered what he had been when God preferred him (Gen. xxxii. 10) ; "With my staff I passed over this Jordan, and now I am become two bands ; " so do you say, I am a worthless creature, it is God that hath taken me into his grace, praised be the Lord that hath chosen me. Then consider how many are left to perish in the wide world. Some live out of the church's pale that never heard of Christ, and many others have only a loose general form of Christianity. Oh ! blessed be God that hath chosen me to be of the number of his peculiar people. It is said (Zech. xiii. 8), "And it shall come to pass in all the land, saith the Lord, that two parts shall be cut off and die, but the third shall be left therein." We pass through many bolters before we come to be God's peculiar people, as the corn is ground, bolted, searched before it comes to be fine flour. Many have not the knowledge of God, and others live in the church but are carnal ; and for me to be one of his peculiar people, a member of Christ's mystical body, oh ! what a privilege is this ! And then what moved him to all this ? Nothing but his own free grace. Therefore praise the Lord.—*Thomas Manton.*

Verse 4.—"*His peculiar treasure.*" The Hebrew word *segullah* signifieth God's special jewels, God's proper ones, or God's secret ones, that he keeps in store for himself, and for his own special service and use. Princes lock up with their own hands in secret their most precious and costly jewels ; and so doth God his : "*For the* LORD *hath chosen Jacob unto himself, and Israel for his peculiar treasure,*" or for his secret gain.—*Thomas Brooks.*

Verse 4.—"*His peculiar treasure.*" Will not a man that is not defective in his prudentials secure his jewels ? "They shall be mine in that day when I make up my jewels, and I will spare them as a father his son that serveth him : " Malachi iii. 17. If a house be on fire, the owner of it will first take care of his wife and children, then of his jewels, and last of all, of his lumber and rubbish. Christ secures first his people, for they are his jewels ; the world is but lumber and rubbish.—*Richard Mayhew.*

Verse 5.—" *For I know.*" The word "*I*" is made emphatic in the original. Whatever may be the case with others, I have had personal and precious experience of the greatness of Jehovah's power, and of his infinite supremacy above all other gods. The author of the psalm may either speak for all Israel as a unit, or he may have framed his song so that every worshipper might say this for himself as his own testimony.—*Henry Cowles.*

Verse 5.—" *For I know that the* LORD *is great,*" etc. On what a firm foundation does the Psalmist plant his foot—"*I know!*" One loves to hear men of God speaking in this calm, undoubting, and assured confidence, whether it be of the Lord's goodness or of the Lord's greatness. You may perhaps say, that it required no great stretch of faith or knowledge, or any amount of bravery, to declare that God was great ; but I think that not many wise nor mighty had in the Psalmist's days attained unto his knowledge or made his confession, that Jehovah, the God of Israel, was "*above all gods.*" Baal and Chemosh, and Milcom and Dagon, claimed the fealty of the nations round about ; and David, in the Court of Achish, would have found his declaration as unwelcome, as it would have been rejected as untrue. Moses once carried a message from Jehovah to the king of Egypt, and his reply was, " Who is the Lord, that I should obey his voice ? I know not the Lord ;" and even of Jehovah's peculiar treasure, all were not Israel that were of Israel.

There is a knowledge that plays round the head, like lightning on a mountain's summit, that leaves no trace behind ; and there is a knowledge that, like the fertilizing stream, penetrates into the very recesses of the heart, and issues forth in all the fruits of holiness, of love, and peace, and joy for evermore.—*Barton Bouchier.*

Verse 6.—" *Whatsoever the* LORD *pleased, that did he,*" etc. He was not forced to make all that he made, but *all that he willed he made.* His will was the cause of all things which he made. Thou makest a house, because if thou didst not make it thou wouldest be left without a habitation : necessity compels thee to make a home, not free-will. Thou makest a garment, because thou wouldest go about naked if thou didst not make it ; thou art therefore led to making a garment by necessity, not by free-will. Thou plantest a mountain with vines, thou sowest seed, because if thou didst not do so, thou wouldest not have food ; all such things thou doest of necessity. God has made all things of his goodness. He needed nothing that he made ; and therefore he hath made all things that he willed.

He did whatsoever he willed in the heaven and earth : dost thou do all that thou willest even in thy field ? Thou willest many things, but canst not do all thou wishest in thy own house. Thy wife, perchance, gainsays thee, thy children gainsay thee, sometimes even thy servant contumaciously gainsays thee, and thou doest not what thou willest. But thou sayest, I do what I will, because I punish the disobedient and gainsayer. Even this thou doest not when thou willest.—*Augustine.*

Verse 6.—" *Whatsoever the* LORD *pleased, that did he,*" etc. God's will obtains and hath the upper hand everywhere. Down man, down pope, down devil ; you must yield ; things shall not be as you will, but as God will ! We may well say, " Who hath resisted his will ?" Rom. ix. 19. Many, indeed, disobey, and sin against the will of his precept ; but none ever did, none ever shall, frustrate or obstruct the will of his purpose ; for he will do all his pleasure, and in his way mountains shall become a plain.—*William Slater* (—1704), *in* " *The Morning Exercises.*"

Verse 6.—Upon the Arminian's plan (if absurdity can deserve the name of a plan), the glorious work of God's salvation, and the eternal redemption of Jesus Christ, are not complete, unless a dying mortal lends his arm ; that is, unless he, who of himself can do nothing, vouchsafe to begin and accomplish that which all the angels in heaven cannot do ; namely, to convert the soul from Satan to God. How contrary is all this to the language of Scripture—how repugnant to the oracles of truth ! " Whatsoever the Lord pleased, that did he in heaven and in earth."—*Ambrose Serle* (—1815), *in "Horæ Solitariæ."*

Verse 6.—*" In heaven and in the earth,"* etc. His power is infinite. He can do what he will do everywhere ; all places are there named but purgatory ; perhaps he can do nothing there, but leaves all that work for the Pope.—*Thomas Adams.*

Verse 6.—*" In the seas, and all deep places."* He did wonders in the mighty waters : more than once he made the boisterous sea a calm, and walked upon the surface of it ; and as of old he broke up the fountains of the great deep, and drowned the world ; and at another time dried up the sea, and led his people through the depths, as through a wilderness ; so he will hereafter bind the old serpent, the devil, and cast him into the abyss, into the great deep, the bottomless pit, where he will continue during the thousand-years' reign of Christ with his saints.—*John Gill.*

Verse 6.—The word *" pleaseth"* limits the general note or particle *" all "* unto all works which in themselves are good, or else serve for good use, and so are pleasing to the Lord for the use sake. He doth not say that the Lord doth all things which are done, but all things which he pleaseth, that is, he doth not make men sinful and wicked, neither doth he work rebellion in men, which is displeasing unto him ; but he doth whatsoever is pleasing, that is, all things which are agreeable to his nature. And whatsoever is according to his will and good pleasure, that he doth, for none can hinder it. This is the true sense and meaning of the words.—*George Walker, in " God made visible in his Works,"* 1641.

Verse 6.—*" Whatsoever the* LORD *pleased, that did he,"* etc. With reference to the government of Providence, it is said of God, that " he doeth according to his will in the army of heaven, and among the inhabitants of the earth." Even insensible matter is under his control. Fire and hail, snow and vapour, and stormy wind, fulfil his word : and with reference to intelligent agents, we are told that he maketh the most refractory, even the wrath of man, to praise him, and the remainder of wrath he restrains. The whole Bible exhibits Jehovah as so ordering the affairs of individuals, and of nations, as to secure the grand purpose he had in view in creating the world,—viz., the promotion of his own glory, in the salvation of a multitude which no man can number, of all nations, and kindreds, and tribes, and peoples, and tongues. One of the most prominent distinctions between divine revelation and ordinary history is, that when the same general events are narrated, the latter exhibits—(it is its province so to do—it is not able indeed to do more,) the agency of man, the former, the agency of God. Profane history exhibits the instruments by which Jehovah works ; the finger of divine revelation points to the unseen but almighty hand which wields and guides the instrument, and causes even Herod and Pontius Pilate, together with the Jews and the people of Israel, to do what the hand and the counsel of God determined before to be done.—*George Payne, in " Lectures on Christian Theology,"* 1850.

Verse 7.—*" He causeth the vapours to ascend,"* etc. Dr. Halley made a number of experiments at St. Helena as to the quantity of water that is daily evaporated from the sea, and he found that ten square inches of the ocean's surface yielded one cubic inch of water in twelve hours—a square mile therefore yields 401,448,960 cubic inches, or 6,914 tons of water. From the surface of the Mediterranean Sea during a summer's day there would pass off in invisible vapour five thousand millions of tons of water. This being only for one day, the quantity evaporated in a year would be 365 times greater, and in two thousand years it would amount to four thousand billions of tons, which evaporation would in time empty the Mediterranean Sea ; but we have good reason for believing that there is as much water there now as in the time of the Romans, therefore the balance is kept up by the downpour of rain, the influx of the rivers, and the currents from the Atlantic.

Now let us consider the amount of power required for all this evaporation. Mr. Joule, whose experiments have given to the world so much valuable information, says that if we had a pool of water one square mile and six inches in depth to be evaporated by artificial heat, it would require the combustion of 30,000 tons of coal to effect it ; therefore to evaporate all the water that ascends from the earth it would take 6,000,000,000,000 (six billion) tons, or more than all the coal that could be stowed away in half-a-dozen such worlds as this ; and yet silently and surely has the process of evaporation been going on for millions of years.—*Samuel Kinns, in "Moses and Geology," 1882.*

Verse 7.—" *He causeth the vapours to ascend,*" etc.   There is no physical necessity that the boiling-point of water should occur at two hundred and twelve degrees of the Fahrenheit scale.   As far as we know, it might have been the same with the boiling-points of oil of turpentine, alcohol or ether.   We shall see the benevolence of the present adjustment by noticing some of the consequences which would follow if any change were made.

The amount of vapor given off at ordinary temperatures by any liquid depends on the temperature at which it boils.   If the boiling-point of water were the same as that of alcohol, the vapour given off by the ocean would be two and a half times as much as at present.   Such an excess of aqueous vapour would produce continual rains and inundations, and would make the air too damp for animal, and too cloudy for vegetable, life.   If water boiled at the same temperature as ether, the vapour rising from the ocean would be more than twenty-five times as much as at present.   In such a state of things no man could see the sun on account of the clouds ; the rain would be so excessive as to tear up the soil and wash away plants ; inundations would be constant, and navigation would be impossible in the inland torrents which would take the place of our rivers.   In winter the snow of one day might bury the houses.   If, on the other hand, water boiled at the same temperature with oil of turpentine, the vapour given off by the ocean would be less than one-fourth of its present amount.   In this case rain would be a rarity, like an eclipse of the sun, the dryness of the desert of Sahara would be equalled in a large part of the globe, which would, therefore, be bare of vegetation, and incapable of sustaining animal life.   Plants would be scorched by unclouded sunshine, springs and rivulets would be dry, and inland navigation would cease ; for nearly all the rain would be absorbed by the porous earth.

We see, then, that the boiling-point of water has been adjusted to various relations.   It is adjusted to the capacity of space to contain aqueous vapour in a transparent state ; if it were higher than two hundred and twelve degrees, the earth would be scorched by an unclouded sun ; if it were lower, it would droop under continual shade.   It is suited to the demand of plants for water ; if it were higher, they would suffer from drought ; if it were lower, they would be torn up by floods.   It is in harmony with the texture of the soil : if it were higher, the earth would absorb all the rain which falls ; if it were lower, the soil would often be washed away by the surface torrents after a shower.   It is adapted to the elevation of the continents above the sea ; if it were higher, rivers with their present inclination would be so shallow as to be often dry ; if it were lower, most rivers would be so deep as to be torrents, while the land would be covered with floods.—*Professor Hemholtz.*

Verse 7.—" *To ascend from the ends of the earth.*"   Rains in England are often introduced by a south-east wind.   " Vapour brought to us by such a wind must have been generated in countries to the south and east of our island.   It is therefore, probably, in the extensive valleys watered by the Meuse, the Moselle, and the Rhine, if not from the more distant Elbe, with the Oder and the Weser, that the water rises, in the midst of sunshine, which is soon afterwards to form *our* clouds, and pour down *our* thunder-showers."   " Drought and sunshine in one part of Europe may be necessary to the production of a wet season in another."*
—*William Whewell* (1795—1866), *in " The Bridgewater Treatise" [Astronomy and General Physics]*, 1839.

Verse 7.—" *From the surface of the earth raising the vapours.*"   The whole description is beautifully exact and picturesque.   Not " the ends," or even " the summits " or " extreme mountains," for the original is in the singular number

---

* Howard on the Climate of London.

(קצה), but from the whole of the *extreme layer*, the *superficies* or *surface* of the earth ; from every point of which the great process of exhalation is perpetually going on to supply the firmament with refreshing and fruitful clouds.—*John Mason Good.*

Verse 7.—" *He maketh lightnings for the rain.*" When the electrical clouds are much agitated, the rain generally falls heavily, and if the agitation is excessive, it hails. As the electricity is dissipated by the frequent discharges the cloud condenses, and there comes a sudden and heavy rain ; but the greater the accumulation of electricity, the longer is the rain delayed. Thus connected as the electrical phenomena of the atmosphere are with clouds, vapour, and rain, how forcibly are we struck with these appropriate words in the Scriptures.—*Edwin Sidney, in* " *Conversations on the Bible and Science,*" 1866.

Verse 7.—" *He maketh lightnings for the rain.*" Dr. Russell, in his description of the weather at Aleppo, in September, tells us, that seldom a night passes without much *lightning* in the north-west quarter, but not attended with *thunder ;* and that when this *lightning* appears in the west or south-west points, it is a *sure sign* of the approaching rain, which is *often followed* with thunder. This last clause, which is not perfectly clear, is afterwards explained in his more enlarged account of the weather of the year 1746, when he tells us that though it began to be cloudy on the 4th of September, and continued so for a few days, and *even thundered*, yet no rain fell till the 11th, which shows that his meaning was, that the *lightning* in the west or south-west points, which is often followed with thunder, is a sure sign of the approach of rain. I have before mentioned that a squall of wind and clouds of dust are the usual forerunners of these first rains. Most of these things are taken notice of in Ps. cxxxv. 7 ; Jer. x. 13 ; li. 16 ; and serve to illustrate them. Russell's account determines, I think, that the Nesiim, which our translators render *vapours*, must mean, as they elsewhere translate the word, *clouds*. It shows that God " *maketh lightnings for the rain*," they, in the west and south-west points, being at Aleppo the sure *prognostics* of rain. The squalls of wind bring on these refreshing showers, and are therefore " precious things " of the " treasures " of God.—*Thomas Harmer.*

Verse 7.—" *He maketh lightnings for the rain.*" The Psalmist mentions it as another circumstance calling for our wonder, that *lightnings are mixed with rain*, things quite opposite in their nature one from another. Did not custom make us familiar with the spectacle, we would pronounce this mixture of fire and water to be a phenomenon altogether incredible. The same may be said of the phenomena of the winds. Natural causes can be assigned for them, and philosophers have pointed them out ; but the winds, with their various currents, are a wonderful work of God. He does not merely assert the power of God, be it observed, in the sense in which philosophers themselves grant it, but he maintains that not a drop of rain falls from heaven without a divine commission or dispensation to that effect. All readily allow that God is the author of rain, thunder, and wind, in so far as he originally established this order of things in nature ; but the Psalmist goes farther than this, holding that when it rains, this is not effected by a blind instinct of nature, but is the consequence of the decree of God, who is pleased at one time to darken the sky with clouds, and at another to brighten it again with sunshine.—*John Calvin.*

Verse 7.—" *He maketh lightnings for the rain.*" It is a great instance of the divine wisdom and goodness, that lightning should be accompanied by rain, to soften its rage, and prevent its mischievous effects. Thus, in the midst of judgment, does God remember mercy. The threatenings in his word against sinners are like lightning ; they would blast and scorch us up, were it not for his promises made in the same word to penitents, which, as a gracious rain, turn aside their fury, refreshing and comforting our affrighted spirits.—*George Horne.*

Verse 7.—" *He bringeth the wind out of his treasuries.*" That is, say some, out of the caves and hollow places of the earth ; but I rather conceive that because the wind riseth many times on a sudden, and as our Saviour saith (John iii. 8), ' we cannot tell whence it cometh,' therefore God is said here to bring it forth, as if he had it locked up in readiness in some secret and hidden treasuries or store-houses.—*Arthur Jackson.*

Verse 7.—"*He bringeth the wind.*" The winds are, with great beauty, repre-sented as laid up by him as jewels in a treasure house. Indeed, few verses better express creative control, than those in which the winds, which make sport of man's efforts and defy his power, are represented as thus ready to spring forth at God's bidding from the quarters where they quietly sleep. The occasion comes, the thoughts of Jehovah find expression in his providence, and his ready servants leap suddenly forth : "*He bringeth the winds out of his treasuries.*" But this bringing forth is not for physical purposes only ; it is for great moral and spiritual ends also. Take one illustration out of many. His people were on the edge of deepest and most brutish idolatry. They were ready to fall into a most degraded form of idol worship, when he offered to them that ever yearning heart of Fatherly love :

"Thus saith the Lord, Learn not the way of the heathen." Their god is only " the tree cut out of the forest," silvered over, or decked with gold ; " upright as the palm tree, but speaks not : the stock is a doctrine of vanities ; but the Lord is the true God ; he maketh lightnings with rain ; he bringeth the wind out of his treasuries." Jer. x. 2—16. Thus, too, the words of Agur to Ithiel and Ucal, " He hath gathered the wind in his fists." Prov. xxx. 4.—*John Duns, in " Science and Christian Thought,"* 1868.

Verse 8.—"*Who smote the firstborn of Egypt.*" The first born only were smit-ten ; these were singled out in every family with unerring precision, the houses of the Israelities, wherever the blood of the lamb was sprinkled on the door-posts, being passed over. The death of all those thousands, both of man and beast, took place at the same instant—" at midnight."

Is God unrighteous, then, that taketh vengeance ? No ; this is an act of retri-bution. The Egyptians had slain the children of the Israelites, casting their infants into the river. Now the affliction is turned upon themselves ; the delight of their eyes is taken from them ; all their firstborn are dead, from the firstborn of Pharaoh that sat upon his throne, unto the firstborn of the captive that was in the dungeon.—*Thomas S. Millington, in " Signs and Wonders in the Land of Ham,"* 1873.

Verse 8.—"*And beast.*" The Egyptians worshipped many animals, and when the firstborn of the sacred animals died the circumstance greatly increased the impressiveness of the plague as an assault upon the gods of Egypt.—*C. H. S. Suggested by Otto Von Gerlach.*

Verses 8, 9, 10—12.—Worthy is Jahve to be praised, for he is the Redeemer out of Egypt. Worthy is he to be praised, for he is the Conqueror of the Land of Promise.—*Franz Delitzsch.*

Verse 9.—'*Who sent tokens and wonders.*'—" *Tokens,*" that is, signs or evidences of the Divine power. " *Wonders,*" things fitted to impress the mind with awe ; things outside of the ordinary course of events ; things not produced by natural laws, but by the direct power of God. The allusion here is, of course, to the plagues of Egypt, as recorded in Exodus.—*Albert Barnes.*

Verse 10.—" *Who smote great nations,*" etc. It is better that the wicked should be destroyed a hundred times over than that they should tempt those who are as yet innocent to join their company. Let us but think what might have been our fate, and the fate of every other nation under heaven at this hour, had the sword of the Israelites done its work more sparingly. Even as it was, the small por-tions of the Canaanites who were left, and the nations around them, so tempted the Israelites by their idolatrous practices that we read continually of the whole people of God turning away from his service. But, had the heathen lived in the land in equal numbers, and, still more, had they intermarried largely with the Israelites, how was it possible, humanly speaking, that any sparks of the light of

God's truth should have survived to the coming of Christ? Would not the Israelites have lost all their peculiar character; and if they had retained the name of Jehovah as of their God, would they not have formed as unworthy notions of his attributes, and worshipped him with a worship as abominable as that which the Moabites paid to Chemosh or the Philistines to Dagon?

But this was not to be, and therefore the nations of Canaan were to be cut off utterly. The Israelites' sword, in its bloodiest executions, wrought a work of mercy for all the countries of the earth to the very end of the world. They seem of very small importance to us now, those perpetual contests with the Canaanites, and the Midianites, and the Ammonites, and the Philistines, with which the Books of Joshua and Judges and Samuel are almost filled. We may half wonder that God should have interfered in such quarrels, or have changed the course of nature, in order to give one of the nations of Palestine the victory over another. But in these contests, on the fate of one of these nations of Palestine the happiness of the human race depended. The Israelites fought not for themselves only, but for us. It might follow that they should thus be accounted the enemies of all mankind,—it might be that they were tempted by their very distinctness to despise other nations; still they did God's work,—still they preserved unhurt the seed of eternal life, and were the ministers of blessing to all other nations, even though they themselves failed to enjoy it.—*Thomas Arnold*, 1795—1842.

Verse 10.—"*Who smote great nations,*" etc. Let us not stand in fear of any enemies that rise up against us, and conspire to hinder the peace of the church, and stop the passage of the gospel; when God beginneth to take the cause of his people into his own hand, and smiteth any of his enemies on the jaw-bone, the rest are reserved to the like destruction. For wherefore doth God punish his adversaries, and enter into judgment with them? Wherefore doth he visit them, and strike them down with his right hand? Is it only to take vengeance, and to show his justice in their confusion? No, it serveth for the comfort and consolation of his servants, that howsoever God be patient, yet in the end they shall not escape. —*William Attersoll*, 1618.

Verse 11.—"*Sihon king of the Amorites, and Og.*" Notice is taken of two kings, Sihon and Og, not as being more powerful than the rest, but because shutting up the entrance to the land in front they were the most formidable enemies met with, and the people, besides, were not as yet habituated to war.—*John Calvin.*

Verse 11.—"*Sihon king of the Amorites.*" When Israel arrived on the borders of the Promised Land they encountered Sihon. (Numb. xxi. 21.) He was evidently a man of very great courage and audacity. Shortly before the time of Israel's arrival he had dispossessed the Moabites of a splendid territory, driving them south of the natural bulwark of the Arnon with great slaughter and the loss of a great number of captives (xxi. 26—29). When the Israelite host appears, he does not hesitate or temporize like Balak, but at once gathers his people together and attacks them. But the battle was his last. He and all his host were destroyed, and their district from Arnon to Jabbok became at once the possession of the conqueror.

Josephus (Ant. iv. 5, § 2) has preserved some singular details of the battle, which have not survived in the text either of the Hebrew or LXX. He represents the Amorite army as containing every man in the nation fit to bear arms. He states that they were unable to fight when away from the shelter of their cities, and that being especially galled by the slings and arrows of the Hebrews, and at last suffering severely from thirst, they rushed to the stream and to the recesses of the ravine of the Arnon. Into these recesses they were pursued by their active enemy and slaughtered in vast numbers.

Whether we accept these details or not, it is plain, from the manner in which the name of Sihon fixes itself in the national mind, and the space which his image occupies in the official records, and in the later poetry of Israel, that he was a truly formidable chieftain.—*George Grove, in Smith's Dictionary of the Bible,* 1863.

Verse 11.—*Sihon*, although conqueror of Moab, and much more formidable than the Canaanites whom Israel had feared at Kadesh, fell easily because Israel fought in faith. There is no adversary that can really offer any effectual opposition to our onward march if assailed in the strength of Christ with a cheerful courage.

Og the King of Bashan was much more formidable even than *Sihon*, but he seems to have fallen yet more easily, judging from the brief notice of the conquest. Even so, when once we have overcome a difficulty or conquered an evil habit in the strength of faith, other conquests open out before us readily and naturally which we should not have dared to contemplate before. It is most true in religion that "nothing succeeds like success."—*R. Winterbotham, in " The Pulpit Commentary,"* 1881.

Verse 11.—" *Og king of Bashan.*" The task was not an easy one, for Edrei—" *the strong* "—Og's capital, was in ordinary circumstances almost unassailable, since it was, strange to say, built in a hollow artificially scooped out of the top of a hill, which the deep gorge of the Hieromax isolates from the country round. Its streets may still be seen running in all directions beneath the present town of Adraha. But Kenath, in the district called Argob—" *the stony* "—was still stronger, for it was built in the crevices of a great island of lava which has split, in cooling, into innumerable fissures, through whose labyrinth no enemy could safely penetrate. In these were its streets and houses, some of which, of a later date, with stone doors, turning on hinges of stone, remain till this day. . . . . Nor were these the only fastnesses. No fewer than sixty cities " fenced with high walls, gates, and bars " (Deut. iii. 5), had to be taken ; but they all fell, sooner or later, before the vigorous assaults of the invaders, and, long afterwards, there might be seen, in the capital of their allies, the Ammonites, one of the trophies of the campaign—the gigantic iron bedstead of King Og, or as some think, the huge sarcophagus he had prepared for himself, as was the custom with Canaanite kings. —*Cunningham Geikie, in " Hours with the Bible,"* 1881.

Verse 12.—" *Their land for an heritage.*" The land was given to them to be transmitted from father to son, by hereditary right and succession.—*Joseph Addison Alexander.*

Verse 13.—" *Thy name, O* LORD, *endureth for ever,*" etc. Immutability is a glory belonging to all the attributes of God. It is not a single perfection of the Divine nature, nor is it limited to particular objects thus and thus disposed. Mercy and justice have their distinct objects and distinct acts : mercy is conversant about a penitent, justice about an obstinate sinner. In our conceptions of the Divine perfections, his perfections are different. The wisdom of God is not his power, nor his power his holiness ; but immutability is the centre wherein they all unite. There is not one perfection which may not be said to be, and truly is, immutable ; none of them will appear so glorious without this beam, the sun of immutability, which renders them highly excellent, without the least shadow of imperfection. How cloudy would his blessedness be, if it were changeable ; how dim his wisdom, if it might be obscured ; how feeble his power, if it were capable of becoming sickly and languishing ; how would mercy lose much of its lustre, if it could change into wrath, and justice much of its dread, if it could be turned into mercy ; while the object of justice remains unfit for mercy, and one that hath need of mercy continues only fit for the Divine fury ? But unchangeableness is the thread that runs through the whole web ; it is the enamel of all the rest ; none of them without it could look with a triumphant aspect.—*Stephen Charnock.*

Verse 13.—" *Thy name, O* LORD, *endureth for ever.*" God is, and will be always the same to his church, a gracious, faithful, wonder-working God ; and his church is, and will be the same to him, a thankful, praising people ; and thus his name *endures for ever.*—*Matthew Henry.*

Verse 13.—" *Thy memorial, O* LORD, *throughout all generations ;* " or, *the remembrance of them to generation and generation ;* to every age. The love of

Christ is remembered by his people in every age, as they enjoy the blessings of his grace in redemption, justification, pardon, etc.   It cannot be forgotten as long as the gospel is preached, the ordinances of Baptism and the Lord's Supper administered, and the Lord has a people in the world ; all which will be as long as the sun and moon endure, and there will therefore always be a memorial of him.— *John Gill.*

Verse 14.—" *For the* LORD *will judge his people,*" etc.   Is it so, that all providence is for the good of the church ?   This is comfort in the low estate of the church at any time.   God's eye is upon his people even whilst he seems to have forsaken them.   If he seem to be departed, it is but in some other part of the earth, to show himself strong for them ; wherever his eye is fixed in any part of the world, his church hath his heart, and his church's relief is his end.   Though the church may sometimes lie among the pots in a dirty condition, yet there is a time of resurrection, when God will restore it to its true glory, and make it as white as a dove with its silver wings : Ps. lxviii. 13.   The sun is not always obscured by a thick cloud, but it will be freed from the darkness of it.   " *God will judge his people, and he will repent himself concerning his servants* " [the original is, *Comfort himself*].   It is a comfort to God to deliver his people, and he will do it when it shall be most comfortable to his glory and to their hearts.—*Stephen Charnock.*

Verse 14.—" *He will repent himself.*"   The original word " *repent himself* " here has a very extensive signification, which cannot be expressed by any one English rendering.   It implies taking compassion upon them, with the intention of being comforted in their future, and of taking vengeance on their oppressors.   Such are the several meanings in which the word is used.   Language fails to express the mind of God toward his faithful people.   How dear ought his counsels to be to us, and the consideration of all his ways !   This reflection was continually urged upon the nation of Israel, so liable as they were to fall away to idolatry.— *W. Wilson.*

Verse 15.—" *The idols of the heathen.*"   The shrines on the hill-tops were very rude affairs, enclosures formed by rough stone walls, and containing ragamuffin gods—stocks of weather-beaten wood, blocks of battered stone, and lumps of rusty old iron.   The carved wooden gods were so much the worse for the weather, that their features, if they ever had any, were altogether defaced.   One, not made of a single piece, like the rest, but built together by joiner work, had fared worse than its more humble neighbours.   His arms were gone, and his breast, heart, and stomach had all fallen out ; strange to say, his head remained, and it was laughable to see such a hollow mockery stare at you with a solemn face.   The stone images were sadly battered by tumbling about among the rubbish, and the cast-metal gods mostly had their heads broken off and set carefully on again, to stand there till the next storm would send them rolling.   Thus God is not only robbed in the valley, but men climb up as near to heaven as they can, and insult him to his face.—*James Gilmour, in* " *Among the Mongols,*" 1883.

Verse 15.—" *The idols,*" etc.   Herodotus telleth us that Amasis had a large laver of gold, wherein both he and his guests used to wash their feet.   This vessel he brake and made a god of it, which the Egyptians devoutly worshipped.   And the like idolomania is at this day found among Papists, what distinction soever they would fain make betwixt an *idol* and an *image*, which indeed (as they use them) are all one.—*John Trapp.*

Verse 15.—" *Silver and gold.*"   By singling out these metals, the most precious materials of which the idols were framed, and pouring contempt upon even these costly images, the psalmist heightens the scorn which he implies for such as were of inferior price, and which had not the one element of costliness in their favour.   And when we bear in mind the Apostle's saying that covetousness is idolatry, we shall be warned that we, too, may need this lesson against worshipping silver and gold, or the worldly wisdom and specious eloquence which may be compared to these metals.—*Neale and Littledale.*

Verse 15.—" *The work of men's hands.*" Therefore they should rather, if it were possible, worship man, as their creator and lord, than be worshipped by him.—*Matthew Pool,* 1624—1679.

Verses 15, 16, 17.—The Rev. John Thomas, a missionary in India, was one day travelling alone through the country, when he saw a great number of people waiting near an idol temple. He went up to them, and as soon as the doors were opened, he walked into the temple. Seeing an idol raised above the people, he walked boldly up to it, held up his hand, and asked for silence. He then put his fingers on its eyes, and said, "It has eyes, but it cannot see ! It has ears, but it cannot hear ! It has a nose, but it cannot smell ! It has hands, but it cannot handle ! It has a mouth, but it cannot speak ! Neither is there any breath in it !" Instead of doing injury to him for affronting their god and themselves, the natives were all surprised ; and an old Brahmin was so convinced of his folly by what Mr. Thomas said, that he also cried out, "It has feet, but cannot run away !" The people raised a shout, and being ashamed of their stupidity, they left the temple, and went to their homes.—*From* " *The New Cyclopædia of Illustrative Anecdote,*" 1875.

Verses 16, 17.—" *Mouths,*" " *eyes,*" " *ears.*" So many members as the images have, serving to represent perfections ascribed to them, so many are the lies.—*David Dickson.*

Verses 16—17.—They can neither *speak* in answer to your prayers and inquiries, nor *see* what you do or what you want, nor *hear* your petitions, nor *smell* your incenses and sacrifices, nor use their *hands* either to take anything from you, or to give anything to you ; nor so much as *mutter*, nor give the least sign of apprehending your condition or concerns.—*Matthew Pool.*

Verses 16—17.—" *Mouths, but they speak not :* " " *ears, but they hear not.*"

> A heated fancy or imagination
> May be mistaken for an inspiration.
> True ; but is this conclusion fair to make—
> That inspiration must be all mistake ?
> A pebble-stone is not a diamond : true ;
> But must a diamond be a pebble too ?
> *To own a God who does not speak to men,*
> *Is first to own, and then disown again ;*
> *Of all idolatry the total sum*
> *Is having gods that are both deaf and dumb.*
>
> John Byrom, 1691—1763.

Verse 18.—" *Like them shall be those making them, every one who (is) trusting in them.*" If the meaning had been simply, those who make them *are* like them, Hebrew usage would have required the verb to be suppressed. Its insertion, therefore, in the future form (יִהְיוּ) requires it to be rendered strictly *shall be*, i.e., in fate as well as character. Idolaters shall perish with their perishable idols. See Isai. i. 31.—*Joseph Addison Alexander.*

Verse 18.—People never rise above the level of their gods, which are to them their better nature.—*Andrew Robert Faussett.*

Verse 18.—" *They that make them are like unto them.*" Idolatry is a benumbing sin, which bereaveth the idolater of the right use of his senses.—*David Dickson.*

Verse 18.—" *They that make them,*" etc. Teacheth us, that the idol, the idol-maker, and all such also as serve idols, are not only beastly and blockish before men, but shall before God, in good time, come to shame and confusion.—*Thomas Wilcocks,* 1549—1608.

Verses 18. —" *Like unto them.*" A singular phenomenon, known as the Spectre of the Brocken, is seen on a certain mountain in Germany. The traveller who at dawn stands on the topmost ridge beholds a colossal shadowy spectre. But in fact it is only his own shadow projected upon the morning mists by the rising sun ; and it imitates, of course, every movement of its creator. So heathen nations have mistaken their own image for Deity. Their gods display human frailties and passions and scanty virtues, projected and magnified upon the heavens, just as the small figures on the slide of a magic-lantern are projected, magnified, and illuminated upon a white sheet.—*From Elan Foster's New Cyclopædia of Illustrations*, 1870.

Verse 18. — "*Like unto them.*" How many are like idol-images, when they have eyes, ears, and mouths as though they had none : that is, when they do not use them when and how they should !—*Christoph Starke.*

Verse 19. – "*Bless the* LORD." Blessing of God is to wish well to, and speak well of God, out of good-will to God himself, and a sense of his goodness to ourselves. God loves your good word, that is, to be spoken of well by you ; he rejoiceth in your well-wishes, and to hear from you expressions of rejoicings in his own independent blessedness. Though God hath an infinite ocean of all blessedness, to which we can add nothing, and he is therefore called by way of eminency, "The Blessed One" (Mark xiv. 61), a title solely proper and peculiar to him, yet he delights to hear the *amen* of the saints, his creatures, resounding thereto ; he delights to hear us utter our "so be it."—*Thomas Goodwin.*

Verse 19.—"*Bless the* LORD." And not an idol (Isai. lxvi. 3), as the Philistines did their Dagon, and as Papists still do their he-saints and she-saints. —*John Trapp.*

Verse 20.—"*Bless the* LORD, *O house of Levi.*" In Ps. cxv. the exhortation given is to *trust* or *hope* in the Lord ; here, to *bless* him. The *Levites* are mentioned in addition to the house of Aaron, there being two orders of priesthood. Everything else in the two psalms is the same, except that, in the last verse, the psalmist here joins himself, along with the rest of the Lord's people, in blessing God.—*Franz Delitzsch.*

Verse 20.—"*Ye that fear the* LORD, *bless the* LORD." These are distinct from the Israelites, priests, and Levites, and design the proselytes among them of other nations that truly feared God, as Jarchi notes ; and all such persons, whoever and wherever they are, have reason to bless the Lord for the fear of him they have, which is not from nature but from grace ; and for the favours shown them, the blessings bestowed upon them, the good things laid up for them, and the guard that is about them, which the Scriptures abundantly declare, and experience confirms.—*John Gill.*

Verse 20.—"*Ye that fear the* LORD, *bless the* LORD." In Scripture it is quite common to find this "*fear*" put for holiness itself, or the sum of true religion. It is not, therefore, such a fear as seized the hearts of our first parents when, hearing the voice of the Lord God, they hid themselves amongst the trees of the garden ; nor such as suddenly quenched the noise of royal revelry in the night of Babylon's overthrow ; nor such as, on some day yet future, shall drive despairing sinners to the unavailing shelter of the mountains and rocks. It is not the fear of guilty distrust, or of hatred, or of bondage—that fear which hath torment, and which perfect love casteth out ; but a fear compatible with the highest privileges, attainments, and hopes of the Christian life. It is the fear of deep humility and reverence, of filial subjection, and adoring gratitude ; the fear which "blesseth the Lord," saying, "*His mercy endureth for ever.*"— *John Lillie* (1812—1867), *in* "*Lectures on the Epistles of Peter.*"

Verse 21.—The conclusion, verse 21, alludes to the conclusion of the preceding psalm. There, the Lord blesses thee out of Zion ; here, let him be blessed out of Zion. The praise proceeds from the same place from which the blessing issues. For Zion is the place where the community dwells with God.—*E. W. Hengstenberg.*

Verse 21.—"*Praise ye the* LORD." When the song of praise is sung unto God, the work of his praise is not ended, but must be continued, renewed, and followed still : "*Praise ye the* LORD."—*David Dickson.*

Verse 21.—"*Bless,*" "*Praise.*" We are not only to bless God, but to praise him : "All thy works shall praise thee, O LORD ; and thy saints shall bless thee."

Blessing relateth to his benefits, praise to his excellencies. We bless him for what he is to us, we praise him for what he is in himself. Now, whether we bless him, or praise him ; it is still to increase our love to him, and delight in him ; for God is not affected with the flattery of empty praises ; yet this is an especial duty, which is of use to you, as all other duties are. It doth you good to consider him as an infinite and eternal Being, and of glorious and incomprehensible majesty. It is pleasant and profitable to us.—*Thomas Manton.*

HINTS TO THE VILLAGE PREACHER.

Verses 1—4.—I. The Employment. Praise three times commended, and in three respects. 1. With respect to God : not his works merely, but himself. 2. With respect to ourselves : it is pleasant and profitable. 3. With respect to others : it best recommends our religion to all who hear it. All others are religions of fear, ours of joy and praise. II. The Persons : servants in attendance at his house, who stand there by appointment, ready to hear, ready to obey. III. The Motives. 1. In general. It is due to God, because he is good ; and it is pleasant to us : verse 3. 2. In particular. Those who are specially privileged by God should specially praise him : verse 4. " This people have I formed for myself ; they shall show forth my praise."—*G. R.*

Verse 1.—*"Praise ye the* Lord." I. The Lord ought to be praised. II. He ought to be praised *by you.* III. He ought to be praised *now :* let us remember his present favours. IV. He ought to be praised in everything for ever.

Verse 1.—*"Praise him, O ye servants of the* Lord." I. Praise him for the privilege of serving him. II. Praise him for the power to serve him. III. Praise him for the acceptance of your service. IV. Praise him as the chief part of your service. V. Praise him that others may be induced to engage in his service.— *W. H. J. P.*

Verse 2.—What is at this day " the house of the Lord " ? Who may be said to stand in it ? What special reasons have they for praise ?

Verse 2.—The nearer to God, the dearer to God ; and the better our place, the sweeter our praise.— *W. B. H.*

Verses 2—5.—*"Our* God," *"Our* Lord." Sweet subject. See our Exposition.

Verse 3.—Praise the Lord, I. For the excellence of his nature. II. For the revelation of his name. III. For the pleasantness of his worship.

Verse 4.—It is a song of praise, and therefore election is mentioned because it is a motive for song. I. *The Choice*—" The Lord hath chosen." Divine. Sovereign. Gracious. Immutable. II. *The Consecration*—" Chosen Jacob to himself." To know him. To preserve his truth. To maintain his worship. To manifest his grace. To keep alive the hope of the Coming One. III. *The Separation*—implied in the special choice. By being taken into covenant : Abraham and his seed. By receiving the covenant inheritance : Canaan. By redemption. By power and by blood out of Egypt. Wilderness separation. Settled establishment in their own land. IV. *The Elevation.* In name—from Jacob to Israel. In value—from worthless to precious. In purpose and use—crown jewels. In preservation—kept as treasures. In delight—God rejoices in his people as his heritage.

Verse 5.—*"I know that the* Lord *is great."* I. By observing nature and providence. II. By reading his word. III. By my own conversion, comfort, and regeneration. IV. By my after-experience. V. By my overpowering communion with him.

Verse 5.—Delicious dogmatism. *"I know,"* etc. I. What I know. 1. The Lord. 2. That he is great. 3. That he is above all. II. Why I know it. 1. Because he is " our Lord." 2. By his operations in nature, providence, and grace (vers. 6—13). III. My incorrigible obstinacy in this regard is proof against worshippers of all other gods : which gods are effeminate ; without sovereignty ; no god, or any god.— *W. B. H.*

Verse 6.—"*Whatsoever the* LORD *pleased, that did he.*" *God's good pleasure in the work of grace.* Seen, *not* in the death of the wicked, Ezek. xxxiii. 11 ; but in the election of his people, 1 Sam. xii. 22 ; in the infliction of suffering on the substitute, Isa. liii. 10 ; in the provision of all fulness for his people in Christ, Col. i. 19 ; in the arrangement of salvation by faith in Christ, John vi. 39 ; in instituting preaching as the means of salvation, 1 Cor. i. 21 ; in the adoption of believers as his children, Eph. i. 5 ; in their sanctification, 1 Thess. iv. 3 ; in their ultimate triumph and reign, Luke xii. 32.— *C. A. D.*

Verse 6·(*last words*).—The power of God in places of trouble, change, and danger—*seas ;* and in conditions of sin, weakness, despair, perplexity—in all *deep places.*

Verses 6—12.—The Resistless Pleasure of Jehovah.   I. Behold it as here exemplified : 1. Ruling all nature.   2. Overturning a rebellious nation.   3. Making sport of kings and crowns.   4. Laying a fertile country at the feet of the chosen. II. Be wise in view thereof.   1. Submit to it : it sweeps the seas, and lays hands on earth and heaven.   2. Think not to hide from it : the " ends of the earth" and " all deep places" are open to it ; it is swifter than its own lightnings.   3. Be awed by its majesty : God's way is strewn with crowns and the bones of kings.   4. Seek its protection : its mightiest efforts are in defence of those it favours.   5. Let the Lord's people fear not with so great a God, and so exhaustless an armoury.— *W. B. H.*

Verse 13.—"*Thy name, O* LORD, *endureth for ever.*"   I. As *the embodiment of perfection :* God's attributes and glory.   II. As *the object of veneration :* " Holy and reverent is his name."   III. As *the cause of salvation :* " For my name's sake," etc.   IV. As *the centre of attraction :* " In his name shall the Gentiles trust."   " Our desire is to the remembrance of thy name."   " Where two or three are gathered in my name," etc.   V. As *a plea in supplication :* " For thy name's sake, pardon," etc.   " Hitherto ye have asked nothing in my name." VI. As *a warrant for action :* " Whatsoever ye do, do all in the name," etc.   VII. As *a refuge in tribulation :* " The name of the Lord is a strong tower : the righteous runneth into it, and is safe."   " I have kept them in thy name."   VIII. As *a mark of glorification :* " I will write upon him the name of my God."   IX. As *a terror to transgressors :* " My name is dreadful among the heathen."— *W. J.*

Verse 14.—"*The* LORD *will judge his people.*"   Others would like to do it, but must not.   The world has seven judgment-days in every week, but shall not be able to condemn the saints.   He himself will judge.   How will he judge them ? 1. Their persons, as to whether they are in or out of Christ.   2. Their principles, as to whether they are genuine or spurious.   3. Their prayers, as to whether they are availing or useless.   4. Their profession, as to whether it is true or false. 5. Their procedure, as to whether it is good or bad.— *W. J.*

Verse 14.—I. The position of believers—" his people," " his servants."   II. The discipline of God's family.   III. The tenderness of the Lord to them.   IV. The safety of believers : they are still the Lord's.

Verse 15.—"*Silver and gold.*"   These are idols in our own land, among worldlings, and with some professors.   Show the folly and wickedness of loving riches, and the evils which come of it.

Verses 16, 17.—The Portrait of many,   I. "*Mouths, but they speak not.*"   No prayer, praise, confession.   II. "*Eyes, but they see not.*"   Discern not, understand not, take no warning ; do not look to Christ.   III. "*Ears, but they hear not.*" Attend no ministry, or are present but unaffected ; hear not God.   IV. "*Neither is there any breath in their mouths.*"   No life, no tokens of life, no prayer and praise which are the breath of spiritual life.

Verse 18.—I. Men make idols like themselves.   II. The idols make their makers like themselves.   Describe both processes.

Verse 19.—"*House of Israel.*"   The Lord's great goodness to all his people, perceived and proclaimed, and the Lord praised for it.

Verse 19.—"*House of Aaron.*"   God's blessing on Aaron's house typical of his grace to those who are priests unto God.

Verses 19—21.—I. The Exhortation.   1. To bless the Lord.   2. To bless him in his own house.   II. To whom it is addressed.   1. To the house of Israel, or the whole church.   2. To the house of Aaron, or ministers of the sanctuary.   3. To the house of Levi, or the attendants upon ministers, and assistants in the services.   4. To all who fear God, wherever they may be.   Even they who fear God are invited to praise him, which is a sure sign that he delighteth in mercy.—*G. R.*

Verse 20.—The Levites, their history, duties, rewards, and obligations to bless God.

Verse 20 (second clause).—I. The fear of God includes all religion.   II. The fear of the Lord suggests praise.   III. The fear of the Lord renders praise acceptable.

Verse 21.—1. The double fact.   1. Blessing perpetually ascending from Zion to God.   2. God perpetually blessing his people by dwelling with them in Zion.   II. The double reason for praise, which is found in the double fact, and concerns overy member of the church.

PSALM CXXXVI.

We know not by whom this psalm was written, but we do know that it was sung in Solomon's temple (2 Chron. vii. 3, 6), and by the armies of Jehoshaphat when they sang themselves into victory in the wilderness of Tekoa. From the striking form of it we should infer that it was a popular hymn among the Lord's ancient people. Most hymns with a solid, simple chorus become favourites with congregations, and this is sure to have been one of the best beloved. It contains nothing but praise. It is tuned to rapture, and can only be fully enjoyed by a devoutly grateful heart.

It commences with a three-fold praise to the Triune Lord (1—3), then it gives us six notes of praise to the Creator (4—9), six more upon deliverance from Egypt (10—15), and seven upon the journey through the wilderness and the entrance into Canaan. Then we have two happy verses of personal gratitude for present mercy (23 and 24), one (verse 25) to tell of the Lord's universal providence, and a closing verse to excite to never-ending praise.

EXPOSITION.

O GIVE thanks unto the LORD ; for *he is* good : for his mercy *endureth* for ever.

2 O give thanks unto the God of gods : for his mercy *endureth* for ever.

3 O give thanks to the Lord of lords : for his mercy *endureth* for ever.

1. "*O give thanks unto the* LORD." The exhortation is intensely earnest : the Psalmist pleads with the Lord's people with an " O," three times repeated. Thanks are the least that we can offer, and these we ought freely to give. The inspired writer calls us to praise Jehovah for all his goodness to us, and all the greatness of his power in blessing his chosen. We thank our parents, let us praise our heavenly Father ; we are grateful to our benefactors, let us give thanks unto the Giver of all good. "*For he is good.*" Essentially he is goodness itself, practically all that he does is good, relatively he is good to his creatures. Let us thank him that we have seen, proved, and tasted that he is good. He is good beyond all others : indeed, he alone is good in the highest sense ; he is the source of good, the good of all good, the sustainer of good, the perfecter of good, and the rewarder of good. For this he deserves the constant gratitude of his people. "*For his mercy endureth for ever.*" We shall have this repeated in every verse of this song, but not once too often. It is the sweetest stanza that a man can sing. What joy that there is mercy, mercy with Jehovah, enduring mercy, mercy enduring for ever. We are ever needing it, trying it, praying for it, receiving it : therefore let us for ever sing of it.

> " When all else is changing within and around,
> In God and his mercy no change can be found."

2. "*O give thanks unto the God of gods.*" If there be powers in heaven or on earth worthy of the name of gods he is the God of them ; from him their dominion comes, their authority is derived from him, and their very existence is dependent upon his will. Moreover, for the moment assuming that the deities of the heathen were gods, yet none of them could be compared with our Elohim, who is infinitely beyond what they are fabled to be. Jehovah is our God, to be worshipped and adored, and he is worthy of our reverence to the highest degree. If the heathen cultivate the worship of their gods with zeal, how much more intently should we seek the glory of the God of gods—the only true and real God. Foolish persons have gathered from this verse that the Israelites believed in the exist-

ence of many gods, at the same time believing that their Jehovah was the chief among them ; but this is an absurd inference, since gods who have a God over them cannot possibly be gods themselves.   The words are to be understood after the usual manner of human speech, in which things are often spoken of not as they really are, but as they profess to be.   God as God is worthy of our warmest thanks, "*for his mercy endureth for ever.*"   Imagine supreme Godhead without everlasting mercy !   It would then have been as fruitful a source of terror as it is now a fountain of thanksgiving.   Let the Highest be praised in the highest style, for right well do his nature and his acts deserve the gratitude of all his creatures.

> Praise your God with right good will,
> For his love endureth still.

3. "*O give thanks to the Lord of lords.*"   There are lords many, but Jehovah is the Lord of them.   All lordship is vested in the Eternal.   He makes and administers law, he rules and governs mind and matter, he possesses in himself all sovereignty and power.   All lords in the plural are summed up in this Lord in the singular ; he is more lordly than all emperors and kings condensed into one.   For this we may well be thankful, for we know the superior Sovereign will rectify the abuses of the underlings who now lord it over mankind.   He will call these lords to his bar, and reckon with them for every oppression and injustice.   He is as truly the Lord of lords as he is Lord over the meanest of the land, and he rules with a strict impartiality, for which every just man should give heartiest thanks. "*For his mercy endureth for ever.*"   Yes, he mingles mercy with his justice, and reigns for the benefit of his subjects.   He pities the sorrowful, protects the helpless, provides for the needy, and pardons the guilty ; and this he does from generation to generation, never wearying of his grace, " because he delighteth in mercy."   Let us arouse ourselves to laud our glorious Lord !   A third time let us thank him who is our Jehovah, our God, and our Lord ; and let this one reason suffice us for three thanksgivings, or for three thousand—

> " For his mercy shall endure,
> Ever faithful, ever sure."

4 To him who alone doeth great wonders ; for his mercy *endureth* for ever.

5 To him that by wisdom made the heavens : for his mercy *endureth* for ever.

6 To him that stretched out the earth above the waters : for his mercy *endureth* for ever.

7 To him that made great lights : for his mercy *endureth* for ever :

8 The sun to rule by day : for his mercy *endureth* for ever :

9 The moon and stars to rule by night : for his mercy *endureth* for ever.

4. "*To him who alone doeth great wonders.*"   Jehovah is the great Thaumaturge, the unrivalled Wonderworker.   None can be likened unto him, he is alone in wonder-land, the Creator and Worker of true marvels, compared with which all other remarkable things are as child's play.   His works are all great in wonder even when they are not great in size ; in fact, in the minute objects of the microscope we behold as great wonders as even the telescope can reveal.   All the works of his unrivalled skill are wrought by him alone and unaided, and to him, therefore, must be undivided honour.   None of the gods or the lords helped Jehovah in creation, or in the redemption of his people : his own right hand and his holy arm have wrought for him these great deeds.   What have the gods of the heathen done ?   If the question be settled by doings, Jehovah is indeed " alone."   It is exceedingly wonderful that men should worship gods who can do nothing, and forget the Lord who alone doeth great wonders.   Even when the

Lord uses men as his instruments, yet the wonder of the work is his alone ; therefore let us not trust in men, or idolize them, or tremble before them.   Praise is to be rendered to Jehovah, "*for his mercy endureth for ever.*"   The mercy of the wonder is the wonder of the mercy ; and the enduring nature of that mercy is the central wonder of that wonder.   The Lord causes us often to sit down in amazement as we see what his mercy has wrought out and prepared for us : " wonders of grace to God belong," yea, great wonders and unsearchable.   Oh the depth !   Glory be to his name world without end !

> Doing wondrous deeds alone,
> Mercy sits upon his throne.

5. "*To him that by wisdom made the heavens.*"   His goodness appears in creating the upper regions.   He set his wisdom to the task of fashioning a firmament, or an atmosphere suitable for a world upon which mortal men should dwell.   What a mass of wisdom lies hidden in this one creating act !   The discoveries of our keenest observers have never searched out all the evidences of design which are crowded together in this work of God's hands.   The lives of plants, animals, and men are dependent upon the fashioning of our heavens : had the skies been other than they are we had not been here to praise God.   Divine foresight planned the air and the clouds, with a view to the human race.   "*For his mercy endureth for ever.*"   The Psalmist's details of mercy begin in the loftiest regions, and gradually descend from the heavens to " our low estate" (verse twenty-three) ; and this is an ascent, for mercy becomes greater as its objects become less worthy. Mercy is far-reaching, long-enduring, all-encompassing.   Nothing is too high for its reach, as nothing is beneath its stoop.

> High as heaven his wisdom reigns,
> Mercy on the throne remains.

6. "*To him that stretched out the earth above the waters.*"   Lifting it up from the mingled mass, the dank morass, the bottomless bog, of mixed land and sea ; and so fitting it to be the abode of man.   Who but the Lord could have wrought this marvel ?   Few even think of the divine wisdom and power which performed all this of old ; yet, if a continent can be proved to have risen or fallen an inch within historic memory, the fact is recorded in the "transactions" of learned societies, and discussed at every gathering of philosophers.   "*For his mercy endureth for ever,*" as is seen in the original upheaval and perpetual upstanding of the habitable land, so that no deluge drowns the race.   By his strength he sets fast the mountains and consolidates the land upon which we sojourn.

> From the flood he lifts the land :
> Firm his mercies ever stand.

7. "*To him that made great lights.*"   This also is a creating miracle worthy of our loudest thanks.   What could men have done without light ?   Though they had the heavens above them, and dry land to move upon, yet what could they see, and where could they go without light ?   Thanks be to the Lord, who has not consigned us to darkness.   In great mercy he has not left us to an uncertain, indistinct light, floating about fitfully, and without order ; but he has concentrated light upon two grand luminaries, which, as far as we are concerned, are to us " great lights."   The Psalmist is making a song for common people, not for your critical savans,—and so he sings of the sun and moon as they appear to us, —the greatest of lights.   These the Lord created in the beginning ; and for the present age of man made or constituted them light-bearers for the world.   "*For his mercy endureth for ever.*"   Mercy gleams in every ray of light, and it is most clearly seen in the arrangement by which it is distributed with order and regularity from the sun and moon.

> Lamps he lit in heaven's heights,
> For in mercy he delights.

8. "*The sun to rule by day.*"   We cannot be too specific in our praises ; after mentioning great lights, we may sing of each of them, and yet not outwear our

theme. The influences of the sun are too many for us to enumerate them all, but untold benefits come to all orders of beings by its light, warmth, and other operations. Whenever we sit in the sunshine, our gratitude should be kindled. The sun is a great ruler, and his government is pure beneficence, because by God's mercy it is moderated to our feebleness ; let all who rule take lessons from the sun which rules to bless. By day we may well give thanks, for God gives cheer. The sun rules because God rules ; it is not the sun which we should worship, like the Parsees ; but the Creator of the sun, as he did who wrote this sacred song. *"For his mercy endureth for ever."* Day unto day uttereth speech concerning the mercy of the Lord ; every sunbeam is a mercy, for it falls on undeserving sinners who else would sit in doleful darkness, and find earth a hell. Milton puts it well :

> " He, the golden tressèd sun
> Caused all day his course to run ;
> For his mercy shall endure
> Ever faithful, ever sure."

9. *"The moon and stars to rule by night."* No hour is left without rule. Blessed be God, he leaves us never to the doom of anarchy. The rule is one of light and benediction. The moon with her charming changes, and the stars in their fixed spheres gladden the night. When the season would be dark and dreary because of the absence of the sun, forth come the many minor comforters. The sun is enough alone ; but when he is gone a numerous band cannot suffice to give more than a humble imitation of his radiance. Jesus, the Sun of Righteousness, alone, can do more for us than all his servants put together. He makes our day. When he is hidden, it is night, and remains night, let our human comforters shine at their full. What mercy is seen in the lamps of heaven gladdening our landscape at night ! What equal mercy in all the influences of the moon upon the tides, those life-floods of the earth ! The Lord is the Maker of every star, be the stars what they may ; he calleth them all by their names, and at his bidding each messenger with his torch enlightens our darkness. *" For his mercy endureth for ever."* Let our thanks be as many as the stars, and let our lives reflect the goodness of the Lord, even as the moon reflects the light of the sun. The nightly guides and illuminators of men on land and sea are not for now and then, but for all time.

They shone on Adam, and they shine on us. Thus they are tokens and pledges of undying grace to men ; and we may sing with our Scotch friends—

> "For certainly
> His mercies dure
> Most firm and sure
> Eternally."

10 To him that smote Egypt in their firstborn : for his mercy *endureth* for ever :

11 And brought out Israel from among them : for his mercy *endureth* for ever :

12 With a ·strong hand, and with a stretched out arm : for his mercy *endureth* for ever.

13 To him which divided the Red sea into parts : for his mercy *endureth* for ever :

14 And made Israel to pass through the midst of it : for his mercy *endureth* for ever :

15. But overthrew Pharaoh and his host in the Red sea : for his mercy *endureth* for ever.

10. We have heard of the glory of the world's creation, we are now to praise the Lord for the creation of his favoured nation by their Exodus from Egypt. Because the monarch of Egypt stood in the way of the Lord's gracious purposes it became needful for the Lord to deal with him in justice ; but the great design

was mercy to Israel, and through Israel mercy to succeeding ages, and to all the world. "*To him that smote Egypt in their firstborn.*" The last and greatest of the plagues struck all Egypt to the heart. The sorrow and the terror which it caused throughout the nation it is hardly possible to exaggerate. From king to slave each one was wounded in the tenderest point. The joy and hope of every household was struck down in one moment, and each family had its own wailing. The former blows had missed their aim compared with the last; but that "smote Egypt." The Lord's firstborn had been oppressed by Egypt, and at last the Lord fulfilled his threatening, "I will slay thy son, even thy firstborn." Justice lingered but it struck home at last. "*For his mercy endureth for ever.*" Yes, even to the extremity of vengeance upon a whole nation the Lord's mercy to his people endured. He is slow to anger, and judgment is his strange work; but when mercy to men demands severe punishments he will not hold back his hand from the needful surgery. What were all the firstborn of Egypt compared with those divine purposes of mercy to all generations of men which were wrapt up in the deliverance of the elect people? Let us even when the Lord's judgments are abroad in the earth continue to sing of his unfailing grace.

> "For evermore his love shall last,
> For ever sure, for ever fast."

11. "*And brought out Israel from among them.*" Scattered as the tribes were up and down the country, and apparently held in a grasp which would never be relaxed, the Lord wrought their deliverance, and severed them from their idolatrous task-masters. None of them remained in bondage. The Lord brought them out; brought them all out; brought them out at the very hour when his promise was due; brought them out despite their being mingled among the Egyptians; brought them out never to return. Unto his name let us give thanks for this further proof of his favour to the chosen ones, "*For his mercy endureth for ever.*" Once the Israelites did not care to go out, but preferred to bear the ills they had rather than risk they knew not what; but the Lord's mercy endured that test also, and ceased not to stir up the nest till the birds were glad to take to their wings. He turned the land of plenty into a house of bondage, and the persecuted nation was glad to escape from slavery. The unfailing mercy of the Lord is gloriously seen in his separating his elect from the world. He brings out his redeemed, and they are henceforth a people who show forth his praise.

> "For God doth prove
> Our constant friend;
> His boundless love
> Shall never end."

12. "*With a strong hand, and with a stretched out arm.*" Not only the matter but the manner of the Lord's mighty acts should be the cause of our praise. We ought to bless the Lord for adverbs as well as adjectives. In the Exodus the great power and glory of Jehovah were seen. He dashed in pieces the enemy with his right hand. He led forth his people in no mean or clandestine manner. "He brought them forth also with silver and gold, and there was not one feeble person in all their tribes." Egypt was glad when they departed. God worked with great display of force, and with exceeding majesty; he stretched out his arm like a workman intent on his labour, he lifted up his hand as one who is not ashamed to be seen. Even thus was it in the deliverance of each one of us from the thraldom of sin; "according to the working of his mighty power which he wrought in Christ when he raised him from the dead and set him at his own right hand in the heavenly places." "*For his mercy endureth for ever*"—therefore his power is put forth for the rescue of his own. If one plague will not set them free there shall be ten; but free they shall all be at the appointed hour; not one Israelite shall remain under Pharaoh's power. God will not only use his hand but his arm—his extraordinary power shall be put to the work sooner than his purpose of mercy shall fail.

> See, he lifts his strong right hand,
> For his mercies steadfast stand.

13. "*To him which divided the Red sea into parts.*" He made a road across the sea-bottom, causing the divided waters to stand like walls on either side. Men deny miracles ; but, granted that there is a God, they become easy of belief. Since it requires me to be an atheist that I may logically reject miracles, I prefer the far smaller difficulty of believing in the infinite power of God. He who causes the waters of the sea ordinarily to remain as one mass can with equal readiness divide them. He who can throw a stone in one direction can with the same force throw it another way ; the Lord can do precisely what he wills, and he wills to do anything which is for the deliverance of his people. "*For his mercy endureth for ever,*" and therefore it endures through the sea as well as over the dry land. He will do a new thing to keep his old promise. His way is in the sea, and he will make a way for his people in the same pathless region.

> Lo, the Red Sea he divides,
> For his mercy sure abides.

14. "*And made Israel to pass through the midst of it.*" He gave the people courage to follow the predestined track through the yawning abyss, which might well have terrified a veteran host. It needed no little generalship to conduct so vast and motley a company along a way so novel and apparently so dangerous. He made them to pass, by the untrodden road ; he led them down into the deep and up again on the further shore in perfect order, keeping their enemies back by the thick darkness of the cloudy pillar. Herein is the glory of God set forth, as all his people see it in their own deliverance from sin. By faith we also give up all reliance upon works and trust ourselves to pass by a way which we have not known, even by the way of reliance upon the atoning blood : thus are we effectually sundered from the Egypt of our former estate, and our sins themselves are drowned. The people marched dry shod through the heart of the sea. Hallelujah ! "*For his mercy endureth for ever.*" Mercy cleared the road, mercy cheered the host, mercy led them down, and mercy brought them up again. Even to the depth of the sea mercy reaches,—there is no end to it, no obstacle in the way of it, no danger to believers in it, while Jehovah is all around. "Forward !" be *our* watchword as it was that of Israel of old, for mercy doth compass us about.

> Through the fire or through the sea
> Still his mercy guardeth thee.

15. "*But overthrew Pharaoh and his host in the Red sea.*" Here comes the thunder-clap. Though we hear them sounding peal upon peal, yet the judgments of the Lord were only loud-mouthed mercies speaking confusion to the foe, that the chosen might tremble before him no longer. The chariots were thrown over, the horses were overthrown. The King and his warriors were alike overwhelmed ; they were hurled from their chariots as locusts are tossed to and fro in the wind. Broken was the power and conquered was the pride of Egypt. Jehovah had vanquished the enemy. "Art thou not it which cut Rahab and wounded the crocodile ?" None are too great for the Lord to subdue, none too high for the Lord to abase. The enemy in his fury drove after Israel into the sea, but there his wrath found a terrible recompense beneath the waves. "*For his mercy endureth for ever.*" Yes, mercy continued to protect its children, and therefore called in the aid of justice to fulfil the capital sentence on their foes. Taken red-handed, in the very act of rebellion against their sovereign Lord, the audacious adversaries met the fate which they had themselves invited. He that goes down into the midst of the sea asks to be drowned. Sin is self-damnation. The sinner goes downward of his own choice, and if he finds out too late that he cannot return, is not his blood upon his own head ? The finally impenitent, however terrible their doom, will not be witnesses against mercy ; but rather this shall aggravate their misery, that they went on in defiance of mercy, and would not yield themselves to him whose mercy endureth for ever. To the Israelites as they sung this song their one thought would be of the rescue of their fathers from the fierce oppressor. Taken like a lamb from between the teeth of the lion, Israel justly praises her Deliverer and chants aloud :

> Evermore his love shall reign ;
> Pharaoh and his host are slain.

16 To him which led his people through the wilderness : for his mercy *endureth* for ever.

17 To him which smote great kings : for his mercy *endureth* for ever :

18 And slew famous kings : for his mercy *endureth* for ever :

19 Sihon king of the Amorites : for his mercy *endureth* for ever :

20 And Og the king of Bashan : for his mercy *endureth* for ever :

21 And gave their land for an heritage : for his mercy *endureth* for ever.

22 *Even* an heritage unto Israel his servant : for his mercy *endureth* for ever.

16. " *To him which led his people through the wilderness.*" He led them into it, and therefore he was pledged to lead them through it. They were " his people," and yet they must go into the wilderness, and the wilderness must remain as barren as ever it was ; but in the end they must come out of it into the promised land. God's dealings are mysterious, but they must be right, simply because they are his. The people knew nothing of the way, but they were led ; they were a vast host, yet they were all led ; there were neither roads nor tracks, but being led by unerring wisdom they never lost their way. He who brought them out of Egypt, also led them through the wilderness. By Moses, and Aaron, and Jethro, and the pillar of cloud he led them. What a multitude of mercies are comprehended in the conduct of such an enormous host through a region wherein there was no provision even for single travellers ; yet the Lord by his infinite power and wisdom conducted a whole nation for forty years through a desert land, and their feet did not swell, neither did their garments wax old in all the journey. " *For his mercy endureth for ever.*" Their conduct in the wilderness tested his mercy most severely, but it bore the strain ; many a time he forgave them ; and though he smote them for their transgressions, yet he waited to be gracious and speedily turned to them in compassion. *Their* faithfulness soon failed, but *his* did not : the fiery, cloudy pillar which never ceased to lead the van was the visible proof of his immutable love—

> " For his mercy, changing never,
> Still endureth, sure for ever."

17. " *To him which smote great kings.*" Within sight of their inheritance Israel had to face powerful enemies. Kings judged to be great because of the armies at their back blocked up their road. This difficulty soon disappeared, for the Lord smote their adversaries, and a single stroke sufficed for their destruction. He who had subdued the really mighty ruler of Egypt made short work of these petty sovereigns, great though they were in the esteem of neighbouring princes. " *For his mercy endureth for ever.*" Mercy, which had brought the chosen tribes so far, would not be baulked by the opposition of boastful foes. The Lord who smote Pharaoh at the beginning of the wilderness march, smote Sihon and Og at the close of it. How could these kings hope to succeed when even mercy itself was in arms against them.

> Evermore his mercy stands
> Saving from the foeman's hands.

18. " *And slew famous kings.*" What good was their fame to them ? As they opposed God they became infamous rather than famous. Their deaths made the Lord's fame to increase among the nations while their fame ended in disgraceful defeat. " *For his mercy endureth for ever.*" Israelitish patriots felt that they could never have too much of this music ; God had protected their nation, and they chanted his praises with unwearied iteration.

> Kings he smote despite their fame,
> For his mercy's still the same.

19. "*Sihon king of the Amorites.*" Let the name be mentioned that the mercy may be the better remembered. Sihon smote Moab, but he could not smite Israel, for the Lord smote *him.* He was valiant and powerful, so as to be both great and famous ; but as he wilfully refused to give a peaceful passage to the Israelites, and fought against them in malice, there was no choice for it but to let him run into that destruction which he courted. His fall was speedy and final, and the chosen people were so struck with it that they sung of his overthrow in their national songs. "*For his mercy endureth for ever.*" His mercy is no respecter of persons, and neither the greatness nor the fame of Sihon could protect him after he had dared to attack Israel. The Lord will not forsake his people because Sihon blusters.

> Come what may
> By night or day,
> Still most sure,
> His love shall dure.

20. "*And Og the king of Bashan.*" He was of the race of the giants, but he was routed like a pigmy when he entered the lists with Israel's God. The Lord's people were called upon to fight against him, but it was God who won the victory. The fastnesses of Bashan were no defence against Jehovah. Og was soon ousted from his stronghold when the captain of the Lord's host led the war against him. He had to exchange his bedstead of iron for a bed in the dust, for he fell on the battle-field. Glory be to the divine conqueror, "*for his mercy endureth for ever.*"

> Giant kings before him yield,
> Mercy ever holds the field.

If Sihon could not turn the Lord from his purpose we may be sure that Og could not. He who delivers us out of one trouble will rescue us out of another, and fulfil all the good pleasure of his grace in us.

21. "*And gave their land for an heritage.*" As Lord of the whole earth he transferred his estate from one tenant to another. The land did not become the property of the Israelites by their own sword and bow, but by a grant from the throne. This was the great end which all along had been aimed at from Egypt to Jordan. He who brought his people out also brought them in. He who had promised the land to the seed of Abraham also saw to it that the deed of gift did not remain a dead letter. Both our temporal and our spiritual estates come to us by royal charter. What God gives us is ours by the best of titles. Inheritance by God's gift is a tenure which even Satan cannot dispute. "*For his mercy endureth for ever.*" Faithful love endures without end, and secures its own end. "Thou wilt surely bring them in," said the prophet poet ; and here we see the deed complete.

> Till they reach the promised land
> Mercy still the same must stand.

22. "*Even an heritage unto Israel his servant.*" Repetitions are effective in poetry, and the more so if there be some little variation in them, bringing out into fuller light some point which else had not been noticed. The lands of the heathen kings were given to "Israel," the name by which the chosen seed is here mentioned for the third time in the psalm, with the addition of the words, "his servant." The leasehold of Canaan to Israel after the flesh was made dependent upon suit and service rendered to the Lord-of-the-manor by whom the lease was granted. It was a country worth singing about, richly justifying the two stanzas devoted to it. The division of the country by lot, and the laws by which the portions of ground were reserved to the owners and their descendants for a perpetual inheritance were fit subjects for song. Had other nations enjoyed land-laws which ensured to every family a plot of ground for cultivation, much of the present discontent would never have arisen, beggary would soon have become uncommon, and poverty itself would have been rare. *" For his mercy endureth for ever."* Yes, mercy fights for the land, mercy divides the spoil among its favoured ones, and mercy secures each man in his inheritance. Glory be to God the faithful One.

> " For his mercy full and free,
> Wins us full felicity."

23 Who remembered us in our low estate : for his mercy *endureth* for ever :

24 And hath redeemed us from our enemies : for his mercy *endureth* for ever.

23. *" Who remembered us in our low estate."* Personal mercies awake the sweetest song—" he remembered *us.*" Our prayer is, "Lord, remember me," and this is our encouragement—he has remembered us. For the Lord even to think of us is a wealth of mercy. Ours was a sorry estate,—an estate of bankruptcy and mendicancy. Israel rested in its heritage, but we were still in bondage, groaning in captivity : the Lord seemed to have forgotten us, and left us in our sorrow ; but it was not so for long : he turned again in his compassion, bethinking himself of his afflicted children. Our state was once so low as to be at hell's mouth ; since then it has been low in poverty, bereavement, despondency, sickness, and heart-sorrow, and we fear, also, sinfully low in faith, and love, and every other grace ; and yet the Lord has not forgotten us as a dead thing out of mind ; but he has tenderly remembered us still. We thought ourselves too small and too worthless for his memory to burden itself about us, yet he remembered us. *" For his mercy endureth for ever."* Yes, this is one of the best proofs of the immutability of his mercy, for if he could have changed towards any, it would certainly have been towards us who have brought ourselves low, kept ourselves low, and prepared ourselves to sink yet lower. It is memorable mercy to remember us in our low estate : in our highest joys we will exalt Jehovah's name, since of this we are sure,—he will not now desert us—

> For his mercy full and free
> Lasteth to eternity.

24. *" And hath redeemed us from our enemies."* Israel's enemies brought the people low ; but the Lord intervened, and turned the tables by a great redemption. The expression implies that they had become like slaves, and were not set free without price and power ; for they needed to be *" redeemed."* In our case the redemption which is in Christ Jesus is an eminent reason for giving thanks unto the Lord. Sin is our enemy, and we are redeemed from it by the atoning blood ; Satan is our enemy, and we are redeemed from him by the Redeemer's power ; the world is our enemy, and we are redeemed from it by the Holy Spirit. We are ransomed, let us enjoy our liberty ; Christ has wrought our redemption, let us praise his name.

" For his mercy endureth for ever." Even to redemption by the death of his Son did divine mercy stretch itself. What more can be desired ? What more can be imagined ? Many waters could not quench love, neither could the floods drown it.

> E'en to death upon the tree
> Mercy dureth faithfully.

25 Who giveth food to all flesh : for his mercy *endureth* for ever.

25. *" Who giveth food to all flesh."* Common providence, which cares for all living things, deserves our devoutest thanks. If we think of heavenly food, by which all saints are supplied, our praises rise to a still greater height ; but meanwhile the universal goodness of God in feeding all his creatures is as worthy of praise as his special favours to the elect nation. Because the Lord feeds all life therefore we expect him to take special care of his own family. *" For his mercy*

endureth for ever.'' Reaching downward even to beasts and reptiles, it is, indeed, a boundless mercy, which knows no limit because of the meanness of its object.

> " All things living he doth feed,
> His full hand supplies their need ;
> For his mercy shall endure,
> Ever faithful, ever sure."

26 O give thanks unto the God of heaven : for his mercy *endureth* for ever.

26. " *O give thanks unto the God of heaven.''* The title is full of honour. The Lord is God in the highest realms, and among celestial beings. His throne is set in glory, above all, out of reach of foes, in the place of universal oversight. He who feeds ravens and sparrows is yet the glorious God of the highest realms. Angels count it their glory to proclaim his glory in every heavenly street. See herein the greatness of his nature, the depth of his condescension, and the range of his love. Mark the one sole cause of his bounty—" *For his mercy endureth for ever.''* He hath done all things from this motive ; and because his mercy never ceases, he will continue to multiply deeds of love world without end. Let us with all our powers of heart and tongue give thanks unto the holy name of Jehovah for ever and ever.

> " Change and decay in all around I see,
> O thou who changest not, abide with me."

EXPLANATORY NOTES.

Whole Psalm.—This psalm was very probably composed by David, and given to the Levites to sing every day : 1 Chron. xvi. 41. Solomon his son followed his example, and made use of it in singing at the dedication of the Temple (2 Chron vii. 3—6) ; as Jehoshaphat seems to have done when he went out to war against his enemies (2 Chron. xx. 21).—*John Gill.*

Whole Psalm.—The grand peculiarity of form in this psalm . . . is the regular recurrence, at the close of every verse, of a burden or *refrain.* . . . It has been a favourite idea with interpreters that such repetitions necessarily imply alternate or responsive choirs. But the other indications of this usage in the Psalter are extremely doubtful, and every exegetical condition may be satisfied by simply supposing that the singers, in some cases, answered their own questions, and that in others, as in that before us, the people united in the burden or chorus, as they were wont to do in the Amen.—*Joseph Addison Alexander.*

Whole Psalm.—The psalm is called by the Greek church *Polyeleos*, from its continual mention of the mercy of God.—*Neale and Littledale.*

Whole Psalm.—In the liturgical language this psalm is called *par excellence* the great Hallel, for according to its broadest compass the great Hallel comprehends Ps. cxx. to cxxxvi., whilst the Hallel which is absolutely so called extends from Ps. cxiii. to cxviii.—*Franz Delitzsch.*

Whole Psalm.—" *Praise ye* (הורו) *Jehovah* ''; not as in Ps. cxxxv. 1, " Hallelujah," but varying the words,—" Be ye *Judahs* to the Lord !"

Praise him for what he is (ver. 1—3).
Praise him for what he is able to do (ver. 4).
Praise him for what he has done in creation (ver. 5—9).
Praise him for what he did in redeeming Israel from bondage (ver. 10—15).
Praise him for what·he did in his providence toward them (ver. 16—22).
Praise him for his grace in times of calamity (ver. 23, 24).
Praise him for his grace to the world at large (ver. 25).
Praise him at the remembrance that this God is the God of heaven (ver. 26).—*Andrew A. Bonar.*

Whole Psalm.—When, in the time of the Emperor Constantius, S. Athanasius was assaulted by night in his church at Alexandria by Syrianus and his troops, and many were wounded and murdered, the Bishop of Alexandria sat still in his chair, and ordered the deacon to begin this psalm, and the people answered in prompt alternation, *" For his mercy endureth for ever."—Christopher Wordsworth.*

Verse 1.—" O give thanks unto the LORD.*"* When we have praised God for reasons offered unto us in one psalm, we must begin again, and praise him for other reasons ; and even when we have done this, we have not overtaken our task, the duty lieth still at our door, to be discharged afresh, as this psalm doth show. —*David Dickson.*

Verse 1.—" For he is good." Observe what we must give thanks for : not as the Pharisee that made all his thanksgivings terminate in his own goodness— "God, I thank thee" that I am so and so—but directing them all to God's glory : *"for he is good."—Matthew Henry.*

Verse 1.—" His mercy endureth for ever." This appears four times in Ps. cxviii. 1—4. This sentence is the wonder of Moses, the sum of revelation, and the hope of man.—*James G. Murphy.*

Verse 1.—" His mercy." Many sweet things are in the word of God, but the name of mercy is the sweetest word in all the Scriptures, which made David harp upon it twenty-six times in this psalm : *" For his mercy endureth for ever."* It was such a cheerful note in his ears when he struck upon mercy, that, like a bird that is taught to pipe, when he had sung it, he sang it again, and when he had sung it again, he recorded it again, and made it the burden of his song : *" For his mercy endureth for ever."* Like a nightingale which, when she is in a pleasant vein, quavers and capers, and trebles upon it, so did David upon his mercy : *" For his mercy endureth for ever."—Henry Smith.*

Verse 1.—" Mercy." By *" mercy "* we understand the Lord's disposition to compassionate and relieve those whom sin has rendered miserable and base ; his readiness to forgive and to be reconciled to the most provoking of transgressors, and to bestow all blessings upon them ; together with all the provision which he has made for the honour of his name, in the redemption of sinners by Jesus Christ. —*Thomas Scott.*

Verse 1.—" His mercy endureth for ever." It is everlasting, Everlastingness, or eternity, is a perfect possession, all at once, of an endless life (saith Boëthius). Everlasting mercy, then, is perfect mercy, which shuts out all the imperfections of time, beginning, end, succession, and such is God's mercy. First, his *essential mercy* is everlastingness itself ; for it is himself, and God hath not, but *is*, things. He is beginning, end, being ; and that which is of himself and even himself is eternity itself. Secondly, his *relative mercy* (which respects us, and makes impression on us), is everlasting, too, in a sense ; for the creatures, ever since they had being in him, or existence in their natural causes, ever did and ever will need mercy, either preserving or conserving. Preventing or continuing mercy in the first sense is *negatively endless*, that is, incapable of end, because unboundable for being : in the second sense, it is *privatively endless*, it shall never actually take end, though in itself it may be, and in some ways is, bounded ; the first is included in the latter, but the latter is chiefly here intended ; and therefore the point arises to be this,—*God's mercy (chiefly to his church) is an endless mercy ;* it knows no end, receives no interruption. Reasons hereof from the word are these (for as touching testimony this psalm shall be our security), first, from *God's nature, " he is good "* Mercy pleaseth him. It is no trouble for him to exercise mercy. It is his delight : we are never weary of receiving, therefore he cannot be of giving ; for it is a more blessed thing to give than to receive ; so God takes more content in the one than we in the other.—*Robert Harris,* 1578—1658.

Verse 1.—"His mercy endureth for ever." God's goodness is a fountain ; it is never dry. As grace is from the world's beginning (Ps. xxv. 6), so it is to the world's end, *à seculo in seculum*, from one generation to another. Salvation is no termer ; grace ties not itself to times. Noah as well as Abel, Moses as well as Jacob, Jeremy as well as David, Paul as well as Simeon hath part in this salvation. God's gracious purpose the Flood drowned not, the smoke of Sinai smothered not, the Captivity ended not, the ends of the world (Saint Paul calls them so) determined not. For Christ, by whom it is, was slain from the beginning,—Saint John saith so. He was before Abraham, he himself saith so. And *Clemens Alexandrinus* [tom. v. page 233] doth Marcion wrong, though otherwise an heretic, in blaming him for holding that Christ saved those also that believed in him before his incarnation. The blood of the beasts under the law was a type of his. And the scars of his wounds appear yet still, and will for ever, till he cometh to judgment. The Apostle shall end this : he is *heri,* and *hodi,* and *semper idem :* Christ is the same yesterday and to-day and for ever.—*Richard Clerke,* —1634.

Verses 1—3.—The three first verses of this Psalm contain the three several names of the Deity, which are commonly rendered *Jehovah, God,* and *Lord,* respectively ; the first having reference to his essence as *self-existent,* and being his proper name ; the second designating him under the character of *a judge* or of an all-powerful being, if Aleim be derived from *Al;* and the third, *Adoni,* representing him as *exercising rule.—Daniel Cresswell.*

Verses 1—3.—"*O give thanks.*"

> What ! give God thanks for everything,
>   Whatever may befall—
> Whatever the dark clouds may bring?
>   Yes, give God thanks for all ;
> For safe he leads thee, hand in hand,
> To thy blessèd Fatherland.
>
> What ! thank him for the lonely way
>   .He to me hath given—
> For the path which, day by day
>   Seems farther off from heaven ?
> Yes, thank him, for he holds thy hand
> And leads thee to thy Fatherland.
>
> Close, close he shields thee from all harm ;
>   And if the road be steep,
> Thou know'st his everlasting arm
>   In safety doth thee keep,
> Although thou canst not understand
> The windings to thy Fatherland.
>
> What blessing, thinkest thou, will he,
>   Who knows the good and ill,
> Keep back, if it is good for thee,
>   While climbing up the hill ?
> Then trust him, and keep fast his hand,
> He leads thee to thy Fatherland.

B. S., in "The Christian Treasury," 1865.

Verses 1—9.—Like the preceding psalm, this psalm allies itself to the Book of Deuteronomy. The first clauses of verses 2 and 3 ("*God of gods*" and "*Lord of lords*") are taken from Deut. x. 17 ; verse 12, first clause ("*with a strong hand and stretched out arm*") from Deut. iv. 34, and v. 15. Verse 16, first clause, is like Deut. viii. 15 (cf. Jer. ii. 6).—*Franz Delitzsch.*

Verses 1—26.—All repetitions are not vain, nor is all length in prayer to be accounted babbling. For repetitions may be used, 1. When they express *fervency* and *zeal :* and so we read, Christ prayed over the same prayer thrice (Matt. xxvi. 44) ; "O my Father, if it be possible, let this cup pass from me." And another evangelist showeth that he did this out of special fervency of spirit (Luke xxii. 44) ; "Being in an agony, he prayed more earnestly." 2. This repetition is not to be disapproved when there is *a special emphasis,* and spiritual elegancy in it, as in Psalm cxxxvi. you have it twenty-six times repeated, "*For his mercy endureth for ever,*" because there was a special reason in it, the Psalmist's purpose there being to show the unweariedness, and the unexhausted riches of God's free grace ; that notwithstanding all the former experiences they had had, God is where he was at first. We waste by giving, our drop is soon spent ; but God is not wasted by bestowing, but hath the same mercy to do good to his creatures, as before.   Though he had done all those wonders for them, yet his mercy was as ready to do good to them still.   All along God saved and blessed his people, *"For his mercy endureth for ever."—Thomas Manton.*

Verse 2.—"The God of gods."   *"God of gods"* is an Hebrew superlative, because he is far above all gods, whether they be so reputed or deputed.—*Robert Harris.*

Verse 2.—"The God of gods."   One, as being Creator, infinitely higher than all others, his creatures, who have at any time been regarded as gods.—*French and Skinner,* 1842.

Verses 2, 3.—Before proceeding to recite God's works, the Psalmist declares his supreme Deity, and dominion : not that such comparative language implies that there is anything approaching Deity besides him, but there is a disposition in men, whenever they see any part of his glory displayed, to conceive of a God separate from him, thus impiously dividing the Godhead into parts, and even proceeding so far as to frame gods of wood and stone.   There is a depraved tendency in all to take delight in a multiplicity of gods.   For this reason, apparently, the Psalmist uses the plural number not only in the word *Elohim* but in the word *Adonim,* so that it reads literally, *Praise ye the Lords of lords :* he would intimate, that the fullest perfection of all dominion is to be found in the one God.—*John Calvin.*

Verse 3.—"The Lord of lords."   The meaning of the title *"Lord,"* as distinct from " Jehovah " and " God," is " Governor."   And in this view also he is eminently entitled to praise and thanksgiving, in that his rule and government of the world are also eminently marked by " *mercy*" and " *goodness :*" not the display of power only, but of power declared chiefly in showing mercy and pity : as again all subject to that rule are witnesses.   Such is God *in himself.*   Nor is it without intention that the doxology is threefold, indicating, doubtless, like the threefold invocation of the Name of the Lord in the blessing of the people (Num. vi. 24—26)—God in Trinity, " Father, Son, and Holy Ghost," as now fully revealed.—*William De Burgh.*

Verse 4.—"To him who alone doeth great wonders."   God hath preserved to himself the power of miracles, as his prerogative : for the devil does no miracles ; the devil and his instruments do but hasten nature or hinder nature, antedate nature or postdate nature, bring things sooner to pass or retard them ; and however they pretend to oppose nature, yet still it is but upon nature and by natural means that they work.   Only God shakes the whole frame of nature in pieces, and in a miracle proceeds so, as if there were no creation yet accomplished, no course of nature yet established.   *Facit mirabilia magna solus,* says David here. There are *mirabilia parva,* some lesser wonders, that the devil and his instruments, Pharaoh's sorcerers can do ; but when it comes to *mirabilia magna,* great wonders, so great that they amount to the nature of a miracle, *facit solus,* God and God only does them.—*Abraham Wright.*

Verse 4.—"To him who alone doeth great wonders."   Does he " *alone*" do great wonders ?   that means, he does so by himself, unaided, needing nothing from others, asking no help from his creatures.   As the Nile from Nubia to the Mediterranean rolls on 1,300 miles in solitary grandeur, receiving not one tributary, but itself alone dispensing fertility and fatness wherever it comes ; so our God " alone" does wonders. (See Deut. xxxii. 12 ; Ps. lxxii. 18, etc.)   No prompter, no helper ; spontaneously he goes forth to work, and all he works is worthy of God.   Then we have no need of any other ; we are independent of all others ; all our springs are in him.—*Andrew A. Bonar.*

Verse 4.—"Who alone doeth great wonders."   There are three things here declared of God ; that he doeth *wonders,* that the wonders he doeth are *great ;* that he *only* doeth them.—*Augustine, in Neale and Littledale.*

Verse 4.—"Who alone doeth great wonders."   Whatsoever instruments the Lord is pleased to use in any of his wonderful works, he alone is the worker, and will not share the glory of the work with any creature.—*David Dickson.*

Verse 4.—It becomes the great God to grant great things. *"To him who alone doeth great wonders."* When you ask great things, you ask such as it becomes God to give, " whose mercy is great above the heavens !" Nothing under heaven can be too great for him to give. The greater things he bestows, the greater glory redounds to his Name.—*David Clarkson,* 1622—1686.

Verse 4.—Christians should not be ashamed of the mysteries and *miracles* of their religion. Sometimes of late years there has been manifested a disposition to recede from the defence of the supernatural in religion. This is a great mistake. Give up all that is miraculous in true religion and there is nothing left of power sufficient to move any heart to worship or adore ; and without worship there is no piety.—*William Swan Plumer.*

Verse 4.—The longer I live, O my God, the more do I wonder at all the works of thy hands. I see such admirable artifice in the very least and most despicable of all thy creatures, as doth every day more and more astonish my observation. I need not look so far as heaven for matter of marvel; though therein thou art infinitely glorious ; while I have but a spider in my window, or a bee in my garden, or a worm under my foot : every one of these overcomes me with a just amazement : yet can I see no more than their very outsides ; their inward form, which gives their being and operations, I cannot pierce into. The less I can know, O Lord, the more let me wonder ; and the less I can satisfy myself with marvelling at thy works, the more let me adore the majesty and omnipotence of thee, that wroughtest them.—*Joseph Hall.*

Verse 5.—*"To him that by wisdom made the heavens."* We find that God has built the heavens in wisdom, to declare his glory, and to show forth his handi-work. There are no iron tracks, with bars and bolts, to hold the planets in their orbits. Freely in space they move, ever changing, but never changed ; poised and balancing ; swaying and swayed ; disturbing and disturbed, onward they fly, fulfilling with unerring certainty their mighty cycles. The entire system forms one grand complicated piece of celestial machinery ; circle within circle, wheel within wheel, cycle within cycle ; revolutions so swift as to be completed in a few hours ; movements so slow, that their mighty periods are only counted by millions of years.—*From "The Orbs of Heaven,"* 1859.

Verse 5.—*"To him that by wisdom made the heavens."* Not only the firmament, but the third heavens, too, where all is felicity, where is the throne of glory. Then, I infer, that if the *mercy* which visits earth is from the same Jehovah who built that heaven and filled it with glory, there must be in his *mercy* something of the same *"understanding"* or *"wisdom."* It is wise, prudent mercy ; not rashly given forth ; and it is the mercy of him whose love has filled that heaven with bliss. The same architect, the same skill, the same love !—*Andrew A. Bonar.*

Verse 6.—*"Stretched out the earth above the waters."* The waters of the great deep (Gen. vii. 11) are meant ; above which the crust of the earth is outspread. In Prov. viii. 27 the great deep encircles the earth.—*"Speaker's Commentary."*

Verse 7.—*"Great lights."* The luminaries of heaven are unspeakable blessings to the children of men. The sun, in the greatness of his strength, measures their day, and exerts an influence over animal and vegetable life, which surrounds them with innumerable comforts ; and the moon and stars walking forth in their brightness, give direction to them amidst the sable hours of night, and both by land and sea proclaim the wisdom, and benignity, and gracious arrangement of the adorable Creator. By these luminaries, day and night, heat and cold, summer and winter are continually regulated : so that God's covenant with the earth is maintained through their medium. How truly, then, may we exclaim, " His mercy endureth for ever !"—*John Morison.*

Verse 7.—*"To him that made great lights."* Light is the life and soul of the universe, the noblest emblem of the power and glory of God, who, in the night season, leaves not himself without witness, but gives us some portion of that light reflected, which by day we behold flowing from its great fountain in the heart of heaven. Thy church and thy saints, O Lord, " are the moon and the stars," which, by the communication of doctrine, and the splendour of example, guide our feet, while we travel on in the night that hath overtaken us, waiting for the dawn of everlasting day. Then we shall behold thy glory, and see thee as thou art.—*George Horne.*

Verse 8.—"*The sun to rule by day.*" This verse showeth that the sun shineth in the day, by the order which God hath set, and not for any natural cause alone, as some imagine and conjecture.—*Thomas Wilcocks.*

Verse 8.—"*The sun.*" The *lantern of the world* (*lucerna Mundi*), as Copernicus names the sun, enthroned in the centre — according to Theon of Smyrna, the all-vivifying, pulsating *heart of the universe*, is the primary source of light and of radiating heat, and the generator of numerous terrestrial, electro-magnetic processes, and indeed of the greater part of the organic vital activity upon our planet, more especially that of the vegetable kingdom. In considering the expression of solar force, in its widest generality, we find that it gives rise to alterations on the surface of the earth,—partly by gravitative attraction,—as in the ebb and flow of the ocean (if we except the share taken in the phenomenon by lunar attraction), partly by light and heat-generating transverse vibrations of ether, as in the fructifying admixture of the aërial and aqueous envelopes of our planet, from the contact of the atmosphere with the vaporizing fluid element in seas, lakes, and rivers. The solar action operates, moreover, by differences of heat, in exciting atmospheric and oceanic currents ; the latter of which have continued for thousands of years (though in an inconsiderable degree) to accumulate or waste away alluvial strata, and thus change the surface of the inundated land ; it operates in the generation and maintenance of the electro-magnetic activity of the earth's crust, and that of the oxygen contained in the atmosphere ; at one time calling forth calm and gentle forces of chemical attraction, and variously determining organic life in the endosmose of cell-walls and in tissue of muscular and nervous fibres ; at another time evoking light processes in the atmosphere, such as the coloured coruscations of the polar light, thunder and lightning, hurricanes and waterspouts.

Our object in endeavouring to compress in one picture the *influences of solar action*, in as far as they are independent of the orbit and the position of the axis of our globe, has been clearly to demonstrate, by an exposition of the connection existing between great, and at first sight heterogeneous, phenomena, how physical nature may be depicted in the *History of the Cosmos* as a whole, moved and animated by internal and frequently self-adjusting forces. But the waves of light not only exert a decomposing and combining action on the corporeal world ; they not only call forth the tender germs of plants from the earth, generate the green colouring matter (chlorophyll) within the leaf, and give colour to the fragrant blossom—they not only produce myriads of reflected images of the Sun in the graceful play of the waves, as in the moving grass of the field—but the rays of celestial light, in the varied gradations of their intensity and duration, are also mysteriously connected with the inner life of man, his intellectual susceptibilities, and the melancholy or cheerful tone of his feelings. This is what Pliny the elder referred to in these words, "*Cœli tristram discutit sol, et humani nubila animi serenat.*" ["The sun chases sadness from the sky, and dissipates the clouds which darken the human heart."]—*F. H. Alexander Von Humboldt* (1769—1859), *in "Cosmos."*

Verse 8.—"*The sun.*"

> O sun ! what makes thy beams so bright ?
> The word that said, " Let there be light."
> —*James Montgomery.*

Verse 9.—"*The moon and stars to rule by night.*" While the apparent revolution of the sun marks out the year and the course of the seasons, the revolution of the

moon round the heavens marks out our months ; and by regularly changing its
figure at the four quarters of its course, subdivides the months into two periods
of weeks, and thus exhibits to all the nations of the earth a "watch-light," or
signal, which every seven days presents a form entirely new, for marking out the
shorter periods of duration.   By its nearness to the earth, and the consequent
increase of its gravitating power, it produces currents in the atmosphere, which
direct the course of the winds, and purify the aerial fluid from noxious exhala-
tions ; it raises the waters of the ocean, and perpetuates the regular returns of
ebb and flow, by which the liquid element is preserved from filth and putrefac-
tion.   It extends its sway even over the human frame, and our health and
disorders are sometimes partially dependent on its influence.   Even its eclipses,
and those it produces of the sun, are not without their use.   They tend to arouse
mankind to the study of astronomy, and the wonders of the firmament ; they
serve to confirm the deductions of chronology, to direct the navigator, and to
settle the geographical position of towns and countries ; they assist the
astronomer in his celestial investigations, and exhibit an agreeable variety of
phenomena in the scenery of the heavens.   In short, there are terrestrial scenes
presented in moon-light, which, in point of solemnity, grandeur, and picturesque
beauty, far surpass in interest, to a poetic imagination, all the brilliancy and
splendours of noon-day.   Hence, in all ages, a moonlight scene has been regarded,
by all ranks of men, with feelings of joy and sentiments of admiration.   The
following description of Homer, translated into English verse by Pope, has been
esteemed one of the finest night-pieces in poetry :—

> "Behold the moon, refulgent lamp of night,
>   O'er Heaven's clear azure spreads her sacred light,
>   When not a breath disturbs the deep serene,
>   And not a cloud o'ercasts the solemn scene ;
>   Around her throne the vivid planets roll,
>   And stars unnumbered gild the glowing pole ;
>   O'er the dark trees a yellower verdure shed,
>   And tip with silver every mountain's head ;
>   Then shine the vales ; the rocks in prospect rise ;
>   A flood of glory bursts from all the skies ;
>   The conscious swains, rejoicing in the sight,
>   Eye the blue vault, and bless the useful light."

Without the light of the moon, the inhabitants of the polar regions would be for
weeks and months immersed in darkness.   But the moon, like a kindly visitant,
returns at short intervals, in the absence of the sun, and cheers them with her
beams for days and weeks together.   So that, in this nocturnal luminary, as in
all the other arrangements of nature, we behold a display of the paternal care
and beneficence of that Almighty Being who ordained "the moon and the stars
to rule by night," as an evidence of his superabundant goodness, and of "his
mercy which endureth for ever."—*Thomas Dick* (1774—1857), *in* "*Celestial
Scenery.*"

Verse 9.—"*Stars to rule by night.*"   The purpose of the sacred narrative being
to describe the adaption of the earth to the use of man, no account is taken of
the nature of the stars, as suns or planets, but merely as signs in the heavens.—
"*Speaker's Commentary.*"

Verse 9.—"*Stars.*"   The stars not only adorn the roof of our sublunary mansion,
they are also in many respects *useful* to man.   Their influences are placid and
gentle.   Their rays, being dispersed through spaces so vast and immense, are
entirely destitute of heat by the time they arrive at our abode ; so that we enjoy
the view of a numerous assemblage of luminous globes without any danger of
their destroying the coolness of the night or the quiet of our repose.   They serve
to guide the traveller both by sea and land ; they direct the navigator in tracing
his course from one continent to another through the pathless ocean.   They serve
" for signs and for seasons, and for days and years."   They direct the labours of
the husbandman, and determine the return and conclusion of the seasons.   They
serve as a magnificent " timepiece," to determine the true length of the day and

of the year, and to mark with accuracy all their subordinate divisions. They assist us in our commerce, and in endeavouring to propagate religion among the nations, by showing us our path to every region of the earth. They have enabled us to measure the circumference of the globe, to ascertain the *density* of the materials of which it is composed, and to determine the exact position of all places upon its surface. They cheer the long nights of several months in the polar regions, which would otherwise be overspread with impenetrable darkness. Above all, they open a prospect into the regions of other worlds, and tend to amplify our views of the Almighty Being who brought them into existence by his power, and "whose kingdom ruleth over all." In these arrangements of the stars in reference to our globe, the Divine wisdom and goodness may be clearly perceived. We enjoy all the advantages to which we have alluded as much as if the stars had been created solely for the use of our world, while, at the same time, they serve to diversify the nocturnal sky of other planets, and to diffuse their light and influence over ten thousands of other worlds with which they are more immediately connected, so that, in this respect, as well as in every other, the Almighty produces the most sublime and diversified effects by means the most simple and economical, and renders every part of the universe subservient to another, and to the good of the whole.—*Thomas Dick*.

Verse 9.—"*Stars.*" When the First Consul crossed the Mediterranean on his Egyptian expedition, he carried with him a cohort of *savans*, who ultimately did good service in many ways. Among them, however, as might be expected at that era, were not a few philosophers of the Voltaire-Diderot school. Napoleon, for his own instruction and amusement on shipboard, encouraged disputation among these gentlemen ; and on one occasion they undertook to show, and, according to their own account, *did* demonstrate, by infallible logic and meta-physic, that there is no God. Bonaparte, who hated all idealogists, abstract reasoners, and logical demonstrators, no matter what they were demonstrating, would not fence with these subtle dialecticians, but had them immediately on deck, and, pointing to the stars in the clear sky, replied, by way of counter-argument, "Very good, messieurs ! but who made all these ?"—*George Wilson, in "Religio Chemici,"* 1862.

Verse 10.—"*To him that smote Egypt in their first-born.*" The Egyptians are well said to have been *smitten in their first-born ;* because they continued in their outrageous obstinacy under the other plagues, though occasionally terrified by them, but were broken and subdued by this last plague, and submitted.—*John Calvin*.

Verse 10.—"*To him that smote Egypt in their first-born, for his mercy,*" etc. Remember his sovereign grace, when righteousness would show itself upon the guilty. There was mercy even then to Israel—drops of that mercy that for ever endureth—at the very time when judgment fell on others. Should not this give emphasis to our praises ? The dark background makes the figures in the fore-ground more prominent.—*Andrew A. Bonar*.

Verse 11.—"*And brought out Israel from among them.*" Such an emigration as this the world never saw. On the lowest computation, the entire multitude must have been above two millions, and in all probability the number exceeded three millions. Is the magnitude of this movement usually apprehended ? Do we think of the emigration of the Israelites from Egypt as of the emigration of a number of families twice as numerous as the population of the principality of Wales, or considerably more than the whole population of the British Metropolis (in 1841), with all their goods, property, and cattle ? The collecting together of so immense a multitude—the arranging the order of their march—the provision of the requisite food even for a few days, must, under the circumstances, have been utterly impossible, unless a very special and overruling Providence had graciously interfered to obviate the difficulties of the case. To the most super-ficial observer it must be evident, that no man, or number of men, having nothing but human resources, could have ventured to undertake this journey. Scarcely any wonder, wrought by Divine power in Egypt, appears greater than this emigration of a nation, when fairly and fully considered.—*George Smith, in "Sacred Annals,"* 1850.

Verse 12.—"*With a stretched-out arm.*" The figure of *an outstretched arm* is appropriate, for we stretch out the arm when any great effort is required; so that this implies that God put forth an extraordinary and not a common or slight display of his power in redeeming his people.—*John Calvin.*

Verse 13.—"*Divided the Red Sea into parts.*" The entire space between the mountains of Ataka and Abon Deradj was dry. At the former point the gulf is eight miles across, at the latter more than double that distance. The waters that had filled this broad and deep chasm stood in two huge mounds on the right hand and on the left. The light of God shone brightly on the astonished multitude. The word was given, they advanced abreast; awe-stricken, but quiet and confident. . . . "Then the Egyptians pursued and went in after them into the midst of the sea, all Pharaoh's horses, even his chariots and his fleet horses" : Exod. xiv. 23.—*William Osburn, in "Israel in Egypt,"* 1856.

Verse 14.—"*And made Israel to pass through the midst of it,*" etc. Willingly, without reluctance ; with great spirit and courage, fearless of danger, and with the utmost safety, so that not one was lost in the passage ; see Ps. lxxviii. 53 ; and thus the Lord makes his people willing to pass through afflictions, he being with them ; and able to bear them, he putting underneath the everlasting arms, even when in the valley of the shadow of death. He carries them safely through them, so that they are not hurt by them ; the waters do not overflow them, nor the flames kindle upon them ; nor are any suffered to be lost : but all come safe to land.—*John Gill.*

Verse 14.—"*And made Israel to pass through the midst of it.*" It is a work of no less mercy and power to give his people grace to make use of an offered means of delivery, than to prepare the deliverance for them ; but the constancy of God's mercy doth not only provide the means, but also giveth his people grace to make use thereof in all ages.—*David Dickson.*

Verse 14.—"*And made Israel to pass through the midst of it.*" It is many times *hail* with the saints, when *ill* with the wicked. Abraham from the hill seeth Sodom on fire.—*John Trapp.*

Verse 15.—"*But overthrew Pharaoh,*" etc. Thus fell Sethos II. It was his terrible destiny to leave to after-times the strongest exemplification of daring wickedness and mad impiety in his life, and of the vengeance of God in his death, that ever was enacted on the earth. Never had such a judgment befallen any nation, as his reign in Egypt. Accordingly the memory of this fearful event has never departed from among men. The gulf in which he perished is named Bahr-Kolzoum, "the sea of destruction," to this day.

The memory and name of Sethos II. were infamous in Egypt. His tomb was desecrated, and his sarcophagus publicly and judicially broken. The vault seems to have been used as a burying-place for slaves. The distinctive title of his name, *Sethos*, has been mutilated on all the monuments of Egypt. In Lower Egypt the mutilation has even been extended to the same title in the rings of his great-grandfather (Sethos I.), such was the deep abhorrence in which the name had fallen, after it had been borne by this wicked king. His is the only one in the whole range of the kings of Egypt which has suffered this mark of public infamy.—*William Osburn.*

Verse 15.—"*But overthrew Pharaoh,*" etc. Margin, as in Hebrew, *shaked off.* The word is applicable to a tree shaking off its foliage, Isa. xxxiii. 9. The same word is used in Ex. xiv. 27 : "And the Lord overthrew (Margin, *shook off*) the Egyptians in the midst of the sea." He shook them off as if he would no longer protect them. He left them to perish.—*Albert Barnes.*

Verse 15.—"*But shook off Pharaoh.*" This translation gives an image of locusts. They fell into the sea like a swarm of locusts.—*Zachary Mudge*—1769.

Verse 15.—"*But overthrew Pharaoh,*" etc. I know that the Gospel is a book of mercy ; I know likewise that in the prophets there are many expressions of mercy ; I know likewise that in the ten commandments, which are the ministration of death, there is made express mention of mercy, " I will have mercy on thousands" : yet, notwithstanding all this, if every leaf, and every line, and every word in the Bible were nothing but mercy, it would nothing avail the presumptuous sinner. Our God is not an impotent God with one arm ; but as he is slow to anger, so is he great in power. And therefore though in this psalm there is nothing but " *his mercy endureth for ever,*" which is twenty-six times in twenty-six verses : yet mark what a rattling thunder-clap is here in this verse. In our addresses therefore unto God, let us so look upon him as a just God, as well as a merciful ; and not either despair of or presume upon his mercy.— *Abraham Wright.*

Verse 16.—"*Led his people through the wilderness.*"

When Israel, of the Lord beloved,
    Out of the land of bondage came,
Her father's God before her moved,
    An awful guide, in smoke and flame.
By day, along the astonished lands,
    The cloudy pillar glided slow ;
By night Arabia's crimsoned sands
    Returned the fiery column's glow.

—*Sir Walter Scott,* 1771—1832.

Verse 16.—"*He led his people through the wilderness.*" It was an astonishing miracle of God to support so many hundreds of thousands of people in a wilderness totally deprived of all necessaries for the life of man, and that for the space of forty years.—*Adam Clarke.*

Verse 16.—"*He led his people through the wilderness,*" etc. It is a very sweet truth which is enunciated in this verse, and one which I think we need very much to realize. His own people, his peculiar people, his chosen, loved, and favoured ones, whom he cherished as the apple of his eye, who were graven on the palms of his hands, and loved with an everlasting love, even these he led through the wilderness ; and all this *because* " His mercy endureth for ever." In another psalm it is said, " He leadeth them beside the still waters, he maketh them to lie down in green pastures" ; but the barren wilderness has no green pastures, the parched and arid desert has no still waters. And yet " in the wilderness shall waters break out, and streams in the desert, and an highway shall be there ; and the ransomed of the Lord shall return, and come to Zion with songs and everlasting joy upon their heads." " Who is this that cometh up from the wilderness, leaning upon her beloved ?" It is one of the Lord's sweet truths that so perplex those that are without, but which are so full of consolation to his own children, that the wilderness and mercy are linked together of God in indissoluble union here. " I will allure her," saith the Lord, " and bring her into the wilderness, and speak comfortably unto her."—*Barton Bouchier.*

Verse 16.—" *Who led his people.*" Note that in what precedes this, in this verse itself, and in what follows, God's three ways of leading are set forth. He leads *out,* he leads *through,* and he leads *into ;* out of sin, through the world, into heaven ; out by faith, through by hope, into by love.—*Michael Ayguan* (1416), *in Neale and Littledale.*

Verse 17.—" *Great kings.*" *Great,* as those times accounted them, when every small city almost had her king. Canaan had thirty and more of them. *Great* also in regard of their stature and strength ; for they were of the giants' race. Deut. iii.; Amos. ii.—*John Trapp.*

Verses 18, 20.—The profane of our times may hence learn to take heed how they wrong the faithful. God is " wise in heart and mighty in strength :" Job ix. 4. Who ever waxed fierce against his people and hath prospered ? For their sakes he hath destroyed great kings and mighty, "*Sihon king of the Amorites, and Og the king of Bashan.*" He can pluck off thy chariot wheels, strike thee in the hinder parts, cause thy heart to fail thee for fear, and in a moment fetch thy soul from thee : better were it for thee to have a millstone hanged about thy neck, and thou to be cast into the bottom of the sea, than to offend the least of these faithful ones ; they are dear in his sight, tender to him, as the apple of his eye. —*John Barlow*, 1632.

Verse 19.—"*Sihon*" occupied the whole district between the Arnon and Jabbok, through which the approach to the Jordan lay. He had wrested it from the predecessor of Balak, and had established himself, not in the ancient capital of Moab-Ar, but in the city still conspicuous to the modern traveller from its wide prospect and its cluster of stone pines—Heshbon. The recollection of his victory survived in a savage war-song, which passed into a kind of proverb in after-times :—

> " Come home to Heshbon ;
> Let the city of Sihon be built and prepared,
> For there is gone out a fire from Heshbon,
> A flame from the city of Sihon.
> It hath consumed Ar of Moab,
> And the lords of the high places of Arnon :
> Woe to thee, Moab; thou art undone, thou people of Chemosh !
> He hath given his sons that escaped, and his daughters, into captivity
> To the king of the Amorites, Sihon."*

The decisive battle between Sihon and his new foes took place at Jahaz, probably on the confines of the rich pastures of Moab and the desert whence the Israelites emerged. It was the first engagement in which they were confronted with the future enemies of their nation. The slingers and archers of Israel, afterwards so renowned, now first showed their skill. Sihon fell ; the army fled † (so ran the later tradition), and devoured by thirst, like the Athenians in the Assinarus on their flight from Syracuse, were slaughtered in the bed of one of the mountain streams. The memory of this battle was cherished in triumphant strains, in which, after reciting, in bitter irony, the song just quoted of the Amorites' triumph, they broke out into an exulting contrast of the past greatness of the defeated chief and his present fall :—

> " We have shot at them : Heshbon is perished :
> We have laid them waste : even unto Nophah :
> With fire : even unto Medeba."‡

—*Arthur Penrhyn Stanley, in "The History of the Jewish Church."*

Verse 20.—"*Og the king of Bashan.*" There is continued victory. The second hindrance disappears after the first. "*Og, king of Bashan,*" last of the giants (Deut. iii. 11), fared no better for all his strength than *Sihon*. It was not some peculiar weakness of Sihon that overthrew him. All enemies of God, however different in resource they may appear when they measure themselves among themselves, are alike to those who march in the strength of God. The power by which the Christian conquers one foe will enable him to conquer all. And yet because Og did *look* more formidable than Sihon, God gave his people special encouragement in meeting him : Numb. xxi. 34. God remembers that even the most faithful and ardent of his people cannot get entirely above the deceitfulness of outward appearances.—*Pulpit Commentary.*

Verse 20.—When "*Og king of Bashan*" took the field—a giant, a new and more terrific foe—he, too, fell. And the *mercy* that thus dealt with enemies so great, enemies so strong, one after another, "*endureth for ever.*" When Antichrist

---

* Num. xxi. 27—29, repeated, as is well known, in Jer. xlviii. 45, 46.
† Joseph. Ant. iv. 5, § 2.   ‡ Num. xxi. 30.

raises up his hosts in the latter days, one after another—when the great, the famous, the mighty, the noble, the gigantic men, in succession assail the Church, they shall perish : " For his *mercy* endureth for ever.—*Andrew A. Bonar.*

Verse 22.— "*Israel his servant.*" He speaks of all that people as of one man, because they were united together in one body, in the worship of one and the same God. Thus God calleth them all his " first-born" : Exod. iv. 22.—*Matthew Pool.*

Verse 23.—"*Who remembered us.*" We should echo in our thankfulness the first intimation that God gives in his providence of an approaching mercy. If you do but hear when the king is on his road towards your town you raise your bells to ring him in, and stay not till he be entered the gates. The birds rise betimes in the morning, and are saluting the rising sun with their sweet notes in the air. Thus should we strike up our harps in praising God at the first appearance of a mercy.— *William Gurnall.*

Verse 23.—"*Who remembered us.*" The word "*remembered*" is a pregnant word, it bears twins twice told, it is big of a six-fold sense, as so many degrees of mercy in it. 1. *To remember* signifies to think upon, in opposition to forgetfulness. We may dwell in man's thoughts and not be the better for it, but we cannot be in God's remembering thoughts but we shall be the better for it. 2. To remember (as the second degree of the mercy) signifies to take notice of a thing, in opposition to neglect ; so it is used in Exod. xx. 8 : "*Remember* the Sabbath-day, to keep it holy :" take notice, that is, neglect it not, "remember" to keep holy the Sabbath-day. So God "*remembered*" us in our low estates : how ? Why, he did not barely think upon us, but he did observe and take notice of us, and considered what our case was. But, 3. It signifies (as the third degree of mercy), to lay to heart, to pity and compassionate persons in such a case. What am I better for anybody's thinking of me, if he do not take notice of me, so as to pity me in my low estate ? So God doth, as in Jer. xxxi. 20. 4. *To remember*, signifies yet more (as the fourth degree of mercy) to be well pleased with a person in such a case, to accept of a person in such a case ; so the word is used in Ps. xx. 3 : " The Lord *remember* all thy offerings, and accept thy burnt sacrifice" ; remember, that is, accept. 5. *To remember* signifies (as the fifth degree of mercy) to hear and to grant a request ; so it is used in 1 Sam. i. 19, 20, 27 : " God *remembered* Hannah," and the next word is, " He gave her what she asked." 6. *To remember* signifies (as the sixth degree of mercy) to help and succour, or to redeem and deliver from that which we were appointed to, from the low estate ; and so it is in Gal. ii. 10 : " Only they would that we should *remember* the poor." Remembering the poor is not barely a thought, but a relieving thought ; therefore saith the Psalmist in the following verse, " who hath redeemed us from our enemies :" this was the *remembrance* of God, *redemption* from enemies.

I might draw considerations [for thanksgiving] from the *Author* of the mercy, *God ;* a God that was offended by us, a God that needed us not, and a God that gains nothing by us ; and yet this God remembered us in our low estate ; that should engage us. I might also draw obligations from *the objects*, and that is *us* that were not only an undeserving but an ill-deserving, and are not a suitable returning people. I might draw arguments from *the mercy*, itself,—that God *remembered* us . . . and I might draw arguments from *the season*, "in our low estate," and from *the excellency of the duty* of thanksgiving ; 'tis a comely thing ; it makes us like the angels, whose whole employment and liturgy is to give and live praise to God. And from this also I might enlarge the discoveries of the obligation, that " his mercy endureth for ever."

"*For his mercy endureth for ever.*" There is no reason to be given for grace but grace ; there is no reason to be given for mercy but mercy : who remembered us : "*for his mercy endureth for ever.*"—*Ralph Venning* (1620—1673), *in "Mercies Memorial."*

Verse 24.—*"And."* If the end of one mercy were not the beginning of another, we were undone.—*Philip Henry*, 1631—1696.

Verse 24.—*"And hath redeemed us."* Or, *broken us off*, pulled us away, as by violence ; for they would never else have loosed us.—*John Trapp.*

Verse 25.—*"Who giveth food to all flesh,"* etc. The very air we breathe in, the bread we eat, our common blessings, be they never so mean, we have them all from grace, and all from the tender mercy of the Lord. Ps. cxxxvi. 25, you have there the story of the notable effects of God's mercy, and he concludes it thus : *"Who giveth food to all flesh : for his mercy endureth for ever."* Mark, the Psalmist doth not only ascribe those mighty victories, those glorious instances of his love and power, to his unchangeable mercy, but he traces our daily bread to the same cause. In eminent deliverances of the church we will acknowledge mercy ; yea, but we should do it in every bit of meat we eat ; for the same reason is rendered all along. What is the reason his people smote Sihon king of the Amorites, and Og the king of Bashan, and that they were rescued so often out of danger ? "For his mercy endureth for ever." And what is the reason he giveth food to all flesh ? "For his mercy endureth for ever." It is not only mercy which gives us Christ, and salvation by Christ, and all those glorious deliverances and triumphs over the enemies of the church ; but it is mercy which furnisheth our tables, it is mercy that we taste with our mouths and wear at our backs. It is notable, our Lord Jesus, when there were but five barley loaves and two fishes (John vi. 11), "He lift up his eyes and gave thanks." Though our provision be never so homely and slender, yet God's grace and mercy must be acknowledged.—*Thomas Manton.*

Verse 25.—*"Who giveth food to all flesh."* We might fancy that they who have so much to sing of in regard to themselves, so much done for their own souls, would have little care for others. We might fear that they would be found selfish. But not so ; the love of God felt by a man makes the man feel as God does toward men ; and as God's love is ever going forth to others, so is the heart of the man of God. We see how it is even as to patriotism—a man's intensest patriotic feelings do not necessarily make him indifferent to the good of other countries, but rather make him wish all countries to be like his own ; so it is, much more certainly and truly, with the Lord's people in their enjoyment of blessing. Their heart expands towards others ; they would fain have all men share in what they enjoy. They therefore cannot close their song without having this other clause—Praise him who is *"the giver of bread to all flesh."* Not to Israel only does he give blessing. Israel had their manna ; but, at the same time, the earth at large has its food. So in spiritual things. Israel's God is he who giveth himself as the Bread of Life to the world. Perhaps at this point the Psalmist's eye may be supposed to see *earth in its state of blessedness*, after Israel is for the last time redeemed from all enemies, and become "life from the dead" to the world—when Christ reigns and dispenses the bread of life to the New Earth, as widely as he gave common food—"the feast of fat things to all nations" (Isai. xxv. 6) ; for his mercy will not rest till this is accomplished.—*Andrew A. Bonar.*

Verse 25.—*"Who giveth food to all flesh."* In the close the psalmist speaks of the paternal providence of God as extending not only to all mankind, but to every living creature, suggesting that we have no reason to feel surprise at his sustaining the character of a kind and provident father to his own people, when he condescends to care for the cattle, and the asses of the field, and the crow, and the sparrow. Men are much better than brute beasts, and there is a great difference between some men and others, though not in merit, yet as regards the privilege of the divine adoption, and the psalmist is to be considered as reasoning from the less to the greater and enhancing the incomparably superior mercy which God shows to his own children.—*John Calvin.*

Verse 25.—*"Who giveth food to all flesh."* Of Edward Taylor, better known as "Father Taylor," the Sailor Preacher of Boston, it is said that his prayers were more like the utterances of an Oriental, abounding in imagery, than a son of these colder western climes. The Sunday before he was to sail for Europe, he was entreating the Lord to care well for his church during his absence. All at once he stopped and ejaculated, "What have I done? Distrust the providence of heaven! A God that gives a whale a ton of herrings for a breakfast, will he not care for my children?" and then went on, closing his prayer in a more confiding strain.—*C. H. Spurgeon, in "Eccentric Preachers,"* 1880.

Verse 26.—*"The God of heaven."* The phrase *"God of heaven"* is not found in the earlier Scriptures. We meet it nowhere else in the psalms ; but we meet it in 2 Chron. xxxvi. 23 ; Ezra i. 2 ; v. 11, 12 ; vi. 9 ; vii. 12, 23 ; Neh. i. 4 ; ii. 4 ; Dan. ii. 18, 19, 44 ; Jonah i. 9. It is twice found in the Apocalypse, Rev. xi. 13 ; xvi. 11. It is a sublime and appropriate designation of the true God, expressive of his glorious elevation above the passions and perturbations of earth. To him all flesh should give thanks, for all receive his mercy in many forms and ways. His favours come down on generation after generation, and to his willing, obedient people they shall flow on during eternal ages.—*William Swan Plumer.*

Verse 26.—My brethren, God's mercies are from everlasting ; and it is a treasure that can never be spent, never exhausted, unto eternity. In Isa. lxiv. 5, we read, "In thy mercy is continuance." If God will but continue to be merciful to me, will a poor soul say, I have enough. Why, saith he, "in his mercies is continuance, and we shall be saved." Hath God pardoned their hitherto? but hast thou sinned again? Can he stretch his goodness and mercy a little further? Why, he will stretch them out unto eternity, unto everlasting ; and if one *everlasting* be not enough, there are twenty-six everlastings in this one psalm. In Isa. liv. 8, "In a little wrath I hid my face from thee, but with everlasting kindness will I have mercy on thee."—*Thomas Goodwin.*

Verse 26.—*"O give thanks unto the God of heaven."* His mercy in providing heaven for his people is more than all the rest.—*John Trapp.*

HINTS TO THE VILLAGE PREACHER.

Verse 1.—I. Consider his name—"Jehovah." II. Carry out your joyful duty : "O give thanks." III. Contemplate the two reasons given—goodness and enduring mercy.

Verse 1.—I. Many subjects for praise. 1. For the goodness of God : "He is good" (verse 1). 2. For his supremacy : "God of gods ; Lord of lords" (verses 2, 3). 3. For his works in general (verse 4). 4. For his works of creation in particular (verses 5—9). 5. For his works of Providence (verses 10—26). II. The chief subject for praise :—"For his mercy endureth for ever." 1. For mercy. This is the sinner's principal need. 2. For mercy in God. This is the sinner's attribute, and is as essential to God as justice. 3. For mercy enduring for ever. If they who have sinned need mercy for ever, they must exist for ever ; and their guilt must be for ever.—*G. R.*

Verse 1.—*"The* LORD *is good."* God is originally good—good of himself. He is infinitely good. He is perfectly good, because infinitely good. He is immutably good.—*Charnock.*

Verses 1—3.—I. The triplet of names : "Jehovah," "the God of gods," "the Lord of lords." II. The threefold adjuration, "O give thanks." III. The irrepressible attribute and argument—"for his mercy," etc.—*W. B. H.*

Verses 1—26.—"For his mercy endureth for ever." See "Spurgeon's Sermons," No. 787 : "A Song, a Solace, a Sermon, and a Summons."

Verse 4.—I. The Lord does great wonders of mercy. II. He does them unaided. III. He does them as none else can do. IV. He should have unique praise.

Verse 4.—*The great lone Wonderworker.* I. God was alone in the wonderwork of Creation : Gen. i. II. Alone in the wonderwork of Redemption : Isa. lxiii. 5.

III. Is alone in the wonderwork of Providence : Ps. civ. 27, 28. IV. Alone in the wonderwork of Sanctification : 1 Thess. v. 23, 24. V. Will be alone in the wonderwork of Universal Triumph : 1 Cor. xv. 25.—*C. A. D.*

Verse 4.—The merciful in the wonderful. The wonderful in the merciful.

Verse 7.—The mercy which dwells in the creation and distribution of light.

Verses 7—9.—I. The constancy of rule. II. The association of light with rule. III. The perpetuity of mercy in this matter.

Verses 8, 9.—I. The glory of the day of joy. II. The comforts of the night of sorrow. III. The hand of God in each.

Verse 10.—Mercy and judgment. In the stroke that filled Egypt with anguish there was conspicuous mercy. I. Even to Egypt ; the sharp stroke should have wrought repentance. So God still strives with men. II. Evidently to Israel ; they being thus delivered ; their firstborn saved. III. Emphatically to the who world : power made known, Christ foreshadowed, an important link in the chain of redemption.—*W. B. H.*

Verse 11.—The bringing out of God's people from their natural state, from their misery, and from association with the ungodly, a great marvel of everlasting mercy.

Verse 11.—Effectual calling ; the intervention at the determined moment of the mercy of infinite ages.—*W. B. H.*

Verse 12.—Displays of divine power in the history of the saints a reason for song.

Verses 13, 14.—God to be praised not only, I. For clearing our way ; but also, II. For giving faith to traverse it. The last as great a mercy as the first.

Verses 13—15.—Mercy queen of the Exodus. I. Her sceptre upon the sea. What cannot Love divine conquer for its chosen ! II. Her standard in the van. Whither shall saints fear to follow her ? III. Her frown upon the pursuers ; life to the beloved, fatal to the foe. IV. To her let there be brought the chaplet of our praises.—*W. B. H.*

Verse 15.—Final victory. I. Battalions of evil annihilated. II. Love unharmed mounting immortal above the wave : "for his mercy endureth for ever." III. Heaven resonant with the song of Moses and the Lamb : to him give thanks. —*W. B. H.*

Verse 16.—I. Personal care : "To him which led." II. Peculiar interest : "His people." III. Persevering goodness : ". Through the wilderness."

Verse 16.—*Led through the Wilderness.* I. God's people must enter the wilderness for trial, for self-knowledge, for development of graces, for preparation for Canaan. II. God leads his people while in the wilderness. Their route, their provision, their discipline, their protection. III. God will bring his people out of the wilderness.—*C. A. D.*

Verses 17—22.—See "Spurgeon's Sermons," No. 1285 : "Sihon and Og ; or, Mercies in Detail."

Verse 21.—I. Our portion, a heritage. II. Our title-deed, a royal grant : "And gave." III. Our praise, due to enduring mercy.

Verse 23.—Prayer of the dying thief turned into a song.

Verses 23, 24.—The gracious remembrance and the glorious redemption.— *C. A. D.*

Verse 24.—Our enemies, our accomplished redemption, the author of it, and his reason for effecting it.

Verse 24.—The multiplied redemptions of the Christian life, and their inexhaustible spring.—*W. B. H.*

Verse 25.—Divine housekeeping. I. The Royal Commissariat. II. Its spiritual counterpart : God's august provisioning for our immortal nature. III. The queenly grace that hath the keeping of the keys : "for his mercy," etc.— *W. B. H.*

Verse 26.—Consider, I. How he rules in heaven. II. How he rules earth from heaven. III. How mercy is the eternal element of that rule, and therefore he is the eternal object of praise.

PSALM CXXXVII.

This plaintive ode is one of the most charming compositions in the whole Book of Psa'ms for its poetic power. If it were not inspired it would nevertheless occupy a high place in poesy, especially the former portion of it, which is tender and patriotic to the highest degree. In the later verses (7, 8, 9), we have utterances of burning indignation against the chief adversaries of Israel,—an indignation as righteous as it was fervent. Let those find fault with it who have never seen their temple burned, their city ruined, their wives ravished, and their children slain; they might not, perhaps, be quite so velvet-mouthed if they had suffered after this fashion. It is one thing to talk of the bitter feeling which moved captive Israelites in Babylon, and quite another thing to be captives ourselves under a savage and remorseless power, which knew not how to show mercy, but delighted in barbarities to the defenceless. The song is such as might fitly be sung in the Jews' wailing-place. It is a fruit of the Captivity in Babylon, and often has it furnished expression for sorrows which else had been unutterable. It is an opalesque psalm within whose mild radiance there glows a fire which strikes the beholder with wonder.

EXPOSITION.

BY the rivers of Babylon, there we sat down, yea, we wept, when we remembered Zion.

2 We hanged our harps upon the willows in the midst thereof.

3 For there they that carried us away captive required of us a song ; and they that wasted us *required of us* mirth, *saying*, Sing us *one* of the songs of Zion.

4 How shall we sing the LORD'S song in a strange land ?

5 If I forget thee, O Jerusalem, let my right hand forget *her cunning*.

6 If I do not remember thee, let my tongue cleave to the roof of my mouth ; if I prefer not Jerusalem above my chief joy.

1. *"By the rivers of Babylon, there we sat down."* Water-courses were abundant in Babylon, wherein were not only natural streams but artificial canals : it was a place of broad rivers and streams. Glad to be away from the noisy streets, the captives sought the river side, where the flow of the waters seemed to be in sympathy with their tears. It was some slight comfort to be out of the crowd, and to have a little breathing room, and therefore they sat down, as if to rest a while and solace themselves in their sorrow. In little groups they sat down and made common lamentation, mingling their memories and their teais. The rivers were well enough, but, alas, they were the rivers of Babylon, and the ground whereon the sons of Israel sat was foreign soil, and therefore they wept. Those who came to interrupt their quiet were citizens of the destroying city, and their company was not desired. Everything reminded Israel of her banishment from the holy city, her servitude beneath the shadow of the temple of Bel, her helplessness under a cruel enemy ; and therefore her sons and daughters sat down in sorrow.

"Yea, we wept, when we remembered Zion." Nothing else could have subdued their brave spirits ; but the remembrance of the temple of their God, the palace of their king, and the centre of their national life, quite broke them down. Destruction had swept down all their delights, and therefore they wept—the strong men wept, the sweet singers wept ! They did not weep when they remembered the cruelties of Babylon ; the memory of fierce oppression dried their

tears and made their hearts burn with wrath : but when the beloved city of their solemnities came into their minds they could not refrain from floods of tears. Even thus do true believers mourn when they see the church despoiled, and find themselves unable to succour her : we could bear anything better than this. In these our times the Babylon of error ravages the city of God, and the hearts of the faithful are grievously wounded as they see truth fallen in the streets, and unbelief rampant among the professed servants of the Lord. We bear our protests, but they appear to be in vain ; the multitude are mad upon their idols. Be it ours to weep in secret for the hurt of our Zion : it is the least thing we can do ; perhaps in its result it may prove to be the best thing we can do. Be it ours also to sit down and deeply consider what is to be done. Be it ours, in any case, to keep upon our mind and heart the memory of the church of God which is so dear to us. The frivolous may forget, but Zion is graven on our hearts, and her prosperity is our chief desire.

2. "*We hanged our harps upon the willows in the midst thereof.*" The drooping branches appeared to weep as we did, and so we gave to them our instruments of music ; the willows could as well make melody as we, for we had no mind for minstrelsy. In the midst of the willows, or in the midst of the rivers, or in the midst of Babylon, it matters little which, they hung their harps aloft—those harps which once in Zion's halls the soul of music shed. Better to hang them up than to dash them down : better to hang them on willows than profane them to the service of idols. Sad indeed is the child of sorrow when he grows weary of his harp, from which in better days he had been able to draw sweet solaces. Music hath charms to give unquiet spirits rest ; but when the heart is sorely sad it only mocks the grief which flies to it. Men put away their instruments of mirth when a heavy cloud darkens their souls.

3. "*For there they that carried us away captive required of us a song.*" It was ill to be a singer at all when it was demanded that this talent should go into bondage to an oppressor's will. Better be dumb than be forced to please an enemy with forced song. What cruelty to make a people sigh, and then require them to sing ! Shall men be carried away from home and all that is dear to them, and yet chant merrily for the pleasure of their unfeeling captors ? This is studied torture : the iron enters into the soul. It is indeed " woe to the conquered " when they are forced to sing to increase the triumph of their conquerors. Cruelty herein reached a refinement seldom thought of. We do not wonder that the captives sat them down to weep when thus insulted. "*And they that wasted us required of us mirth.*" The captives must not only sing but smile, and add merriment to their music. Blind Samson in former days must be brought forth to make sport for Philistines, and now the Babylonians prove themselves to be loaves of the same leaven. Plundered, wounded, fettered, carried into captivity and poverty, yet must the people laugh as if it were all a play, and they must sport as if they felt no sorrow. This was wormwood and gall to the true lovers of God and his chosen land. "*Saying, Sing us one of the songs of Zion.*" Nothing would serve their turn but a holy hymn, and a tune sacred to the worship of Jehovah. Nothing will content the Babylonian mockers but one of Israel's psalms when in her happiest days she sang unto the Lord whose mercy endureth for ever : this would make rare fun for their persecutors, who would deride their worship and ridicule their faith in Jehovah. In this demand there was an insult to their God as well as a mockery of themselves, and this made it the more intensely cruel. Nothing could have been more malicious, nothing more produc-tive of grief. These wanton persecutors had followed the captives into their retirement, and had remarked upon their sorrowful appearance, and " there" and then they bade the mourners make mirth for them. Could they not let the sufferers alone ? Were the exiles to have no rest ? The daughter of Babylon seemed determined to fill up her cup of iniquity, by torturing the Lord's people. Those who had been the most active agents of Israel's undoing must needs follow up their ferocities by mokeries. " The tender mercies of the wicked are cruel." Worse than the Egyptians, they asked not labour which their victims could have

rendered, but they demanded mirth which they could not give, and holy songs which they dared not profane to such a purpose.

4. "*How shall we sing the* LORD's *song in a strange land ?*" How shall they sing at all ? sing in a strange land ? sing Jehovah's song among the uncircumcised ? No, that must not be ; it shall not be. With one voice they refuse, but the refusal is humbly worded by being put in the form of a question. If the men of Babylon were wicked enough to suggest the defiling of holy things for the gratification of curiosity, or for the creation of amusement, the men of Zion had not so hardened their hearts as to be willing to please them at such a fearful cost. There are many things which the ungodly could do, and think nothing of the doing thereof, which gracious men cannot venture upon. The question " How can I ?" or " How shall we ?" comes of a tender conscience and denotes an inability to sin which is greatly to be cultivated.

5. "*If I forget thee, O Jerusalem, let my right hand forget her cunning.*" To sing Zion's songs for the pleasure of Zion's foes, would be to forget the Holy City. Each Jew declares for himself that he will not do this ; for the pronoun alters from " we" to " I." Individually the captives pledge themselves to fidelity to Jerusalem, and each one asserts that he had sooner forget the art which drew music from his harp-strings than use it for Babel's delectation. Better far that the right hand should forget its usual handicraft, and lose all its dexterity, than that it should fetch music for rebels out of the Lord's instruments, or accompany with sweet skill a holy psalm desecrated into a common song for fools to laugh at. Not one of them will thus dishonour Jehovah to glorify Belus and gratify his votaries. Solemnly they imprecate vengeance upon themselves should they so false, so faithless prove.

6. "*If I do not remember thee, let my tongue cleave to the roof of my mouth.*" Thus the singers imprecate eternal silence upon their mouths if they forget Jerusalem to gratify Babylon. The players on instruments and the sweet songsters are of one mind : the enemies of the Lord will get no mirthful tune or song from them. "*If I prefer not Jerusalem above my chief joy.*" The sacred city must ever be first in their thoughts, the queen of their souls ; they had sooner be dumb than dishonour her sacred hymns, and give occasion to the oppressor to ridicule her worship. If such the attachment of a banished Jew to his native land, how much more should we love the church of God of which we are children and citizens. How jealous should we be of her honour, how zealous for her prosperity. Never let us find jests in the words of Scripture, or make amusement out of holy things, lest we be guilty of forgetting the Lord and his cause. It is to be feared that many tongues have lost all power to charm the congregations of the saints because they have forgotten the gospel, and God has forgotten *them.*

7 Remember, O LORD, the children of Edom in the day of Jerusalem ; who said, Rase *it*, rase *it*, *even* to the foundation thereof.

8 O daughter of Babylon, who art to be destroyed ; happy *shall he be*, that rewardeth thee as thou hast served us.

9 Happy *shall he be*, that taketh and dasheth thy little ones against the stones.

7. "*Remember, O* LORD, *the children of Edom in the day of Jerusalem.*" The case is left in Jehovah's hands. He is a God of recompenses, and will deal out justice with impartiality. The Edomites ought to have been friendly with the Israelites, from kinship ; but there was a deep hatred and cruel spite displayed by them. The elder loved not to serve the younger, and so when Jacob's day of tribulation came, Esau was ready to take advantage of it. The captive Israelites being moved by grief to lodge their plaints with God, also added a prayer for his visitation of the nation which meanly sided with their enemies, and even urged the invaders to more than their usual cruelty. "*Who said, Rase it, rase it, even to the foundation thereof.*" They wished to see the last of Jerusalem and the Jewish state ; they would have no stone left standing, they desired to see a clean

sweep of temple, palace, wall, and habitation. It is horrible for neighbours to be enemies, worse for them to show their enmity in times of great affliction, worst of all for neighbours to egg others on to malicious deeds. Those are responsible for other men's sins who would use them as the tools of their own enmity. It is a shame for men to incite the wicked to deeds which they are not able to perform themselves. The Chaldeans were ferocious enough without being excited to greater fury ; but Edom's hate was insatiable. Those deserve to be remembered by vengeance who in evil times do not remember mercy ; how much more those who take advantage of calamities to wreak revenge upon sufferers. When Jerusalem's day of restoration comes Edom will be remembered and wiped out of existence.

8. *"O daughter of Babylon, who art to be destroyed."* Or the destroyer : let us accept the word either way, or both ways : the destroyer would be destroyed, and the Psalmist in vision saw her as already destroyed. It is usual to speak of a city as a virgin daughter. Babylon was in her prime and beauty, but she was already doomed for her crimes. *"Happy shall he be that rewardeth thee as thou hast served us."* The avenger would be fulfilling an honourable calling in overthrowing a power so brutal, so inhuman. Assyrian and Chaldean armies had been boastfully brutal in their conquests ; it was meet that their conduct should be measured back into their own bosoms. No awards of punishment can be more unanswerably just than those which closely follow the *lex talionis*, even to the letter. Babylon must fall, as she caused Jerusalem to fall ; and her sack and slaughter must be such as she appointed for other cities. The patriot-poet sitting sorrowfully in his exile, finds a solace in the prospect of the overthrow of the empress city which holds him in bondage, and he accounts Cyrus right happy to be ordained to such a righteous work. The whole earth would bless the conqueror for ridding the nations of a tyrant ; future generations would call him blessed for enabling men to breathe again, and for once more making liberty possible upon the earth.

We may rest assured that every unrighteous power is doomed to destruction, and that from the throne of God justice will be measured out to all whose law is force, whose rule is selfishness, and whose policy is oppression. Happy is the man who shall help in the overthrow of the spiritual Babylon, which, despite its riches and power, is " to be destroyed." Happier still shall he be who shall see it sink like a millstone in the flood, never to rise again. What that spiritual Babylon is none need enquire. There is but one city upon earth which can answer to the name.

9. *"Happy shall he be, that taketh and dasheth thy little ones against the stones."* Fierce was the heart of the Jew who had seen his beloved city the scene of such terrific butchery. His heart pronounced like sentence upon Babylon. She should be scourged with her own whip of wire. The desire for righteous retribution is rather the spirit of the law than of the gospel ; and yet in moments of righteous wrath the old fire will burn ; and while justice survives in the human breast it will not lack for fuel among the various tyrannies which still survive. We shall be wise to view this passage as a prophecy. History informs us that it was literally fulfilled : the Babylonian people in their terror agreed to destroy their own offspring, and men thought themselves happy when they had put their own wives and children to the sword. Horrible as was the whole transaction, it is a thing to be glad of if we take a broad view of the world's welfare ; for Babylon, the gigantic robber, had for many a year slaughtered nations without mercy, and her fall was the rising of many people to a freer and safer state. The murder of innocent infants can never be sufficiently deplored, but it was an incident of ancient warfare which the Babylonians had not omitted in their massacres, and, therefore, they were not spared it themselves. The revenges of providence may be slow, but they are ever sure ; neither can they be received with regret by those who see God's righteous hand in them. It is a wretched thing that a nation should need an executioner ; but yet if men will commit murders tears are more fitly shed over their victims than over the assassins them-

selves. A feeling of universal love is admirable, but it must not be divorced from a keen sense of justice.

The captives in Babylon did not make music, but they poured forth their righteous maledictions, and these were far more in harmony with their surroundings than songs and laughter could have been. Those who mock the Lord's people will receive more than they desire, to their own confusion : they shall have little enough to make mirth for them, and more than enough to fill them with misery. The execrations of good men are terrible things, for they are not lightly uttered, and they are heard in heaven. "The curse causeless shall not come ;" but is there not a cause ? Shall despots crush virtue beneath their iron heel and never be punished ? Time will show.

EXPLANATORY NOTES.

Whole Psalm.—Observe that this very psalm in which the question is asked, "How can we sing ?" is itself a song, one of the Lord's songs, still. Nothing can be more sad, more desponding. It speaks of weeping in the remembrance of Zion ; it speaks of harps hung upon the willows by exiles who have no heart to use them ; and yet the very telling of these sorrows, of this incapacity for song, is a song still. We chant it in our congregations now, hundreds and thousands of years after its composition, as one of the Church's melodies, as one of the Lord's songs. It gives us a striking example of the variety, of the versatility of worship, even in that department which might seem to be all joyous, all praise. The very refusal to sing may be itself a song. Any real utterance of good thoughts, whether they be thoughts of gladness or thoughts of sorrow, may be a true hymn, a true melody for the congregation, even though it may not breathe at every moment the very thought of all the worshippers. "How shall we sing ?" is itself a permanent hymn, an inspired song, for all the churches.—*C. J. Vaughan.*

Whole Psalm.—This psalm is composed of two parts. The first is, an heavy complaint of the church, unto verse 7. The other is an heavy imprecation and a prophetical denunciation against the enemies of the church, unto the end of the psalm.—*Robert Rollock.*

Whole Psalm.—What a wonderful mixture is the psalm of soft melancholy and fiery patriotism ! The hand which wrote it must have known how to smite sharply with the sword, as well as how to tune the harp. The words are burning words of a heart breathing undying love to his country, undying hate to his foe. The poet is indeed

> "Dower'd with the hate of hate, the scorn of scorn,
> The love of love."

—*J. J. Stewart Perowne.*

Whole Psalm.—Several of the psalms obviously refer to the time of the Babylonian captivity. . . . The captives' mournful sentiments of pensive melancholy and weary longing during its long and weary continuance constitute the burden of the hundred and thirty-seventh. It was probably written by some gifted captive Levite at the time. Some suppose it to have been composed by Jeremiah, the prophet of tears, and sent to his countrymen in the land of their exile, in order to awaken fond memories of the past and sustain a lively hope for the future ; and certainly the ode is worthy even of his pen, for it is one of the sweetest, most plaintive, and exquisitely beautiful elegies in any language. It is full of heart-melting, tear-bringing pathos. The moaning of the captive, the wailing of the exile, and the sighing of the saints are heard in every line.—*W. Ormiston, in "The Study," 1874.*

Whole Psalm.—Here, I. The melancholy captives cannot enjoy themselves, verses 1, 2. II. They cannot humour their proud oppressors, verses 3, 4. III. They cannot forget Jerusalem, verses 5, 6. IV. They cannot forget Edom and Babylon, verses 7, 8, 9.—*Matthew Henry.*

Verse 1.—"*By the rivers of Babylon.*" The canals of Babylon itself, probably (comp. verse 2.)—*William Kay.*

Verse 1.—"*By the rivers.*" Euphrates, Tigris, Chaboras, etc., and the canals which intersected the country. The exiles would naturally resort to the banks of the streams as shady, cool and retired spots, where they could indulge in their sorrowful remembrances. The prophets of the exile saw their visions by the river. Ezek. i. 1 ; Dan. viii. 2 ; x. 4.—"*Bibliotheca Sacra and Theological Review,*" 1848.

Verse 1.—"*By the rivers.*" The bank of a river, like the seashore, is a favourite place of sojourn of those whom deep grief drives forth from the bustle of men into solitude. The boundary line of the river gives to solitude a safe back ; the monotonous splashing of the waves keeps up the dull, melancholy alternation of thoughts and feelings ; and at the same time the sight of the cool, fresh water exercises a soothing influence upon the consuming fever within the heart.—*Franz Delitzsch.*

Verse 1.—"*By the rivers.*" The peculiar reason for the children of Israel being represented as sitting at the streams is the *weeping*. An internal reference of the weeping to the streams, must therefore have been what gave rise to the representation of the sitting. Nor is this reference difficult to be discovered. All languages know of brooks, or streams of tears, compare in Scripture, Lam. ii. 18 ; " Let tears run down like a river day and night" ; iii. 48 ; also Job xxviii. 11, where inversely the gushing of the floods is called *weeping* (Marg.). The children of Israel placed themselves beside the streams of Babel because they saw in them the image and symbol of their floods of tears.—*E. W. Hengstenberg.*

Verse 1.—"*We sat down.*" Among the poets, sitting on the ground is a mark of misery or captivity.

> Multos illa dies incomtis mœsta capillis
> Sederat.—*Propertius.*
> With locks unkempt, mournful, for many days
> She sat.

> O utinam ante tuos sedeam captiva penates.—*Propertius.*
> O might I sit a captive at thy gate !

You have the same posture in an old coin that celebrates a victory of Lucius Verus over the Parthians.

We find Judea on several coins of Vespasian and Titus in the posture that denotes sorrow and captivity. —*From Joseph Addison's Dialogues on Medals.*

Verse 1.—"*Sat down*" implies that the burst of grief was a long one, and also that it was looked on by the captives as some relaxation and repose.—*Chrysostom.*

Verse 1.—" *We wept when we remembered Zion.*" A godly man lays to heart the miseries of the church. I have read of certain trees, whose leaves if cut or touched, the other leaves contract and shrink up themselves, and for a space hang down their heads : such a spiritual sympathy is there among Christians ; when other parts of God's church suffer, they feel themselves, as it were, touched in their own persons. Ambrose reports, that when Theodosius was sick unto death, he was more troubled about the church of God than about his own sickness. When Æneas would have saved Anchises' life, saith he, " Far be it from me that I should desire to live when Troy is buried in its ruins." There are in music two unisons ; if you strike one, you shall perceive the other to stir, as if it were affected : when the Lord strikes others a godly heart is deeply affected, Isai. xvi. 11 : " My bowels shall sound like an harp." Though it be well with a child of God in his own particular, and he dwells in an house of cedar, yet he grieves to see it go ill with the public. Queen Esther enjoyed the king's favour, and all the delights of the court, yet when a bloody warrant was signed for the death of the Jews she mourns and fasts, and ventures her own life to save theirs.—*Thomas Watson.*

Verse 1.—For *Sion* only they wept, unlike many who weep with the weeping and rejoice with the joy of Babylon, because their whole interests and affections are bound up in the things of this world.—*Augustine.*

Verse 1.—Let us weep, because in this life we are forced to sit by the waters of Babylon, and are yet strangers and as it were banished and barred from being satisfied with the pleasures of that river which gladdeth the city of God. Alas, if we did consider that our country were heaven, and did apprehend this place here below to be our prison, or place of banishment, the least absence from our country would draw tears from our eyes and sighs from our hearts, with David (Ps. cxx. 5) : " Woe is me that I sojourn in Mesech, and am constrained to dwell in the tents of Kedar."

Do you remember how the Jews behaved themselves in the time of their exile and captivity, while they sat by the rivers and waters of Babylon ? They wept, would not be comforted ; hanged up their harps and instruments. What are the waters of Babylon but the pleasures and delights of the world, the waters of confusion, as the word signifies ? Now when the people of God sit by them, that is to say, do not carelessly, but deliberately, with a settled consideration, see them slide by and pass away, and compare them with Sion, that is to say, with the inconceivable rivers of pleasure, which are permanent in the heavenly Jerusalem ; how can they choose but weep, when they see themselves sitting by the one, and sojourning from the other ? And it is worthy your observing, that notwithstanding the Jews had many causes of tears, the Chaldeans had robbed them of their goods, honours, countries, liberty, parents, children, friends : the chief thing, for all this, that they mourn for is their absence from Sion,—" *We wept when we remembered thee, O Sion*"—for their absence from Jerusalem. What should we then do for our absence from another manner of Jerusalem ? Theirs was an earthly, old, robbed, spoiled, burned, sacked Jerusalem ; ours a heavenly, new one, into which no arrow can be shot, no noise of the drum heard, nor sound of the trumpet, nor calling unto battle : who would not then weep, to be absent from thence ?"—*Walter Balcanqual, in "A Sermon Preached at St. Maries Spittle,"* 1623.

Verse 1.—"*We remembered Zion.*" It necessarily implies they had *forgot*, else how could they now remember ? In their peace and plenty they had but little regard of Zion then.—*John Whincop, in a Sermon entitled, "Israel's Tears for Distressed Zion,"* 1645.

Verse 1.—Nothing could present a more striking contrast to their native country than the region into which the Hebrews were transplanted. Instead of their irregular and picturesque mountain city, crowning its unequal heights, and looking down into its deep and precipitous ravines, through one of which a scanty stream wound along, they entered the vast, square, and level city of Babylon, occupying both sides of the broad Euphrates ; while all around spread immense plains, which were intersected by long straight canals, bordered by rows of willows. How unlike their national temple—a small but highly finished and richly adorned fabric, standing in the midst of its courts on the brow of a lofty precipice—the colossal temple of the Chaldean Bel, rising from the plain, with its eight stupendous stories or towers, one above the other, to the perpendicular height of a furlong ! The palace of the Babylonian kings was more than twice the size of their whole city ; it covered eight miles, with its hanging gardens built on arched terraces, each rising above the other, and rich in all the luxuriance of artificial cultivation. How different from the sunny cliffs of their own land, where the olive and the vine grew spontaneously, and the cool, shady, and secluded valleys, where they could always find shelter from the heat of the burning noon ! No wonder then that, in the pathetic words of their own hymn, " *by the waters of Babylon they sat down and wept, when they remembered thee, O Zion.*" Of their general treatment as captives we know little. The psalm above quoted seems to intimate that the Babylonians had taste enough to appreciate the poetical and musical talent of the exiles, and that they were summoned occasionally to amuse the banquets of their masters, though it was much against their will that they sang the songs of Zion in a strange land. In general it seems that the Jewish exiles were allowed to dwell together in considerable bodies, not sold as household or personal or prædial slaves, at least not those of the better order of whom the Captivity chiefly consisted. They were colonists rather than captives, and became by degrees possessed of considerable property. They had taken the advice of the prophet Jeremiah (who gave them no hopes of speedy return to their homes) : they had built houses, planted gardens, married and brought up children, submitted themselves as peaceful subjects to the local authorities : all which implies a certain freedom, a certain degree of prosperity and comfort. They had free enjoyment of their religion, such at least as adhered faithfully to their belief in Jehovah. We hear of no special and general religious persecution. —*Henry Hart Milman* (1791—1868), *in "The History of the Jews."*

Verse 1.—They sat in silence ; they remembered in silence ; they wept in silence.—*J. W. Burgon.*

Verses 1—6.—Israel was a typical people. 1. They were typical of God's church in all ages of the world. And, 2. They were typical of the soul of every individual believer.

This psalm is composed for Israel in her captivity. Let us go over it, taking its typical meaning.

I. *When a believer is in captivity he has a sorrowful remembrance of Zion.* So it was with God's ancient people : "By the rivers of Babylon, there we sat down, yea, we wept, when we remembered Zion" (verse 1). In the last chapter of 2 Chron. (14—20), we find the melancholy tale of Judah's captivity. Many of their friends had been slain by the sword—the house of God was burned—the walls of Jerusalem were broken down—and they themselves were captives in a foreign land. No wonder that they sat down and wept when they remembered Zion.

So it is often with the believer when led captive by sin—he sits down and weeps when he remembers Zion. Zion is the place where God makes himself known. When a poor awakened sinner is brought to know the Saviour, and to enter through the rent veil into the holiest of all, then he becomes one of the people of Zion : "A day in thy courts is better than a thousand." He dwells in Zion ; and the people that dwell therein are forgiven their iniquity. But when a believer falls into sin he falls into darkness—he is carried a captive away from Zion. No more does he find entrance within the veil ; no more is he glad when they say to him, "Let us go up to the house of the Lord." He sits down and weeps when he remembers Zion.

II. *The world derides the believer in his captivity.* So it was with ancient Israel. The Chaldeans were cruel conquerors. God says by his prophet,—"I was but a little displeased, and they helped forward the affliction." Not only did they carry them away from their temple, their country, and their homes, but they made a mock of their sorrows. When they saw them sit down to shed bitter tears by the rivers of Babylon, they demanded mirth and a song, saying, "Sing us one of the songs of Zion."

So is it with the world and the captive Christian. There are times when the world does not mock at the Christian. Often the Christian is filled with so strange a joy that the world wonders in silence. Often there is a meek and quiet spirit in the Christian, which disarms opposition. The soft answer turneth away wrath ; and his very enemies are forced to be at peace with him. But stop till the Christian's day of darkness comes—stop till sin and unbelief have brought him into captivity—stop till he is shut out from Zion, and carried afar off, and sits and weeps ; then will the cruel world help forward the affliction—then will they ask for mirth and song ; and when they see the bitter tear trickling down the cheek, they will ask with savage mockery, "Where is your psalm-singing now ?" "Sing us one of the songs of Zion." Even Christ felt this bitterness when he hung upon the cross.

III. *The Christian cannot sing in captivity.* So it was with ancient Israel. They were peculiarly attached to the sweet songs of Zion. They reminded them of the times of David and Solomon—when the temple was built, and Israel was in its greatest glory. They reminded them, above all, of their God, of their temple, and the services of the sanctuary.   Three times a-year they came up from the country in companies, singing these sweet songs of Zion—lifting their eyes to the hills whence came their help.   But now, when they were in captivity, they hanged their harps upon the willows ; and when their cruel spoilers demanded mirth and a song, they said : " How shall we sing the Lord's song in a strange land ?"   So is it with the believer in darkness.   He hangs his harp upon the willows, and cannot sing the song of the Lord.   Every believer has got a harp. Every heart that has been made new is turned into a harp of praise.   The mouth is filled with laughter—the tongue with divinest melody.   Every true Christian loves praise—the holiest Christians love it most.   But when the believer falls into sin and darkness, his harp is on the willows, and he cannot sing the Lord's song, for he is in a strange land.

1. *He loses all sense of pardon.*   It is the sense of pardon that gives its sweetest tones to the song of the Christian.   But when a believer is in captivity he loses this sweet sense of forgiveness, and therefore cannot sing.

2. *He loses all sense of the presence of God.*   It is the sweet presence of God with the soul that makes the believer sing.   But when that presence is away, the Lord's house is but a howling wilderness ; and you say, " How can we sing the Lord's song in a strange land ?"

3. *He loses sight of the heavenly Canaan.*   The sight of the everlasting hills draws forth the heavenly melodies of the believing soul.   But when a believer sins, and is carried away captive, he loses this hope of glory.   He sits and weeps —he hangs his harp upon the willows, and cannot sing the Lord's song in a strange land.

4. *The believer in darkness still remembers Zion, and prefers it above his chief joy.* He often finds, when he has fallen into sin and captivity, that he has fallen among worldly delights and worldly friends.   A thousand pleasures tempt him to take up his rest here ; but if he be a true child of Zion he will never settle down in a strange land.   He will look over all the pleasures of the world and the pleasures of sin, and say, " A day in thy courts is better than a thousand "—" If I forget thee, O Jerusalem, let my right hand forget her cunning."—*Condensed from Robert Murray M' Cheyne,* 1813—1843.

Verses 1, 2.—The psalm is universally admired.   Indeed, nothing can be more exquisitely beautiful.   It is written in a strain of sensibility that must touch every soul that is capable of feeling.   It is remarkable that Dr. Watts, in his excellent versification, has omitted it.   He has indeed some verses upon it in his Lyrics ; and many others have written on this ode.   We have seen more than ten productions of this kind ; the last, and perhaps the best, of which is Lord Byron's.   But who is satisfied with any of these attempts ?   Thus it begins : " By the rivers of Babylon, there we sat down, yea, we wept, when we remembered Zion."   These rivers were probably some of the streams branching off from the Euphrates and Tigris.   Here it is commonly supposed these captive Jews were placed by their task-masters, to preserve or repair the water-works.   But is it improper to conjecture that the Psalmist refers to their being here ; not constantly, but occasionally ; not by compulsion, but choice ?   Hither I imagine their retiring, to unbend their oppressed minds in solitude.   " Come," said one of these pious Jews to another, " come, let us for a while go forth, from this vanity and vileness.   Let us assemble together by ourselves under the refreshing shade of the willows by the watercourses.   And let us take our harps with us, and solace ourselves with some of the songs of Zion."   But as soon as they arrive, and begin to touch the chords, the notes—such is the power of association —awaken the memory of their former privileges and pleasures.   And, overwhelmed with grief, they sit down on the grass ; and weep when they remember Zion ; their dejected looks, averted from each other, seeming to say, " If I forget thee, O Jerusalem, let my right hand forget her cunning.   If I do not remember thee, let my tongue cleave to the roof of my mouth ; if I prefer not Jerusalem above my chief joy."   But what do they with their harps ?   The voice of mirth is heard no more, and all the daughters of music are brought low.   Melody is not in season to a distressed spirit. "Is any afflicted? Let him pray. Is any merry? Let him sing psalms." "As he that taketh away a garment in cold weather, and as vinegar upon nitre, so is he that singeth songs to a heavy heart." They did not, however, break them to pieces, or throw them into the stream—but *hanged* them up only. They hoped that what they could not use at present they might be able to resume at some happier period. To be cast down is not to be destroyed. Distress is not despondency.

"Beware of desperate steps : the darkest day,
Live till to-morrow, will have passed away."

"*We hanged our harps upon the willows in the midst thereof.*" Let us pass from the Jew to the Christian ; and let us survey the Christian in his SPIRITUAL SORROWS. He who would preach well, says Luther, must distinguish well. It is peculiarly necessary to discriminate, when we enter upon the present subject. For all the sorrows of the Christian are not of the same kind or descent. Let us consider four sources of his moral sadness.

I. The first will be *physical.* II. The second will be *criminal.* III. The third will be *intellectual.* IV. The fourth will be *pious.—William Jay, in "The Christian Contemplated.*"

Verse 2.—"*Our harps.*" Many singers were carried captives: Ezra ii. 41. These would of course carry their instruments with them, and be insulted, as here. Their songs were sacred, and unfit to be sung before idolaters.—*From "Anonymous Notes" in James Merrick's Annotations,* 1768.

Verse 2.—"*Willows.*" All the flat, whereon Babylon stood, being by reason of so many rivers and canals running through it made in many places marshy, especially near the said rivers and canals, this caused it to abound much in *willows,* and therefore it is called in Scripture the "Valley of Willows" ; for so the words in Isaiah xv. 7, which we translate "the brook of the willows," ought to be rendered.—*Humphrey Prideaux* (1648—1724), *in "The Old and New Testament Connected,"* etc.

Verse 2.—"*Willows.*" The *Weeping Willow* of Babylon will grow to be a large tree ; its branches being long, slender, and pendulous, makes it proper to be planted upon the banks of rivers, ponds, and over springs ; the leaves, also, are long and narrow ; and when any mist or dew falls, a drop of water is seen hanging at their extremities, which, together with their hanging branches, cause a most lugubrious appearance. Lovers' garlands are said to have been made of a species of this willow, the branches of which are very slender and pliable ; and the plant itself has always been sought after for ornamental plantations, either to mix with others of the like growth in the largest quarters, or to be planted out singly over springs, or in large opens, for the peculiar variety occasioned by its mournful look.—*John Evelyn* (1620—1706), *in "Silva ; or, A Discourse of Forest-Trees.*"

Verse 2.—"*Willows.*" It is a curious fact, that during the Commonwealth of England, when Cromwell, like a wise politician, allowed them to settle in London and to have synagogues, the Jews came hither in sufficient numbers to celebrate the feast of Tabernacles in booths, among the *Willows* on the borders of the Thames. The disturbance of their comfort from the innumerable spectators, chiefly London apprentices, called for some protection from the local magistrates. Not that any insult was offered to their persons, but a natural curiosity, excited by so new and extraordinary a spectacle, induced many to press too closely round their camp, and perhaps intrude upon their privacy.—*Maria Callcott* (1788—1842), *in "A Scripture Herbal,"* 1842.

Verse 2.—"*Willows.*" There is a pretty story told about the way in which the Weeping Willow was introduced into England.* Many years ago, the well-

---

* The two preceding extracts would seem to prove that this story is not true ; at least Evelyn's willow is evidently the weeping willow, and would seem to have long been known.

known poet, Alexander Pope, who resided at Twickenham, received a basket of figs as a present from Turkey. The basket was made of the supple branches of the Weeping Willow, the very same species under which the captive Jews sat when they wept by the waters of Babylon. "*We hanged our harps upon the willows.*" The poet valued highly the small slender twigs as associated with so much that was interesting, and he untwisted the basket, and planted one of the branches in the ground. It had some tiny buds upon it, and he hoped he might be able to rear it, as none of this species of willow was known in England. Happily the willow is very quick to take root and grow. The little branch soon became a tree, and drooped gracefully over the river, in the same manner that its race had done over the waters of Babylon. From that one branch all the Weeping Willows in England are descended.—*Mary and Elizabeth Kirby, in "Chapters on Trees,"* 1873.

Verse 2.—"*In the midst thereof.*" This is most naturally understood of the *city* of Babylon ; which was nearly as large as Middlesex, and had parks and gardens inside it.—*William Kay.*

Verse 3.—"*They that carried us away captive required of us a song* " ; or rather, as it should be rendered, " *the words* of a song." They see no inconsistency in a religion which freely mixes with the world. In their ignorance they only require " *the words* of a song" ; its heavenly strain they have never caught. " They that *wasted us* required of us mirth." Remember, it is this worldly element which wasteth, or lays on heaps, whether so far as our own hearts or the church of God is concerned. But, true to his spiritual instincts, the child of God replies, " How shall we sing *Jehovah's* song in the land of a *stranger?*" and then, so far from being utterly cast down or overcome, rises with fresh outburst of resolution and intenseness of new vigour, to utter the vows of verses 5 and 6. For, after having passed through such a spiritual conflict, we come forth, not wearied, but refreshed ; not weaker, but stronger. It is one of the seeming contradictions of the gospel, that the cure of weariness, and the relief of heavy-ladenness, lies in this—*to take the cross upon ourselves.* After the night-long conflict of Israel, " as he passed over Peniel, *the sun rose upon him,*" and that though " he halted upon his thigh."—*Alfred Edersheim.*

Verse 3.—"*Sing us one of the songs of Zion.*" It is variously set down as simple curiosity to hear something of the famous melodies of the Hebrew people ; as well-meaning counsel to the exiles to reconcile themselves to their inevitable situation, and to resume their former habits in social harmony with the inhabitants of the land ; or, most generally as a fresh aggravation of their misery, in requiring them to make sport for their new masters.—*Genebrardus, Chrysostom, and Cocceius, in Neale and Littledale.*

Verse 3.—"*Sing us one of the songs of Zion.*" No music will serve the epicures in the prophet but temple music : Amos vi. 5, " They invent to themselves instruments of music like David." As choice and excellent as David was in the service of the temple, so would they be in their private feasts. Belshazzar's draughts are not half so sweet in other vessels as in the utensils of the temple : Dan. v. 2, " He commanded to bring forth the golden and silver vessels that were taken out of the house of God." So the Babylonian humour is pleased with nothing so much as with " *one of the songs of Zion ;*" not an ordinary song, but " Sing us *one of your songs of Zion.*" No jest relisheth with a profane spirit so well as when Scripture is abused, and made to lackey to their sportive jollity. Vain man thinketh he can never put honour enough upon his pleasures, and scorn enough upon God and holy things.—*Thomas Manton.*

Verse 3.—"*Sing us one of the songs of Zion.*" The insulting nature of the demand will become the more conspicuous, if we consider, that the usual subjects of these songs were the omnipotence of Jehovah, and his love towards his chosen people.—*William Keatinge Clay,* 1839.

Verse 3.—The Babylonians asked them in derision for one of the songs of Zion. They loaded with ridicule their pure and venerable religion, and aggravated the sufferings of the weary and oppressed exiles by their mirth and their indecency. We are sorry to say that the resemblance still holds betwixt the Jews in a state of captivity and the Christians in the state of their pilgrimage. We have also to sustain the mockery of the profane and the unthinking. Ridicule and disdain are often the fate of sincere piety in this world. Fashion and frivolity and false philosophy have made a formidable combination against us ; and the same truth, the same honesty, the same integrity of principle, which in any other cause would be esteemed as manly and respectable, is despised and laughed at when attached to the cause of the gospel and its sublime interests.—*Thomas Chalmers.*

Verses 3, 4.—St. John Chrysostom observes the improvement such tribulation effected in the Jews, who previously derided, nay, even put to death, some of the prophets ; but now that they were captives in a foreign land, they would not attempt to expose their sacred hymns to the ridicule of the Gentiles.—*Robert Bellarmine.*

Verse 4.—*"How shall we sing the* LORD's *song in a strange land ?"* Now, is it not true that, in many senses, we, like the Jewish exiles, have to sing the Lord's song in a strange land ? If not a land strange to *us*, then, all the more strange to *it*—a land foreign, so to say, and alien to the Lord's song. The very life which we live here in the body is a life of sight and sense. Naturally we walk by sight ; and to sing the Lord's song is possible only to faith. Faith is the soul's sight : faith is seeing the Invisible : this comes not of nature, and without this we cannot sing the Lord's song, because we are in a land strange to it.

Again, the feelings of the present life are often adverse to praise. The exiles in Babylon could not sing because they were in heaviness. God's hand was heavy upon them. He had a controversy with them for their sins. Now the feelings of many of us are in like manner adverse to the Lord's song. Some of us are in great sorrow. We have lost a friend ; we are in anxiety about one who is all to us ; we know not which way to turn for to-morrow's bread or for this day's comfort. How can we sing the Lord's song ?

And there is another kind of sorrow, still more fatal, if it be possible, to the lively exercise of adoration. And that is, a weight and burden of unforgiven sin. Songs may be heard from the prison-cell of Philippi ; songs maybe heard from the calm death-bed, or by the open grave ; but songs cannot be drawn forth from the soul on which the load of God's displeasure, real or imagined, is lying, or which is still powerless to apprehend the grace and the life for sinners which is in Christ Jesus. That, we imagine, was *the* difficulty which pressed upon the exile Israelite ; that certainly is an impediment now, in many, to the outburst of Christian praise. And again, there is a land yet more strange and foreign to the Lord's song even than the land of unforgiven guilt—and that is the land of unforsaken sin.— *Condensed from C. J. Vaughan.*

Verse 4.—*"The Lord's song—in a strange land."* It was the contrast, it was the incongruity which perplexed them. The captives in Babylon—that huge, unwieldy city, with its temple of the Chaldean Bel towering aloft on its eight stupendous stories to the height of a furlong into the sky—the Israelite exiles, bidden there to an idolatrous feast, that they might make sport for the company by singing to them one of the far-famed Hebrew melodies, for the gratification of curiosity or the amusement of the ear—how could it be done ? *The Lord's song*— one of those inspired compositions of Moses or David, in which the saintly soul of the king or the prophet poured itself forth in lowliest, loftiest adoration, before the one Divine Creator, Redeemer, and Sanctifier—how *could* it be sung, they ask, in a scene so incongruous ? The words would languish upon the tongue, the notes would refuse to sound upon the disused harp. Such psalmody requires its accompaniment and its adaptation—if not actually in the Temple-courts of Zion, yet at least in the balmy gales of Palestine and the believing atmosphere of Israel.—*C. J. Vaughan, in "The Family Prayer and Sermon Book."*

Verse 4.—*"The Lord's song."* These songs of old, to distinguish them from heathenish songs, were called God's songs, the Lord's songs ; because taught by him, learned of him, and commanded by him to be sung to his praise.—*John Bunyan.*

Verse 4.—Many were the sad thoughts which the remembrance of Zion would call up : the privileges they had there enjoyed ; the solemn feasts and happy meetings of their tribes to worship there before the Lord ; the Temple—" the beautiful house where their fathers had worshipped "—now laid waste.

But the one embittering thought that made them indeed heavy at heart, silenced their voices, and unstrung their harps, was the cause of this calamity— their sin. Paul and Silas could sing in a dungeon, but it was not their sin brought them there : and so the saints suffering for the name of Christ could say, " we are exceeding joyful in all our tribulation." There is no real sorrow in any circumstances into which God brings us, or where he leads and goes with us ; but where sin is, and suffering is felt to be—not persecution, but—judgment, there is and can be no joy ; the soul refuses to be comforted. Israel cannot sing beside the waters of Babylon.— *William De Burgh.*

Verse 4.—There is a distinction between us and God's ancient people ; for at that time the worship of God was confined to one place ; but now he has his temple wherever two or three are met together in Christ's name, if they separate themselves from all idolatrous profession, and maintain purity of Divine worship. —*John Calvin.*

Verse 4.—It is one of the pathetic touches about the English captivity of King John II. of France, that once sitting as a guest to see a great tournament held in his honour, he looked on sorrowfully, and being urged by some of those about him to be cheerful and enjoy the splendid pageant, he answered with a mournful smile, " *How shall we sing the* LORD'S *song in a strange land ?*"—*Polydore Virgil,* —1555.

Verse 5.—" *If I forget thee, O Jerusalem.*" Calvary, Mount of Olives, Siloam, how fragrant are ye with the Name that is above every name ! " *If I forget thee, O Jerusalem !* " Can I forget where he walked so often, where he spake such gracious words, where he died ? Can I forget that his feet shall stand on that " Mount of Olives, which is before Jerusalem, on the east ?" Can I forget that there stood the Upper Room, and there fell the showers of Pentecost ?—*Andrew A. Bonar.*

Verse 5.—" *Let my right hand forget her cunning.*" There is a striking and appropriate point in this, which has been overlooked. It is, that, as it is customary for people in the East to swear by their professions, so one who has no profession—who is poor and destitute, and has nothing of recognized value in the world—swears by his right hand, which is his sole stake in society, and by the " *cunning* " of which he earns his daily bread. Hence the common Arabic proverb (given by Burckhardt) reflecting on the change of demeanour produced by improved circumstances :—" He was wont to swear ' by the cutting off of his right hand !' He now swears ' by the giving of money to the poor.' " The words, " *her cunning,*" are supplied by the translators, in whose time *cunning* (from the Saxon *cannan*, Dutch *konnen*, " to know ") meant " skill " ; and a cunning man was what we should now call a skilful man. In the present case the skill indicated is doubtless that of playing on the harp, in which particular sense it occurs so late as Prior :—

> " When Pedro does the lute command,
>   She guides the cunning artist's hand."

Modern translators substitute " skill" ; but perhaps a term still more general would be better—such as, " May my right hand lose its power."—*John Kitto, in* " *The Pictorial Bible.*"

Verse 5.—" *Let my right hand forget.*" Something must be supplied from the context . . . the playing on the stringed instrument, verse 2, whether the right hand should be applied to the purpose or not, was the point in question. Then, the punishment also perfectly accords with the misdeed, as in Job xxxi.

22 : If I, misapplying my right hand to the playing of joyful strains on my instrument, forget thee, Jerusalem, let my right hand, as a punishment, forget the noble art ; and then also verse 6 fits admirably to what goes before : May my misemployed hand lose its capacity to play, and my tongue, misemployed in singing cheerful songs, its capacity to sing.—*E. W. Hengstenberg.*

Verse 6.—" *If I do not remember thee.*" Either our beds are soft, or our hearts hard, that can rest when the church is at unrest, that feel not our brethren's hard cords through our soft beds.—*John Trapp.*

Verse 6.—" *If I prefer not Jerusalem above my chief joy.*" Literally, " *if I advance not Jerusalem above the head of my joy.*" If I set not Jerusalem as a diadem on the head of my rejoicing, and crown all my happiness with it.—*Christopher Wordsworth.*

Verse 7.—" *Remember, O* LORD, *the children of Edom,*" etc.   The Jews were their brethren : Obad. 10 ; Amos i. 11.   They were their neighbours, Idumea and Judea bordered upon one another : Mark iii. 8.   They were confederates with the Jews (Jer. xxvii. 3 : an Edomitish ambassador was at Jerusalem), who, together with the ambassadors of the other kings there mentioned, were strengthening themselves with Zedekiah against Nebuchadnezzar ; see Obad. 7. For them, therefore, to revenge themselves for former wrongs done them upon the Jews, and that in the day of their calamity, this made their sin exceedingly sinful—*William Greenhill,* 1591—1677.

Verse 7.—" *Remember, O* LORD, *the children of Edom,*" etc. Or all kinds of evil speaking against our brother, this sin of Edom, to sharpen an enemy against our brother in the day of his sorrow and distress, this opening of the mouth wide against him, to exult over him in his calamity, is most barbarous and unchristian. . . . Observe how the cruelty of the Edomites is aggravated by this time ; the wofullest time that ever Jerusalem had, called therefore " *the day of Jerusalem.*" When all things conspired to make their sorrow full, then, in the anguish and fit of their mortal disease, then did Edom arm his eye, his tongue his heart, his hand, and join all those with the enemy against his brother. Learn, that God taketh notice not only *what* we do against another, but *when ;* for he will set these things in order before us ; for the God of mercy cannot abide cruelty.—*Edward Marbury,* 1649.

Verse 7.—" *Remember, O* LORD, *the children of Edom.*" Edom shall be remembered for the mischievous counsel he gave ; and the daughter of Babylon shall be for ever razed out of memory for razing Jerusalem to the ground. And let all the secret and open enemies of God's church take heed how they employ their tongues and hands against God's secret ones : they that presume to do either may here read their fatal doom written in the *dust* of Edom, and in the *ashes* of Babylon.—*Daniel Featley* (1582—1645), *in " Clavis Mystica."*

Verse 7.—In Herod, the Idumean, Edom's hatred ·found its concentrated expression. *His* attempt was to destroy him whom God had laid in Zion as the " sure foundation."—*William Kay.*

Verse 7.—It may be observed that the Jews afterward acted the same part toward the Christian church which the Edomites had acted toward them, encouraging and stirring up the Gentiles to persecute and destroy it from off the face of the earth. And God " remembered " them for the Christians' sakes, as they prayed him to " remember Edom" for their sakes. Learn we hence, what a crime it is, for Christians to assist the common enemy, or call in the common enemy to assist them, against their brethren.—*George Horne.*

Verse 7.—We are not to regard the imprecations of this psalm in any other light than as prophetical. They are grounded on the many prophecies which had already gone forth on the subject of the destruction of Babylon, if, as we may admit, the psalm before us was written after the desolation of Jerusalem. But these prophecies have not yet been fulfilled in every particular, and remain to be accomplished in mystic Babylon, when the dominion of Antichrist shall be for

ever swept away, and the true church introduced into the glorious liberty of the
sons of God, at the appearing of their Lord and Saviour Jesus Christ in his own
kingdom.— *William Wilson.*

Verse 7.—Edom's hatred was the hatred with which the carnal mind in its
natural enmity against God always regards whatever is the elect object of his
favour. Jerusalem was the city of *God.* " Rase it, rase it even to the ground,"
is the mischievous desire of every unregenerate mind against every building that
rests on the elect Stone of Divine foundation. For God's election never pleases
man until, through grace, his own heart has become an adoring receiver of that
mercy which while in his natural state he angrily resented and refused to own
in its effects on other men From Cain to Antichrist this solemn truth holds
always good.—*Arthur Pridham.*

Verses 7—9.—I do not know if the same feeling has occurred to others, but I
have often wished the latter verses of this psalm had been disjoined from this
sweet and touching beginning. It sounds as if one of the strings on their well-
tuned harps was out of melody, as if it struck a jarring note of discord. And
yet I know the feeling is wrong, for it is no more than what the Lord himself had
foretold and declared should be the final desolation of proud Babylon itself : yet
one longs more intensely for the period when the nations of the earth shall learn
war no more ; and every harp and every voice, even those of the martyred ones
beneath God's altar loudest and sweetest of all, shall sing the Lord's songs, the
song of Moses, and the Lamb, in that pleasant land, where no sighing and no
tears are seen.—*Barton Bouchier.*

Verse 8.—" *O daughter of Babylon, who art to be destroyed.*" In the beginning
of the fifth year of Darius happened the revolt of the Babylonians which cost him
the trouble of a tedious siege again to reduce them . . . . he besieged the city
with all his forces . . . . As soon as the Babylonians saw themselves begirt by
such an army as they could not cope with in the field, they turned their thoughts
wholly to the supporting of themselves in the siege ; in order whereto they took
a resolution, the most desperate and barbarous that ever any nation practised.
For to make their provisions last the longer, they agreed to cut off all unnecessary
mouths among them, and therefore drawing together all the women and children,
they strangled them all, whether wives, sisters, daughters, or young children
useless for the wars, excepting only that every man was allowed to save one of
his wives, which he best loved, and a maid-servant to do the work of the house.
—*Humphrey Prideaux.*

Verse 8.—" *Who art to be destroyed.*" הַשְּׁדוּדָה has been explained in a variety
of ways. Seventy : ἡ ταλαίπωρος ; Vulg. *misera :* others, *destroyer, powerful,*
violent, or *fierce.* Perhaps it best suits the context to regard it as expressing what
is already accomplished : it is so certain, in the view of the Psalmist, that the ruin
will come, that he uses the past participle, as if the work were now completed.
" O daughter of Babylon, the destroyed !"—" *Bibliotheca Sacra and Theological*
Review."

Verse 8.—He that sows evil shall reap evil ; he that soweth the evil of sin, shall
reap the evil of punishment. So Eliphaz told Job that he had seen (Job iv. 8),
" they that plough iniquity, and sow wickedness, reap the same." And that
either in kind or quality, proportion or quantity. In kind, the very same that
he did to others shall be done to him ; or in proportion, a measure answerable to
it. So he shall reap what he hath sown, in quality or in quantity ; either in portion the same, or in proportion the like. The prophet cursing Edom and Babel
saith thus, " O daughter of Zion, happy shall he be that rewardeth thee as thou
hast served us." The original is, " that recompenseth to thee thy deed which
thou didst to us." . . . Thus is wickedness recompensed *suo genere,* in its own
kind. So often the transgressor is against the transgressor, the thief robs the
thief, *proditoros proditor ;* as in Rome many unchristened emperors, and many
christened popes, by blood and treason got the sovereignty, and by blood and
treason lost it. Evil men drink of their own brewing, are scourged with their

own rod, drowned in the pit which they digged for others, as Haman was hanged on his own gallows, Perillus tormented in his own engine!—*Thomas Adams.*

Verses 8, 9.—The subject of these two verses is the same with that of many chapters in Isaiah and Jeremiah; namely, the vengeance of heaven executed upon Babylon by Cyrus, raised up to be king of the Medes and Persians, united under him for that purpose. The meaning of the words, "*Happy shall he be,*" is, He shall go on and prosper, for the Lord of hosts shall go with him, and fight his battles against the enemy and oppressor of his people, empowering him to recompense upon the Chaldeans the works of their hands, and to reward them as they served Israel.—*George Horne.*

Verses 8, 9.—It needs no record to tell us that, in the siege and carrying away of Jerusalem, great atrocities were committed by the conquerors. We may be sure that

> " Many a chiding mother then
> And new-born baby died,"

for the wars of the old world were always attended by such barbarous cruelties. The apostrophe of verses 8, 9, consequently merely proclaims the certainty of a just retribution—of the same retribution that the prophets had foretold (Isai. xiii. 16; xlvii.; Jer. l.; compare, " who art to be destroyed, verse 8), and the happiness of those who should be its ministers; who should mete out to her what she had measured to the conquered Jew. It was the decree of Heaven that their " children" should " be dashed to pieces before their eyes." The Psalmist simply recognizes the decree as just and salutary; he pronounces the terrible vengeance to have been deserved. To charge him with vindictiveness, therefore, is to impugn the justice and mercy of the Most High. And there is nothing to sustain the charge, for his words are simply a prediction, like that of the prophet. " As thou hast done, it shall be done unto thee; thy reward shall return upon thine own head": Obad. 15.—*Joseph Hammond, in " The Expositor,"* 1876.

Verse 9.—"*Happy shall he be that taketh,*" etc. That is, so oppressive hast thou been to all under thy domination, as to become universally hated and detested; so that those who may have the last hand in thy destruction, and the total extermination of thy inhabitants, shall be reputed " *happy*"—shall be *celebrated* and *extolled* as those who have rid the world of a curse so grievous. These prophetic declarations contain no excitement to any person or persons to commit acts of cruelty and barbarity; but are simply *declarative* of what would take place in the order of the retributive providence and justice of God, and the general opinion that should in consequence be expressed on the subject; therefore *praying for the destruction of our enemies* is totally out of the question.—*Adam Clarke.*

Verse 9.—"*Happy shall he be,*" etc. With all possible might and speed oppose the very first risings and movings of the heart to sin; for these are the buds that produce the bitter fruit; and if sin be not nipped in the very bud, it is not imaginable how quickly it will shoot forth. . . . Now these sins, though they may seem small in themselves, yet are exceedingly pernicious in their effects. These little foxes destroy the grapes as much or more than the greater, and therefore are to be diligently sought out, hunted, and killed by us, if we would keep our hearts fruitful. We should deal with these first streamings out of sin as the Psalmist would have the people of God deal with the brats of Babylon: "*Happy shall he be, that taketh and dasheth thy little ones against the stones.*" And without doubt most happy and successful will that man prove in his spiritual welfare, who puts on no bowels of pity even to his infant corruptions, but slays the small as well as the great; and so not only conquers his enemies by opposing their present force, but also by extinguishing their future race. The smallest children, if they live, will be grown men; and the first motions of sin, if they are let alone, will spread into great, open, and audacious presumptions.—*Robert South,* 1633—1716.

Verse 9.—"*Against the stones.*" That סלע signifies *a rock*, is undubitable, from the concurrent testimony of all the best Hebrew lexicographers. Hence it follows, because there is no rock, nor mountain, nor hill, either in the city or in the province of ancient Babylonia, that the locality against which the malediction of this psalm is hurled cannot be the metropolis of the ancient Assyrian empire, but must be apocalyptic Babylon, or Papal Rome, built upon seven hills, one of which is the celebrated Tarpeian Rock.   But the eighth verse emphatically declares that the retributive justice of God will visit upon apocalyptic Babylon the same infliction which Assyrian Babylon, and also Pagan Rome, inflicted upon Jerusalem. As therefore Nebuchadnezzar as well as Titus " burnt the house of the Lord, and the king's house, and all the houses of Jerusalem, and every great man's house burnt he with fire" (2 Kings xxv. 9), so " the ten horns shall hate the whore, and shall make her desolate and naked, and shall eat her flesh, and burn her with fire ; and she shall be utterly burned with fire" (Rev. xvii. 16 ; xviii. 8).   When the Canaanites had filled up the measure of their iniquity, Israel received a divine commission to exterminate the guilty nation.   When Papal Rome shall have filled up the measure of her iniquity, then " a mighty angel will take up a stone, like a great millstone, and will cast it into the sea, saying, Thus with violence shall that great city Babylon be thrown down" : " For her sins have reached unto heaven, and God hath remembered her iniquities.   Reward her even as she rewarded you, and double unto her double according to her works : in the cup which she hath filled fill to her double" (Rev. xviii. 5, 6).   Then shall issue the divine proclamation : " Rejoice over her, thou heaven, and ye holy apostles and prophets ; for God hath avenged you on her" (Rev. xviii. 20).—*John Noble Coleman, in " The Book of Psalms, with Notes,"* 1863.

Verse 9.—"*He that taketh and dasheth thy little ones against the stones.*"

> My heroes slain, my bridal bed o'erturned,
> My daughters ravish'd, and my city burn'd,
> My bleeding infants dash d against the floor ;
> These have I yet to see, perhaps yet more.

Homer's Iliad, Pope's Translation, Book xxii. 89—91.

HINTS TO THE VILLAGE PREACHER.

Verse 1.—I. A duty once the source of joy : " remember Zion."   II. Circumstances which make the remembrance sorrowful.   III. Peculiar persons who feel this joy or sorrow : " we."

Verse 1.—I. Zion forsaken in prosperity. Its services neglected ; its priests demoralized ; the worship of Baal and of Ashtaroth preferred to the worship of the true God.   II. Zion remembered in adversity.   In Babylon more than in Jerusalem ; on the banks of the Euphrates more than on the banks of Jordan ; with tears when they might have remembered it with joy.   " I spake unto thee in thy prosperity, and thou saidst, I will not hear."   " Lord, in trouble they have visited thee.   They poured out a prayer when thy chastening was upon them." —*G. R.*

Verse 2.—I. Harps—or capacities for praise.   II. Harps on willows, or song suspended.   III. Harps retuned, or joys to come.

Verse 2.—I. A confession of joy being turned into sorrow : " we hanged," etc. The moaning of their harps upon weeping willows better harmonized with their feelings than any tunes which they had been accustomed to play.   II. A hope of sorrow being turned into joy.   They took their harps with them into captivity, and hung them up for future use.—*G. R.*

Verse 2.—" *We hanged our harps,*" etc.   I. In remembrance of lost joys.   Their harps were associated with a glorious past.   They could not afford to forget that past.   They kept up the good old custom.   There are always means of remembrance at hand.   II. In manifestation of present sorrow.   They could not play on account of, 1. Their sinfulness.   2. Their circumstances.   3. Their home. III. In anticipation of future blessing.   They did not dash their harps to pieces.

Term of exile limited. Return expressly foretold. We shall want our harps in the good times coming. Sinners play their harps now, but must soon lay them aside for ever.— *W. J.*

Verse 3 (*last clause*).—Taken away from the text this is a very pleasant and praiseworthy request. Why do we wish for such a song ? 1. It is sure to be pure. 2. It will certainly be elevating. 3. It will probably be gladsome. 4. It will comfort and enliven us. 5. It will help to express our gratitude.

Verses 3, 4.—I. The cruel demand. 1. A song when we are captives. 2. A song to please our adversaries. 3. A holy song for unholy purposes. II. The motive for it. Sometimes mere ridicule ; at others, mistaken kindness seeking by sharpness to arouse us from despondency ; often mere levity. III. The answer to it, " How can ?" etc.

Verses 3, 4.—I. When God calls for joy we ought not to sorrow. The songs of Zion should be sung in Zion. II. When God calls for sorrow we ought not to rejoice. " How shall we sing ?" etc. See Is. v. 12.— *G. R.*

Verses 3, 4.—I. The unreasonable request : " Sing us one of the songs of Zion." This was—1. A striking testimony to the joyful character of Jehovah's worship. Even the heathen had heard of " the songs of Zion." 2. A severe trial of the fidelity of captive Israel. It might have been to their present advantage to have complied with the request. 3. A cruel taunt of the sad and desponding condition of the captives. II. The indignant refusal. " How shall we sing the Lord's song in a strange land ?" There is no singing this song by true Israelites—1. When the heart is out of tune, as it must necessarily be when in " a strange land." 2. In uncongenial society—amongst unsympathetic strangers. 3. For unsanctified purposes—to make mirth for the heathen. Many so-called sacred concerts pain devout Christians as much as the demand to sing the Lord's song did the devout Israelites. The Lord's song must be sung only " to the Lord."— *W. H. J. P.*

Verses 3, 4.—The burlesque of holy things. I. The servants of God are in an unsympathetic world. II. The demand to be amused and entertained. Temple songs to pass an idle hour ! Such the popular demand to-day. Men would have us burlesque religion to tickle them. III. The justly indignant reply of all true men, " How shall we ?" Christian workers have more serious if less popular business on hand.— *W. B. H.*

Verse 5.—The person who remembers ; the thing remembered ; the solemn imprecation.

Verse 5.—No harp but for Jesus.
I. The harp consecrated. At conversion.

> " One sword, at least, thy rights shall guard,
>   One faithful harp shall praise thee."

II. The harp silent :

> " Thy songs were made for the brave and free,
>   They shall never sound in slavery."

III. The harp re-strung above :

> " And I heard the voice of harpers
>   Harping with their harps."

W. B. H.

Verses 5, 6.—I. To rejoice with the world is to forget the church. II. To love the church we must prefer her above everything. III. To serve the church we must be prepared to suffer anything.

Verse 7.—The hatred of the ungodly to true religion. I. Its cause. II. Its extent. " Rase it," etc. III. Its season for display : " in the day of Jerusalem" —trouble, etc. IV. Its reward : " Remember, O Lord."

WORK UPON THE HUNDRED AND THIRTY-SEVENTH PSALM.

" AN EXPOSITION upon some select Psalms of David. . . . Written by that faithful servant of God M. Robert Rollok. . . . And translated out of Latine into English by C[harles] L[umisden] . . . Edinborgh . . . 1600," [8vo.] contains a short exposition on Psalm CXXXVII. [Of little value.]

PSALM CXXXVIII.

TITLE.—A Psalm of David. *This psalm is wisely placed. Whoever edited and arranged these sacred poems, he had an eye to apposition and, contrast; for if in Ps. cxxxvii. we see the need of silence before revilers, here we see the excellence of a brave confession. There is a time to be silent, lest we cast pearls before swine; and there is a time to speak openly, lest we be found guilty of cowardly non-confession. The psalm is evidently of a Davidic character, exhibiting all the fidelity, courage, and decision of that King of Israel and Prince of Psalmists. Of course the critics have tried to rend the authorship from David on account of the mention of the temple, though it so happens that in one of the psalms which is allowed to be David's the same word occurs. Many modern critics are to the word of God what blow-flies are to the food of men: they cannot do any good, and unless relentlessly driven away they do great harm.*

DIVISION.—*In full confidence David is prepared to own his God before the gods of the heathen, or before angels or rulers (1—3); he declares that he will instruct and convert kings and nations, till on every highway men shall sing the praises of the Lord (4 and 5). Having thus spoken, he utters his personal confidence in Jehovah, who will help his lowly servant, and preserve him from all the malice of wrathful foes.*

EXPOSITION.

I WILL praise thee with my whole heart : before the gods will I sing praise unto thee.

2 I will worship toward thy holy temple, and praise thy name for thy lovingkindness and for thy truth : for thou hast magnified thy word above all thy name.

3 In the day when I cried thou answeredest me, *and* strengthenedst me *with* strength in my soul.

1. "*I will praise thee with my whole heart.*" His mind is so taken up with God that he does not mention his name : to him there is no other God, and Jehovah is so perfectly realized and so intimately known, that the Psalmist, in addressing him, no more thinks of mentioning his name than we should do if we were speaking to a father or a friend. He sees God with his mind's eye, and simply addresses him with the pronoun " thee." He is resolved to praise the Lord, and to do it with the whole force of his life, even with his whole heart. He would not submit to act as one under restraint, because of the opinions of others ; but in the presence of the opponents of the living God he would be as hearty in worship as if all were friends and would cheerfully unite with him. If others do not praise the Lord, there is all the more reason why we should do so, and should do so with enthusiastic eagerness. We need a broken heart to mourn our own sins, but a whole heart to praise the Lord's perfections. If ever our heart is whole and wholly occupied with one thing, it should be when we are praising the Lord. "*Before the gods will I sing praise unto thee.*" Why should these idols rob Jehovah of his praises ? The Psalmist will not for a moment suspend his songs because there are images before him, and their foolish worshippers might not approve of his music. I believe David referred to the false gods of the neighbouring nations, and the deities of the surviving Canaanites. He was not pleased that such gods were set up ; but he intended to express at once his contempt of *them*, and his own absorption in the worship of the living Jehovah by continuing most earnestly to sing wherever he might be. It would be paying these dead idols too much respect to cease singing because they were perched aloft. In these days when new religions are daily excogitated, and new gods are set up, it is well to know

how to act. Bitterness is forbidden, and controversy is apt to advertise the heresy ; the very best method is to go on personally worshipping the Lord with unvarying zeal, singing with heart and voice his royal praises. Do they deny the Divinity of our Lord ? Let us the more fervently adore him. Do they despise the atonement ? Let us the more constantly proclaim it. Had half the time spent in councils and controversies been given to praising the Lord, the church would have been far sounder and stronger than she is at this day. The Hallelujah Legion will win the day. Praising and singing are our armour against the idolatries of heresy, our comfort under the depression caused by insolent attacks upon the truth, and our weapons for defending the gospel. Faith, when displayed in cheerful courage, has about it a sacred contagion : others learn to believe in the Most High when they see his servant

> " Calm 'mid the bewildering cry,
> Confident of victory."

2. "*I will worship toward thy holy temple,*" or the place of God's dwelling, where the ark abode. He would worship God in God's own way. The Lord had ordained a centre of unity, a place of sacrifice, a house of his indwelling ; and David accepted the way of worship enjoined by revelation. Even so, the true-hearted believer of these days must not fall into the will-worship of superstition, or the wild worship of scepticism, but reverently worship as the Lord himself prescribes. The idol gods had their temples ; but David averts his glance from them, and looks earnestly to the spot chosen of the Lord for his own sanctuary. We are not only to adore the true God, but to do so in his own appointed way : the Jew looked to the temple, we are to look to Jesus, the living temple of the Godhead. "*And praise thy name for thy loving kindness and for thy truth.*" Praise would be the main part of David's worship ; the name or character of God the great object of his song ; and the special point of his praise the grace and truth which shone so conspicuously in that name. The person of Jesus is the temple of the Godhead, and therein we behold the glory of the Father, " full of grace and truth." It is upon these two points that the name of Jehovah is at this time assailed—his grace and his truth. He is said to be too stern, too terrible, and therefore " modern thought" displaces the God of Abraham, Isaac, and Jacob, and sets up an effeminate deity of its own making. As for us, we firmly believe that God is love, and that in the summing up of all things it will be seen that hell itself is not inconsistent with the beneficence of Jehovah, but is, indeed, a necessary part of his moral government now that sin has intruded into the universe. True believers hear the thunders of his justice, and yet they do not doubt his lovingkindness. Especially do we delight in God's great love to his own elect, such as he showed to Israel as a race, and more especially to David and his seed when he entered into covenant with him. Concerning this there is abundant room for praise. But not only do men attack the lovingkindness of God, but the truth of God is at this time assailed on all sides ; some doubt the truth of the inspired record as to its histories, others challenge the doctrines, many sneer at the prophecies ; in fact, the infallible word of the Lord is at this time treated as if it were the writing of impostors, and only worthy to be carped at. The swine are trampling on the pearls at this time, and nothing restrains them ; nevertheless, the pearls are pearls still, and shall yet shine about our Monarch's brow. We sing the lovingkindness and truth of the God of the Old Testament,—" the God of the whole earth shall he be called." David before the false gods first sang, then worshipped, and then proclaimed the grace and truth of Jehovah ; let us do the same before the idols of the New Theology.

"*For thou hast magnified thy word above all thy name.*" The word of promise made to David was in his eyes more glorious than all else that he had seen of the Most High. Revelation excels creation in the clearness, definiteness, and fulness of its teaching. The name of the Lord in nature is not so easily read as in the Scriptures, which are a revelation in human language, specially adapted to the human mind, treating of human need, and of a Saviour who appeared in human nature to redeem humanity. Heaven and earth shall pass away, but the divine word will not pass away, and in this respect especially it has a pre-eminence over every other form of manifestation. Moreover, the Lord lays all the rest of his name under tribute to his word : his wisdom, power, love, and all his other attributes combine to carry out his word. It is his word which creates, sustains, quickens, enlightens, and comforts. As a word of command it is supreme ; and in the person of the incarnate Word it is set above all the works of God's hands. The sentence in the text is wonderfully full of meaning. We have collected a vast mass of literature upon it, but space will not allow us to put it all into our notes. Let us adore the Lord who has spoken to us by his word, and by his Son ; and in the presence of unbelievers let us both praise his holy name and extol his holy word.

3. *"In the day when I cried thou answeredst me."* No proof is so convincing as that of experience. No man doubts the power of prayer after he has received an answer of peace to his supplication. It is the distinguishing mark of the true and living God that he hears the pleadings of his people, and answers them ; the gods hear not and answer not, but Jehovah's memorial is—" the God that heareth prayer." There was some special day in which David cried more vehemently than usual ; he was weak, wounded, worried, and his heart was wearied ; then like a child he " cried,"—cried unto his Father. It was a bitter, earnest, eager prayer, as natural and as plaintive as the cry of a babe. The Lord answered it ; but what answer can there be to a cry ?—to a mere inarticulate wail of grief ? Our heavenly Father is able to interpret tears, and cries, and he replies to their inner sense in such a way as fully meets the case. The answer came in the same day as the cry ascended : so speedily does prayer rise to heaven, so quickly does mercy return to earth. The statement of this sentence is one which all believers can make, and as they can substantiate it with many facts, they ought boldly to publish it, for it is greatly to God's glory. Well might the Psalmist say, " I will worship" when he felt bound to say " thou answeredst me." Well might he glory before the idols and their worshippers when he had answers to prayer to look back upon. This also is our defence against modern heresies : we cannot forsake the Lord, for he has heard our prayers.

"And strengthenedst me with strength in my soul." This was a true answer to his prayer. If the burden was not removed, yet strength was given wherewith to bear it, and this is an equally effective method of help. It may not be best for us that the trial should come to an end ; it may be far more to our advantage that by its pressure we should learn patience. Sweet are the uses of adversity, and our prudent Father in heaven will not deprive us of those benefits. Strength imparted to the soul is an inestimable boon ; it means courage, fortitude, assurance, heroism. By his word and Spirit the Lord can make the trembler brave, the sick whole, the weary bright. This soul-might will continue : the man having been strengthened for one emergency remains vigorous for life, and is prepared for all future labours and sufferings ; unless, indeed, he throw away his force by unbelief, or pride, or some other sin. When God strengthens, none can weaken. Then is our soul strong indeed when the Lord infuses might into us.

4 All the kings of the earth shall praise thee, O LORD, when they hear the words of thy mouth.

5 Yea, they shall sing in the ways of the Lord : for great *is* the glory of the LORD.

4. *"All the kings of the earth shall praise thee, O LORD, when they hear the words of thy mouth."* Kings have usually small care to hear the word of the Lord ; but King David feels assured that if they do hear it they will feel its power. A little piety goes a long way in courts ; but brighter days are coming, in which rulers will become hearers and worshippers : may the advent of such happy times be hastened. What an assembly !—" all the kings of the earth !" What a purpose ! Gathered to hear the words of Jehovah's mouth. What a preacher ! David him-

self rehearses the words of Jehovah. What praise ! when they all in happy union lift up their songs unto the Lord. Kings are as gods below, and they do well when they worship tne God above. The way of conversion for kings is the same as for ourselves : faith to them also cometh by hearing, and hearing by the word of God. Happy are those who can cause the word of the Lord to penetrate palaces ; for the occupants of thrones are usually the last to know the joyful sounds of the gospel. David, the king, cared for kings' souls, and it will be wise for each man to look first after those who are of his own order. He went to his work of testimony with full assurance of success : he meant to speak only the words of Jehovah's mouth, and he felt sure that the kings would hear and praise Jehovah.

5. "*Yea, they shall sing in the ways of the* LORD." Here is a double wonder—kings in God's ways, and kings singing there. Let a man once know the ways of Jehovah, and he will find therein abundant reason for song ; but the difficulty is to bring the great ones of the earth into ways so little attractive to the carnal mind. Perhaps when the Lord sends us a King David to preach, we shall yet see monarchs converted and hear their voices raised in devout adoration. "*For great is the glory of the* LORD." This glory shall overshadow all the greatness and glory of all kings : they shall be stirred by a sight of it to obey and adore. O that Jehovah's glory were revealed even now ! O that the blind eyes of men could once behold it, then their hearts would be subdued to joyful reverence. David, under a sense of Jehovah's glory, exclaimed, "I will sing" (verse 1), and here he represents the kings as doing the same thing.

6 Though the LORD *be* high, yet hath he respect unto the lowly : but the proud he knoweth afar off.

7 Though I walk in the midst of trouble, thou wilt revive me : thou shalt stretch forth thine hand against the wrath of mine enemies, and thy right hand shall save me.

8 The LORD will perfect *that which* concerneth me : thy mercy, O LORD, *endureth* for ever : forsake not the works of thine own hands.

6. "*Though the* LORD *be high.*" In greatness, dignity, and power, Jehovah is higher than the highest. His nature is high above the comprehension of his creatures, and his glory even exceeds the loftiest soarings of imagination. "*Yet hath he respect unto the lowly.*" He views them with pleasure, thinks of them with care, listens to their prayers, and protects them from evil. Because they think little of themselves he thinks much of them. They reverence him, and he respects them. They are low in their own esteem, and he makes them high in his esteem. "*But the proud he knoweth afar off.*" He does not need to come near them in order to discover their utter vanity : a glance from afar reveals to him their emptiness and offensiveness. He has no fellowship with them, but views them from a distance ; he is not deceived, but knows the truth about them, despite their blustering ; he has no respect unto them, but utterly abhors them. To a Cain's sacrifice, a Pharaoh's promise, a Rabshakeh's threat, and a Pharisee's prayer, the Lord has no respect. Nebuchadnezzar, when far off from God, cried, "Behold this great Babylon which I have builded" ; but the Lord knew him, and sent him grazing with cattle. Proud men boast loudly of their culture and "the freedom of thought," and even dare to criticize their Maker : but he knows them from afar, and will keep them at arm's length in this life, and shut them up in hell in the next.

7. "*Though I walk in the midst of trouble, thou wilt revive me.*" If I am walking there now, or shall be doing so in years to come, I have no cause for fear ; for God is with me, and will give me new life. When we are somewhat in trouble it is bad enough, but it is worse to penetrate into the centre of that dark continent and traverse its midst : yet in such a case the believer makes progress, for he walks ; he keeps to a quiet pace, for he does no more than walk ; and he is not

without the best of company, for his God is near to pour fresh life into him. It is a happy circumstance that, if God be away at any other time, yet he is pledged to be with us in trying hours : " when thou passest through the rivers I will be with thee." He is in a blessed condition who can confidently use the language of David,—" thou wilt revive me." He shall not make his boast of God in vain : he shall be kept alive, and made more alive than ever. How often has the Lord quickened us by our sorrows ! Are they not his readiest means of exciting to fulness of energy the holy life which dwells within us ? If we receive reviving, we need not regret affliction. When God revives us, trouble will never harm us. "*Thou shalt stretch forth thine hand against the wrath of mine enemies, and thy right hand shall save me.*" This is the fact which would revive fainting David. Our foes fall when the Lord comes to deal with them ; he makes short work of the enemies of his people,—with one hand he routs them. His wrath soon quenches their wrath ; his hand stays their hand. Adversaries may be many, and malicious, and mighty ; but our glorious Defender has only to stretch out his arm and their armies vanish. The sweet singer rehearses his assurance of salvation, and sings of it in the ears of the Lord, addressing him with this confident language. He will be saved,—saved dexterously, decidedly, divinely ; he has no doubt about it. God's right hand cannot forget its cunning ; Jerusalem is his chief joy, and he will defend his own elect.

8. "*The* Lord *will perfect that which concerneth me.*" All my interests are safe in Jehovah's hands.

> "The work which his goodness began,
> The arm of his strength will complete ;
> His promise is yea and Amen,
> And never was forfeited yet."

God is concerned in all that concerns his servants. He will see to it that none of their precious things shall fail of completion ; their life, their strength, their hopes, their graces, their pilgrimage, shall each and all be perfected. Jehovah himself will see to this ; and therefore it is most sure. "*Thy mercy, O* Lord, *endureth for ever.*" The refrain of the former psalm is in his ears, and he repeats it as his own personal conviction and consolation. The first clause of the verse is the assurance of faith, and this second one reaches to the full assurance of understanding. God's work in us will abide unto perfection because God's mercy towards us thus abideth. "*Forsake not the works of thine own hands.*" Our confidence does not cause us to live without prayer, but encourages us to pray all the more. Since we have it written upon our hearts that God will perfect his work in us, and we see it also written in Scripture that his mercy changeth not, we with holy earnestness entreat that we may not be forsaken. If there be anything good in us, it is the work of God's own hands : will he leave it ? Why has he wrought so much in us if he means to give us up ?—it will be a sheer waste of effort. He who has gone so far will surely persevere with us to the end. Our hope for the final perseverance of the believer lies in the final perseverance of the believer's God. If the Lord begins to build, and does not finish, it will not be to his honour. He will have a desire to the work of his hands, for he knows what it has cost him already, and he will not throw away a vessel upon which he has expended so much of labour and skill. Therefore do we praise him with our whole heart, even in the presence of those who depart from his Holy Word, and set up another God and another gospel ; which are not another, but there be some that trouble us.

EXPLANATORY NOTES.

Psalms cxxxviii.—cxlv.—These eight psalms are composed in the *first* person, and they follow very happily after the fifteen " Songs of Up-goings," and the three psalms of praise uttered by the chorus of those who have *gone up* to Sion. Those psalms were the united utterances of national devotion. These eight psalms are the devout Israelite's Manual of *private* prayer and praise.—*Christopher Words-worth.*

Whole Psalm.—This is the first of a series of eight psalms (cxxxviii.—cxlv.), probably the last composed by David, a kind of commentary on the great Messianic promise in 2 Sam. vii. They are found in this part of the psalter, in consequence of having been made the basis, or rather the body, of a system or series (cxxxv.—cxlvi.) by a later writer.—*Joseph Addison Alexander.*

Whole Psalm.—If this psalm refers to the promise in 2 Sam. vii., there can be no doubt of the correctness of the superscription, which ascribes it to David. For he, on whom the promise has been conferred, himself stands forth as the speaker. Proof also of David's authorship is found in the union, so characteristic of him, of bold courage, see especially verse 3, and deep humility, see verse 6. And in proof of the same comes, finally, the near relationship in which it stands with the other psalms of David, especially those which likewise refer to the promise of the everlasting kingdom ; and with David's thanksgiving in 2 Sam. vii., the conclusion of which remarkably agrees with the conclusion of our psalm : " And now, Lord God, the word which thou hast spoken upon thy servant and upon his house, that fulfil even to eternity, and do as thou hast spoken."—*E. W. Hengstenberg.*

Verse 1.—"*I* will praise *thee with my whole heart.*" It is a part of our thankfulness to engage our heart to praise God in time to come, since we find that all the thanks we can give for the present are short of our duty or desire to praise him : "*I will praise thee,*" saith David. Sometimes the believer will find his heart set at liberty in God's worship, which at another time he will find to be in bands, and then he should take the opportunity of an enlarged heart to run int he way of God's service, as David doth here : "*I will praise thee with my whole heart.*"—*David Dickson.*

Verse 1.—"*I will praise thee.*" Up, dear soul ! What though thou hast once complained like Israel of thy captivity in Babylon, Ps. cxxxvii. 1, yet now sing once more a song of joy to the Lord. Thou hast been pressed like a cluster of grapes, now give forth thy ripe juice.—*Christoph Starke.*

Verse 1.—"*I will praise thee.*" Alas, for that capital crime of the Lord's people —barrenness in praises ! Oh, how fully I am persuaded that a line of praises is worth a leaf of prayer, and an hour of praises is worth a day of fasting and mourning !—*John Livingstone, 1603—1672.*

Verse 1.—"*With my whole heart.*" This expression, as in Ps. ix. 1, points to the surpassing greatness of the benefit received, which filled the whole heart with thankfulness, and did not proceed, as it were, from some particular corner of it. It corresponds also to the greatness of the benefaction, in the expression, " *before the gods,*"—demanding of these, whether they would verify their godhead by pointing to any such boon conferred by them on their servants. The benefit which could afford such a demonstration, and give occasion and ground for raillery, must have been a surpassingly great one. -*E. W. Hengstenberg.*

Verse 1.—"*Before the gods.*" There is much diversity in the meaning assigned to " *gods*" in this verse. It may mean literally in an idolatrous country, in the very temples of false gods, as so many Christian martyrs bore testimony to the faith. The LXX., Vulgate, Ethiopic, and Arabic translate *angels.* The Chaldee has *judges,* the Syriac *kings,* and the earlier Greek fathers explain it as a reference to the choirs of *Priests and Levites* in the Temple.—*Zigabenus, in Neale and Littledale.*

Verse 1.—"*Before the gods.*" Some (LXX., Luther, Calvin, etc.) interpret these words of the angels, and compare Ps. xxix. 1 ; but it is doubtful if the Hebrew word Elohim, used nakedly and without any explanation, can have this meaning : it is also, as it would seem, in this connection, pointless : others (Rabbins, Flamin., Delitzsch, etc.) interpret " the great ones of the earth," and compare verse 4 below, and Pss. lxxxii. 1, cxix. 46, etc. ; but this interpretation, too, seems to give no special force to the passage. Probably (Aq., Symm., Jer., etc.) the meaning is, " Before, or in the presence of, the gods of the heathen, *i.e.*, in scorn of, in sight of, the idols, who can do nothing, I will praise Jehovah, who does miracles for me and his people." For a similar expression, see Ps. xxiii. 5, Heb. : see also Pss. xcv. 3, xcvi. 5, for places in which the Hebrew word " *gods*" is used probably for idols.—*Speaker's Commentary.*

Verse 1.—"*Before the gods,*" etc. The Vulgate hath, *in conspectu angelorum,* " before the angels" ; their presence should awe men and women, and keep them from all dishonesty, evil words, acts, gestures, secret grudging, all discontents and distempers. For as they are rejoiced to discern a good frame of spirit in you, to see you keep that order God hath set in the church and state, to walk as Christians to the honour of God ; so they are grieved to see the contrary, and you must answer for your sins against these great officers in the great family of heaven and earth.—*William Greenhill.*

Verse 2.—"*I will worship toward thy holy temple.*" The holy temple was a type and figure of the Lord Jesus Christ. Therefore we find Daniel opening his windows toward the temple, where he prayed three times a day ; and we find Jonah saying, " Yet will I look again toward thy holy temple." So looking to Jesus, he is our temple. There is no acceptable worship except through him ; but we can offer spiritual sacrifices acceptable to God through Jesus Christ. Then, set the Lord Jesus Christ before your eyes, that you may worship God and draw near to the footstool of mercy through him, that you may offer an acceptable sacrifice, and praise his name for his lovingkindness and for his truth.—*Joseph C. Philpot,* 1802—1869.

Verse 2.— "*Thy holy temple.*" This psalm is entitled " a Psalm of David," and Calvin considers him to be its author agreeably to the title ; but the mention of " the temple" in this verse seems to render such an opinion doubtful. If, however, we translate this word by " mansion," which is the proper rendering of the original—" *the mansion of thy sanctity,*"—this objection to its composition by David falls to the ground.—*James Anderson's Note to Calvin in loc.*

Verse 2.—"*I will . . . praise thy name for thy lovingkindness.*" There are two beautiful thoughts brought out here ; one is, " God's condescension in thought" ; the other, " his tenderness in action." These are both included in " *lovingkindness.*" And both of these are shown by God to his own people. He humbleth himself to behold the things of the children of men ; he condescends to men of low estate. Of the blessed Jesus it is said, that " though he was rich, yet for your sakes he became poor, that ye through his poverty might be rich" : 2 Cor. viii. 9. Who can tell the depths to which God condescends in loving thought ? We are told that the very hairs of our head are all numbered ; and if the hairs of our head, then surely all else beside. God, as the Heavenly Father, takes an interest in everything about his people ; he takes this interest in matters which they think beneath his notice, or of which they, from their ignorance, do not know the importance. The mother may draw whole stores of comfort from a realization of the *condescending thoughtfulness of God.* He will be interested about her babe ; if she commit it to him, he who made the universe will, with his infinite mind, think upon her cradle and the helpless creature that is rocked to sleep therein. The sick man may draw whole stores of comfort from the same source, for he can believe the ONE by whom the body was fearfully and wonderfully made will think over the sufferings of that body, and alleviate them, or give strength for the endurance of them if they must be borne. Condescension of thought marks all the dealings of God with his people. And hard following upon it comes *tenderness in action.* Now this " tenderness in action" is a great part of the lovingkindness of God ; it is meet that a thoughtful mind and tender hand should go together in the perfection of love. God is not only energetic, but tender also in action ; he is the God of the dew-drops, as well as the God of the thunder showers ; the God of the tender grass blade, as much as of the mountain oak. We read of great machines, which are able to crush iron bars, and yet they can touch so gently as not to break the shell of the smallest egg ; as it is with them, so is it with the hand of the Most High ; he can crush a world, and yet bind up a wound. And great need have we of tenderness in our low estate ; a little thing would crush us : we have such bruised and feeble souls, that unless we had One who would deal tenderly with us we must soon be destroyed.—*Philip Bennett Power, in "The 1 Wills' of the Psalms,"* 1861.

Verse 2.—"Thou hast magnified thy word above all thy name." His *" word "* being here annexed to *" lovingkindness* and *truth,"* must needs be that part of his word to which these two are applicable, *i.e.,* his promise, the matter whereof is *mercy* or *lovingkindness,* and in the performance of which is *truth* or *fidelity.* And then to *" magnify"* this *" word "* of promise seems to signify two things ; 1, the making very great and excellent promises, and then, 2, the performing them most punctually ; and the doing it *above all his name* is promising and performing most superlative mercies above all that is famed or spoken or believed of God. Then thus it will run ; *I will worship,* etc., *and praise thy name above thy lovingkindness and above thy truth" ;* i.e., it will be too low, too short a compellation, to call thee merciful or veracious, or style thee after any other of thy attributes ; thou art all these, and more than so, *" thou hast magnified thy word,"* given and performed most glorious promises, *" above all thy name,"* above all that men have apprehended or spoken of thee.

This verse and psalm may easily be interpreted of God's mercies in Christ, so far above what could be famed, or said, or believed, or apprehended of him.— *Condensed from H. Hammond.*

Verse 2.—"Thou hast magnified thy word above all thy name." Beyond all question there are higher and clearer manifestations of himself, of his being, of his perfection, of his purposes in the volume of revelation, than any which his works have disclosed or can disclose. There are very many points in relation to God, of the highest interest to mankind, on which the disclosures of science shed no light ; there are many things which it is desirable for man to know, which cannot be learned in the schools of philosophy ; there are consolations which man needs in a world of trouble which cannot be found in nature ; there is especially a knowledge of the method by which sin may be pardoned, and the soul saved, which can never be disclosed by the blow-pipe, the telescope, or the microscope. These things, if learned at all, must be learned from revelation, and these are of more importance to man as a traveller to another world than all the learning which can be acquired in the schools of philosophy—valuable as that learning is. —*Albert Barnes.*

Verse 2.—"For thou hast magnified thy word above all thy name," etc. This is a dark sentence at the first view, but as a judicious expositor upon the place well observes, the words may be thus read, and will better agree with the Hebrew ; *" thou hast magnified thy name above all things, in thy word,"* that is, in fulfilling thy word thou hast magnified thy name above all things, in that thou hast fulfilled thy word. What thou freely promisedst, thou hast faithfully performed ; what thou hast spoken with thy mouth thou hast fulfilled with thy hand ; for which thy name is wonderfully to be magnified.—*James Nalton,* 1664.

Verse 2.—"Thou hast magnified thy word above all thy name." Every creature bears the name of God ; but in his word and truth therein contained it is written at length, and therefore he is more choice of this than of all his other works ; he cares not much what becomes of the world and all in it, so that he keeps his word, and saves his truth. Ere long we shall see the world in flames ; the heavens and earth shall pass away, *" but the word of the Lord endures for ever."* When God will, he can make more such worlds as this ; but he cannot make another truth, and therefore he will not lose one jot thereof. Satan, knowing this, sets all his wits to work to deface this and disfigure it by unsound doctrine. The word is the glass in which we see God, and seeing him are changed into his likeness by his Spirit. If this glass be cracked, then the conceptions we have of God will misrepresent him unto us ; whereas the word, in its native clearness, sets him out in all his glory unto our eye.— *William Gurnall.*

Verse 2.—"Thou hast magnified thy word above all thy name." Thou hast bestowed the promise of perpetuity to my house and to my kingdom, which rises in grandeur and goodness above all thy past manifestations of thyself in behalf of thy people (2 Sam. vii. 10, 12, 13, 15, 16, 21, 22, 24—26, 29 : ver. 21 especially, " For thy *Word's* sake . . . hast thou done all these *great* things " ; ver. 26, " And let thy name be *magnified* for ever"—an undesigned coincidence of language between the history and the psalm). In the Messiah alone the greatness of the promise finds, and shall hereafter more fully find, its realization for Israel and the whole world.—*Andrew Robert Fausset.*

Verse 2.—"*Thou hast magnified thy word above all thy name.*" God has sent his word to us,

1. As *a mirror*, to reflect his glory. " The heavens declare the glory of God ; and the firmament sheweth his handy-work" ; from them may his eternal power and Godhead be clearly seen. Ps. xix. 1, 3, 4. In his providential dealings, also, is much of his wisdom and goodness exhibited. But of his perfections, generally, we can form no idea from these things ; of his purposes we can know nothing. The state of the Heathen world clearly attests this ; for they behold the wonders of Creation and Providence, as well as we : " There is no speech nor language where *their* voice is not heard. Their line is gone out through all the earth, and their words to the end of the world " : Ps. xix. 3, 4. But in the sacred volume all the glory of the Godhead shines : there we are admitted, so to speak, even to the council-chamber of the Most High ; to hear the covenant entered into between the Father and the Son ; the Father engaging to give to him a seed, whom he should have for his inheritance, if he, on his part, would " make his soul an offering for their sins," and, in their nature, expiate the guilt of their iniquities. This mysterious transaction having taken place in the incarnation and death of the Lord Jesus Christ, we behold all the perfections of God united and harmonizing in a way that they never did, or could, by any other means : we see justice more inexorable, than if it had executed vengeance on the whole human race ; and mercy more abundant, than if it had spared the whole human race without any such atonement. There, as it is well expressed, " Mercy and truth are met together ; righteousness and peace have kissed each other" : Ps. lxxxv. 10. Of this great mystery we find not a trace in the whole creation besides ; but in the word it is reflected, as in a mirror (2 Cor. iii. 18) ; and it shines so brightly, that the very angels around the throne are made wiser by the revelation of it to the Church : Eph. iii. 10.

2. As *a standard*, to which everything may be referred. Of God's will we know nothing, but from the word : " we know neither good nor evil from all that is before us." What God requires of us, nothing in Creation or Providence can inform us : what he will do for us, we cannot ascertain : how he will deal with us, we cannot ascertain. But, in the sacred volume, all is written as with a sunbeam. There is nothing which God expects us to do for him, which is not there most explicitly declared : nothing which he engages to do for us, that does not form the subject of a distinct promise. The whole of his procedure in the day of judgment is there laid open : the laws by which we shall be judged : the manner in which the testimony, whether against us or in our favour, shall be produced ; the grounds on which the sentence of condemnation or acquittal shall be passed ; yea, the very state to which every person, either as acquitted or condemned, shall be consigned ; all is so clearly made known, that every person, who will judge himself with candour now, may assuredly anticipate his fate. There is nothing left to conjecture. Every man has a standard to which he may refer, for the rectifying of his judgment in every particular : so that nothing can be added for the instruction of our minds, or the regulation of our future expectations.

3. As *a fountain*, from whence all his blessings emanate. Great blessings, beyond all doubt, flow down to us through the works of Creation and Providence : in fact, they are incessantly administering to our welfare ; for " God opens his hands, and fills all things living with plenteousness." Still, however, the benefits derived from them are only temporal ; whereas those which the inspired volume

imparts are spiritual and eternal ; from whence we derive all our knowledge of Divine truth, and all our hopes of everlasting salvation. Nor is it the knowledge only of truth that we obtain, but the operation and efficacy of it on our souls. There is in Divine truth, when applied by the Holy Spirit, a power to wound, to sanctify, to save : Ps. xix. 7—11. When it comes to the soul with power, the stoutest heart in the universe is made to tremble : when it is poured out as balm, the most afflicted creature under heaven is made to leap for joy. Look over the face of the globe, and see how many, who were once under the unrestrained dominion of sin, are now transformed into the image of their God. And then ascend to heaven, and behold the myriads of the redeemed around the throne of God, uniting their hallelujahs to God and to the Lamb : to this state were they all brought by that blessed word, which alone could ever prevail for so great a work. Thus it is that God has magnified his word ; and thus it is that he *will* magnify it, to the end of time ; yea, through eternity will it be acknowledged as the one source of all blessings that shall ever be enjoyed.—*Charles Simeon, in Horæ Homileticæ.*

Verse 2.—"For thou hast magnified thy word above all thy name." This is one of those expressions of Scripture that seem so comprehensive, and yet so amazing. To my mind it is one of the most remarkable expressions in the whole book of God. *"Thou hast magnified thy word above all thy name."* The *name* of God includes all the perfections of God ; everything that God is, and which God has revealed himself as having—his justice, majesty, holiness, greatness, and glory, and whatever he is in himself, that is God's name. And yet he has " *magnified* " something " *above his name*"—his *word*—his *truth*. This may refer to the Incarnate Word, the Son of God, who was called " *the Word.*" " There are three that bear record in heaven, the Father, the *Word*, and the Holy Ghost, and these three are one" : 1 John v. 7, " In the beginning was the *Word*, and the *Word* was with God " : John i. 1. You may take the words either as meaning that God has magnified his *Word*, his eternal Son—above all his great name, that is, he has set Jesus on high above all the other perfections of his majesty ; or take it as meaning his written word, which is written in the sacred Scriptures. So, in that case, not only the Incarnate *Word* in the person of Jesus ; but also the written word in the Scriptures of truth. He has magnified it above all his name in the fulfilment of it : God's faithfulness being so dear to him, he has exalted his faithfulness above all his other perfections. We see this in nature. Here is a man so to be depended upon, so faithful to his word, that he will sacrifice anything sooner than depart from it : that man will give up his property, or life itself, rather than forfeit his word. So God has spoken of magnifying his word above all his name. He would sooner allow all his other perfections to come to naught, than for his faithfulness to fail. He has so magnified his faithfulness, that his love, his mercy, his grace, would all sooner fail than his faithfulness—the word of his mouth and what he has revealed in the Scripture. What a firm salvation, then, is ours, which rests upon his word, when God has magnified that word above all his name ! What volumes of blessedness and truth are contained therein ! so that, if God has revealed his truth to your soul, and given you faith to anchor in the world of promise, sooner than that should fail, he would suffer the loss of all ; for, he has magnified his word above all his name.—*Joseph C. Philpot.*

Verse 2.—"Thou hast magnified thy word above all thy name." God has a *greater* regard unto the words of his mouth, than to the works of his hand : heaven and earth shall pass away, but one jot or tittle of what he hath spoken shall never fall to the ground. Some do understand this of Christ the essential Word, in whom he has set his name, and whom he has so highly exalted, that he has given him " a name above every name."—*Ebenezer Erskine, 1680—1754.*

Verse 2.—"Thou hast magnified thy word above all thy name." Meaning that his word or promise shall have, as it were, and exercise a kind of sovereignty over all his prerogatives and attributes, wisdom, justice, power, etc. So that men need not fear that any of them shall at any time, or in any case whatsoever, move in the least contrariety thereunto.—*John Goodwin, 1593—1665.*

Verse 2.—"*Thou hast magnified thy word above all thy name.*" It may be when there are some extraordinary works of God in the world, thunder and lightning, etc., we are ready to be afraid, and oh ! the great God that doth appear in these great works ! Were our hearts as they ought to be when we read the *Word*, we would tremble at that more than at any manifestation of God since the world began in all his works ; and if so be thou dost not see more of the glory of God in his *Word* than in his works, it is because thou hast little light in thee.—*Jeremiah Burroughs*, 1599—1646.

Verse 2.—"*Thou hast magnified thy word above all thy name.*" " By the word of the Lord were the heavens made, and all the host of them by the breath of his mouth." But mightier far is the word by which a lost world is redeemed. This is the " *word* " that he hath " *magnified above all his name*," as displaying at once the exceeding greatness of his power, the resources of his manifold wisdom, and the blended glories of holiness and love.—*John Lillie.*

Verse 2.—It is not with the truth merely excogitated, but with the truth expressed, that we have any concern ; not with the truth as seen by our inspired teacher, but with the truth as by him spoken to us. It is not enough that the Spirit hath made him to see it aright—this is not enough if he have not also made him to speak it aright. A pure influx into the mind of an apostle is no sufficient guarantee for the instruction of the world, unless there be a pure efflux also ; for not the doctrine that has flowed in, but the doctrine that has flowed out, is truly all that we have to do with. Accordingly, it is to the doctrine in efflux, that is to the *word*, that we are bidden to yield ourselves. It is the word that is a light unto our feet and a lamp unto our path ; it is his word that God hath exalted above all his name; it is the word that he hath settled fast in heaven, and given to it a stability surer and more lasting than to the ordinances of nature. We can take no cognizance of the doctrine that is conveyed from heaven to earth, when it has only come the length of excogitation in the mind of an apostle ; and it is not till brought the farther length of expression, either by speech or by writing, that it comes into contact with us. In short our immediate concern is with, not what apostles conceive inwardly, but what they bring forth outwardly—not with the schemes or the systems which they have been made to apprehend, but with the books which they have written ; and had the whole force and effect of this observation been sufficiently pondered, we feel persuaded that the advocates of a mitigated inspiration would not have dissevered, as they have done, the inspiration of sentiment from the inspiration of language.—*Thomas Chalmers.*

Verse 2.—"*Thy word,*" or, "*Thy promise.*" So great are God's promises, and so faithful and complete is his performance of them, as even to surpass the expectations which the greatness of his name has excited.—*Annotated Paragraph Bible.*

Verse 3.—"*In the day when I cried,*" etc. God granted him a speedy answer ; for it was in the very day that he cried that he was heard.: and it was a spiritual answer ; he was *strengthened with strength in his soul.* Would you have soul strength for the work you have in view ? then cry unto him who is the " strength of Israel " for it ; for " he giveth power to the faint, and he increaseth strength to them that have no might."—*Ebenezer Erskine.*

Verse 3.—" *In the day when I cried thou answeredst me,*" etc. That part of an army which is upon action in the field is sure to have their pay, if their masters have any money in their purse, or care of them ; yea, sometimes when their fellows left in their quarters are made to wait. I am sure there is more gold and silver (spiritual joy, I mean, and comfort) to be found in Christ's camp, among his suffering ones, than their brethren at home in peace and prosperity ordinarily can show. What are the promises but vessels of cordial wine, tunned on purpose against a groaning hour, when God usually broacheth them ! " Call upon me," saith God, " in the day of trouble." Ps. l. 15. And may we not do so in the day of peace ? Yes ; but he would have us most bold with him in the day of trouble. None find such quick despatch at the throne of grace as suffering saints. "*In the day that I cried,*" saith David, " *thou answeredst me, and strengthenedst me with strength in my soul."* He was now in a strait, and God comes in haste to him. Though we may keep a well friend waiting should he send for us, yet we will give a sick friend leave to call us up at midnight. In such extremities we usually go with the messenger that comes for us ; and so doth God with the prayer. Peter knocked at their gate, who were assembled to seek God for him, almost as soon as their prayer knocked at heaven gate in his behalf. And truly it is no more than needs, if we consider the temptations of our afflicted condition ; we are prone then to be suspicious that our best friends forget us, and to think every stay a delay, and neglect of us ; therefore God chooseth to show himself most kind at such a time. " As the sufferings of Christ abound in us, so our consolation also aboundeth by Christ" : 2 Cor. i. 5. As man laid on trouble, so Christ laid in consolation : both tides rose and fell together ; when it was spring-tide with him in affliction, it was so with him in his joy. We relieve the poor as their need increaseth ; so Christ comforts his people as their troubles multiply. And now, Christian, tell me, doth not thy dear Lord deserve a ready spirit in thee to meet any suffering with, for, or from him, who gives his sweetest comforts where his people are put to bear their saddest sorrows ? Well may the servant do his work cheerfully when his master is so careful of him as with his own hands to bring him his breakfast into the fields. The Christian stays not till he comes to heaven for all his comfort. There indeed shall be the full supper, but there is a breakfast, Christian, of previous joys, more or less, which Christ brings to thee into the field, to be eaten on the place where thou endurest thy hardship.—*William Gurnall.*

Verse 3.—"*Thou answeredst me, and strengthenedst me with strength in my soul."* It is one gracious way of answering our prayers when God doth bestow upon us spiritual strength in our souls ; if he do not give the things we desire, yet if he gives us strength in our souls, he graciously answers our prayers. What is this spiritual strength ? I answer, it is a work of the Spirit of God, enabling a man to do and suffer what God would have him without fainting or backsliding.—*James Nalton.*

Verse 3.—"*Thou strengthenedst me with strength in my soul."* Other masters cut out work for their servants, but do not help them in their work ; but our Master in heaven doth not only give us work, but strength. God bids us serve him, and he will enable us to serve him, Ezek. xxxvi. 27 : "I will cause you to walk in my statutes." The Lord doth not only fit work for us, but fits us for our work ; with his command he gives power.—*Thomas Watson.*

Verse 3.—"*Thou makest me brave in my soul (with) strength."* The common version of this clause (" *strengthenedst me with strength in my soul* ") contains a paronomasia not in the original, where the verb and noun have not even a letter in common. The verb is by some translated *made me proud, i.e.,* elated me, not with a vain or selfish pride, but with a lofty and exhilarating hope.—*Joseph Addison Alexander.*

Verse 4.—"*All the kings of the earth shall praise thee."* In a sense sufficiently striking this promise was fulfilled to David, and to the nation of Israel, as surrounding monarchs beheld the wonderful dispensations of divine providence which attended their steps (2 Sam. v. 11 ; viii. 10) ; but in its completest sense, it shall realize its accomplishment in the future conquests of Messiah, when the princes and potentates of the earth receive his word, learn by divine grace to celebrate the glorious methods of his love, and see in the light of faith the greatness of Jehovah's glory as the God of salvation. "*All the kings of the earth*" shall yet praise the Lord, and shall hasten with their numerous subjects to hail the triumphs of his grace.—*John Morison.*

Verse 5.—"*Yea, they shall sing in the ways of the* Lord." There will come a time when the praise of Jahve, which according to cxxxvii. 4 was obliged to be dumb in the presence of the heathen, will be sung by the kings of the heathen themselves.—*Franz Delitzsch.*

Verse 5.—"*Yea, they shall sing in the ways of the* LORD." Walking with God is a pleasant walk : the ways of wisdom are called "ways of pleasantness" : Prov. iii. 17. Is not the light pleasant ? Ps. lxxxix. 15 : "They shall walk, O LORD, in the light of thy countenance." Walking with God is like walking among beds of spices, which send forth a fragrant perfume. This is it which brings peace, Acts ix. 31 : "Walking in the fear of the Lord, and in the comfort of the Holy Ghost." While we walk with God, what sweet music doth the bird of conscience make in our breast ! "*They shall sing in the ways of the Lord.*"—*Thomas Watson.*

Verse 6.—"*Though the* LORD *be high.*" We have here God's transcendent greatness ; he is the *high Lord,* or Jehovah : he is "the high and lofty One, who inhabits eternity, and who dwells in the high and lofty place, to which no man can approach." Who can think or speak of his highness in a suitable manner ? It dazzles the eyes of sinful mortal worms to behold "the place where his honour dwells." Oh how infinite is the distance between him and us ! "There are none of the sons of the mighty that can be compared unto him" ; yea, "the inhabitants of the earth are before him but as the drop in the bucket, and the small dust in the balance." He is not only "*high*" above men, but above angels : cherubims and seraphims are his ministering spirits. He is "*high*" above the heavens ; for "the heaven, yea, the heaven of heavens cannot contain him" ; and he "humbleth himself" when "he beholds things that are in heaven." Oh, sirs, study to entertain high and admiring thoughts and apprehensions of the glorious majesty of God ; for "honour and majesty are before him ; strength and beauty are in his sanctuary."—*Ebenezer Erskine.*

Verse 6.—"*The* LORD *hath respect unto the lowly.*" God has such a respect unto the lowly, not as if this frame of soul were meritorious of any good at his hand, but because,

1. This is a disposition that best serves God's great design of lifting up and glorifying his free grace. What think you, sirs, was God's design in election, in redemption, in the whole of the gospel dispensation, and in all the ordinances thereof ? His grand design in all was to rear up a glorious high throne, from which he might display the riches of his free and sovereign grace ; this is that which he will have magnified through eternity above all his other name. Now, this lowliness and humility of spirit suits best unto God's design of exalting the freedom of his grace. It is not the legalist, or proud Pharisee, but the poor humble publican, who is smiting on his breast, and crying, "God be merciful to me, a sinner," that submits to the revelation of grace.

2. God has such respect unto the humble soul because it is a fruit of the Spirit inhabiting the soul, and an evidence of the soul's union with the Lord Jesus Christ, in whom alone we are accepted.

3. This is a disposition that makes the soul like Christ ; and the liker that a person is to Christ, God loves him ay the better. We are told that Christ was "meek and lowly" ; "he did not cry, nor lift up, nor cause his voice to be heard in the streets" ; though he was "the brightness of his Father's glory," yet he was content to appear "in the form of a servant" ; though he was rich, yet he was content to become poor, that we through his poverty might be rich. Now, the humble soul, being the image of Christ, who is the express image of his Father, God cannot but have a regard unto him.—*Ebenezer Erskine.*

Verse 6.—"*He hath respect unto the lowly.*" Give me the homely vessel of humility, which God shall preserve, and fill with the wine of his grace ; rather than the varnished cup of pride, which he will dash in pieces, like a potter's vessel. Where humility is the corner stone, there glory shall be the topstone.— *William Secker, in "The Nonsuch Professor in his Meridian Splendour,"* 1660.

Verse 6.—"*The proud he knoweth afar off.*" He that meets a spectacle or person which he cannot endure to look upon, avoids it, or turns from it while he is yet afar off ; whereas, if the object be delightful, he draweth near and comes as close as he can. When therefore it is said, *The Lord knoweth a proud man afar off*, it shows his disdain of him : he will scarce touch him with a pair of tongs (as we say) ; he cannot abide to come near him. He knows well enough how vile he is even at the greatest distance.—*Joseph Caryl.*

Verse 6.—"*The proud he knoweth afar off.*" By punishing them in hell.—*Richard Rolle*, 1340.

Verse 7.—"*Though I walk in the midst of trouble, thou wilt revive me.*" So as to the three youths in the fiery furnace, their persecutor, Nebuchadnezzar, said, " Lo, I see four men loose, *walking in the midst of the fire,* and they have no hurt, and the form of the fourth is like the Son of God."—*Andrew Robert Fausset.*

Verse 7.—"*In the midst of trouble thou wilt revive me.*" The wisdom of God is seen in helping in desperate cases. God loves to show his wisdom when human help and wisdom fail. Exquisite lawyers love to wrestle with niceties and difficulties in the law, to show their skill the more. God's wisdom is never at a loss ; but when providences are darkest, then the morning star of deliverance appears. Sometimes God melts away the spirits of his enemies. Josh. ii. 24. Sometimes he finds them other work to do, and sounds a retreat to them, as he did to Saul when he was pursuing David. " The Philistines are in the land." " In the mount God will be seen." When the church seems to be upon the altar, her peace and liberty ready to be sacrificed, then the angel comes.—*Thomas Watson.*

Verse 7.—"*Thou shalt stretch forth thine hand,*" etc. Thou shalt interpose thine help betwixt me and them, and save me harmless ; as the poets feign their gods did those whom they favoured. *Thou shalt strike them with thy left hand, and save me with thy right ;* so Tremellius senseth it.—*John Trapp.*

Verse 8.—"*The* LORD *will perfect,*" etc. God's work is perfect, man's is clumsy and incomplete. God does not leave off till he has finished. When he rests, it is because, looking on his work, he sees it all " very good." His Sabbath is the Sabbath of an achieved purpose, of a fulfilled counsel. The palaces which we build are ever like that in the story, where one window remains dark and unjewelled, while the rest blaze in beauty. But when God builds none can say, " He was not able to finish." In his great palace he makes her " windows of agates," and *all* her " borders of pleasant stones."

I suppose that if the mediæval dream had ever come true, and an alchemist had ever turned a grain of lead into gold, he could have turned all the lead in the world, in time, and with crucibles and furnaces enough. The first step is all the difficulty, and if you and I have been changed from enemies into sons, and had one spark of love to God kindled in our hearts, that is a mightier change than any that yet remains to be effected in order to make us perfect. One grain has been changed, the whole mass will be in due time.—*Alexander Maclaren, Sermon in* " *Wesleyan Methodist Magazine,*" 1879.

Verse 8.—"*Forsake not the works of thine own hands.*" When we are under such afflictions as threaten to ruin us, 'tis seasonable to tell the Lord he made us. David strengthens prayer upon this argument : "*Forsake not the works of thine own hands.*" All men love their own works, many dote upon them : shall we think God will forsake his ? See how the people of God plead with God in greatest distress (Isai. lxiv. 8) : " But now, O LORD, thou art our father ; we are the clay, and thou our potter ; and we are all the work of thy hand. Be not wroth very sore, O LORD."—*Joseph Caryl.*

Verse 8.—" *Forsake not the works of thine own hands.*" Look upon the wounds of thine hands, and forsake not the works of thine hands, prayed Queen Elizabeth. And Luther's usual prayer was, Confirm, O God, in us that thou hast wrought, and perfect the work that thou hast begun in us, to thy glory. So be it.—*John Trapp.*

Verse 8.—"*Forsake not the works of thine own hands.*" Behold in me thy work, not mine : for mine, if thou seest, thou condemnest ; thine, if thou seest, thou crownest. For whatever good works there be of mine, from thee are they to me ; and so they are more thine than mine. For I hear from thine apostle, " By grace are ye saved through faith ; and that not of yourselves : it is the gift of God .

Not of works, lest any man should boast. For we are his workmanship, created in Christ Jesus" : Eph. ii. 8—10.—*Augustine*.

Verse 8.—"*Thine own hands.*" His creating hands formed our souls at the beginning ; his nail-pierced hands redeemed them on Calvary ; his glorified hands will hold our souls fast and not let them go for ever. Unto his hands let us commend our spirits, sure that even though the works of our hands have made void the works of his hands, yet his hands will again make perfect all that our hands have unmade.—*J. W. Burgon.*

HINTS TO THE VILLAGE PREACHER.

Verses 1, 2, 3.—David vexed with rival gods, as we are with rival gospels. How will he act ? I. *Sing with whole-hearted praise.* 1. It would generously show his contempt of the false. 2. It would evince his strong faith in the true. 3. It would declare his joyful zeal for God. 4. It would shield him from evil from those about him. II. *Worship by the despised rule.* 1. Quietly ignoring all will-worship. 2. Looking to the person of Christ, which was typified by the temple. 3. Trusting in sacrifice. 4. Realizing God himself, for it is to God he speaks. III. *Praise the questioned attributes.* 1. Lovingkindness in its universality, in its speciality. Grace in everything. 2. Truth. Historic accuracy. Certainty of promises. Correctness of prophecies. Assured of the love of God and the truth of his word, let us cling the closer to these. IV. *Reverence the honoured word.* It is beyond all revelation by creation and providence, for it is—1. More clear. 2. More sure. 3. More sovereign. 4. More complete, unique. 5. More lasting. 6. More glorifying to God. V. *Prove it by experience.* 1. By offering prayer. 2. By narrating the answer. 3. By exhibiting the strength in soul which was given in answer to prayer.

Verse 2.—The Christward position. I. Worship and praise are to be blended. II. They are to be presented with an eye to God in Christ, for he is the temple : the place of divine indwelling, sacrifice, intercession, priesthood, oracle, and manifestation.

Verse 2 (first clause).—I. The soul's noblest attitude : "Toward thy holy temple." II. The soul's noblest exercise : "worship," "praise."— *W. W.*

Verse 2.—I. *The worshipper's contemplation.* Gaze fixed on Holy Temple. Material temple not yet built. Christ the sanctuary. Heb. viii. 2. All worship through him. Eye of worshippers fixed on him. II. *The worshipper's song.* Love and truth. Note the combination. Truth by Moses. Grace and truth by Jesus Christ. III. *The worshipper's argument.* Because Christ "The Word " is the embodiment and most glorious manifestation of God. Heb. i. 2, 3.—*Archibald G. Brown.*

Verse 3.—I. Prayer answered *in* the day. II. Prayer answered by giving strength *for* the day. See 2 Cor. xii. 8, 9.—*A. G. B.*

Verse 3.—I. Answers to prayer should be noted and acknowledged : "Thou answeredst me." II. Speedy answers should have special praise : "In the day when I cried, thou," etc. III. A strengthened soul is sometimes the best answer to prayer : "Strengthened me with strength."—*J. F.*

Verse 3.—Remarkable answer to prayer. I. The prayer : feeble, earnest, sorrowful, inarticulate. II. The answer : prompt, divine, effectual, certain. III. The praise deserved by such grace. See preceding verses.

Verse 3.—I. A special day. II. A specific form of prayer : "I cried." III. A special method of response.— *W. W.*

Verse 4.—I. A royal audience. II. A royal orchestra.

Verses 4, 5.—I. They who hear the words of God will know God. II. They who know God will praise him, however exalted they may be amongst men : " All the kings," etc. III. They who praise God will walk in his ways. IV.

They who walk in the ways of the Lord will glorify him, and he will be glorified in them.—*G. R.*

Verse 5.—See " Spurgeon's Sermons," No. 1615 : " Singing in the Ways of the Lord."

Verse 5.—This is spoken of kings, but it is true of the humblest pilgrims. The Lord hath respect unto the lowly, and will make them sing. I. *They shall sing in the ways.* 1. They take pleasure in them. 2. They do not go out of them to find pleasure. 3. They sing as they proceed in service, in worship, in holiness, in suffering. 4. They are in a case for singing. They have strength, safety, guidance, provision, comfort. II. *They sing of the ways of the Lord.* 1. Of God's ways to them. 2. Of their way to God. They know whence they came out. They know where they are going. It is a good road ; prophets went by it, and the Lord of the prophets. Therein we have good company, good accommodation, good prospects, good daylight. III. *They sing of the Lord of the way.* His lovingkindness. His truth. Answers to prayer. His condescension. His reviving us in trouble. His delivering us. His perfecting us. His everlasting mercy. IV. *They shall sing to the Lord of the way.* 1. To his honour. 2. To the extending of that honour. 3. As a preparation to eternally honouring him.

Verse 6.—Divine inversions. I. Lowliness honoured to its great surprise. II. Pride passed by to its eternal mortification.—*W. B. H.*

Verse 7 (first clause).—I. The psalmist's dismal excursion : walking " in the midst of trouble" ; this is not a spectator, but one assailed. Troubles—personal, social, ecclesiastical, national. II. His cheering anticipation—of revival, defence, deliverance.—*W. J.*

Verse 7.—I. Good men are sometimes in the midst of troubles : these are many, and continue long. II. They interfere not with their progress. They " walk in the midst" of them ; faint, yet pursuing ; sometimes they " run with patience," etc. III. They have comfort in them : " Though I walk," etc., " thou wilt revive me." IV. They are benefited by them. 1. Their enemies are overthrown. 2. Their deliverance is complete.—*G. R.*

Verse 7.—The child of God often revived *out* of trouble ; more frequently *in* trouble ; not seldom *through* trouble. Delivered from, sustained in, sanctified through, trouble.—*A. G. B.*

Verse 7.—An incident of the road to the city. I. Pilgrims beset by thieves and struck down. II. The arrival of Greatheart and flight of the enemy. III. The flask to the lips : " thou wilt revive me." Sweet awakening to know the beauty of his face and strength of his hand !—*W. B. H.*

Verse 7 (third clause).—Right-hand salvation. I. It shall be wrought of God. II. He shall throw his strength into the deed. III. His utmost dexterity shall be displayed.

Verse 8 (first clause).—I. A wide subject—" That which concerneth me." Not necessarily that which gives me concern. II. A promise that covers it : " the Lord will perfect."—*A. G. B.*

Verse 8 (first and last clauses).—Faith in divine purpose no hindrance to prayer, but rather an encouragement in it : " The Lord will perfect." " Forsake not." —*A. G. B.*

Verse 8.—See " Spurgeon's Sermons," Nos. 231 and 1506 : " Faith in Perfection," and, " Choice Comfort for a Young Believer."

Verse 8.—The grace of God makes a man thoughtful, and leads him to concern about himself, his life, his future, and the completeness of the work of grace. This might lead us to sadness and despair, but the Lord worketh in us for other ends. I. *He fills us with assurance.* 1. That the Lord will work for us. 2. That he will complete his work. 3. That he will do this in providence ; if it be properly a concern of ours. 4. That he will do this within us. Our graces shall grow. Our soul shall become Christly. Our whole nature perfect. 5. That he will do this with our work for him. II. *He gives us rest in his mercy.* 1. Thou wilt forgive my sins. 2. Thou wilt bear with my nature. 3. Thou wilt support me in suffering. 4. Thou wilt supply me in need. 5. Thou wilt succour me in death. III. *He puts prayer into our hearts.* 1. That he will not forsake me. 2. That he will not leave his own work in me undone. 3. Nor his work by me unfinished. Why did he begin ? Why carry so far ? Why not complete ?

Verse 8.—I. Faith's full assurance : " The Lord will perfect that which concerneth me." II. Faith's firm foundation : " Thy mercy, O Lord, endureth for ever." III. Faith's fervent prayer : " Forsake not the works of thine own hands."—*W. H. J. P.*

PSALM CXXXIX.

One of the most notable of the sacred hymns. It sings the omniscience and omnipresence of God, inferring from these the overthrow of the powers of wickedness, since he who sees and hears the abominable deeds and words of the rebellious will surely deal with them according to his justice. The brightness of this psalm is like unto a sapphire stone, or Ezekiel's "terrible crystal"; it flames out with such flashes of light as to turn night into day. Like a Pharos, this holy song casts a clear light even to the uttermost parts of the sea, and warns us against that practical atheism which ignores the presence of God, and so makes shipwreck of the soul.

TITLE.—To the Chief Musician. *The last time this title occurred was in Psalm cix. This sacred song is worthy of the most excellent of the singers, and is fitly dedicated to the leader of the Temple psalmody, that he might set it to music, and see that it was devoutly sung in the solemn worship of the Most High.* A Psalm of David. *It bears the image and superscription of King David, and could have come from no other mint than that of the son of Jesse. Of course the critics take this composition away from David, on account of certain Aramaic expressions in it. We believe that upon the principles of criticism now in vogue it would be extremely easy to prove that Milton did not write Paradise Lost. We have yet to learn that David could not have used expressions belonging to "the language of the patriarchal ancestral house." Who knows how much of the antique speech may have been purposely retained among those nobler minds who rejoiced in remembering the descent of their race? Knowing to what wild inferences the critics have run in other matters, we have lost nearly all faith in them, and prefer to believe David to be the author of this psalm, from internal evidences of style and matter, rather than to accept the determination of men whose modes of judgment are manifestly unreliable.*

EXPOSITION.

O LORD, thou hast searched me, and known *me.*

2 Thou knowest my downsitting and mine uprising, thou understandest my thought afar off.

3 Thou compassest my path and my lying down, and art acquainted *with* all my ways.

4 For *there is* not a word in my tongue, *but,* lo, O LORD, thou knowest it altogether.

5 Thou hast beset me behind and before, and laid thine hand upon me.

6 *Such* knowledge *is* too wonderful for me ; it is high, I cannot *attain* unto it.

1. "*O* LORD, *thou hast searched me, and known me.*" He invokes in adoration Jehovah the all-knowing God, and he proceeds to adore him by proclaiming one of his peculiar attributes. If we would praise God aright we must draw the matter of our praise from himself—"O Jehovah, thou hast." No pretended god knows aught of us ; but the true God, Jehovah, understands us, and is most intimately acquainted with our persons, nature, and character. How well it is for us to know the God who knows us ! The divine knowledge is extremely thorough and searching ; it is as if he had searched us, as officers search a man for contraband goods, or as pillagers ransack a house for plunder. Yet we must not let the figure run upon all fours, and lead us further than it is meant to do : the Lord knows all things naturally and as a matter of course, and not by any effort on his part. Searching ordinarily implies a measure of ignorance which is removed by

observation ; of course this is not the case with the Lord ; but the meaning of the psalmist is, that the Lord knows us as thoroughly as if he had examined us minutely, and had pried into the most secret corners of our being. This infallible knowledge has always existed—" Thou hast searched me " ; and it continues unto this day, since God cannot forget that which he has once known. There never was a time in which we were unknown to God, and there never will be a moment in which we shall be beyond his observation. Note how the psalmist makes his doctrine personal : he saith not, " O God, thou knowest all things" ; but, " thou hast known *me*." It is ever our wisdom to lay truth home to ourselves. How wonderful the contrast between the observer and the observed ! Jehovah and me ! Yet this most intimate connection exists, and therein lies our hope. Let the reader sit still a while and try to realize the two poles of this statement,—the Lord and poor puny man—and he will see much to admire and wonder at.

2. "*Thou knowest my downsitting and mine uprising.*" *Me* thou knowest, and all that comes of me. I am observed when I quietly sit down, and marked when I resolutely rise up. My most common and casual acts, my most needful and necessary movements, are noted by thee, and thou knowest the inward thoughts which regulate them. Whether I sink in lowly self-renunciation, or ascend in pride, thou seest the motions of my mind, as well as those of my body. This is a fact to be remembered every moment : sitting down to consider, or rising up to act, we are still seen, known, and read by Jehovah our Lord. "*Thou understandest my thought afar off.*" Before it is my own it is foreknown and comprehended by thee. Though my thought be invisible to the sight, though as yet I be not myself cognizant of the shape it is assuming, yet thou hast it under thy consideration, and thou perceivest its nature, its source, its drift, its result. Never dost thou misjudge or wrongly interpret me : my inmost thought is perfectly understood by thine impartial mind. Though thou shouldst give but a glance at my heart, and see me as one sees a passing meteor moving afar, yet thou wouldst by that glimpse sum up all the meanings of my soul, so transparent is everything to thy piercing glance.

3. "*Thou compassest my path and my lying down.*" My path and my pallet, my running and my resting, are alike within the circle of thine observation. Thou dost surround me even as the air continually surrounds all creatures that live. I am shut up within the wall of thy being ; I am encircled within the bounds of thy knowledge. Waking or sleeping I am still observed of thee. I may leave thy path, but thou never leavest mine. I may sleep and forget thee, but thou dost never slumber, nor fall into oblivion concerning thy creature. The original signifies not only surrounding, but winnowing and sifting. The Lord judges our active life and our quiet life ; he discriminates our action and our repose, and marks that in them which is good and also that which is evil. There is chaff in all our wheat, and the Lord divides them with unerring precision. "*And art acquainted with all my ways.*" Thou art familiar with all I do ; nothing is concealed from thee, nor surprising to thee, nor misunderstood by thee. Our paths may be habitual or accidental, open or secret, but with them all the Most Holy One is well acquainted. This should fill us with awe, so that we sin not ; with courage, so that we fear not ; with delight, so that we mourn not.

4. "*For there is not a word in my tongue, but lo, O* LORD, *thou knowest it altogether.*" The unformed word, which lies within the tongue like a seed in the soil, is certainly and completely known to the Great Searcher of hearts. A negative expression is used to make the positive statement all the stronger : not a word is unknown is a forcible way of saying that every word is well known. Divine knowledge is perfect, since not a single word is unknown, nay, not even an unspoken word, and each one is " altogether" or wholly known. What hope of concealment can remain when the speech with which too many conceal their thoughts is itself transparent before the Lord ? O Jehovah, how great art thou ! If thine eye hath such power, what must be the united force of thine whole nature !

5. *"Thou hast beset me behind and before."* As though we were caught in an ambush, or besieged by an army which has wholly beleaguered the city walls, we are surrounded by the Lord. God has set us where we be, and beset us wherever we be. Behind us there is God recording our sins, or in grace blotting out the remembrance of them ; and before us there is God foreknowing all our deeds, and providing for all our wants. We cannot turn back and so escape him, for he is behind ; we cannot go forward and outmarch him, for he is before. He not only beholds us, but he besets us ; and lest there should seem any chance of escape, or lest we should imagine that the surrounding presence is yet a distant one, it is added,—*"And laid thine hand upon me."* The prisoner marches along surrounded by a guard, and gripped by an officer. God is very near ; we are wholly in his power ; from that power there is no escape. It is not said that God *will* thus beset us and arrest us, but it is done—" Thou hast beset me." Shall we not alter the figure, and say that our heavenly Father has folded his arms around us, and caressed us with his hand ? It is even so with those who are by faith the children of the Most High.

6. *"Such knowledge is too wonderful for me."* I cannot grasp it. I can hardly endure to think of it. The theme overwhelms me. I am amazed and astounded at it. Such knowledge not only surpasses my comprehension, but even my imagination. *"It is high, I cannot attain unto it."* Mount as I may, this truth is too lofty for my mind. It seems to be always above me, even when I soar into the loftiest regions of spiritual thought. Is it not so with every attribute of God ? Can we attain to any idea of his power, his wisdom, his holiness ? Our mind has no line with which to measure the Infinite. Do we therefore question ? Say, rather, that we therefore believe and adore. We are not surprised that the Most Glorious God should in his knowledge be high above all the knowledge to which we can attain : it must of necessity be so, since we are such poor limited beings ; and when we stand a-tip-toe we cannot reach to the lowest step of the throne of the Eternal.

7 Whither shall I go from thy spirit ? or whither shall I flee from thy presence ?

8 If I ascend up into heaven, thou *art* there : if I make my bed in hell, behold, thou *art there.*

9 *If* I take the wings of the morning, *and* dwell in the uttermost parts of the sea ;

10 Even there shall thy hand lead me, and thy right hand shall hold me.

11 If I say, Surely the darkness shall cover me ; even the night shall be light about me.

12 Yea, the darkness hideth not from thee ; but the night shineth as the day : the darkness and the light *are* both alike *to thee.*

Here omnipresence is the theme,—a truth to which omniscience naturally leads up. *" Whither shall I go from thy spirit ?"* Not that the Psalmist wished to go from God, or to avoid the power of the divine life ; but he asks this question to set forth the fact that no one can escape from the all-pervading being and observation of the Great Invisible Spirit. Observe how the writer makes the matter personal to himself—" Whither shall *I* go ?" It were well if we all thus applied truth to our own cases. It were wise for each one to say—The spirit of the Lord is ever around *me :* Jehovah is omnipresent *to me.* *"Or whither shall I flee from thy presence ?"* If, full of dread, I hastened to escape from that nearness of God which had become my terror, which way could I turn ? " Whither ?" " Whither ?" He repeats his cry. No answer comes back to him. The reply to his first " Whither ?" is its echo,—a second " Whither ?" From the sight of God he cannot be hidden, but that is not all,—from the immediate, actual, constant presence of God he cannot be withdrawn. We must be, whether we will it or not, as near to God as our soul is to our body. This makes it dreadful work to sin ; for we offend the Almighty to his face, and commit acts of treason at the very foot of his throne. *Go* from him, or *flee* from him we cannot : neither by patient travel nor by hasty flight can we withdraw from the all-surrounding Deity. His mind is in our mind ; himself within ourselves. His spirit is over our spirit ; our presence is ever in his presence.

8. "*If I ascend up into heaven, thou art there.*" Filling the loftiest region with his yet loftier presence, Jehovah is in the heavenly place, at home, upon his throne. The ascent, if it were possible, would be unavailing for purposes of escape ; it would, in fact, be a flying into the centre of the fire to avoid the heat. There would he be immediately confronted by the terrible personality of God. Note the abrupt words—" THOU, THERE." "*If I make my bed in hell, behold, thou art there.*" Descending into the lowest imaginable depths among the dead, there should we find the Lord. THOU ! says the Psalmist, as if he felt that God was the one great Existence in all places. Whatever Hades may be, or whoever may be there, one thing is certain, *Thou*, O Jehovah, art there. Two regions, the one of glory and the other of darkness, are set in contrast, and this one fact is asserted of both—" thou art there." Whether we rise up or lie down, take our wing or make our bed, we shall find God near us. A "*behold*" is added to the second clause, since it seems more a wonder to meet with God in hell than in heaven, in Hades than in Paradise. Of course the presence of God produces very different effects in these places, but it is unquestionably in each ; the bliss of one, the terror of the other. What an awful thought, that some men seem resolved to take up their night's abode in hell, a night which shall know no morning.

9. "*If I take the wings of the morning, and dwell in the uttermost parts of the sea.*" If I could fly with all swiftness, and find a habitation where the mariner has not yet ploughed the deep, yet I could not reach the boundaries of the divine presence. Light flies with inconceivable rapidity, and it flashes far afield beyond all human ken ; it illuminates the great and wide sea, and sets its waves gleaming afar ; but its speed would utterly fail if employed in flying from the Lord. Were we to speed on the wings of the morning breeze, and break into oceans unknown to chart and map, yet there we should find the Lord already present. He who saves to the uttermost would be with us in the uttermost parts of the sea.

10. "*Even there shall thy hand lead me.*" We could only fly from God by his own power. The Lord would be leading, covering, preserving, sustaining us even when we were fugitives from him. "*And thy right hand shall hold me.*" In the uttermost parts of the sea my arrest would be as certain as at home : God's right hand would there seize and detain the runaway. Should we be commanded on the most distant errand, we may assuredly depend upon the upholding right hand of God as with us in all mercy, wisdom, and power. The exploring missionary in his lonely wanderings is led, in his solitary feebleness he is held. Both the hands of God are with his own servants to sustain them, and against rebels to overthrow them ; and in this respect it matters not to what realms they resort, the active energy of God is around them still.

11. "*If I say, Surely the darkness shall cover me.*" Dense darkness may oppress me, but it cannot shut me out from thee, or thee from me. Thou seest as well without the light as with it, since thou art not dependent upon light which is thine own creature, for the full exercise of thy perceptions. Moreover, thou art present with me whatever may be the hour ; and being present thou discoverest all that I think, or feel, or do. Men are still so foolish as to prefer night and darkness for their evil deeds ; but so impossible is it for anything to be hidden from the Lord that they might just as well transgress in broad daylight.

> Darkness and light in this agree;
> Great God, they're both alike to thee.
> Thine hand can pierce thy foes as soon
> Through midnight shades as blazing noon.

A good man will not wish to be hidden by the darkness, a wise man will not expect any such thing. If we were so foolish as to make sure of concealment because the place was shrouded in midnight, we might well be alarmed out of our security by the fact that, as far as God is concerned, we always dwell in the light ; for even the night itself glows with a revealing force,—"*even the night shall be light about me.*" Let us think of this if ever we are tempted to take license from the dark—it is light about us. If the darkness be light, how great is that light in which we dwell ! Note well how David keeps his song in the first person ; let us mind that we do the same as we cry with Hagar, "Thou God seest *me.*"

12. "*Yea,*" of a surety, beyond all denial. "*The darkness hideth not from thee*"; it veils nothing, it is not the medium of concealment in any degree what ever. It hides from men, but not from God. "*But the night shineth as the day*" : it is but another form of day : it shines, revealing all ; it "shineth as the day," —quite as clearly and distinctly manifesting all that is done. "*The darkness and the light are both alike to thee.*" This sentence seems to sum up all that went before, and most emphatically puts the negative upon the faintest idea of hiding under the cover of night. Men cling to this notion, because it is easier and less expensive to hide under darkness than to journey to remote places ; and therefore the foolish thought is here beaten to pieces by statements which in their varied forms effectually batter it. Yet the ungodly are still duped by their grovelling notions of God, and enquire, "How doth God know ?" They must fancy that he is as limited in his powers of observation as they are, and yet if they would but consider for a moment they would conclude that he who could not see in the dark could not be God, and he who is not present everywhere could not be the Almighty Creator. Assuredly God is in all places, at all times, and nothing can by any possibility be kept away from his all-observing, all-comprehending mind. The Great Spirit comprehends within himself all time and space, and yet he is infinitely greater than these, or aught else that he has made.

13 For thou hast possessed my reins : thou hast covered me in my mother's womb.

14 I will praise thee ; for I am fearfully *and* wonderfully made : marvellous *are* thy works ; and *that* my soul knoweth right well.

15 My substance was not hid from thee, when I was made in secret, *and* curiously wrought in the lowest parts of the earth.

16 Thine eyes did see my substance, yet being unperfect ; and in thy book all *my members* were written, *which* in continuance were fashioned, when *as yet there was* none of them.

17 How precious also are thy thoughts unto me, O God ! how great is the sum of them !

18 *If* I should count them, they are more in number than the sand : when I awake, I am still with thee.

13. "*For thou hast possessed my reins.*" Thou art the owner of my inmost parts and passions : not the indweller and observer only, but the acknowledged lord and possessor of my most secret self. The word "reins" signifies the kidneys, which by the Hebrews were supposed to be the seat of the desires and longings ; but perhaps it indicates here the most hidden and vital portion of the man ; this God doth not only inspect, and visit, but it is his own ; he is as much at home there as a landlord on his own estate, or a proprietor in his own house. "*Thou hast covered me in my mother's womb.*" There I lay hidden—covered by thee. Before I could know thee, or aught else, thou hadst a care for me, and didst hide me away as a treasure till thou shouldst see fit to bring me to the light. Thus the Psalmist describes the intimacy which God had with him. In his most secret part—his reins, and in his most secret condition—yet unborn, he was under the control and guardianship of God.

14. "*I will praise thee*": a good resolve, and one which he was even now carrying out. Those who are praising God are the very men who *will* praise him. Those who wish to praise have subjects for adoration ready to hand. We too seldom remember our creation, and all the skill and kindness bestowed upon our frame : but the sweet singer of Israel was better instructed, and therefore he prepares for the chief musician a song concerning our nativity and all the fashioning which precedes it. We cannot begin too soon to bless our Maker, who began so soon to bless us : even in the act of creation he created reasons for our praising his name. "*For I am fearfully and wonderfully made.*" Who can gaze even upon a model of our anatomy without wonder and awe ? Who could dissect a portion of the human frame without marvelling at its delicacy, and trembling at its frailty ? The Psalmist had scarcely peered within the veil which hides the nerves, sinews, and blood-vessels from common inspection ; the science of anatomy was quite unknown to him ; and yet he had seen enough to arouse his admiration of the work and his reverence for the Worker. "*Marvellous are thy works.*" These parts of my frame are all *thy* works ; and though they be home works, close under my own eye, yet are they wonderful to the last degree. They are works within my own self, yet are they beyond my understanding, and appear to me as so many miracles of skill and power. We need not go to the ends of the earth for marvels, nor even across our own threshold ; they abound in our own bodies. "*And that my soul knoweth right well.*" He was no agnostic—he knew ; he was no doubter—his soul knew ; he was no dupe—his soul knew right well. Those know indeed and of a truth who first know the Lord, and then know all things in him. He was made to know the marvellous nature of God's work with assurance and accuracy, for he had found by experience that the Lord is a masterworker, performing inimitable wonders when accomplishing his kind designs. If we are marvellously wrought upon even before we are born, what shall we say of the Lord's dealings with us after we quit his secret workshop, and he directs our pathway through the pilgrimage of life ? What shall we not say of that new birth which is even more mysterious than the first, and exhibits even more the love and wisdom of the Lord.

15. "*My substance was not hid from thee.*" The substantial part of my being was before thine all-seeing eye ; the bones which make my frame were put together by thine hand. The essential materials of my being before they were arranged were all within the range of thine eye. I was hidden from all human knowledge, but not from thee : thou hast ever been intimately acquainted with me. "*When I was made in secret.*" Most chastely and beautifully is here described the formation of our being before the time of our birth. A great artist will often labour alone in his studio, and not suffer his work to be seen until it is finished ; even so did the Lord fashion us where no eye beheld as, and the veil was not lifted till every member was complete. Much of the formation of our inner man still proceeds in secret : hence the more of solitude the better for us. The true church also is being fashioned in secret, so that none may cry, " Lo, here !" or " Lo, there !" as if that which is visible could ever be identical with the invisibly growing body of Christ. "*And curiously wrought in the lowest parts of the earth.*" " Embroidered with great skill," is an accurate poetical description of the creation of veins, sinews, muscles, nerves, etc. What tapestry can equal the human fabric ? This work is wrought as much in private as if it had been accomplished in the grave, or in the darkness of the abyss. The expressions are poetical, beautifully veiling, though not absolutely concealing, the real meaning. God's intimate knowledge of us from our beginning, and even before it, is here most charmingly set forth. Cannot he who made us thus wondrously when we were not, still carry on his work of power till he has perfected us, though we feel unable to aid in the process, and are lying in great sorrow and self-loathing, as though cast into the lowest parts of the earth ?

16. "*Thine eyes did see my substance, yet being unperfect.*" While as yet the vessel was upon the wheel the Potter saw it all. The Lord knows not only our shape, but our substance : this is substantial knowledge indeed. The Lord's

observation of us is intent and intentional,—" Thine eyes did see." Moreover, the divine mind discerns all things as clearly and certainly as men perceive by actual eye-sight. His is not hearsay acquaintance, but the knowledge which comes of sight. *"And in thy book all my members were written, which in continuance were fashioned, when as yet there was none of them."* An architect draws his plans, and makes out his specifications ; even so did the great Maker of our frame write down all our members in the book of his purposes. That we have eyes, and ears, and hands, and feet, is all due to the wise and gracious purpose of heaven : it was so ordered in the secret decree by which all things are as they are. God's purposes concern our limbs and faculties. Their form, and shape, and everything about them were appointed of God long before they had any existence. God saw us when we could not be seen, and he wrote about us when there was nothing of us to write about. When as yet there were none of our members in existence, all those members were before the eye of God in the sketch-book of his foreknowledge and predestination.

This verse is an exceedingly difficult one to translate, but we do not think that any of the proposed amendments are better than the rendering afforded us by the Authorized Version. The large number of words in italics will warn the English reader that the sense is hard to come at, and difficult to express, and that it would be unwise to found any doctrine upon the *English* words ; happily there is no temptation to do so.

The great truth expressed in these lines has by many been referred to the formation of the mystical body of our Lord Jesus. Of course, what is true of man, as man, is emphatically true of Him who is the representative man. The great Lord knows who belong to Christ ; his eye perceives the chosen members who shall yet be made one with the living person of the mystical Christ. Those of the elect who are as yet unborn, or unrenewed, are nevertheless written in the Lord's book. As the form of Eve grew up in silence and secrecy under the fashioning hand of the Maker, so at this hour is the Bride being fashioned for the Lord Jesus ; or, to change the figure,—a body is being prepared in which the life and glory of the indwelling Lord shall for ever be displayed. The Lord knoweth them that are his : he has a specially familiar acquaintance with the members of the body of Christ ; he sees their substance, unperfect though they be.

17. *"How precious also are thy thoughts unto me, O God !"* He is not alarmed at the fact that God knows all about him ; on the contrary, he is comforted, and even feels himself to be enriched, as with a casket of precious jewels. That God should think upon him is the believer's treasure and pleasure. He cries, " How costly, how valued are thy thoughts, how dear to me is thy perpetual attention !" He thinks upon God's thoughts with delight ; the more of them the better is he pleased. It is a joy worth worlds that the Lord should think upon us who are so poor and needy : it is a joy which fills our whole nature to think upon God ; returning love for love, thought for thought, after our poor fashion. *"How great is the sum of them !"* When we remember that God thought upon us from old eternity, continues to think upon us every moment, and will think of us when time shall be no more, we may well exclaim, " How great is the sum !" Thoughts such as are natural to the Creator, the Preserver, the Redeemer, the Father, the Friend, are evermore flowing from the heart of the Lord. Thoughts of our pardon, renewal, upholding, supplying, educating, perfecting, and a thousand more kinds perpetually well up in the mind of the Most High. It should fill us with adoring wonder and reverent surprise that the infinite mind of God should turn so many thoughts towards us who are so insignificant and so unworthy ! What a contrast is all this to the notion of those who deny the existence of a personal, conscious God ! Imagine a world without a thinking, personal God ! Conceive of a grim providence of machinery !—a fatherhood of law ! Such philosophy is hard and cold. As well might a man pillow his head upon a razor edge as seek rest in such a fancy. But a God always thinking of us makes a happy world, a rich life, a heavenly hereafter.

18. *"If I should count them, they are more in number than the sand."* This figure

shows the thoughts of God to be altogether innumerable ; for nothing can surpass in number the grains of sand which belt the main ocean and all the minor seas. The task of counting God's thoughts of love would be a never-ending one. If we should attempt the reckoning we must necessarily fail, for the infinite falls not within the line of our feeble intellect. Even could we count the sands on the sea-shore, we should not then be able to number God's thoughts, for they are " more in number than the sand." This is not the hyperbole of poetry, but the solid fact of inspired statement : God thinks upon us infinitely : there is a limit to the act of creation, but not to the might of divine love.

" *When I awake, I am still with thee.*" Thy thoughts of love are so many that my mind never gets away from them, they surround me at all hours. I go to my bed, and God is my last thought ; and when I wake I find my mind still hovering about his palace-gates ; God is ever with me, and I am ever with him. This is life indeed. If during sleep my mind wanders away into dreams, yet it only wanders upon holy ground, and the moment I wake my heart is back with its Lord. The Psalmist does not say, " When I awake, I return to thee," but, " I am still with thee " ; as if his meditations were continuous, and his communion unbroken. Soon we shall lie down to sleep for the last time : God grant that when the trumpet of the archangel shall waken us we may find ourselves still with him.

19 Surely thou wilt slay the wicked, O God : depart from me therefore, ye bloody men.

20 For they speak against thee wickedly, *and* thine enemies take *thy name* in vain.

21 Do not I hate them, O LORD, that hate thee ? and am not I grieved with those that rise up against thee ?

22 I hate them with perfect hatred : I count them mine enemies.

23 Search me, O God, and know my heart : try me, and know my thoughts.

24 And see if *there be any* wicked way in me, and lead me in the way everlasting.

19. "*Surely thou wilt slay the wicked, O God.*" There can be no doubt upon that head, for thou hast seen all their transgressions, which indeed have been done in thy presence ; and thou hast long enough endured their provocations, which have been so openly manifest before thee. Crimes committed before the face of the Judge are not likely to go unpunished. If the eye of God is grieved with the presence of evil, it is but natural to expect that he will remove the offending object. God who sees all evil will slay all evil. With earthly sovereigns sin may go unpunished for lack of evidence, or the law may be left without execution from lack of vigour in the judge ; but this cannot happen in the case of God, the living God. He beareth not the sword in vain. Such is his love of holiness and hatred of wrong, that he will carry on war to the death with those whose hearts and lives are wicked. God will not always suffer his lovely creation to be defaced and defiled by the presence of wickedness : if anything is sure, this is sure, that he will ease him of his adversaries. "*Depart from me therefore, ye bloody men.*" Men who delight in cruelty and war are not fit companions for those who walk with God. David chases the men of blood from his court, for he is weary of those of whom God is weary. He seems to say—If God will not let you live with him I will not have you live with me. You would destroy others, and therefore I want you not in my society. You will be destroyed yourselves, I desire you not in my service. Depart from me, for you depart from God. As we delight to have the holy God always near us, so would we eagerly desire to have wicked men removed as far as possible from us. We tremble in the society of the ungodly lest their doom should fall upon them suddenly, and we

should see them lie dead at our feet. We do not wish to have our place of intercourse turned into a gallows of execution, therefore let the condemned be removed out of our company.

20. "*For they speak against thee wickedly.*" Why should I bear their company when their talk sickens me ? They vent their treasons and blasphemies as often as they please, doing so without the slightest excuse or provocation ; let them therefore begone, where they may find a more congenial associate than I can be. When men speak against God they will be sure to speak against us, if they find it serve their turn ; hence godless men are not the stuff out of which true friends can ever be made. God gave these men their tongues, and they turn them against their Benefactor, wickedly, from sheer malice, and with great perverseness. "*And thine enemies take thy name in vain.*" This is their sport : to insult Jehovah's glorious name is their amusement. To blaspheme the name of the Lord is a gratuitous wickedness in which there can be no pleasure, and from which there can be no profit. This is a sure mark of the " enemies" of the Lord, that they have the impudence to assail his honour, and treat his glory with irreverence. How can God do other than slay them ? How can we do other than withdraw from every sort of association with them ? What a wonder of sin it is that men should rail against so good a Being as the Lord our God ! The impudence of those who talk wickedly is a singular fact, and it is the more singular when we reflect that the Lord against whom they speak is all around them, and lays to heart every dishonour which they render to his holy name. We ought not to wonder that men slander and deride us, for they do the same with the Most High God.

21. "*Do not I hate them, O* LORD, *that hate thee?*" He was a good hater, for he hated only those who hated good. Of this hatred he is not ashamed, but he sets it forth as a virtue to which he would have the Lord bear testimony. To love all men with benevolence is our duty ; but to love any wicked man with complacency would be a crime. To hate a man for his own sake, or for any evil done to us, would be wrong ; but to hate a man because he is the foe of all goodness and the enemy of all righteousness, is nothing more nor less than an obligation. The more we love God the more indignant shall we grow with those who refuse him their affection. " If any man love not the Lord Jesus Christ let him be Anathema Maranatha." Truly, " jealousy is cruel as the grave." The loyal subject must not be friendly to the traitor. "*And am not I grieved with those that rise up against thee?*" He appeals to heaven that he took no pleasure in those who rebelled against the Lord ; but, on the contrary, he was made to mourn by a sight of their ill behaviour. Since God is everywhere, he knows our feelings towards the profane and ungodly, and he knows that so far from approving such characters the very sight of them is grievous to our eyes.

22. "*I hate them with perfect hatred.*" He does not leave it a matter of question. He does not occupy a neutral position. His hatred to bad, vicious, blasphemous men is intense, complete, energetic. He is as whole-hearted in his hate of wickedness as in his love of goodness. "*I count them mine enemies.*" He makes a personal matter of it. They may have done him no ill, but if they are doing despite to God, to his laws, and to the great principles of truth and righteousness, David proclaims war against them. Wickedness passes men into favour with unrighteous spirits ; but it excludes them from the communion of the just. We pull up the drawbridge and man the walls when a man of Belial goes by our castle. His character is a *casus belli ;* we cannot do otherwise than contend with those who contend with God.

23. "*Search me, O God, and know my heart.*" David is no accomplice with traitors. He has disowned them in set form, and now he appeals to God that he does not harbour a trace of fellowship with them. He will have God himself search him, and search him thoroughly, till every point of his being is known, and read, and understood ; for he is sure that even by such an investigation there will be found in him no complicity with wicked men. He challenges the fullest investigation, the innermost search : he had need be a true man who can put him-

self deliberately into such a crucible. Yet we may each one desire such search-ing ; for it would be a terrible calamity to us for sin to remain in our hearts un-known and undiscovered. *"Try me, and know my thoughts."* Exercise any and every test upon me. By fire and by water let me be examined. Read not alone the desires of my heart, but the fugitive thoughts of my head. Know with all-penetrating knowledge all that is or has been in the chambers of my mind. What a mercy that there is one being who can know us to perfection ! He is intimately at home with us. He is graciously inclined towards us, and is willing to bend his omniscience to serve the end of our sanctification. Let us pray as David did, and let us be as honest as he. We cannot hide our sin : salvation lies the other way, in a plain discovery of evil, and an effectual severance from it.

24. *"And see if there be any wicked way in me."* See whether there be in my heart, or in my life, any evil habit unknown to myself. If there be such an evil way, take me from it, take it from me. No matter how dear the wrong may have become, nor how deeply prejudiced I may have been in its favour, be pleased to deliver me therefrom altogether, effectually, and at once, that I may tolerate nothing which is contrary to thy mind. As I hate the wicked in their way, so would I hate every wicked way in myself. *"And lead me in the way everlasting."* If thou hast introduced me already to the good old way, be pleased to keep me in it, and conduct me further and further along it. It is a way which thou hast set up of old, it is based upon everlasting principles, and it is the way in which im-mortal spirits will gladly run for ever and ever. There will be no end to it world without end. It lasts for ever, and they who are in it last for ever. Conduct me into it, O Lord, and conduct me throughout the whole length of it. By thy providence, by thy word, by thy grace, and by thy Spirit, lead me evermore.

EXPLANATORY NOTES.

Whole Psalm.—Aben Ezra observes, that this is the most glorious and excellent psalm in all the book : a very excellent one it is ; but whether the most excellent, it is hard to say.—*John Gill.*

Whole Psalm.—There is one psalm which it were well if Christians would do by it as Pythagoras by his Golden Precepts,—every morning and evening repeat it. It is David's appeal of a good conscience unto God, against the malicious sus-picions and calumnies of men, in Psalm cxxxix.—*Samuel Annesley* (1620—1696), *in "The Morning Exercises."*

Whole Psalm.—This psalm is one of the sublimest compositions in the world. How came a shepherd boy to conceive so sublime a theme, and to write in so sub-lime a strain ? Holy men of God spake as they were moved by the Holy Ghost. What themes are more sublime than the Divine attributes ? And which of these attributes is more sublime than Omnipresence ? Omniscience, spirituality, in-finity, immutability and eternity are necessarily included in it.—*George Rogers.*

Whole Psalm.—Let the modern wits, after this, look upon the honest shepherds of Palestine as a company of *rude and unpolished clowns ;* let them, if they can, produce from profane authors thoughts that are more sublime, more delicate, or better turned ; not to mention the sound divinity and solid piety which are appar-ent under these expressions.—*Claude Fleury,* 1640—1723.

Whole Psalm.—Here the poet inverts his gaze, from the blaze of suns, to the strange atoms composing his own frame. He stands shuddering over the preci-pice of himself. Above is the All-encompassing Spirit, from whom the morning wings cannot save ; and below, at a deep distance, appears amid the branching forest of his animal frame, so fearfully and wonderfully made, the abyss of his spiritual existence, lying like a dark lake in the midst. How, between mystery and mystery, his mind, his wonder, his very reason, seem to rock like a little boat between the sea and sky. But speedily does he regain his serenity ; when he throws himself, with childlike haste and confidence, into the arms of that

Fatherly Spirit, and murmurs in his bosom, "How precious also are thy thoughts unto *me*, O God ; how great is the sum of them" ; and looking up at last in his face, cries—"Search me, O Lord. I cannot search thee ; I cannot search myself ; I am overwhelmed by those dreadful depths ; but search me as thou only canst ; see if there be any wicked way in me, and lead me in the way everlasting."— *George Gilfillan* (1813—1878), *in "The Bards of the Bible."*

Whole Psalm.—The psalm has an immediately practical aim, which is unfolded near the close. It is not an abstract description of the Divine attributes, with a mere indirect purpose in view. If God is such a being, if his vital agency reaches over all his creation, pervades all objects, illumines the deepest and darkest recesses ; if his knowledge has no limits, piercing into the mysterious processes of creation, into the smallest and most elemental germs of life ; if his eye can discern the still more subtle and recondite processes of mind, comprehending the half-formed conception, the germinating desire "afar off" ; if, anterior to all finite existence, his predetermining decree went forth ; if in those ancient records of eternity man's framework, with all its countless elements and organs, in all the ages of his duration, were inscribed—then for his servant, his worshipper on earth, two consequences follow, most practical and momentous : *first*, the ceasing to have or feel any complacency with the wicked, any sympathy with their evil ways, any communion with them as such ; and, *secondly*, the earnest desire that God would search the psalmist's soul, lest in its unsounded depths there might be some lurking iniquity, lest there might be, beyond the present jurisdiction of his conscience, some dark realm which the Omniscient eye only could explore.— *Bela B. Edwards* (1802—1852), *in H. C. Fish's "Masterpieces of Pulpit Eloquence."*

Whole Psalm. —

> Searcher of hearts ! to thee are known
> The inmost secrets of my breast ;
> At home, abroad, in crowds, alone,
> Thou mark'st my rising and my rest,
> My thoughts far off, through every maze,
> Source, stream, and issue—all my ways.
>
> How from thy presence should I go,
> Or whither from thy Spirit flee,
> Since all above, around, below,
> Exist in thine immensity ?
> If up to heaven I take my way,
> I meet thee in eternal day.
>
> If in the grave I make my bed
> With worms and dust, lo ! thou art there !
> If, on the wings of morning sped,
> Beyond the ocean I repair,
> I feel thine all-controlling will,
> And thy right hand upholds me still.
>
> "Let darkness hide me," if I say,
> Darkness can no concealment be ;
> Night, on thy rising, shines like day ;
> Darkness and light are one with thee :
> For thou mine embryo-form didst view,
> Ere her own babe my mother knew.
>
> In me thy workmanship display'd,
> A miracle of power I stand :
> Fearfully, wonderfully made,
> And framed in secret by thine hand ;
> I lived, ere into being brought,
> Through thine eternity of thought.
>
> How precious are thy thoughts of peace,
> O God, to me ! how great the sum !
> New every morn, they never cease :
> They were, they are, and yet shall come,
> In number and in compass more
> Than ocean's sands or ocean's shore.

Search me, O God! and know my heart;
Try me, my inmost soul survey;
And warn thy servant to depart
From every false and evil way:
So shall thy truth my guidance be
To life and immortality.

                                                        James Montgomery.

Whole Psalm.—The psalm may be thus summarized. Verse 1. "*O* LORD, *thou hast searched me, and known me.*"—As though he said, "O LORD, thou art the heart-searching God, who perfectly knowest all the thoughts, counsels, studies, endeavours, and actions of all men, and therefore mine." Verse 2. "*Thou knowest my downsitting and mine uprising, thou understandest my thought afar off.*"—As if he had said, "Thou knowest my rest and motion, and my plodding thoughts of both." Verse 3. "*Thou compassest my path and my lying down, and art acquainted with all my ways.*"—As if he had said, "Thou fannest and winnowest me," that is, "Thou discussest and triest me to the utmost." Verse 4. "*For there is not a word in my tongue, but, lo, O* LORD, *thou knowest it altogether.*"—As if he had said, "I cannot speak a word, though never so secret, obscure, or subtle, but thou knowest what, and why, and with what mind it was uttered." Verse 5. "*Thou hast beset me behind and before, and laid thine hand upon me.*"—As if he had said, "Thou keepest me within the compass of thy knowledge, like a man that will not let his servant go out of his sight. I cannot break away from thee." Verse 6. "*Such knowledge is too wonderful for me; it is high, I cannot attain unto it.*"—As if he had said, "The knowledge of thy great and glorious majesty and infiniteness is utterly past all human comprehension." Verse 7. "*Whither shall I go from thy spirit? or whither shall I flee from thy presence?*"—As if he had said, "Whither can I flee from thee, whose essence, presence, and power is everywhere?" Verse 8. "*If I ascend up into heaven, thou art there: if I make my bed in hell, behold, thou art there.*"—As if he had said, "There is no height above thee, there is no depth below thee." Verse 9. "*If I take the wings of the morning, and dwell in the uttermost parts of the sea.*"—As if he had said, "If I had wings to fly as swift as the morning light, from the east to the west, that I could in a moment get to the furthest parts of the world." Verse 10. "*Even there shall thy hand lead me, and thy right hand shall hold me.*"—As if he had said, "Thence shall thy hand lead me back, and hold me fast like a fugitive." Verse 11. "*If I say, Surely the darkness shall cover me; even the night shall be light about me.*"—As if he had said, "Though darkness hinders man's sight, it doth not thine." In a word, look which way you will, there is no hiding-place from God. "For his eyes are upon the ways of man, and he seeth all his goings. There is no darkness nor shadow of death, where the workers of iniquity may hide themselves": Job xxxiv. 21, 22. Therefore, Christians, do nothing but what you are willing God should take notice of; and judge in yourselves whether this be not the way to have a good and quiet conscience.—*Samuel Annesley.*

Whole Psalm.—In this Aramaizing Psalm what the preceding psalm says in verse 6 comes to be carried into effect, viz.: "*For Jahve is exalted and he seeth the lowly, and the proud he knoweth from afar.*" This psalm has manifold points of contact with its predecessor.—*Franz Delitzsch.*

"*To the Chief Musician.*"—As a later writer could have no motive for prefixing the title, "*To the Chief Musician,*" it affords an incidental proof of antiquity and genuineness.—*Joseph Addison Alexander.*

"*A Psalm of David.*"—How any critic can assign this psalm to other than David I cannot understand. Every line, every thought, every turn of expression and transition, is his, and his only. As for the arguments drawn from the two Chaldaisms which occur, this is really nugatory. These Chaldaisms consist merely in the substitution of one letter for another, very like it in shape, and easily to be mistaken by a transcriber, particularly by one who had been used to the Chaldee idiom; but the moral arguments for David's authorship are so strong as to overwhelm any such verbal, or rather *literal* criticism, were even the objections more formidable than they actually are.—*John Jebb.*

Verse 1.—"*O* LORD, *thou hast searched me, and known (me).*" There is no "*me*" after "*known*" in the Hebrew ; therefore it is better to take the object after "*known*" in a wider sense. The omission is intentional, that the believing heart of all who use this psalm may supply the ellipsis. Thou hast known and knowest *all that concerns the matter in question,* as well whether I and mine are guilty or innocent (Ps. xliv. 21) ; also my exact circumstances, my needs, my sorrows, and the precise time when to relieve me.—*A. R. Fausset.*

Verse 1.—"*O* LORD, *thou hast searched me, and known me.*" The godly may sometimes be so overclouded with calumnies and reproaches as not to be able to find a way to clear themselves before men, but must content and comfort themselves with the testimony of a good conscience and with God's approbation of their integrity, as here David doth.—*David Dickson.*

Verse 1.—"*O* LORD, *thou hast searched me, and known me.*" David here lays down the great doctrine, that God has a perfect knowledge of us, First, *in the way of an address to God :* he saith it to him, acknowledging it to him, and giving him the glory of it. Divine truths look full as well when they are prayed over as when they are preached over : and much better than when they are disputed over. When we speak of God to him himself, we find ourselves concerned to speak with the utmost degree both of sincerity and reverence, which will be likely to make the impressions the deeper. Secondly, he lays it down *in a way of application to himself :* not thou hast known all, but "thou hast known *me*" *;* that is it which I am most concerned to believe, and which it will be most profitable for me to consider. Then we know things for our good when we know them for ourselves. Job v. 27. . . . David was a king, and "the hearts of kings are unsearchable" to their subjects (Prov. xxv. 3), but they are not so to their sovereign.—*Matthew Henry.*

Verse 1.—"*O* LORD, *thou hast searched me.*" I would have you observe how thoroughly in the very first verse he brings home the truth to his own heart and his own conscience : "O LORD, thou hast searched *me.*" He does not slur it over as a general truth, in which such numbers shared that he might hope to escape or evade its solemn appeal to himself ; but it is, "Thou hast searched *me.*"—*Barton Bouchier.*

Verse 1.—"*Searched.*" The Hebrew word originally means *to dig,* and is applied to the search for precious metals (Job xxviii. 3), but metaphorically to a moral inquisition into guilt.—*Joseph Addison Alexander.*

Verses 1—5.—God knows everything that passes in our inmost souls better than we do ourselves : he reads our most secret thoughts : all the cogitations of our hearts pass in review before him ; and he is as perfectly and entirely employed in the scrutiny of the thoughts and actions of an individual, as in the regulation of the most important concerns of the universe. This is what we cannot comprehend ; but it is what, according to the light of reason, must be true, and, according to revelation, is indeed true. God can do nothing imperfectly ; and we may form some idea of his superintending knowledge, by conceiving what is indeed the truth, that all the powers of the Godhead are employed, and solely employed, in the observation and examination of the conduct of one individual. I say, this is indeed the case, because all the powers of the Godhead are employed upon the least as well as upon the greatest concerns of the universe ; and the whole mind and power of the Creator are as exclusively employed upon the formation of a grub as of a world. God knows everything perfectly, and he knows everything perfectly at once. This, to a human understanding, would breed confusion ; but there can be no confusion in the Divine understanding, because confusion arises from imperfection. Thus God, without confusion, beholds as distinctly the actions of every man, as if that man were the only created being, and the Godhead were solely employed in observing him. Let this thought fill your mind with awe and with remorse.—*Henry Kirke White,* 1785—1806.

Verses 1—12.—

O Lord, in me there lieth nought
 But to thy search revealed lies ;
  For when I sit
  Thou markest it ;
 No less thou notest when I rise ;
Yea, closest closet of my thought
 Hath open windows to thine eyes.

Thou walkest with me when I walk ;
 When to my bed for rest I go,
  I find thee there,
  And everywhere :
 Not youngest thought in me doth grow,
No, not one word I cast to talk
 But, yet unuttered, thou dost know.

If forth I march, thou goest before ;
 If back I turn, thou com'st behind :
  So forth nor back
  Thy guard I lack ;
 Nay, on me, too, thy hand I find.
Well, I thy wisdom may adore,
 But never reach with earthly mind.

To shun thy notice, leave thine eye,
 O whither might I take my way ?
  To starry sphere ?
  Thy throne is there.
 To dead men's undelightsome stay ?
There is thy walk, and there to lie
 Unknown, in vain I should assay.

O sun, whom light nor flight can match !
 Suppose thy lightful flightful wings
  Thou lend to me,
  And I could flee
 As far as thee the evening brings :
Ev'n led to west he would me catch,
 Nor should I lurk with western things.

Do thou thy best, O secret night,
 In sable veil to cover me :
  Thy sable veil
  Shall vainly fail :
 With day unmasked my night shall be ;
For night is day, and darkness light,
 O Father of all lights, to thee.

     —*Sir Philip Sidney*, 1554—1586.

Verse 2.—"*Thou.*" David makes the personal pronoun the very frontispiece of the verse, and so says expressly and distinctively to Jehovah, "*Thou* knowest" ; thus marking the difference between God and all others, as though he said, "Thou, and thou alone, O God, in all the universe, knowest altogether all that can be known concerning me, even to my inmost thought, as well as outward act."—*Martin Geier.*

Verse 2.—"*Thou knowest my downsitting and mine uprising.*" *Does* God care ? *Is* he our Friend ? Even in such little matters as these, does he watch over us "to do us good " ? . . . When we "sit down" he sees ; when we rise up he is there. Not an action is lost or a thought overlooked. No wonder that, as these tiny miracles of care are related by David, he adds the words, "*Such knowledge is too wonderful for me ; it is high, I cannot attain unto it.*" We get accustomed to the thought that God made the sun and sky, the " moon and stars which he hath ordained," and we bow to the fact that they are " the work of his fingers." Let us go further ! The " *coming in* " and " *going out* "of the Christian is mentioned several times in Scripture as though it were very important. So much hinges on these little words. " David went out and came in before the people. And David

behaved himself wisely in all his ways ; and the Lord was with him" : 1 Sam.
xviii. 13, 14.   " The LORD shall preserve thy going out and thy coming in from
this time forth, and even for evermore" : Ps. cxxi. 8.   David was given both
preservation and *wisdom* in his " goings out " and " comings in."   Perhaps the
latter was both cause and effect of the first.   It was needed, for many eyes were
upon him, and many eyes are upon us : are they not ?   Perhaps more than we
think.—*Lady Hope, in "Between Times,"* 1884.

Verse 1.—"Downsitting and uprising." "Uprising" following " *downsitting*" is
in the order of right sequence ; for action ought to follow meditation.   Jacob
saw the angels ascending to God before they descended to service among mortals.
Hence we are taught first to join ourselves to God by meditation, and afterwards
to repair to the aid of our fellows.—*Thomas Le Blanc.*

Verse 2.—"Uprising" may respect either rising *from bed,* when the Lord knows
whether the heart is still with him (ver. 18) ; what sense is had of the Divine
protection and sustentation, and what thankfulness there is for the mercies of the
night past ; and whether the voice of prayer and praise is directed to him in the
morning, as it should be (Ps. iii. 5 ; v. 3) ; or else rising *from the table,* when the
Lord knows whether a man's table has been his snare, and with what thankfulness he rises from it for the favours he has received.   The Targum interprets this
of rising up to go to war ; which David did, in the name and strength, and by
the direction of the Lord.—*John Gill.*

Verse 2.—"Thou understandest my thought afar off." "My thought" : that is,
every thought, though innumerable thoughts pass through me in a day.   The
divine knowledge reaches to their source and fountain, before they are our
thoughts.   If the Lord knows them before their existence, before they can be
properly called ours, much more doth he know them when they actually spring up
in us ; he knows the tendency of them, where the bird will alight when it is in
flight ; he knows them exactly ; he is therefore called a " discerner" or criticiser
of the heart : Heb. iv. 2. —*Stephen Charnock.*

Verse 2.—"Thou understandest my thought afar off."   Not that God is at a distance from our thoughts ; but he understands them while they are far off from us,
from our knowledge, while they are potential, as gardeners know what weeds
such ground will bring forth, when nothing appears.   Deut. xxxi. 21.   " I know
their imagination which they go about, even now, before I have brought them
into the land which I sware" : God knew their thoughts before they came into
Canaan, what they would be there.   And how can it be, but that God should
know all our thoughts, seeing he made the heart, and it is in his hand (Prov. xxi.
1), seeing, " we live, and move, and have our being" in God (Acts xvii. 28) ; seeing he is through us all, and in us all (Eph. iv. 6).   Look well to your hearts,
thoughts, risings, whatever comes into your mind ; let no secret sins, or corruptions, lodge there ; think not to conceal anything from the eye of God.— *William
Greenhill.*

Verse 2.—"Thou understandest my thought afar off."   Though my thoughts be
never so foreign and distant from one another, thou understandest the chain of
them, and canst make out their connexion, when so many of them slip my notice
that I myself cannot.—*Matthew Henry.*

Verse 2.—"My thought."   The רע, *rea,* which we have rendered " *thought,*"
signifies also a *friend* or *companion,* on which account some read—*thou knowest
what is nearest me afar off,* a meaning more to the point than any other, if it
could be supported by example.   The reference would then be very appropriately
to the fact that the most distant objects are contemplated as near by God.   Some
for " *afar off* " read *beforehand,* in which signification the Hebrew word is elsewhere taken ; as if he had said, O Lord, every thought which I conceive in my
heart is already known to thee beforehand.—*John Calvin.*

Verse 2.—"Thought."   In all affliction, in all business, a man's best comfort is
this, that all he does and even all he thinks, God knows.   In the Septuagint we
read διαλογισμούς, that is, " reasonings."   God knows all our inner ratiocination,
all the dialogues, all the colloquies of the soul with itself.—*Thomas Le Blanc.*

Verse 2.—"Thou understandest my thought." Before men we stand as opaque bee-hives. They can see the thoughts go in and out of us, but what work they do inside of a man they cannot tell. Before God we are as glass bee-hives, and all that our thoughts are doing within us he perfectly sees and understands.—*Henry Ward Beecher.*

Verse 2. —"Thou understandest my thought afar off."

> Man may not see thee do an impious deed ;
> But God thy very inmost thought can read."
>
> —*Plutarch.*

Verse 2.—"Afar off." This expression is, as in Ps. cxxxviii. 6, to be understood as contradicting the delusion (Job xxii. 12—14) that God's dwelling in heaven prevents him from observing mundane things.—*Lange's Commentary.*

Verse 2.—"Afar off." Both in distance, however far off a man may seek to hide his thoughts from God ; and in time, for God knows the human thought before man conceives it in his heart, in his eternal prescience. The Egyptians called God the " eye of the world."—*Thomas Le Blanc.*

Verses 2—4.—Do not fancy that your demeanour, posture, dress, or deportment are not under God's providence. You deceive yourself. Do not think that your thoughts pass free from inspection. The Lord understands them afar off. Think not that your words are dissipated in the air before God can hear. Oh, no ! He knows them even when still upon your tongue. Do not think that your ways are so private and concealed that there is none to know or censure them. You mistake. God knows all your ways.—*Johann David Frisch,* 1731.

Verse 3. —"Thou compassest my path and my lying down," etc. The words that I have read unto you, seem to be a metaphor, taken from soldiers surrounding the ways with an ambush, or placing scouts and spies in every corner, to discover the enemy in his march ; *"Thou compassest my path "* : thou hast (as it were) thy spies over me, wheresoever I go. By *"path"* is meant the outward actions and carriage of his ordinary conversation. By *" lying down "* is signified to us the private and close actions of his life ; such as were attended only by darkness and solitude. In Psal. xxxvi. verse 4, it is said of the wicked that " he deviseth mischief upon his bed," to denote not only his perverse diligence, but also his secresy in it : and God is said to " hide his children in the secret of his pavilion," so that these places of rest and lying down are designed for secresy and withdrawing. When a man retires into his chamber, he does in a manner, for a while, shut himself out of the world. And that this is the fine sense of that expression of *lying down* appears from the next words, *"Thou art acquainted with all my ways"* ; where he collects in one word what he had before said in two ; or, it may come in by way of entrance and deduction, from the former. As if he should say, Thou knowest what I do in my ordinary converse with men, and also how I behave myself when I am retired from them ; therefore thou knowest *all* my actions, since a man's actions may be reduced either to his public or private deportment. By the other expression of *" my ways "* is here meant the total of a man's behaviour before God, whether in thoughts, words, or deeds, as is manifest by comparing this with other verses.—*Robert South.*

Verse 3.—"Thou compassest my path." This is a metaphor either from huntsmen watching all the motions and lurking-places of wild beasts, that they may catch them ; or from soldiers besieging their enemies in a city, and setting round about them.—*Matthew Pool.*

Verse 3.—"Thou compassest," or *fannest,* or *winnowest, " my path "* ; that is, discussest or triest out to the utmost, even tracing the footsteps, as the Greek signifieth. Compare Job xxxi. 4.—*Henry Ainsworth.*

Verse 3.—"Thou art acquainted with all my ways." God takes notice of every step we take, every right step, and every by-step. He knows what rule we walk by, what end we walk toward, what company we walk with.—*Religious Tract Society's Commentary.*

Verse 3.—"Art acquainted," as by most familiar intercourse, as if thou hadst always lived with me [Hebrew] and thus become entirely familiar with my ways. —*Henry Cowles.*

Verse 3.—The Psalmist mentions four modes of human existence ; *stationis, sessionis, itionis, cubationis ;* because man never stayeth long in one mood, but in every change the eyes of the Lord cease not to watch him.—*Geier.*

Verse 4.—"*For there is not a word in my tongue,*" etc. The words admit a double meaning. Accordingly some understand them to imply that God knows what we are about to say before the words are formed on our tongue ; others, that though we speak not a word, and try by silence to conceal our secret intentions, we cannot elude his notice. Either rendering amounts to the same thing, and it is of no consequence which we adopt. The idea meant to be conveyed is, that while the tongue is the index of thought to man, being the great medium of communication, God, who knows the heart, is independent of words. And use is made of the demonstrative particle *lo !* to indicate emphatically that the innermost recesses of our spirit stand present to his view.—*John Calvin.*

Verse 4.—"*For there is not a word in my tongue,*" etc. How needful it is to set a watch before the doors of our mouth, to hold that unruly member of ours, the tongue, as with bit and bridle. Some of you feel at times that you can scarcely say a word, and the less you say the better. Well, it way be as well ; for great talkers are almost sure to make slips with their tongue. It may be a good thing that you cannot speak much ; for in the multitude of words there lacketh not sin. Wherever you go, what light, vain, and foolish conversations you hear ! I am glad not to be thrown into circumstances where I can hear it. But with you it may be different. You may often repent of speaking, you will rarely repent of silence. How soon angry words are spoken ! How soon foolish expressions drop from the mouth ! The Lord knows it all, marks it all, and did you carry about with you a more solemn recollection of it you would be more watchful than you are.—*Joseph C. Philpot.*

Verse 4.—"*When there is not a word in my tongue, O* LORD, *thou knowest all* ";* so some read it ; for thoughts are words to God.—*Matthew Henry.*

Verse 4.—"*Thou knowest it.*" The gods know what passes in our minds without the aid of eyes, ears, or tongues ; on which divine omniscience is founded the feeling of men that, when they wish in silence, or offer up a prayer for anything, the gods hear them.—*Cicero.*

Verse 5.—"*Thou hast beset me behind and before,*" etc. There is here an insensible transition from God's omniscience to his omnipresence, out of which the Scriptures represent it as arising. "*Behind and before,*" i.e., on all sides. The idea of *above* and *below* is suggested by the last clause. "*Beset,*" besiege, hem in, or closely surround. "*Thy hand,*" or the palm of thy hand, as the Hebrew word strictly denotes.—*Joseph Addison Alexander.*

Verse 5.—"*Thou hast beset me behind and before.*" What would you say if, wherever you turned, whatever you were doing, whatever thinking, whether in public or private, with a confidential friend telling your secrets, or alone planning them—if, I say, you saw an eye constantly fixed on you, from whose watching, though you strove ever so much, you could never escape. . . . that could perceive your every thought ? The supposition is awful enough. There is such an Eye.—*De Vere.*

Verse 5.—"*Thou hast beset me behind and before.*" One who finds the way blocked up turns back ; but David found himself hedged in *behind* as well as *before.*—*John Calvin.*

Verse 5.—"*Thou hast . . . laid thine hand upon me.*" As by an arrest ; so that I am thy prisoner, and cannot stir a foot from thee.—*John Trapp.*

Verse 5.—"*And laid thine hand upon me.*" To make of me one acceptable to thyself. To rule me, to lead me, to uphold me, to protect me ; to restore me ; in my growth, in my walk, in my failures, in my affliction, in my despair.—*Thomas Le Blanc.*

Verse 6.—"*Such knowledge is too wonderful for me,*" etc.   When we are about to look upon God's perfections, we should observe our own imperfections, and thereby learn to be the more modest in our searching of God's unsearchable perfection : "*Such knowledge,*" saith David, " *is too high for me, I cannot attain unto it.*"   Then do we see most of God, when we see him incomprehensible, and do see ourselves swallowed up in the thoughts of his perfection, and are forced to fall in admiration of God, as here.   "*Such knowledge is too wonderful for me ; it is high, I cannot attain unto it.*"—*David Dickson.*

Verse 6.— "*Such knowledge is too wonderful for me.*"   Compared with our stinted knowledge, how amazing is the knowledge of God !   As he made all things, he must be intimately acquainted, not only with their properties, but with their very essence.   His eye, at the same instant, surveys all the works of his immeasurable creation.   He observes, not only the complicated system of the universe, but the slightest motion of the most microscopic insect ;—not only the sublimest conception of angels, but the meanest propensity of the most worthless of his creatures. At this moment he is listening to the praises breathed by grateful hearts in distant worlds, and reading every grovelling thought which passes though the polluted minds of the fallen race of Adam. . . . At one view, he surveys the past, the present, and the future.   No inattention prevents him from observing ; no defect of memory or of judgment obscures his comprehension.   In his remembrance are stored not only the transactions of this world, but of all the worlds in the universe ;—not only the events of the six thousand years which have passed since the earth was created, but of a duration without beginning.   Nay, things to come, extending to a duration without end, are also before him.   An eternity past and an eternity to come are, at the same moment, in his eye ; and with that eternal eye he surveys infinity.   How amazing !   How inconceivable !—*Henry Duncan* (1774—1846), *in "Sacred Philosophy of the Seasons."*

Verse 6.—"*Such knowledge is too wonderful for me.*"   There is a mystery about the Divine Omnipresence, which we do not learn to solve, after years of meditation.   As God is a simple spirit, without dimensions, parts, or susceptibility of division, he is equally, that is, fully, present at all times in all places.   At any given moment he is not present partly here and partly in the utmost skirt of the furthest system which revolves about the dimmest telescopic star, as if like a galaxy of perfection he stretched a sublime magnificence through universal space, which admitted of separation and partition; but he is present, with the totality of his glorious properties in every point of space.   This results undeniably from the simple spirituality of the Great Supreme.   All that God is in one place he is in all places.   All there is of God is in every place.   Indeed, his presence has no dependence on space or matter.   His attribute of essential presence were the same if universal matter were blotted out.   Only by a figure can God be said to be in the universe ; for the universe is comprehended by him.   All the boundless glory of the Godhead is essentially present at every spot in his creation, however various may be the manifestations of this glory at different times and places.

Here we have a case which ought to instruct and sober those, who, in their shallow philosophy, demand a religion without mystery.   It would be a religion without God ; for " who by searching can find out God ?"—*James W. Alexander,* *in "The [American] National Preacher,"* 1860.

Verse 7.—" *Whither shall I go from thy spirit ?*"   By the " *spirit of God* " we are not here, as in several other parts of Scripture, to conceive of his power merely, but his understanding and knowledge.   In man the spirit is the seat of intelligence, and so it is here in reference to God, as is plain from the second part of the sentence, where by " *the face of God* " is meant his knowledge or inspection. —*John Calvin.*

Verse 7.—" *Whither shall I go from thy spirit ?*"   That is, either from thee, who art a spirit, and so canst pierce and penetrate me ; be as truly and essentially in the very bowels and marrow of my soul, as my soul is intimately and essentially in my body : "*from thy spirit*"; that is, from thy knowledge and thy power ;

thy knowledge to detect and observe me, thy power to uphold or crush me.—*Ezekiel Hopkins*, 1633—1690.

Verse 7.—We may elude the vigilance of a human enemy and place ourselves beyond his reach. God fills all space—there is not a spot in which his piercing eye is not on us, and his uplifted hand cannot find us out. Man must strike soon if he would strike at all ; for opportunities pass away from him, and his victim may escape his vengeance by death. There is no passing of opportunity with God, and it is this which makes his long-suffering a solemn thing. God can wait, for he has a whole eternity before him in which he may strike. " All things are open and naked to him with whom we have to do."—*Frederick William Robertson*, 1816—1853.

Verse 7.—"*Whither shall I go*," etc. A heathen philosopher once asked, " Where is God ?" The Christian answered, " Let me first ask you, Where is he not ?"—*John Arrowsmith*, 1602—1659.

Verse 7.—"*Whither shall I flee from thy presence ?*" That exile would be strange that could separate us from God. I speak not of those poor and common comforts, that in all lands and coasts it is his sun that shines, his elements of earth or water that bear us, his air we breathe ; but of that special privilege, that his gracious presence is ever with us ; that no sea is so broad as to divide us from his favour ; that wheresoever we feed, he is our host ; wheresoever we rest, the wings of his blessed providence are stretched over us. Let my soul be sure of this, though the whole world be traitors to me.—*Thomas Adams.*

Verse 7.—"*Whither shall I flee ?*" etc. Surely no whither : they that attempt it, do but as the fish which swimmeth to the length of the line, with a hook in the mouth.—*John Trapp.*

Verse 7.—"'*Thy presence.*" The presence of God's glory is in heaven ; the presence of his power on earth ; the presence of his justice in hell ; and the presence of his grace with his people. If he deny us his powerful presence, we fall into nothing ; if he deny us his gracious presence, we fall into sin ; if he deny us his merciful presence, we fall into hell.—*John Mason.*

Verse 7.—"*Thy presence.*" The celebrated Linnæus testified in his conversation, writings, and actions, the greatest sense of God's presence. So strongly indeed was he impressed with the idea, that he wrote over the door of his library : "*Innocuè vivite, Numen adest—Live innocently : God is present.*"—*George Seaton Bowes, in "Information and Illustration,* 1884.

Verses 7—11.—You will never be neglected by the Deity, though you were so small as to sink into the depths of the earth, or so lofty as to fly up to heaven ; but you will suffer from the gods the punishment due to you, whether you abide here, or depart to Hades, or are carried to a place still more wild than these.—*Plato.*

Verses 7—12.—The psalm was not written by a Pantheist. The Psalmist speaks of God as a Person everywhere present in creation, yet distinct from creation. In these verses he says, "*Thy* spirit . . . *thy* presence . . . *thou* art there . . . *thy* hand . . . *thy* right hand . . . darkness hideth not from *thee.*" God is everywhere, but he is not everything.—*William Jones, in "A Homiletic Commentary on the Book of Psalms,*" 1879.

Verse 8.—"*If I make my bed.*" Properly, " If I strew or spread my couch." If I should seek that as a place to lie down.—*Albert Barnes.*

Verse 8.—"*Hell*" in some places in Scripture signifies the lower parts of the earth, without relation to punishment : "*If I ascend up into heaven, thou art there ; if I make my bed in hell, behold, thou art there.*" By " *heaven*" he means the upper region of the world, without any respect to the state of blessedness ; and " *hell* " is the most opposite and remote in distance, without respect to misery. As if he had said, Let me go whither I will, thy presence finds me out.—*Joseph Caryl.*

Verse 8.—"*Thou art there.*" Or, more emphatically and impressively in the original, "*Thou !*" That is, the Psalmist imagines himself in the highest heaven, or in the deepest abodes of the dead,—and lo ! God is there also ; he has not gone from *him !* he is still in the presence of the same God !—*Albert Barnes.*

Verse 8.—"*Thou art there.*" This is not meant of his knowledge, for that the Psalmist had spoken of before : verses 2, 3, " Thou understandest my thought afar off : thou art acquainted with all my ways." Besides, " thou art there" ; not thy wisdom or knowledge, but *thou*, thy essence, not only thy virtue. For having before spoken of his omniscience, he proves that such knowledge could not be in God unless he were present in his essence in all places, so as to be excluded from none. He fills the depths of hell, the extension of the earth, and the heights of the heavens. When the Scripture mentions the power of God only, it expresseth it by hand or arm ; but when it mentions the spirit of God, and doth not intend the third person of the Trinity, it signifies the nature and essence of God ; and so here, when he saith, " *Whither shall I go from thy spirit ?*" he adds exegetically," *whither shall I flee from thy presence ?*" or Hebrew, "*face*" *;* and the face of God in Scripture signifies the essence of God : Exod. xxxiii. 20, 23, " Thou canst not see my face," and " my face shall not be seen" ; the effects of his power, wisdom, providence, are seen, which are his back-parts, but not his face. The effects of his power and wisdom are seen in the world, but his essence is invisible, and this the Psalmist elegantly expresseth.—*Stephen Charnock.*

Verse 9.—"*The wings of the morning,*" is an elegant metaphor ; and by them we may conjecture is meant the sunbeams, called " *wings*" because of their swift and speedy motion ; making their passage so sudden and instantaneous, as that they do prevent the observation of the eye ; called " *the wings of the morning* " because the dawn of the morning comes flying in upon these wings of the sun, and brings light along with it ; and, by beating and fanning of these wings, scatters the darkness before it. ."Now," saith the Psalmist, " if I could pluck these wings of the morning," the sunbeams, if I could imp [graft] my own shoulders with them ; if I should fly as far and as swift as light, even in an instant, to the uttermost parts of the sea ; yea, if in my flight I could spy out some solitary rock, so formidable and dismal as if we might almost call in question whether ever a Providence had been there ; if I could pitch there on the top of it, where never anything had made its abode, but coldness, thunders, and tempests ; yet there shall thy hand lead me, and thy right hand shall hold me."—*Ezekiel Hopkins.*

Verse 9.—"*The wings of the morning.*" This figure to a Western is not a little obscure. For my part, I cannot doubt that we are to understand certain beautiful light clouds as thus poetically described. I have observed invariably, that in the late spring-time, in summer, and yet more especially in the autumn, white clouds are to be seen in Palestine. They only occur at the earliest hours of morning, just previous to and at the time of sunrise. It is the total absence of clouds at all other parts of the day, except during the short period of the winter rains, that lends such striking solemnity and force to those descriptions of the Second Advent where our Lord is represented as coming in the clouds. This feature of his majesty loses all its meaning in lands like ours, in which clouds are of such common occurrence that they are rarely absent from the sky. The morning clouds of summer and autumn are always of a brilliant silvery white, save at such times as they are dyed with the delicate opal tints of dawn. They hang low upon the mountains of Judah, and produce effects of undescribable beauty, as they float far down in the valleys, or rise to wrap themselves around the summit of the hills. In almost every instance, by about seven o'clock the heat has dissipated these fleecy clouds, and to the vivid Eastern imagination morn has folded her outstretched wings.—*James Neil.*

Verse 9.—"*If I take the wings of the morning.*" The point of comparison appears to be the incalculable velocity of light.—*Joseph Addison Alexander.*

Verses 9, 10.—When we think that we fly from God, in running out of one place into another, we do but run from one hand to the other ; for there is no place where God is not, and whithersoever a rebellious sinner doth run, the hand of God will meet with him to cross him, and hinder his hoped-for good success, although he securely prophesieth never so much good unto himself in his journey.

What! had Jonah offended the winds or the waters, that they bear him such enmity? The winds and the waters and all God's creatures are wont to take God's part against Jonah, or any rebellious sinner. For though God in the beginning gave power to man over all creatures to rule them, yet when man sins, God giveth power and strength to his creatures to rule and bridle man. Therefore even he that now was lord over the waters, now the waters are lord over him.—*Henry Smith.*

Verses 9, 10.—

Should fate command me to the farthest verge
Of the green earth, to distant barbarous climes,
Rivers unknown to song; where first the sun
Gilds Indian mountains, or his setting beam
Flames on the Atlantic isles; 'tis nought to me:
Since GOD is ever present, ever felt,
In the void waste as in the city full;
And where he vital breathes, there must be joy.
When e'en at last the solemn hour shall come,
And wing my mystic flight to future worlds,
I cheerful will obey; there with new powers,
Will rising wonders sing: I cannot go
Where universal love smiles not around,
Sustaining all yon orbs, and all their sons:
From seeming evil still deducing good,
And better thence again, and better still,
In infinite progression.
                                    —*James Thomson,* 1700—1748.

Verse 11.—"*If I say, Surely the darkness shall cover me,*" etc. The foulest enormities of human conduct have always striven to cover themselves with the shroud of night. The thief, the counterfeiter, the assassin, the robber, the murderer, and the seducer, feel comparatively safe in the midnight darkness, because no human eye can scrutinize their actions. But what if it should turn out that sable night, to speak paradoxically, is an unerring photographist! What if wicked men, as they open their eyes from the sleep of death, in another world, should find the universe hung round with faithful pictures of their earthly enormities, which they had supposed for ever lost in the oblivion of night! What scenes for them to gaze at for ever! They may now, indeed, smile incredulously at such a suggestion; but the disclosures of chemistry may well make them tremble. Analogy does make it a scientific probability that every action of man, however deep the darkness in which it was performed, has imprinted its image on nature, and that there may be tests which shall draw it into daylight, and make it permanent so long as materialism endures.—*Edward Hitchcock, in "The Religion of Geology,"* 1851.

Verse 12.—"*The darkness hideth not from thee.*" Though the place where we sin be to men as dark as Egypt, yet to God it is as light as Goshen.—*William Secker.*

Verse 13.—"*Thou hast possessed my reins.*" From the sensitiveness to pain of this part of the body, it was regarded by the Hebrews as the seat of sensation and feeling, as also of desire and longing (Ps. lxxii. 21; Job xvi. 13; xix. 27). It is sometimes used of the inner nature generally (Ps. xvi. 7, Jer. xx. 12), and specially of the judgment or direction of reason (Jer. xi. 20, xii. 2).—*William Lindsay Alexander, in Kitto's Cyclopædia.*

Verse 13.—"*Thou hast possessed my reins.*" The *reins* are made specially prominent in order to mark them, the seat of the tenderest, most secret emotions, as the work of him who trieth the heart and the reins.—*Franz Delitzsch.*

Verse 13.—"*Thou hast covered me in my mother's womb.*" The word here rendered *cover* means properly to interweave; to weave; to knit together, and the literal translation would be, "Thou hast *woven* me in my mother's womb," meaning that God had put his parts together, as one who weaves cloth, or who makes a basket. So it is rendered by De Wette and by Gesenius (*Lex.*). The original word has, however, also the idea of protecting, as in a booth or hut, woven or knit together,—to wit, of boughs and branches. The former signification best suits the connection ; and then the sense would be, that as God had made him— as he had formed his members, and united them in a bodily frame and form before he was born—he must be able to understand all his thoughts and feelings. As he was not concealed from God before he saw the light, so he could not be anywhere.—*Albert Barnes.*

Verse 14.—"*I will praise thee,*" etc. All God's works are admirable, man wonderfully wonderful. "Marvellous are thy works ; and that my soul knoweth right well." What infers he on all this ? Therefore "*I will praise thee.*" If we will not praise him that made us, will he not repent that he made us ? Oh that we knew what the saints do in heaven, and how the sweetness of that doth swallow up all earthly pleasures ! They sing honour and glory to the Lord. Why ? Because he hath created all things : Rev. iv. 11. When we behold an exquisite piece of work, we presently enquire after him that made it, purposely to commend his skill : and there is no greater disgrace to an artist, than having perfected a famous work, to find it neglected, no man minding it, or so much as casting an eye upon it. All the works of God are considerable, and man is bound to this contemplation. "When I consider the heavens," etc., I say, "What is man ?" Ps. viii. 3, 4. He admires the heavens, but his admiration reflects upon man. *Quis homo ?* There is no workman but would have his instruments used, and used to that purpose for which they were made. . . . Man is set like a little world in the midst of the great, to glorify God ; this is the scope and end of his creation.—*Thomas Adams.*

Verse 14.—"*I am fearfully and wonderfully made.*" The term "*fearful*" is sometimes to be taken subjectively, for our being possessed of fear. In this sense it signifies the same as timid. Thus the prophet was directed to say to them that were of a "fearful heart, be strong." At other times it is taken objectively, for that property in an object the contemplation of which excites fear in the beholder. Thus it is said of God that he is "fearful in praises," and that it is a "fearful thing to fall into the hands of the living God." In this sense it is manifestly to be understood in the passage now under consideration. The human frame is so admirably constructed, so delicately combined, and so much in danger of being dissolved by innumerable causes, that the more we think of it the more we tremble, and wonder at our own continued existence.

> "How poor, how rich, how abject, how august,
> How complicate, how wonderful is man !
> How passing wonder he who made him such,
> Who mingled in our make such strange extremes
> Of different natures, marvellously mixed !
> Helpless immortal, insect infinite,
> A worm, a god—I tremble at myself !

To do justice to the subject, it would be necessary to be well acquainted with anatomy. I have no doubt that a thorough examination of that "substance which God hath curiously wrought" (verse 15), would furnish abundant evidence of the justness of the Psalmist's words ; but even those things which are manifest to common observation may be sufficient for this purpose. In general it is observable that the human frame abounds with avenues at which enter every thing conducive to preservation and comfort, and every thing that can excite alarm. Perhaps there is not one of these avenues but what may become an inlet to death, nor one of the blessings of life but what may be the means of accomplishing it. We live by inhalation, but we also die by it. Diseases and death in innumerable forms are conveyed by the very air we breathe. God hath given us a relish for divers aliments, and rendered them necessary to our subsistence : yet, from the abuse of them, what a train of disorders and premature deaths are found amongst men ! And, when there is no abuse, a single delicious morsel may, by the evil design of another, or even by mere accident, convey poison through all our veins, and in one hour reduce the most athletic form to a corpse.

The elements of fire and water, without which we could not subsist, contain properties which in a few moments would be able to destroy us; nor can the utmost circumspection at all times preserve us from their destructive power. A single stroke on the head may divest us of reason or of life. A wound or a bruise of the spine may instantly deprive the lower extremities of all sensation. If the vital parts be injured, so as to suspend the performance of their mysterious functions, how soon is the constitution broken up! By means of the circulation of the blood, how easily and suddenly are deadly substances diffused throughout the frame! The putridity of a morbid subject has been imparted to the very hand stretched out to save it. The poisoned arrow, the envenomed fang, the hydrophobic saliva, derive from hence their fearful efficacy. Even the pores of the skin, necessary as they are to life, may be the means of death. Not only are poisonous substances hereby admitted, but, when obstructed by surrounding damps, the noxious humours of the body, instead of being emitted, are retained in the system, and become productive of numerous diseases, always afflictive, and often fatal to life.

Instead of wondering at the number of premature deaths that are constantly witnessed, there is far greater reason to wonder that there are no more, and that any of us survive to seventy or eighty years of age.

> " Our life contains a thousand springs,
>   And dies if one be gone:
> Strange that a harp of thousand strings
>   Should keep in tune so long."

Nor is this all. If we are "*fearfully made*" as to our animal frame, it will be found that we are much more so considered as moral and accountable beings. In what relates to our animal nature, we are in most instances constructed like other animals; but, in what relates to us as moral agents, we stand distinguished from all the lower creation. We are made for eternity. The present life is only the introductory part of our existence. It is that, however, which stamps a character on all that follows. How fearful is our situation! What innumerable influences is the mind exposed to from the temptations which surround us! Not more dangerous to the body is the pestilence that walketh in darkness than these are to the soul. Such is the construction of our nature that the very word of life, if heard without regard, becomes a savour of death unto death. What consequences hang upon the small and apparently trifling beginnings of evil! A wicked thought may issue in a wicked purpose, this purpose in a wicked action, this action in a course of conduct, this course may draw into its vortex millions of our fellow-creatures, and terminate in perdition, both to ourselves and them. The whole of this process was exemplified in the case of Jeroboam, the son of Nebat. When placed over the ten tribes, he first *said in his heart*, " If this people go up to sacrifice at Jerusalem, their hearts will turn to Rehoboam; and thus shall the kingdom return to the house of David." 1 Kings xii. 26 —30. On this he took counsel, and made the calves of Dan and Bethel. This engaged him in a course of wickedness, from which no remonstrances could reclaim him. Nor was it confined to himself; for he " made all Israel to sin." The issue was, not only their destruction as a nation, but, to all appearance, the eternal ruin of himself and great numbers of his followers. Such were the fruits of an evil thought!

Oh, my soul, tremble at thyself! Tremble at the fearfulness of thy situation; and commit thine immortal all into his hands " who is able to keep thee from falling, and to present thee faultless before the presence of his glory with exceeding joy."—*Andrew Fuller.*

Verse 14.—"*I am fearfully and wonderfully made.*" Never was so terse and expressive a description of the physical conformation of man given by any human being. So "*fearfully*" are we made, that there is not an action or gesture of our bodies, which does not, apparently, endanger some muscle, vein, or sinew, the rupture of which would destroy either life or health. We are so "*wonderfully*" made, that our organization infinitely surpasses, in skill, contrivance, design, and adaptation of means to ends, the most curious and complicated piece of mechanism, not only ever executed "by art and man's device," but ever conceived by human imagination.—*Richard Warner,* 1828.

Verse 14.—"*I am wonderfully made.*" Take notice of the curious frame of the body. David saith, "*I am wonderfully made*"; *acu pictus sum,* so the Vulgate rendereth it, "painted as with a needle," like a garment of needlework, of divers colours, richly embroidered with nerves and veins. What shall I speak of the eye, wherein there is such curious workmanship, that many upon the first sight of it have been driven to acknowledge God? Of the hand, made to open and shut, and to serve the labours and ministries of nature without wasting and decay for many years? If they should be of marble or iron, with such constant use they would soon wear out; and yet now they are of flesh they last so long as life lasteth. Of the head? fitly placed to be the seat of the senses, to command and direct the rest of the members. Of the lungs? a frail piece of flesh, yet, though in continual action, of a long use. It were easy to enlarge upon this occasion; but I am to preach a sermon, not to read an anatomy lecture. In short, therefore, every part is so placed and framed, as if God had employed his whole wisdom about it. But as yet we have spoken but of the casket wherein the jewel lieth. The soul, that divine spark and blast, how quick, nimble, various, and indefatigable in its motions! how comprehensive in its capacities! how it animateth the body, and is like God himself, all in every part! Who can trace the flights of reason? What a value hath God set upon the soul! He made it after his image, he redeemed it with Christ's blood.—*Thomas Manton.*

Verse 14.—What is meant by saying that the soul is *in* the body, any more than saying that a thought or a hope is in a stone or a tree? *How* is it joined to the body? what keeps it one with the body? what keeps it in the body? what prevents it any moment from separating from the body? When two things which we see are united, they are united by some connexion which we can understand. A chain or cable keeps a ship in its place; we lay the foundation of a building in the earth, and the building endures. But what is it which unites soul and body? how do they touch? how do they keep together? how is it we do not wander to the stars or the depths of the sea, or to and fro as chance may carry us, while our body remains where it was on earth? So far from its being wonderful that the body one day dies, how is it that it is made to live and move at all? how is it that it keeps from dying a single hour? Certainly it is as uncomprehensible as anything can be, how soul and body can make up one man; and, unless we had the instance before our eyes, we should seem in saying so to be using words without meaning. For instance, would it not be extravagant and idle to speak of time as deep or high, or of space as quick or slow? Not less idle, surely, it perhaps seems to some races of spirits to say that thought and mind have a body, which in the case of man they have, according to God's marvellous will.—*John Henry Newman, in Parochial Sermons,* 1839.

Verse 14.—Moses describes the creation of man (Gen. ii. 7): "The Lord God formed man of the dust of the ground, and breathed into his nostrils the breath of life; and man became a living soul." Now what God did then immediately, he doth still by means. Do not think that God made man at first, and that ever since men have made one another. No (saith Job), "he that made me in the womb made him": ch. xxxi. 15. David will inform us: "*I am fearfully and wonderfully made: marvellous are thy works,*" etc. As if he had said, Lord, I am wonderfully made, and thou hast made me. I am a part or parcel of thy marvellous works, yea, the breviate or compendium of them all. The frame of the body (much more the frame of the soul, most of all the frame of the new creature in the soul) is God's work, and it is a wonderful work of God. And therefore David could not satisfy himself in the bare affirmation of this, but enlargeth in the explication of it in verses 15 and 16. David took no notice of father or mother, but ascribed the whole efficiency of himself to God. And indeed David was as much made by God as Adam ; and so is every son of Adam. Though we are begotten and born of our earthly parents, yet God is the chief parent and the only fashioner of us all. Thus graciously spake Jacob to his brother Esau, demanding, " Who are those with thee ? And he said, The children which God hath graciously given thy servant " : Gen. xxxiii. 5. Therefore, as the Spirit of God warns, " Know ye that the LORD he is God : it is he that hath made us, and not we ourselves " (Ps. c. 3) ; which as it is true especially of our spiritual making, so 'tis true also of our natural.—*Joseph Caryl.*

Verse 14.—Those who were skilful in Anatomy among the ancients, concluded, from the outward and inward make of a human body, that it was the work of a Being transcendently wise and powerful. As the world grew more enlightened in this art, their discoveries gave them fresh opportunities of admiring the conduct of Providence in the formation of a human body. Galen was converted by his dissections, and could not but own a Supreme Being upon a survey of this his handiwork. There are, indeed, many parts, of which the old anatomists did not know the certain use ; but as they saw that most of those which they examined were adapted with admirable art to their several functions, they did not question but those whose uses they could not determine, were contrived with the same wisdom for respective ends and purposes. Since the circulation of the blood has been found out, and many other great discoveries have been made by our modern anatomists, we see new wonders in the human frame, and discern several important uses for those parts, which uses the ancients knew nothing of. In short, the body of man is such a subject as stands the utmost test of examination. Though it appears formed with the nicest wisdom upon the most superficial survey of it, it still mends upon the search, and produces our surprise and amazement in proportion as we pry into it.—*The Spectator.*

Verses 14—16.—The subject, from the 14th verse to the 16th inclusive, might have been much more particularly illustrated ; but we are taught, by the peculiar delicacy of expression in the Sacred Writings, to avoid, as in this case, the entering too minutely into *anatomical* details.—*Adam Clarke.*

Verse 15.—"*My substance was not hid from thee,*" etc. What deeper solitude, what state of concealment more complete, than that of the babe as yet unborn ? Yet the Psalmist represents the Almighty as present even there. "*My substance was not hid from thee, when I was made in secret, and curiously wrought in the lowest parts of the earth.*" The whole image and train of thought is one of striking beauty. We see the wonderful work of the human body, with all its complex tissue of bones, and joints, and nerves, and veins, and arteries growing up, and fashioned, as it had been a piece of rich and curious embroidery under the hand of the manufacturer. But it is not the work itself that we are now called on to admire. The contexture is indeed fearful and wonderful ; but how much more when we reflect that the divine Artificer wrought within the dark and narrow confines of the womb. Surely the darkness is no darkness with him who could thus work. Surely the blackest night, the closest and most artificial recess, the subtlest disguises and hypocrisies are all seen through, are all naked and bare before him whose " *eyes did see our substance yet being imperfect.*" The night is as clear as the day ; and secret sins are set in the light of his countenance, no less than those which are open and scandalous, committed before the sun or on the house-top. And if " in his book all our members are written, which day by day were fashioned, when as yet there was none of them," surely the actions of these members, now that they are grown, or growing, to maturity, and called upon to fulfil the functions for which they were created, shall be all noted down ; and none be contrived so secretly, but that when the books are opened at the last day, it shall be found written therein to justify or to condemn us. Such is the main lesson which David himself would teach us in this psalm,—the *omnipresence* and *omniscience* of Almighty God. My brethren, let us reflect for a little upon this deep mystery ; that he, " the High and Lofty One that inhabiteth eternity," is about our path and about our bed, and spieth out all our ways ; that go whither

we will he is there ; that say what we will, there is not a word on our tongue but
he knoweth it altogether. The reflection is, indeed, mysterious, but it is also
most profitable.—*Charles Wordsworth, in "Christian Boyhood," 1846.*

Verse 15.—"*My substance was not hid from thee.*" Should an artisan intend
commencing a work in some dark cave where there was no light to assist him,
how would he set his hand to it ? in what way would he proceed ? and what kind
of workmanship would it prove ? But God makes the most perfect work of all in
the dark, for he fashions man in the mother's womb.—*John Calvin.*

Verse 15.—"*When I was made in secret,*" etc. The author uses a metaphor derived from the most subtle art of the Phrygian workman :

> " When I was formed in the secret place,
> *When* I was wrought with a needle in the depths of the earth."

Whoever observes this (in truth he will not be able to observe it in the common
translations), and at the same time reflects upon the wonderful mechanism of the
human body ; the various implications of the veins, arteries, fibres, and mem-
branes ; the " undescribable texture" of the whole fabric—may, indeed, feel the
beauty and gracefulness of this well-adapted metaphor, but will miss much of its
force and sublimity, unless he be apprised that the art of designing in needlework
was wholly dedicated to the use of the sanctuary, and, by a direct precept of the
divine law, chiefly employed in furnishing a part of the sacerdotal habit, and the
vails for the entrance of the Tabernacle. Exod. xxviii. 39 ; xxvi. 36 ; xxvii. 16.
Thus the poet compares the wisdom of the divine Artificer with the most estima-
ble of human arts—that art which was dignified by being consecrated altogether
to the use of religion ; and the workmanship of which was so exquisite, that even
the sacred writings seem to attribute it to a supernatural guidance. See Exod.
xxxv. 30—35.—*Robert Lowth (1710—1787), in "Lectures on the Sacred Poetry of the
Hebrews."*

Verse 15.—"*Curiously wrought in the lowest parts of the earth,*" that is, in the
womb : as curious workmen, when they have some choice piece in hand, they
perfect it in private, and then bring it forth to light for men to gaze at. What a
wonderful piece of work is man's head (God's masterpiece in this little world),
the.chief seat of the soul, that *cura Divini ingenii*, as Favorinus calls it. Many
locks and keys argue the value of the jewel that they keep, and many papers
wrapping the token within them, the price of the token. The tables of the testament, first laid up in the ark, secondly, the ark bound about with pure gold ;
thirdly, overshadowed with cherubim's wings ; fourthly, enclosed within the vail
of the Tabernacle ; fifthly, with the compass of the Tabernacle ; sixthly, with a
court above all ; seventhly, with a treble covering of goats', rams', and badgers'
skins above all ; they must needs be precious tables. So when the Almighty
made man's head (the seat of the reasonable soul), and overlaid it with hair, skin,
and flesh, like the threefold covering of the Tabernacle, and encompassed it with
a skull and bones like boards of cedar, and afterwards with divers skins like
silken curtains ; and lastly, enclosed it with the yellow skin that covers the brain
(like the purple veil), he would doubtless have us to know it was made for some
great treasure to be put therein. How and when the reasonable soul is put into
this curious cabinet philosophers dispute many things, but can affirm nothing of
certainty.—*Abraham Wright.*

Verse 15.—"*In the lowest parts of the earth.*" From this remarkable expression,
which, in the original, and as elsewhere used, denotes the region of the dead—
Sheol, or *Hades*—it would appear that it is not only his formation in the womb the
Psalmist here contemplates, but also—regarding the region of the dead as the
womb of resurrection life—the refashioning of the body hereafter, and its new
birth to the life immortal, which will be no less " marvellous" a work, but rather
more so, than the first fashioning of man's " substance." Confirmed by the
words of verse 18—" When I awake, I am still with thee"—the same language
before employed to express the resurrection hope, Ps. xvii. 15 ; when there shall
be a further illustration of God's mindfulness of his purposes and " precious

counsels" with respect to his redeemed, in anticipation of which they may repeat this psalm with renewed feelings of wonder and admiration.—*William De Burgh.*

Verses 15, 16.—The word " *substance*" represents different words in these verses. In verse 15 it is " my strength," or " my bones" ; in verse 16 the word is usually rendered " embryo" : but " clew" (life a ball yet to be unwound) finds favour with great scholars.

"*In the lowest parts of the earth* " denotes no subterranean limbo or workshop ; but is a poetical parallel to " in secret."

"*Which in continuance were fashioned* " is wrong. The margin, though also wrong, indicates the right way : " my days were determined before one of them was."—*David M'Laren, in "The Book of Psalms in Metre,"* 1883.

Verse 16.—"*Thine eyes did see my substance, yet being unperfect,*" ˙etc. From whence we may learn, first, not to be proud of what we are ; all's the work of God. How beautiful or comely, how wise or holy soever you are, 'tis not of yourselves. What hath any man, either in naturals or supernaturals, which he hath not received ? Secondly, despise not what others are or have, though they are not such exact pieces, though they have not such excellent endowments as yourselves ; yet they are what God hath made them. Thirdly, despise not what yourselves are. Many are ashamed to be seen as God made them ; few are ashamed to be seen what the devil hath made them. Many are troubled at small defects in the outward man ; few are troubled at the greatest deformities of the inward man : many buy artificial beauty to supply the natural ; few spiritual, to supply the defects of the supernatural beauty of the soul.—*Abraham Wright.*

Verse 16.—"*My substance yet being unperfect.*" One word in the original, which means strictly anything *rolled together* as a ball, and hence is generally supposed to mean here the fœtus or embryo. Hupfeld, however, prefers to understand it of the ball of life, as consisting of a number of different threads (" the days" of verse 16—see margin) which are first a compact mass as it were, and which are then unwound as life runs on.—*J. J. Stewart Perowne.*

Verse 16.—A skilful architect before he builds draws a model, or gives a draught of the building in his book, or upon a table ; there he will show you every room and contrivance : in his book are all the parts of the building written, while as yet there are none of them, or before any of them are framed and set up. In allusion to architects and other artisans, David speaks of God, "*In thy book all my members were written*" ; that is, Thou hast made me as exactly as if thou hadst drawn my several members and my whole proportion with a pen or pencil in a book, before thou wouldst adventure to form me up. The Lord uses no book, no pen to decipher his work. He had the perfect idea of all things in himself from everlasting ; but he may well be said to work as by pattern, whose work is the most perfect pattern.—*Joseph Caryl.*

Verse 17.—"*How precious also are thy thoughts unto me,*" etc. So far from thinking it a hardship to be subject to this scrutiny, he counts it a most valuable privilege. However others may regard this truth, " *to me,*" my judgment and my feelings, " *how costly,*" valuable " *are thy thoughts,*" i.e. thy perpetual attention to me.—*Joseph Addison Alexander.*

Verse 17.—"*How precious also are thy thoughts unto me, O God !*" How cold and poor are *our* warmest thoughts towards God ! How unspeakably loving and gloriously rich are *his* thoughts towards us ! Compare Eph. i. 18 : " The riches of the glory of his inheritance in the saints."—*A. R. Fausset.*

Verse 17.—"*How precious . . . how great is the sum of them !*" Our comforts vie with the number of our sorrows, and win the game. The mercies of God passed over in a gross sum breed no admiration ; but cast up the particulars, and then arithmetic is too dull an art to number them. As many dusts as a man's hands can hold, is but his handful of so many dusts ; but tell them one by one, and they exceed all numeration. It was but a crown which king Solomon wore ;

but weigh the gold, tell the precious stones, value the richness of them, and what was it then ?—*Thomas Adams.*

Verses 17, 18.—Behold David's love to God ; sleeping and waking his mind runs upon him. There needs no arguments to bring those to our remembrance whom we love. We neglect ourselves to think upon them. A man in love wastes his spirits, vexes his mind, neglects his meat, regards not his business, his mind still feeds on that he loves. When men love that they should not, there is more need of a bridle to keep them from thinking of it, than of spurs to keep them to it. Try thy love of God by this. If thou thinkest not often of God, thou lovest him not. If thou canst not satisfy thyself with profits, pleasures, friends, and other worldly objects, but thou must turn other businesses aside, that thou mayest daily think of God, then thou lovest him.—*Francis Taylor, in "God's Glory in Man's Happiness,"* 1654.

Verses 17, 18.—Mercies are either ordinary or extraordinary—our common necessaries, or the remarkable supplies which we receive now and then at the hand of God. Thou must not only praise him for some extraordinary mercy, that comes with such pomp and observation that all thy neighbours take notice of it with thee, as the mercy which Zacharias and Elizabeth had in their son, that was noised about all the country (Luke i. 65) ; but also for ordinary every-day mercies : for first, we are unworthy of the least mercy (Gen. xxxii. 10), and therefore God is worthy of praise for the least, because it is more than he owes us. Secondly, these common, ordinary mercies are many. Thus David enhanceth the mercies of this kind,—"*O God, how great is the sum of them!* If I should count them, they are more in number than the sand ; when I wake I am still with thee." As if he had said, There is not a point of time wherein thou art not doing me good ; as soon as I open my eyes in the morning I have a new theme, in some fresh mercies given since I closed them over-night, to employ my praiseful meditations. Many little items make together a great sum. What is lighter than a grain of sand, yet what is heavier than the sand upon the sea-shore ? As little sins (such as vain thoughts and idle words), because of their multitude, arise to a great guilt, and will bring in a long bill, a heavy reckoning at last ; so, ordinary mercies, what they want in their size of some other great mercies, have compensated it in their number. Who will not say that a man shows greater kindness in maintaining one at his table with ordinary fare all the year than in entertaining him at a great feast twice or thrice in the same time ?—*William Gurnall.*

Verse 18.—"*They are more in number than the sand.*" Pindar says, that sand flies number (*Olymp. Ode* 2). The Pythian oracle indeed boastingly said, I know the number of the sand, and the measure of the sea (*Herodot. Clio.* l. i. c. 47). It is to this that Lucan may refer when he says, measure is not wanting to the ocean, or number to the sand (*Pharsal.* l. 5, v. 182).—*Samuel Burder.*

Verse 18.—"*If I should count them, they are more in number than the sand.*"

> If all his glorious deeds my song would tell,
> The shore's unnumbered stones I might recount as well.
>
> *Pindar,* B.C. 518—442.

Verse 18.—"*When I awake, I am still with thee.*" It is the great advantage of a Christian, which he has above other men, that he has his friends always about him, and (if the fault be not his own) need never to be absent from them. In the friendship and converse of the world, we use to say, "Friends must part," and those who have delight and satisfaction in one another's society must be content to leave it, and to be taken off from it. But this is the privilege of a believer that undertakes communion with God, that it is possible for him always to be with him. Again, in human converse and society we know it is ordinary for friends to dream that they are in company with one another ; but when they awake they are a great way off. But a Christian that converses with God, and has his thoughts fastened upon him, when he awakes he is still with him, which is that which is here exhibited to us in the example of the prophet David.

A godly soul should fall asleep in God's arms, like a child in the mother's lap ; it should be sung and lulled to sleep with " songs of the night." And this will make him the fitter for converse with God the next day after. This is the happiness of a Christian that is careful to lie down with God, that he finds his work still as he left it, and is in the same disposition when he rises as he was at night when he lay down to rest. As a man that winds up his watch over night, he finds it going the next morning ; so is it also, as I may say, with a Christian that winds up his heart. This is a good observation to be remembered, especially in the evening afore the Sabbath.—*Thomas Horton,* —1673.

Verse 18.—" *When I awake, I am still with thee.*" It is no small advantage to the holy life to " begin the day with God." The saints are wont to leave their hearts with him over night, that they may find them with him in the morning. Before earthly things break in upon us, and we receive impressions from abroad, it is good to season the heart with thoughts of God, and to consecrate the early and virgin operations of the mind before they are prostituted to baser objects. When the world gets the start of religion in the morning, it can hardly overtake it all the day ; and so the heart is habituated to vanity all the day long. But when we begin with God, we take him along with us to all the business and comforts of the day ; which, being seasoned with his love and fear, are the more sweet and savoury to us.—*Thomas Case* (1598—1682), *in the Epistle Dedicatory to* " *The Morning Exercise.*"

Verse 18.—"*When I awake.*" Accustom yourself to a serious meditation every morning. Fresh airing our souls in heaven will engender in us a purer spirit and nobler thoughts. A morning seasoning will secure us for all the day. Though other necessary thoughts about our calling will and must come in, yet when we have dispatched them, let us attend to our morning theme as our chief companion. As a man that is going with another about some considerable business, suppose to Westminster, though he meets with several friends on the way, and salutes some, and with others with whom he has some affairs he spends some little time, yet he quickly returns to his companion, and both together go to their intended stage. Do thus in the present case. Our minds are active and will be doing something, though to little purpose ; and if they be not fixed upon some noble object, they will, like madmen and fools, be mightily pleased in playing with straws. The thoughts of God were the first visitors David had in the morning. God and his heart met together as soon as he was awake, and kept company all the day after.—*Stephen Charnock.*

Verse 19.—"*Depart from me therefore, ye bloody men.*" The expression, " *bloody men,*" or " *men of blood,*" includes not only homicides, who shed human blood, but all other wicked and evil doers, who injure, or seek to injure others, or who slay their own souls by sin, or the souls of others by scandal ; all of whom may be truly called homicides ; for hatred may be called the mainspring of homicide, and thus St. John says, " Whoso hateth his brother is a homicide."—*Robert Bellarmine.*

Verse 19.—"*Therefore.*" When we have a controversy with the wicked we should take heed that private spleen do not rule us, but that only our interest in God's quarrel with them doth move us, as the Psalmist doth here.—*David Dickson.*

Verse 20.—"*Thine enemies take thy name in vain.*" In every action three things are considerable,—the *end*, the *agent*, the *work*. These three duly weighed, we shall soon see what it is to take God's name in vain.

I. That which hath no end proposed, or is done to no end, may truly be said to be done in vain. As the sowing of seed without reaping the fruit, the planting a vineyard without a vintage, or feeding a flock without eating the milk of it. These are labours in vain. So he that taketh the name of God to no end, neither to God's glory, nor the private or public good, taketh it in vain. *Cui bono?* is a question in all undertakings. If to no good, as good and better not undertaken at all ; it is to no end, it is in vain. If a man have well-fashioned legs, and they be lame, *frustra pulchras habet tibia claudus,* the lame man hath them in vain. The chief end, therefore, in taking this name must be, 1. The glory of God, otherwise we open our mouths in vain, as it is in Job. God is willing to impart all his blessings to us, and requires nothing of us again but glory, which if we return not, he may say, as David did of Nabal, for whom he had done many good turns, in securing his shepherds and flocks, etc. ; and when he desired nothing but a little meat for the young men he denied it : All that I have done for this fellow is in vain ; in vain have I kept all he hath. So, God having done so much for us, and expecting nothing but the glory of his name, if we be defective herein, he may well say all that he hath done for us is in vain.

2. Next to God's glory is the good of ourselves and others ; and so to take God's name without reference to this end, if we neither promote our own good nor the good of others, it is in vain, *ex privatione finis,* because it wants a right end ; therefore Saint Paul rejoiced, having by his preaching laboured for the saving of souls, I rejoice, saith he, that I have not run in vain, neither laboured in vain.

II. In the *agent* the heart and soul is to be considered, which in the person acting is the chief mover. If the soul be *Rachah,* vain and light, as when we take God's name without due advice and reverence, though we propound a right end, yet we take his name in vain. Therefore the wise man advises " not to be rash with our mouth" (Eccl. v. 2) ; and the Psalmist professeth that his heart was fixed when he praised God (Ps. lvii. 7) : the heart ought to be fixed and stablished by a due consideration of God's greatness when we speak of him. This is opposed to rashness, inconstancy, and lightness, such as are in chaff and smoke, which are apt to be carried away with every blast, and such as are so qualified do take God's name in vain.

III. In the *work* itself may be a twofold vanity, which must be avoided. Firstly, Falsehood. Secondly, Injustice.

1. If it be *false,* then is it also vain, as theirs in Isaiah (ch. xxviii. 15) : " We have made a covenant with death, and with hell are we at agreement ; when the overflowing scourge shall pass through, it shall not come unto us : for we have made lies our refuge, and under falsehood have we hid ourselves." And this is that *actio erroris,* work of error, of which Jeremiah speaketh. *Vanitas opponitur veritati,* vanity is opposed to verity and truth ; therefore a thing is said to be vain when it is false or erroneous. " They are vanity, the work of errors," saith the prophet (Jer. x. 15) ; and as there is truth in natural things, so is there a truth in moral things, which if it be wanting, our speech is vain.

2. If *unjust* it is vain too. " If I be wicked, why then labour I in vain ?" saith holy Job (ch. ix. 29) ; and, " The very hope of unjust men perisheth," saith the wise man (Prov. xi. 7) ; and, " They walk in a vain shadow, and disquiet themselves in vain" (Ps. xxxix. 6). If justice be wanting in our actions, or truth in our assertions and promises, they are vain ; and to use God's name in either is to take his name in vain. So that if either we take the name of God to no end, but make it common, and take it up as a custom till it come to a habit, not for any good end ; or if our hearts be not stable or fixed, but light and inconstant when we take it ; or if we take it to colour or bolster up any falsehood or any unjust act, we take it in vain, and break the commandment.—*Lancelot Andrews.*

Verse 21.—*"Do not I hate them, O* LORD, *that hate thee ?"* The simple future in the first clause comprehends several distinct shades of meaning. Do I not, may I not, must I not, hate those hating thee ? Hate them, not as man hates, but as God hates.—*Joseph Addison Alexander.*

Verse 21.—*"Do not I hate them, O* LORD, *that hate thee ?"* Can he who thinks good faith the holiest thing in life, avoid being an enemy to that master who, as quæstor, dared to despoil, desert, and betray ? Can he who wishes to pay due honours to the immortal gods, by any means avoid being an enemy to that man who has plundered all their temples ?—*Cicero.*

Verse 21.—*"And am not I grieved with those that rise up against thee ?"* The expression here—"*grieved*"—explains the meaning of the word "*hate*" in the former member of the verse. It is not that hatred which is followed by malignity or ill-will ; it is that which is accompanied with grief, pain of heart, pity, sorrow. So the Saviour looked on men : Mark iii. 5 : "And when he had looked round about on them with *anger*, being *grieved* for the hardness of their hearts." The Hebrew word used here, however, contains *also* the idea of being disgusted with ; of loathing ; of nauseating. The feeling referred to is anger—conscious disgust —at such conduct ; grief, pain, sorrow, that men should evince such feelings towards their Maker.—*Albert Barnes*.

Verse 21.—"*Am not I grieved ?*" etc. Acted upon by mingled feelings of sorrow for them, and loathing at their evil practices. Thus our Lord "looked round about on them with *anger*, being *grieved* for the hardness of their hearts" : Mark iii. 5.—*French and Skinner*.

Verse 21.—It is said that Adam Smith disliked nothing more than that moral apathy—that obtuseness of moral perception—which prevents man from not only seeing clearly, but feeling strongly, the broad distinction between virtue and vice, and which, under the pretext of liberality, is all indulgent even to the blackest crimes. At a party at Dalkeith Palace, where Mr. ——, in his mawkish way, was finding palliations for some villainous transactions, the doctor waited in patient silence until he was gone, then exclaimed : "Now I can breathe more freely. I cannot bear that man ; he has no indignation in him."

Verses 21, 22.—A faithful servant hath the same interests, the same friends, the same enemies, with his master, whose cause and honour he is, upon all occasions, in duty bound to support and maintain. A good man hates, as God himself doth ; he hates not the persons of men, but their sins ; not what God made them, but what they have made themselves. We are neither to hate the men, on account of the vices they practise ; nor to love the vices, for the sake of the men who practise them. He who observeth invariably this distinction, fulfilleth the perfect law of charity, and hath the love of God and of his neighbour abiding in him.—*George Horne*.

Verses 21, 22.—First, we must hate the company and society of manifest and obstinate sinners, who will not be reclaimed. Secondly, all their sins, not communicating with any man in his sin, we must have no fellowship (as with the workers so) with the unfruitful works of darkness. Thirdly, all occasions and inducements unto these sins. Fourthly, all appearances of wickedness (1 Thess. v. 22), that is, which men in common judgment account evil ; and all this must proceed from a good ground, even from a good heart hating sin perfectly, that is all sin, as David, "*I hate them with perfect hatred*"; and not as some, who can hate some sin, but cleave to some other : as many can hate pride, but love covetousness or some other darling sin : but we must attain to the hatred of all, before we can come to the practice of this precept [Jude 23] ; besides that, all sins are hateful even in themselves.—*William Perkins*, 1558—1602.

Verses 21, 24.—The temper of mourning for public sins, for the sins of others, is the greatest note of sincerity. When all other signs of righteousness may have their exceptions, this temper is the utmost term, which we cannot go beyond in our self-examination. The utmost prospect David had of his sincerity, when he was upon a diligent enquiry after it, was his anger and grief for the sin of others. When he had reached so far, he was at a stand, and knew not what more to add : "Am not I grieved with those that rise up against thee ? I hate them with perfect hatred : I count them mine enemies. Search me, O God, and know my heart : try me, and know my thoughts : and see if there be any wicked way in me." If there be anything that better can evidence my sincerity than this, Lord, acquaint me with it ; "know my heart," *i.e.*, make me to know it. He whose sorrow is only for matter confined within his own breast, or streams with it in his life, has reason many times to question the truth of it ; but when a man cannot behold sin as sin in another without sensible regret, it is a sign he hath savingly felt the bitterness of it in his own soul. It is a high pitch and growth, and a consent between the Spirit of God and the soul of a Christian, when he can

lament those sins in others whereby the Spirit is grieved ; when he can rejoice
with the Spirit rejoicing, and mourn with the Spirit mourning. This is a clear
testimony that we have not self-ends in the service of God ; that we take not up
religion to serve a turn ; that God is our aim, and Christ our beloved.—*Stephen
Charnock.*

Verse 22.—"I hate them with perfect hatred." What is *" with a perfect hatred "* ?
I hated in them their iniquities, I loved thy creation. This it is to hate with a
perfect hatred, that neither on account of the vices thou hate the men, nor on
account of the men love the vices. For see what he addeth, *"They became my
enemies."* Not only as God's enemies, but as his own too doth he now describe
them. How then will he fulfil in them both his own saying, *"Have not I hated
those that hated thee, Lord,"* and the Lord's command, *"Love your enemies"* ?
How will he fulfil this, save with that perfect hatred, that he hate in them that
they are wicked, and love that they are men ? For in the time even of the Old
Testament, when the carnal people was restrained by visible punishments, how
did Moses, the servant of God, who by understanding belonged to the New Testament, how did he hate sinners when he prayed for them, or how did he not hate
them when he slew them, save that he *" hated them with a perfect hatred "* ? For
with such perfection did he hate the iniquity which he punished, as to love the
manhood for which he prayed.—*Augustine.*

Verse 23.—"Try me." True faith is precious ; it is like gold, it will endure a
trial. Presumption is but a counterfeit, and cannot abide to be tried : 1 Pet. i. 7.
A true believer fears no trial. He is willing to be tried by God. He is willing to
have his faith tried by others, he shuns not the touchstone. He is much in test-
ing himself. He would not take anything upon trust, especially that which is of
such moment. He is willing to hear the worst as well as the best. That preaching pleases him best which is most searching and distinguishing : Heb. iv. 12.
He is loath to be deluded with vain hopes. He would not be flattered into a false
conceit of his spiritual state. When trials are offered, he complies with the apostle's advice, 2 Cor. xiii. 5.—*David. Clarkson.*

Verse 23.—What fearful dilemma have we here ? The Holiest changeth not,
when he comes a visitant to a human heart. He is the same there that he is in
the highest heaven. He cannot look upon sin ; and how can a human heart welcome him into its secret chambers ? How can the blazing fire welcome the
quenching water ? It is easy to commit to memory the seemly prayer of an ancient penitent, *"Search me, O God, and know my heart ; try me, and know my
thoughts."* The dead letters, worn smooth by frequent use, may drop freely from
callous lips, leaving no sense of scalding on the conscience; and yet, truth of God
though they are, they may be turned into a lie in the act of utterance. The
prayer is not true, although it is borrowed from the Bible, if the suppliant invite
the All-seeing in, and yet would give a thousand worlds, if he had them, to keep
him out for ever.
    Christ has declared the difficulty, and solved it : "I am the way, the truth,
and the life : no man cometh unto the Father, but by me." When the Son has
made the sinner free, he is free indeed. The dear child, pardoned and reconciled,
loves and longs for the Father's presence. What ! is there neither spot nor
wrinkle now upon the man, that he dares to challenge inspection by the Omniscient, and to offer his heart as Jehovah's dwelling-place ? He is not yet so pure ;
and well he knows it. The groan is bursting yet from his broken heart : " O
wretched man that I am ! who shall deliver me from the body of this death ?"
Many stains defile him yet ; but he loathes them now, and longs to be free. The
difference between an unconverted and a converted man is not that the one has
sins, and the other has none ; but that the one takes part with his cherished sins
against a dreaded God, and the other takes part with a reconciled God against
his hated sins. He is out with his former friends, and in with his former adversary. Conversion is a turning, and it is one turning only ; but it produces simul-

taneously and necessarily two distinct effects. Whereas his face was formerly turned away from God, and toward his own sins ; it is now turned away from his own sins, and toward God. This one turning, with its twofold result, is in Christ the Mediator, and through the work of the Spirit.

As long as God is my enemy, I am his. I have no more power to change that condition than the polished surface has to refrain from reflecting the sunshine that falls upon it. It is God's love, from the face of Jesus shining into my dark heart, that makes my heart open to him, and delight to be his dwelling-place. The eyes of the just Avenger I cannot endure to be in this place of sin ; but the eye of the compassionate Physician I shall gladly admit into this place of disease ; for he comes from heaven to earth that he may heal such sin-sick souls as mine. When a disciple desires to be searched by the living God, he does not thereby intimate that there are no sins in him to be discovered : he intimates rather that his foes are so many and so lively, that nothing can subdue them except the presence and power of God.— *William Arnot* (—1875), *in "Laws from Heaven, for Life on Earth."*

Verses 23, 24.—There are several things worthy of notice in the Psalmist's appeal, in the words before us. First, notice *the Psalmist's intrepidity.* Here is a man determined to explore the recesses of his own heart. Did Buonaparte, did Nelson, did Wellington, ever propose to do this ? Were all the renowned heroes of antiquity present, I would ask them all if they ever had courage to enter into their own hearts. David was a man of courage. When he slew a lion in the way, when he successfully encountered a bear, when he went out to meet the giant Goliath, he gave undoubted proofs of courage ; but never did he display such signal intrepidity as when he determined to look into his own heart. If you stood upon some eminence, and saw all the ravenous and venomous creatures that ever lived collected before you, it would not require such courage to combat them as to combat with your own heart. Every sin is a devil, and each may say, " My name is Legion, for we are many." Who knows what it is to face himself ? And yet, if we would be saved, this must be done.

Secondly, notice *the Psalmist's integrity.* He wished to know all his sins, that he might be delivered from them. As every individual must know his sins at some period, a wise man will seek to know them here, because the present is the only time in which to glorify God, by confessing, by renouncing, by overcoming them. One of the attributes of sin is to hide man from himself, to conceal his deformity, to prevent him from forming a just conception of his true condition. It is a solemn fact, that there is not an evil principle in the bosom of the devil himself which does not exist in ours, at the present moment, unless we are fully renewed by the power of the Holy Spirit. That these evil principles do not continually develop themselves, in all their hideous deformity, is entirely owing to the restraining and forbearing mercy of God.

Thirdly, notice *the Psalmist's wisdom.* He presents his prayer to God himself. God is the only Being in the universe that knows himself—that peruses himself in his own light. In the same light he sees all other beings ; and hence it follows that, if other beings see themselves truly, it must be in the light of God. If the sun were an intelligent being, I would ask him, " How do you see yourself ? In your own light ?" And he would reply, " Yes." " And how do you see the planets that are continually revolving around you ?" " In my own light also, for all the light that is in them is borrowed from me."

You will observe that the Psalmist begins with his principles : his desire is to have these tried by a competent judge, and to have every thing that is evil removed from them. This is an evidence of his wisdom. The heart and its thoughts must be made right, before the actions of the life can be set right. Those who are most eminent for piety are most conversant with God ; and, for this reason, they become most conversant with themselves. David says, elsewhere, " Who can understand his errors ? Cleanse THOU me from *secret* faults." And Job says, " If I wash myself with snow water, and make me never so clean, yet shalt THOU plunge me in the ditch, and mine own clothes shall abhor me."

When these holy men perused themselves in God's light, they saw their sins of omission and commission, and prayed earnestly to be delivered from all.— *William Howels*, 1832.

Verses 23, 24.—The text is a prayer, and it indicates, as we think, three great facts in regard to the suppliant : the first, that David thoroughly wished to become acquainted with himself ; the second, that he felt conscious that God could see through all disguises ; and the third, that he desired to discover, in order that by Divine help he might correct, whatsoever was wrong in his conduct.

Now, the first inference which we draw from the text, when considered as indicating the feelings of the petitioner is, that he was thoroughly honest, that it was really his wish to become acquainted with his own heart. And is there, you may say, anything rare or remarkable in this ? Indeed we think there is. It would need, we believe, a very high degree of piety to be able to put up with sincerity the prayers of our text. For, will you tell me that it does not often happen, that even whilst men are carrying on a process of self-examination, there is a secret wish to remain ignorant of certain points, a desire not to be proved wrong when interest and inclination combine in demanding an opposite verdict ? . . . In searching into yourselves, you know where the tender points are, and those points you will be apt to avoid, so as not to put yourselves to pain, nor make it evident how much you need the caustic and the knife. Indeed, we may be sure that we state nothing but what experience will prove, when we declare it a high attainment in religion to be ready to know how bad we are. . . . And this had evidently been reached by the Psalmist, for he pleads very earnestly with God that he would leave no recess of his spirit unexplored, that he would bring the heart and all its thoughts, the life and all its ways, under a most searching examination, so that no form and no degree of evil might fail to be detected.— *Henry Melvill.*

Verses 23, 24.—Self-examination is not the simple thing which, at first sight, it might appear. No Christian who has ever really practised it has found it easy. Is there any exercise of the soul which any one of us has found so unsatisfactory, so almost impossible, as self-examination ? The fact is this, that the heart is so exceedingly complicated and intricate, and it is so very near the eye which has to investigate it, and both it and the eye are so restless and so shifting, that its deep anatomy baffles our research. Just a few things, here and there, broad and open, and floating upon the surface, a man discovers ; but there are chambers receding within chambers, in that deepest of all deep things, a sinner's heart, which no mere human investigation ever will reach, . . . it is the prerogative of God alone to " *search*" the human heart.

To the child of God—the most intimate with himself in all the earth—I do not hesitate to say—" There are sins latent at this moment in you, of which you have no idea ; but it only requires a larger measure of spiritual illumination to impress and unfold them. You have no idea of the wickedness that is now in you." But while I say this, let every Christian count well the cost before he ventures on the bold act of asking God to " search" him. For be sure of this, if you do really and earnestly ask God to " *search* " you, he will do it. And he will search you most searchingly ; and if you ask him to " *try* " you, he will try you,—and the trial will be no light matter !

I am persuaded that we often little calculate what we are doing—what we are asking God to do—when we implore him to give us some spiritual attainment, some growth in grace, some increase in holiness, or peace. To all these things there is a condition, and that condition lies in a discipline, and that discipline is generally proportionate to the strength and the measure of the gift that we ask.

I do not know what may have been the state of the Psalmist at the period when he indited this psalm ; but I should think either one of Saul's most cruel persecutions, or the rebellion of his son Absalom, followed quick upon the traces of that prayer,—" *Search me, O God, and know my heart : try me, and know my thoughts,*" etc.

Still, whatever his attainment, every child of God will desire, at any sacrifice, to know his own exact state before God ; for, as he desires in all things to have a mind conformed to the mind of God, so he is especially jealous lest he should, by any means, be taking a different view, or estimate, of his own soul from that which God sees it.—*Condensed from James Vaughan.*

Verses 23, 24.—Hypocrisy at the fashionable end of the town is very different from hypocrisy in the city. The modish hypocrite endeavours to appear more vicious than he really is, the other kind of hypocrite more virtuous. The former is afraid of everything that has the show of religion in it, and would be thought engaged in many criminal gallantries and amours which he is not guilty of. The latter assumes a face of sanctity, and covers a multitude of vices under a seeming religious deportment.

But there is another kind of hypocrisy, which differs from both of these : I mean that hypocrisy by which a man does not only deceive the world, but very often imposes on himself ; that hypocrisy which conceals his own heart from him, and makes him believe he is more virtuous than he really is, and either not attend to his vices, or mistake even his vices for virtues. It is this fatal hypocrisy and self-deceit which is taken notice of in those words, " Who can understand his errors ? cleanse thou me from secret faults."

These two kinds of hypocrisy, namely, that of deceiving the world, and that of imposing on ourselves, are touched with wonderful beauty in the hundred and thirty-ninth psalm. The folly of the first kind of hypocrisy is there set forth by reflections on God's omniscience and omnipresence, which are celebrated in as noble strains of poetry as any other I ever met with, either sacred or profane. The other kind of hypocrisy, whereby a man deceives himself, is intimated in the two last verses, where the Psalmist addresses himself to the great Searcher of hearts in that emphatical petition ; " Try me, O God, and seek the ground of my heart : prove me, and examine my thoughts. Look well if there be any way of wickedness in me, and lead me in the way everlasting."—*Joseph Addison* (1672— 1719), *in " The Spectator."*

Verses 23, 24.—How beautiful is the humility of David ! He cannot speak of the wicked but in terms of righteous indignation ; he cannot but hate the haters of his God ; yet, he seems immediately to recollect, and to check himself—" Try *me*, O Lord, and seek the ground of *my* heart." Precisely in the same spirit of inward humility and self-recollection, Abraham, when pleading before God in prayer for guilty depraved Sodom, fails not to speak of *himself*, as being dust and ashes : Gen. xviii. 27.—*James Ford*, 1871.

Verses 23, 24.—Why did David pray thus to God, *"Search me, O God, and know my heart,"* having said before, in the first verse, *"Thou hast searched me, and known me"* ? Seeing David knew that God had searched him, what needed he to pray that God would search him ? why did he beg God to do that which he had done already ? The answer is at hand. David was a diligent self-searcher, and therefore he was so willing to be searched, yea, he delighted to be searched by God ; and that not (as was said) because himself had done it already, but also because he knew God could do it better. He knew by his own search that he did not live in any way of wickedness against his knowledge, and yet he knew there might be some way of wickedness in him that he knew not of. And there-fore he doth not only say, *"Search me, O God, and know my thoughts";* but he adds, *"See if there be any wicked way* (or *any way of pain and grief*) *in me ";* (the same word signifies both, because wicked ways lead in the end to pain and grief) ; *" and lead me in the way everlasting."* As if he had said, Lord, I have searched myself, and can see no wicked way in me ; but, Lord, thy sight is in-finitely clearer than mine, and if thou wilt but search me thou mayest see some wicked way in me which I could not see, and I would fain see and know the worst of myself, that I might amend and grow better ; therefore, Lord, if there be any such way in me, cause me to know it also. O take that way out of me, and take me out of that way ; *" lead me in the way everlasting."* David had tried himself, and he would again be tried by God, that he, being better tried, might become yet better. He found himself gold upon his own trial, and yet he feared there might be some dross in him that he had not found ; and now he would be re-tried that he might come forth purest gold. Pure gold fears neither the furnace nor the fire, neither the test nor the touchstone ; nor is weighty gold afraid of the balance. He that is weight will be weight, how often soever he is weighed ; he that is gold will be gold, how often soever he is tried, and the oftener he is tried the purer gold he will be ; what he is he will be, and he would be better than he is.—*Joseph Caryl.*

Verse 24.—"*See if there be any wicked way in me.*" This is a beautiful and impressive *prayer* for the commencement of every day. It is, also, a great sentiment to *admonish* us at the beginning of each day.

There is the way of *unbelief* within, to which we are very prone. There is the way of *vanity* and pride, to which we often accustom ourselves. There is the way of *selfishness* in which we frequently walk. There is the way of *worldliness* we often pursue—empty pleasures, shadowy honours, etc. There is the way of *sluggishness.* What apathy in prayer, in the examination and application of God's Word, we manifest ! There is the way of *self-dependence,* by which we often dishonour God and injure ourselves. There is, unhappily, the way of *disobedience,* in which we often walk. At any rate, our obedience is cold, reluctant, uncertain —not simple, entire, fervent. How necessary is it, then, to go to God at once, and earnestly to prefer the petition, "*Lord, see if there be any wicked way in me.*" Let nothing that is wrong, that is opposed to thy character, repugnant to thy word, or injurious and debasing to ourselves, remain, or be harboured within us. —*Condensed from T. Wallace, in "Homiletic Commentary."*

Verse 24.—"*See if there be any wicked way in me.*" To what a holiness must David have attained ere he could need, if we may so speak, Divine scrutiny, in order to his being informed of errors and defects ! Is there one of us who can say that he has corrected his conduct up to the measure of his knowledge, and that now he must wait the being better informed before he can do more towards improving his life ? I do not know how to define a higher point in religious attainment than supposing a man warranted in offering up the prayer of our text. I call upon you to be cautious in using this prayer. It is easy to mock God, by asking him to search you whilst you have made but little effort to search yourselves, and perhaps still less to act upon the result of the scrutiny.—*Henry Melvill.*

Verse 24.—"*See if there be any wicked way in me,*" etc.—

Think and be careful what thou art within,
For there is sin in the desire of sin :
Think and be thankful, in a different case,
For there is grace in the desire of grace.

John Byrom, 1691—1763.

Verse 24.—"*The way everlasting.*" *Way of eternity,* or *of antiquity, the old way,* as Jer. vi. 16 ; meaning the way of faith and godliness, which God taught from the beginning, and which continueth for ever ; contrary to "the way of the wicked," which perisheth : Ps. i. 6.—*Henry Ainsworth.*

HINTS TO THE VILLAGE PREACHER.

Verses 1 and 23.—A matter of fact made a matter of prayer.

Verse 1.—1. A cheering thought for sinners. If God knew them not perfectly, how could he have prepared a perfect salvation for them ? 2. A comfortable truth for saints. "Your heavenly Father knoweth that ye have need of all these things."—*G. R.*

Verses 1—5.—In these verses we have God's Omniscience, I. Described. 1. As observing minute and comparatively unimportant actions : "My downsitting and uprising." 2. As taking note of our thoughts and the motives behind them : "Understandest my thought." 3. As investigating all our ways : "Thou compassest," etc. ; better rendered, " Thou triest my walking and lying down," *i.e.*, my activities and restings. 4. Accurately estimating every word at the instant of its utterance : " For there is not a word," etc. 5. As being " behind " men, remembering their past, and " before" men, acquainted with their future : " Thou hast beset me," etc. 6. As every instant holding men under watchful scrutiny : " And laid," etc. II. Personally realized and pondered : " Thou hast searched *me.*" *Me* and *my* run through the whole set of statements. Thus felt and used, the fact of God's omniscience, 1. Begets reverence. 2. Inspires confidence. 3. Produces carefulness of conduct.—*J. F.*

Verses 2—4.—The knowledge of God extends, I. To our movements, our " down sitting and uprising"—when we sit down to read, write, or converse, and when we rise up to active service. II. To our thoughts : " Thou understandest my thoughts afar off." What they have been, what they now are, what they will be, what under all circumstances they would have been. He who made minds knows what their thoughts will be at all times, or he could not predict future events, or govern the world. He can know our thoughts without being the Author of them. III. To our actions : verse 3. Every step we take by day, and all we purpose to do in wakeful hours of the night : all our private, social, and public ways, are compassed or sifted by him, to distinguish the good from the bad, as wheat from the chaff. IV. To our words : verse 4. It has been said that the words of all men and from all time are registered in the atmosphere, and may be faithfully recalled. Whether it be so or not, they are phonographed in the mind of God.—*G. R.*

Verse 2 (*first clause*).—The importance of the commonest acts of life.

Verse 2 (*second clause*).—The serious nature of thoughts. Known to God ; seen through, their drift perceived ; and attention given to them while as yet in the distance.

Verse 3.—The encircling Presence, in our activities, meditations, secrecies, and movements.

Verse 4.—I. Words on the tongue first *in* it, and in that stage known to God. II. Words on the tongue very numerous, yet all known. III. Words on the tongue have wide meaning, yet known " altogether." Lesson : Take heed of your words not yet spoken.

Verse 5.—A soul captured. Stopped, overtaken, arrested. What has it done ? What shall it do ?

Verse 6.—I. God imperfectly known to man. II. Man perfectly known to God. It has been said that wise men never wonder ; to us it appears they are always wondering.—*G. R.*

Verse 6.—Theme : the facts of our religion, too wonderful to understand, are just those in which we have most reason to rejoice. I. Prove it. 1. The incomprehensible attributes of God give unspeakable value to his promises. 2. The Incarnation is at once the most complete and most endearing manifestation of God we possess, yet it is the most inexplicable. 3. Redemption by the death of Christ is the highest guarantee of salvation we can conceive ; but who can explain it ? 4. Inspiration makes the Bible the word of God, though none can give an account of its mode of operation in the minds of those " moved by the Holy Ghost." 5. The resurrection of the body, and its glorification, satisfy the deepest yearning of our soul (Rom. viii. 23 ; 2 Cor. v. 2—4) ; but none can conceive the how. II. Apply its lessons. 1. Let us not stumble at doctrines simply because they are mysterious. 2. Let us be thankful God has not kept back the great mysteries of our religion simply because there would be some offended at them. 3. Let us readily receive all the joy which the mysteries bring, and calmly wait the light of heaven to make them better understood.—*J. F.*

Verses 7—10.—I. God is wherever I am. I fill but a small part of space ; he fills all space. II. He is wherever I shall be. He does not move with me, but I move in him. " In him we live, and move," etc. III. God is wherever I could be. " If I ascend to heaven," etc. " If I descend to Sheol," etc. If I travel with the sunbeams to the most distant part of the earth, or heavens, or the sea, I shall be in thy hand. No mention is here made of annihilation, as though that were possible ; which would be the only escape from the Divine Presence ; for he is not the God of the dead, of the annihilated, in the Sadducean meaning of the word, but of the living. Man is always somewhere, and God is always everywhere.—*G. R.*

Verse 8.—The glory of heaven and the terror of hell : " THOU."

Verses 9, 10.—I. The greatest security and encouragement to a sinner supposed. 1. The place—the remotest part of the sea ; by which you are to understand the most obscure nook in the creation. 2. His swift and speedy flight after the commission of sin, to this supposed refuge and sanctuary : " If I take the wings of the morning." II. This supposed security and encouragement is utterly destroyed (verse 10).—*See Flavel's "Seaman's Preservative in Foreign Countries."*

Verses 11, 12.—Darkness and light are both alike to God. I. Naturally. " I form the light, and I create the darkness." II. Providentially. Providential dispensations that are dark to us are light to him. We change with respect to him, not he to us. III. Spiritually. "Let him that walketh in darkness," etc. " Yea, though I walk," etc. He went before them in a pillar of cloud to guide them by day, and a pillar of fire to guide them by night. It was the same God in the day-cloud and in the night-light.—*G. R.*

Verse 14.—" I am fearfully and wonderfully made." This is true of man in his fourfold state. I. In his primitive integrity. II. In his deplorable depravity. III. In his regeneration. IV. In his fixed state in hell or heaven.—*W. W.*

Verses 17, 18.—The psalm dilates upon the omniscience of God. In no mournful manner, but the reverse. I. *God's thoughts of us.* 1. How certain. 2. How numerous. 3. How condescending. 4. How tender. 5. How wise. 6. How practical. 7. How constant. II. *Our thoughts upon his thoughts.* 1. How rare and yet how due to the subject. 2. How delightful. 3. How consoling. 4. How strengthening to faith. 5. How arousing to love. III. *Our thoughts upon God himself.* 1. They place us near God. 2. They keep us near God. 3. They restore us to him. We are with God when we awake from sleep, from lethargy, from death.

Verses 17, 18.—I. The saint precious to God. He thinks of him tenderly ; in countless ways ; perpetually. II. God precious to the saints. Noting God's loving-kindnesses, numbering them, newly awakening to them. III. The mingling of these loves : " I am still with thee."—*W. B. H.*

Verse 18.—"*When I awake I am still with thee.*" Awaking is sometimes, yea, most commonly, taken in the *natural signification*, for the recovery from bodily sleep. 2. *Morally*, for recovery from sin. 3. *Mystically ;* " when I shall awake," that is, from the sleep of death.—*T. Horton.*

Verse 18.—" A Christian on Earth still in Heaven" [an Appendix to " A Christian on the Mount ; or, A Treatise concerning Meditation"], by *Thomas Watson,* 1660.

Verse 18.—"*I am still with thee.*" 1. By way of meditation. 2. In respect to communion. 3. In regard of action, and the businesses which are done by us.—*T. Horton.*

Verse 19.—I. The doctrine of punishment the necessary outcome of omniscience. II. Inevitable judgment an argument for separation from sinners.—*W. B. H.*

Verse 20.—Two scandalous offences against God. I. To speak slanderously of him. II. To speak irreverently of him. These are committed only by his enemies.

Verses 21, 22.—I. Such hatred one need not be ashamed of. II. Such hatred one should be able to define : " grieved." III. Such hatred one must labour to keep right. " Perfect hatred " is a form of hate consistent with all the virtues.

Verses 23, 24.—The language, I. Of self-examination. 1. As in the sight of God. 2. With a desire for the help of God : verse 23. Look me through, and through, and tell me what thou thinkest of me. II. Of self-renunciation : " See if," etc. (verse 24) ; any sin unpardoned, any evil disposition unsubdued, any evil habit unrestrained, that I may renounce it.   III. Of self-dedication : " Lead me," etc. : a submission entirely to divine guidance in the future.—*G. R.*

Verse 24.—I. The evil way.   Naturally in us ; may be of different kinds ; must be removed ; removal needs Divine help.   II. The everlasting way.   There is but one, we need leading in it.   It is the good old way, it does not come to an end, it leads to blessedness without end.

Verse 24 (*last clause*).—See " Spurgeon's Sermons," No. 903 : " The Way Everlasting."

PSALM CXL.

This Psalm is in its proper place, and so fitly follows cxxxix. that you might almost read right on, and make no break between the two. Serious injury would follow to the whole Book of Psalms if the order should be interfered with as certain wiseacres propose. It is THE CRY OF A HUNTED SOUL, *the supplication of a believer incessantly persecuted and beset by cunning enemies, who hungered for his destruction. David was hunted like a partridge upon the mountains, and seldom obtained a moment's rest. This is his pathetic appeal to Jehovah for protection, an appeal which gradually intensifies into a denunciation of his bitter foes. With this sacrifice of prayer he offers the salt of faith; for in a very marked and emphatic manner he expresses his personal confidence in the Lord as the Protector of the oppressed, and as his own God and Defender. Few short psalms are so rich in the jewelry of precious faith.*

"To the Chief Musician."—The writer wished this experimental hymn to be under the care of the chief master of song, that it might neither be left unsung, nor chanted in a slovenly manner. Such trials and such rescues deserved to be had in remembrance, and to be set up among the choicest memorials of the Lord's goodness. We, too, have our songs which are of no ordinary kind, and these must be sung with our best powers of heart and tongue. We will offer them to the Lord by no other hand than that of "the Chief Musician."

"A Psalm of David."—The life of David wherein he comes in contact with Saul and Doeg is the best explanation of this psalm; and surely there can be no reasonable doubt that David wrote it, and wrote it in the time of his exile and peril. The tremendous outburst at the end has in it the warmth which was so natural to David, who was never lukewarm in anything; yet it is to be noticed that concerning his enemies he was often hot in language through indignation, and yet he was cool in action, for he was not revengeful. His was no petty malice, but a righteous anger: he foresaw, foretold, and even desired the just vengeance of God upon the proud and wicked, and yet he would not avail himself of opportunities to revenge himself upon those who had done him wrong. It may be that his appeals to the great King cooled his anger, and enabled him to leave his wrongs unredressed by any personal act of violence. "Vengeance is mine; I will repay, saith the Lord"; and David when most wounded by undeserved persecution and wicked falsehood was glad to leave his matters at the foot of the throne, where they would be safe with the King of kings.

EXPOSITION.

DELIVER me, O LORD, from the evil man : preserve me from the violent man ;

2 Which imagine mischiefs in *their* heart ; continually are they gathered together *for* war.

3 They have sharpened their tongues like a serpent ; adders' poison *is* under their lips. Selah.

1. "*Deliver me, O* LORD, *from the evil man.*" It reads like a clause of the Lord's prayer, "Deliver us from evil." David does not so much plead against an individual as against the species represented by him, namely, the being whose best description is—"the evil man." There are many such abroad ; indeed we shall not find an unregenerate man who is not in some sense an evil man, and yet all are not alike evil. It is well for us that our enemies are evil : it would be a horrible thing to have the good against us. When "the evil man" bestirs himself against the godly he is as terrible a being as a wolf, or a serpent, or even a devil. Fierce, implacable, unpitying, unrelenting, unscrupulous, he cares for nothing but the indulgence of his malice. The persecuted man turns to God in prayer ; he could not do a wiser thing. Who can meet the evil man and defeat him save Jehovah himself, whose infinite goodness is more than a match for all

the evil in the universe ? We cannot of ourselves baffle the craft of the enemy, but the Lord knoweth how to deliver his saints. He can keep us out of the enemy's reach, he can sustain us when under his power, he can rescue us when our doom seems fixed, he can give us the victory when defeat seems certain ; and in any and every case, if he do not save us from the man he can keep us from the evil. Should we be at this moment oppressed in any measure by ungodly men, it will be better to leave our defence with God than to attempt it ourselves.

"*Preserve me from the violent man.*" Evil in the heart simmers in malice, and at last boils in passion. Evil is a raging thing when it getteth liberty to manifest itself ; and so "the evil man" soon develops into "the violent man." What watchfulness, strength, or valour can preserve the child of God from deceit and violence ? There is but one sure Preserver, and it is our wisdom to hide under the shadow of his wings. It is a common thing for good men to be assailed by enemies : David was attacked by Saul, Doeg, Ahithophel, Shimei, and others ; even Mordecai sitting humbly in the gate had his Haman ; and our Lord, the Perfect One, was surrounded by those who thirsted for his blood. We may not, therefore, hope to pass through the world without enemies, but we may hope to be delivered out of their hands, and preserved from their rage, so that no real harm shall come of their malignity. This blessing is to be sought by prayer, and expected by faith.

2. "*Which imagine mischiefs in their heart.*" They cannot be happy unless they are plotting and planning, conspiring and contriving. They seem to have but one heart, for they are completely agreed in their malice ; and with all their heart and soul they pursue their victim. One piece of mischief is not enough for them ; they work in the plural, and prepare many arrows for their bow. What they cannot actually do they nevertheless like to think over, and to rehearse on the stage of their cruel fancy. It is an awful thing to have such a heart-disease as this. When the imagination gloats over doing harm to others, it is a sure sign that the entire nature is far gone in wickedness. "*Continually are they gathered together for war.*" They are a committee of opposition in permanent session : they never adjourn, but perpetually consider the all-absorbing question of how to do the most harm to the man of God. They are a standing army always ready for the fray : they not only go to the wars, but dwell in them. Though they are the worst of company, yet they put up with one another, and are continually in each other's society, confederate for fight. David's enemies were as violent as they were evil, as crafty as they were violent, and as persistent as they were crafty. It is hard dealing with persons who are only in their element when they are at daggers-drawn with you. Such a case calls for prayer, and prayer calls on God.

3. "*They have sharpened their tongues like a serpent.*" The rapid motion of a viper's tongue gives you the idea of its sharpening it ; even thus do the malicious move their tongues at such a rate that one might suppose them to be in the very act of wearing them to a point, or rubbing them to a keen edge. It was a common notion that serpents inserted their poison by their tongues, and the poets used the idea as a poetical expression, although it is certain that the serpent wounds by his fangs and not by his tongue. We are not to suppose that all authors who used such language were mistaken in their natural history any more than a writer can be charged with ignorance of astronomy because he speaks of the sun's travelling from east to west. How else can poets speak but according to the appearance of things to an imaginative eye. The world's great poet puts it in " King Lear " :

> " She struck me with her tongue,
> Most serpent-like, upon the very heart."

In the case of slanderers, they so literally sting with their tongues, which are so nimble in malice, and withal so piercing and cutting, that it is by no means un-just to speak of them as sharpened. "*Adders' poison is under their lips.*" The deadliest of all venom is the slander of the unscrupulous. Some men care not what they say so long as they can vex and injure. Our text, however, must not be confined in its reference to some few individuals, for in the inspired epistle to the Romans it is quoted by the apostle as being true of us all. So depraved are we by nature that the most venomous creatures are our fit types. The old serpent has not only inoculated us with his venom, but he has caused us to be ourselves producers of the like poison : it lies under our lips, ready for use, and, alas, it is all too freely used when we grow angry, and desire to take vengeance upon any who have caused us vexation. It is sadly wonderful what hard things even good men will say when provoked ; yea, even such as call themselves " perfect" in cool blood are not quite as gentle as doves when their claims to sinlessness are bluntly questioned. This poison of evil-speaking would never fall from our lips, however much we might be provoked, if it were not there at other times ; but by nature we have as great a store of venomous words as a cobra has of poison. O Lord, take the poison-bags away, and cause our lips to drop nothing but honey. " *Selah.*" This is heavy work. Go up, go up, my heart ! Sink not too low. Fall not into the lowest key. Lift up thyself to God.

4 Keep me, O LORD, from the hands of the wicked ; preserve me from the violent man ; who have purposed to overthrow my goings.

5 The proud have hid a snare for me, and cords ; they have spread a net by the wayside ; they have set gins for me.　Selah.

4. "*Keep me, O* LORD, *from the hands of the wicked.*" To fall into their hands would be a calamity indeed. David in his most pitiable plight chose to fall into the hand of a chastising God rather than to be left in the power of men. No creature among the wild beasts of the wood is so terrible an enemy to man as man himself when guided by evil, and impelled by violence. The Lord by providence and grace can keep us out of the power of the wicked. He alone can do this, for neither our own watchfulness nor the faithfulness of friends can secure us against the serpentine assaults of the foe. We have need to be preserved from the smooth as well as the rough hands of the ungodly, for their flatteries may harm us as much as their calumnies. The hands of their example may pollute us, and so do us more harm than the hands of their oppression. Jehovah must be our keeper, or evil hands will do what evil hearts have imagined and evil lips have threatened. "*Preserve me from the violent man.*" His intense passion makes him terribly dangerous. He will strike anyhow, use any weapon, smite from any quarter : he is so furious that he is reckless of his own life if he may accomplish his detestable design. Lord, preserve us by thine omnipotence when men attack us with their violence. This prayer is a wise and suitable one. "*Who have purposed to overthrow my goings.*" They resolve to turn the good man from his resolve, they would defeat his designs, injure his integrity, and blast his character. Their own goings are wicked, and therefore they hate those of the righteous, seeing they are a standing rebuke to them. This is a forcible argument to use in prayer with God : he is the patron of holiness, and when the pure lives of his people are in danger of overthrow, he may be expected to interpose. Never let the pious forget to pray, for this is a weapon against which the most determined enemy cannot stand.

5. "*The proud have hid a snare for me.*" Proud as they are, they stoop to this mean action : they use a snare, and they hide it away, that their victim may be taken like a poor hare who is killed without warning—killed in its usual run, by a snare which it could not see. David's enemies wished to snare him in his path of service, the usual way of his life. Saul laid many snares for David, but the Lord preserved him. All around us are snares of one sort or another, and he will be well kept, ay, divinely kept, who never falls into one of them. "*And cords.*" With these they pull the net together and with these they bind their captive. Thus fowlers do, and trappers of certain large animals. The cords of

love are pleasant, but the cords of hate are cruel as death itself. "*They have spread a net by the wayside.*" Where it will be near their prey ; where the slightest divergence from the path will bring the victim into it. Surely the common wayside ought to be safe : men who go out of the way may well be taken in a net, but the path of duty is proverbially the path of safety ; yet it is safe nowhere when malicious persons are abroad. Birds are taken in nets, and men are taken by deceit. Satan instructs his children in the art of fowling, and they right speedily learn how to spread nets : perhaps they have been doing that for us already ; let us make our appeal to God concerning it. "*They have set gins for me.*" One instrument of destruction is not enough ; they are so afraid of missing their prey that they multiply their traps, using differing devices, so that one way or another they may take their victim. Those who avoid the snare and the net may yet be caught in a gin, and accordingly gins are placed in all likely places. If a godly man can be cajoled, or bribed, or cowed, or made angry, the wicked will make the attempt. Ready are they to twist his words, misread his intentions, and misdirect his efforts ; ready to fawn, and lie, and make themselves mean to the last degree so that they may accomplish their abominable purpose. "*Selah.*" The harp needs tuning after such a strain, and the heart needs lifting up towards God.

6 I said unto the LORD, Thou *art* my God : hear the voice of my supplications, O LORD.

7 O GOD the Lord, the strength of my salvation, thou hast covered my head in the day of battle.

8 Grant not, O LORD, the desires of the wicked : further not his wicked device ; *lest* they exalt themselves. Selah.

6. "*I said unto the LORD, Thou art my God.*" Here was David's stay and hope. He was assured that Jehovah was his God, he expressed that assurance, and he expressed it before Jehovah himself. That had need be a good and full assurance which a man dares to lay before the face of the heart-searching Lord. The Psalmist when hunted by man, addressed himself to God. Often the less we say to our foes, and the more we say to our best Friend the better it will fare with us : if we say anything, let it be said unto the Lord. David rejoiced in the fact that he had already said that Jehovah was his God : he was content to have committed himself, he had no wish to draw back. The Lord was David's own by deliberate choice, to which he again sets his seal with delight. The wicked reject God, but the righteous receive him as their own, their treasure, their pleasure, their light and delight. "*Hear the voice of my supplications, O LORD.*" Since thou art mine, I pray thee hear my cries. We cannot ask this favour of another man's god, but we may seek it from our own God. The prayers of saints have a voice in them ; they are expressive pleadings even when they sound like inarticulate moanings.

The Lord can discern a voice in our wailings, and he can and will hearken thereto. Because he is God he can hear us ; because he is *our* God he will hear us. So long as the Lord doth but hear us we are content : the answer may be according to his own will, but we do entreat to be heard : a soul in distress is grateful to any one who will be kind and patient enough to hearken to its tale, but specially is it thankful for an audience with Jehovah. The more we consider his greatness and our insignificance, his wisdom and our folly, the more shall we be filled with praise when the Lord attends unto our cry.

7. "*O GOD the Lord, the strength of my salvation, thou hast covered my head in the day of battle.*" When he looked back upon past dangers and deliverances, the good man felt that he should have perished had not the Lord held a shield over his head. In the day of the clash of arms, or of the putting on of armour (as some read it), the glorious Lord had been his constant Protector. Goliath had his armour-bearer, and so had Saul, and these each one guarded his master ; yet

the giant and the king both perished, while David, without armour or shield, slew the giant and baffled the tyrant. The shield of the Eternal is a better protection than a helmet of brass. When arrows fly thick and the battle-axe crashes right and left, there is no covering for the head like the power of the Almighty. See how the child of providence glorifies his Preserver ! He calls him not only his salvation, but the strength of it, by whose unrivalled force he had been enabled to outlive the cunning and cruelty of his adversaries. He had obtained a deliverance in which the strength of the Omnipotent was clearly to be seen. This is a grand utterance of praise, a gracious ground of comfort, a prevalent argument in prayer. He that has covered our head aforetime will not now desert us. Wherefore let us fight a good fight, and fear no deadly wound : the Lord God is our shield, and our exceeding great reward.

8. "*Grant not, O* Lord, *the desires of the wicked.*" Even they are dependent upon thee · they can do no more than thou dost permit. Thou dost restrain them ; not a dog of them can move his tongue without thy leave and license. Therefore I entreat thee not to let them have their way. Even though they dare to pray to thee, do not hear their prayers against innocent men. Assuredly the Lord Jehovah will be no accomplice with the malevolent ; their desires shall never be his desires ; if they thirst for blood he will not gratify their cruelty. "*Further not his wicked device.*" They are so united as to be like one man in their wishes ; but do not hear their prayers. Though hand join in hand, and they desire and design as one man, yet do not thou lend them the aid of thy providence. Do not permit their malicious schemes to succeed. The Lord may allow success to attend the policy of the wicked for a time for wise reasons unknown to us, but we are permitted to pray that it be not so. The petition " Deliver us from evil " includes and allows such supplication. "*Lest they exalt themselves.*" If successful, the wicked are sure to grow proud, and insult the righteous over whom they have triumphed, and this is so great an evil, and so dishonouring to God, that the Psalmist uses it in his pleading as an argument against their being allowed to prosper. The glory of the wicked is opposed to the glory of God. If God seems to favour them they grow too high for this world, and their heads strike against the heavens. Let us hope that the Lord will not suffer this to be. "*Selah.*" Here let us exalt our thoughts and praises high over the heads of self-exalting sinners. The more they rise in conceit the higher let us rise in confidence.

9 As for the head of those that compass me about, let the mischief of their own lips cover them.

10 Let burning coals fall upon them ; let them be cast into the fire ; into deep pits, that they rise not up again.

11 Let not an evil speaker be established in the earth : evil shall hunt the violent man to overthrow *him.*

9. "*As for the head of those that compass me about, let the mischief of their own lips cover them.*" To the Lord who had covered his head amid the din of arms the Psalmist appeals against his foes, that their heads may be covered in quite another sense—covered with the reward of their own malice. David's foes were so many that they hemmed him in, encircling him as hunters do their prey. It is little wonder that he turns to the Lord in his dire need. The poet represents his adversaries as so united as to have but one head ; for there is often a unanimity among evil spirits which makes them the more strong and terrible for their vile purposes. The *lex talionis*, or law of retaliation, often brings down upon violent men the evil which they planned and spoke of for others : their arrows fall upon themselves. When a man's lips vent curses they will probably, like chickens, come home to roost. A stone hurled upward into the air is apt to fall upon the thrower's head.

David's words may be read in the future as a prophecy ; but in this verse, at any rate, there is no need to do so in order to soften their tone. It is so just that the mischief which men plot and the slander which they speak should recoil upon themselves that every righteous man must desire it : he who does not desire it may wish to be considered humane and Christlike, but the chances are that he has a sneaking agreement with the wicked, or is deficient in a manly sense of right and wrong. When evil men fall into pits which they have digged for the innocent we believe that even the angels are glad ; certainly the most gentle and tender of philanthropists, however much they pity the sufferers, must also approve the justice which makes them suffer. We suspect that some of our excessively soft-spoken critics only need to be put into David's place, and they would become a vast deal more bitter than he ever was.

10. *"Let burning coals fall upon them."* Then will they know that the scattering of the firebrands is not the sport they thought it to be. When hailstones and coals of fire descend upon them, how will they escape ? Even the skies above the wicked are able to deal out vengeance upon them. *"Let them be cast into the fire."* They have kindled the flames of strife, and it is fair that they should be cast therein. They have heated the furnace of slander seven times hotter than it was wont to be heated, and they shall be devoured therein. Who would have pitied Nebuchadnezzar if he had been thrown into his own burning fiery furnace ? *"Into deep pits, that they rise not up again."* They made those ditches or fosses for the godly, and it is meet that they should themselves fall into them and never escape. When a righteous man falls he rises again ; but when the wicked man goes down " he falls like Lucifer, never to hope again." The Psalmist in this passage graphically depicts the Sodom of the wicked persecutor : fire falls upon him from heaven ; the city blazes, and he is cast into the conflagration ; the vale of Siddim is full of slime-pits, and into these he is hurried. Extraordinary judgment overtakes the extraordinary offender : above, around, beneath, all is destruction. He would have consumed the righteous, and now he is consumed himself. So shall it be : so let it be.

11. *"Let not an evil speaker be established in the earth."* For that would be an established plague, a perpetual curse. Men of false and cruel tongues are of most use when they go to fatten the soil in which they rot as carcases : while they are alive they are the terror of the good, and the torment of the poor. God will not allow the specious orators of falsehood to retain the power they temporarily obtain by their deceitful speaking. They may become prominent, but they cannot become permanent. They shall be disendowed and disestablished in spite of all that they can say to the contrary. All evil bears the element of decay within itself ; for what is it but corruption ? Hence the utmost powers of oratory are insufficient to settle upon a sure foundation the cause which bears a lie within it. *"Evil shall hunt the violent man to overthrow him."* He hunted the good, and now his own evil shall hunt him. He tried to overthrow the goings of the righteous, and now his own unrighteousness shall prove his overthrow. As he was violent, so shall he be violently assaulted and hunted down. Sin is its own punishment ; a violent man will need no direr doom than to reap what he has sown. It is horrible for a huntsman to be devoured by his own hounds ; yet this is the sure fate of the persecutor.

12 I know that the LORD will maintain the cause of the afflicted, *and* the right of the poor.

13 Surely the righteous shall give thanks unto thy name : the upright shall dwell in thy presence.

12. *"I know that the* LORD *will maintain the cause of the afflicted, and the right of the poor."* All through the psalm the writer is bravely confident, and speaks of things about which he had no doubt : in fact, no psalm can be more grandly positive than this protest against slander. The slandered saint knew Jehovah's care for the afflicted, for he had received actual proofs of it himself. " I will maintain it" is the motto of the great Defender of the rights of the needy. What

confidence this should create within the bosoms of the persecuted and poverty-stricken ! The prosperous and wealthy can maintain their own cause, but those who are otherwise shall find that God helps those who cannot help themselves. Many talk as if the poor had no rights worth noticing, but they will sooner or later find out their mistake when the Judge of all the earth begins to plead with them.

13. *"Surely the righteous shall give thanks unto thy name."* The former psalm had its "surely," but this is a more pleasing one. As surely as God will slay the wicked he will save the oppressed, and fill their hearts and mouths with praises. Whoever else may be silent, the righteous will give thanks ; and whatever they may suffer, the matter will end in their living through the trial, and magnifying the Lord for his delivering grace. On earth ere long, and in heaven for ever, the pure in heart shall sing unto the Lord. How loud and sweet will be the songs of the redeemed in the millennial age, when the meek shall inherit the earth, and delight themselves in the abundance of peace !

"The upright shall dwell in thy presence." Thus shall they give thanks in the truest and fullest manner. This abiding before the Lord shall render to him "songs without words," and therefore all the more spiritual and true. Their living and walking with their God shall be their practical form of gratitude. Sitting down in holy peace, like children at their father's table, their joyful looks and language shall speak their high esteem and fervent love to him who has become their dwelling-place. How high have we climbed in this psalm—from being hunted by the evil man to dwelling in the divine presence ; so doth faith upraise the saint from the lowest depths to heights of peaceful repose. Well might the song be studded with Selahs, or uplifters.

EXPLANATORY NOTES.

Whole Psalm.—Another Psalm " *of David,*" to be sung by all saints, even as it was used by their Head, David's Son. In it we have (verses 1—3) the *picture of the wicked*, with a *"Selah,"* that bids us pause over its dark colours. Then we have (verses 4, 5) *a view of the snares spread by the wicked*, with another " Selah"-pause. Thereafter, we see a soul in *the attitude of faith* (verses 6—8). They are laying the snares, but calm as Elisha beholding the Syrian host assembling (2 Kings vi. 15), the stayed soul sings—

" *I have said to the Lord, My God art thou* " ;

and then he prays, putting a *"Selah"* at the close, that we may again pause and survey the scene.—*Andrew A. Bonar.*

Whole Psalm.—There is no doubt that this psalm expresses the feelings of David on the first intelligence of Saul's setting out *anew* in pursuit of him (comp. verse 2). And then, in Psalm cxli, we have his supplication at the time when this danger was ever approaching nearer. Various things are said in this psalm (according to the Hebrew) primarily of a single person (Saul :) thus *e.g.,* verses 1, 4 ; and the numerous tongues of which David complains (verse 3) are just the tongues of traitors who again informed Saul of this new place of David's residence in the wilderness of Engedi, where he might have imagined himself so secure. The laying of snares (verse 5) agrees perfectly in part with this treachery, and in part with the search after David by Saul and his numerous army, mentioned in 1 Samuel xxiv. 2. In the same way might the burning coals, spoken of in verse 10, and likewise the deep pits (German, floods) mentioned there, have suggested themselves most naturally to David upon the rocks of Engedi, where he had the Dead Sea just before him. Verse 10 seems also to allude to the events which happened on the night before the destruction of Sodom.—*T. C. Barth, in* "*The Bible Manual.*"

Whole Psalm.—As in Psalm cxxxviii. David set before his seed God's promise as the anchor of hope (2 Sam. vii.) ; and in Psalm cxxxix., God's omniscience as our consolation in danger and motive for shunning evil ; so in this psalm he sets forth the danger from calumnious enemies, and our only safety in Jehovah, our strength.—*Andrew Robert Fausset.*

Verses 1, 4, 6, 8.— Good men live by prayer. He who gets to the throne of grace is covered by the cloud of glory, through which no sun can smite by day, nor moon by night.— *William Swan Plumer.*

Verses 1, 7—11.—On the first reading of this psalm one is inclined to think that there is somewhat of fierceness and bitterness in it, which is hardly consistent with the character of a child of God, and therefore unbecoming in David . . . And yet I really think that a little more examination of the language of this psalm will lead us to believe that we are doing David wrong in affixing anything like a meaning or desire of vindictiveness to his words.

Assuredly we can find no fault with one who takes his wrongs in prayer to God ; who, like Hezekiah, takes the roll of his cares, and sorrows, and trials, and spreads it before the Lord. And this is what David does in the very first verse : "*Deliver me, O LORD, from the evil man ; preserve me from the violent man.*" I do not think a person who does this, who, when smarting under a sense of injury and wrong, goes at once to God and lays open his heart to him, is likely to go very far wrong ; for even though he may have begun in somewhat of an unkindly spirit, yet prayer opens before us such a sight and sense of our own guiltiness and wrongs towards God, and thereby exercises such an abasing, as well as healing and soothing, influence over our feelings towards others, that we might almost be assured that he whose prayer might begin even with a vehement enumeration of his own wrongs, would end with something very like a determination to bless them that cursed, and to do good to them that hated him.

You will observe, too, how, from first to last, David leaves his cause in God's hands ; it is not " my sword and my bow that shall help me " ; he counted them vain things to help a man ; and therefore, as he had so often said in other psalms ; " The Lord was his shield and his defence," and as God had already shielded his head in the day of battle, so he prays for the same protection against his enemies now.—*Barton Bouchier.*

Verses 1, 11.—Three special forms of Satanic energy are individualized. The *evil* or wicked man, the *violent* man, and the *man of tongue* are severally appealed from by the suppliant speaker of the prayer of faith.—*Arthur Pridham.*

Verse 2.—"*Continually are they gathered together for war.*" Literally, this clause reads, " *who gather wars,*" and so some understand it. But it is well known that the prepositions are often omitted in the Hebrew, and no doubt he means that they stirred up general enmity by their false information which acted as a trumpet sounding to battle.—*John Calvin.*

Verses 2, 3.—The wicked assault the righteous with three weapons :—with the heart, by conspiracy ; with the tongue, by lying ; and with the hand, by violence.—*John Lorinus,* 1569—1634.

Verse 3.—"*They have sharpened their tongues like a serpent.*" To sharpen or whet the tongue imports the keenest and extremest kind of talkativeness, much more to sharpen the tongue " *like a serpent.*" Naturalists tell us that no living creature stirs his tongue so swiftly as a serpent, and serpents are therefore said to have a treble tongue, because, moving their tongue so fast, they seem to have three tongues.   The Psalmist means—the wicked speak thick and threefold, they sting and poison me with their tongues.—*Joseph Caryl.*

Verse 3.—"*They have sharpened their tongues like a serpent.*" This is an exact description of the way in which a serpent darts out his tongue before he inflicts the wound. See him : his head is erect, and his piercing eye is wildly and fiercely fixed on the object ; the tongue rapidly appears and disappears, as if by that process it would be sharpened for the contest. Thus were the enemies of

David making sharp their tongues for his destruction.—*Joseph Roberts, in "Oriental Illustrations of the Sacred Scriptures,"* 1835.

Verse 3.—"They have sharpened their tongues like a serpent," etc.   Is it not a fact, that there are many men, the very existence of whom is a baneful poison, as it were ?   They dart their livid tongue like the tongue of a serpent ; and the venom of their disposition corrodes every object upon which it concentrates itself ; ever vilifying and maligning, like the ill-omened bird of night.—*Pliny.*

Verse 3.—"They have sharpened their tongues like a serpent."   As the adder skilfully prepares herself for her work of death, so do the unhappy children of slander and falsehood prepare themselves, by every possible effort, for injuring their unoffending victims.—*John Morison.*

Verse 3.—In St. James's day, as now, it would appear that there were idle men and idle women, who went about from house to house, dropping slander as they went, and yet you could not take up that slander and detect the falsehood there. You could not evaporate the truth in the slow process of the crucible, and then show the residuum of falsehood glittering and visible.   You could not fasten upon any word or sentence, and say that it was calumny ; for in order to constitute slander, it is not necessary that the word spoken should be false—half-truths are often more calumnious than whole falsehoods.   It is not even necessary that a word should be distinctly uttered ; a dropped lip, an arched eyebrow, a shrugged shoulder, a significant look, an incredulous expression of countenance, nay, even an emphatic silence, may do the work ; and when the light and trifling thing which has done the mischief has fluttered off, the venom is left behind, to work and rankle, to inflame hearts, to fever human existence, and to poison human society at the fountain springs of life.   Very emphatically was it said by one whose whole being had smarted under such affliction, *"Adders' poison is under their lips."*—*Frederick William Robertson.*

Verse 3.—Slander and calumny must always precede and accompany persecution, because malice itself cannot excite people against a good man, as such ; to do this, he must first be represented as a bad man.   What can be said of those who are busied in this manner, but that they are a " generation of vipers," the brood of the old " Serpent," that grand accuser and calumniator of the brethren, having under their tongues a bag of " poison," conveying instant death to the reputation on which they fasten.   Thus David was hunted as a rebel, Christ was crucified as a blasphemer, and the primitive Christians were tortured as guilty of incest and murder.—*George Horne.*

Verse 3.—Man consists of soul and body ; the body is but the shadow, or at best but the bearer of the soul : it's the soul that bears God's image ; it's the soul especially for which Christ died.   Now, by how much the soul is more precious than the body, by so much are the helps more excellent, and the enemies more dangerous than the body's.   The body is fed with meat ; but it is perishing meat (1 Cor. vi. 13) ; but the food of the soul is the heavenly manna (John vi. 27). Answerably, the enemies are more hurtful, for that that hurts or kills the body toucheth not the soul ; but what hurts or kills the soul kills the body with it, and destroys the whole man.   The conclusion is, that therefore the bane or poison of the soul is much more hideous, horrible and hateful than that of the body ; and of that poison speaks the present Scripture : *"adders' poison is under their lips."* A strange text, some may say, and 'tis true ; but it is the fitter for these strange times, wherein the poison both of soul and body so far prevails.   The words do describe in part the malignant and malicious nature of the unregenerate and sinful man ; and to that purpose are they cited by the apostle to the Romans (ch. iii. 13).   The *asp* is but a little creature ; but not a little poisonful.   So little a creature hath been the bane and death of many a great person ; let one suffice for all. That royal and renowned Cleopatra, queen of Egypt, chose rather to die by the biting of two asps than to be carried in triumph at Rome by Augustus.   The manner of their poisoning is this,—he that is bitten by the asp falls forthwith into a gentle sweat and a sweet sleep, and his strength and vital spirits decay and weaken by little till he die ; thus the present pain is little, but the stroke is deadly. And even such stings are the tongues, and such swords the words of wicked men. And no marvel; for what can come but poisonful words and actions from them whose very inward nature is all poison within!

The poison of the soul is only *sin*, and this is like to poison in many respects. Poison, wherever it enters, stays not there, but diffuseth itself all over the body, and never ceaseth till it has infected all. Such is the nature of sin; enter where it will it creeps from one member of the body to another, and from the body to the soul, till it has infected the whole man; and then from man to man, till a whole family; and stays not there, but runs like a wildfire, from family to family, till it has poisoned a whole town, and so a whole country, and a whole kingdom. Woeful experience proves this true, both for Popish opinions, idle fashions, vain customs, and ill-examples of all sorts, which once set on foot, spread themselves over the politic body of church and commonwealth, like a gangrene or a leprosy over the natural body, or like a poison through all the blood. Poison, having entered anywhere, as it seeks to creep presently over all, so desires it especially to seize upon the heart; such a malice and pride lies in the malignant nature of it, that it aspires to the heart; and such a craft and cunning lurks in it, that having once entered, it creeps closely and unfelt till it gets to the heart; but having possessed itself of that sovereign part of man, then like a tyrant it reigns and rages, and infecting first the vital blood and noble parts, it diffuseth itself over all and every part. And such is the nature of sin, the spiritual poison of the soul; enter where it will, it is the heart it aims at, and it will never stay till it comes there. The truth of this is so clear that proofs are needless; for who knows not that the senses are but the doors or windows, but the heart is the throne, and the soul itself the seat of sin: and hence it is that Solomon adviseth, —"My son, keep thy heart with all diligence": Prov. iv. 23.—*William Crashaw, in "The Parable of Poyson,"* 1618.

Verse 3.—"*Adders' poison is under their lips.*" The word rendered "*adder*," עַכְשׁוּב, *achsub*, occurs here only; and it is perhaps impossible to determine what species is intended. As the word, in its proper signification, seems to express coiling, or bending back—an act common to most serpents—the name has perhaps no determinate reference; or it may be another name for the *pethen*, mentioned under Job xx.; which seems also to have been the opinion of the Seventy, as they render both words by ἀσπίς, and are followed by the Vulgate (*aspis*).

As to the *poison*, it will be observed, that in the venomous serpents there is a gland under the eye secreting the poisonous matter, which is conveyed, in a small tube or canal, to the end of a fang which lies concealed at the roof of the mouth. This fang is moveable at the pleasure of the serpent, and is protruded when it is about to strike at an antagonist. The situation of this poison, which is, in a manner, behind the upper lip, gives great propriety to the expression, "*adders' poison is under their lips.*" The usage of the Hebrew language renders it by no means improbable that the fang itself is called לָשׁוֹן *lashon*, a tongue, in the present text; and a serpent might then be said to sharpen its tongue, when, in preparing to strike, it protruded its fangs. We do not see any explanation by which a more consistent meaning may be extracted from the expression here employed. —*John Kitto, in the "Pictorial Bible."*

Verse 3.—Often the tongue of the serpent is spoken of as the seat of its venom. This is popular, not scientific language.—*William Swan Plumer.*

Verse 3.—"*Adder.*" The word *acshub* (pronounced ăk-shoob), only occurs in this one passage. The precise species represented by this word is unknown. Buxtorf, however, explains the word as the Spitter, "illud genus quod venenum procul exspuit." Now, if we accept this derivation, we must take the word *acshub* as a synonym for *pethen*. We have already identified the Pethen with the Naja haje, a snake which has the power of expelling the poison to some distance, when it is out of reach of its enemy. Whether the snake really intends to eject the poison, or whether it is merely flung from the hollow fangs by the force of the suddenly-checked stroke, is uncertain. That the Haje cobra can expel its poison is an acknowledged fact, and the Dutch colonists of the Cape have been so familiarly acquainted with this habit, that they have called this reptile by the name of Spuugh-Slange, or Spitting-Snake, a name which, if we accept Buxtorf's etymology, is precisely equivalent to the word *acshub.—J. G. Wood, in "Bible Animals."*

Verses 3, 5, 8.—*"Selah."* We meet with *Selah* here for the first time since Psalm lxxxix. From Psalm xc. to Psalm cxl. no *Selah* occurs. Why omitted in these fifty we cannot tell any more than why so often recurring in others. However, there are only about forty psalms in all in which it is used.—*Andrew A. Bonar.*

Verse 4.—*"Keep me,"* etc. From doing as they do, or as they would have me do, or as they promise themselves I will do.—*Matthew Henry.*

Verse 4.—*"Preserve me from the violent man."* The second clause of the first versicle of this verse is the same as the second versicle of verse 1, which seems the burden of the song.—*"Speaker's Commentary."*

Verse 4.—*"To overthrow my goings."* To take my feet from under me, to destroy the basis of belief, the power of advance in good works, that we may turn back from the way of salvation, or fall upon it, or, at any rate, may go very slowly along it.—*Neale and Littledale.*

Verse 5.—*"The proud have hid a snare for me, and cords."* The following story illustrates how *cords* have been used by thieves so lately as the year 1822 :— "Two skilful leaders of Dacoits, having collected some forty followers, and distributed among them ten matchlocks, ten swords, and twenty-five spears, waylaid a treasure going from the native Collector's treasury at Budrauna to Goruckpore. The prize consisted of £1,200, and was guarded by a Naik, or corporal, with four sepoys and five troopers. It had to pass through a dense jungle, and it was settled—said one of them in after years—'that the attack should take place there ; that we should have strong ropes tied across the road in front and festooned to trees on both sides, and, at a certain distance behind, similar ropes festooned to trees on one side, and ready to be fastened on the other, as soon as the escort of horse and foot should get well in between them.' Having completed these preparations the gang laid down on either side of the road patiently awaiting their prey. 'About five in the morning,' continued the narrator, ' we heard a voice as if calling upon the name of God (Allah), and one of the gang started up at the sound, and said, " Here comes the treasure !" We put five men in front with their match-locks loaded—not with ball but shot, that we might, if possible, avoid killing anybody. When we got the troopers, infantry, and treasure all within the space, the hind ropes were run across the road, and made fast to the trees on the opposite side, and we opened a fire in upon the party from all sides. The foot soldiers got into the jungle at the sides of the road, and the troopers tried to get over the ropes at both ends, but in vain.' The corporal and a horse were killed ; two troopers wounded, and the treasure carried off in spite of a hot pursuit."—*From James Hutton's "Popular Account of the Thugs and Dacoits of India,"* 1857.

Verse 5.—*"The proud have hid a snare for me, and cords."* There was " a trap hidden for him with cords" ; a trap being sunk into some frequented path, and always covered over with grass or brushwood, and having long cords attached to each side, by which the hunter, lurking at a little distance, might close it whenever he saw the game stepping on the spot. But the net spread for him by his enemies extended to the very " side of the encampment," which indicates, that even among the soldiers lying around him, there were some who had been bribed and persuaded to watch and betray him.—*Benjamin Weiss, in "A New Translation of the Psalms, with Notes,"* 1858.

Verse 5.—*"Snare." "Net." "Gins."* The several uses to which the contrivances denoted by the Hebrew words thus rendered were respectively applied, do not appear to be well ascertained. In general the Psalmist alludes to the artifices employed for capturing birds or beasts. It is, however, a curious circumstance, as noticed by Thevenot, that artifices of this kind are literally employed against men as well as other animals by some of the Orientals. "The cunningest robbers in the world," says he, "are in this country. They use a certain slip with a running noose, which they cast with so much sleight about a man's neck when they are within reach of him, that they never fail, so that they strangle him in a trice."—*Richard Mant.*

Verse 6.—"*The voice of my supplications.*" The one safety for simple and unlearned people when assailed by the crafty arguments of heretics and infidels is not controversy, but prayer, a weapon their adversaries seldom use. and cannot understand.—*Bruno of Aste,* 1123.

Verse 7.—"*Thou hast covered my head in the day of battle.*" Hebrew, *of armour.* For David had never indeed any battle with Saul, but declined it ; but Saul often armed against him ; but then God's providence covered him as a shield : but the *head* is only spoken of to set forth his whole body, because that is chiefly aimed at by the enemy, as where the life principally lieth.—*John Mayer.*

Verse 7.—"*Thou hast covered my head,*" etc. That is, I had no other helmet or armour but thy Almighty power in the day when I fought with Goliath. 1 Sam. xvii. 39, 40, 50.—*Thomas Fenton.*

Verse 7.—"*Thou hast covered my head in the day of battle.*" A captain or prince had always beside him in battle an armour-bearer, whose duty it was "to cover his master's head," that is, to ward off with the shield the blows aimed at his head, and which, in the heat of the fight, had escaped his own notice.—*Benjamin Weiss.*

Verse 8.—"*His wicked device*"; which is to destroy me. "*Exalt themselves*"; not only against me, but against thee also, as if by their power and policy they had frustrated thy design and promise made to me.—*M. Pool.*

Verse 9.—"*As for the head of those that compass me about,*" etc. God, he saith, had covered his head in the day of battle : now contrariwise he showeth what should cover the head of his enemies, viz., it should come to them as with their lips they had maliciously spoken against him ; for it may be thus rendered— "The head of my besieger, let the trouble of his lips cover it" : for cursing, let him be covered with cursing as with a cloak."—*John Mayer.*

Verse 9.—"*Those that compass me about.*" For an explanation of this expression we would refer the reader to "The Treasury of David," vol. i. p. 387, where he will find two very pertinent extracts from J. Stevenson and Dr. Shaw.

Verse 9.—"*The mischief of their own lips.*" The pride and hauteur of the Jews in our Lord's day brought the Roman arms upon them, and caused them to fall into irremediable ruin. They invoked their own fate by exposing themselves to an invasion from Rome at all ; but they did it still more in that terrific cry— "His blood be upon us and on our children."—*William Hill Tucker, in "The Psalms, with Notes, Shewing their Prophetic and Christian Character,*" 1840.

Verses 9, 10.—Such passages admit of translation in the future, and are rather predictions than imprecations.—*Ingram Cobbin,* 1839.

Verses 9—11.—The prophet, in these three verses, predicted those just judgments which heaven will inflict on the slanderers and persecutors of the righteous. Their lips, which uttered mischief against others, shall be the means of covering themselves with confusion, when out of their own mouths they shall be judged. Those tongues which have contributed to set the world on fire, shall be tormented with the hot burning coals of eternal vengeance : and they, who, with so much eagerness and diligence have prepared pits for the destruction of their brethren, shall be cast into a deep and bottomless pit, out of which they will not rise up again any more for ever. Evil speakers and false accusers shall gain no lasting establishment, but punishment shall hunt sin through all its doubles, and seize it at last as its legal prey. Let these great truths be firmly rooted in our hearts, and they will keep us steady in the worst of times.—*George Horne.*

Verse 10.—*"Let burning coals fall upon them,"* etc. The Psalmist seems here to allude to the destruction of the Sodomites. In these imprecations he considered his enemies as the enemies of God, rather than as his own ; and he thus cursed them, as knowing, in the quality of a prophet, that God himself had cursed them : and therefore these sorts of imprecations do not authorize other persons to curse their enemies.—*Thomas Fenton.*

Verse 10.—*"Let burning coals fall upon them,"* etc. An imprecation which (with the similar previous one, Psalm ix. 6, etc.) is a prophecy ; and one which, while it has had no fulfilment in the case of David's enemies, or any persecutors of the church in times past, brings again vividly before the mind the fiery judgment of the Lord's coming, and the awful sentence already pronounced against " the beast and false prophet," the leaders of the confederation of the kings of the earth and their armies, then " gathered together to make war against him"—" these were cast alive into the lake of fire burning with brimstone" : Rev. xix. 19, 20. So before, Psalm lv. 15 ; lxiii. 9.—*William De Burgh.*

Verse 11.—*"Let not an evil speaker* [*a man full of tongue*] *be established,"* etc. The man given to talk, the liar, the flatterer, the detractor, the scold, the brawler, " shall not be established in the earth," for such people are abhorred by the wicked as well as by the good.—*Robert Bellarmine.*

Verse 11.—*"Let not an evil speaker be established,"* etc. The positions laid down in this verse will find abundant illustration in every age of the church. *"An evil speaker,"* who takes delight in wounding the reputation of others, is seldom established or prospered in the earth. Providence fights against such an unhappy wretch. *"The violent man,"* the Ishmaelite whose hand is against every man, is in general overthrown by the very same weapons which he wields against others. —*John Morison.*

Verse 11.—*"An evil speaker."* By " a man of the tongue," as the original has it, the Hebrews express a *detractor* or *sycophant ;* one who gives his tongue the liberty to vent what mischief he pleases. The Chaldee here expresses it by *a delator* or vile informer with a *threefold* or *three-forked tongue ;* because such a man wounds *three* at once ; the receiver, the sufferer, and himself.—*Thomas Fenton.*

Verse 11.—*"Evil shall hunt the violent man to overthrow him."* 'Tis an allusion to hounds that are of a quick scent, and pursue the game with pleasure ; they do not see the deer or the hare, yet they follow upon the scent ; and though they have sometimes a very cold and dead scent, yet they will follow and work it out. Thus " evil shall hunt the violent man to overthrow him "; and though sometimes he hath, as it were, got out of the view or sight of evil, and thinks himself under covert, yet these evils, like a company of greedy hounds, will pursue till they have overtaken and overthrown him.—*Joseph Caryl.*

Verse 12.—*"I know."* For I have a promise of it, and that's infallible.—*John Trapp.*

Verses 12, 13.—*"I know that the* LORD *will maintain the cause,"* etc. Why, how comes the Psalmist so confident ? *"Surely the righteous shall give thanks unto thy name":* as if he had said, Thou hast a name for a gracious and faithful God in thy promise, and this thou wilt never suffer to be blotted by failing in thy work. Christian, thou mayest venture all thou art worth on the public faith of Heaven : " His words are pure, as silver tried seven times in a furnace." He that will not suffer a liar or covenant-breaker to set foot on his holy hill, will much less suffer any one thought of falseness or unfaithfulness to enter into his own most holy heart.—*William Gurnall.*

Verse 13.—*"Surely the righteous shall give thanks unto thy name,"* etc. Teacheth us two things, first, that it becometh the godly to show themselves continually thankful, because God is continually merciful to them ; secondly, what is the excellent estate and condition of God's children, which, though it do not yet appear, yet shall it in the end break forth with fulness of glory."—*Thomas Wilcocks.*

Verse 13.—"*The upright shall dwell in thy presence.*" "*Sit in thy presence,*" as thy friends or guests or favoured servants. Perhaps it may mean *sit* (*enthroned*) *before thee.* Compare Matt. xix. 28. Some understand the sense to be *shall dwell* (in the land) *before thee,* i.e., under thy protection and inspection.—*Joseph Addison Alexander.*

HINTS TO THE VILLAGE PREACHER.

Verses 1—5.—I. The particular source of David's affliction : it was from men. In this he was a type of Christ. 1. Their wickedness : "the evil man." 2. Their violence : "the violent man." 3. Their malicious designs : "which imagine mischiefs in their heart." 4. Their confederacy : "continually are they gathered together for war." 5. Their false accusations : "They have sharpened their tongues like a serpent," etc. (verse 3). 6. Their avowed design : "they have purposed to overthrow my goings" (verse 4). 7. Their intrigues (verse 5). II. His universal remedy : "Deliver me, O LORD " ; "preserve" and help me. His defence is, 1. In God. 2. In prayer to God.—*G. R.*

Verses 1—5.—In our position, age, and country, we are not in danger of violence from men, as was David ; still, no man is absolutely safe from the danger. I. Mention some cases not yet impossible. 1. A Christian workman, because he cannot comply with unrighteous customs, excites the animosity of his fellow workers. They will do him mischief, spoil his work, steal his tools, speak evil of him, until his employer discharges him to restore peace in the factory. 2. A Christian clerk or shop assistant, because his presence is a check upon his sinful companions, may have snares laid for him, etc. II. Suggest advice, useful, should such a case arise. 1. Resort to God with a " Deliver me," and a " Preserve me." 2. Maintain integrity and uprightness. 3. Should the mischievous ones succeed, still trust in God, who can make their mischief lead to your profit, and make his goodness outwit their devices.—*J. F.*

Verse 3.—The depraved state of the natural man as to his speech.

Verse 4 (*first clause*).—A wise prayer. The wicked will slander, and oppress, or mislead, flatter and defile. No one can keep us but the Lord.

Verse 5.—The Dangers of Society. I. The secrecy of the attacks of the ungodly : "hid a snare." II. The variety of their weapons : "and cords." III. The cunning choice of position : "by the wayside." IV. The object of their designs : "for me" : they desire to destroy the man himself.

Verse 5.—"The Net by the Wayside," or, covert temptations ; temptations brought near, and made applicable to daily life.

Verse 6.—I. The language of assurance. II. The plea for acceptance in prayer.

Verses 6, 7.—David comforted himself, 1. In his interest in God : "I said . . . thou art my God." 2. In his access to God : he had leave to speak to him, and might expect an answer of peace : " Hear," etc. 3. In the assurance he had of help from God, and happiness in him (verse 7). 4. In the experience he had formerly of God's care of him : " Thou hast covered my head in the day of battle."—*Matthew Henry.*

Verses 6—8.—Three arguments to be pleaded in a prayer for protection. I. The believer's covenanted property in God. " I said . . . thou art my God." II. The past mercies of God. " Thou hast covered," etc. III. The impropriety of the wicked being encouraged in their wickedness, ver. 8.—*J. F.*

Verses 6, 7—12.—The Consolations of the Believer in Time of Trouble. I. What he can say. II. What he can remember. III. What he is assured of.

Verses 6, 7, 12, 13.—Times of Assault, Slander, and Temptation should be special times of Prayer and Faith. David here makes prominent five things. I. *Possession asserted.* 1. The Possession : " My God." Opposed to idols. Beloved by self. 2. The Claim published. 3. The Witness selected. Secret.

Sacred. Searching. 4. The Occasion chosen. II. *Petition presented.* 1. His prayers were frequent. 2. His prayers were full of meaning. 3. His prayers were meant for God. 4. His prayers needed divine attention. III. *Preservation experienced.* 1. God had been his Armour-bearer. 2. God had guarded his most vital part. 3. God had saved him. 4. God's strength had been displayed. IV. *Protection expected.* 1. God is a righteous Judge. 2. God is a compassionate Friend. 3. God is a well-known Guardian. V. *Praise predicted.* 1. Praise assured by gratitude. 2. Praise expressed by words. 3. Praise implied by confidence. 4. Praise practised by communion.

Verse 9.—How the sin of evil-speakers comes home to them.—*W. B. H.*

Verse 11 (first clause).—I. Notice a few varieties of evil speakers. 1. Liars ; the common liar, the trade liar, the stock-exchange liar, the political liar, etc. 2. Scandal-mongers. 3. Blasphemers and swearers. 4. Libertines and seducers. 5. Sceptics and new theology inventors. II. The propriety of the prayer. 1. Because evil speaking is intrinsically an evil thing. 2. It is an extensively injurious thing. 3. He who would have God's truth established must needs desire that evil speaking must fail. III. The limitation of the prayer : " In the earth." 1. It is certain an evil speaker cannot be established in heaven, nor in hell. 2. The earth is the only sphere of his influence ; but, alas ! men on the earth are too prone to be influenced by him. 3. Then, become righteous and true, by faith in the Righteous One and the " Truth."—*J. F.*

Verse 11 (second clause).—The Cruel Hunter pursued by his own Dogs.

Verse 11 (second clause).—Theme—Sins committed, and not repented of, pursue men to their ruin. I. Illustrate. 1. They may raise a force of opposition from men. Tarquin, Napoleon, etc. 2. They may precipitate ruin, as Haman was hunted by his own sin to the gallows. 3. They may arouse destructive remorse, as in Judas. 4. Certainly they will pursue to the judgment-seat, and hunt the soul into hell. II. Apply. 1. How fearful a thing must sin be. 2. The more terrible because self-created. 3. Flee from the avenging pursuers to Christ, the only and safe refuge.—*J. F.*

Verse 11 (second clause).—The hunt and pursuit of the violent sinner. I. The progress of the chase. 1. At first the victim is ignorant of it. 2. But ere long he finds Scripture, conscience, God, Death, at his heels. 3. His own sins cry loudest after him. II. The issue of the hunt. Hemmed in, overthrown, lost for ever, unless he repent. III. Another Huntsman. " The Son of man is come to seek and save that which was lost."—*W. B. H.*

Verse 12.—I. The known fact. II. The reasons for being so assured of it. III. The conduct arising out of the knowledge.

Verse 12.—Something worth knowing. I. By the afflicted and the poor who trust in the Lord. II. By the oppressors who afflict and do the wrong. III. By all men, that they may trust in the Lord, and praise him for his compassion towards the needy, and for his even-handed justice.—*J. F.*

Verses 12, 13.—I. Trust under all circumstances (verse 12). II. Gratitude for all things : " The righteous shall give thanks unto thy name." III. Safety at all times : " The upright shall dwell in thy presence."—*G. R.*

Verse 13.—One of the noblest forms of praise,—dwelling in the presence of God. Or, reverent regard to God's presence, holy communion with the Lord, confiding rest in God's dealings, obedient doing of the heavenly will—the best way of giving thanks to God.

Verse 13.—Two assertions beyond contradiction. I. The righteous are sure to give thanks to God, let others be as thankless as they will. For, 1. They recognise all their good as coming from God. 2. They realise themselves as unworthy of the good they receive. 3. They are anxious to do right, because they are righteous ; and that involves thanksgiving. 4. Thankfulness is a part of the joy derived from what they enjoy. II. The upright are sure to dwell in God's presence. 1. In the sense of setting the Lord before them. 2. In the sense of an abiding present fellowship with God. 3. In the sense of enjoying God's approval. 4. In the sense of dwelling in heaven for ever.—*J. F.*

PSALM CXLI.

TITLE.—A PSALM OF DAVID. *Yes, David under suspicion, half afraid to speak lest he should speak unadvisedly while trying to clear himself; David slandered and beset by enemies; David censured even by saints, and taking it kindly; David deploring the condition of the godly party of whom he was the acknowledged head: David waiting upon God with confident expectation. The Psalm is one of a group of four, and it bears a striking likeness to the other three. Its meaning lies so deep as to be in places exceedingly obscure, yet even upon its surface it has dust of gold. In its commencement the psalm is lighted up with the evening glow as the incense rises to heaven; then comes a night of language whose meaning we cannot see; and this gives place to morning light in which our eyes are unto the Lord.*

DIVISION.—*The Psalmist cries for acceptance in prayer (verses 1, 2); then he begs to be kept as to his speech, preserved in heart and deed, and delivered from every sort of fellowship with the ungodly. He prefers to be rebuked by the gracious rather than to be flattered by the wicked, and consoles himself with the confident assurance that he will one day be understood by the godly party, and made to be a comfort to them (verses 3—6). In the last verses the slandered saint represents the condition of the persecuted church, looks away to God and pleads for rescue from his cruel enemies, and for the punishment of his oppressors.*

EXPOSITION.

L ORD, I cry unto thee : make haste unto me ; give ear unto
my voice, when I cry unto thee.

2 Let my prayer be set forth before thee *as* incense ; *and* the
lifting up of my hands *as* the evening sacrifice.

1. "LORD, *I cry unto thee.*" This is my last resort : prayer never fails me.
My prayer is painful and feeble, and worthy only to be called a cry ; but it is a
cry unto Jehovah, and this ennobles it. I have cried unto thee, I still cry to
thee, and I always mean to cry to thee. To whom else could I go ? What else
can I do ? Others trust to themselves, but I cry unto thee. The weapon of all
prayer is one which the believer may always carry with him, and use in every
time of need. "*Make haste unto me.*" His case was urgent, and he pleaded that
urgency. God's time is the best time, but when we are sorely pressed we may
with holy importunity quicken the movements of mercy. In many cases, if help
should come late, it would come too late ; and we are permitted to pray against
such a calamity. "*Give ear unto my voice, when I cry unto thee.*" See how a second time he talks of crying : prayer had become his frequent, yea, his constant
exercise : twice in a few words he says, "I cry ; I cry." How he longs to be
heard, and to be heard at once ! There is a voice to the great Father in every
cry, and groan, and tear of his children : he can understand what they mean
when they are quite unable to express it. It troubles the spirit of the saints
when they fear that no favourable ear is turned to their doleful cries : they cannot rest unless their "unto thee" is answered by an "unto me." When prayer
is a man's only refuge, he is deeply distressed at the bare idea of his failing
therein.

> "That were a grief I could not bear,
> Didst thou not hear and answer prayer ;
> But a prayer-hearing, answering God
> Supports me under every load."

2. "*Let my prayer be set forth before thee as incense.*" As incense is carefully
prepared, kindled with holy fire, and devoutly presented unto God, so let my
prayer be. We are not to look upon prayer as easy work requiring no thought.

it needs to be "set forth"; what is more, it must be set forth "before the Lord," by a sense of his presence and a holy reverence for his name: neither may we regard all supplication as certain of divine acceptance, it needs to be set forth before the Lord "as incense," concerning the offering of which there were rules to be observed, otherwise it would be rejected of God. "*And the lifting up of my hands as the evening sacrifice.*" Whatever form his prayer might take his one desire was that it might be accepted of God. Prayer is sometimes presented without words by the very motions of our bodies: bended knees and lifted hands are the tokens of earnest, expectant prayer. Certainly work, or the lifting up of the hands in labour, is prayer if it be done in dependence upon God and for his glory: there is a hand-prayer as well as a heart-prayer, and our desire is that this may be sweet unto the Lord as the sacrifice of eventide. Holy hope, the lifting up of hands that hang down, is also a kind of worship: may it ever be acceptable with God. The Psalmist makes a bold request: he would have his humble cries and prayers to be as much regarded of the Lord as the appointed morning and evening sacrifices of the holy place. Yet the prayer is by no means too bold, for, after all, the spiritual is in the Lord's esteem higher than the ceremonial, and the calves of the lips are a truer sacrifice than the calves of the stall.

So far we have a prayer about prayer: we have a distinct supplication in the two following verses.

3 Set a watch, O LORD, before my mouth; keep the door of my lips.

4 Incline not my heart to *any* evil thing, to practise wicked works with men that work iniquity: and let me not eat of their dainties.

5 Let the righteous smite me; *it shall be* a kindness: and let him reprove me; *it shall be* an excellent oil, *which* shall not break my head: for yet my prayer also *shall be* in their calamities.

6 When their judges are overthrown in stony places, they shall hear my words; for they are sweet.

3. "*Set a watch, O* LORD, *before my mouth.*" That mouth had been used in prayer, it would be a pity it should ever be defiled with untruth, or pride, or wrath; yet so it will become unless carefully watched, for these intruders are ever lurking about the door. David feels that with all his own watchfulness he may be surprised into sin, and so he begs the Lord himself to keep him. When Jehovah sets the watch the city is well guarded: when the Lord becomes the guard of our mouth the whole man is well garrisoned. "*Keep the door of my lips.*" God has made our lips the door of the mouth, but we cannot keep that door of ourselves, therefore do we entreat the Lord to take the rule of it. O that the Lord would both open and shut our lips, for we can do neither the one nor the other aright if left to ourselves. In times of persecution by ungodly men we are peculiarly liable to speak hastily, or evasively, and therefore we should be specially anxious to be preserved in that direction from every form of sin. How condescending is the Lord! We are ennobled by being door-keepers for him, and yet he deigns to be a door-keeper for us.

"*Incline not my heart to any evil thing.*" It is equivalent to the petition, "Lead us not into temptation." O that nothing may arise in providence which would excite our desires in a wrong direction. The Psalmist is here careful of his heart. He who holds the heart is lord of the man: but if the tongue and the heart are under God's care all is safe. Let us pray that he may never leave us to our own inclinings, or we shall soon decline from the right.

"*To practise wicked works with men that work iniquity.*" The way the heart inclines the life soon tends: evil things desired bring forth wicked things practised. Unless the fountain of life is kept pure the streams of life will soon be polluted. Alas, there is great power in company : even good men are apt to be swayed by association ; hence the fear that we may practise wicked works when we are with wicked workers. We must endeavour not to be with them lest we sin with them. It is bad when the heart goes the wrong way alone, worse when the life runs in the evil road alone ; but it is apt to increase unto a high degree of ungodliness when the backslider runs the downward path with a whole horde of sinners around him. Our practice will be our perdition if it be evil : it is an aggravation of sin rather than an excuse for it to say that it is our custom and our habit. It is God's practice to punish all who make a practice of iniquity. Good men are horrified at the thought of sinning as others do ; the fear of it drives them to their knees. Iniquity, which, being interpreted, is a want of equity, is a thing to be shunned as we would avoid an infectious disease. *"And let me not eat of their dainties."* If we work with them we shall soon eat with them. They will bring out their sweet morsels, and delicate dishes, in the hope of binding us to their service by the means of our palates. The trap is baited with delicious meats that we may be captured and become meat for their malice. If we would not sin with men we had better not sit with them, and if we would not share their wickedness we must not share their wantonness.

5. *"Let the righteous smite me ; it shall be a kindness."* He prefers the bitters of gracious company to the dainties of the ungodly. He would rather be smitten by the righteous than feasted by the wicked. He gives a permit to faithful admonition, he even invites it—" let the righteous smite me." When the ungodly smile upon us their flattery is cruel ; when the righteous smite us their faithfulness is kind. Sometimes godly men rap hard ; they do not merely hint at evil, but hammer at it ; and even then we are to receive the blows in love, and be thankful to the hand which smites so heavily. Fools resent reproof ; wise men endeavour to profit by it. *"And let him reprove me ; it shall be an excellent oil, which shall not break my head."* Oil breaks no heads, and rebuke does no man any harm ; rather, as oil refreshes and perfumes, so does reproof when fitly taken sweeten and renew the heart. My friend must love me well if he will tell me of my faults : there is an unction about him if he is honest enough to point out my errors. Many a man has had his head broken at the feasts of the wicked, but none at the table of a true-hearted reprover. The oil of flattery is not excellent ; the oil so lavishly used at the banquet of the reveller is not excellent ; head-breaking and heart-breaking attend the anointings of the riotous ; but it is otherwise with the severest censures of the godly : they are not always sweet, but they are always excellent ; they may for the moment bruise the heart, but they never break either it or the head. *"For yet my prayer also shall be in their calamities."* Gracious men never grow wrathful with candid friends so as to harbour an ill-feeling against them ; if so, when they saw them in affliction, they would turn round upon them and taunt them with their rebukes. Far from it ; these wisely grateful souls are greatly concerned to see their instructors in trouble, and they bring forth their best prayers for their assistance. They do not merely pray for them, but they so closely and heartily sympathize that their prayers are " in their calamities," down in the dungeon with them. So true is Christian brotherhood that we are with our friends in sickness or persecution, suffering their griefs ; so that our heart's prayer is in their sorrows. When we can give good men nothing more, let us give them our prayers, and let us do this doubly to those who have given us their rebukes.

6. This is a verse of which the meaning seems far to seek. Does it refer to the righteous among the Israelites ? We think so. David surely means that when their leaders fell never to rise again, they would then turn to him and take delight in listening to his voice. *"When their judges are overthrown in stony places, they shall hear my words ; for they are sweet."* And so they did : the death of Saul made all the best of the nation look to the son of Jesse as the Lord's anointed ; his words became sweet to them. Many of those good men who had spoken severely of David's quitting his country, and going over to the Philistines, were nevertheless dear to his heart for their fidelity, and to them he

returned nothing but good-will, loving prayers, and sweet speeches, knowing that by-and-by they would overlook his faults, and select him to be their leader. They smote him when he erred, but they recognized his excellences. He, on his part, bore no resentment, but loved them for their honesty. He would pray for them when their land lay bleeding at the feet of their foreign enemies ; he would come to their rescue when their former leaders were slain ; and his words of courageous hopefulness would be sweet in their ears. This seems to me to be a good sense, consistent with the context. At the same time, other and more laboured interpretations have their learned admirers, and to these we will refer in our notes from other authors.

7 Our bones are scattered at the grave's mouth, as when one cutteth and cleaveth *wood* upon the earth.

8 But mine eyes *are* unto thee, O GOD the Lord : in thee is my trust ; leave not my soul destitute.

9 Keep me from the snares *which* they have laid for me, and the gins of the workers of iniquity.

10 Let the wicked fall into their own nets, whilst that I withal escape.

7. David's case seemed hopeless : the cause of God in Israel was as a dead thing, even as a skeleton broken, and rotten, and shovelled out of the grave, to return as dust to its dust. "*Our bones are scattered at the grave's mouth.*" There seemed to be no life, no cohesion, no form, order, or headship among the godly party in Israel : Saul had demolished it, and scattered all its parts, so that it did not exist as an organized whole. David himself was like one of these dried bones, and the rest of the godly were in much the same condition. There seemed to be no vitality or union among the holy seed ; but their cause lay at death's door. "*As when one cutteth and cleaveth wood upon the earth.*" They were like wood divided and thrown apart : not as one piece of timber, nor even as a bundle, but all cut to pieces, and thoroughly divided. Leaving out the word "wood," which is supplied by the translators, the figure relates to cleaving upon the earth, which probably means ploughing, but may signify any other form of chopping and splitting, such as felling a forest, tearing up bushes, or otherwise causing confusion and division. How often have good men thought thus of the cause of God ! Wherever they have looked, death, division, and destruction have stared them in the face. Cut and cloven, hopelessly sundered ! Scattered, yea, scattered at the grave's mouth ! Split up and split for the fire ! Such the cause of God and truth has seemed to be. "Upon the earth" the prospect was wretched ; the field of the church was ploughed, harrowed, and scarified : it had become like a wood-chopper's yard, where everything was doomed to be broken up. We have seen churches in such a state, and have been heart-broken. What a mercy that there is always a place above the earth to which we can look ! There lives One who will give a resurrection to his cause, and a reunion to his divided people. He will bring up the dead bones from the grave's mouth, and make the dried faggots live again. Let us imitate the Psalmist in the next verse, and look up to the living God.

8. "*But mine eyes are unto thee, O GOD the Lord.*" He looked upward and kept his eyes fixed there. He regarded duty more than circumstances ; he considered the promise rather than the external providence ; and he expected from God rather than from men. He did not shut his eyes in indifference or despair, neither did he turn them to the creature in vain confidence, but he gave his eyes to his God, and saw nothing to fear. Jehovah his Lord is also his hope. Thomas called Jesus Lord and God, and David here speaks of his God and Lord. Saints delight to dwell upon the divine names when they are adoring or appealing. "*In thee is my trust.*" Not alone in thine attributes or in thy promises, but in thyself. Others might confide where they chose, but David kept to his God : in him

he trusted always, only, confidently, and unreservedly. "*Leave not my soul destitute*"; as it would be if the Lord did not remember and fulfil his promise. To be destitute in circumstances is bad, but to be destitute in soul is far worse ; to be left of friends is a calamity, but to be left of God would be destruction. Destitute of God is destitution with a vengeance. The comfort is that God hath said, " I will never leave thee nor forsake thee."

9. "*Keep me from the snares which they have laid for me.*" He had before asked, in verse 3, that the door of his mouth might be kept ; but his prayer now grows into " Keep *me*." He seems more in trouble about covert temptation than concerning open attacks. Brave men do not dread battle, but they hate secret plots. We cannot endure to be entrapped like unsuspecting animals ; therefore we cry to the God of wisdom for protection. "*And the gins of the workers of iniquity.*" These evil workers sought to catch* David in his speech or acts. This was in itself a piece of in-equity, and so of a piece with the rest of their conduct. They were bad themselves, and they wished either to make him like themselves, or to cause him to seem so. If they could not catch the good man in one way, they would try another ; snares and gins should be multiplied, for anyhow they were determined to work his ruin. Nobody could preserve David but the Omniscient and Omnipotent One : he also will preserve us. It is hard to keep out of snares which you cannot see, and to escape gins which you cannot discover. Well might the much-hunted Psalmist cry, " Keep me."

10. "*Let the wicked fall into their own nets, whilst that I withal escape.*" It may not be a Christian prayer, but it is a very just one, and it takes a great deal of grace to refrain from crying *Amen* to it ; in fact, grace does not work towards making us wish otherwise concerning the enemies of holy men. Do we not all wish the innocent to be delivered, and the guilty to reap the result of their own malice ? Of course we do, if we are just men. There can be no wrong in desiring that to happen in our own case which we wish for all good men. Yet is there a more excellent way.

EXPLANATORY NOTES.

Whole Psalm.—This psalm, like the one before it, is distinguished by a pregnant brevity and the use of rare expressions, while at the same time it is full of verbal and real coincidences with the other psalms of David. These indications are so clear and undeniable, that a sceptical critic of great eminence (De Wette) pronounces it one of the oldest psalms in the collection.—*Joseph Addison Alexander.*

Whole Psalm.—Few psalms in so small a compass crowd together so many gems of precious and holy truth.—*Barton Bouchier.*

Whole Psalm.—Many commentators are strongly of opinion that this psalm was written as a memorial of that very interesting scene in the life of David recorded in 1 Sam. xxiv., relating to his generous treatment of Saul. Though he had an opportunity of putting his cruel persecutor to death in the cave of Engedi, yet he spared his life, only cutting off his skirt, and not suffering his followers to touch him ; and when Saul had gone out of the cave, David, going out after him, remonstrated with him from some distance in the gentlest and most respectful language in regard to the injustice of his conduct towards him. It is thought that the sixth verse contains so express a reference to this very remarkable occurrence in David's history, as to leave little doubt that it was the occasion on which the psalm was composed.—*James Anderson's Note to Calvin, in loc.*

Whole Psalm.—The imagery and allusions of the psalm are in keeping ; viz., the oil which had lately anointed him ; and the watch before his mouth, etc., suggested by the watching at the mouth of the cave, though ultimately referring to the tabernacle service.—*John Jebb.*

Verse 1.—" LORD, *I cry unto thee.*" Misbelief doth seek many ways for delivery from trouble ; but faith hath but one way,—to go to God, to wit, by prayer, for whatsoever is needful. — *David Dickson.*

Verse 1.—" LORD, *I cry unto thee.*" No distress or danger, how great soever, shall stifle my faith or stop my mouth, but it shall make me more earnest, and my prayers, like strong streams in narrow straits, shall bear down all before them.— *John Trapp.*

Verse 1.—"*Unto thee . . . unto me.*" Our prayer and God's mercy are like two buckets in a well ; while the one ascends, the other descends. —*Ezekiel Hopkins.*

Verse 1.—Note that the difference of tense, "*I have cried* " (Heb., LXX., and Vulgate) followed by " *when I cry,*" signifies the earnest perseverance of the saint in prayer, never ceasing, so long as trouble lasts. And trouble does last so long as we are in the world ; wherefore the apostle teaches us to " Pray without ceasing."—*Augustine and Bruno, in Neale and Littledale.*

Verses 1—5.—That the Psalmist was now in some distress, whereof he was deeply sensible, is evident from the vehemency of his spirit, which he expresseth in the reiteration of his request or supplication (verse 1) ; and by his desire that his " prayer might come before the Lord like incense, and the lifting up of his hands as the evening sacrifice" (verse 2). The Jewish expositors guess, not improbably, that in that allusion he had regard unto his present exclusion from the holy services of the tabernacle, which in other places he deeply complains of.

For the matter of his prayer in this beginning of the psalm, it respecteth himself, and his deportment under his present condition, which he desireth may be harmless and holy, becoming himself, and useful to others. And whereas he was two ways liable to miscarry ; first, by too high an exasperation of spirit against his oppressors and persecutors ; and, secondly, by a fraudulent and pusillanimous compliance with them in their wicked courses ;—which are the two extremes which men are apt sinfully to run into in such conditions : he prays earnestly to be delivered from them both. The first he hath respect unto in verse 3, "*Set a watch, O* LORD, *before my mouth ; keep the door of my lips* " : namely, that he might not, under those great provocations which were given him, break forth into an unseemly intemperance of speech against his unjust oppressors, which sometimes fierce and unreasonable cruelties will wrest from the most sedate and moderate spirits. But it was the desire of this holy Psalmist, as in like cases it should be ours, that his heart might be always preserved in such a frame, under the conduct of the Spirit of God, as not to be surprised into an expression of distempered passion in any of his words or sayings. The other he regards in his earnest supplication to be delivered from it, verse 4 : "*Incline not my heart to any evil thing, to practise wicked works with men that work iniquity : and let me not eat of their dainties.*" There are two parts of his request unto the purpose intended. 1. That by the power of God's grace influencing his mind and soul, his heart might not be inclined unto any communion or society with his wicked adversaries in their wickedness. 2. That he might be preserved from a liking of, or a longing after those things, which are the baits and allurements whereby men are apt to be drawn into societies and conspiracies with the workers of iniquity ; "*And let me not eat of their dainties.*" See Prov. i. 10—14. For he here describeth the condition of men prospering for a season in a course of wickedness ; they first jointly give up themselves unto the practice of iniquity, and then together solace themselves in those satisfactions of their lusts, with which their power and interest in the world do furnish them.

These are the " *dainties,*" for which an impotent longing and desire do betray the minds of unstable persons unto a compliance with ways of sin and folly : for I look on these " *dainties* " as comprising whatever the lust of the eyes, the lust of the flesh, or the pride of life can afford. All these David prays to be delivered from any inclination unto ; especially when they are made the allurements of a course of sin. In the enjoyment of these " *dainties,*" it is the common practice of wicked men to soothe up, and mutually encourage one another in the way and course wherein they are engaged. And this completes that poor felicity which in this world so many aspire unto, and whereof alone they are capable. The whole of it is but a society in perishing sensual enjoyments, without control, and with mutual applauses from one another. This the Psalmist had a special regard unto when casting his eye towards another communion and society which he longed after (verse 5). He saw there not dainties but rebukes : he discerned that which is most opposite unto those mutual applauses and rejoicings in one another, which is the salt and cement of all evil societies, for he noticed rebukes and reproofs for the least miscarriages that shall be observed. Now whereas the dainties which some enjoy in a course of prosperous wickedness, are that alone which seems to have anything in it amongst them that is desirable, and on the other side rebukes and reproofs are those alone which seem to have any sharpness, or matter of un-easiness and dislike in the society of the godly, David balanceth that which seem-eth to be sharpest in the one society, against that which seems to be sweetest in the other, and, without respect unto other advantages, prefers the one above the other. Hence, some read the beginning of the words, " Let the righteous *rather* smite me," meaning, " rather than that I should eat of the dainties of the un-godly."—*John Owen.*

Verse 2.—*"Let my prayer be set forth before thee."* Margin, *directed.* The He-brew word means to fit ; to establish ; to make firm. The Psalmist desires that his prayer should not be like that which is feeble, languishing, easily dissipated ; but that it should be like that which is firm and secure.—*Albert Barnes.*

Verse 2.—*"Let my prayer be set forth before thee as incense."* Literally, Let my prayer, incense, be set in order before Thee,—implying that prayer was in the reality what incense was in the symbol. . . . Passing to New Testament Scrip-ture, though still only to that portion which refers to Old Testament times, we are told of the people without being engaged in prayer, while Zacharias was offering incense within the Sanctuary (Luke i. 10) ; they were in spirit going along with the priestly service. And in the book of Revelation the prayers of saints are once and again identified with the offering of incense on the golden altar before the throne. Rev. v. 8 ; viii. 3, 4.—*Patrick Fairbairn, in " The Typology of Scripture."*

Verse 2.—*"Set forth."* Prayer is, knowing work, believing work, thinking work, searching work, humbling work, and nothing worth if heart and hand do not join in it.—*Thomas Adam,* 1701—1784.

Verse 2.—*"Set forth before thee as incense,"* whose fragrant smoke still ascends upwards. But many times in the very ascent, whilst it strives up higher and higher, *infimo phantasmate verberatur,* saith Gregory, " it is beaten back again by earthly imaginations which intervene," and then is extenuated by degrees, and vanisheth to nothing. Therefore the prophet prays *ut dirigatur oratio,* " that his prayer may be set before God," *ut stabiliatur ;* so some render it out of the He-brew, " that it may be established," that it may neither evaporate itself nor be whiffed about with the wind of vain and contrary imaginations, which come *ab extrinseco* [from without], and may corrupt it.—*Anthony Farindon.*

Verse 2.—*"As incense."* That in general by *incense* prayer is signified, the Scripture expressly testifieth. And there is a fourfold resemblance between them : 1. In that *it was beaten and pounded* before it was used. So doth accept-able prayer proceed from a broken and contrite heart : Ps. li. 17. 2. *It was of no use until fire was put under it,* and that taken from the altar. Nor is that prayer of any virtue or efficacy which is not kindled by the fire from above, the Holy Spirit of God, which we have from our altar, Christ Jesus. 3. *It naturally ascended upwards towards heaven,* as all offerings in the Hebrew are called נלוֹת, " ascensions," risings up. And this is the design of prayer, to ascend unto the throne of God : " I will direct unto thee, and will look up" ; that is, pray : Ps. v. 3. 4. *It yielded a sweet savour ;* which was one end of it in temple services, wherein there was so much burning of flesh and blood. So doth prayer yield a sweet savour unto God ; a savour of rest, wherein he is well pleased.—*John Owen.*

Verse 2.—*"As incense . . . as the evening sacrifice."* Though this address of mine must necessarily want all that solemnity of preparation required in the service of thy holy Tabernacle, the cloud of incense and perfume, etc., the mincha or oblation of fine flour, etc., yet let the purity and fervour of my heart, and the innocency of my hands, now lifted up to thee in this sad hour of my distress, be accepted instead of all these, and prevail for deliverance and a safe retreat to me and my companions.— *Charles Peters* (—1777), *in "A Critical Dissertation on the Book of Job,"* 1751.

Verse 2.—*"As the evening sacrifice."* This should be our daily service, as a lamb was offered up morning and evening for a sacrifice. But, alas! how dull and dead are our devotions! Like Pharaoh's chariots, they drive on heavily. Some, like Balaam's ass, scarce ever open their mouths twice.—*Thomas Adams.*

Verse 2.—*"My hands."* Spreading forth our hands in believing and fervent prayer is the only way of grasping mercy.—*F. E., in "The Saints Ebenezer,"* 1667.

Verse 2.—In the gorgeous ceremonial worship of the Hebrews, none of the senses were excluded from taking part in the service. . . . The sense of smell occupied, perhaps, the most prominent place; for the acceptance of the worship was always indicated by a symbol borrowed from this sense: "The Lord smelled a sweet savour." The prayer of the people ascended as incense, and the lifting up of their hands as the evening sacrifice. The offering of incense formed an essential part of the religious service. The altar of incense occupied one of the most conspicuous and honoured positions in the tabernacle and temple. . . . On this altar a censer full of incense poured forth its fragrant clouds every morning and evening; and yearly, as the day of atonement came round, when the high priest entered the holy of holies, he filled a censer with live coals from the sacred fire on the altar of burnt offerings, and bore it into the sanctuary, where he threw upon the burning coals the "sweet incense beaten small," which he had brought in his hand. Without this smoking censer he was forbidden, on pain of death, to enter into the awful shrine of Jehovah. Notwithstanding the washing of his flesh, and the linen garments with which he was clothed, he dare not enter the holiest of all with the blood of atonement, unless he could personally shelter himself under a cloud of incense.

It has been supposed by some writers that incense was invented for the purpose of concealing or neutralizing the noxious effluvia caused by the number of beasts slaughtered every day in the sanctuary. Other writers have attached a mystical import to it, and believed that it was a symbol of the breath of the world arising in praise to the Creator, the four ingredients of which it was composed representing the four elements. While a third class, looking upon the tabernacle as the palace of God, the theocratic King of Israel, and the ark of the covenant as his throne, regarded the incense as merely corresponding to the perfume so lavishly employed about the person and appointments of an Oriental monarch. It may doubtless have been intended primarily to serve these purposes and convey these meanings, but it derived its chief importance in connection with the ceremonial observances of the Mosaic ritual from the fact of its being the great symbol of prayer. It was offered at the time when the people were in the posture and act of devotion; and their prayers were supposed to be presented to God by the priest, and to ascend to him in the smoke and odour of that fragrant offering. Scripture is full of allusions to it, understood in this beautiful symbolical sense. Acceptable, prevailing prayer was a sweet-smelling savour to the Lord; and prayer that was unlawful, or hypocritical, or unprofitable, was rejected with disgust by the organ of smell.

Doubtless the Jews felt, when they saw the soft white clouds of fragrant smoke rising slowly from the altar of incense, as if the voice of the priest were silently but eloquently pleading in that expressive emblem in their behalf. The association of sound was lost in that of smell, and the two senses were blended in one. And this symbolical mode of supplication, as Dr. George Wilson has remarked, has this one advantage over spoken or written prayer, that it appealed to those who were both blind and deaf, a class that are usually shut out from social worship by their affliction. Those who could not hear the prayers of the priest could join in devotional exercises symbolized by incense, through the medium of their sense of smell ; and the hallowed impressions shut out by one avenue were admitted to the mind and heart by another.

The altar of incense stood in the closest connection with the altar of burnt-offerings. The blood of the sin offering was sprinkled on the horns of both on the great day of annual atonement. Morning and evening, as soon as the sacrifice was offered, the censer poured forth its fragrant contents, so that the perpetual incense within ascended simultaneously with the perpetual burnt-offering outside. Without the live coals from off the sacrificial altar, the sacred incense could not be kindled ; and without the incense previously filling the holy place, the blood of atonement from the altar of burnt-offering could not be sprinkled on the mercy-seat. Beautiful and expressive type of the perfect sacrifice and the all-prevailing intercession of Jesus—of intercession founded upon atonement, of atonement preceded and followed by intercession ! Beautiful and expressive type, too, of the prayers of believers kindled by the altar-fire of Christ's sacrifice, and perfumed by his merits !—*Hugh Macmillan, in "The Ministry of Nature,"* 1871.

Verse 3.—*"Set a watch, O* LORD, *before my mouth,"* etc. 1. A man would never use this language without a conviction of *the importance of the subject*. . . . Everything is transacted by speech, in natural, civil, and religious concerns : how much, therefore, depends on the good or evil management of the tongue ! What an ardour of holy love and friendship, or of anger and malice, may a few words fan into a flame ! The tongue is the principal instrument in the cause of God ; and it is the chief engine of the devil ; give him this, and he asks no more—there is no mischief or misery he will not accomplish by it. The use, the influence of it, therefore, is inexpressible ; and words are never to be considered only as *effects*, but as *causes*, the operation of which can never be fully imagined. Let us suppose a case, a case, I fear, but too common. You drop, in the thoughtlessness of conversation, or for the sake of argument or wit, some irreligious, sceptical expression—it lodges in the memory of a child, or a servant—it takes root in a soil favourable to such seed—it gradually springs up, and brings forth fruit, in the profanation of the Sabbath ; the neglect of the means of grace ; in the reading of improper books ; in the choice of dangerous companions ;—who can tell where it will end ? But there is a Being who knows where it began. It will be acknowledged that some have it in their power, by reason of their office, talents, and influence, to do much more injury than others ; but none are so insignificant as to be harmless.

2 A man would never use this language without a conviction that *he is in danger of transgression*. And if David was conscious of a liableness to err, shall we ever presume on our safety ? Our danger arises from the depravity of our nature. "The heart is deceitful above all things, and desperately wicked " ; and " who can bring a clean thing out of an unclean ?" Our danger arises from the contagion of example. There is nothing in which mankind are more universally culpable than in the disorders of speech. Yet with these we are constantly surrounded ; and to these we have been accustomed from our impressible infancy. We are in danger from the frequency of speech. "In the multitude of words there wanteth not sin." We must of necessity speak often ; but we often speak without necessity. Duty calls us to intermingle much with our fellow-creatures ; but we are too little in the closet, and too much in the crowd—and when we are in company we forget the admonition, " Let every man be swift to hear, and slow to speak."

3. A man would never use this language without a conviction of *inability to preserve himself*. The Bible teaches us this truth, not only doctrinally, but historically. The examples of good men, and men eminent in godliness, confirm it in the very article before us. Moses, the meekest man in the earth, " spake unadvisedly with his lips." You have heard of the patience of Job, but he " cursed the day of his birth" ; and Jeremiah, the prophet of the Lord, did the same. Peter said, " Though all men should be offended because of thee, I will never be offended ; though I should die with thee, yet will I not deny thee." But how

did he use his tongue a few hours after ? Then " began he to curse and to swear, saying, " I know not the man !' '

4. A man would never use this language without a conviction of *the wisdom of applying to God for the assistance he needs.* Prayer is the effect of our weakness, and the expression of our dependence. It confesses the agency of God. 1. In the first place—God is equal to our preservation. 2. His succours are not to be obtained without prayer. 3. Prayer always brings the assistance it implores.— *Condensed from W. Jay's Sermon on "The Regulation of the Tongue."*

Verse 3.—"*Set a watch, O* LORD, *before my mouth,*" etc. Watching and prayer are often joined together. We are best kept when recommended into God's hand. I do observe here, First, That unadvised and passionate speeches do easily drop from us in our troubles, especially in our persecution. Secondly, That a godly, conscientious man is very tender of these, as of all evil. He that would live in communion with God for the present, and hope to appear with comfort before him hereafter, is sensible of the least thing that tends to God's displeasure, and God's dishonour : this is the true spirit of one that will be owned by Christ at the last day. Thirdly, There is no way to prevent being provoked to impatience and rashness of speech, or any evil, but by keeping a watch, and renewing our obligations to God. Fourthly, Whoever would keep a watch must call in the aid and assistance of God's grace ; "*Lord, set a watch before my mouth.*"—*Thomas Manton.*

Verse 3.—"*Set a watch, O* LORD, *before my mouth,*" etc. Thus holy men have kept the sessions at home, and made their hearts the foremen of the jury, and examined themselves as we examine others. The fear of the Lord stood at the door of their souls, to examine every thought before it went in, and at the door of their lips, to examine every word before it went out, whereby they escaped a thousand sins which we commit, as though we had no other work.—*Henry Smith.*

Verse 3.—"*Set a watch, O* LORD, *before my mouth.*" Nature having made my lips to be a door to my words, let grace keep that door, that no word may be suffered to go out which may any way tend to the dishonour of God, or the hurt of others.—*Matthew Henry.*

Verse 3.—"*Set a watch,*" etc. Let a seal for words not to be spoken lie on the tongue. A watch over words is better than over wealth.—*Lucian.*

Verse 3.—"*Keep the door of my lips.*" That it move not creaking and complaining, as on rusty hinges, for want of the oil of joy and gladness. David had somewhat to do with his tongue, as we see (Ps. xxxix. 1, 3) ; and when he had carted the ark, how untowardly he spake, as if the fault were more in God than himself, that there was such a breach made in Uzzah (1 Chron. xiii. 12). It was but need thus to pray.—*John Trapp.*

Verse 4.—"*Incline not my heart to any evil thing,*" etc. The present pleasure and commodity of sin is in high estimation with the sinner, and much sweeter to him than what he may lawfully enjoy ; the pleasures of sin are his delicates. No man can keep himself from being taken with the allurements of a sinful course, except the Lord preserve him : "*Let me not eat of their dainties.*" The holiest men in Scripture have been most sensible of the impotency of their own free will, and of their inability to resist temptations, or to bring the principles of grace into action ; most diffident of themselves, most dependent upon God, most careful to make use of means, and conscientious in following of ordinances, as their prayers do testify : "*Incline not my heart to any evil thing,*" etc.—*David Dickson.*

Verse 4.—"*Incline not my heart.*" Heb. Let not be inclined my heart.—*John Jebb.*

Verse 4.—"*My heart.*" That man is like Esau which had an inheritance, which had a heart but now he hath not possession of his own ; therefore, give God thy heart, that he may keep it ; and not a piece of thy heart, not a room in thy heart, but thy heart. The heart divided, dieth. God is not like the mother which would have the child divided, but like the natural mother, which said, rather than it should be divided, let her take all. Let the devil have all, if he which gave it be not worthy of it. God hath no cope-mate, therefore he will have no parting of stakes, but all or none ; and therefore he which asks here thy heart, in the sixth of Deuteronomy and the fifth verse, asketh " all thy heart, all thy soul, and all thy strength" ; thrice he requireth *all*, lest we should keep a thought behind. Yet it is *thy* heart, that is, a vain heart, a barren heart, a sinful heart, until thou give it unto God, and then it is the spouse of Christ, the temple of the Holy Ghost, and the image of God, so changed, and formed, and refined, that God calls it a new heart.

There is such strife for the heart as there was for Moses's body. " Give it me," saith the Lord ; " give it me," saith the tempter ; " give it me," saith the pope ; " give it me," saith riches ; " give it me," saith pleasure ; as though thou must needs give it to some one. Now here is the choice, whether thou wilt give it to God or the devil ; God's heart or the devil's heart ; whose wilt thou be ?—*Henry Smith.*

Verse 4.—"*Let me not eat of their dainties.*" Sin is not only meat, but sweet meat, not only bread, but pleasant bread to an evil heart. Daniel for some weeks ate no pleasant bread ; he ate bread to keep life and soul together, but he forbare feasting or good cheer. Sin is a feast to a carnal man, it is his good cheer, yea, it is " *dainties* " to him. David, speaking of wicked men, says, "*Incline not my heart to any evil thing, to practise wicked works with men that work iniquity : and let me not eat of their dainties.*" These " *dainties* " may be expounded either for the prosperity that comes in by wicked practices (some by wicked ways get not only their ordinary food but " *dainties* ") ; or those " *dainties* " are sin itself : they feasted themselves in doing evil : " LORD, *let me not eat of their dainties.*" If that be their food I had rather starve than eat with them.—*Joseph Caryl.*

Verse 4.—"*Their dainties.*" The enemies of David were sensual and luxurious ; and they would have gladly admitted him to share in their banquets, if his character had resembled their own. He entreats to be preserved from inducement so to do.—*William Walford.*

Verse 5.—"*Let the righteous smite me,*" etc. This verse is so obscure as to be almost unintelligible. According to the English versions, it expresses his willingness to be rebuked by good men for his benefit. But this sense is not only hard to be extracted from the words, but foreign from the context. Of the many contradictory interpretations which have been proposed the most probable is that which makes the sentence mean, that the sufferings endured by the good man, even at the hand of the wicked, are chastisements inflicted by a righteous God in justice and with mercy, and as such may be likened to a festive ointment, which the head of the sufferer should not refuse, as he will still have need of consolation and occasion to invoke God, in the midst of trials and of mischiefs yet to be experienced.—*Joseph Addison Alexander.*

Verse 5.—"*Let the righteous smite me.*" The word הַלַם is seldom used in Scripture but to signify a severe stroke which shakes the subject smitten, and causeth it to tremble ; see Prov. xxiii. 35 ; 1 Sam. xiv. 16 ; Ps. lxxiv. 6 ; and it is used for the stroke of the hammer on the anvil in fashioning of the iron (Isai. xli. 7). Wherefore the word חֶסֶד following may be taken adverbially, as a lenitive of that severity which this word importeth : " Let him smite me, but" *leniter, benignè, misericorditer,* " gently, kindly, friendly, mercifully ": and so some translations read the words, " Let the righteous smite me friendly, or kindly."—*John Owen.*

Verse 5.—"*Let the righteous smite me ; it shall be a kindness,*" etc. Grace will teach a Christian to take those potions which are wholesome, though they be not toothsome. Faithful reproof is a token of love, and therefore may well be esteemed a kindness. Such wounding of a friend is healing, and so David might well call it " *an excellent oil.*" And he did not only say so, which is easy and ordinary, but acted accordingly. He did not as the papists, who highly commend holy water, but turn away their faces when it comes to be sprinkled on them. When he had by sin, and continuance in it, so gangrened his flesh, and corrupted himself, that he was in danger of death, he suffered his sores to be thoroughly searched without regret. Nathan was the chirurgeon whom God employed to search that wound which had divers mouths for festering in his soul ; and truly he did not dally with his patient, though he were a prince, but thrust his instrument to the bottom ; yet whatever pain it put him to, he took it patiently, and was so far from being angry with the prophet, that he made him one of his privy council. It is a sign of a polluted nature for a man, like a serpent, if he be but touched, to gather poison, and vomit it up at the party. " Rebuke a wise man, and he will love thee" : Prov. ix. 8.—*George Swinnock.*

Verse 5.—"*Let the righteous smite me,*" etc. If the righteous smite us by reproofs, it must be taken as a kindness, and as a precious balsam, which doth not break our head, but heal us. Not that we are bound to belie ourselves in compliance with every man's censorious humour that will accuse us ; but we must be readier to censure ourselves than others, and readier to confess a fault than to expect a confession from others whom we reprove. Sincerity and serious repentance will be honourable in that person who is most careful to avoid sin, and most ready penitently to confess it when he hath been overcome, and truly thankful to those that call him to repentance ; as being more desirous that God and his laws and religion should have the glory of their holiness, than that he himself should have the undue glory of innocency ; and escape the deserved shame of his sin.

It is one of the most dangerous diseases of professors, and one of the greatest scandals of this age, that persons taken for eminently religious are more impatient of plain, though just, reproof than many a drunkard, swearer, or fornicator ; and when they have spent hours or days in the seeming earnest confession of their sin, and lament before God and man that they cannot do it with more grief and tears, yet they take it for a heinous injury in another that will say half so much against them, and take him for a malignant enemy of the godly who will call them as they call themselves.—*Richard Baxter* (1615—1691), *in "The Morning Exercises."*

Verse 5.—"*Let the righteous smite me.*" If a righteous or a right-wise man smite and reprove, he will do it, 1. *Sine felle,* without gall, without bitterness. 2. *Sine publicatione,* without publishing, divulging, or telling it to the world. 3. *Sine contumelia,* without disgrace—to reform his friend, not to disgrace him. 4. *Sine adulatione,* without flattery. 5. *Non sine Deo,* not without God.—*John Gore, in a Sermon entitled "Unknowne Kindnesse,"* 1635.

Verse 5.—"*The righteous,*" etc. The minister cannot be always preaching ; two or three hours, may be, in a week, he spends among his people in the pulpit, holding the glass of the gospel before their faces ; but the lives of professors, these preach all the week long : if they were but holy and exemplary, they would be as a repetition of the preacher's sermon to their families and neighbours among whom they converse, and keep the sound of his doctrine continually ringing in their ears. This would give Christians an amiable advantage in doing good to their carnal neighbours by counsel and reproof, which now is seldom done, and when done it proves to little purpose, because not backed with their own exemplary walking. " It behoves him," saith Tertullian, " that would counsel or reprove another, to guard his speech with the authority of his own conversation, lest, wanting that, what he says puts himself to the blush." We do not love one that hath a stinking breath to come very near us ; such, therefore, had need have a sweet-scented life.

Reproofs are good physic, but they have an unpleasant reception ; it is hard for men not to throw them back on the face of him that gives them. Now nothing is more powerful to keep a reproof from thus coming back than the holiness of the person that reproves. "*Let the righteous smite me,*" saith David, " *it shall be a kindness : and let him reprove me ; it shall be an excellent oil, which shall not break my head.*" See how well it is taken from such a hand, from the authority that holiness carries with it. None but a vile wretch will smite a righteous man with reproach for smiting him with a reproof, if softly laid on, and like oil fermented, and wrought into him, as it should, with compassion and love to his soul ! Thus we see how influential the power of holiness would be unto the wicked, neither

would it be less upon our brethren and fellow-Christians. Holy David professed
he would take it as a kindness for the righteous man to smite him ; yea, as kindly
as if he broke a box of precious oil upon his head, which was amongst the Jews a
high expression of love.—*William Gurnall.*

Verse 5.—"*It shall be a kindness.*" 1. It is a kindness *reducere erratum,* to bring
back the wandering. 2. *Senare ægrotum,* to recover the sick. 3. *Suscitare lethar-
gum,* to awake, to stir up the lethargic, the sleepy. 4. *Ligare insanum,* to bind a
madman. 5. *Liberare perditum,* to save a lost man, one in imminent danger.—
John Gore.

Verse 5.—"*It shall be an excellent oil, which shall not break my head.*" Some persons pride themselves on being blunt, or, as they call it, "honest" ; but very
blunt people do little good to others, and get little love to themselves. The
Scriptures recommend gentleness and kindness. Reproof should fall like the
dew, and not like the rushing hail-storm. The "oil" insinuates itself ; the stone
wounds and then rebounds. Christians should take heed of getting fond of the
work of "rebuking." Such "spiritual constables" do a great deal of mischief
without intending it. They are in a church what a very witty and sarcastic person is in society, or what a tell-tale is in a school ; and approximate very closely
to that class which the apostle terms "busybodies in other men's matters."
Our manner must be tender and winning. The nail of reproof, says an old writer,
must be well oiled in kindness before it is driven home. Meddling with the
faults of others is like attempting to move a person afflicted with the rheumatic
gout : it must be done slowly and tenderly, nor must we be frightened by an outcry or two. The great thing is to show the person that you really love him ; and
if you manifest this in the sight of God, he will bless your efforts, and give you
favour in the sight of an erring brother.—*Christian Treasury.*

Verse 5.—"*It shall be an excellent oil.*" Certain oils are said to have a most
salutary effect on the head ; hence in fevers, or any other complaints which affect
the head, the medical men always recommend oil. I have known people who
were deranged, cured in a very short time by nothing more than the application
of a peculiar kind of oil to the head. There are, however, other kinds which are
believed, when thus applied, to produce delirium. Thus the reproofs of the
righteous were compared to "*excellent oil,*" which produced a most salutary effect
on the head. So common is this practice of anointing the head, that all who can
afford it do it every week.

But, strange as it may appear, the crown of their heads is the place selected for
chastisement ; thus owners of slaves, or husbands, or school-masters, beat the
heads of the offenders with their knuckles. Should an urchin come late to
school, or forget his lesson, the pedagogue says to some of the other boys, "Go
beat his head !" "Begone, fellow ! or I will beat thy head." Should a man be
thus chastized by an inferior, he quotes the old proverb : "If my head is to be
beaten, let it be done with the fingers that have rings on" ; meaning a man of
rank. "Yes, yes ; let a holy man smite my head ! and what of that ? it is an
excellent oil." "My master has been beating my head, but it has been good oil
for me."—*Joseph Roberts.*

Verse 5.—"*Oil, which shall not break my head.*" When I first took this text in
hand, this seemed unto me a very strange and uncouth expression. If the Psalmist had said, It shall be a stone that shall not break my head, etc., we had easily
understood him ; but to speak of an oil, or a balm, which we know to be so soft,
so supple, so lithe and gentle an ointment, that he should speak of breaking his
head with oil, it is strange. I confess it troubled me a while, till at length I conceived it might be spoken by contraries ; as when a physician gives a patient
some pectoral, or cordial, and saith, Take this, it will not hurt you ; his meaning
is, it will help and do him good. So this oil *shall not break my head ;* that is, it
shall heal it, being broken by my own corruption, by Satan's temptations, and by
the evil influence of such as flatter me in my sins.—*John Gore.*

Verse 5.—If David could say of his enemy that cursed him, "Let him alone,
for God hath bidden him to curse" ; much more safely mayest thou say of thy

friend that reproves thee, "Let him alone, for God hath bidden him to smite." And as the apostle saith of ministers, that God "doth entreat you by us"; so persuade yourselves that God doth reprove you by them.—*John Gore.*

Verse 5.—It was the saying of a heathen, though no heathenish saying, "That he who would be good, must either have a faithful friend to instruct him, or a watchful enemy to correct him." Should we murder a physician because he comes to cure us; or like him worse, because he would make us better? The flaming sword of *reprehension* is but to keep us from the forbidden fruit of *transgression.* "*Let the righteous smite me; it shall be a kindness: and let him reprove me; it shall be an excellent oil, which shall not break my head.*" Let him smite me as with a *hammer*, for so the word signifies. A Boanerges is as necessary as a Barnabas.—*William Secker.*

Verse 5.—"*Yet my prayer also shall be in their calamities.*" That is, if ever they who are my reprovers fall into calamity, though they may think they provoked me so by reproving me, that they have lost my love, and have cast themselves out of my prayers, or that I will never speak well of them or for them again; yet I will pray for them with all my heart, as their matter shall require. I will pray for them when they have most need of prayer, even "*in their calamities.*" Some heighten the sense thus,—The more they sharpen their reproof, the more I think myself bound to pray for them. It shows an excellent spirit, not to be hindered from doing good to others by anything they do or speak against us, nor by their sharpest (though perhaps mistaken) reproofs of us. Thus it was that that good man Job "*prayed for his friends,*" who had spoken much against him, and not only reproved him without cause, but reproached him without charity.—*Joseph Caryl.*

Verse 6.—"*When their judges are overthrown,*" etc. When the judgments in reserve for the leaders of my enemies shall come upon them, they will perceive too late how reasonable are my words, and wish that they had hearkened to them sooner.—*Joseph Addison Alexander.*

Verse 6.—"*Overthrown.*" The verb rendered "*overthrown*" is used of Jezebel in 2 Kings ix. 33; "Throw her down. So they threw her down."—*Speaker's Commentary.*

Verse 6.—"*They shall hear my words; for they are sweet.*" This is especially true of all the words which David spake by inspiration, or the Spirit of God spake to him; particularly in his book of Psalms, concerning the Messiah, the covenant of grace, and the blessings of it; of the rich experiences of grace he had, and the several doctrines of the gospel declared by him; which were sweet, delightful, and entertaining to those who have ears to hear such things; or whose ears are opened to hear them, so as to understand them and distinguish them, but to others not.—*John Gill.*

Verse 6.—"*They shall hear my words; for they are sweet.*" Those that slighted the word of God before, will relish it and be glad of it when they are in affliction; for that opens the ear to instruction. When the world is bitter the word is sweet. Oppressed innocency cannot gain a hearing with those that live in pomp and pleasure; but when they come to be overthrown themselves, they will have more compassionate thoughts of the afflicted.—*Matthew Henry.*

Verse 6.—"*For they are sweet.*" They shall be pleasant; mild; gentle; equitable; just. After the harsh and severe enactments of Saul, after enduring his acts of tyranny, the people will be glad to welcome me, and to live under the laws of a just and equal administration. The passage, therefore, expresses confidence that Saul and his hosts would be overthrown, and that the people of the land would gladly hail the accession to the throne of one who had been anointed to reign over them.—*Albert Barnes.*

Verses 6, 7.—The mild and dutiful behaviour of David towards Saul and his friends are set together by way of contrast, in the strongest light, from the instances of each sort here produced. The first is, David's humanity towards Saul, in giving him his life at two several times, when he had it in his power to destroy him as he pleased. "*Their judges have been dismissed in the rocky places ; and have heard my words that they are sweet* " *;* that is, "Their princes have been dismissed in safety, when I had them at an advantage in those rocky deserts ; and only heard me expostulate with them in the gentlest words."

The other is, Saul's barbarity and cruelty towards David (or his friends, which is much the same) in the horrid massacre of Ahimelech and the priests, by the hand of Doeg the Edomite, done in such a savage manner, that he compares it to the chopping and cleaving wood ; "*Like as when one cutteth and cleaveth, so have our bones been scattered on the earth at the command of Saul* " *;* for so I read the Hebrew words, *le-pi Saul, at the mouth,* that is, the command *of Saul.*

Should we suppose this passage to refer to the first time of David's sparing Saul, viz., when he had him in his power in the cave of *Engedi* (here called *jedé selay*), the sides of the rock, or the rocky places, the speech he made on this occasion when he called after Saul (and which is recorded in 1 Sam. xxiv., from the eighth to the sixteenth verse) might well be called *sweet* or *pleasant words.* For they set his own innocence and the king's unjust behaviour to him in so strong a light, and with all that gentleness and mildness, and even this hard-hearted prince could not forbear being greatly affected with it for the present ; and we are told (verses 16, 17) that "he lifted up his voice and wept."—*Charles Peters.*

Verse 7.—"*Our bones are scattered at the grave's mouth,*" etc. The primary reference may be to the slaughter of the priests by the command of Saul, 1 Sam. xxii. 16—19. The language, however, may be illustrative of the many massacres like that on the eve of St. Bartholomew, so numerous as to be scattered on the face of the earth, marking the passage of pious martyrs from this world to a better, and testifying where the blood of the slain shall be disclosed for the judgment of their murderers.—*W. Wilson.*

Verse 7.—"*Our bones are scattered at the grave's mouth,*" etc. Assuming the very extreme, it is a look of hope into the future : should his bones and the bones of his followers be even scattered about the mouth of Sheôl (cf. the Syrian picture of Sheôl : " the dust upon its threshold, '*al-escúfteh,*" *Deutsche Morgenländ. Zeitschrift,* xx. 513), their soul below, their bones above—it would nevertheless be only as when one in ploughing cleaves the earth ; *i.e.,* they do not lie there in order that they may continue lying, but that they may rise up anew, as the seed that is sown sprouts up out of the upturned earth.—*Franz Delitzsch.*

Verse 7.—"*Our bones are scattered at the grave's mouth.*" That is to say, I and my company are in a dying condition, free among the dead ; yea, if taken we should be put to most cruel deaths, hewn in pieces, or pulled limbmeal, and left unburied ; and our dead bodies mangled by a barbarous inhumanity, as woodcleavers make the shivers fly hither and thither. This is the perilous case of me and my partisans.—*John Trapp.*

Verse 7.—"*Our bones are scattered at the grave's mouth.*" This seems to be strong eastern painting, and almost figurative language ; but that it may be strictly true, the following extract demonstrates : " At five o'clock we left Garigana, our journey being still to the eastward of north ; and, at a quarter past six in the evening, arrived at the village of that name, whose inhabitants had all perished with hunger the year before ; their wretched bones being all unburied, and scattered upon the surface of the ground, where the village formerly stood. We encamped among the bones of the dead, as no space could be found free from them ; and on the 23rd, at six in the morning, full of horror at this miserable spectacle, we set out for Teawa."—(*James Bruce's Travels.*) To the Jews such a spectacle must have been very dreadful, as the want of burial was esteemed one of the greatest calamities which could befal them.—*Burder's "Oriental Customs."*

Verse 7.—"*Like one ploughing and cleaving in the earth.*" This clause may be explained not of cleaving wood but ploughing, to which the first verb is applied in Arabic. *Like* (one) *ploughing and cleaving* (making furrows) *in the earth,* not for the sake of mangling its surface, but to make it fruitful and productive, (so) *our bones are scattered at the mouth of hell* as the necessary means of a glorious resurrection.—*Joseph Addison Alexander.*

Verse 7.—Who can attend the digging of a grave, and view the ruins then disclosed, without exclaiming, "*Our bones are scattered at the grave's mouth, as when one cutteth and cleaveth wood upon the earth*"?—*George Horne.*

Verse 8.—"*Mine eyes are unto thee, O* GOD *the Lord.*" If you would keep your mind fixed in prayer, keep your *eye* fixed. Much vanity comes in at the eye. When the eyes wander in prayer, the heart wanders. To think to kee pthe heart fixed in prayer, and yet let the eyes gaze abroad, is as if one should think to keep his house safe, yet let the windows be open.— *Thomas Watson.*

Verse 8.—"*Leave not my soul destitute.*" The literal Hebrew is, *Pour not out my soul,* but keep it in thy cup of salvation.—*Agellius.* [Compare Isaiah liii. 12 : " He hath poured out his soul unto death."]

Verse 8.—"*Leave not my soul destitute,*" or, "*Cast not out my soul.*" That is, cast not my life away, as water, which is of no account, is cast out of a vessel containing it.—*Daniel Cresswell.*

Verse 8.—"*Leave not my soul destitute.*" His soul knew what it was to be "*destitute*"; he had known the misery of spiritual beggary and soul poverty. It was not with him as natural poverty is with the rich, a matter of speculation, a mere matter of theory ; but a matter of personal and painful experience. . . . It is in the margin "*Make not my soul bare*"; Strip me not of every hope ; leave me not completely naked ; abandon me not to nature's beggary and misery ; let me not go down into the pit with all my sins upon my head ; leave not my soul destitute of pardon and peace.—*Joseph C. Philpot.*

Verses 8—10.—

> O pour not out my soul, I pray,
> From the dark snare preserve my way,
> The chambers of the blind entangling net,
> Which by my path the powers of evil set.
>
> Behold them laid, the godless crew,
> Low in the toils they darkly drew :
> The while, with gathering heart and watchful eye,
> I wait mine hour to pass victorious by.
>
> —*John Keble.*

Verses 9, 10.—"*Snares,*" "*Gins,*" "*Nets.*" The usual method of capturing or killing the lion in Palestine was by pitfalls or nets, to both of which there are many references in the Scriptures. The mode of hunting the lion with nets was identical with that which is practised in India at the present time. The precise locality of the lion's dwelling-place having been discovered, a circular wall of net is arranged round it, or if only a few nets can be obtained, they are set in a curved form, the concave side being towards the lion. They then send dogs into the thicket, hurl stones and sticks at the den, shoot arrows into it, fling burning torches at it, and so irritate and alarm the animal that it rushes against the net, which is so made that it falls down and envelops the animal in its folds. If the nets be few, the drivers go to the opposite side of the den, and induce the lion to escape in the direction where he sees no foes, but where he is sure to run against the treacherous net. Other large and dangerous animals were also captured by the same means. Another and more common, because an easier and a cheaper method, was, by digging a deep pit, covering the mouth with a slight covering of sticks and earth, and driving the animal upon the treacherous covering. It is an easier method than the net, because after the pit is once dug, the only trouble lies in throwing the covering over its mouth. But it is not so well adapted for taking beasts alive, as they are likely to be damaged, either by the fall into the pit, or by the means used in getting them out again. Animals, therefore, that are caught in pits are generally, though not always, killed before they are taken out. The net, however, envelops the animal so perfectly, and renders it so helpless, that it can be easily bound and taken away. The hunting net is very expensive, and requires a large staff of men to work it, so that none but a rich man could use the net in hunting.

Besides the net, several other modes of bird-catching were used by the ancient Jews, just as is the case at the present day. Boys, for example, who catch birds for their own consumption, and not for the market, can do so by means of various traps, most of which are made on the principle of the noose, or snare. Sometimes a great number of hair-nooses are set in places to which the birds are decoyed, so that in hopping about, many of them are sure to be entangled in the snares. Sometimes the noose is ingeniously suspended in a narrow passage which the birds are likely to traverse, and sometimes a simple fall-trap is employed.— *J. G. Wood.*

Verse 10.—"*Into their own nets.*" The word rendered "*nets*" occurs only in this place, as the closely corresponding word in Ps. cxl. 10, which is rendered "*deep pits,*" occurs there only.—*Speaker's Commentary.*

HINTS TO THE VILLAGE PREACHER.

Verse 1.—I. The Perpetuity of Prayer : "I cry. I cry." II. The Personality : "unto thee," "unto me." III. The Practicalness : "Make haste ; give ear."

Verse 1.—Holy haste. I. The saint hasting to God. II. The saint hastening God. III. God's sure hastening to his help.—*W. B. H.*

Verses 1, 2.—I. Prayer put forth : 1. With urgency : "Make haste unto me." 2. With fervency : "Give ear," etc. II. Prayer set forth : "Let my prayer be set forth," etc. When hearing is obtained there is composure and order in prayer. When the fire is kindled the incense rises. III. Prayer held forth : "The lifting up of my hands as the evening sacrifice," as constant and accepted. —*G. R.*

Verse 2.—True prayer acceptable as incense and as the evening sacrifice. It is spiritual, solemn, ordained of God, brings Christ to remembrance.

Verse 3.—I. The mouth a door. II. A watchman needed. III. The Lord fulfilling that office.

Verse 4.—Total abstinence from evil desires, practices, and delights.

Verse 4.—A prayer, I. For the repression of every evil tendency in the heart : "Incline not my heart," etc. II. For the prevention of any association with the wicked in their sinful works : "To practise," etc. III. For a holy contempt of the temporal pleasure or profit placed in our way through the sin of others : "Let me not eat," etc. Note, many who will not engage in a wicked act do not object to participate in its gains.—*J. F.*

Verse 4.—Deprecation of, I. Devil's desires. II. Devil's deeds. III. Devil's dainties.—*W. B. H.*

Verse 5.—Rebukes of good men. I. Invited. II. Appreciated : "it shall be a kindness." III. Utilized : "an excellent oil." IV. Cheerfully endured : "not break my head." V. Repaid, by our prayers for them in time of trouble.

Verse 5 (last clause).—"Intercessory Prayer." See "Spurgeon's Sermons," No. 1,049.

Verse 6.—I. Times of trouble will come to the careless. II. Then they will be more ready to hear the gospel. III. Then they will find sweetness in that which they formerly refused.

Verse 6.—A Desert Oasis. I. The world is a stony place, hard, barren. II. Often pride and self-trust suffer overthrowing there. III. Then words of God by his sent servant make an oasis in the desert.—*W. B. H.*

Verses 7, 8.—A cemetery scene. I. Dry bones of the dead about the grave. II. Weary bones of the aged and sick around the grave. III. All bones being from day to day made ready for the grave. IV. Bones finding rest in God : "mine eyes are unto thee, O God," etc.

Verse 8.—Expectation. Supplication.

Verse 9.—The snares. Who lay them? Why? Who so many? How are we to escape? "Keep me."

Verses 9, 10.—David prays, 1. That he may see God in his deliverance from his enemies, and, 2. That they may see God in the frustration of their designs.—*G. R.*

Verse 10.—Great pains to little purpose. I. The making of nets, etc. II. The taking of God's antagonists in their own nets. III. The invariable escape of God's friends. Lesson : Nothing can prosper sin, or hurt godliness.—*W. B. H.*

WORK UPON THE HUNDRED AND FORTY-FIRST PSALM.

In Charles Peters's " Critical Dissertation on the Book of Job," 4to, 1751, pp. 332—357, there is a very learned exposition, with a paraphrase of this psalm ; of it Bishop Horne in his Commentary says :—" Many parts of the Exposition of this psalm given by the late learned Mr. Peters . . . have been adopted in the ensuing comment."

PSALM CXLII.

TITLE.—Maschil of David. *This Maschil is written for our instruction. It teaches us principally by example how to order our prayer in times of distress. Such instruction is among the most needful, practical, and effectual parts of our spiritual education. He who has learned how to pray has been taught the most useful of the arts and sciences. The disciples said unto the Son of David, "Lord, teach us to pray"; and here David gives us a valuable lesson by recording his own experience as to supplication from beneath a cloud.*

A Prayer when he was in the cave. *He was in one of his many lurking places, either Engedi, Adullam, or some other lone cavern wherein he could conceal himself from Saul and his blood hounds. Caves make good closets for prayer ; their gloom and solitude are helpful to the exercise of devotion. Had David prayed as much in his palace as he did in his cave, he might never have fallen into the act which brought such misery upon his later days.*

SUBJECT.—*There can be little doubt that this song dates from the days when Saul was sorely persecuting David, and David himself was in soul-trouble, probably produced by that weakness of faith which led him to associate with heathen princes. His fortunes were evidently at their lowest, and, what was worse, his repute had fearfully fallen ; yet he displayed a true faith in God, to whom he made known his pressing sorrows. The gloom of the cave is over the psalm, and yet as if standing at the mouth of it the prophet-poet sees a bright light a little beyond.*

EXPOSITION.

I CRIED unto the LORD with my voice ; with my voice unto the LORD did I make my supplication.

2 I poured out my complaint before him ; I shewed before him my trouble.

3 When my spirit was overwhelmed within me, then thou knewest my path. In the way wherein I walked have they privily laid a snare for me.

4 I looked on *my* right hand, and beheld, but *there was* no man that would know me : refuge failed me ; no man cared for my soul.

5 I cried unto thee, O LORD : I said, Thou *art* my refuge *and* my portion in the land of the living.

6 Attend unto my cry ; for I am brought very low : deliver me from my persecutors ; for they are stronger than I.

7 Bring my soul out of prison, that I may praise thy name : the righteous shall compass me about ; for thou shalt deal bountifully with me.

1. "*I cried unto the* LORD *with my voice.*" It was a cry of such anguish that he remembers it long after, and makes a record of it. In the loneliness of the cave he could use his voice as much as he pleased ; and therefore he made its gloomy vaults echo with his appeals to heaven. When there was no soul in the cavern seeking his blood, David with all his soul was engaged in seeking his God. He felt it a relief to his heart to use his voice in his pleadings with Jehovah. There was a voice *in* his prayer when he used his voice *for* prayer : it was not *vox et præterea nihil.* It was a prayer *vivo corde* as well as *vivâ voce.* "*With my voice unto the* LORD *did I make my supplication.*" He dwells upon the fact that he spoke aloud in prayer ; it was evidently well impressed upon his memory, hence he doubles the word and says, " with my voice ; with my voice." It is well when

our supplications are such that we find pleasure in looking back upon them. He that is cheered by the memory of his prayers will pray again. See how the good man's appeal was to Jehovah only : he did not go round about to men, but he ran straight forward to Jehovah, his God. What true wisdom is here ! Consider how the Psalmist's prayer grew into shape as he proceeded with it. He first poured out his natural longings,—" I cried " ; and then he gathered up all his wits and arranged his thoughts,—" I made supplication." True prayers may differ in their diction, but not in their direction : an impromptu cry and a preconceived supplication must alike ascend towards the one prayer-hearing God, and he will accept each of them with equal readiness. The intense personality of the prayer is noteworthy : no doubt the Psalmist was glad of the prayers of others, but he was not content to be silent himself. See how everything is in the first person,—"*I* cried with *my* voice ; with *my* voice did *I* make *my* supplication." It is good to pray in the plural—" Our Father," but in times of trouble we shall feel forced to change our note into " Let this cup pass from *me*."

2. "*I poured out my complaint before him.*" His inward meditation filled his soul : the bitter water rose up to the brim ; what was to be done ? He must pour out the wormwood and the gall, he could not keep it in ; he lets it run away as best it can, that so his heart may be emptied of the fermenting mixture. But he took care *where* he outpoured his complaint, lest he should do mischief, or receive an ill return. If he poured it out before man he might only receive contempt from the proud, hard-heartedness from the careless, or pretended sympathy from the false ; and therefore he resolved upon an outpouring before God alone, since *he* would pity and relieve. The word is scarcely " complaint " ; but even if it be so we may learn from this text that our complaint must never be of a kind that we dare not bring before God. We may complain *to* God, but not *of* God. When we complain it should not be before men, but before God alone. "*I shewed before him my trouble.*" He exhibited his griefs to one who could assuage them : he did not fall into the mistaken plan of so many who publish their sorrows to those who cannot help them. This verse is parallel with the first ; David first pours out his complaint, letting it flow forth in a natural, spontaneous manner, and then afterwards he makes a more elaborate show of his affliction ; just as in the former verse he began with crying, and went on to " make supplication." Praying men can pray better as they proceed. Note that we do not show our trouble before the Lord that *he* may see *it*, but that *we* may see *him*. It is for *our* relief, and not for his information that we make plain statements concerning our woes : it does us much good to set out our sorrow in order, for much of it vanishes in the process, like a ghost which will not abide the light of day ; and the rest loses much of its terror, because the veil of mystery is removed by a clear and deliberate stating of the trying facts. Pour out your thoughts and you will see what they are ; show your trouble and the extent of it will be known to you : let all be done before the Lord, for in comparison with his great majesty of love the trouble will seem to be as nothing.

3. "*When my spirit was overwhelmed within me, then thou knewest my path.*" The bravest spirit is sometimes sorely put to it. A heavy fog settles down upon the mind, and the man seems drowned and smothered in it ; covered with a cloud, crushed with a load, confused with difficulties, conquered by impossibilities. David was a hero, and yet his spirit sank : he could smite a giant down, but he could not keep himself up. He did not know his own path, nor feel able to bear his own burden. Observe his comfort : he looked away from his own condition to the ever-observant, all-knowing God : and solaced himself with the fact that all was known to his heavenly Friend. Truly it is well for us to know that God knows what we do not know. We lose our heads, but God never closes his eyes : our judgments lose their balance, but the eternal mind is always clear.

"*In the way wherein I walked have they privily laid a snare for me.*" This the Lord knew at the time, and gave his servant warning of it. Looking back, the sweet singer is rejoiced that he had so gracious a Guardian, who kept him from unseen dangers. Nothing is hidden from God ; no secret snare can hurt the man who dwells in the secret place of the Most High, for he shall abide under the shadow of the Almighty. The use of concealed traps is disgraceful to our enemies, but they care little to what tricks they resort for their evil purposes. Wicked men must find some exercise for their malice, and therefore when they dare not openly assail they will privately ensnare. They watch the gracious man to see where his haunt is, and there they set their trap ; but they do it with great caution, avoiding all observation, lest their victim being forewarned should escape their toils. This is a great trial, but the Lord is greater still, and makes us to walk safely in the midst of danger, for he knows us and our enemies, our way and the snare which is laid in it. Blessed be his name.

4. "*I looked on my right hand, and beheld, but there was no man that would know me.*" He did not miss a friend for want of looking for him, nor for want of looking in a likely place. Surely some helper would be found in the place of honour ; some one would stand at his right hand to undertake his defence. He looked steadily, and saw all that could be seen, for he " beheld " ; but his anxious gaze was not met by an answering smile. Strange to say, all were strange to David. He had known many, but none would know him. When a person is in ill odour it is wonderful how weak the memories of his former friends become : they quite forget, they refuse to know. This is a dire calamity. It is better to be opposed by foes than to be forsaken by friends. When friends look for us they affect to have known us from our birth, but when we look for friends it is wonderful how little we can make them remember : the fact is that in times of desertion it is not true that no man did know us, but no man *would* know us. Their ignorance is wilful. "*Refuge failed me.*" Where in happier days I found a ready harbour I now discovered none at all. My place of flight had taken to flight. My refuge gave me a refusal. "*No man cared for my soul.*" Whether I lived or died was no concern of anybody's. I was cast out as an outcast. No soul cared for my soul. I dwelt in No-man's land, where none cared to have me, and none cared about me. This is an ill-plight—no place where to lay our head, and no head willing to find us a place. How pleased were his enemies to see the friend of God without a friend ! How sad was he to be utterly deserted in his utmost need ! Can we not picture David in the cave, complaining that even the cave was not a refuge for him, for Saul had come even there ? Hopeless was his looking out, we shall soon see him looking up.

5. "*I cried unto thee, O* Lord." As man would not regard him, David was driven to Jehovah, his God. Was not this a gain made out of a loss ? wealth gained by a failure ? Anything which leads us to cry unto God is a blessing to us. This is the second time that in this short psalm we find the same record, " I cried unto thee, O Lord " : the saintly man is evidently glad to remember his cry and its results. We hear often of the bitter cry of outcast London, here is another bitter cry, and it comes from an outcast, in wretched lodgings, forgotten by those who should have helped him. "*I said, Thou art my refuge and my portion in the land of the living.*" There is a sort of progressive repetition all through this sacred song ; he *cried* first, but he *said* afterwards : his cry was bitter, but his saying was sweet ; his cry was sharp and short, but his saying was fresh and full. It gives a believer great pleasure to remember his own believing speeches : he may well desire to bury his unbelieving murmurings in oblivion, but the triumphs of grace in working in him a living faith, he will not dream of forgetting. What a grand confession of faith was this ! David spoke to God, and of God— " Thou art my refuge." Not thou hast provided me a refuge, but thou, thyself, art my refuge. He fled to God alone ; he hid himself beneath the wings of the Eternal. He not only believed this, but said it, and practised it. Nor was this all ; for David, when banished from his portion in the promised land, and cut off from the portion of goods which he by right inherited, found his portion in God, yea, God *was* his portion. This was so not only in reference to a future state, but here among living men. It is sometimes easier to believe in a portion in heaven than in a portion upon earth : we could die more easily than live, at least we think so. But there is no living in the land of the living like living upon the liv-

ing God. For the man of God to say these precious things in the hour of his dire distress was a grand attainment. It is easy to prate bravely when we dwell at ease, but to speak confidently in affliction is quite another matter.

Even in this one sentence we have two parts, the second rising far above the first. It is something to have Jehovah for our refuge, but it is everything to have him for our portion. If David had not *cried* he would not have *said;* and if the Lord had not been his *refuge* he would never have been his *portion.* The lower step is as needful as the higher; but it is not necessary always to stop on the first round of the ladder.

6. "*Attend unto my cry.*" Men of God look upon prayer as a reality, and they are not content without having an audience with God; moreover, they have such confidence in the Lord's condescending grace, that they hope he will even attend to that poor broken prayer which can only be described as a cry. "*For I am brought very low,*" and therefore all the prayer I can raise is a mournful cry. This is his argument with God: he is reduced to such a sad condition that if he be not rescued he will be ruined. Gracious men may not only be low, but very low; and this should not be a reason for their doubting the efficacy of their prayers, but rather a plea with the Lord why they should have special attention. "*Deliver me from my persecutors.*" If he did not get out of their hands, they would soon kill him out of hand, and as he could not himself effect an escape, he cried to God, "deliver me." "*For they are stronger than I.*" As he before found a plea in his sadness, so now in his feebleness: Saul and his courtiers were in power, and could command the aid of all who sought royal favour; but poor David was in the cave, and every Nabal girded at him. Saul was a monarch, and David a fugitive; Saul had all the forms of law on his side, while David was an outlaw: so that the prayer before us comes from the weak, who proverbially go to the wall,—a good place to go to if they turn their faces to it in prayer, as Hezekiah did in his sickness. The Lord is wont to take the side of the oppressed, and to show his power by baffling tyrants; David's supplication was therefore sure to speed. In these sentences we see how explicitly the man of God described his case in his private communings with his Lord: in real earnest he poured out his complaint before him and showed before him his trouble.

7. "*Bring my soul out of prison, that I may praise thy name.*" That God may be glorified is another notable plea for a suppliant. Escaped prisoners are sure to speak well of those who give them liberty. Soul-emancipation is the noblest form of liberation, and calls for the loudest praise: he who is delivered from the dungeons of despair is sure to magnify the name of the Lord. We are in such a prison that only God himself can bring us out of it, and when he does so he will put a new song into our mouths. The cave was not half such a dungeon to David's body as persecution and temptation made for his soul. To be exiled from the godly is worse than imprisonment, hence David makes it one point of his release that he would be restored to church fellowship—"*The righteous shall compass me about.*" Saints gather around a child of God when his Father smiles upon him; they come to hear his joyful testimony, to rejoice with him, and to have their own faith encouraged. All the true believers in the twelve tribes were glad to rally to David's banner when the Lord enlarged his spirit; they glorified God for him and with him and through him. They congratulated him, consorted with him, crowned him, and championed him. This was a sweet experience for righteous David, who had for awhile come under the censure of the upright. He bore their smiting with patience, and now he welcomes their sanction with gratitude. "*For thou shalt deal bountifully with me.*" God's bountiful dealing is sure to bring with it the sympathy and alliance of all the favourites of the Great King. What a change from looking for a friend and finding none to this enthusiastic concourse of allies around the man after God's own heart! When we can begin a psalm with crying, we may hope to close it with singing. The voice of prayer soon awakens the voice of praise.

EXPLANATORY NOTES.

Title.—He calls this prayer *Maschil*, "a psalm of instruction," because of the good lessons he had himself learned in the cave, learned on his knees, and so learned that he desired to teach others.—*Matthew Henry.*

Title.—"*A prayer when he was in the cave.*" Every part of this psalm shows the propriety of its inscription or title. He expressly mentions his being in a place where he was entirely shut up, where he saw no possible method of escaping, as having no friends that dared to own him and appear for his deliverance, and when every one seemed to desert him, and to have abandoned all care of his safety and life. This he pathetically describes, and in such terms as cannot fail to move the tender affections of every one who considers them. On the first sense of his danger, shut up in a cave, surrounded by three thousand chosen soldiers, closely observed by a watchful enemy who would spare no art or pains to apprehend him, he seems almost to have despaired of himself, and declares that his spirit is quite overwhelmed with the greatness of his distress. At length, recollecting his principles, and the promises that God had made him, he earnestly supplicates the protection of God, and assures himself that he should yet praise God for his deliverance, and that good men should share his joy, and encompass the altar of God with thanksgiving for the mercy that he had shown him.—*Samuel Chandler.*

Title.—"*The cave.*" Leaving our horses in charge of some Arabs, and taking one for our guide, we started for the cave now known as Mughâret Khureitûn, which is believed to be the cave Adullam, having a fearful gorge below, gigantic cliffs above, and the path winding along a narrow shelf of the rock. At length, from a great rock hanging on the edge of the shelf, we entered by a long leap a low window which opened into the perpendicular face of the cliff. We were then within the traditional hold of David, and, creeping half doubled through a narrow crevice for a few rods, we stood beneath the dark vault of the first grand chamber of this mysterious and oppressive cavern, 1 Sam. xxii. 1, 2 ; 2 Sam. xxiii. 13—17. Our whole collection of lights did little more than make the damp darkness visible. After groping about as long as we had time to spare, we returned to the light of day, fully convinced that, with David and his lionhearted followers inside, all the strength of Israel under Saul could not have forced an entrance—would not have even attempted it.—*William M. Thompson.*

Verse 1.—"*I cried unto the* LORD." Thou hast posted me over to no deputy for the hearing of my prayer, neither dost thou require that I should bring a spokesman for the presenting of it ; but thou hast commanded me to come myself, and to come to thee thyself.—*Sir Richard Baker on the Lord's Prayer.*

Verse 1.—"*With my voice.*" The Lord needs not the tongue to be an interpreter between him and the hearts of his children. He that hears without ears can interpret prayers though not uttered by the tongue. Our desires are cries in the ears of the Lord of hosts. The vehemency of the affections may sometimes cause the outcrying of the voice ; but alas ! without this it is but a tinkling cymbal. . . . There is a use of words in prayer, to excite, and convey, and give vent to, affection : Hosea xiv. 2, "Take with you words, and turn to the LORD : say unto him, Take away all iniquity, and receive us graciously." The prophet doth not only prescribe that they should take affections, but take with them words.—*Thomas Manton.*

Verse 2.—"*I poured out my complaint before him.*" Literally, my meditation ; that is—what so much occupied my thoughts at the time I expressed aloud. The word "*complaint*" does not express the idea. The meaning is, not that he *complained* of God or of man ; but that his mind *meditated* on his condition.—*Albert Barnes.*

Verse 2.—"*I poured out*," etc. I did it fully, and fervently, and confidently.—*Matthew Pool.*

Verse 2.—"*Poured out . . . before him.*" Those words teach us that in prayer we should not try to keep anything back from God, but should show him all that is in our hearts, and that in his presence in our closet, with the door shut, but not before men. The Carmelite adds that there is much force in the words "*with my voice*," twice repeated (as in Heb., A. V., Vulgate, etc.) to show us that we ought to pray to God directly for ourselves, and in person, and not be contented with an *Ora pro me* addressed to some one else.—*Cassiodorus and Ayguan, in Neale and Littledale.*

Verse 2.—"*I shewed before him my trouble.*" Be very particular in secret prayer, both as to sins, wants, and mercies . . . Be not ashamed to open out all thy necessities. David argues because he is "poor and needy"; four several times he presses his wants and exigencies before God, like an earnest but holy beggar (Ps. xl. 17 ; lxx. 5 ; lxxxvi. 1 ; cix. 22). He "*shewed before him*" his trouble. He presents "*before*" God his ragged condition, and spreads open his secret wounds ; as Job said, he "would order" his "cause before him" : Job xxiii. 4. . . . Before God we may speak out our minds fully, and name the persons that afflict, affront, and trouble us ; and woe to them that a child of God upon a mature judgment names in prayer ! I find not that such a prayer in Scripture ever returned empty . . . A great reason why we reap so little benefit in prayer is, because we rest too much in generals ; and if we have success, it is but dark, so that often we cannot tell what to make of the issues of prayer. Besides, to be particular in our petitions would keep the spirit much from wandering when we are intent upon a weighty case, and the progress of the soul in grace would manifest its gradual success in prayer.—*Samuel Lee* (1625—1691), *in "The Morning Exercises."*

Verse 2.—The committing of our cause to God is at once our duty, our safety, and our ease.—*Abraham Wright.*

Verse 3.—"*When my spirit was overwhelmed within me.*" "*When even my spirit* (the higher faculty) is *wrapped* in *darkness upon me*" ; that is, when even my spirit (*ruach*), which ought to elevate my *soul* (*nephesh*) falls heavily upon me, as in a swoon.

> "When heavy, like a veil of woe,
> My spirit on me lay."

What is here said of the *spirit*, is oftener predicted of the *soul*, the seat of the passions. See Psalms xlii. 6 ; xliii. 5 ; cxxxi. 2. The dejection of the *spirit* represents a still more sorrowful and downcast condition, than the fainting of the *soul*. See Psalm cxliii. 3, 4, and compare our Lord's words, "My *soul* is troubled" (John xii. 27) with the Evangelist's statement, "Jesus was troubled in spirit" (John xiii. 21 ; xi. 33).—*Christopher Wordsworth.*

Verse 3.—"*When my spirit was overwhelmed within me.*" Literally, *in the muffling upon me of my spirit.* When my spirit was so wrapped in trouble and gloom, so "muffled round with woe," that I could not see the path before me, was distracted and unable to choose a line of conduct, "*Thou* (emphatic) knewest my path."—*A. S. Aglen, in "An Old Testament Commentary for English Readers,"* 1884.

Verse 3.—I wish you much comfort from David's thought : "*When my spirit was overwhelmed within me, then thou knewest my path.*" The Lord is not withdrawn to a great distance, but his eye is upon you. He sees you not with the indifference of a mere spectator ; but he observes with attention, he knows, he considers your path : yea, he appoints it, and every circumstance about it is under his direction. Your trouble began at the hour he saw best,—it could not come before ; and he has marked the degree of it to a hair's breadth, and its duration to a minute. He knows likewise how your spirit is affected ; and such supplies of grace and strength, and in such seasons as he sees needful, he will afford in

due season. So that when things appear darkest, you shall still be able to say,
Though chastened, not killed. Therefore hope in God, for you shall yet praise
him.—*John Newton* (1725—1807), *in "Cardiphonia."*
Verse 3.—"Thou knewest."

> From human eyes 'tis better to conceal
> Much that I suffer, much I hourly feel;
> But, oh, this thought can tranquillize and heal,
> All, all is known to thee.
>
> Nay, all by thee is ordered, chosen, planned,
> Each drop that fills my daily cup, thy hand
> Prescribes for ills, none else can understand,
> All, all is known to thee.
>   —*Charlotte Elliott.*

Verse 3.—Although we as Christians possess the full solution of the problem of
suffering, yet we frequently find ourselves in the position of Job, in regard to this
or that particular affliction. There are sorrows so far reaching, so universal;
there are losses so absolute, and blows so terrible and inexplicable, that it seems
for a time as if we were wrapped in thickest gloom, and as if the secret of the
Lord had not been revealed. Why was this man stricken, and that man spared?
Why was such and such a being, in whom so many hopes centred, or who had
already realised so many pleasant expectations, why was he withdrawn? Why
was that other person left, a useless encumbrance to earth? Why was that voice,
which found echo in so many hearts, suddenly silenced? Why have I been smitten? Why have I lost that which rendered my moral life beautiful and useful?
Oftentimes the soul seems lost for awhile in thoughts which overwhelm it, it loses
its foothold, it tumbles about helplessly amid the deep waters of affliction. It
seems as if all were over. Do not believe it. Remember Job; you cannot go to
greater lengths of despair than he, and yet God had pity on him. There is much
comfort for you in this example of indescribable suffering, exasperated to the
highest degree, and yet pardoned and consoled. Cling to the memory of this
blessed fact as to a cable of deliverance, a board or a plank amidst the shipwreck.
And then remember that affliction forms part of God's plan, and that he also
asks you to manifest ready and absolute confidence in him.—*E. De Pressensé,
D. D., in "The Mystery of Suffering,"* 1869.

Verse 3.—"They have privily laid a snare for me." Snares on the right hand,
and snares on the left : snares on the right hand, worldly prosperity ; snares on
the left hand, worldly adversity ; snares on the right hand, flattery ; snares on
the left hand, alarm. Do thou walk in the midst of the snares : depart not from
the way : let neither flattery ensnare thee, nor alarm drive thee off it.—*Augustine.*

Verse 4.—"I looked on my right hand, and beheld." The first two verbs must be
translated as imperatives, as in the margin of the English Bible. ["Look on the
right hand, and see."] The right hand is mentioned as the post of a protector.
—*Joseph Addison Alexander.*

Verse 4.—"I looked on my right hand." The allusion here, it is supposed, is to
the observance of the ancient Jewish courts of judicature, in which the advocate,
as well as the accuser, stood on the *right hand* of the accused (Psalm cx. 5). The
Psalmist felt himself in the condition of one who had nobody to plead his cause,
and to protect him in the dangerous circumstances in which he was placed.—
James Anderson's Note to Calvin in loc.

Verse 4.—"There was no man that would know me." The fact that David,
although surrounded by a band of loyal subjects, confesses to having no true
friend, is to be understood similarly to the language of Paul when he says in Phil.
ii. 20 : "I have no man like-minded." All human love, since sin has taken possession of humanity, is more or less selfish, and all fellowship of faith and of love
imperfect ; and there are circumstances in life in which these dark sides make
themselves felt overpoweringly, so that a man seems to himself to be perfectly
isolated, and turns all the more urgently to God, who alone is able to supply the

soul's want of some object to love, whose love is absolutely unselfish, and unchangeable, and unbeclouded, to whom the soul can confide without reserve whatever burdens it, and who not only honestly desires its good, but is able also to compass it in spite of every obstacle. Surrounded by bloodthirsty enemies, and misunderstood, or at least not thoroughly understood by his friends, David feels himself broken off from all created beings.—*Franz Delitzsch.*

Verse 4.—"*There was no man that would know me.*" Teacheth us of what little estimation God's children be, with the world and worldly men.—*Thomas Wilcocks.*

Verse 4.—"*There was no man that would know me.*" Persecution from the side of our enemies presses sorely, but abandonment by our friends, who should have stood by one's side as helpers and defenders, presses more sorely still.—*Taube, in Lange's Commentary.*

Verse 4.—Observe the beautiful opposition between "Thou knewest" (verse 3) and "no man would know me." "*Refuge failed me,*"—literally "*perished*" from me (Jer. xxv. 35 ; Amos ii. 14). But "thou hast been my *refuge* in the day of my trouble" ; Ps. lix. 16.—*Andrew Robert Fausset.*

Verses 4, 5.—"*Refuge failed me. . . . Thou art my refuge.*" Travellers tell us that they who are at the top of the Alps can see great showers of rain fall under them, but not one drop of it falls on them. They who have God for their portion are in a high tower, and thereby safe from all troubles and showers. A drift-rain of evil will beat in at the creature's windows, be they never so well pointed ; all the garments this world can make up cannot keep them that travel in such weather from being wet to the skin. No creature is able to bear the weight of its fellow-creature ; but as reeds, they break under the pressure, and as thorns, they run into the sides of those who lean on them. The bow drawn beyond its compass breaks in sunder, and the string wound above its strength snaps in pieces. Such are outward helps to all that trust to them in hardships.—*George Swinnock.*

Verses 4, 5.—"*Refuge failed me. . . . Thou art my refuge.*" Are there any among us to whom the world's face is quite changed, and the brooks of comfort in it are dried up, and they are so tossed, chased, and harassed in it that they have forgotten their resting-place ? Are any of you "become a stranger unto your brethren and an alien unto your mother's children" ? Ps. lxix. 8. Is it grown such a strange world, that even "your own familiar friend, in whom you trusted, which did eat of your bread, hath lifted up his heel against you" ? (Ps. xli. 9) ; and that wherever you turn yourselves in it, to find rest and refuge, the door is shut in your face ? Here is a refuge for you ; here is one open door ; come in, thou blessed of the Lord : "the Lord gathereth the outcasts of Israel " : Ps. cxlvii. 2. It seems the Lord minds to have you in : he is doing with you as a father with a stubborn son who ran away from his father's house, thinking to shift for himself among his friends, and not come back : the father sends peremptory word through them all, saying, "In whosoever house my son is skulking, presently turn him out of doors, and let none of you take him in ; and if he come to you give him not one night's lodging, nay, let him not eat in your house." Wherefore is all this but just to get him back again to his father's house ?— *Thomas Boston, 1676—1732.*

Verses 4, 5.—When all slighted him, when none took care of him ; what doth David in this case ? The words in verse 5 tell us what. "*I cried unto thee, O LORD : I said, Thou art my refuge and my portion in the land of the living.*" As if he had said, Upon these unkindnesses, disrespects, and slightings which I found in the world, I took occasion, yea, I was stirred in my spirit to cry unto thee, O Lord, and to say, "*Thou art my refuge,*" that is, then I made thee my refuge more than ever. Having made thee my choice in my best times, when men honoured and embraced me, I am much encouraged in these evil times when men regard me not to shelter my weather-beaten self in thy name and power. When we have most friends in the world, then God is our best friend, but when the world hates us, and frowns upon us, especially when (as the prophet speaks of some, Isai. lxvi. 5) "our brethren hate us, and cast us out for the name's sake of God himself," saying, "Let the Lord be glorified," when 'tis thus with us (I say) our souls are even forced into the presence of God, to renew our interests in his love, and to assure our souls that we are accepted with him.—*Joseph Caryl.*

Verse 5.—"*I have cried unto thee, Jehovah, I have said,*" etc.   I have cried and still cry ; I have said and still say.—*Joseph Addison Alexander.*

Verse 5.—"*I said.*"   This imports, I. A REMEMBRANCE OF THE SOLEMN TRANSACTION, Ps. ciii. 18.   This is a deed never to be forgotten, but always to be kept in remembrance.   But, O ye who have said this, remember, 1. *What* you said.   You said that God in Christ should be your refuge, that under the shade of his wings you hid yourselves, and that, renouncing all other refuges, as refuges of lies, you did betake yourselves to the covert of Christ's righteousness, and that there ye would abide for your portion ; which was a formal acceptance of and laying hold on the covenant.   2. *To whom* you said it.   To God in Christ speaking to you in the gospel-offer, and inviting you into the refuge.   What men say to their superiors, they think themselves specially concerned to mind.   And surely what ye have said to God, ye ought in a peculiar manner to remember, and awe your hearts with the consideration of the majesty of the party to whom ye said it, Ps. xvi. 2 : " O my soul, thou hast said unto the Lord, Thou art my Lord " ; for he is not one with whom we may deal falsely.   3. *How* ye said it.   Did ye not say it in your hearts, while God in Christ was held out as a refuge for you ?   And the language of the heart is plain language with a heart-searching God.   Did not some of you say it with your mouths ? and did not all communicants say it solemnly before the world, angels, and men, by their receiving the elements of bread and wine ?   4. *Upon what grounds* you said it.   Did you not see a necessity of a refuge for you, and a necessity of taking God in Christ for your refuge ?   Ye had rational grounds for it, and lasting grounds that can never fail ; so that ye can never have ground to retract nor shift about for another refuge.   Jer. ii. 31. 5. *Where* ye said it.   Remember the spot of ground where ye said it in prayer, where ye said it at the communion-table.   Ps. xlii. 6.   The stones of the place will be witnesses of your saying it.   Josh. xxiv. 27.

II. A STANDING TO IT, without regretting that we said it, remembering what is said, John vi. 66—69 : " From that time many of his disciples went back, and walked no more with him.   Then said Jesus unto the twelve, Will ye also go away ?   Then Simon Peter answered him, Lord, to whom shall we go ? thou hast the words of eternal life.   And we believe and are sure that thou art that Christ, the Son of the living God."   Men often repent what they have said, and therefore will not own that they have said it.   But gracious souls will not repent their saying this, but will abide by it.   If they were to make their choice a thousand times, having chosen God in Christ for their refuge and portion, they would not alter ; Jer. iii. 19 : " I said, Thou shalt call me, My Father ; and shalt not turn away from me."   Many alterations may be in men's circumstances in the world, but there can never be one that will afford ground for retracting this saying.

III. AN OWNING OF THE OBLIGATION OF IT : "*I said,*" and am obliged thereby to stand to it, " For I have opened my mouth unto the Lord and I cannot go back," Judg. xi. 35.   God in Christ is yours, and ye are his by his own consent ; ye are no more your own ; ye have said the word, and must own that it is binding on you ; and ye must beware that after vows ye make not enquiry.   Whoever may pretend they have their choice yet to make of a refuge and portion to themselves, ye cannot : ye are engaged already, and ye are not at liberty to hearken to any other proposals, any more than a woman who has already signed her contract with one man.

IV. A PROFESSING OF IT CONFIDENTLY without being ashamed of it ; as though you should say, " I own it before all men, and am not ashamed of my choice."   Antichrist allows some of his vassals to carry his mark in their right hand.   Rev. xiii. 16.   But all the followers of the Lamb have their mark on their foreheads, where it will not hide, Rev. xiv. 1.   The world would put the people of God to shame on the head of their refuge and portion, as if they had made a foolish bargain of it, Psal. xiv. 6 : " Ye have shamed the counsel of the poor, because the

LORD is his refuge." But sincerity will make men despise that shame, as David said, "And I will yet be more vile than thus, and will be base in mine own sight."

V. A SATISFACTION OF HEART IN IT : as though you should say, "I said it, and, Oh, but I am well pleased that ever I said it ; it was the best saying I could ever say. Ps. xvi. 2, 5, 6, 7. And this is in effect to say it over again. And good reason there is for them who have sincerely said it to be well satisfied in their refuge, and to rejoice in their portion. The reflecting upon it may afford solid delight and content of heart. Ye who have taken the Lord for your refuge may with much satisfaction reflect upon what you have done.—*Thomas Boston.*

Verse 6.—"Attend unto my cry."—

Can I see another's woe,
And not be in sorrow too?
Can I see another's grief,
And not seek for kind relief?

Can I see a falling tear,
And not feel my sorrow's share?
Can a father see his child
Weep, nor be with sorrow filled?

Can a mother sit and hear
An infant groan, an infant fear?
No, no; never can it be!
Never, never can it be!

And can he, who smiles on all,
Hear the wren, with sorrows small—
Hear the small bird's grief and care,
Hear the woes that infants bear,

And not sit beside the nest,
Pouring pity in its breast?
And not sit the cradle near,
Weeping tear on infant's tear?

And not sit both night and day
Wiping all our tears away?
Oh, no! never can it be!
Never, never can it be!

He doth give his joy to all;
He becomes an infant small;
He becomes a man of woe;
He doth feel the sorrow too.

Think not thou canst sigh a sigh,
And thy Maker is not by;
Think not thou canst weep a tear,
And thy Maker is not near.

Oh! he gives to us his joy,
That our grief he may destroy:
Till our grief is fled and gone,
He doth sit by us and moan.

—William Blake (1757—1828), in "Songs of Innocence," 1789.

Verse 6.—"I am brought very low," etc. However true this may have been of David lurking in a cave, while his enemy, Saul, was at the head of a powerful army, it is more literally true of Christ, who could truly say, *"I am brought very low,"* because " he himself became obedient unto death, even to the death of the cross." He was also *" brought very low,"* when he, that had the right of sitting on the cherubim, hung between two robbers. Truly also were his enemies *" stronger than he"* when " their hour came," and " power was given to darkness," so as to appear, for awhile, to eclipse the sun of justice itself.—*Robert Bellarmine.*

Verse 6.—*"For they are stronger than I."*　But they are not stronger than THOU. Thou canst make us "stronger than our enemies" : Ps. cv. 24.　He who is stronger than the strong man armed (Luke xi. 22), Israel's oppressor, and whose very "weakness is stronger than men" (1 Cor. i. 25), shall "ransom" her "from him that was stronger than" she : Jer. xxxi. 11 ; Ps. xviii. 17.—*Andrew Robert Fausset.*

Verse 7.—*"Bring my soul out of prison,"* etc.　As if he should say, O Lord, I confess I am a poor prisoner to sin and Satan, I would fain be set at liberty to believe thy word, and to do thy will ; but, alas, I cannot.　I find many a door fast shut upon me in this prison, and many a lock upon the doors, many lets and impediments which I am never able to remove ; and therefore, gracious Lord, do that for me, which neither I myself nor all the friends I can make are ever able to do for me ; pay the debts of thy poor prisoner in my blessed Surety, and set open the prison doors : *"Bring my soul out of prison, O* LORD, *that I may praise thy name!"*—*Matthew Lawrence, in "The Use and Practice of Faith,"* 1657.

Verse 7.—*"The righteous shall compass me about."*　In a circle, like a crown, as the word signifies ; when delivered they should flock to him and come about him to see him and look at him, as a miracle of mercy, whose deliverance was marvellous ; and to congratulate him upon it, and to join with him in praise unto God for it.　The Targum is, "For my sake the righteous will make to thee a crown of praise."—*John Gill.*

Verse 7.—*"For thou shalt deal bountifully with me."*　Others' mercies ought to be the matter of our praises to God ; and others' praises to God on our behalf ought to be both desired and rejoiced in by us.—*Matthew Henry.*

HINTS TO THE VILLAGE PREACHER.

Verse 1.—I. A vivid memory—of what he did, and how, and when. II. A public declaration ; from which we infer that his prayer cheered him, brought him succour in trouble, and deliverance out of it. III. A reasonable inference : he prays again.

Verses 1, 2.—I. Special seasons for prayer : times of complaint and trouble. II. Special prayer on such occasions ; "I cried," "I make my supplication," "I poured out my complaint," "I showed before him my trouble." Spread the whole case before God, as Hezekiah did the letter from Sennacherib.—*G. R.*

Verse 2.—I. The true place for prayer—"before him." II. The freedom of prayer—"poured out." III. The unveiling of the heart in prayer—"shewed before him my trouble."

Verse 3 (*first clause*).—I. When. II. Then.

Verse 3 (*latter clause*).—Temptations. I. What form they take ?—"snares." II. Who lay them ?—"they." III. How do they lay them ? Secretly, craftily—"in the way," frequently. IV. What becomes of the tempted believer ? He lives to tell the tale, to warn others, to glorify God.

Verse 4 (*last clause*).—The soul considered of no value. I. Consider the worth of the soul. 1. The soul will continue for ever. 2. The righteous will grow more happy, and the wicked more miserable. 3. A great price has been paid for it. II. Contrast the care we take of our souls, and our anxiety about worldly objects. 1. The solicitude we manifest for riches. 2. Our care in educating the intellects of our children. 3. Eagerness in pursuit of business, honour—even trifles. 4. How anxious about a human life ! Describe the search for a lost child. 5. Contrast our care for souls and our Saviour's care for them : Paul's, Luther's, Whitefield's. III. Remember some things which show that this care does not exist. 1. If you do not statedly observe secret prayer. 2. If your soul is not burdened with the souls of others.   3. If you neglect family prayer, or observe it as a mere form.   4. If you do not regularly go to prayer-meetings.   Remark : The great responsibility resting upon every Christian.—*Jacob Knapp, in "The Homiletic Monthly,"* 1882.

Verse 4 (*last clause*).—The burden of souls.   I. What is meant by care for souls ?   1. To have a firm conviction of their value.   2. To cherish tender solicitude for their welfare.   3. To feel alarming apprehensions of their danger.   4. To make zealous exertions for their salvation.   II. Who ought specially to exercise this care ?   1. Parents.   2. Teachers.   3. Ministers.   4. Members.   III. The criminality of neglect.   1. It is ungrateful.   2. It is cruel.   3. It is fatal.— *W. W. Wythe, in "The Pulpit Analyst,"* 1870.

Verses 4, 5.—I. A terrible plight ; no friend, no helper, no pitying heart.   II. A touching prayer.   A cry and a saying.

Verses 4, 5.—I. Human help fails most when most needed.   1. In outward troubles : " I looked," etc.   2. In soul troubles : " No man cared for my soul." II. Divine help is most given when most needed.   A refuge and a portion when all others fail.   Man has many friends in prosperity, one only in adversity.—*G. R.*

Verses 4, 5.—I. Why the saints make God their refuge, and the object of their faith and hope in their greatest afflictions.   1. God has given himself to the saints, in the covenant of grace, to be their God, and has promised that they shall be his people.   2. God stands in a most near relation to the saints, and condescends to sustain many endearing characters of love, which he fulfils to their advantage.   3. The saints, through the power of God's grace upon their souls, have chosen him for their portion, and their highest felicity.   II. What perfections there are in God that render him a safe refuge for the saints, and a proper object of their confidence.   1. God is infinite in mercy.   2. God is infallible in wisdom. 3. God is boundless in power.   4. God is omniscient and omnipresent.   5. God is a Being whose love never changes.   6. God is an independent Being, and the Governor and Director of all things.   III. The many sweet advantages, arising to the saints, from this practice of making God their refuge, in their greatest troubles.   1. They have been preserved from fainting under their heavy burdens.   2. They have derived from God new and seasonable supplies of divine grace and strength for service.   3. God has refreshed his saints with divine consolations for the future.—*John Farmer,* 1744.

Verse 5.—The soul choosing God.   I. Deliberately : " I cried unto thee, I said."   II. For all in all : " refuge," " portion."   III. Before every other " in the land of the living."—*W. B. H.*

Verse 5.—" How we may bring our Hearts to bear Reproofs."   See John Owen's Sermon in " The Morning Exercises," vol. ii. page 600, etc. ; and in his " Works," vol. xvi. p. 23, etc.

Verse 6.—Two petitions and two arguments.

Verses 6, 7.—I. The language of Despondency.   " I am brought very low." " My enemies are stronger than I."   " My soul is in prison."   II. Of Prayer. " Attend unto me."   " Deliver me."   " Bring me out of prison."   III. Of Praise.   1. For the congratulation of others.   2. For his own deliverance and prosperity. —*G. R.*

Verse 6.—Low and Lowly.   Here is David, I. In a low place ; the depths of a cave.   II. In a low way : " very low" ; " stronger than I."   III. But see,— " with the lowly is wisdom" (Prov. xi. 2) ; he prays.   IV. The Lord " hath respect to the lowly," Ps. cxxxviii. 6.   He will not pray in vain.—*W. B. H.*

Verse 7.—A prisoner.   A freed-man.   A singer.   A centre.   A wonder.

Verse 7.—Prison Dreams.   I. What we image in our fetters.   1. Christ's brow girt about with rare praise.   2. Christ's people compassing and companying us in costliest service.   3. A new life of bounty and blessing—when we get out.   II. How far do our dreamings come true ?   Before peril and after ; under conviction, and after conversion ; sick room, and active service.   III. The duty of fidelity to prison vows and lessons.—*W. B. H.*

Verse 7 (*middle clause*).—A Queen Bee.   An under-shepherd.   A warm hearth.

A Museum of wonders. Or, they shall surround me, interested in my story—
" out of prison" ; drawn by my song—" praise thy name" ; attracted by likeness
of character, and admiring the goodness of the Lord.

Verse 7 (*last clause*).—Take this with Ps. cxvi. 7. " The Lord hath dealt bountifully with thee." Infer the future from the past.

WORK UPON THE HUNDRED AND FORTY-SECOND PSALM.

In Chandler's " Life of David," vol. i. pp. 157—160, there is an Exposition of
this Psalm.

PSALM CXLIII.

TITLE.—*A Psalm of David. It is so much like other Davidic psalms that we accept the title without a moment's hesitation. David's history illustrates it, and his spirit breathes in it.* Why it has been set down as one of the seven Penitential Psalms we can hardly tell; for it is rather a vindication of his own integrity, and an indignant prayer against his slanderers, than a confession of fault. *It is true the second verse proves that he never dreamed of justifying himself before the Lord; but even in it there is scarcely the brokenness of penitence. It seems to us rather martial than penitential, rather a supplication for deliverance from trouble than a weeping acknowledgment of transgression. We suppose that seven penitentials were needed by ecclesiastical rabbis, and therefore this was impressed into the service. In truth, it is a mingled strain, a box of ointment composed of divers ingredients, sweet and bitter, pungent and precious.* It is the outcry of an overwhelmed spirit, *unable to abide in the highest state of spiritual prayer, again and again descending to bewail its deep temporal distress; yet evermore struggling to rise to the best things. The singer moans at intervals; the petitioner for mercy cannot withhold his cries for vindication. His hands are outstretched to heaven, but at his girdle hangs a sharp sword, which rattles in its scabbard as he closes his psalm.*

DIVISION.—*This psalm is divided by the Selah. We prefer to follow the natural cleavage, and therefore have made no other dissection of it. May the Holy Spirit lead us into its inner meaning.*

EXPOSITION.

HEAR my prayer, O LORD, give ear to my supplications: in thy faithfulness answer me, *and* in thy righteousness.

2 And enter not into judgment with thy servant: for in thy sight shall no man living be justified.

3 For the enemy hath persecuted my soul; he hath smitten my life down to the ground; he hath made me to dwell in darkness, as those that have been long dead.

4 Therefore is my spirit overwhelmed within me; my heart within me is desolate.

5 I remember the days of old; I meditate on all thy work; I muse on the work of thy hands.

6 I stretch forth my hands unto thee: my soul *thirsteth* after thee, as a thirsty land. Selah.

1. "*Hear my prayer, O* LORD, *give ear to my supplications.*" In the preceding psalm he began by declaring that he had cried unto the Lord; here he begs to be favourably regarded by Jehovah the living God, whose memorial is that he heareth prayer. He knew that Jehovah did hear prayer, and therefore he entreated him to hear his supplication, however feeble and broken it might be. In two forms he implores the one blessing of gracious audience:—"hear" and "give ear." Gracious men are so eager to be heard in prayer that they double their entreaties for that boon. The Psalmist desires to be heard and to be considered; hence he cries, "hear," and then "give ear." Our case is difficult, and we plead for special attention. Here it is probable that David wished his suit against his adversaries to be heard by the righteous Judge; confident that if he had a hearing in the matter whereof he was slanderously accused, he would be triumphantly acquitted. Yet while somewhat inclined thus to lay his case before the Court of King's Bench, he prefers rather to turn it all into a petition, and

present it before the Court of Requests, hence he cries rather " hear my prayer " than " hear my suit." Indeed David is specially earnest that he himself, and the whole of his life, may not become the subject of trial, for in that event he could not hope for acquittal. Observe that he offered so much pleading that his life became one continual *prayer ;* but that petitioning was so varied in form that it broke out in many *supplications.*

"*In thy faithfulness answer me, and in thy righteousness.*" Saints desire to be answered as well as heard : they long to find the Lord faithful to his promise and righteous in defending the cause of justice. It is a happy thing when we dare appeal even to righteousness for our deliverance ; and this we can do upon gospel principles, for " if we confess our sins he is faithful and just to forgive us our sins." Even the sterner attributes of God are upon the side of the man who humbly trusts, and turns his trust into prayer. It is a sign of our safety when our interests and those of righteousness are blended. With God's faithfulness and righteousness upon our side we are guarded on the right hand and on the left. These are active attributes, and fully equal to the answering of any prayer which it would be right to answer. Requests which do not appeal to either of these attributes it would not be for the glory of God to hear, for they must contain desires for things unpromised, and unrighteous.

2. "*And enter not into judgment with thy servant.*" He had entreated for audience at the mercy-seat, but he has no wish to appear before the judgment-seat. Though clear before men, he could not claim innocence before God. Even though he knew himself to be the Lord's servant, yet he did not claim perfection, or plead merit ; for even as a servant he was unprofitable. If such be the humble cry of a servant, what ought to be the pleading of a sinner ? "*For in thy sight shall no man living be justified.*" None can stand before God upon the footing of the law. God's sight is piercing and discriminating ; the slightest flaw is seen and judged ; and therefore pretence and profession cannot avail where that glance reads all the secrets of the soul. In this verse David told out the doctrine of universal condemnation by the law long before Paul had taken his pen to write the same truth. To this day it stands true even to the same extent as in David's day : no man living even at this moment may dare to present himself for trial before the throne of the Great King on the footing of the law. This foolish age has produced specimens of a pride so rank that men have dared to claim perfection in the flesh ; but these vain-glorious boasters are no exception to the rule here laid down : they are but men, and poor specimens of men. When their lives are examined they are frequently found to be more faulty than the humble penitents before whom they vaunt their superiority.

3. "*For the enemy hath persecuted my soul.*" He has followed me up with malicious perseverance, and has worried me as often as I have been within his reach. The attack was upon the soul or life of the Psalmist : our adversaries mean us the worst possible evil, their attacks are no child's play, they hunt for the precious life. "*He hath smitten my life down to the ground.*" The existence of David was made bitter by the cruelty of his enemy ; he was as one who was hurled down and made to lie upon the ground, where he could be trampled on by his assailant. Slander has a very depressing effect upon the spirits ; it is a blow which overthrows the mind as though it were knocked down with the fist. "*He hath made me to dwell in darkness, as those that have been long dead.*" The enemy was not content with felling his life to the ground—he would lay him lower still, even in the grave ; and lower than that, if possible, for the enemy would shut up the saint in the darkness of hell if he could. David was driven by Saul's animosity to haunt caverns and holes, like an unquiet ghost ; he wandered out by night, and lay hid by day like an uneasy spirit which had long been denied the repose of the grave. Good men began to forget him, as though he had been long dead ; and bad men made ridicule of his rueful visage as though it belonged not to a living man, but was dark with the shadow of the sepulchre. Poor David ! He was qualified to bless the house of the living, but he was driven to consort with the dead ! Such may be our case, and yet we may be

very dear to the Lord. One thing is certain, the Lord who permits us to dwell in darkness among the dead, will surely bring us into light, and cause us to dwell with those who enjoy life eternal.

4. *"Therefore is my spirit overwhelmed within me; my heart within me is desolate."* David was no stoic: he felt his banishment, and smarted under the cruel assaults which were made upon his character. He felt perplexed and overturned, lonely and afflicted. He was a man of thought and feeling, and suffered both in spirit and in heart from the undeserved and unprovoked hostility of his persecutors. Moreover, he laboured under the sense of fearful loneliness; he was for a while forsaken of his God, and his soul was exceeding heavy, even unto death. Such words our Lord Jesus might have used: in this the Head is like the members, and the members are as the Head.

5. *"I remember the days of old."* When we see nothing new which can cheer us, let us think upon old things. We once had merry days, days of deliverance, and joy and thanksgiving; why not again? Jehovah rescued his people in the ages which lie back, centuries ago; why should he not do the like again? We ourselves have a rich past to look back upon; we have sunny memories, sacred memories, satisfactory memories, and these are as flowers for the bees of faith to visit, from whence they may make honey for present use. *"I meditate on all thy works."* When my own works reproach me, thy works refresh me. If at the first view the deeds of the Lord do not encourage us, let us think them over again, ruminating and considering the histories of divine providence. We ought to take a wide and large view of *all* God's works; for as a whole they work together for good, and in each part they are worthy of reverent study. *"I muse on the work of thy hands."* This he had done in former days, even in his most trying hours. Creation had been the book in which he read of the wisdom and goodness of the Lord. He repeats his perusal of the page of nature, and counts it a balm for his wounds, a cordial for his cares, to see what the Lord has made by his skilful hands. When the work of our own hand grieves us, let us look to the work of God's hands. Memory, meditation, and musing are here set together as the three graces, ministering grace to a mind depressed and likely to be diseased. As David with his harp played away the evil spirit from Saul, so does he here chase away gloom from his own soul by holy communion with God.

6. *"I stretch forth my hands unto thee."* He was eager for his God. His thoughts of God kindled in him burning desires, and these led to energetic expressions of his inward longings. As a prisoner whose feet are bound extends his hands in supplication when there is hope of liberty, so does David. *"My soul thirsteth after thee, as a thirsty land."* As the soil cracks, and yawns, and thus opens its mouth in dumb pleadings, so did the Psalmist's soul break with longings. No heavenly shower had refreshed him from the sanctuary: banished from the means of grace, his soul felt parched and dry, and he cried out, "My soul to thee"; nothing would content him but the presence of his God. Not alone did he extend his hands, but his heart was stretched out towards the Lord. He was athirst for the Lord. If he could but feel the presence of his God he would no longer be overwhelmed or dwell in darkness; nay, everything would turn to peace and joy.

Selah.—It was time to pause, for the supplication had risen to agony point. Both harp-strings and heart-strings were strained, and needed a little rest to get them right again for the second half of the song.

7 Hear me speedily, O LORD: my spirit faileth: hide not thy face from me, lest I be like unto them that go down into the pit.

8 Cause me to hear thy lovingkindness in the morning; for in thee do I trust: cause me to know the way wherein I should walk; for I lift up my soul unto thee.

9 Deliver me, O LORD, from mine enemies: I flee unto thee to hide me.

10 Teach me to do thy will ; for thou *art* my God : thy spirit *is* good : lead me into the land of uprightness.

11 Quicken me, O LORD, for thy name's sake: for thy righteousness' sake bring my soul out of trouble.

12 And of thy mercy cut off mine enemies, and destroy all them that afflict my soul : for I *am* thy servant.

7. *"Hear me speedily, O* LORD : *my spirit faileth."* If long delayed, the deliverance would come too late. The afflicted suppliant faints, and is ready to die. His life is ebbing out ; each moment is of importance ; it will soon be all over with him. No argument for speed can be more powerful than this. Who will not run to help a suppliant when his life is in jeopardy ? Mercy has wings to its heels when misery is in extremity. God will not fail when our spirit fails, but the rather he will hasten his course and come to us on the wings of the wind. *"Hide not thy face from me, lest I be like unto them that go down into the pit."* Communion with God is so dear to a true heart that the withdrawal of it makes the man feel as though he were ready to die and perish utterly. God's withdrawals reduce the heart to despair, and take away all strength from the mind. Moreover, his absence enables adversaries to work their will without restraint ; and thus, in a second way, the persecuted one is like to perish. If we have God's countenance we live, but if he turns his back upon us we die. When the Lord looks with favour upon our efforts we prosper, but if he refuses to countenance them we labour in vain.

8. *"Cause me to hear thy lovingkindness in the morning ; for in thee do I trust."* Lord, my sorrow makes me deaf,—cause me to hear : there is but one voice that can cheer me—cause me to hear thy lovingkindness ; that music I would fain enjoy at once—cause me to hear it in the morning, at the first dawning hour. A sense of divine love is to the soul both dawn and dew ; the end of the night of weeping, the beginning of the morning of joy. Only God can take away from our weary ears the din of our care, and charm them with the sweet notes of his love. Our plea with the Lord is our faith : if we are relying upon him, he cannot disappoint us : " in thee do I trust" is a sound and solid argument with God. He who made the ear will cause us to hear : he who is love itself will have the kindness to bring his lovingkindness before our minds. *"Cause me to know the way wherein I should walk ; for I lift up my soul unto thee."* The Great First Cause must cause us to hear and to know. Spiritual senses are dependent upon God, and heavenly knowledge comes from him alone. To know the way we ought to take is exceedingly needful, for how can we be exact in obedience to a law with which we are not acquainted ? or how can there be an ignorant holiness ? If we know not the way, how shall we keep in it ? If we know not wherein we should walk, how shall we be likely to follow the right path ? The Psalmist lifts up his soul : faith is good at a dead lift : the soul that trusts will rise. We will not allow our hope to sink, but we will strive to get up and rise out of our daily griefs. This is wise. When David was in any difficulty as to his way he lifted his soul towards God himself, and then he knew that he could not go very far wrong. If the soul will not rise of itself we must lift it, lift it up unto God. This is good argument in prayer : surely the God to whom we endeavour to lift up our soul will condescend to show us what he would have us to do. Let us attend to David's example, and when our heart is low, let us heartily endeavour to lift it up, not so much to comfort as to the Lord himself.

9. *"Deliver me, O* LORD, *from mine enemies."* Many foes beset us, we cannot overcome them, we cannot even escape from them ; but Jehovah can and will rescue us if we pray to him. The weapon of all-prayer will stand us in better stead than sword and shield. *"I flee unto thee to hide me."* This was a good result from his persecutions. That which makes us flee to our God may be an ill wind, but it blows us good. There is no cowardice in such flight, but much holy courage. God can hide us out of reach of harm, and even out of sight of it. He

is our hiding-place ; Jesus has made himself the refuge of his people : the sooner, and the more entirely we flee to him the better for us. Beneath the crimson canopy of our Lord's atonement believers are completely hidden ; let us abide there and be at rest. In the seventh verse our poet cried, "Hide not thy face," and here he prays, "Hide me." Note also how often he uses the words "unto thee" ; he is after his God ; he must travel in that direction by some means, even though he may seem to be beating a retreat ; his whole being longs to be near the Lord. Is it possible that such thirstings for God will be left unsupplied ? Never, while the Lord is love.

10. "*Teach me to do thy will.*" How childlike—"teach me" ! How practical "Teach me to do" ! How undivided in obedience—"to do thy will" ! To do all of it, let it be what it may. This is the best form of instruction, for its source is God, its object is holiness, its spirit is that of hearty loyalty. The man is hidden in the Lord, and spends his peaceful life in learning the will of his Preserver. A heart cannot long be desolate which is thus docile. "*For thou art my God.*" Who else can teach me as thou canst ? Who else will care to do it but my God ? Thou hast given me thyself, thou wilt surely give me thy teaching. If I have thee, may I not ask to have thy perfect mind ? When the heart can sincerely call Jehovah "my God," the understanding is ready to learn of him, the will is prepared to obey him, the whole man is eager to please him. "*Thy spirit is good.*" God is all spirit and all good. His essence is goodness, kindness, holiness : it is his nature to do good, and what greater good can he do to us than to hear such a prayer as that which follows—"*Lead me into the land of uprightness*" ? David would fain be among the godly, in a land of another sort from that which had cast him out. He sighed for the upland meadows of grace, the table-lands of peace, the fertile plains of communion. He could not reach them of himself ; he must be led there. God, who is good, can best conduct us to the goodly land. There is no inheritance like a portion in the land of promise, the land of precept, the land of perfectness. He who teaches us must put us into leading-strings, and guide and conduct us to his own dwelling-place in the country of holiness. The way is long, and steep, and he who goes without a divine leader will faint on the journey ; but with Jehovah to lead it is delightful to follow, and there is neither stumbling nor wandering.

11. "*Quicken me, O* LORD, *for thy name's sake.*" Oh for more life as well as more light ! Teaching and leading call for invigoration, or we shall be dull scholars and slow pilgrims. Jehovah, the Lord and giver of life, is the only one from whom life can come to renew and revive us ;—hence, the prayer is to him only. Perchance a servant might teach and lead, but only the Master can enliven. We are often near to death, and hence each one may fitly cry, "Quicken *me*"; but what is there in us which we can plead as a reason for such a favour ? Nothing, literally nothing. We must beg it for his name's sake. He must quicken us because he is the living God, the loving God; the Lord who delighteth in mercy. What blessed arguments lie clustered together in his glorious name ! We need never cease praying for want of acceptable pleas ; and we may always fall back upon the one before us—"thy name's sake." It will render the name of Jehovah the more glorious in the eyes of men if he creates a high degree of spiritual life in his servants ; and this is a reason for his doing so, which we may urge with much confidence.

"*For thy righteousness' sake bring my soul out of trouble.*" Let men see that thou art on the side of right, and that thou wilt not allow the wicked to ride roughshod over those who trust in thee. Thou hast promised to succour thy people ; thou art not unrighteous to forget their work of faith ; thou art, on the contrary, righteous in answering sincere prayer, and in comforting thy people. David was heavily afflicted. Not only was there trouble in his soul, but his soul was in trouble ; plunged in it as in a sea, shut up in it as in a prison. God could bring him out of it, and especially he could at once lift up his soul or spirit out of the ditch. The prayer is an eager one, and the appeal a bold one. We may be sure that trouble was soon over when the Lord heard such supplications.

12. "*And of thy mercy cut off mine enemies, and destroy all them that afflict my soul.*" He believes that it will be so, and thus prophesies the event ; for the words may be read as a declaration, and it is better so to understand them. We could not *pray* just so with our Christian light ; but under Old Testament arrangements the spirit of it was congruous to the law. It is a petition which justice sanctions, but the spirit of love is not at home in presenting it. *We*, as Christians, turn the petition to spiritual use only. Yet David was of so generous a mind, and dealt so tenderly with Saul, that he could hardly have meant all that his words are made in our version to say. "*For I am thy servant*"; and therefore I hope that my Master will protect me in his service, and grant me victory while I fight his battles. It is a warrior's prayer, and smells of the dust and smoke of battle. It was heard, and therefore it was not asking amiss. Still there is a more excellent way.

EXPLANATORY NOTES.

Whole Psalm.—This psalm of David most aptly answereth to that psalm which precedeth it ; for in Ps. cxlii. he showeth that he prayed, repeating it twice (verse 1) ; and here he twice saith, " Hear my prayer, give ear to my supplication." In Psalm cxlii. (verse 3) he saith, " When my spirit was overwhelmed within me " ; here (verse 4), " My spirit is overwhelmed within me."—*John Mayer.*

Whole Psalm.—The promise referred to throughout this octave of Psalms [cxxxviii—cxlv.] is that recorded in 2 Sam. vii. 12, etc., " When thy days be fulfilled . . . I will set up thy seed after thee . . . and I will establish his kingdom . . . If he commit iniquity, I will chasten him . . . But my mercy shall not depart away from him ; and thine house and thy kingdom shall be established for ever." What fixes the connection of the psalm with the history is the frequent application of the term "*Thy* (Jehovah's) *servant*," by David to himself in the latter, as in verses 2 and 12 of the former. Jehovah had first used it of David, " Tell to my servant, to David "; David therefore fastens on it as his plea again and again (2 Sam. vii. 5, 9—21, 25—29). David's plea, " For I am thy servant," is no boast of his service, but a magnifying of God's electing grace : " Who am I, O Lord God ? and what is my house, that thou hast brought me hitherto ?" 2 Sam. vii. 18.

The cry (verse 6) "*My soul thirsteth after thee as a thirsty land*," answers to David's own words in Psalm lxiii. 1, when he was fleeing from Absalom, and still in the wilderness of Judah (title, Ps. lxiii.) on the near side of Jordan : " My soul *thirsteth* for thee." The history here again is an undesigned agreement with the psalm(2 Sam. xvi. 2, 14) : " The King, and all the people with him, came *weary*, and refreshed themselves " with Ziba's fruits ; also xvii. 2. The Hebrew for "*thirsty*" in Psalm cxliii. is the same as for "*weary*" in lxiii. 1, and in 2 Sam. xvi. 14, and means " panting," " weary," " thirsting."—*Andrew Robert Fausset, in "Studies in the CL. Psalms,"* 1876.

Whole Psalm.—At the making of this psalm (as it plainly appeareth) David was cast into some desperate danger ; whether by Saul when he was forced to flee into the cave, as in the former psalm, or by Absalom his son, or by any other, it is uncertain. Howsoever, in this he complaineth grievously to God of the malice of his enemies, and desireth God to hear his prayers, he acknowledgeth that he suffereth those things by God's just judgment, most humbly craving mercy for his sins ; desiring not only to be restored, but also to be governed by God's Spirit, that he may dedicate and consecrate the rest of his life to God's service. This worthy psalm, then, containeth these three things. First, a confession of his sins. Secondly, a lamentation over his injuries. Thirdly, a supplication for temporal deliverance and spiritual graces.—*Archibald Symson.*

Whole Psalm.—It is not without some use to observe in this psalm how the heart of its devout composer turned alternately from spiritual to temporal, and again from temporal to spiritual subjects. He first complains of *his sins*, and begs for *mercy ;* then of *his enemies,* and prays for *deliverance.* Then he laments his darkness, and pleads for the light of God's countenance, and for wisdom, and understanding. After this, the thought of his enemies rushes in again upon his soul, and he flees to God for protection. Lastly, he again puts up his prayer for wisdom and holiness : "Teach me to do thy will ; for thou art my God : thy spirit is good ; lead me into the land of uprightness." This is a peculiarly important petition : before he had prayed to know the way in which he should walk, he now prays that he may walk in it.—*John Fawcett,* 1769—1851.

Whole Psalm.—This is appointed by the Church for Ash-Wednesday, and is the seventh and last of the Penitential Psalms. These seven Penitential Psalms are also sometimes called "the Special Psalms," and have long been used in the Church as the completest and most spiritual acts of repentance which she possesses. They have sometimes been considered as directed against the seven deadly sins ; as, for instance, Psalm vi. against Wrath ; Ps. xxxii. against Pride ; Ps. xxxviii. against Gluttony ; Ps. li. against Impurity ; Ps. cii. against Covetousness ; Ps. cxxx. against Envy ; and the present Psalm against Indifference, or Carelessness.—*J. W. Burgon.*

Verse 1.—"*Hear my prayer, O* LORD," etc. Alas, O Lord, if thou hear not my prayer, I were as good not pray at all ; and if thou hear it, and give not ear unto it, it were as good thou didst not hear it at all. O, therefore, "*hear my prayer, O God, and give ear to my supplications*" *;* that neither my praying may be lost for want of thy hearing it, nor thy hearing it be lost for want of thy attending it. When I only make a prayer to God, it seems enough that he hear it ; but when I make a supplication, it requires that he give ear unto it : for seeing a supplication hath a greater intention in the setting out, it cannot without a greater attention be entertained.

But what niceness of words is this ? as though it were not all one "*to hear*" and "*to give ear*"? or as though there were any difference between a prayer and a supplication ? Is it not perhaps so indeed ? for hearing sometimes may be only passive, where giving ear is always active ; and seeing Christ, we doubt not, heard the woman of Canaan's first cry, while it was a prayer ; but gave no ear till her second cry, when it was grown to a supplication. However it be, as thy hearing, O God, without giving ear would be to no purpose, so thy giving ear without giving answer would do me no good ; O, therefore, "*answer me,*" O God : for if thou answer not my prayer, how canst thou answer my expectation ? My prayer is but the seed ; it is thy answer that makes the harvest. If thou shouldst not answer me at all, I could not hope for any harvest at all ; and if thou shouldst answer me, and not "*in thy righteousness,*" that would be a harvest indeed, but nothing but of blasted corn. Therefore, answer me, O God, but "in thy righteousness" ; for thy righteousness never made an unpleasing answer. It was an answer in thy righteousness which thou madest to Noah : "My spirit shall not always strive with man ; for the imagination of man's heart is evil from his infancy." It was an answer in thy righteousness which thou madest to Abraham : "Fear not ; I will be thy shield, and thy exceeding great reward." It was an answer in thy righteousness which thou madest to the thief upon the cross : "This day thou shalt be with me in paradise." Oh, then, answer me also in thy righteousness, O God, and then the harvest of my hope will be as plentiful as the seven years of plenty foretold by Joseph.—*Sir Richard Baker.*

Verse 1.—"*Hear my prayer,*" . . . "*give ear to my supplications,*" . . . "*answer me.*" He doth here three times repeat his earnest desire to be heard, as in the fifth psalm four times he doubleth and ingeminateth this same suit to be heard. . . . When he doubleth his request of hearing, he would have God hear him with both his ears, that is, most attentively and readily : so instant is a troubled mind that he desireth the prayer he putteth up to be remembered, as was said by the angel to the centurion : "Thy prayer and almsdeeds are come up before God " : Acts x. 4.—*Archibald Symson.*

Verse 1.—"*In thy faithfulness answer me, and in thy righteousness.*" It was thy righteousness that thou didst make the promise, but it is thy faithfulness that thou wilt keep thy promise : and seeing I am certain of thy making it, how can I be doubtful of thy keeping it ? If thou shouldst not answer me in thy righteousness, yet thou shouldst be righteous still ; but if thou shouldst not answer me in thy faithfulness, thou shouldst not be faithful still.—*Sir Richard Baker.*

Verse 1.—"*Answer me in thy righteousness.*" Forgiveness is not inconsistent with truth or righteousness, and the pardon which in mercy God bestows upon the sinner is bestowed in justice to the well-beloved Son who accepted and discharged the sinner's obligations. This is an infinitely precious truth, and the hearts of thousands in every age have been sustained and gladdened by it. A good old Christian woman in humble life so fully realized this, that when a revered servant of God asked her, as she lay on her dying pillow, the ground of her hope for eternity, she replied, with great composure, " I rely on the justice of God " ; adding, however, when the reply excited surprise, " justice, not to me, but to my Substitute, *in whom I trust.*"—*Robert Macdonald, in "From Day to Day ; or, Helpful Words for Christian Life,"* 1879.

Verse 2.—"*Enter not into judgment with thy servant.*" The Divine justice has just been invoked in the first verse ; and now the appellant suddenly seems to deprecate it. These verses really sum up the apparent paradox of the Book of Job (see Job iv. 17, ix. 2, 32, xiv. 3, *seq.*, xv. 14, xxii. 4, etc.). In one breath Job frequently pours forth pathetic protestations of his innocence, and a dread lest God should take him at his word, and arraign him for trial. The godly man, in his desire to have his character vindicated before man, appeals to the just Judge, but instantly falls back with a guilty sense that before his tribunal none can stand :

> " For merit lives from man to man,
>   And not from man, O Lord, to thee."

—*A. S. Aglen.*

Verse 2.—He doth not pray absolutely that God " would not enter into judgment with him," for this were to forego his government of the world ; but that he would not do so on account of his own duties and obedience. But if so be these duties and obedience did answer, in any sense or way, what is required of us as a righteousness unto justification, there was no reason why he should deprecate a trial by them, or upon them.—*John Owen.*

Verse 2.—He doth not say, " with an enemy, a rebel, a traitor, an impenitent sinner"; but " *with thy servant,*" one that is devoted to thy fear, one that is consecrated to thy service, one that is really and indeed " wholly thine, as much and as fully as he can be." As if he had said, " Lord, if the holiest, purest, best of men should come and stand before thee in judgment, or plead with thee, they must needs be cast in their cause. ' If thou, Lord, shouldest mark iniquities,' alas ! ' O Lord, who shall stand ? ' " Psalm cxxx. 3.—*Thomas Lye* (1621—1684), *in "The Morning Exercises."*

Verse 2.—"*Enter not into judgment with thy servant,*" for thou hast already entered into judgment with thy Son, and laid upon him the iniquity of us all. "*Enter not into judgment with thy servant,*" for thy servant enters into judgment with himself ; and " if we will judge ourselves we shall not be judged."—*Matthew Henry.*

Verse 2.—Not the proudest philosopher among the Gentiles, nor the most precise Pharisee among the Jews ; we may go yet further and say, not the holiest saint that ever lived, can stand righteous before that bar. God hath nailed that door up, that none can for ever enter by a law-righteousness into life and happiness. This way to heaven is like the northern passage to the Indies, whoever attempts it is sure to be frozen up before he gets half way thither.—*William Gurnall.*

Verse 2.—"*Enter not into judgment,*" etc. Some years ago I visited a poor young woman dying with consumption. She was a stranger in our town, and had been there a few weeks before, some time in her girlhood, and had attended my Sabbath-school class. What did I find was her only stay, and hope, and comfort in the view of the dark valley of the shadow of death, which was drawing down upon her ? One verse of a psalm she had learned at the class, and never forgot. She repeated it with clasped hands, piercing eyes, and thin voice trembling from her white lips.

> "Thy servant also bring thou not
> In judgment to be tried :
> Because no living man can be
> In thy sight justify'd."

No—no sinner can endure sight of thee, O God, if he tries to be self-justified. —*James Comper Gray, in "The Biblical Museum,"* 1879.

Verse 2.—"*Enter not into judgment with thy servant.*" We read of a certain Dutch divine, who being to die, was full of fears and doubts. And when some said to him, " You have been so active and faithful, why should you fear ?" Oh, said he, the judgment of man and the judgment of God are different.—*John Trapp.*

Verse 2.—"*Enter not into judgment.*" A metaphor taken from the course pursued by those who seek to recover the very utmost to which they are entitled by strict legal process. Compare Job xxii. 4, 5. In a similar sense we are commanded to pray to God that he will forgive us our debts.—*Daniel Cresswell.*

Verse 2.—There is probably here a tacit reference to the great transgression, the consequences of which followed David all his days.— *William Walford.*

Verse 2.—"*Thy servant.*" A servant is one who obeys the will of another. . . . There were these four ways in which one might come to be a servant—by birth, by purchase, by conquest, and by voluntary engagement. Some were servants in one of the ways, and some in another. There were servants who were born in the master's house, servants who were bought with the master's money, servants who were the captives of his sword and bow, and servants who had freely engaged themselves to do his work. . . . In the case of the believer there is something that is peculiar and remarkable. He is God's servant by birth. But he is more —he is God's servant by purchase. And that is not all : he is God's servant by conquest. Yes, and by voluntary engagement too. He is the servant of God, not in some one of the four ways, but in all of them together.—*Andrew Gray* (1805—1861), *in "Gospel Contrasts and Parallels."*

Verse 2.—Not only the worst of my sins, but the best of my duties speak me a child of Adam.— *William Beveridge.*

Verse 2.—So far from being able to answer for my sins, I cannot answer even for my righteousness.—*Bernard of Clairvaux,* 1091—1153.

Verse 2.—A young man once said to me : " I do not think I am a sinner." I asked him if he would be willing his mother or sister should know all he had done, or said, or thought,—all his motions and all his desires. After a moment he said : " No, indeed, I should not like to have them know ; no, not for the world." " Then can you dare to say, in the presence of a holy God, who knows every thought of your heart, ' I do not commit sin ' ?"—*John B. Gough, in "Sunlight and Shadow,"* 1881.

Verse 3.—"*For the enemy,*" etc. If ever trouble be just cause for calling upon thee, how can mine be more just, when " *the enemy hath persecuted my soul, hath smitten my life down to the ground, and hath made me to dwell in darkness, as those that have been long dead* " ? All this " *the enemy* " hath done unto me : but what enemy ? Is it not the enemy of all mankind, who hath singled me out, as it were to a duel ? And can *I* resist him myself alone, whom the whole army of mankind cannot ? But is it not the enemy of thyself, O God, who is but my enemy because I am thy servant ? And wilt thou see thy servants persecuted—in thy cause persecuted—and not protect them ? Shall I suffer, grievously suffer, for thy sake, and wilt thou forsake me ? Alas, O Lord ; if they were but some light evils that are inflicted upon me I would bear them without complaining, and never make my moan to thee about them ; but they are the three greatest miseries that can be thought of ; the greatest persecution, the greatest overthrow, and the greatest captivity. For what persecution so grievous as to be persecuted in my soul ? for he plays no less a game than for souls : he casts indeed at the body sometimes, and sometimes at goods, yet these are but the bye ; the main of his aim is at the soul ; for if he can otherwise win the soul he cares not much for either body or goods, but rather makes use of them to keep men in security ; for whatsoever he doth, whatsoever he leaves undone, it is all done but in persecution of the soul ; and he can persecute as well with prosperity as with adversity, and knows how to fit their several application. It seems as if he takes me for another Job ; he sees he can do no good upon me with fawning and clawing, and therefore falls now to quarrelling and striking : and he strikes no light blows ; for " *he hath stricken my life down to the ground* " ; and lower would have struck it, if thou, God, hadst not broken his blow. He strikes me downward, to keep me from heaven, as much as he can : and now that he sees me down, he lets not me rest so neither ; but seizeth upon me, and being himself the prince of darkness, hath kept me in darkness ; not for a night or two, as men stay at their inn, but for a much longer time, as at their dwelling ; and it is no ordinary darkness that he hath made me to dwell in, but even the darkness of dead men ; and that in the highest degree, as those that have been long dead. They that have been dead but a while are yet remembered sometimes, and sometimes talked of ; but they that have been long dead are as quite forgotten as if they had never been ; and such, alas, am I. So long have I been made to dwell in darkness, as if I had been dead many years ago, that he that would seek to find me out must be fain to look for me amongst the tombs and monuments. Indeed, to dwell in darkness is no better than the house of death : for as long as we are in life, if we want sometimes the light of the sun, yet the light of a candle will serve to supply it ; but I, alas, am kept in such darkness that neither the sunshine of thy gospel nor the lantern of thy law gives any light unto me. I cannot with confidence say, as once I did, " Thou, O Lord, shalt light my candle for me" ; and as a body being dead grows cold and stiff, and is not to be bowed, so my soul with continuance in sinning is grown hardened, and, as it were, stiff in sin ; that it is as hard a matter to make me flexible to any goodness as to bring a body long dead to life again.—*Sir Richard Baker.*

Verse 3.—"*To dwell in darkness.*" To seek my safety in holes and obscure places in the wilderness. See 2 Sam. xvii. 16. "*As those that have been long dead.*" That is, where I seem to be buried alive, and to have no more hopes of being restored to a happy condition in this world than those that have been long dead have of living again in it.—*Thomas Fenton.*

Verse 4.—"*Therefore is my spirit overwhelmed,*" etc. David was not only a great saint, but a great soldier, and yet even he was sometimes ready to faint in the day of adversity. " Howl, fir trees, if the cedars be shaken."—*Matthew Henry.*

Verse 4 (second clause).—"*Within me*"—literally, " *in the midst of me* " ; imply-ing how *deeply* the feeling had penetrated. "*Is desolate,*" or rather, " is *stupe-fied,*" in a similar sense to that of the Hebrew (Isai. lix. 16 ; lxiii. 5 ; Dan. viii. 27). So the Chaldaic, The LXX., Vulgate, Arabic, and Syriac, " *is agitated.*"—*Andrew Robert Fausset.*

Verse 4.—"*Is desolate.*" Or rather, " is full of amazement," literally, " aston-ishes itself " ; seeks to comprehend the mystery of its sufferings, and is ever beaten back upon itself in its perplexity : such is the full force of the reflexive conjugation here employed.—*J. J. Stewart Perowne.*

Verses 4, 5.—How poor a judgment can be formed of a man's state from the considerations of comfort only. A holy man, we clearly see, may be void of comfort ; his spirit may be overwhelmed, and his heart desolate. Nay, was it not so even with the holy Jesus himself ? was he not very heavy, and his soul exceeding sorrowful even unto death ? But never did the Saviour's faith and submission to his Father's will shine more brightly than in that hour of darkness. And David's faith also rises to meet the occasion. His trial is great, and his faith is great also. Hardly when he is on the mount of praise, and singing his songs of Zion in the most triumphant strain, does he appear more admirable than when struggling through this painful conflict. He is troubled on every side, yet not removed ; perplexed, but not in despair ; persecuted, but not forsaken ; cast down, but not destroyed. He has no arm of flesh to trust to, and nothing within himself to support his hope ; but with what simplicity, and energy of trust, does he betake himself to God, revolving in his memory past seasons of deliverance, and staying his mind on the power and truth of Jehovah ! " I remember the days of old ; I meditate on all thy works ; I muse on the work of thy hands."— *John Fawcett.*

Verse 5.—"*I remember the days of old ; I meditate,*" etc. This meditation gives an ease to the overwhelming of my spirits, a comfort to the desolateness of my heart ; for I am thinking sometimes upon Jonah, how he was overwhelmed with waters and swallowed up of a whale, and yet at last delivered ; sometimes I am thinking of Joseph, how he was bound and left desolate in a pit, and yet at last relieved ; and then I meditate thus with myself,—Is God's power confined to persons ? could he deliver them in their extremities, and can he not deliver me in mine ?—*Sir Richard Baker.*

Verse 5.—"*I meditate on all thy works.*" Let us look for God in the future more earnestly than we have done in the past,—look for him in vineyards and orchards and harvest fields,—in the bright plumage of birds, and the delicate bloom of fruit, and the sweet gracefulness of flowers,—in the dense foliage of the forest, and the sparse heather of the moor,—in the rich luxuriance of fertile valleys, and the rugged grandeur of the everlasting hills, -- in the merry dance of the rivulet, and the majestic tides of the ocean—in the gay colours of the rainbow, and the splendour of the starry heavens,—in the gentle radiance of the moon, and the gorgeous light of setting suns,—in the clear azure sky, and the weird pageantry of clouds,—in the snow-mantled wintry landscape, and the brilliant effulgence of a summer's noon,—in the virgin loveliness of spring, and in the pensive fading beauty of autumn,—let us look for him with an earnest, eager, and unwearied gaze, till we see him to be a God of wisdom as well as power, of love as well as sovereignty, of beauty as well as glory.—*A. W. Momerie, in "The Origin of Evil, and other Sermons,"* 1881.

Verses 5, 6.—"*I meditate.*" "*I stretch forth my hands.*" Meditation is prayer's handmaid to wait on it, both before and after the performance of supplication. It is as the plough before the sower, to prepare the heart for the duty of prayer ; and as the harrow after the sower, to cover the seed when 'tis sown. As the hopper feeds the mill with grist, so does meditation supply the heart with matter for prayer.—*William Gurnall.*

Verse 6.—"*I stretch forth my hands unto thee.*" As a poor beggar for an alms. Beggary here is not the easiest and poorest trade. but the hardest and richest of all other.—*John Trapp.*

Verse 6.—"*I stretch forth my hands unto thee,*" as if I were in hope thou wouldst take me by the hand and draw me to thee.—*Sir Richard Baker.*

Verse 6.—"*My soul thirsteth after thee,*" etc. Alas ! this thirst is rare to be found. Worldly thirsts there are in many : the drunkard's thirst, Deut. xxix. 19 ; the worldling's thirst, Hab. ii. 5 ; the epicure's thirst, whose belly is his god, Phil. iii. 19 ; the ambitious man's thirst—Diotrephes, 3 John 9 ; and the malicious man's thirst, the blood thirsty, Ps. v. 6. Thirst after these things doth keep away that thirst after grace without which we shall never escape Dives' thirst in hell, Luke xvi. 24. If we have a godly thirst, it will appear by diligence in frequenting the place and means of grace, Prov. viii. 34 ; brute beasts for want of water will break through hedges, and grace-thirsty souls will make their ways through all encumbrances to come where they may have satisfaction.—*Thomas Pierson, 1570—1633.*

Verse 6.—*"My soul thirsteth after thee, as a thirsty land."* He declareth his vehement affection to God by a very pretty similitude, taken from the ground which is thirsty by the long drought of summer, wherein the earth, rent in pieces, as it were, and with open mouth through long thirst, seeketh drink from heaven. By which he showeth that he came to God as destitute of natural substance, and therefore seeketh from above that which he lacked. So in all his extremities he looked ever upward ; from above he seeketh help and comfort. Albeit we be in extremity, and as it were rent asunder, yet here is comfort,—there are waters in heaven which will refresh us, if we gape after them. Here is a blessing—those that thirst shall be satisfied. If we thirst for mercy, for deliverance, for spiritual or temporal comfort, we shall be satisfied therewith ; for if God heard the prayers of Hagar and Ishmael being athirst in the wilderness, and opened unto them a fountain (Gen. xxi. 17, 19), will he forsake Isaac, the child of promise ? If he heard Samson in the bitterness of his heart, when he said, "I die from thirst," and opened a spring out of the jawbone of an ass (Jud. xv. 19), will he forsake us in time of our distress, if we thirst aright ?—*Archibald Symson.*

Verse 6.—*"My soul thirsteth after thee, as a thirsty land."* Sir John Chardin, in his MSS. says :—"The lands of the East, which the great dryness there causes to crack, are the ground of this figure, which is certainly extremely beautiful ; for these dry lands have chinks too deep for a person to see the bottom of : this may be observed in the Indies more than anywhere, a little before the rains fall, and wherever the lands are rich and hard."—*Harmer's Observations.*

Verse 6.—*"I stretch forth my hands unto thee,"* etc. It is not a strange thing, then, for the soul to find its life in God. This is its native air : God as the Environment of the soul has been from the remotest age the doctrine of all the deepest thinkers in religion. How profoundly Hebrew poetry is saturated with this high thought will appear when we try to conceive of it with this left out. True poetry is only science in another form. And long before it was possible for religion to give scientific expression to its greatest truths, men of insight uttered themselves in psalms which could not have been truer to Nature had the most modern light controlled the inspiration. "As the hart panteth after the water-brooks, so panteth my soul after thee, O God." What fine sense of the natural analogy of the natural and spiritual does not underlie these words. As the hart after its environment, so man after his ; as the water-brooks are fitly designed to meet the natural wants, so fitly does God implement the spiritual need of man. It will be noticed that in the Hebrew poets the longing for God never strikes one as morbid, or unnatural to the men who uttered it. It is as natural for them to long for God as for the swallow to seek her nest. Throughout all their images no suspicion rises within us that they are exaggerating. We feel how truly they are reading themselves, their deepest selves. No false note occurs in all their aspiration. There is no weariness even in their ceaseless sighing, except the lover's weariness for the absent—if they would fly away, it is only to be at rest. Men who have no soul can only wonder at this. Men who have a soul, but with little faith, can only envy it. How joyous a thing it was to the Hebrews to seek their God ! How artlessly they call upon him to entertain them in his pavilion, to cover them with his feathers, to hide them in his secret place, to hold them in the hollow of his hand, or stretch around them the everlasting arms ! These men were true children of nature. As the humming-bird among its own palm-trees, as the ephemera in the sunshine of a summer evening, so they lived their joyous lives. And even the full share of the sadder experiences of life which came to all of them but drove them the further into the secret place, and led them with more consecration to make, as they expressed it, "*the Lord their portion.*" All that has been said since from Marcus Aurelius to Swedenborg, from Augustine to Schleiermacher, of a besetting God as the full complement of humanity is but a repetition of the Hebrew poets' faith. And even the New Testament has nothing higher to offer man than this. The Psalmist's "God is our refuge and strength" is only the earlier form, less defined, less practicable, but not less noble, of Christ's " Come unto me, and I will give you rest."—*Henry Drummond, in "Natural Law in the Spiritual World,"* 1884.

Verses 6, 7.—*"I stretch forth my hands.* . . . *Hear me,"* etc. So will the weary hands be raised yet again, through faith in him who stretched forth his hands upon the cross. So will the fainting soul wait and long for the outpouring of his grace, who upon the cross said, " I thirst." We shall thirst for our salvation, even as the parched-up fields and dying herbs seem to gasp and pant like living things for the sweet and cheering showers in the fierce heat of summer. So will the soul cry to be heard, and that soon, lest its faith grow faint with delay ; and the hiding of God's face, the denying of his smile of pardon, will press on the spirit like sickness, and weigh it down like the heaviness of death.—*J. W. Burgon.*

Verse 7.—*"Hear me speedily."* David is in trouble, and he betakes himself to prayer. Prayer is the sovereign remedy the godly fly to in all their extremities. The saints in sorrows have fled for comfort and healing unto prayers and supplications. Heaven is a shop full of all good things—there are stored up blessings and mercies ; this the children of God know who fly to this shop in their troubles, begging for help from this holy sanctuary. " In the day of my trouble I sought the Lord " : Ps. lxxvii. 2. When any vexation makes our life grievous unto us, what should we seek but help ? of whom should we seek, but of the Lord ? how should we seek, but by prayer ? . . . *"Speedily."* His request is not only for hearing, but for speedy hearing : *"Hear me, and hear me speedily ";* answer, and answer quickly. This is the tone and tune of men in distress. Man in misery earnestly sues for speedy delivery. In our afflictions and troubles, deliverance, though it should come with wings, we never think it comes soon enough. Weak man cannot content himself to know he shall have help, unless it be present help.—*Thomas Calvert,* 1647.

Verse 7.—*"My spirit faileth."* This is David's first reason to move the Lord ; he is at the last cast and even giving up the ghost with long waiting for help : from his low condition we may see what is often the condition of God's children, —and the best of God's servants have waited for comfort and the feelings of his Spirit, to the very failing of their own spirit. David, a man after God's own heart, is yet brought low with the faintness and failing of his heart, in waiting for help from God. " In the sweat of thy face shalt thou eat bread " (Gen. iii. 19) ; this lies upon the sons of men. But here, not sweat of face only, that were but small ; but sighs and fainting of the heart lie upon the sons of God, in seeking and hungering after a taste of God's bread of life, inward comfort, assurance, and joy of the Holy Ghost. Thus the Church was brought to this sick bed ere her comfort came : " For these things I weep ; mine eye, mine eye runneth down with water, because the comforter that should relieve my soul is far from me :" Lam. i. 16. The disciples' spirits were even failing in the tempest, when Christ slept and seemed to neglect them, as if he cared not though they perished. How should our spirits do other but fail, when our Comforter sleeps, when our only friend seems to be our enemy ?

Failing of spirit is both a motive which God means to yield unto and to be won by withal ; and it is also his opportunity, when he usually helps. It is a strong motive in our prayers to move him, for he is pitiful, and will not let his children utterly fail and perish ; he is a pitiful Spirit to failing spirits. " I will not contend (saith the Lord) for ever, neither will I be always wroth ;" why ? we deserve his wrath should last and take fire for ever against us ; yea, but (saith the Lord) this is the reason, " The spirit should fail before me, and the souls which I have made" (Isaiah lvii. 16) : I love and pity the fainting souls and spirits of men : I will help my children ; how can I see my creatures whom I made and do love, to perish for want of my help ? David knew the Lord's nature, and that this was a speeding argument in prayer, which made him here and elsewhere so often use it. A pitiful father will not see the spirit of his children utterly fail. It is his opportunity ; he usually helps when all other helps fail, that we may the more strongly cleave to him, and ground ourselves upon him, as knowing how infirm we are, if he confirm us not.   When man's cruse of oil is dry, and fails, and can drop no more, then is God's time to prepare his.   Thus helped he the Israelites at the Red Sea, when all man's strength and wisdom was at a stand.   He loves to be seen in the mount, in extremities.—*Condensed from Thomas Calvert.*

Verse 7.—The prayer of David becomes, as he proceeds, both more spiritual and more fervent.   In the sixth verse we find him thirsting after God ; and now that thirst is become so intense that it admits of no delay.   In the beginning of the psalm he was content to say, " Hear my prayer "; but now he cries, " Hear me *speedily.*"   This is not the language of sinful impatience : it is, indeed, good that a man should both hope and quietly wait for the salvation of God ; yet a man may desire, not only an answer, but also a speedy answer, without incurring the charge of impatience.   Whatever a man desires to have he desires to have soon ; nor can he be otherwise than grieved at anything which delays the accomplishment of his wishes.   In such desire or grief there is nothing sinful, provided it do not lead to murmuring or distrust of God.   Hence this petition for *speedy* relief, and manifestation of God's presence and favour is very frequent with the Psalmist.   He often prays, " Make haste, O Lord, to deliver ; make haste to help me, O Lord."   Nay, if a man does not desire the light of God's countenance soon, it is a certain proof that he does not desire it at all.   If the natural language of his heart be not, " hear me speedily," delay is to him no exercise of patience.   The very idea of patience implies that something is contrary to our wish ; and the stronger the desire is, the more difficult will that exercise of patience become.

" Hope deferred maketh the heart sick " ; and therefore David adds, " my spirit faileth."   He believed verily to see the goodness of the Lord in the land of the living ; yet so intense was his desire, that faith could hardly keep his spirit from fainting, while the blessing, which he so eagerly pursued, seemed still distant, and fled before him.   He is afraid lest if God should long delay, and withdraw himself, faith and hope could hold out no longer.   He therefore pleads, " hide not thy face from me, lest I become like them that go down into the pit "; and urges the failing of his spirit before him who " will not contend for ever, lest the spirit should fail before him."—*John Fawcett.*

Verses 7, 8, 10, 11.—Observe how David mixes together prayers for joy, for guidance, and for sanctification—" Hide not thy face from me."   " Cause me to know the way wherein I should walk."   " Teach me to do thy will."   " Cause me to hear thy loving-kindness in the morning."   " Quicken me, O Lord, for thy name's sake."   Now this is exactly right : our prayers, as well as our other obedience, must be without partiality ; nay, we should desire comfort for the sake of holiness, rather than holiness for the sake of comfort.—*John Fawcett.*

Verse 8.—"*Cause me to hear thy lovingkindness.*"   Here he craveth God's favour and kindness, as he doth in many other psalms.   Because in his favour is life, wealth, and grace, all good things, and pleasure for evermore, so that if he look kindly to us we need be afraid of nothing.   But how shall he be assured of his favour ?   Even by *hearing* it, as he saith in the fifty-first psalm : " Make me to hear joy and gladness."   The voice which is heard is the word of God, which, being apprehended by faith, is able to comfort our souls in whatsoever temptation.   It is no marvel that such atheists and papists who altogether refuse the word of God, live comfortless and die without comfort, because they refuse that instrument which should carry joy to them.   Good reason they die athirst, since they reject that vessel, the word of God, by which they might be refreshed. Therefore since faith cometh by hearing of God's word, and all our comfort cometh by it, let us pray God to bore our ears and our hearts, that we may receive the glad tidings of reconciliation from God.

"*Cause me to know the way wherein I should walk.*"   The second petition ariseth very well from the first.   For when we have obtained an assurance of God's favour, as he is reconciled to us in Jesus Christ, it followeth next that we should desire to conform our lives to the obedience of his commandments. For no man will frame himself to walk in God's ways till he be assured of God's favour. Therefore faith in God's promises is the most effectual cause to bring forth good works ; and an assurance of justification the surest means to produce sanctification.

"*For I lift up my soul unto thee.*" Behold what a wonderful effect God worketh by afflictions : they depress and cast down the outward man, and our inward man by them is elevated and raised aloft ; yea, the more we are afflicted, the more we are stirred up. The oftener the messenger of Satan is sent to buffet us, the more earnestly (with Paul) we cry unto the Lord to be delivered (2 Cor. xii. 8). So if we be cast down to hell in our feelings, what the worse are we if by that we be raised up to heaven ?—*Archibald Symson.*

Verse 8.—"*Cause me to hear thy lovingkindness in the morning,*" etc. To hear thy lovingkindness in the morning makes my waking to be saluted, as it were, with music ; makes my troubles seem as if they were but dreams ; makes me find it true that though " weeping may endure for a night, yet joy cometh in the morning " : Ps. xxx. 5. . . . It may well be said we hear this lovingkindness in the morning, seeing it makes it morning to us whensoever we hear it.—*Sir Richard Baker.*

Verse 8.—"*Cause me to hear thy lovingkindness in the morning.*" If evil fall upon us in the night, we would have it removed ere the morning : if in the morning, we would not have it our bed-fellow in the evening. We would have the Lord's promise run thus,—Your sorrows shall not endure the whole night, your joy shall come long before the morning. The luxurious Emperor [? Smyndirides the Sybarite] and his drunken mates sat and drank all the night, and slept all the day, insomuch that it was said of them, they never saw sun-set nor sun-rise. Such would we have the evils we suffer—of so short continuance that neither sun-set nor sun-rise might see us in our misery. This makes me wonder at that strange Egyptian beast called Pharaoh, who being demanded of Moses when he would have God's plague of the frogs removed, answered, "*To-morrow.*" Surely, here he spake not as a man, to whom one hour's trouble is accounted a day, a day a month, a month a year. For in leaving of two things we change our desires, and are much different.

1. In leaving of sin, then we procrastinate and put off ; and when God says, " To-day hear my voice," we answer, " To-morrow," and are like the Levite's wife's father (Judg. xix. 6), too kind hosts to such bad guests : saying to our sins, " tarry till the morning." Our pace to repentance is slow, we are far from haste in that matter.

2. But for afflictions to leave us, then we wish they had feet like hinds' feet, to run away from us, or we the wings of a dove to fly away from them, and be at rest. . . . What prisoner desires not to be presently set free, and that liberty's soft hand may loose his iron knots ? What mariner wishes a long storm ? What servant sighs not over his hard apprenticeship ? Yea, who is he, that if there were an appearance of an offering to take the cup of calamity from his mouth, saying, " Thou shalt drink no more," would answer, " This cup shall not yet pass from me, I delight to carouse and drink deeply of these bitter waters" ? Yea, this desire extends so far that it comes to the Son of man, the blessed Seed of the woman, who was so clad with human weakness that he earnestly prayed for speedy help from his heavy anguish ; and that not once, but often,— " Oh, my Father, if it be possible," etc. ; and when his Father answers not, he cries like one ready to fall under the burden, " My God, my God, why hast thou forsaken me ?" The reason for Christ's thus complaining is to be fetched from thence, whence his flesh came ; even from us. It was our human flesh, not his Divine spirit, which was so weary of suffering ; his spirit was willing, it was our flesh that was so weak.—*Thomas Calvert.*

Verse 8.—"*Cause me to hear thy lovingkindness in the morning.*" This is a short and sweet morning prayer. God hears early prayer, and lovingly responds to it.

The smiles of his face, the sweetness of his voice, the gifts of his hand, bless the morning, bless all the day. Do we write and read experimentally? Then we know the blessedness of divine love. The subject is truly pleasant and precious. *"Lovingkindness"* is a favourite expression, is a choice theme of David's. It is used more in the Book of Psalms than in any other book in the Scriptures. Lovingkindness is love showing kindness; it is the sun of love shining with rays of kindness; the river of love sending forth streams of kindness; it is the heart of love uttering itself by words of kindness, doing deeds, and giving gifts of kindness.

Here it is the *voice* of the lovingkindness of the Lord that David desires to hear. This voice is the music of heaven, the joyful sound of the gospel, and it makes a jubilee in the Christian's heart. To him there is beauty, sweetness, fulness in the theme; it is his joy and rejoicing. This is the voice that speaks *pardon.* Pardon is through Jesus the medium of this kindness. Apart from this there is no hope of forgiveness. We plead this and realize pardon. "Have mercy upon me, O God, according to thy lovingkindness: according unto the multitude of thy tender mercies blot out my transgressions": Ps. li. 1. It is the Lord's lovingkindness that pardons me. This voice speaks *peace:* "The Lord will speak peace unto his people." Precious peace is the result of pardoning kindness. This voice also speaks *joy.* This is the alone and all-sufficient source of joy. It is sought elsewhere, but found only here. It sweetens every bitter, and makes sweeter every sweet. It is a balsam for every wound, a cordial for every fear. The present is but a taste, but a drop of the future fulness of joy. How sweetly refreshing is the joy of the Lord's lovingkindness. This voice speaks *hope.* With the sweet music of this voice falling upon our ears, the night of hopelessness passes away, and the morning of expectation opens upon us. It assures us of supplies for our wants, of safety in danger, of endurance to the end, and of a glorious portion in eternity.

"The morning" is the season in which David desires to hear the voice of the lovingkindness of the Lord. The morning is a season often mentioned by him, and as a time of devotion is much prized by him. "My voice shalt thou hear in the morning, O LORD; in the morning will I direct my prayer unto thee, and will look up": Ps. v. 3. *"Cause me to hear thy lovingkindness in the morning":* let it engage my thoughts and affections. It is well to have a subject like this to occupy our waking thoughts, and to take hold of our first desires. If other thoughts get into our hearts in the morning, we may not be able to turn them out all the day. Prayer and praise, reading and meditation, will be sweet with such a subject occupying and influencing our minds. They will be exercises of cheerfulness, freedom, and blessedness.

"Cause me to hear" this voice. It speaks every morning, but many ears are deaf to it. But while others are indifferent to it, cause me to hear it; let me not lose the opportunity: waken my ear morning by morning, so that I may hail the season and enjoy the privilege. And when the morning of eternity shall come, "cause me to hear the voice of thy lovingkindness" welcoming me to its joys.— *W. Abbot, in "The Baptist Messenger,"* 1870.

Verse 8. —*"Cause me to know the way wherein I should walk."* The whole valley is surrounded by ranges of regal crags; but the mountain of the Gemmi, apparently absolutely inaccessible, is the last point to which you would turn for an outlet. A side gorge that sweeps up to the glaciers and snowy pyramids flashing upon you in the opposite direction is the route which you suppose your guide is going to take; and visions of pedestrians perilously scaling icy precipices, or struggling up to the middle through ridges of snow, begin to surround you, as the prospect of your own experience in this day's expedition. So convinced was I that the path *must* go in that direction, that I took a short cut, which I conceived would bring me again into the mule path at a point under the glaciers; but after scaling precipices and getting lost in a wood of firs in the valley, I was glad to rejoin my friend with the guide, and to clamber on in pure ignorance and wonder. . . . Now what a striking symbol is this of things that sometimes take place in our spiritual pilgrimage. We are often brought to a stand, hedged up and hemmed in by the providence of God so that there seems no way out. A man is sometimes thrown into difficulties in which he sits down beginning to despair, and says to himself, " Well, this time it is all over with me "; like Sterne's starling, or, worse, like Bunyan's man in the cage, he says, " I cannot get out." Then when God has drawn him from all self-confidence and self-resource, a door opens in the wall and he rises up, and walks at liberty, praising God.—*George Barrell Cheever*, 1807—.

Verses 8—10.—After thou hast prayed, observe what God doth towards thee ; especially how he doth guide thy feet and heart after prayer ; there is much in that. That which was the spirit of supplication in a man when he prayed, rests upon him as the spirit of obedience in his course. That dependence which he hath upon God for the mercy he seeks for is a special motive and means to keep him fearful of offending, and diligent in duty. He looks to his paths, and endeavours to behave himself as becomes a suitor, as well as to pray as a suitor. David walked by this principle when he said (Ps. lxvi. 18), " If I regard iniquity in my heart, the Lord will not hear me" ; that consideration still came in as a curb unto sin. Therefore David, in these verses, when he was to pray, even as for his life, for deliverance from his enemies, he specially prays God to direct him and keep him, that he might not sin against him ; for he knew that by sinning he should enervate and spoil all his prayers. He cries not only *"Hear me speedily,"* but also, *" Cause me to know the way wherein I should walk ; teach me to do thy will."* This he especially prays for, more than for deliverance, for else he knew God would not hear him. Therefore when thou art in treaty with God for any mercy, observe, doth God still after praying keep thee in a more obedient frame of spirit ? If so, it is a sign he intends to answer thee. The same is true when he keeps thee from using ill means, etc. When he meant to give David the kingdom, he kept him innocent, and made his heart tender, so that it smote him but for cutting off the lap of Saul's garment.—*Thomas Goodwin.*

Verse 9.—*"Deliver me, O* Lord, *from mine enemies."* In the former verse he desireth God's mercy and lovingkindness, and that he might be showed the way wherein he should walk : now he desireth to be free of temporal danger. This is a good method in prayer, first to seek the kingdom of God and spiritual graces, for then all other things shall be added to us. We seek in vain temporal deliverances of God if we neglect to seek spiritual graces, which are most necessary for us.

As for *enemies,* the church and her members neither have wanted nor shall want innumerable foes, against whom we can only oppose God's protection. In number, in power, in policy and subtilty they are ever above us. There is no help for us against them all but our gracious God. Esau came with four hundred against Jacob, a naked man, with his wife, children, and droves of cattle. But Mahanaim was with him ; he was guarded by God's angels. And, therefore, since the church of God in France, Germany, and elsewhere is in danger of the Leviathan and the sons of Anak, let us run to the Lord, and cry unto him,—O God Jehovah, deliver thy church from her enemies, who art one against all, deliver thy church from her enemies, who likewise are thy enemies.—*Archibald Symson.*

Verse 9.—*"I flee unto thee to hide me."* Is David's valour come to this, that he is come now to be glad to fly ? Had he not done better to have died valiantly than to fly basely ? O my soul, to fly is not always a sign of baseness ; it is not always a point of valour to stand to it ; but then to fly when we feel our own weakness, and to him to fly, in whom is our strength—this is, if not valour, at least wisdom, but it is, to say true, both wisdom and true valour. And now, O God, seeing I find my own weakness, and know thy strength, what should I do but fly, and whither fly but only to thee ?—to thee, a strong fortress to all that build upon thee ; to thee, a safe sanctuary to all that fly unto thee.—*Sir Richard Baker.*

Verse 9.—*"I flee unto thee to hide me."* This implies, 1. *Danger:* the Christian may be in danger from sin, self, foes. 2. *Fear:* his fears may be groundless, but they are often very painful. 3. *Inability*—to defend himself or overcome his opposers. 4. *Foresight :* he sees the storm in the distance, and looks out for the covert. 5. *Prudence :* he hides before the storm, ere the enemy comes upon him. 6. A laudable *concern* for safety and comfort. The believer, if wise, will at all times flee to Jehovah. Jacob flies to Laban ; the manslayer to the refuge ; the bird to his mountain ; and the Christian to his God. Asa may seek to physicians ; Ephraim to king Jareb ; and Saul to the witch ; but the believer looks to his God. The Lord receives, befriends, and secures him. Let us flee to him by prayer, in faith, with hope, for salvation ; and he will receive us, shelter us, and be our refuge and strength. Flee from sin, from self, from the world ; but flee to Jesus. His heart is ever toward us, his ear is open to us, and his hand is ready to help, protect, and deliver us. His throne is our asylum. His promise is our comfort, and his omnipotence is our guard.

> Happy soul, that, free from harms,
> Rests within his Shepherd's arms !
> Who his quiet shall molest ?
> Who shall violate his rest ?
> He who found the wandering sheep,
> Loves, and still delights to keep.

James Smith, in "The Believer's Daily Remembrancer."

Verse 9.—"*I flee unto thee to hide me.*" The Lord hid the prophets so that Ahab could not find them out : 1 Kings xviii. 13. If we will creep under his wings he will surely keep us.—*Archibald Symson.*

Verse 9.—"*I flee unto thee to hide me.*" It may be rendered, " *With thee have I hid* " ; that is, myself : so Arama gives the sense. "*I have hid myself with thee.*" Jarchi, Aben Ezra, and Kimchi interpret it to this purpose, " I have hid my affairs, my straits and troubles, my difficulties and necessities, from men, and have revealed them unto thee, who alone can save." The Targum is, " I have appointed thy Word to be (my) Redeemer.—*John Gill.*

Verses 9, 10.—Be persuaded actually to hide yourselves with Jesus Christ. To have a hiding-place and not to use it is as bad as to want one : fly to Christ ; run into the holes of this rock. Three things must be done by all those that would hide themselves with Christ.

1. You must put away sin by repentance. Jesus Christ will not be a sanctuary for rebels, he will not protect evil-doers. Christ will never hide the devil, nor any of his servants. Isai. lv. 6, 7 : " Let the ungodly forsake his way," etc. David knew this, therefore he prays that God would teach him to do his will : "*Deliver me, etc. I fly unto thee to hide me.' Teach me to do thy will.*" He that will not do the will of Christ shall receive no protection from Christ. *Protectio sequitur allegiantiam.* You must be his liege people if you will have him to defend you. Job xxii. 23, 25.

2. You must pray that he would hide you. The promise is made to prayer : Isa. lxv. 10, " Sharon shall be a fold of flocks, and the valley of Achor a place for the herds to lie down in, for my people that have sought me." He that prays most fervently is like to be hid most securely. And then,

3. You must believe in him. Faith is the key that opens the door of this hiding-place, and locks it again. One word in the Hebrew signifies to trust and to make a refuge. Ps. lvii. 1. He that doth not make Christ his trust shall not have Christ for his hiding-place ; he will hide none but those that commit themselves to him : " I will set him on high, because he hath known my name" : Ps. xci. 9, 14.—*Ralph Robinson.*

Verse 10.—"*Teach me to do thy will.*" He saith not, Teach me to *know* thy will, but to *do* thy will. God teaches us in three ways. First, by his word. Secondly, he illuminateth our minds by the Spirit. Thirdly, he imprinteth it in our hearts and maketh us obedient to the same ; for the servant who knoweth the will of his master, and doeth it not, shall be beaten with many stripes : Luke xii. 47.—*Archibald Symson.*

Verse 10.—*"Teach me to do thy will."* We are to pray that God would teach us to know, and then teach us to do, his will. Knowledge without obedience is lame, obedience without knowledge is blind ; and we must never hope for acceptance if we offer the blind and the lame to God.—*Vincent Alsop* (—1703), in *"The Morning Exercises."*

Verse 10.—*"Teach me to do thy will."* The Lord doth no sooner call his people to himself, but as soon as ever he hath thus crowned them with these glorious privileges, and given them any sense and feeling of them, then they immediately cry out, O Lord, what shall I now do for thee ? How shall I now live to thee ? They know now that they are no more their own, but his ; and therefore should now live to him.

It is true indeed obedience to the law is not required of us now as it was of Adam ; it was required of him as a condition antecedent to life, but of those that be in Christ it is required only as a duty consequent to life, or as a rule of life, that seeing he hath purchased our lives in redemption, and actually given us life in vocation and sanctification, we should now live unto him, in all thankful and fruitful obedience, according to his will revealed in the moral law. It is a vain thing to imagine that our obedience is to have no other rule but the Spirit, without an attendance to the law : the Spirit is indeed the efficient cause of our obedience, and hence we are said to be "led by the Spirit" (Rom. viii. 14) ; but it is not properly the rule of our obedience, but the will of God revealed in his word, especially in the law, is the rule ; the Spirit is the wind that drives us in our obedience ; the law is our compass, according to which it steers our course for us : the Spirit and the law, the wind and the compass, can stand well together. *"Teach me to do thy will ; for thou art my God"* (there is David's rule, viz., God's will revealed) ; *"Thy Spirit is good"* (there is David's wind, that enabled him to steer his course according to it). The Spirit of life doth free us from the law of sin and death ; but not from the holy, and pure, and good, and righteous law of God. Rom. viii. 1—3.—*Thomas Shepherd, in "The Sound Believer,"* 1671.

Verse 10.—*"Teach me to do thy will,"* etc. We are inclined and enabled [to good] by the sanctifying Spirit. In the Christian religion, not only the precepts are good, but there goeth along with them the power of God to make us good. *"Teach me to do thy will ; for thou art my God : thy Spirit is good."* The Spirit's direction hath strength joined with it. And he is a good Spirit, as he doth incline us to good. The Spirit is the only fountain of all goodness and holiness : Neh. ix. 20, "Thou gavest also thy good Spirit to instruct them." Why is he so often called the good Spirit, but that all his operations tend to make men good and holy ? Eph. v. 9, "The fruit of the Spirit is in all goodness and righteousness and truth."—*Thomas Manton.*

Verse 10.—*"Thy Spirit is good ; lead me,"* says the Psalmist. And therefore it is a usual phrase in Rom. viii. and Gal. iv., our being *led* by the Spirit.—*Thomas Goodwin.*

Verse 10.—*"Lead me into the land of uprightness,"* into the communion of saints, that pleasant land of the upright ; or into a settled course of holy living, which will lead to heaven, that land of uprightness, where holiness will be in perfection, and he that is holy will be holy still. We should desire to be led and kept safe to heaven, not only because it is a land of blessedness, but because it is a land of uprightness ; it is the perfection of grace.—*Matthew Henry.*

Verse 10.—*"Lead me."* Man by nature is as a cripple and blind, he cannot go upright unless he be led by a superior spirit ; yea, he must be carried as an eagle carrieth her little ones, or as a mother her tender child. Think not that we can step one right step to heaven but by the conduct and convoy of God's Holy Spirit. Miserable are those who go without his conduction.—*Archibald Symson.*

Verse 10.—*"The land of uprightness." Mishor* is the name for the smooth upland downs of Moab (Deut. iii. 10 ; Josh. xiii. 17 ; xx. 8 ; Jer. xlviii. 8, 21). Derived from the root *yashar,* "even, level plain," it naturally came to be used figuratively for equity, right, righteous, and uprightness. Mal. ii. 6 ; Isai. xi. 4 ; Ps. xlv. 7 ; lxvii. 5 ; cxliii. 10.—*Cunningham Geikie, in "Hours with the Bible,"* 1884.

Verse 10.—"*The land of uprightness.*" The land of plainness, a land where no wickedness of men, and malice of Satan, vex the soul from day to day ; a land where no rough paths and crooked turns lengthen out the traveller's weary journey (see verse 5) ; but where all is like the smooth pasture-lands of Reuben (Deut. iii. 10 ; Josh. xiii. 9), a fit place for flocks to lie down.—*Andrew A. Bonar.*

Verse 11.—"*Quicken me, O* LORD, *for thy name's sake.*" For the sake of thine own glory, that thou mayest show thyself to be the God of lovingkindness and power which thou art esteemed to be. —*Andrew Robert Fausset.*

Verse 11.—"*For thy righteousness' sake.*" It is worthy of observation that the Psalmist pleads God's righteousness as the foundation on which he bases his supplication for the deliverance of his soul from trouble, and God's lovingkindness or mercy as that on which he grounds his prayer, or his conviction, that God will destroy his enemies. This is not the language of a revengeful and bloodthirsty spirit. —*Speaker's Commentary.*

Verse 11.—"*Bring my soul out of trouble.*" I can bring it in, but thou only canst bring it out.—*John Trapp.*

Verses 11, 12.—"*Thy name's sake . . . thy righteousness' sake . . . And of thy mercy.*" Mark here, my soul, with what three cords David seeks to draw God to grant him his suits : for his name's sake, for his righteousness' sake, and for his mercy's sake,—three such motives, that it must be a very hard suit that God will deny, if either of them be used. But though all the three be strong motives, yet as David riseth in his suits, so he may seem also to rise in his motives ; and by this account ; for his righteousness' sake will prove a motive of a higher degree than for his name's sake, and for his mercy's sake the highest of them all—as indeed his mercy-seat is the highest part of all his ark, if it be not rather that as the attributes of God, so these motives, that are drawn from the attributes, are of equal pre-eminence. But if the three motives be all of them so strong, being each of them single, how strong would they be if they were all united, and twisted, I may say, into one cord ? And united they are all, indeed, into a motive, which God hath more clearly revealed to us than he did to David (although it be strange, seeing it was his Lord ; and yet not strange, seeing it was his son) ; and this is the motive : for thy Son Christ Jesus' sake ; for he is the *verbum abbreviatum* [the Word in brief], in whom are included all the motives—all the powerful motives—that can be used to God for obtaining our suits.—*Sir Richard Baker.*

Verses 11, 12.—The verbs in these two last verses, as Dr. Hammond hath noted, should be rendered in the future ; "*Thou shalt quicken,*" etc., and then the psalm will end, as usual, with an act of faith and assurance, that all those mercies, which have been asked, shall be obtained ; that God, for the sake of his " *name,*" and his " *righteousness,*" of his glory, and his faithfulness in the performance of his promises, will not fail to be favourable and gracious to his servants, "*quickening*" them, even when dead in trespasses and sins, and bringing them, by degrees, "*out of all their troubles*"*:* going forth with them to the battle against their spiritual " *enemies,*" and enabling them to vanquish the authors of their " *affliction* " and misery, to mortify the flesh, and to overcome the world ; that so they may triumph with their Redeemer, in the day when he shall likewise quicken their mortal bodies, and put all enemies under their feet.—*George Horne.*

Verse 12.—"*Of thy mercy cut off mine enemies.*" He desireth God to slay his enemies in his mercy, when rather their destruction was a work of his justice ? I answer, that the destruction of the wicked is a mercy to the church. As God showed great mercy and kindness to his church by the death of Pharaoh, Sennacherib, Herod, and other troublers thereof.—*Archibald Symson.*

Verse 12.—"*Cut off mine enemies,*" etc. When you find these imprecations to be prophecies of events which the Psalmist himself could not understand ; but were to be fulfilled in persons whom the Psalmist could not know, as they were to live in distant future ages,—for instance, Judas, and the Romans, and leaders of the Jewish nation,—who would make these imprecations proofs of a revengeful spirit ?—*James Bennet* (1774—1862), *in "Lectures on the Acts of the Apostles,"* 1847.

Verse 12.—"*I am thy servant.*" David the king professeth himself one of God's pensioners. Paul, when he would blaze his coat of arms, and set forth his best heraldry, he doth not call himself Paul, an Hebrew of the Hebrews, or Paul of the tribe of Benjamin, but Paul " a servant of Christ" : Rom. i. 1. Theodosius thought it a greater dignity to be God's servant than to be an emperor. Christ himself, who is equal with his Father, yet is not ashamed of the title *servant :* Isai. liii. 11. Every servant of God is a son, every subject a prince : it is more honour to serve God than to have kings to serve us : the angels in heaven are servitors to the saints.—*Thomas Watson.*

HINTS TO THE VILLAGE PREACHER.

Verse 1.—Three threes. I. As to his devotions,—prayers, supplications, requests. II. As to his success,—hear, give ear, answer me. III. As to his argument,—because thou art Jehovah, faithful, righteous.

Verses 1, 2.—A suitable prayer for a believer who has reason to suppose that he is suffering chastening for sin. I. Here is earnest importunity, as of one depending entirely upon divine favour for a hearing. II. Here is believing fervency laying hold of divine faithfulness and justice ; see 1 John i. 9. III. Here is a deep consciousness of the vanity of self-justification pleading for pure mercy, ver. 2.—*J. F.*

Verse 2.—I. Who he is. " Thy servant." II. What he knows. " In thy sight shall no man living be justified." III. What he asks. " Enter not into judgment."

Verses 3—6.—Consider, I. The great lengths God may sometimes permit the enemy to go, ver. 3. The case of Job a good illustration. II. The deep depression of spirit he may even permit his saints to experience, ver. 4. III. The good things he has provided for their meditation when even at their worst, ver. 5. IV. The two things his grace will never suffer to die, whose existence is a pledge of near approaching joy,—1. The thirsting after himself. 2. The practice of prayer. The whole is a good text for a lecture on the life and experience of Job.—*J. F.*

Verses 4, 5, 6.—I. Down in Despondency. II. Deep in Meditation. III. Determined in Supplication.

Verses 5, 6.—"*I muse on the work of thy hands. I stretch forth my hands unto thee.*" Hand in hand : or the child of God admiring the work of God's hands, and praying with uplifted hands to be wrought upon by the like power.

Verse 5.—David's method. I. He gathered materials ; facts and evidence concerning God : " I remember." II. He thought out his subject and arranged his matter : " I meditate." III. He discoursed thereon, and was brought nearer to God : " I muse"—discourse. IV. Let us close by viewing all this as an example for preachers and others.—*W. B. H.*

Verse 6.—God alone the desire of his people.

Verse 6.—Deep calling to deep. I. The insatiable craving of the heart. II. The vast riches in glory. III. The rushing together of the seas : " My soul is to thee."—*W. B. H.*

Verse 7.—Reasons for speedy answers.

Verse 7.—Never despair. I. Because you have the Lord to plead with. II. Because you may freely tell him the desperateness of your case. III. Because you may be urgent with him for deliverance.—*J. F.*

Verse 7.—Cordial for the swooning heart. I. God's beloved fainting. II. The best restorative ; her Lord's face. III. She has the presence of mind to call him as she falls.—*W. B. H.*

Verse 8.—The two prayers—"*Cause me to hear,*" and "*Cause me to know.*" The two pleas—"*In thee do I trust,*" and "*I lift up my soul unto thee.*"

Verse 8, Ps. cxlii. 3.—"*Thou knewest my path.*" Ps. cxliii. 8.—"*Cause me to know the way."* I. Trusting Omniscience in everything. II. Following conscience in everything.

Verse 8.—On fixing a time for the answering of our prayer. I. By whom it may be done. Not by all believers, but by those who through dwelling with God have attained to a holy boldness. II. When it may be done. 1. When the case is specially urgent. 2. When God's honour is concerned. III. What renders it pleasing to God when done. Great faith. "For in thee do I trust."—*J. F.*

Verse 8.—Listening for Lovingkindness. I. Where to listen. At the gates of Scripture ; in the halls of meditation ; nigh the footsteps of Jesus. II. When to listen. "In the morning" ; as early and as often as possible. III. How to listen. In trustful dependence : "Cause me to hear thy lovingkindness in the morning, for in thee do I trust." IV. Why to listen. To "know the way wherein I should walk."—*W. B. H.*

Verse 9.—Admirable points in this prayer to be imitated by us. There is, I. A sense of danger. II. A confession of weakness. III. A prudent foresight. IV. A solid confidence :—he expects to be hidden from his foes.

Verse 9.—I. Looking up. II. Lying close.—*W. B. H.*

Verse 10.—Two childlike requests—"Teach me . . . lead me."

Verse 10.—See "Spurgeon's Sermons," No. 1519, "At School."

Verse 10 (first half).—I. The best instructions : "Teach me to do thy will." Not merely to know, but "to do." II. The only efficient Instructor. III. The best reason for asking and expecting instruction : "For thou art my God."—*J. F.*

Verse 10.—*"Teach me to do thy will."* We may call this sentence a description of David's school ; and it is a very complete one ; at least, it hath in it the three best things that belong to a school. I. The best teacher. II. The best scholar. III. The best lesson ; for who so good a teacher as God ? who so good a scholar as David ? what so good a lesson as to do God's will ?—*Sir Richard Baker.*

Verse 10 (latter half).—I. Utopia—"the land of uprightness." Describe it, and declare its glories. II. The difficult paths to that upland country. III. The divine Guide,—"thy Spirit is good."

Verse 11 (first clause).—I. What is this blessing? "Quicken me." II. In what way will it glorify God, so that we may plead for the sake of his name ?

Verse 11 (second clause).—How is the righteousness of God concerned in our deliverance from trouble ?

Verse 12.—I. To the Master : "I am thy servant." II. For the servant : he seeks protection because he belongs to his master.

WORKS ON THE HUNDRED AND FORTY-THIRD PSALM.

MEDITATIONS AND DISQVISITIONS UPON The Three last Psalms of DAVID [Pss. CII., CXXX., CXLIII.]. *By* SR. RICHARD BAKER, *Knight, LONDON. . . .* **1639.** [The above is scarce, but will be found in Mr. Higham's Reprint of Sir R. Baker on the Psalms.]

A SACRED SEPTENARIE, OR, A GODLY AND FRVITFVLL EXPOSITION ON THE SEVEN PSALMS OF REPENTANCE. . . . by Mr. Archibald Symson. . . . *LONDON,* 1638 [4to.], contains an Exposition of this Psalm, pp. 276—308.

There is an Exposition of Psalm CXLIII., in Vol. I., pp. 35—66, of "Sermons chiefly designed for the Use of Families, by John Fawcett, A.M. [2 Vols. 8vo, second edition], Carlisle : 1818."

PSALM CXLIV.

Albeit that this Psalm is in some measure very similar to Psalm xviii., yet it is a new song, and in its latter portion it is strikingly so. Let the reader accept it as a new psalm, and not as a mere variation of an old one, or as two compositions roughly joined together. It is true that it would be a complete composition if the passage from verse 12 to the close were dropped; but there are other parts of David's poems which might be equally self-contained if certain verses were omitted; and the same might be said of many uninspired sonnets. It does not, therefore, follow that the latter part was added by another hand, nor even that the latter part was a fragment by the same author, appended to the first song merely with the view of preserving it. It seems to us to be highly probable that the Psalmist, remembering that he had trodden some of the same ground before, felt his mind moved to fresh thought, and that the Holy Spirit used this mood for his own high purposes. Assuredly the addendum is worthy of the greatest Hebrew poet, and it is so admirable in language, and so full of beautiful imagery, that persons of taste who were by no means over-loaded with reverence have quoted it times without number, thus confessing its singular poetical excellence. To us the whole psalm appears to be perfect as it stands, and to exhibit such unity throughout that it would be a literary Vandalism, as well as a spiritual crime, to rend away one part from the other.

Title.—*Its title is "Of David," and its language is of David, if ever language can belong to any man. As surely as we could say of any poem, This is of Tennyson, or of Longfellow, we may say, This is of David. Nothing but the disease which closes the eye to manifest fact and opens it to fancy, could have led learned critics to ascribe this song to anybody but David. Alexander well says, "The Davidic origin of this psalm is as marked as that of any in the Psalter."*

It is to God the devout warrior sings when he extols him as his strength and stay (verses 1 and 2). Man he holds in small account, and wonders at the Lord's regard for him (verses 3 and 4); but he turns in his hour of conflict to the Lord, who is declared to be "a man of war," whose triumphant interposition he implores (verses 5 to 8). He again extols and entreats in verses 9, 10 and 11; and then closes with a delightful picture of the Lord's work for his chosen people, who are congratulated upon having such a God to be their God.

EXPOSITION.

BLESSED *be* the LORD my strength, which teacheth my hands to war, *and* my fingers to fight :

2 My goodness, and my fortress ; my high tower, and my deliverer ; my shield, and *he* in whom I trust ; who subdueth my people under me.

1. "*Blessed be the* LORD *my strength.*" He cannot delay the utterance of his gratitude, he bursts at once into a loud note of praise. His best word is given to his best friend—"Blessed be Jehovah." When the heart is in a right state it must praise God, it cannot be restrained ; its utterances leap forth as waters forcing their way from a living spring. With all his strength David blesses the God of his strength. We ought not to receive so great a boon as strength to resist evil, to defend truth, and to conquer error, without knowing who gave it to us, and rendering to him the glory of it. Not only does Jehovah give strength to his saints, but he is their strength. The strength is made theirs because God is theirs. God is full of power, and he becomes the power of those who trust him. In him our great strength lieth, and to him be blessings more than we are able to utter. It may be read, "*My Rock*" ; but this hardly so well consorts with the following words : "*Which teacheth my hands to war, and my fingers to fight.*" The word *rock* is the Hebrew way of expressing strength ; the grand old language is

full of such suggestive symbols. The Psalmist in the second part of the verse sets forth the Lord as teacher in the arts of war. If we have strength we are not much the better unless we have skill also. Untrained force is often an injury to the man who possesses it, and it even becomes a danger to those who are round about him ; and therefore the Psalmist blesses the Lord as much for teaching as for strength. Let us also bless Jehovah if he has in anything made us efficient. The tuition mentioned was very practical, it was not so much of the brain as of the hands and fingers ; for these were the members most needful for conflict. Men with little scholastic education should be grateful for deftness and skill in their handicrafts. To a fighting man the education of the hands is of far more value than mere book-learning could ever be ; he who has to use a sling or a bow needs suitable training, quite as much as a scientific man or a classical professor. Men are too apt to fancy that an artisan's efficiency is to be ascribed to himself ; but this is a popular fallacy. A clergyman may be supposed to be taught of God, but people do not allow this to be true of weavers or workers in brass ; yet these callings are specially mentioned in the Bible as having been taught to holy women and earnest men when the tabernacle was set up at the first. All wisdom and skill are from the Lord, and for them he deserves to be gratefully extolled. This teaching extends to the smallest members of our frame ; the Lord teaches fingers as well as hands ; indeed, it sometimes happens that if the finger is not well trained the whole hand is incapable.

David was called to be a man of war, and he was eminently successful in his battles ; he does not trace this to his good generalship or valour, but to his being taught and strengthened for the war and the fight. If the Lord deigns to have a hand in such unspiritual work as fighting, surely he will help us to proclaim the gospel and win souls ; and then we will bless his name with even greater intensity of heart. We will be pupils, and he shall be our Master, and if we ever accomplish anything we will give our Instructor hearty blessing.

This verse is full of personality ; it is mercy shown to David himself which is the subject of grateful song. It has also a presentness about it ; for Jehovah is now his strength, and is still teaching him ; we ought to make a point of presenting praise while yet the blessing is on the wing. The verse is also pre-eminently practical, and full of the actual life of every day ; for David's days were spent in camps and conflicts. Some of us who are grievously tormented with rheumatism might cry, " Blessed be the Lord, my Comforter, who teacheth my knees to bear in patience, and my feet to endure in resignation" ; others who are on the look out to help young converts might say, " Blessed be God who teaches my eyes to see wounded souls, and my lips to cheer them" ; but David has his own peculiar help from God, and praises him accordingly. This tends to make the harmony of heaven perfect when all the singers take their parts ; if. we all followed the same score, the music would not be so full and rich.

2. Now our royal poet multiplies metaphors to extol his God. "*My goodness, and my fortress.*" The word for *goodness* signifies *mercy.* Whoever we may be, and wherever we may be, we need mercy such as can only be found in the infinite God. It is all of mercy that he is any of the other good things to us, so that this is a highly comprehensive title. O how truly has the Lord been mercy to many of us in a thousand ways ! He is goodness itself, and he has been unbounded goodness to us. We have no goodness of our own, but the Lord has become goodness to us. So is he himself also our *fortress* and safe abode : in him we dwell as behind impregnable ramparts and immovable bastions. We cannot be driven out, or starved out ; for our fortress is prepared for a siege ; it is stored with abundance of food, and a well of living water is within it. Kings usually think much of their fenced cities, but King David relies upon his God, who is more to him than fortresses could have been. "*My high tower, and my deliverer.*" As from a lofty watch-tower the believer, trusting in the Lord, looks down upon his enemies. They cannot reach him in his elevated position ; he is out of bowshot ; he is beyond their scaling ladders ; he dwells on high. Nor is this all ; for Jehovah is our Deliverer as well as our Defender. These different figures set

forth the varied benefits which come to us from our Lord. He is every good thing which we can need for this world or the next. He not only places us out of harm's way full often, but when we must be exposed, he comes to our rescue, he raises the siege. routs the foe, and sets us in joyous liberty. *"My shield, and he in whom I trust."* When the warrior rushes on his adversary, he bears his targe upon his arm, and thrusts death aside ; thus doth the believer oppose the Lord to the blows of the enemy, and finds himself secure from harm. For this and at thousand other reasons our trust rests in our God for everything ; he never fails us, and we feel boundless confidence in him. *"Who subdueth my people under me."* He keeps my natural subjects subject, and my conquered subjects peaceful under my sway. Men who rule others should thank God if they succeed in the task. Such strange creatures are human beings, that if a number of them are kept in peaceful association under the leadership of any one of the Lord's servants, he is bound to bless God every day for the wonderful fact. The victories of peace are as much worthy of joyful gratitude as the victories of war. Leaders in the Christian church cannot maintain their position except as the Lord preserves to them the mighty influence which ensures obedience and evokes enthusiastic loyalty. For every particle of influence for good which we may possess let us magnify the name of the Lord.

Thus has David blessed Jehovah for blessing him. How many times he has appropriated the Lord by that little word *My!* Each time he grasps the Lord, he adores and blesses him ; for the one word *Blessed* runs through all the passage like a golden thread. He began by acknowledging that his strength for fighting foreign enemies was of the Lord, and he concluded by ascribing his domestic peace to the same source. All round as a king he saw himself to be surrounded by the King of kings, to whom he bowed in lowly homage, doing suit and service on bended knee, with grateful heart admitting that he owed everything to the Rock of his salvation.

3 LORD, what *is* man, that thou takest knowledge of him ! *or* the son of man, that thou makest account of him !

4 Man is like to vanity : his days *are* as a shadow that passeth away.

3. *"LORD, what is man, that thou takest knowledge of him !"* What a contrast between Jehovah and man ! The Psalmist turns from the glorious all-sufficiency of God to the insignificance and nothingness of man. He sees Jehovah to be everything, and then cries, "Lord, what is man !" What is man in the presence of the Infinite God ? . What can he be compared to ? He is too little to be described at all ; only God, who knows the most minute object, can tell what man is. Certainly he is not fit to be the rock of our confidence : he is at once too feeble and too fickle to be relied upon. The Psalmist's wonder is that God should stoop to know him, and indeed it is more remarkable than if the greatest archangel should make a study of emmets, or become the friend of mites. God knows his people with a tender intimacy, a constant, careful observation : he foreknew them in love, he knows them by care, he will know them in acceptance at last. Why and wherefore is this ? What has man done ? What has he been ? What is he now that God should know him, and make himself known to him as his goodness, fortress, and high tower ? This is an unanswerable question. Infinite condescension can alone account for the Lord stooping to be the friend of man. That he should make man the subject of election, the object of redemption, the child of eternal love, the darling of infallible providence, the next of kin to Deity, is indeed a matter requiring more than the two notes of exclamation found in this verse.

"Or the son of man, that thou makest account of him !" The son of man is a weaker being still,—so the original word implies. He is not so much *man* as God made him, but man as his mother bore him ; and how can the Lord think of him, and write down such a cipher in his accounts ? The Lord thinks much of man,

and in connection with redeeming love makes a great figure of him : this can be believed, but it cannot be explained. Adoring wonder makes us each one cry out, Why dost thou take knowledge of me ? We know by experience how little man is to be reckoned upon, and we know by observation how greatly he can vaunt himself, if is therefore meet for us to be humble and to distrust ourselves ; but all this should make us the more grateful to the Lord, who knows man better than we do, and yet communes with him, and even dwells in him. Every trace of the misanthrope should be hateful to the believer ; for if God makes account of man it is not for us to despise our own kind.

4. "*Man is like to vanity.*" Adam is like to Abel. He is like that which is nothing at all. He is actually vain, and he resembles that unsubstantial empty thing which is nothing but a blown-up nothing,—a puff, a bubble. Yet he is not vanity, but only like it. He is not so substantial as that unreal thing ; he is only the likeness of it. Lord, what is a man ? It is wonderful that God should think of such a pretentious insignificance. "*His days are as a shadow that passeth away.*" He is so short-lived that he scarcely attains to years, but exists by the day, like the ephemera, whose birth and death are both seen by the self-same sun. His life is only like to a shadow, which is in itself a vague resemblance, an absence of something rather than in itself an existence. Observe that human life is not only as a shade, but as a shade which is about to depart. It is a mere mirage, the image of a thing which is not, a phantasm which melts back into nothing. How is it that the Eternal should make so much of mortal man, who begins to die as soon as he begins to live ?

The connection of the two verses before us with the rest of the psalm is not far to seek : David trusts in God and finds him everything ; he looks to man and sees him to be nothing ; and then he wonders how it is that the great Lord can condescend to take notice of such a piece of folly and deceit as man.

5 Bow thy heavens, O LORD, and come down : touch the mountains, and they shall smoke.

6 Cast forth lightning, and scatter them : shoot out thine arrows, and destroy them.

7 Send thine hand from above ; rid me, and deliver me out of great waters, from the hand of strange children ;

8 Whose mouth speaketh vanity, and their right hand *is* a right hand of falsehood.

5. "*Bow thy heavens, O* LORD, *and come down.*" The heavens are the Lord's own, and he who exalted them can bow them. His servant is struggling against bitter foes, and he finds no help in men, therefore he entreats Jehovah to come down to his rescue. It is, indeed, a coming down for Jehovah to interfere in the conflicts of his tried people. Earth cries to heaven to stoop ; nay, the cry is to the Lord of heaven to bow the heavens, and appear among the sons of earth. The Lord has often done this, and never more fully than when in Bethlehem the Word was made flesh and dwelt among us : now doth he know the way, and he never refuses to come down to defend his beloved ones. David would have the real presence of God to counterbalance the mocking appearance of boastful man : eternal verity could alone relieve him of human vanity. "*Touch the mountains, and they shall smoke.*" It was so when the Lord appeared on Sinai ; the strongest pillars of earth cannot bear the weight of the finger of God. He is a consuming fire, and his touch kindles the peaks of the Alps, and makes them smoke. If Jehovah would appear, nothing could stand before him ; if the mighty mountains smoke at his touch, then all mortal power which is opposed to the Lord must end in smoke. How long-suffering he is to his adversaries, whom he could so readily consume. A touch would do it ; God's finger of flame would set the hills on fire, and consume opposition of every kind.

6. "*Cast forth lightning, and scatter them.*" The Eternal can hurl his lightnings

wheresoever he pleases, and effect his purpose instantaneously.   The artillery of heaven soon puts the enemy to flight : a single bolt sets the armies running hither and thither in utter rout.   "*Shoot out thine arrows, and destroy them.*"   Jehovah never misses the mark ; his arrows are fatal to his foes when he goes forth to war. It was no common faith which led the poet-king to expect the Lord to use his thunderbolts on behalf of a single member of that race which he had just now described as " like to vanity."   A believer in God may without presumption expect the Almighty Lord to use on his behalf all the stores of his wisdom and power : even the terrible forces of tempest shall be marshalled to the fight, for the defence of the Lord's chosen.   When we have once mastered the greater difficulty of the Lord's taking any interest in us, it is but a small thing that we should expect him to exert his great power on our behalf.   This is far from being the only time in which this believing warrior had thus prayed : the eighteenth Psalm is specially like the present ; the good man was not abashed at his former boldness, but here repeats himself without fear.

7. "*Send thine hand from above.*"   Let thy long and strong arm be stretched out till thine hand seizes my foes, and delivers me from them.   "*Rid me, and deliver me out of great waters.*"   Make a Moses of me,—one drawn out of the waters.   My foes pour in upon me like torrents, they threaten to overwhelm me ; save me from their force and fury ; take them from me, and me from them. "*From the hand of strange children.*"   From foreigners of every race ; men strange to me and thee, who therefore must work evil to me, and rebellion against thyself.   Those against whom he pleaded were out of covenant with God ; they were Philistines and Edomites ; or else they were men of his own nation of black heart and traitorous spirit, who were real strangers, though they bore the name of Israel.   Oh to be rid of those infidel, blaspheming beings who pollute society with their false teachings and hard speeches !   Oh to be delivered from slanderous tongues, deceptive lips, and false hearts !   No wonder these words are repeated, for they are the frequent cry of many a tried child of God ;—"*Rid me, and deliver me.*"   The devil's children are strange to us : we can never agree with them, and they will never understand us : they are aliens to us, and we are despised by them.   O Lord, deliver us from the evil one, and from all who are of his race.

8. "*Whose mouth speaketh vanity.*"   No wonder that men who are vanity speak vanity.   " When he speaketh a lie, he speaketh of his own.   " They cannot be depended upon, let them promise as fairly as they may : their solemn declarations are light as the foam of the sea, in no wise to be depended upon.   Good men desire to be rid of such characters : of all men deceivers and liars are among the most disgusting to true hearts.   "*And their right hand is a right hand of falsehood.*" So far their hands and their tongues agree, for they are vanity and falsehood. These men act as falsely as they speak, and prove themselves to be all of a piece. Their falsehood is right-handed, they lie with dexterity, they deceive with all their might.   It is a dreadful thing when a man's expertness lies more in lies than in truth ; when he can neither speak nor act without proving himself to be false. God save us from lying mouths, and hands of falsehood.

9   I will sing a new song unto thee, O God : upon a psaltery *and* an instrument of ten strings will I sing praises unto thee.

10   *It is he* that giveth salvation unto kings : who delivereth David his servant from the hurtful sword.

11   Rid me, and deliver me from the hand of strange children, whose mouth speaketh vanity, and their right hand *is* a right hand of falsehood :

9. "*I will sing a new song unto thee, O God.*"   Weary of the false, I will adore the true.   Fired with fresh enthusiasm, my gratitude shall make a new channel for itself.   I will sing as others have done ; but it shall be a new song, such as

no others have sung. That song shall be all and altogether for my God : I will extol none but the Lord, from whom my deliverance has come. "*Upon a psaltery and an instrument of ten strings will I sing praises unto thee.*" His hand should aid his tongue, not as in the case of the wicked, co-operating in deceit ; but his hand should unite with his mouth in truthful praise. David intended to tune his best instruments as well as to use his best vocal music : the best is all too poor for so great a God, and therefore we must not fall short of our utmost. He meant to use many instruments of music, that by all means he might express his great joy in God. The Old Testament dispensation abounded in types, and figures, and outward ritual, and therefore music dropped naturally into its place in the "worldly sanctuary" ; but, after all, it can do no more than represent praise, and assist our expression of it ; the real praise is in the heart, the true music is that of the soul. When music drowns the voice, and artistic skill takes a higher place than hearty singing, it is time that instruments were banished from public worship ; but when they are subordinate to the song, as here, it is not for us to prohibit them, or condemn those who use them, though we ourselves greatly prefer to do without them, since it seems to us that the utmost simplicity of praise is far more congruous with the spirit of the gospel than pomp of organs. The private worshipper, singing his solo unto the Lord, has often found it helpful to accompany himself on some familiar instrument, and of this David in the present psalm is an instance, for he says, " I will sing praise unto thee,"—that is, not so much in the company of others as by himself alone. He saith not " we," but " I."

10. "*It is he that giveth salvation unto kings.*" Those whom the Lord sets up he will keep up. Kings, from their conspicuous position, are exposed to special danger, and when their lives and their thrones are preserved to them they should give the Lord the glory of it. In his many battles David would have perished had not almighty care preserved him. He had by his valour wrought salvation for Israel, but he lays his laurels at the feet of his Lord and Preserver. If any men need salvation kings do, and if they get it the fact is so astonishing that it deserves a verse to itself in the psalm of praise. "*Who delivereth David his servant from the hurtful sword.*" He traces his escape from death to the delivering hand of God. Note, he speaks in the present tense—*delivereth*, for this was an act which covered his whole life. He puts his name to the confession of his indebtedness : it is David who owns without demur to mercy given to himself. He styles himself the Lord's servant, accepting this as the highest title he had attained or desired.

11. Because of what the Lord had done, David returns to his pleading. He begs deliverance from him who is ever delivering him. "*Rid me, and deliver me from the hand of strange children.*" This is in measure the refrain of the song, and the burden of the prayer. He desired to be delivered from his open and foreign adversaries, who had broken compacts, and treated treaties as vain things. "*Whose mouth speaketh vanity, and their right hand is a right hand of falsehood.*" He would not strike hands with those who carried a lie in their right hand : he would be quit of such at once, if possible. Those who are surrounded by such serpents know not how to deal with them, and the only available method seems to be prayer to God for a riddance and deliverance. David in the seventh verse, according to the original, had sought the help of both the Lord's hands, and well he might, for his deceitful enemies, with remarkable unanimity, were with one mouth and one hand seeking his destruction.

12 That our sons *may be* as plants grown up in their youth ; *that* our daughters *may be* as corner stones, polished *after* the similitude of a palace :

13 *That* our garners *may be* full, affording all manner of store : *that* our sheep may bring forth thousands and ten thousands in our streets :

14 *That* our oxen *may be* strong to labour ; *that there be* no breaking in, nor going out ; that *there be* no complaining in our streets.

15 Happy *is that* people, that is in such a case : *yea,* happy *is that* people, whose God *is* the LORD.

Riddance from the wicked and the gracious presence of the Lord are sought with a special eye to the peace and prosperity which will follow thereupon. The sparing of David's life would mean the peace and happiness of a whole nation. We can scarcely judge how much of happiness may hang upon the Lord's favour to one man.

12. God's blessing works wonders for a people. "*That our sons may be as plants grown up in their youth.*" Our sons are of first importance to the state, since men take a leading part in its affairs ; and what the young men are the older men will be. He desires that they may be like strong, well-rooted, young trees, which promise great things. If they do not grow in their youth, when will they grow ? If in their opening manhood they are dwarfed, they will never get over it. O the joys which we may have through our sons ! And, on the other hand, what misery they may cause us ! Plants may grow crooked, or in some other way disappoint the planter, and so may our sons. But when we see them developed in holiness, what joy we have of them ! "*That our daughters may be as corner stones, polished after the similitude of a palace.*" We desire a blessing for our whole family, daughters as well as sons. For the girls to be left out of the circle of blessing would be unhappy indeed. Daughters unite families as corner stones join walls together, and at the same time they adorn them as polished stones garnish the structure into which they are builded. Home becomes a palace when the daughters are maids of honour, and the sons are nobles in spirit ; then the father is a king, and the mother a queen, and royal residences are more than outdone. A city built up of such dwellings is a city of palaces, and a state composed of such cities is a republic of princes.

13. "*That our garners may be full, affording all manner of store.*" A household must exercise thrift and forethought : it must have its granary as well as its nursery. Husbands should husband their resources ; and should not only furnish their tables but fill their garners. Where there are happy households, there must needs be plentiful provision for them, for famine brings misery even where love abounds. It is well when there is plenty, and that plenty consists of " all manner of store." We have occasionally heard murmurs concerning the abundance of grain, and the cheapness of the poor man's loaf. A novel calamity ! We dare not pray against it. David would have prayed for it, and blessed the Lord when he saw his heart's desire. When all the fruits of the earth are plentiful, the fruits of our lips should be joyful worship and thanksgiving. Plenteous and varied may our products be, that every form of want may be readily supplied. "*That our sheep may bring forth thousands and ten thousands in our streets,*" or rather in the open places, the fields, and sheep-walks where lambs should be born. A teeming increase is here described. Adam tilled the ground to fill the garner, but Abel kept sheep, and watched the lambs. Each occupation needs the divine blessing. The second man who was born into this world was a shepherd, and that trade has ever held an important part in the economy of nations. Food and clothing come from the flock, and both are of first consideration.

14. "*That our oxen may be strong to labour* "; so that the ploughing and cartage of the farm may be duly performed, and the husbandman's work may be accomplished without unduly taxing the cattle, or working them cruelly. "*That there be no breaking in, nor going out* "; no irruption of marauders, and no forced emigration ; no burglaries and no evictions. "*That there be no complaining in our streets* "; no secret dissatisfaction, no public riot ; no fainting of poverty, no clamour for rights denied, nor concerning wrongs unredressed. The state of things here pictured is very delightful : all is peaceful and prosperous ; the throne

is occupied efficiently, and even the beasts in their stalls are the better for it. This has been the condition of our own country, and if it should now be changed, who can wonder? for our ingratitude well deserves to be deprived of blessings which it has despised.

These verses may with a little accommodation be applied to a prosperous church, where the converts are growing and beautiful, the gospel stores abundant, and the spiritual increase most cheering. There ministers and workers are in full vigour, and the people are happy and united. The Lord make it so in all our churches evermore.

15. "*Happy is that people that is in such a case.*" Such things are not to be overlooked. Temporal blessings are not trifles, for the miss of them would be a dire calamity. It is a great happiness to belong to a people so highly favoured. "*Yea, happy is that people, whose God is the* LORD." This comes in as an explanation of their prosperity. Under the Old Testament Israel had present earthly rewards for obedience : when Jehovah was their God they were a nation enriched and flourishing. This sentence is also a sort of correction of all that had gone before ; as if the poet would say—all these temporal gifts are a part of happiness, but still the heart and soul of happiness lies in the people being right with God, and having a full possession of him. Those who worship the happy God become a happy people. Then if we have not temporal mercies literally we have something better : if we have not the silver of earth we have the gold of heaven, which is better still.

In this psalm David ascribes his own power over the people, and the prosperity which attended his reign, to the Lord himself. Happy was the nation which he ruled ; happy in its king, in its families, in its prosperity, and in the possession of peace ; but yet more in enjoying true religion and worshipping Jehovah, the only living and true God.

EXPLANATORY NOTES.

Whole Psalm.—The psalm, in its mingled tones of prayer and praise, is a fit connecting link between the supplicatory psalms which go before, and the strains of thanksgiving which follow it.—*Speaker's Commentary.*

Whole Psalm.—After six psalms of sorrowful prayer in distress, we have now a psalm of praise and thanksgiving for God's gracious answer to supplications ; and also a psalm of intercession. The present psalm bears a strong resemblance to David's last song in 2 Sam. xxii. and to Ps. xviii. Here we have a vision of Christ rejoicing ;—after his passion—risen in glory, and having ascended in triumph, and pleading for us at the right hand of God.—*Christopher Wordsworth.*

Whole Psalm.—This psalm is ruled by the numbers ten and seven. Ten verses complete the first part of the psalm, which falls into two divisions. The first portion contains, in verses 1 and 2, ten attributes of God,—three and seven, the seven divided into four and three. In like manner it contains ten requests to God in verses 5—7, divided precisely as the attributes. To this significance of the number ten for the first part, allusion is pointedly made in verse 9. Seven blessings are prayed for in the second part, four in verses 12, 13 (valiant sons, beautiful daughters, full store-houses, numerous flocks), and three in verse 14 (labouring oxen, no breach and diminution, no cry). The whole contains, apart from the closing epiphonem, which, as usual, stands outside the formal arrangement, seven strophes, each of two verses.

An objection has been brought against the Davidic authorship from the " traces of reading " it contains. But one would require to consider more exactly, what sort of reading is here to be thought of. It is only the psalms of David which form the ground-work of this new psalm. But that it is one of David's peculiarities to derive from his earlier productions a foundation for new ones, is evident from a variety of facts, which, if any doubt must still be entertained on the subject, would obtain a firm ground to stand upon in this psalm, which *can* only have been composed by David. The way and manner of the use made of such materials is to be kept in view. This is always of a spirited and feeling nature, and no trace anywhere exists of a dead borrowing. That we cannot think here of such a borrowing ; that the appropriation of the earlier language did not proceed from spiritual impotence, but rested upon deeper grounds, is manifest from the consideration of the second part, where the dependence entirely ceases, and where even the opponents of the Davidic authorship have not been able to overlook the strong poetical spirit of the time of David. They betake themselves to the miserable shift of affirming, that the Psalmist borrowed this part of the psalm from a much older poem now lost.—*E. W. Hengstenberg.*

Verse 1.—"*Blessed be the* LORD." A prayer for further mercy is fitly begun with a thanksgiving for former mercy ; and when we are waiting upon God to bless us, we should stir up ourselves to bless him —*Matthew Henry.*

Verse 1.—"*The* LORD *my strength,*" etc. Agamemnon says to Achilles—

> If tnou hast strength, 'twas heaven that strength bestowed ;
> For know, vain man ! thy valour is from God.
>
> —*Homer.*

Verse 1.—"*My strength*" [Heb. " *my rock*"]. The climax should be noted : the rock, or cliff, comes first as the place of refuge, then the fortress or *fastness*, as a place carefully fortified, then the personal deliverer, without whose intervention escape would have been impossible.—*Speaker's Commentary.*

Verse 1.—"*The* LORD . . . *teacheth*" *:* and not as man teacheth. Thus he taught Gideon to fight with the innumerable host of Midian by sending to their homes two-and-twenty thousand, and retaining but ten thousand of his soldiers : and then again by reducing that remnant to the little band of three hundred who lapped when brought down to the water. Thus he taught Samson by abstaining from strong drink, and by suffering no razor to pass over his head. Thus he taught the three kings in the wilderness to war against their enemies, not by any strength of their armies, but by making ditches in the desert. Thus he taught David himself by waiting for the sound of the going in the tops of the mulberry trees. And so he taught the arms of the True David to fight when stretched on the cross : nailed, to human sight, to the tree of suffering, but, in reality, winning for themselves the crown of glory : helpless in the eyes of Scribes and Pharisees ; in those of archangels, laying hold of the two pillars, sin and death, whereon the house of Satan rested, and heaving them up from their foundation.—*Ayguan, in Neale and Littledale.*

Verse 1—"*The* LORD *my strength, which teacheth my hands to war.*" There were three qualities of a valiant soldier found in Christ, the Captain of our salvation, in his war against Satan, which his followers are bound to emulate : boldness in attack, skill in defence, steadiness in conflict, all which he teaches by his example (Matt. iv. 1, 4, 7, 10, 11). He was *bold in attack*, for he began the combat by going up into the wilderness to defy the enemy. So we, too, should be always beforehand with Satan, ought to fast, even if not tempted to gluttony, and be humble, though not assailed by pride, and so forth. He was *skilful in defence*, parrying every attack with Holy Writ ; where we, too, in the examples of the saints, may find lessons for the combat. He was *steadfast in conflict*, for he persevered to the end, till the devil left him, and angels came and ministered unto him ; and we, too, should not be content with repelling the first attack, but persevere in our resistance until evil thoughts are put to flight, and heavenly resolutions take their place.—*Neale and Littledale.*

Verse 1.—"*Teacheth my hands.*" Used to the hook and harp, and not to the sword and spear ; but God hath apted and abled them to feats of arms and warlike exploits. It is God that giveth skill and success, saith Solomon (Prov. viii.) ; wisdom and ability, saith Daniel (chap. ii). And as in the spiritual warfare, so here ; our weapons are "mighty through God" (2 Cor. x. 4), who promiseth that no weapon formed against his people shall prosper (Isai. liv. 17).—*John Trapp.*

Verse 1.—"*To war, . . . to fight.*" I want to speak of a great defect among us, which often prevents the realization of going "from strength to strength"; viz., the *not using, not trading with*, the strength given. We should not think of going to God for money only to keep it in the bank. But are we not doing this with regard to strength? We are constantly asking for strength for service; but if we are not putting this out in hearty effort, it is of no use to us. Nothing comes of hoarded strength.

"Blessed be the Lord my strength, *which teacheth my hands to war, and my fingers to fight.*" David, you see, was looking for strength for a purpose. Some people seem to expect strength, but never attempt to put forth their hands to war, and their fingers to fight—there is so little venturing upon God, so little use of grace given, partly from fear of man, partly from indolence and worldly-mindedness . . . It is not for us to be merely luxuriating in the power which God supplies. Action strengthens, and before we have a right to ask for an increase, we must use that already given.—*Catherine Pennefather, in "Service,"* 1881.

Verse 2.—Is not the spiritual victory of every believer achieved by God? Truly it is he who teaches his *hands to war and his fingers to fight;* and when the final triumph shall be sung in heaven, the victor's song will be, "Not unto me, O Lord, not unto me, but unto thy name give glory, for thy mercy and for thy truth's sake."—*John Morison.*

Verse 1.—"*My hands for fight, my fingers for war.*" *Fight* and *war* are both verbs and nouns in English, but the Hebrew words are nouns with the article prefixed.—*Joseph Addison Alexander.*

Verse 1.—"*My fingers to fight.*" Probably the immediate reference here is to the use of the bow,—placing the arrow, and drawing the string.—*Albert Barnes.*

Verse 2.—"*My goodness,*" etc. This way of using the word in a passive sense, as in the Hebrew, sounds harshly; just as elsewhere (Ps. xviii. 50) he calls himself "God's king," not in the sense of his having dominion over God, but being made and appointed king by him. Having experienced God's kindness in so many ways, he calls him "*his goodness,*" meaning that whatever good he possessed flowed from him. The accumulation of terms, one upon another, which follows, may appear unnecessary, yet it tends greatly to strengthen faith. We know how unstable men's minds are, and especially how soon faith wavers, when they are assailed by some trial of more than usual severity.—*John Calvin.*

Verse 2.—"*My fortress.*" David calls God by names connected with the chief deliverances of his life. The psalms abound in local references and descriptive expressions, *e.g.* Ps. xviii. 2 [and in this place]. The word translated "*fortress*" is *metzudah* or *masada*. From 1 Sam. xxiii. 29, I have no doubt that he is speaking of Masada, an isolated peak 1500 feet high, on which was a stronghold.—*James Wareing Bardsley, in "Glimpses through the Veil,"* 1883.

Verse 2.—"*My high tower.*" Such *towers* were erected on mountains, on rocks, or on the walls of a city, and were regarded as safe places mainly because they were inaccessible. So the old castles in Europe,—as that at Heidelberg, and generally those along the Rhine,—were built on lofty places, and in such positions as not to be easily accessible.—*Albert Barnes.*

Verse 2.—"*My shield.*" The Hebrew word signifies, not the huge shield which was carried by an armour-bearer, but the handy target with which heroes entered into hand-to-hand conflicts. A warrior took it with him when he used his bow or his sword. It was often made of metal, but still was portable, and useful, and was made to serve as an ornament, being brightened or anointed with oil. David had made abundant use of the Lord, his God, from day to day, in battles many and murderous.—*C. H. S.*

Verse 2.—"*Who subdueth my people under me.*" David, accordingly, having ascribed the victories he had gained over foreign enemies to God, thanks him at the same time for the settled state of the kingdom. Raised indeed as he was from an obscure station, and exposed to hatred from calumnious charges, it was scarcely to have been believed that he would ever obtain a peaceable reign. The people had suddenly, and beyond expectation, submitted to him ; and so surprising a change was eminently God's work.—*John Calvin.*

Verse 3.—"LORD, *what is man,*" etc.

> Now what is man when grace reveals
> The virtues of a Saviour's blood ?
> Again a life divine he feels,
> Despises earth, and walks with God.

> And what in yonder realms above,
> Is ransomed man ordained to be ?
> With honour, holiness, and love,
> No seraph more adorned than he.

> Nearest the throne, and first in song.
> Man shall his hallelujahs raise,
> While wondering angels round him throng,
> And swell the chorus of his praise.
>　　　　　　—*John Newton, in Olney Hymns.*

Verse 3.—" LORD, *what is man ?*"　Take him in his four elements, of earth, air, fire, and water.　In the *earth*, he is as fleeting dust ; in the *air*, he is as a disappearing vapour ; in the *water*, he is as a breaking bubble ; and in the *fire*, he is as consuming smoke.—*William Secker, in " The Nonsuch Professor."*

Verses 3, 4. —" LORD, *what is man,*" etc.　There is no book so well worthy reading as this living one.　Even now David spake as a king of men, of *people subdued under him :* now he speaks as a humble vassal to God : " LORD, *what is man that thou takest knowledge of him ?*"　In 'one breath is both sovereignty and subjugation : an absolute sovereignty over his people : "*My people are subdued under me* "; an humble subjection to the God of kings ; " LORD, *what is man ?*" Yea, in the very same word wherein is the profession of that sovereignty, there is an acknowledgment of subjection : "*Thou hast subdued my people.*"　In that he had a people, he was a king : that they might be his people, a subjection was requisite ; and that subjugation was God's, and not his own : "*Thou hast subdued.*"　Lo, David had not subdued his people, if God had not subdued them for him.　He was a great king, but they were a stiff people : the God that made them swayed them to a due subjection.　The great conquerors of worlds could not conquer hearts, if he, that moulded hearts, did not temper them.　" By me kings reign," saith the Eternal Wisdom ; and he that had courage enough to encounter a bear, a lion, Goliath, yet can say, "*Thou hast subdued my people.*"

Contrarily, in the lowliest subjection of himself, there is an acknowledgment of greatness.　Though he abused himself with, "*What is man ?*" yet, withal he adds, "*Thou takest knowledge of him, thou makest account of him*" : and this knowledge, this account of God, doth more exalt man than his own vanity can depress him.　My text, then, ye see, is David's rapture, expressed in an ecstatical question of sudden wonder ; a wonder at God, and at man : MAN'S VILENESS ; "*What is man ?*" GOD'S MERCY AND FAVOUR, in his knowledge, in his estimation of man. Lo, there are ·but two lessons that we need to take out here, in the world, God and man ; man, in the notion of his wretchedness ; God, in the notion of his bounty.

Let us, if you please, take a short view of both ; and, in the one, see cause of our humiliation ; of our joy and thankfulness in the other : and if, in the former, there be a sad Lent of mortification ; there is, in the latter, a cheerful Easter of our raising and exaltation.

Many a one besides David wonders at himself : one wonders at his own honour ; and, though he will not say so, yet thinks, " What a great man am I ! Is not this great Babel, which I have built ?"　This is Nebuchadnezzar's wonder. Another wonders at his person, and finds, either a good face, or a fair eye, or an exquisite hand, or a well-shaped leg, or some gay fleece, to admire in himself : this was Absalom's wonder.　Another wonders at his wit and learning : " How came I by all this ?　*Turba hæc!*　This vulgar, that knows not the law, is ac-

cursed " : this was the Pharisee's wonder. Another wonders at his wealth ;
" Soul, take thine ease" ; as the epicure in the gospel. David's wonder is as
much above, as against all these : he wonders at his *vileness :* like as the Chosen
Vessel would boast of nothing but his infirmities : " LORD, *what is man ?*"
    How well this hangs together ! No sooner had he said, "*Thou hast subdued my
people under me,*" than he adds, " LORD, *what is man ?*" Some vain heart would
have been lifted up with a conceit of his own eminence ; " Who am I ? I am not
as other men. I have people under me ; and people of my own, and people subdued to me "; this is to be more than a man. I know who hath said, " I said ye
are gods."—*Joseph Hall.*
    Verse 3.—Dr. Hammond refers this psalm to the slaying of Goliath, and thus
understands the appellation " *son of man,*"—" David was but a young stripling,
the youngest and most inconsiderable of all the sons of Jesse, who also was himself an ordinary man."
    Verse 3.—"*Thou takest knowledge of him.*" It is a great word. Alas ! what
knowledge do we take of the gnats that play in the sun ; or the ants, or worms,
that are crawling in our grounds ? Yet the disproportion betwixt us and them is
but finite ; infinite betwixt God and us. Thou, the Great God of Heaven, to take
knowledge of such a thing as man. If a mighty prince shall vouchsafe to spy
and single out a plain homely swain in a throng, as the Great Sultan did lately a
tankard-bearer ; and take special notice of him, and call him but to a kiss of his
hand and nearness to his person ; he boasts of it as a great favour : for thee,
then, O God, who abasest thyself to behold the things in heaven itself, to
cast thine eye upon so poor a worm as man, it must needs be a wonderful
mercy.—*Exigua pauperibus magna ;* as Nazianzen to his Amphilochius.—*Joseph
Hall.*

    Verse 4.—"*Man is like to vanity.*" As he that goeth to a fair, with a purse full
of money, is devising and debating with himself how to lay it out—possibly
thinking that such and such commodities will be most profitable, and bring him
in the greatest gain—when on a sudden a cut-purse comes and easeth him both
of his money and care how to dispose of it. Surely thou mightst have taken
notice how some of thy neighbours or countrymen, when they have been busy in
their contrivances, and big with many plots and projects how to raise their estate
and names and families, were arrested by death in a moment, returned to their
earth, and in that day all their gay, their great thoughts perished, and came to
nothing. The heathen historian could not but observe how Alexander the Great,
when he had to carry on his great designs, summoned a parliament before him of
the whole world, he was himself summoned by death to appear in the other
world. The Dutch, therefore, very wittily to express the world's vanity, picture
at Amsterdam a man with a full-blown bladder on his shoulders, and another
standing by pricking the bladder with a pin, with this motto, QUAM SUBITO, How
soon is all blown down !—*George Swinnock.*
    Verse 4.—"*Man is like to vanity.*" When Cain was born, there was much ado
about his birth ; " I have gotten a man-child from God," saith his mother : she
looked upon him as a great possession, and therefore called his name *Cain,* which
signifies " a possession." But the second man that was born unto the world bare
the title of the world, "*vanity*" ; his name was *Abel,* that is, "*vanity.*" A pre-
monition was given in the name of the second man what would or should be the
condition of all men. In Psalm cxliv. 4 there is an allusion unto those two
names. We translate it, "*Man is like to vanity*" ; the Hebrew is, "*Adam is as
Abel*" ; *Adam,* you know, was the name of the first man, the name of Abel's
father ; but as Adam was the proper name of the first, so it is an appellative, or
common to all men : now *Adam,* that is, man of all men, are *Abel,* vain, and walking in a vain show.—*Joseph Caryl.*
    Verse 4.—"*Man is like to vanity,*" etc. The occasion of the introduction of
these sentiments here is not quite clear. It may be the humility of the warrior
who ascribes all success to God instead of to human prowess, or it may be a reflec-

tion uttered over the corpses of comrades, or, perhaps a blending of the two.—
A. S. Aglen.

Verse 4.—"*Man is like to vanity*," etc. With what idle dreams, what foolish plans, what vain pursuits, are men for the most part occupied! They undertake dangerous expeditions and difficult enterprises in foreign countries, and they acquire fame; but what is it?—*Vanity!* They pursue deep and abstruse speculations, and give themselves to that "much study which is a weariness to the flesh," and they attain to literary renown, and survive in their writings; but what is it?—*Vanity!* They rise up early, and sit up late, and eat the bread of anxiety and care, and thus they amass wealth; but what is it?—*Vanity!* They frame and execute plans and schemes of ambition—they are loaded with honours and adorned with titles—they afford employment for the herald, and form a subject for the historian; but what is it?—*Vanity!* In fact, all occupations and pursuits are worthy of no other epithet, if they are not preceded by, and connected with, a deep and paramount regard to the salvation of the soul, the honour of God, and the interests of eternity. . . . Oh, then, what phantoms, what airy nothings are those things that wholly absorb the powers and occupy the days of the great mass of mankind around us! Their most substantial good perishes in the using, and their most enduring realities are but "the fashion of this world that passeth away."—*Thomas Raffles*, 1788—1863.

Verse 4.—"*A shadow that passeth away.*" The shadows of the mountains are constantly shifting their position during the day, and ultimately disappear altogether on the approach of night: so is it with man who is every day advancing to the moment of his final departure from this world.—*Bellarmine.*

Verse 5.—"*Bow thy heavens.*" This expression is derived from the appearance of the clouds during a tempest: they hang low, so as to obscure the hills and mountains, and seem to mingle earth and heaven together. Such an appearance is figuratively used to depict the coming of God, to execute vengeance upon the enemies of his people. See Ps. xviii. 10, and other instances.—*William Walford.*

Verse 5.—"*Bow thy heavens, O* LORD, *and come down.*" etc. This was never so remarkably fulfilled as in the incarnation of Jesus Christ, when heaven and earth were, as it were, brought together. Heaven itself was, as it were, made to bow that it might be united to the earth. God did, as it were, come down and bring heaven with him. He not only came down to the earth, but he brought heaven down with him to men and for men. It was a most strange and wonderful thing. But this will be more remarkably fulfilled still by Christ's second coming, when he will indeed bring all heaven down with him—viz., all the inhabitants of heaven. Heaven shall be left empty of its inhabitants to come down to the earth; and then the mountains shall smoke, and shall indeed flow down at his presence, as in Isai. lxiv. 1.—*Jonathan Edwards.*

Verse 5.—"*Touch the mountains, and they shall smoke.*" The meaning is, when God doth but lay his hand upon great men, upon the mightiest of the world, he makes them smoke or fume, which some understand of their anger; they are presently in a passion, if God do but touch them. Or we may understand it of their consumption. A *smoking* mountain will soon be a *burnt* mountain. In our language, to make a man smoke is a proverbial expression for destroying or subduing.—*Joseph Caryl.*

Verses 5, 6.—

> Bow thy heavens, Jehovah,
> Come down in thy might,
> Let the rays of thy glory
> The mountain-tops light.

> With the bolts of thy thunder
> Discomfit my foe,
> With the flash of thine arrows
> Their force overthrow.

—William Digby Seymour.

Verse 6.—"*Cast forth lightning.*" The Hebrew here is, "Lighten lightning"; that is, Send forth lightning. The word is used as a verb nowhere else.—*Albert Barnes.*

Verse 7.—"*Send thine hand from above.*" Hebrew, *hands*, both hands, all thy whole power, for I need it.—*John Trapp.*

Verse 7.—"*Rid me, and deliver me.*" Away, you who theorize about suffering, and can do no more than descant upon it, away! for in the time of weeping we cannot endure your reasonings. If you have no means of delivering us, if you have nothing but sententious phrases to offer, put your hands on your mouths; enwrap yourselves in silence! It is enough to suffer; but to suffer and listen to you is more than we can bear. If Job's mouth was nigh unto blasphemy, the blame is yours, ye miserable comforters, who talked instead of weeping. If I must suffer, then I pray for suffering without fine talk!—*E. De Pressensé.*

Verse 7.—"*Rid me, and deliver me . . . from the hand of strange children.*" We must remember that as the Grecians (conceiting themselves the best bred people in the world) called all other nations "barbarians"; so the people of Israel, the stock of Abraham (being God's peculiar covenant people), called all other nations "aliens" or "strangers"; and because they were hated and maligned by all other nations, therefore they called all professed strangers *enemies;* so the word is used (Isai. i. 7). "Your land strangers shall devour"; that is, enemies shall invade and prevail over you. "*Deliver me out of the hand of strange children,*" or out of the hand of strangers; that is, out of the hand of mine enemies. The Latin word *alienus* is often put for *hostis*, and the Roman orator [Cicero] telleth us that "he who is now called a stranger was called an enemy by our ancestors." The reason was because strangers proved unkind to, yea, turned enemies against those that entertained them.—*Joseph-Caryl.*

Verse 7.—"*Strange children.*" He calls them *strangers*, not in respect of generic origin, but character and disposition.—*John Calvin.*

Verse 7.—The "*strange children,*" now the enemies of David, shall be either won to willing subjection, or else shall be crushed under the triumphant Messiah (Ps. ii.). The Spirit by David spake things the deep significance of which reached further than even he understood (1 Pet. i. 11, 12).—*Andrew Robert Fausset.*

Verse 8.—"*Whose mouth speaketh vanity,*" etc. Two things go naturally together in the verse—the lying tongue and deceitful hand. The meaning is that upon the matter in hand nothing was to be looked for from any of their promises, since it was only to deceive that they flattered with their mouth and gave the hand.—*John Calvin.*

Verse 8.—"*Their right hand is a right hand of falsehood.*" The pledge of the right hand, which used to be a witness of good faith, was violated by treachery and wickedness.—*Cicero. Philip. xi. c. 2.*

Verse 9.—"*Psaltery—an instrument of ten strings.*" *Nebel-azor.* We are led to the conclusion that the *nebel* was the veritable *harp* of the Hebrews. It could not have been large, because it is so frequently mentioned in the Bible as being carried in processions. . . . The English translators render *nebel* (apparently without any special reason) by no less than four words; (1) psaltery, (2) psalm, (3) lute, (4) viol. The first of these is by far the most common in the Authorized Version, and is no doubt the most correct translation if the word be understood in its true sense as a *portable harp*. *Nebels* were made of fir-wood, and afterwards of almug, or algum, which was, perhaps, the red sandal-wood of India. . . . With *nebel* is often associated the word *azor*, which is traced to a root signifying *ten*, and which has therefore been rendered in the Septuagint by ἐν δεκαχόρδῳ or as ψαλτηριον δεκάχορδον (*psalterium decem chordarum*), or *in dechachordo psalterio* in the Vulgate. In the Chaldee, Syriac, and Arabic versions also are found words implying the existence of ten strings in the *nebel-azor*. The word *azor* may therefore be considered as qualifying or describing the special kind of *nebel* to be used, much in the same way as we now speak of a *trichord* pianoforte. It is in our English version always rendered by the words "*ten-stringed.*"—*John Stainer, in "The Music of the Bible,"* 1882.

Verse 10.—"*It is he that giveth salvation unto kings.*" Ferdinand, king of Aragon, sending his son against the Florentines, thus bespake him : Believe me, son, victories are not gotten by art or subtlety, but given of God.—*John Trapp.*

Verse 10.—"*It is he that giveth salvation unto kings.*" What a doctrine this for the kings and great men of the earth to remember ! Could they be brought to feel and acknowledge it, they would not trust to the sagacity of their own councils, nor to the strength of their own arm ; but would ever remember that the Most High is the ruler among the nations, and that he putteth down one and raiseth up another according to the dictates of his own all-perfect will. Such remembrances as this would stain the pride of all human glory, and would lead men to feel that the Lord alone is to be exalted.—*John Morison.*

Verse 11.—This psalm is the language of a prince who wished his people's prosperity : that their ' garners might be full of all manner of stores ' ; that their ' sheep might bring forth thousands and ten thousands in their streets ' ; that their ' oxen ' might be fat for slaughter, or ' strong for labour ' ; that there might be neither robbery nor beggary in their streets : no oppressive magistrates, nor complaining people : and as if all these blessings were to be derived from the character of the people, and the character of the people from the education they had received, our text is a prayer for the youth of Judea.—*Robert Robinson* (1735 —1790), *in "The Nature and Necessity of Early Piety."*

Verse 12.—The reminiscences or imitations of Ps. xviii. suddenly cease here, and are followed by a series of original, peculiar, and for the most part no doubt antique expressions. On the supposition that the title is correct in making David the author, this is natural enough. On any other supposition it is unaccountable, unless by the gratuitous assumption, that this is a fragment of an older composition, a mode of reasoning by which anything may be either proved or disproved.—*Joseph Addison Alexander.*

Verse 12.—"*That our sons may be as plants,*" etc. They who have ever been employed in the cultivation of plants of any kind, are continually tempted to wish that the human objects of their care and culture would grow up as rapidly, as straight, as flourishingly, would as uniformly fulfil their specific idea and purpose, as abundantly reward the labour bestowed on them. . . . If our sons are indeed to grow up as young plants, like our English oaks, which according to the analogies of Nature, furnish no inappropriate type of our national character, they must not be stunted or dwarfed or pollarded, for the sake of being kept under the shade of a stranger. They should grow up straight toward heaven, as God had ordained them to grow. . . . There is something so palpable and striking in this type, that five-and-twenty years ago, in speaking of the gentlemanly character, I was led to say, " If a gentleman is to grow up he must grow like a tree : there must be nothing between him and heaven."—*Julius Charles Hare, in a Sermon entitled "Education the Necessity of Mankind,"* 1851.

Verse 12.—"*That our sons may be as plants grown up in their youth,*" etc. Thus David prays for the rising generation. Metaphors seem generally unsuitable to prayer, but they do not wear this aspect in the prayers recorded in the Scriptures. The language of the text is tropical, but the metaphors are suitable and seasonable. *Roots* of vegetables are necessarily invisible. *Tender* plants are insignificant. A plant *grown up*, having height in its stem, width in its branches, abundance in its foliage, and fulness in its bloom, is conspicuous. David prays that the sons of that generation might be in their youth " *as plants grown up,*" that is, that their piety might not only live, but that their godliness might be fully expressed. The stones of a *foundation* are concealed. The stones in the *mid-wall* of a building are also necessarily hid. The stones on the *surface* of a wall are visible, but they are not distinguished. The *corner-stone* of buildings in that day was prominent and eminent. Placed at the angle of the structure, where two walls met, on the top of the walls, and being richly ornamented and polished, it attracted attention. David prays that the daughters of that day might make an open and lovely profession of religion—that both sons and daughters might not only *have* piety but *show* it.—*Samuel Martin, in "Cares of Youth."*

Verse 12.—*"Plants grown up." "Corner-stones polished."* These processes of growth and polish can be carried on in one place only, the church of Christ.—*Neale and Littledale.*

Verse 12.—*That our daughters may be as corner stones,"* etc. *"The polished corners of the temple,"* rather *" the sculptured angles, the ornament, of a palace."* Great care and much ornament were bestowed by the ancients upon the angles of their splendid palaces. It is remarkable that the Greeks made use of pilasters, called Caryatides (carved after the figure of a woman dressed in long robes), to support the entablatures of their buildings.—*Daniel Cresswell.*

Verse 12.—*" That our daughters may be as corner stones, polished after the similitude of a palace" or temple.* By daughters families are united and connected to their mutual strength, as the parts of a building are by the corner-stones; and when they are graceful and beautiful both in body and mind, they are then polished after the similitude of a nice and curious structure. When we see our daughters well established, and stayed with wisdom and discretion, as corner-stones are fastened in the building; when we see them by faith united to Christ, as the chief corner-stone, adorned with the graces of God's Spirit, which are the polishing of that which is naturally rough, and " become women professing godliness "; when we see them purified and consecrated to God as living temples, we think ourselves happy in them.—*Matthew Henry.*

Verse 12.—*" That our daughters may be as corner stones,"* etc. One might perhaps at the first glance have expected that the *daughters* of a household would be as the graceful ornament of the clustering foliage or the fruit-bearing tree, and the *sons* as the corner-stones upholding the weight and burden of the building, and yet it is the reverse here. And I think one may read the love and tenderness of the Lord in this apparently casual but intended expression, and that he meant the nations of the earth to know and understand how much of their happiness, their strength, and their security was dependent on the female children of a family. It has not been so considered in many a nation that knew not God : in polished Greece in times of old, and in some heathen nations even to this day, the female children of a family have been cruelly destroyed, as adding to the burdens and diminishing the resources of a household ; and alas ! too, even in Christian countries, if not destroyed, they are with equal pitiless and remorseless cruelty cut off from all the solace and ties and endearments of life, and immured in that living mockery of a grave, the cloister, that they may not prove incumbrances and hindrances to others ! How contrary all this to the loving purpose of our loving God ! whose Holy Spirit has written for our learning that sons and daughters are alike intended to be the ornament and grace, the happiness and blessing of every household.—*Barton Bouchier.*

Verse 12.—*"After the similitude of a palace."* Most interpreters give the last word the vague sense of " *a palace."* There is something, however, far more striking in the translation *temple,* found in the Prayer Book and the ancient versions. The omission of the article is a poetic license of perpetual occurrence. The temple was the great architectural model and standard of comparison, and particularly remarkable for the great size and skilful elaboration of its foundation-stones, some of which, there is reason to believe, have remained undisturbed since the time of Solomon.—*Joseph Addison Alexander.*

Verses 12—15.—In the former part of the psalm he speaks of such things as concern *his own* happiness : " Blessed be the Lord my strength" (verse 1) ; " Send thine hand from above ; and deliver me out of great waters " (verse 7) ; " Rid me, and deliver me from the hand of strange children" (verse 11). And he might as easily have continued the same strain in the clauses following : "That *my* sons may grow up as plants, *my* daughters may be as the polished corners of the temple, *my* sheep fruitful, *my* oxen strong, *my* garners full and plenteous" ; and accordingly he might have concluded it also—" Happy shall *I* be, if *I* be in such a case." This, I say, he might have done ; nay, this he would have done, if his desires had reflected only upon himself. But being of a diffusive heart, and knowing what belonged to the neighbourhoods of piety, as loth to enjoy this happiness alone, he alters his style, and (being in the height of well-wishes to himself) he turns the singular into a plural—*our sheep, our oxen, our garners, our sons and daughters*, that he might compendiate all in this,— "*Happy are the people.*" Here is a true testimony both of a religious and generous mind, who knew in his most retired thoughts to look out of himself, and to be mindful of the public welfare in his privatest meditations. S. Ambrose observes it as a clear character of a noble spirit, to do what tends to the public good, though to his own disadvantage.—*Richard Holdsworth* (1590—1649), *in* "*The Valley of Vision.*"

Verses 12—15.—These words contain a striking picture of a prosperous and happy nation. We are presented with a view of the *masculine youth* of the nation by the oaks of the forest, become great in the early period of the vigour and excellency of the soil. They are represented in the distinguishing character of their sex, standing abroad the strength of the nation, whence its resources for action must be derived. On the other hand, the *young females* of a nation are exhibited under an equally just and proper representation of their position and distinguishing character. They are not exhibited by a metaphor derived from the hardier tenants of the forest, but they are shown to us by a representation taken from the perpetual accompaniments of the dwelling ; they are the supports and the ornaments of domestic life. *Plenty* of every kind is represented to us in possession and in reasonable expectation. "*No breaking in,*" no invasion by a furious foe, oppresses the inhabitants of this happy country with terror ; neither is there any "*going out.*" The barbarous practice employed by Sennacherib, and other ancient conquerors, of transporting the inhabitants of a vanquished country to some distant, unfriendly, and hated land,—the practice at this moment employed, to the scandal of the name and the sorrow of Europe—they dread not : they fear no "*going out.*" Under circumstances of such a nature causes of distress or complaint exist not ; or, if they do, they are capable of being so modified, and alleviated, and remedied, that *there is no complaining in the streets.* " Happy, then, is that people, that is in such a case."—*John Pye Smith*, 1775—1851.

Verse 13.—"*That our sheep may bring forth thousands,*" etc. The surprising fecundity of the sheep has been celebrated by writers of every class. It has not escaped the notice of the royal Psalmist, who, in a beautiful ascription of praise to the living and the true God, entreats that the sheep of his chosen people might " *bring forth thousands and ten thousands in our streets.*" In another song of Zion, he represents, by a very elegant metaphor, the numerous flocks covering like a garment the face of the field :—" The pastures are clothed with flocks ; the valleys also are covered over with corn ; they shout for joy, they also sing " : Ps. lxv. 13. The bold figure is fully warranted by the prodigious numbers of sheep which whitened the extensive pastures of Syria and Canaan. In that part of Arabia which borders on Judea, the patriarch Job possessed at first seven thousand, and after the return of his prosperity, fourteen thousand sheep ; and Mesha, the king of Moab, paid the king of Israel " a yearly tribute of a hundred thousand lambs, and an equal number of rams with the wool " : 2 Kings iii. 4. In the war which the tribe of Reuben waged with the Hagarites, the former drove away " two hundred and fifty thousand sheep " : 1 Chron. v. 21. At the dedication of the temple, Solomon offered in sacrifice " an hundred and twenty thousand sheep." At the feast of the passover, Josiah, the king of Judah, " gave to the people, of the flock, lambs and kids, all for the passover offerings, for all that were present, to the number of thirty thousand, and three thousand bullocks : these were of the king's substance" : 2 Chron. xxxv. 7. The ewe brings forth her young commonly once a year, and in more ungenial climes, seldom more than one lamb at a time. But twin lambs are as frequent in the oriental regions, as they are rare in other places ; which accounts in a satisfactory manner for the prodigious numbers which the Syrian shepherd led to the mountains. This uncommon fruitfulness seems to be intimated by Solomon in his address to the spouse :—" Thy teeth are like a flock of sheep that are even shorn, which came up from the washing ; whereof every one bear twins, and none is barren among them" : Cant. iv. 2.—*George Paxton* (1762—1837), *in "Illustrations of Scripture."*

Verses 13, 14.—"*Streets,*" though not incorrect, is an inadequate translation of the Hebrew word, which means external spaces, streets as opposed to the inside of houses, fields or country as opposed to a whole town. Here it includes not only roads but fields.—*Joseph Addison Alexander.*

Verse 14.—"*That our oxen may be strong to labour.*" [Margin : "*able to bear burdens,*" or, *loaded* with flesh.] As in the verse before he had ascribed the fruitfulness of the herds and flocks to God's goodness, so now the fattening of their oxen, to show that there is nothing relating to us here which he overlooks.—*John Calvin.*

Verse 14.—"*That our oxen may be strong to labour.*" Oxen were not only used for ploughing, thrashing, and drawing, but also for bearing burdens ; compare 1 Chron. xii. 40, which passage is peculiarly fitted to throw light on the verse before us. Laden oxen presuppose a rich abundance of produce.—*E. W. Hengstenberg.*

Verse 14.—"*That there be no complaining in our streets,*" etc. Rather, " and no cry of sorrow" (comp. Isaiah xxiv. 11 ; Jer. xiv. 2 ; xlvi. 12) " in our open places," *i.e.*, the places where the people commonly assembled near the gate of the city (comp. 2 Chron. xxxii. 6 ; Neh. viii. 1). The word rendered " *complaining* " does not occur elsewhere in the psalter.—*Speaker's Commentary.*

Verse 14.—"*No complaining.*" No outcries but " Harvest-homes."—*John Trapp.*

Verse 15.—"*Happy is that people,*" etc. We have in the text happiness with an echo, or ingemination ; " *happy* " and " *happy.*" From this ingemination arise the parts of the text ; the same which are the parts both of the greater world and the less. As the heaven and earth in the one, and the body and soul in the other ; so are the passages of this Scripture in the two veins of happiness. We may range them as Isaac does the two parts of his blessing (Gen. xxvii. 28) ; the vein of civil happiness, in " the fatness of the earth " ; and the vein of Divine happiness, in " the fatness of heaven." Or (if you will have it out of the gospel), here's Martha's portion in the " many things " of the body ; and Mary's better part in the *unum necessarium* of the soul. To give it yet more concisely, here's the path of *prosperity* in outward comforts, "*Happy is that people, that is in such a case*" ; and the path of *piety* in comforts spiritual : "*Yea, happy is that people, whose God is the* LORD."

In the handling of the first, without any further subdivision, I will only show what it is the Psalmist treats of ; and that shall be by way of gradation, in these three particulars. It is *De* FELICITATE ; *De Felicitate* POPULI ; *De* HAC *Felicitate Populi :* of *happiness ;* of the *people's* happiness ; of the people's happiness, as *in such a case.*

Happiness is the general, and the first : a noble argument, and worthy of an inspired pen, especially the Psalmist's. Of all other there can be none better to speak of *popular* happiness than such a *king ;* nor of *celestial,* than such a *prophet.* Yet I mean not to discourse of it in the full latitude, but only as it hath a peculiar positure in this psalm, very various and different from the order of other psalms. In this psalm it is reserved to the *end,* as the close of the foregoing meditations. In other psalms it is set in the *front*, or first place of all ; as in the xxxii., in the cxii., in the cxix., and in the cxxviii. Again, in this the Psalmist ends with *our* happiness and begins with God's. " Blessed be the LORD my strength." In the 41st Psalm, contrary, he makes his *exordium* from *man's ;* " Blessed is he that considereth the poor" ; his *conclusion* with *God's ;* " Blessed be the LORD God of Israel." I therefore observe these variations, because they are helpful to the understanding both of the *essence* and *splendour* of true happiness. To the knowledge of the *essence* they help, because they demonstrate how our own happiness is enfolded in the glory of God, and subordinate unto it. As we cannot begin with *beatus* unless we end with *benedictus :* so we must begin with *benedictus* that we may end with *beatus.* The reason is this,—because the glory of God is as well the *consummation* as the *introduction* to a Christian's happiness. Therefore as in the other psalm he begins below and ends upwards ; so in this, having begun from above with that which is principal, " Blessed be the LORD " ; he fixeth his second thoughts upon the subordinate, " Blessed, or happy, are the people." He could not proceed in a better order : he first looks up to *God's* kingdom, then reflects upon his own, as not meaning to *take* blessedness before he had *given* it.—*Richard Holdsworth.*

Verse 15—"*Happy is that people, that is in such a case,*" etc. The first part of this text hath relation to temporal blessings, "*Blessed is the people that be so* ": the second to spiritual,-" *Yea, blessed is the people whose God is the* LORD." " His left hand is under my head," saith the spouse (Cant. ii. 6) ; that sustains me from falling into murmuring, or diffidence of his providence, because out of his left hand he hath given me a competency of his temporal blessings ; " But his right hand doth embrace me," saith the spouse there ; his spiritual blessings fill me, possess me so that no rebellious fire breaks out within me, no outward temptation breaks in upon me. So also Solomon says again, " In her left hand is riches and glory" (temporal blessings) " and in her right hand length of days" (Prov. iii. 16), all that accomplishes and fulfils the eternal joys of the saints of heaven. The person to whom Solomon attributes this right and left hand is Wisdom ; and a wise man may reach out his right and left hand, to receive the blessings of both sorts. And the person whom Solomon represents by Wisdom there, is Christ himself. So that not only a worldly wiseman, but a Christian wiseman may reach out both hands, to both kinds of blessings, right and left, spiritual and temporal.

Now, for this first blessedness, as no philosophers could ever tell us amongst the Gentiles what true blessedness was, so no grammarian amongst the Jews, amongst the Hebrews, could ever tell us what the right signification of this word is, in which David expresses blessedness here ; whether *asherei,* which is the word, be a plural noun, and signify *beatitudines,* blessednesses in the plural, and intimate thus much, that blessedness consists not in any one thing, but in a harmony and consent of many ; or whether this *asherei* be an adverb, and signify *beate,* and so be an acclamation, O how happily, how blessedly are such men provided for that are so ; they cannot tell. Whatsoever it be, it is the very first word with which David begins his Book of Psalms ; *beatus vir ;* as the last word of that book is, *laudate Dominum ;* to show that all that passes between God and man, from first to last, is blessings from God to man, and praises from man to God ; and that the first degree of blessedness is to find the print of the hand of God even in his temporal blessednesses, and to praise and glorify him for them in the right use of them. A man that hath no land to hold by it, nor title to recover by it, is never the better for finding, or buying, or having a fair piece of evidence, a fair instrument, fairly written, duly sealed, authentically testified ; a man that hath not the grace of God, and spiritual blessings too, is never the nearer happiness, for all his abundances of temporal blessedness. Evidences are evidences to them who have title. Temporal blessings are evidences to them who have a testimony of God's spiritual blessings in the temporal. Otherwise, as in his hands who hath no title, it is a suspicious thing to find evidences, and he will be thought to have embezzled and purloined them, he will be thought to have forged and counterfeited them, and he will be called to an account for them, how he came by them, and what he meant to do with them : so to them who have temporal blessings without spiritual, they are but useless blessings, they are but counterfeit blessings, they shall not purchase a minute's peace here, nor a minute's refreshing to the soul hereafter ; and there must be a heavy account made for them, both how they were got, and how they were employed.— *John Donne.*

Verse 15.—*"Happy is that people,"* etc. It is only a narrow and one-sided religion that can see anything out of place in this beatitude of plenty and peace. If we could rejoice with the psalms fully and without misgiving, in the temporal blessings bestowed by heaven, we should the more readily and sincerely enter into the depths of their spiritual experience. And the secret of this lies in the full comprehension and contemplation of the beautiful and pleasant as the gift of God.—*A. S. Aglen.*

Verse 15.—*"Yea, happy is that people, whose God is the* LORD.*"   "Yea, happy."* This is the best wine, kept to the last, though all men be not of this opinion. You shall hardly bring a worldly man to think so. The world is willing enough to misconstrue the order of the words, and to give the priority to civil happiness, as if it were first in dignity, because 'tis first named : they like better to hear of the *cui sic* than the *cui Dominus.* To prevent this folly, the Psalmist interposeth a caution in this corrective particle, " *yea, happy.*" It hath the force of a revocation, whereby he seems to retract what went before, not simply and absolutely, but in a certain degree, lest worldly men should wrest it to a misinterpretation. It is not an *absolute* revocation, but a *comparative ;* it doth not simply deny that there is some part of popular happiness in these outward things, but it prefers the spirituals before them : " *Yea,*" that is, *Yea more,* or, *Yea rather ;* like that of Christ in the Gospel, when one in the company blessed the womb that bare him, he presently replies, " Yea, rather blessed are they that hear the word of God and keep it ": Luke xi. 28. In like manner, the prophet David, having first premised the inferior part and outside of a happy condition ; fearing lest any should of purpose mistake his meaning, and, hearing the first proposition, should either there set up their rest, and not at all take up the second ; or if they take it in, do it preposterously, and give it the precedence before the second, according to the world's order, *Virtus post nummos.* In this respect he puts in the clause of revocation, whereby he shows that these outward things, though *named* first, yet they are not to be *reputed* first. The particle "*Yea*" removes them to the second place ; it tacitly transposeth the order ; and the path of piety, which was *locally* after, it placeth *virtually* before. 'Tis as if he had said, Did I call them *happy* who are in such a case ? Nay, miserable are they if they be only in such a case : the temporal part cannot make them so without the spiritual. Admit the windows of the visible heaven were opened, and all outward blessings poured down upon us ; admit we did perfectly enjoy whatsoever the vastness of the earth contains in it ; tell me, What will it profit to gain all and lose God ? If the earth be bestowed upon us, and not heaven ; or the material heaven be opened, and not the beatifical ; or the whole world made ours, and God not ours ; we do not arrive at happiness. All that is in the first proposition is nothing unless this be added, " *Yea, happy are the people which have the Lord for their God.*"—*Richard Holdsworth.*

Verse 15.—

Thrice happy nations, where with look benign
Thine aspect bends ; beneath thy smile divine
The fields are with increasing harvests crown'd,
The flocks grow fast, and plenty reigns around,
Nor sire, nor infant son, black death shall crave,
Till ripe with age they drop into the grave ;
Nor fell suspicion, nor relentless care,
Nor peace-destroying discord enter there,
But friends and brothers, wives and sisters, join
The feast in concord and in love divine.

—*Callimachus.*

Verse 15.—David having prayed for many temporal blessings in the behalf of the people from verse 12 to verse 15, at last concludes, "*Blessed are the people that are in such a case*"; but presently he checks and corrects himself, and eats, as it were, his own words, but rather, "*happy is that people whose God is the Lord.*" The Syriac rendereth it question wise, "Is not the people [happy] that is in such a case?" The answer is, "*No,*" except they have God to boot : Ps. cxlvi. 5. Nothing can make that man truly miserable that hath God for his portion, and nothing can make that man truly happy that wants God for his portion. God is the author of all true happiness ; he is the donor of all true happiness ; he is the maintainer of all true happiness, and he is the centre of all true happiness ; and, therefore, he that hath him for his God, and for his portion, is the only happy man in the world.—*Thomas Brooks.*

Verse 15.—"*Whose God is* JEHOVAH." A word or name well-known to us English, by our translators now often retaining that name in the mention of God in our English Bible, and therefore we shall do well to retain it. *Lord* was a lower word, in common acceptation, than *God.* But JEHOVAH is a higher name than either, and more peculiar, incommunicable, and comprehensive. Exod. vi. 3 : "I appeared " (saith the Lord) "unto Abraham, unto Isaac, and unto Jacob, by the name *God Almighty*, but by my name JEHOVAH was I not known to them."

To have God to be our *Jehovah* is the insurance of happiness to us. For of many, observe but these two things in the name *Jehovah :* First, God's absolute *independency*—that he is of himself omnipotent, Exod. iii. 14 : "And God said, I AM THAT I AM." Secondly, God's *faithfulness*, that he cannot but be as good as his word, Exod. vi. 2, 3, 4, 6 : "And I have also established my covenant with them ; wherefore say unto the children of Israel, I am JEHOVAH (so in the Hebrew), and I will bring you out from under the burdens of the Egyptians." So that this name is our *security* of God's performance. Examine we therefore our bonds, and bills, that is, his promises to us ; behold, they are all the promises of Jehovah ; they must stand good, for they bear his name ; they must reflect his name, and promote both our good and God's grand design.—*Nathanael Homes,* 1678.

With this prayer of Jehovah's anointed One end the prayers of the Book of Psalms. The remaining six psalms consist exclusively of praise and high Hallelujahs.—*Lord Congleton, in "The Psalms : a new Version, with Notes,"* 1875.

HINTS TO THE VILLAGE PREACHER.

Verse 1.—I. Two things needful in our holy war—strength and skill ; for the hands and the fingers, for the difficult and the delicate. II. In what way God supplies us with both. He is the one, and teaches the other. Impartation and Instruction. The teaching comes by illumination, experience, distinct guidance.

Verse 1.—Things not to be forgotten by the Christian Soldier. I. The true source of his strength : "The Lord my strength." If remembered, 1. He will not be found trusting in self. 2. He will never be wanting in courage. 3. He will always anticipate victory. 4. He will never be worsted in the conflict. II. His constant need of instruction, and the Teacher who never forgets him : "Which teacheth my hands," etc. If remembered, 1. He will gird on the armour provided and commended by God. 2. He will select for his weapon the sword of the Spirit. 3. He will study the divinely-given text-book of military tactics and discipline, that he may learn (1) the devices of the enemy ; (2) methods of attack and defence ; (3) how to bear himself in the thick of the fight. 4. He will wait upon God for understanding. III. The praise due to God, both for victories won and skill displayed : "Blessed be," etc. If remembered, 1. He will wear his honours humbly. 2. Glorify the honour of his King. 3. Twice taste the sweets of victory in the happiness of gratitude.—*J. F.*

Verse 2.—Double flowers. I. Good preserved from evil : " goodness " and " fortress." II. Safety enlarged into liberty : " tower," " deliverer." III. Security attended with rest : " shield, in whom I trust." IV. Sufficiency to maintain superiority : " subdueth my people under me.". View God as working all.

Verse 2.—A Group of Titles. Notice, I. Which comes first. " Goodness." *Heb.* " Mercy." 1. It is right and natural that a saved sinner should make the most of " mercy," and place it in the foreground. 2. Mercy is the ground and reason of the other titles named. For whatever God is to us, it is a special manifestation of his mercy. 3. It is a good thing to see a believer ripe in experience making mercy the leading note in his song of praise. II. Which comes last : " He in whom I trust." It suggests, 1. That what God is makes him worthy of trust. 2. That meditation upon what he is strengthens our trust. III. What peculiar force the word " my" gives to each. It makes it, 1. A record of experience. 2. An ascription of praise. 3. A blessed boasting. 4. An incentive, enough to set others longing.—*J. F.*

Verse 3.—A note of interrogation, exclamation, and admiration.

Verse 3.—The question, I. Denies any right in man to claim the regard of God. II. Asserts the great honour God has nevertheless put upon him. III. Suggests that the true reason of God's generous dealings is the graciousness of his own heart. IV. Implies the becomingness of gratitude and humility. V. Encourages the most unworthy to put their confidence in God.—*J. F.*

Verse 3.—I. What was man as he came from the hands of his Creator ? 1. Rational. 2. Responsible. 3. Immortal. 4. Holy and happy. II. What is man in his present condition ? 1. Fallen. 2. Guilty. 3. Sinful. 4. Miserable, and helpless in his misery. III. What is man when he has believed in Christ ? 1. Restored to a right relation to God. 2. Restored to a right disposition toward God. 3. He enjoys the influences of the Holy Spirit. 4. He is in process of preparation for the heavenly world. IV. What shall man be when he is admitted into heaven ? 1. Free from sin and sorrow. 2. Advanced to the perfection of his nature. 3. Associated with angels. 4. Near to his Saviour and his God. —*George Brooks, in " The Homiletic Commentary,"* 1879.

Verse 3.—Worthless man much regarded by the mighty God. Sermon by Ebenezer Erskine. Works iii., pp. 141—162.

Verse 3.—It is a wonder above all wonders, that ever the great God should make such account of such a thing as man. I. It will appear if you consider what a great God the Lord is. II. What a poor thing man is. III. What a great account the great God hath of this poor thing, man.—*Joseph Alleine.*

Verse 4.—He is nothing, he pretends to be something, he is soon gone, he ends in nothing as to this life ; yet there is a light somewhere.

Verse 4.—The Shadow-World. I. Our lives are like shadows. II. But God's light casts these shadows. Our being is of God. The brevity and mystery of life are a part of providence. III. The destiny of the shadows ; eternal night ; or eternal light.—*W. B. H.*

Verse 4.—The brevity of our earthly life. I, A profitable subject for meditation. II. A rebuke to those who provide for this life alone. III. A trumpet-call to prepare for eternity. IV. An incentive to the Christian to make the best of this life for the glory of God.—*J. F.*

Verse 5.—Condescension, visitation, contact, and conflagration.

Verses 7, 8, 11.—Repetitions, not vain. Repetitions in prayer are vain when they result from form, thoughtlessness, or superstition ; but not, *e.g.*, I. When they are the utterance of genuine fervour. II. When the danger prayed against is imminent. III. When the fear which prompts the prayer is urgent. IV. When the repetition is prompted by a new motive, verses 7, 8 ; by God's condescension, verses 3, 11 ; by God's former deliverance, verse 10 ; and by the results which will flow from the answer, verses 12—14.—*C. A. D.*

Verse 8.—What is " a right hand of falsehood " ? Ask the hypocrite, the schemer, the man of false doctrine, the boaster, the slanderer, the man who forgets his promise, the apostate.

Verse 9.—For God's Ear. I. The Singer. A grateful heart. II. The Song. Praiseful. New. III. The Accompaniment : " Psaltery." Helps to devotion. Give God the best. IV. The Auditor and Object of the eulogium : " Thee, O God."—*W. B. H.*

Verse 11.—Persons from whom it is a mercy to escape : those alien to God, vain in conversation, false in deed.

Verses 11, 12.—The Nature and Necessity of early Piety. A Sermon preached to a Society of Young People, at Willingham, Cambridgeshire, on the First Day of the Year M.DCC.LXXII.—*Robert Robinson.*

Verse 12.—Youth attended with development, stability, usefulness, and spiritual health.

Verse 12 (*first clause*).—To Young Men. Consider, I. What is desired on your behalf : " Sons may be as plants," etc. 1. That you may be respected and valued. 2. That you may have settled principles and virtues. Plants are not blown hither and thither. 3. That you may be vigorous and strong in moral power. II. What is requisite on your part to the accomplishment of this desire. 1. A good rootage in Christ. 2. Constant nourishment from the word of God. 3. The dews of divine grace obtained by prayer. 4. A resolute tendency within to answer the God-appointed purpose of your existence.—*J. F.*

Verse 12 (*second clause*).—To Young Women. Consider, I. The important position you may occupy in the social fabric : " As corner-stones." 1. The moral and religious tone of society is determined more by your character and influence than by those of men. 2. The complexion of home life will be a reflex of your conduct and character, either as daughters, sisters, or wives. 3. The moulding of the character of the next generation, remember, begins with the mother's influence. 4. Let these facts weigh with you as a motive in seeking the grace of God, without which you can never fulfil your mission worthily. II. The beauty which ought to belong to you in your position. " Polished after," etc. The beauty of, 1. Heart purity : " The King's daughter is all glorious within." 2., A noble and modest conduct : " wrought gold," no imitation ; real gold. 3. Gracious and gentle demeanour. III. How both the right position and right beauty are obtained. 1. By yielding yourselves to God. 2. By Christ dwelling in your heart. 3. By becoming living stones and polished stones under the workmanship of the Holy Spirit.—*J. F.*

Verse 14.—A prayer for our ministers, and for the security, unity, and happiness of the church.

Verse 14.—The prosperous Church. There—I. Labour is cheerfully performed. II. The enemy is kept without the gate. III. There are few or no departures. IV. Faith and content silence complaint. V. Pray that such may be our case as a church.—*W. B. H.*

Verse 15.—The peculiar happiness of those whose God is the Lord.

PSALM CXLV.

This is one of the alphabetical psalms, composed with much art, and, doubtless, so arranged that the memory might be aided. The Holy Spirit condescends to use even the more artificial methods of the poet, to secure attention, and impress the heart.

Title.—David's Psalm of Praise. It is David's, David's very own, David's favourite. It is David's Praise just as another (Psalm lxxxvi.) is David's Prayer. It is altogether praise, and praise pitched in a high key. David had blessed God many a time in other psalms, but this he regarded as his peculiar, his crown jewel of praise. Certainly David's praise is the best of praise, for it is that of a man of experience, of sincerity, of calm deliberation, and of intense warmth of the heart. It is not for any one of us to render David's praise, for David only could do that, but we may take David's psalm as a model, and aim at making our own personal adoration as much like it as possible: we shall be long before we equal our model. Let each Christian reader present his own praise unto the Lord, and call it by his own name. What a wealth of varied praise will thus be presented through Christ Jesus!

Division.—The psalm does not fall into any marked divisions, but is one and indivisible. Our own translators have mapped out this song with considerable discernment. It is not a perfect arrangement, but it will suit our convenience in exposition. David praiseth God for his fame or glory (1—7), for his goodness (8—10), for his kingdom (11—13), for his providence (14—16), for his saving mercy (17—21).

EXPOSITION.

I WILL extol thee, my God, O king; and I will bless thy name for ever and ever.

2 Every day will I bless thee; and I will praise thy name for ever and ever.

3 Great *is* the LORD, and greatly to be praised; and his greatness *is* unsearchable.

4 One generation shall praise thy works to another, and shall declare thy mighty acts.

5 I will speak of the glorious honour of thy majesty, and of thy wondrous works.

6 And *men* shall speak of the might of thy terrible acts; and I will declare thy greatness.

7 They shall abundantly utter the memory of thy great goodness, and shall sing of thy righteousness.

1. *"I will extol thee, my God, O king."* David as God's king adores God as his king. It is well when the Lord's royalty arouses our loyalty, and our spirit is moved to magnify his majesty. The Psalmist has extolled his Lord many a time before, he is doing so still, and he will do so in the future: praise is for all tenses. When we cannot express all our praise just now, it is wise to register our resolution to continue in the blessed work, and write it down as a bond, " I will extol thee." See how David testifies his devotion and adherence to his God by the pronoun " my," how he owns his allegiance by the title " king," and how he goes on to declare his determination to make much of him in his song.

"And I will bless thy name for ever and ever." David determined that his praise should rise to blessing, should intelligently spend itself upon the name or character of God, and should be continued world without end. He uses the word

" bless" not merely for variation of sound, but also for the deepening and sweetening of the sense. To bless God is to praise him with a personal affection for him, and a wishing well to him : this is a growingly easy exercise as we advance in experience and grow in grace. David declares that he will offer every form of praise, through every form of existence. His notion of duration is a full one— " for ever " has no end, but when he adds another " ever " to it he forbids all idea of a close. Our praise of God shall be as eternal as the God we praise.

2. "*Every day will I bless thee.*" Whatever the character of the day, or of my circumstances and conditions during that day, I will continue to glorify God. Were we well to consider the matter we should see abundant cause in each day for rendering special blessing unto the Lord. All before the day, all in the day, all following the day should constrain us to magnify our God every day, all the year round. Our love to God is not a matter of holy days : every day is alike holy to holy men. David here comes closer to God than when he said, " I will bless thy name" : it is now, " I will bless *thee.*" This is the centre and kernel of true devotion : we do not only admire the Lord's words and works, but himself. Without realizing the personality of God, praise is well-nigh impossible ; you cannot extol an abstraction. "*And I will praise thy name for ever and ever.*" He said he would bless that name, and now he vows to praise it ; he will extol the Lord in every sense and way. Eternal worship shall not be without its variations ; it will never become monotonous. Heavenly music is not harping upon one string, but all strings shall be tuned to one praise. Observe the personal pronouns here : four times he says "*I* will " : praise is not to be discharged by proxy : there must be your very self in it, or there is nothing in it.

3. "*Great is the* LORD, *and greatly to be praised.*" Worship should be somewhat like its object—great praise for a great God. There is no part of Jehovah's greatness which is not worthy of great praise. In some beings greatness is but vastness of evil : in him it is magnificence of goodness. Praise may be said to be great when the song contains great matter, when the hearts producing it are intensely fervent, and when large numbers unite in the grand acclaim. No chorus is too loud, no orchestra too large, no psalm too lofty for the lauding of the Lord of Hosts.

"*And his greatness is unsearchable.*"

> " Still his worth your praise exceeds,
> Excellent are all his deeds."

Song should be founded upon search ; hymns composed without thought are of no worth, and tunes upon which no pains have been spent are beneath the dignity of divine adoration. Yet when we meditate most, and search most studiously we shall still find ourselves surrounded with unknowable wonders, which will baffle all attempts to sing them worthily. The best adoration of the Unsearchable is to own him to be so, and close the eyes in reverence before the excessive light of his glory. Not all the minds of all the centuries shall suffice to search out the unsearchable riches of God ; he is past finding out ; and, therefore, his deserved praise is still above and beyond all that we can render to him.

4. "*One generation shall praise thy works to another.*" There shall be a tradition of praise : men shall hand on the service, they shall make it a point to instruct their descendants in this hallowed exercise. We look back upon the experience of our fathers, and sing of it ; even thus shall our sons learn praise from the Lord's works among ourselves. Let us see to it that we praise God before our children, and never make them think that his service is an unhappy one. "*And shall declare thy mighty acts.*" The generations shall herein unite : together they shall make up an extraordinary history. Each generation shall contribute its chapter, and all the generations together shall compose a volume of matchless character. David began with " I," but he has in this verse soon reached to an inconceivable multitude, comprehending all the myriads of our race of every age. The praise of the Lord enlarges the heart, and as it grows upon us our minds grow with it. God's works of goodness and acts of power make up a subject which all the eras of human story can never exhaust. A praiseful heart seems to

live in all the centuries in delightful companionship with all the good. We are not afraid that the incense will ever cease to burn upon the altars of Jehovah : the priests die, but the adoration lives on. All glory be unto him who remains the same Lord throughout all generations.

5. "*I will speak of the glorious honour of thy majesty.*" 'Tis fit a king should speak of the majesty of the King of kings. David cannot give over the worship of God into the hands of others, even though all generations should undertake to perpetuate it : he must have his own individual share in it, and so he saith, " I will speak." What a speaker ! for he no sooner begins than he heaps up words of honour—" the glorious honour of thy majesty," or " the beauty of the honour of thy majesty." His language labours to express his meaning ; he multiplies the terms by which he would extol Jehovah, his King. Everything which has to do with the Great King is majestic, honourable, glorious. His least is greater than man's greatest, his lowest is higher than man's highest. There is nothing about the infinite Lord which is unworthy of his royalty ; and, on the other hand, nothing is wanting to the splendour of his reign : his majesty is honourable, and his honour is glorious : he is altogether wonderful.

"*And of thy wondrous works.*" All the works of God among men are Godlike, but certain of them are specially calculated to create surprise. Many works of power, of justice, of wisdom, are wonderful ; and his work of grace is wondrous above all. This specially, and all the rest proportionately, should be spoken of by holy men, by experienced men, and by men who have the ability to speak with power. These things must not be permitted to pass away in silence ; if others do not remember them, representative men like David must make a point of conversing upon them in private, and speaking of them in public. Let it be the delight of each one of us according to our position to speak lovingly of our Lord.

6. "*And men shall speak of the might of thy terrible acts.*" If unobservant of other matters these acts of judgment shall seize their attention and impress their minds so that they must talk about them. Did not men in our Saviour's day speak of the falling tower of Siloam and the slaughtered Galileans ? Are there not rumours of wars, when there are not even whispers of other things ? Horrible news is sure to spread : under mercies men may be dumb, but concerning miseries they raise a great outcry. The force of dread is a power which loosens the tongue of the multitude : they are sure to talk of that which makes the ear to tingle and the hair to stand upright.

While they are thus occupied with " fearsome facts," such as the drowning of a world, the destruction of the cities of the plain, the plagues of Egypt, the destruction at the Red Sea, and so forth, David would look at these affairs in another light, and sing another tune. "*And I will declare thy greatness.*" Those acts which were terrible deeds to most men were mighty deeds, or *greatnesses* to our holy poet : these he would publish like a herald, who mentions the titles and honours of his royal master. It is the occupation of every true believer to rehearse the great doings of his great God. We are not to leave this to the common converse of the crowd, but we are personally to make a declaration of what we have seen and known. We are even bound in deep solemnity of manner to warn men of the Lord's greatness in his terrible acts of justice : thus will they be admonished to abstain from provoking him. To fulfil this duty we are already bound by solemn obligations, and we shall do well to bind ourselves further by resolutions, " I will—God helping me, I will."

7. "*They shall abundantly utter the memory of thy great goodness.*" They shall pour forth grateful memories even as springs gush with water, plenteously, spontaneously, constantly, joyously. The Lord's redeemed people having been filled with his great goodness, shall retain the happy recollection of it, and shall be moved often and often to utter those recollections. Not content with a scanty mention of such amazing love, they shall go on to an abundant utterance of such abundant favour. It shall be their delight to speak with one another of God's dealings with them, and to compare notes of their experiences. God has done nothing stintedly ; all his goodness is great goodness, all worthy to be remem-

bered, all suggestive of holy discourse. Upon this subject there is no scarcity of matter, and when the heart is right there is no need to stop from want of facts to tell. Oh, that there were more of these memories and utterances, for it is not meet that the goodness of the living God should be buried in the cemetery of silence, in the grave of ingratitude.

"*And shall sing 'of thy righteousness.*" They shall say and then sing. And what is the theme which impels them to leave the pulpit for the orchestra? What do they sing of? They sing of that righteousness which is the sinner's terror, which even good men mention with deep solemnity. Righteousness received by gospel light is in reality the secret foundation of the believer's hope. God's covenant of grace is our strong consolation, because he who made it is righteous, and will not run back from it. Since Jesus died as our substitute, righteousness requires and secures the salvation of all the redeemed. This attribute is our best friend, and therefore we sing of it.

Modern thinkers would fain expunge the idea of righteousness from their notion of God; but converted men would not. It is a sign of growth in sanctification when we rejoice in the justice, rectitude, and holiness of our God. Even a rebel may rejoice in mercy, which he looks upon as laxity; but a loyal subject rejoices when he learns that God is so just that not even to save his own elect would he consent to violate the righteousness of his moral government. Few men will shout for joy at the righteousness of Jehovah, but those who do so are his chosen, in whom his soul delighteth.

8 The LORD *is* gracious, and full of compassion; slow to anger, and of great mercy.

9 The LORD *is* good to all: and his tender mercies *are* over all his works.

10 All thy works shall praise thee, O LORD; and thy saints shall bless thee.

8. "*The Lord is gracious.*" Was it not in some such terms that the Lord revealed himself to Moses? Is not this Jehovah's glory? To all living men this is his aspect: he is gracious, or full of goodness and generosity. He treats his creatures with kindness, his subjects with consideration, and his saints with favour. His words and ways, his promises and his gifts, his plans and his purposes all manifest his grace, or free favour. There is nothing suspicious, prejudiced, morose, tyrannical, or unapproachable in Jehovah,—he is condescending and kind. "*And full of compassion.*" To the suffering, the weak, the foolish, the despondent, he is very pitiful: he feels for them, he feels with them: he does this heartily, and in a practical manner. Of this pitifulness he is full, so that he compassionates freely, constantly, deeply, divinely, and effectually. In God is fulness in a sense not known among men, and this fulness is all fragrant with sympathy for human misery. If the Lord be full of compassion there is no room in him for forgetfulness or harshness, and none should suspect him thereof. What an ocean of compassion there must be since the Infinite God is full of it. "*Slow to anger.*" Even those who refuse his grace yet share in long-suffering. When men do not repent, but, on the contrary, go from bad to worse, he is still averse to let his wrath flame forth against them. Greatly patient and extremely anxious that the sinner may live, he " lets the lifted thunder drop," and still forbears. " Love suffereth long and is kind," and God is love. "*And of great mercy.*' This is his attitude towards the guilty. When men at last repent, they find pardon awaiting them. Great is their sin, and great is God's mercy. They need great help, and they have it though they deserve it not; for he is greatly good to the greatly guilty.

9. "*The* LORD *is good to all.*" No one, not even his fiercest enemy, can deny this; for the falsehood would be too barefaced, since the very existence of the lips which slander him is a proof that it is slander. He allows his enemies to live, he even supplies them with food, and smooths their way with many com-

forts ; for them the sun shines as brightly as if they were saints, and the rain waters their fields as plentifully as if they were perfect men.   Is not this goodness to all ?   In our own land the gospel sounds in the ears of all who care to listen ; and the Scriptures are within reach of the poorest child.   It would be a wanton wresting of Scripture to limit this expression to the elect, as some have tried to do ; we rejoice in electing love, but none the less we welcome the glorious truth, " Jehovah is good to all."

"*And his tender mercies are over all his works.*"   Not "his new-covenant works," as one read it the other day who was wise above that which is written, yea, contrary to that which is written.   Kindness is a law of God's universe : the world was planned for happiness ; even now that sin has so sadly marred God's handiwork, and introduced elements which were not from the beginning, the Lord has so arranged matters that the fall is broken, the curse is met by an antidote, and the inevitable pain is softened with mitigations.   Even in this sin-stricken world, under its disordered economy, there are abundant traces of a hand skilful to soothe distress and heal disease.   That which makes life bearable is the tenderness of the great Father.   This is seen in the creation of an insect as well as in the ruling of nations.   The Creator is never rough, the Provider is never forgetful, the Ruler is never cruel.   Nothing is done to create disease, no organs are arranged to promote misery ; the incoming of sickness and pain is not according to the original design, but a result of our disordered state.   Man's body as it left the Maker's hand was neither framed for disease, decay, nor death, neither was the purpose of it discomfort and anguish ; far otherwise, it was framed for a joyful activity, and a peaceful enjoyment of God.   Jehovah has in great consideration laid up in the world cures for our ailments, and helps for our feebleness ; and if many of these have been long in their discovery, it is because it was more for man's benefit to find them out himself, than to have them labelled and placed in order before his eyes.   We may be sure of this, that Jehovah has never taken delight in the ills of his creatures, but has sought their good, and laid himself out to alleviate the distresses into which they have guiltily plunged themselves.

The duty of kindness to animals may logically be argued from this verse. Should not the children of God be like their Father in kindness ?

10.   "*All thy works shall praise thee, O Lord.*"   There is a something about every creature which redounds to the honour of God.   The skill, kindness, and power manifested in the formation of each living thing is in itself to the praise of God, and when observed by an intelligent mind the Lord is honoured thereby. Some works praise him by their being, and others by their well-being ; some by their mere existence, and others by their hearty volition.   "*And thy saints shall bless thee.*"   These holy ones come nearer, and render sweeter adoration.   Men have been known to praise those whom they hated, as we may admire the prowess of a warrior who is our foe ; but saints lovingly praise, and therefore are said to " bless."   They wish well to God ; they would make him more blessed, if such a thing were possible ; they desire blessings upon his cause and his children, and invoke success upon his work and warfare.   None but blessed men will bless the Lord.   Only saints or holy ones will bless the thrice holy God.   If we praise Jehovah because of his works around us, we must go on to bless him for his works within us.   Let the two " shalls" of this verse be fulfilled, especially the latter one.

11 They shall speak of the glory of thy kingdom, and talk of thy power.

12 To make known to the sons of men his mighty acts, and the glorious majesty of his kingdom.

13 Thy kingdom *is* an everlasting kingdom, and thy dominion *endureth* throughout all generations.

11.   "*They shall speak of the glory of thy kingdom.*"   Excellent themes for saintly

minds. Those who bless God from their hearts rejoice to see him enthroned, glorified, and magnified in power. No subject is more profitable for humility, obedience, hope, and joy than that of the reigning power of the Lord our God. His works praise him, but they cannot crown him : this remains for holy hands and hearts. It is their high pleasure to tell of the glory of his kingdom in its justice, kindness, eternity, and so forth. Kingdoms of earth are glorious for riches, for extent of territory, for victories, for liberty, for commerce, and other matters ; but in all true glories the kingdom of Jehovah excels them. We have seen a palace dedicated "to all the glories of France" ; but time, eternity, and all space are filled with the glories of God : on these we love to speak. "*And talk of thy power.*" This power supports the kingdom and displays the glory, and we are sure to talk of it when the glory of the divine kingdom is under discussion. God's power to create or to destroy, to bless or to punish, to strengthen or to crush, is matter for frequent rehearsal. All power comes from God. Apart from him the laws of nature would be inoperative. His power is the one source of force—mechanical, vital, mental, spiritual. Beyond the power of God which has been put forth, infinite force lies latent in himself. Who can calculate the reserve forces of the Infinite ? How, then, can his kingdom fail ? We hear talk of the five great powers, but what are they to the One Great Power ? The Lord is " the blessed and only Potentate." Let us accustom ourselves to think more deeply and speak more largely of this power which ever makes for righteousness and works for mercy.

12. "*To make known to the sons of men his mighty acts.*" These glorious deeds ought to be known to all mankind ; but yet few reckon such knowledge to be an essential part of education. As the State cannot teach these holy histories the people of God must take care to do it themselves. The work must be done for every age, for men have short memories in reference to their God, and the doings of his power. They inscribe the deeds of their heroes upon brass, but the glorious acts of Jehovah are written upon the sand, and the tide of time washes them from present memory ; therefore we must repeat the lesson, and yet again repeat it. The saints are the religious instructors of the race ; they ought to be not only the historians of the past, but the bards of the present, whose duty it is to keep the sons of men in memory of the great deeds which the Lord did in the days of their fathers and in the old time before them. Note the contrast between the great deeds of God and the puny sons of Adam, who have even degenerated from their father, though he was as nothing compared with his Maker.

"*And the glorious majesty of his kingdom.*" What a grand subject ! Yet this we are to make known ; the publication of it is left to us who bless the Lord. " The glory of the majesty of his reign." What a theme ! Jehovah's reign as sovereign Lord of all, his majesty in that dominion, and the glory of that majesty ! The threefold subject baffles the most willing mind. How shall we make this known to the sons of men ? Let us first labour to know it ourselves, and then let us make it a frequent subject of discourse, so shall men know it from us, the Holy Spirit attending our word.

13. "*Thy kingdom is an everlasting kingdom.*" His meditation has brought him near to God, and God near to him : he speaks to him in adoration, changing the pronoun from " his" to " thy." He sees the great King, and prostrates himself before him. It is well when our devotion opens the gate of heaven, and enters within the portal, to speak with God face to face, as a man speaketh with his friend. The point upon which the Psalmist's mind rests is the eternity of the divine throne,—" thy reign is a reign of all eternities." The Lord's kingdom is without beginning, without break, without bound, and without end. He never abdicates his throne, neither does he call in a second to share his empire. None can overthrow his power, or break away from his rule. Neither this age, nor the age to come, nor ages of ages shall cause his sovereignty to fail. Herein is rest for faith. " The Lord sitteth King for ever." "*And thy dominion endureth throughout all generations.*" Men come and go like shadows on the wall, but God reigneth eternally. We distinguish kings as they succeed each other by calling

them first and second ; but this King is Jehovah, the First and the Last. Adam in his generation knew his Creator to be King, and the last of his race shall know the same. All hail, Great God ! Thou art ever Lord of lords !

These three verses are a reverent hymn concerning " the kingdom of God " : they will be best appreciated by those who are in that kingdom in the fullest sense, and are most truly loyal to the Lord. It is, according to these verses, a kingdom of glory and power ; a kingdom of light which men are to know, and of might which men are to feel ; it is full of majesty and eternity ; it is the benediction of every generation. We are to speak of it, talk of it, and make it known, and then we are to acknowledge it in the homage directed distinctly to the Lord himself—as in verse thirteen.

14 The LORD upholdeth all that fall, and raiseth up all *those that be* bowed down.

15 The eyes of all wait upon thee ; and thou givest them their meat in due season.

16 Thou openest thine hand, and satisfiest the desire of every living thing.

In these three verses Jehovah is adored for his gracious providence towards men and all other creatures ; this fitly follows the proclamation of his royalty, for we here see how he rules his kingdom, and provides for his subjects.

14. "*The LORD upholdeth all that fall.*" Read this verse in connection with the preceding, and admire the unexpected contrast : he who reigns in glorious majesty, yet condescends to lift up and hold up those who are apt to fall. The form of the verb shows that he is always doing this ; he is Jehovah upholding. His choice of the fallen, and the falling, as the subjects of his gracious help is specially to be noted. The fallen of our race, especially fallen women, are shunned by us, and it is peculiar tenderness on the Lord's part that such he looks upon, even those who are at once the chief of sinners and the least regarded of mankind. The falling ones among us are too apt to be pushed down by the strong : their timidity and dependence make them the victims of the proud and domineering. To them also the Lord gives his upholding help. The Lord loves to reverse things, —he puts down the lofty, and lifts up the lowly.

"*And raiseth up all those that be bowed down.*" Another deed of condescension. Many are despondent, and cannot lift up their heads in courage, or their hearts with comfort ; but these he cheers. Some are bent with their daily load, and these he strengthens. Jesus loosed a daughter of Abraham whom Satan had so bound that she was bowed down, and could by no means lift up herself. In this he proved himself to be the true Son of the Highest. Think of the Infinite bowing to lift up the bowed, and stooping to be leaned upon by those who are ready to fall. The two " alls" should not be overlooked : the Lord has a kindly heart towards the whole company of the afflicted.

15. "*The eyes of all wait upon thee.*" They have learned to look to thee : it has become their nature to turn to thee for all they want. As children look to a father for all they need, so do the creatures look to God, the all-sufficient Provider. It were well if all men had the eye of faith, and if all waited therewith upon the Lord. "*And thou givest them their meat in due season.*" They wait, and God gives. The thought of this brings God so near to our poet-prophet that he is again speaking with God after the style of thee and thou. Is it to be wondered at when the Lord is feeding the hungry all around us,—giving food to all creatures, and to ourselves among them ? Like a flock of sheep the creatures stand around the Lord as their great Shepherd ; all eyes are to his hand expecting to receive their food ; nor are they disappointed, for when the hour comes suitable provender is ready for each creature. Observe the punctuality of the Lord in giving food at meal-time,—in the season when it is due. This he does for all, and each living thing has its own season, so that the Lord of heaven is feeding his great flock both by day and by night, during every moment of time.

16. *"Thou openest thine hand, and satisfiest the desire of every living thing."* Thou alone providest, O Jehovah! Thou doest it liberally, with open hand; thou doest it easily, as if it were only to open thine hand; thou doest this at once as promptly as if all supplies were ready to hand. Living things have needs, and these create desires; the living God has suitable supplies at hand, and these he gives till inward satisfaction is produced, and the creature sighs no longer. In spiritual things, when God has raised a desire, he always gratifies it; hence the longing is prophetic of the blessing. In no case is the desire of the living thing excited to produce distress, but in order that it may seek and find satisfaction.

These verses refer to natural providence; but they may equally well apply to the stores of grace, since the same God is king in both spheres. If we will but wait upon the Lord for pardon, renewing, or whatever else we need, we shall not wait in vain. The hand of grace is never closed while the sinner lives.

17 The LORD *is* righteous in all his ways, and holy in all his works.

18 The LORD *is* nigh unto all them that call upon him, to all that call upon him in truth.

19 He will fulfill the desire of them that fear him : he also will hear their cry, and will save them.

20 The LORD preserveth all them that love him : but all the wicked will he destroy.

21 My mouth shall speak the praise of the LORD : and let all flesh bless his holy name for ever and ever.

In these verses we behold our God in the realm of his free grace dealing well with his believing people.

17. *"The LORD is righteous in all his ways, and holy in all his works."* His ways and works are both worthy to be praised. Jehovah cannot be unjust or impure. Let his doings be what they may, they are in every case righteous and holy. This is the confession of the godly who follow his ways, and of the gracious who study his works. Whatever God is or does must be right. In the salvation of his people he is as righteous and holy as in any other of his ways and works : he has not manifested mercy at the expense of justice, but the rather he has magnified his righteousness by the death of his Son.

18. *"The LORD is nigh unto all them that call upon him."* Not only near by his omnipresence, but to sympathize and favour. He does not leave praying men, and men who call his name, to battle with the world alone, but he is ever at their side. This favour is not for a few of those who invoke him ; but for each one of the pious company. "All" who place themselves beneath the shield of his glorious name by calling themselves by it, and by calling upon it in supplication, shall find him to be a very present help in trouble. *"To all that call upon him in truth ":* for there are many whose formal prayers and false professions will never bring them into communion with the Lord. To pray in truth, we must have a true heart, and the truth in our heart ; and then we must be humble, for pride is a falsehood ; and be earnest, or else prayer is a lie. A God of truth cannot be nigh to the spirit of hypocrisy ; this he knows and hates ; neither can he be far removed from a sincere spirit, since it is his work, and he forsakes not the work of his own hands.

19. *"He will fulfil the desire of them that fear him ":* that is, those who reverence his name and his law. Inasmuch as they have respect unto his will, he will have respect unto their will. They shall have their way for they have his way in their hearts. A holy heart only desires what a holy God can give, and so its desire is filled full out of the fulness of the Lord. *"He also will hear their cry, and will save them."* Divinely practical shall his nearness be, for he will work their deliverance. He will listen to their piteous cry, and then will send salvation from

every ill. This he will do himself personally ; he will not trust them to angels or saints.

20. *"The* LORD *preserveth all them that love him."* They keep him in their love, and he keeps them by his love. See how these favoured ones have advanced from fearing the Lord and crying to him, even to loving him, and in that love they are secure from all danger. Mark the number of " alls" in these later verses of the psalm. In each of these God is all in all. *"But all the wicked will he destroy."* Wickedness is an offence to all holy beings, and therefore those who are determined to continue in it must be weeded out. As good sanitary laws remove all creators of pest and plague, so does the moral government of God mark every evil thing for destruction ; it cannot be tolerated in the presence of a perfectly holy God. What ruins wicked men frequently become in this life ! What monuments of wrath will they be in the world to come ! Like Nineveh and Babylon, and other destroyed places, they shall only exist to declare how thoroughly God fulfils his threatenings.

21. *"My mouth shall speak the praise of the* LORD." Whatever others may do, I will not be silent in the praise of the Lord : whatever others may speak upon, my topic is fixed once for all : I will speak the praise of Jehovah. I am doing it, and I will do it as long as I breathe. *"And let all flesh bless his holy name for ever and ever."* Praise is no monopoly for one, even though he be a David ; others are debtors, let them also be songsters. All men of every race, condition, or generation should unite to glorify God. No man need think that he will be rejected when he comes with his personal note of praise ; all are permitted, invited, and exhorted to magnify the Lord. Specially should his holiness be adored: this is the crown, and in a certain sense the sum, of all his attributes. Only holy hearts will praise the holy name, or character of the Lord ; oh, that all flesh were sanctified, then would the sanctity of God be the delight of all. Once let the song begin and there will be no end to it. It shall go on for ever and a day, as the old folks used to say. If there were two for-evers, or twenty for-evers, they ought all to be spent in the praises of the ever-living, ever-blessing, ever-blessed JEHOVAH. Blessed be the Lord for ever for having revealed to us his name, and blessed be that name as he has revealed it ; yea, blessed be he above all that we can know, or think, or say. Our hearts revel in the delight of praising him. Our mouth, our mind, our lip, our life shall be our Lord's throughout this mortal existence, and when time shall be no more.

EXPLANATORY NOTES.

This has been happily characterized as the " new song" promised in Ps. cxliv. 9. In other words, it is the song of praise, corresponding to the didactic, penitential, and supplicatory psalms of this series.—*Joseph Addison Alexander.*

The ancient Hebrews declare him happy whoever, in after times, utters this psalm thrice each day with the mouth, heart, and tongue.—*Victorinus Bythner, —* 1670.

The last six or seven psalms are the Beulah of the book, where the sun shineth night and day, and the voice of the turtle is heard in the land. Coming at the close after all the mournful, plaintive, penitential, prayerful, varying notes, they unconsciously typify the joy and rest of glory.—*George Gilfillan.*

Title.—The praise of David. Psalms are the praises of God accompanied with song ; psalms are songs containing the praise of God. If there be praise, but not of God, it is not a psalm. If there be praise, and praise of God, if it is not sung, it is not a psalm. To make a psalm there go these three—praise, God's praise, and song.—*Augustine.*

Title.—It is observable concerning David's entitling the psalm "*The Praise of David,*" that in the original no psalm else beareth such a title. It is appropriated to it, because this wholly consists of praise ; he was elevated therein to a frame of spirit made up of the pure praise of God, without any touch of what was particular to himself. It was not thanks, but altogether praise, and wholly praise.—*Thomas Goodwin.*

Title.—This psalm, which is designated a *Tehillah,* or a psalm of *praise,*—a name which has passed from this psalm to the whole Psalter, which is commonly called *Sepher Tehillim,* or "*Book of Praises,*"—is the last of the psalms ascribed to David.

It is remarkable, that although that is the name given to the Psalter (which is entitled in Hebrew *Sepher Tehillim,* or *Book of Praises*), this is the only psalm in the whole number which is designated in the title as a *Tehillah*—a word derived from the same root as *Hallelujah.* It seems as if this name *Tehillah* had been studiously reserved for the *last* of David's psalms, in order to mark more emphatically that all his utterances are consummated in *praise.* And this view is more clearly manifested by the circumstance that the word *Tehillah* is introduced into the *last verse* of this psalm, " My soul shall speak the *praise*" (*tehillah*) " of the Lord " (observe this preparation for Hallelujah, *Praise ye* the Lord) ; " and let all flesh bless his holy name for ever and ever." As much as to say, that though David's voice was now about to be hushed in this life, yet it would never be silent in the world to come, and would ever " praise the Lord " ; and as much, also, as to say that his last exhortation should be to all nations to praise him, " Let all flesh bless his holy name for ever and ever."—*Christopher Wordsworth.*

Title.—This psalm is entitled "*David's praise.*" For howsoever the prayers and the praises (all) in this book, are (for the most part) of David's penning : yet two there are he hath singled out from the rest, and set his own mark on them as proper to himself : the lxxxvi. Psalm, his *Tephilla, David's* own *Prayer ;* and there is here his *Tehilla,* his own *Praise* or thanksgiving. As if he had made the rest for all in common, but reserved these peculiarly for himself.—*Lancelot Andrews.*

Whole Psalm.—In regard to its alphabetic structure, it has one peculiarity, *viz.,* the *nun* is omitted ; the reason of which may be, that (as we have seen in some other psalms of this structure) by means of that or some other such omission, we might be kept from putting stress on the mere form of the composition.—*Andrew A. Bonar.*

Whole Psalm.—Cassiodorus quaintly remarks that the psalms in which the alphabetical order is complete, are especially fitted for the righteous in the Church Triumphant, but those in which one letter is missing, are for the Church Militant here on earth, as still imperfect, and needing to be purified from defect. —*Neale and Littledale.*

Verse 1.—"*I will extol thee, my God, O King.*" To extol is to set pre-eminently on high ; to exalt above all others ; it is the expression of the greatest possible admiration ; it is letting others know our high opinion of a person, and endeavouring to win them over to it. The man who has such a high opinion of another as to induce him to extol him, will not be likely to rest without bringing forth into prominent observation the object of his praise.—*Philip Bennett Power.*

Verse 1.—"*O King* "; or *the King,* by way of eminency ; the King of kings, the God by whom kings reign, and to whom I and all other kings owe subjection and obedience.—*Matthew Pool.*

Verse 1.—"*O king.*" The Psalmist in rapt ecstasy seems as though he saw God incarnate in Christ present to inspire his praise. Christ is our God and King, to be extolled in the heart, with the mouth, and by the life.—*Thomas Le Blanc.*

Verse 1.—"*King.*" God is King in verity ; others are called kings in vanity.— *Martin Geier.*

Verse 1.—"*I will bless thy name for ever and ever.*" The name of God in Scripture is taken, first, for *God himself.* The name of a thing is put for the thing named, Ps. xliv. 5 : " Through thee will we push down our enemies : through thy name will we tread them under that rise up against us." " Through thy *name,*" that is, through *thee.* Secondly, the name of God is often in Scripture put for *the attributes of God.* Thirdly, the name of God is put for *his ordinances of worship.* " Go ye now unto my place which was in Shiloh, where I set my name at the first" (Jer. vii. 12), that is, where I first set up my public worship ; because, as a man is known by his proper name, so is God by his proper worship. Fourthly, the name of God is *that reverence, esteem and honour which angels and men give unto God.* As we know amongst us, the report and reputation that a man hath among men is a man's name ; what men speak of him, that is his name ; such an one hath a good name, we say ; such an one hath an ill name, that is, men speak or think well or ill of such persons. So Gen. vi. 4. When Moses describes the giants, he saith, " They were men of renown" ; the Hebrew is, " They were men of *name,*" because the name of a man is the character he hath amongst men ; as a man is esteemed, so his name is carried, and himself is accepted in the world. So the name of God is that high esteem, those honourable apprehensions, which angels and men have of God ; such as the thoughts and speeches of men are for the celebration of God's glory and praise, such is his name in the world.—*Joseph Caryl.*

Verse 1.—"*For ever and ever.*" לְעוֹלָם וָעֶד, *leolam vaed, for ever and onward,* in this and the coming world. Expressions of this sort are very difficult to be translated, but they are, on the whole, well interpreted by those words of Mr. Addison :—

> " Through all eternity to thee,
> A joyful song I'll raise ;
> But oh, eternity's too short
> To utter all thy praise !

—*Adam Clarke.*

Verse 1.—"*For ever and ever.*" Praise is the only part of duty in which we at present engage, which is lasting. We pray, but there shall be a time when prayer shall offer its last litany ; we believe, but there shall be a time when faith shall be lost in sight ; we hope, and hope maketh not ashamed, but there shall be a time when hope lies down and dies, lost in the splendour of the fruition that God shall reveal. But praise goes singing into heaven, and is ready without a teacher to strike the harp that is waiting for it, to transmit along the echoes of eternity the song of the Lamb. In the party-coloured world in which we live, there are days of various sorts and experiences, making up the aggregate of the Christian's life. There are waiting days, in which, because Providence fences us round, and it seems as if we cannot march, we cannot move, as though we must just wait to see what the Lord is about to do in us and for us ; and there are watching days, when it behoves us never to slumber, but to be always ready for the attacks of our spiritual enemy ; and there are warring days, when with nodding plume, and with ample armour, we must go forth to do battle for the truth ; and there are weeping days, when it seems as if the fountains of the great deep within us were broken up ; and as though, through much tribulation, we had to pass to heaven in tears. But these days shall all pass away by-and-by—waiting days all be passed, warring days all be passed, watching days all be passed ; but

> "Our days of praise shall ne'er be past
> While life, and thought, and being last,
> And immortality endures."

—*William Morley Punshon,* 1824—1881.

Verse 1.—"*For ever and ever.*" To praise God now does not satisfy devout aspiration, for in this age the worshipper's devotion is interrupted by sin, fear, sickness, etc. ; but in eternity praise will proceed in unbroken procession.—*John Lorinus.*

Verses 1, 2.—"*I will bless thee for ever and ever,*" and again, verse 2. This intimates, 1. That he resolved to continue in this work *to the end of his life,* throughout his "for ever" in this world. 2. That the psalms he penned should be made use of in praising God by the church *to the end of time.* 2 Chron. xxix. 30. 3. That he hoped to be praising God *to all eternity* in the other world : they that make it their constant work on earth, shall have it their everlasting bliss in heaven.—*Matthew Henry.*

Verse 2.—"*Every day.*" Then God is to be blessed and praised in dark as well as bright days.—*Johannes Paulus Palanterius,* 1600.

Verse 2.—"*Every day (in the week) will I bless thee,*" the Psalmist seems to signify. As there are "seven spirits" peculiarly existing in nearness to God, David holds the seven days of the week like seven stars in his hand, or like a seven-branched candlestick of gold, burning every day with his devotion. He calls the seven days to be as seven angels with trumpets.—*Thomas Le Blanc.*

Verse 2.—"*I will bless thee : I will praise thy name.*" The repetition intimates the fervency of his affection to this work, the fixedness of his purpose to abound in it, and the frequency of his performances therein.—*Matthew Henry.*

Verse 2.—"*Praise.*" If we are to define it in words, we may say that *praise* is thankful, lowly, loving worship of the goodness and majesty of God. And therefore we often find the word "praise" joined with "blessing" and "thanksgiving" : but though all three are akin to each other, they are not all alike. They are steps in a gradual scale—a song of degrees. Thanksgiving runs up into blessing, and blessing ascends into praise ; for praise comprehends both, and is the highest and most perfect work of all living spirits.—*Henry Edward Manning,* 1850.

Verse 3.—"*Great is the Lord.*" If "*great*" here be referred to God as a king, then a *great* king he is in respect of the breadth of his empire, for all creatures, from the highest angel to the poorest worm, are under him. "Great" for length ; for "his kingdom is an everlasting kingdom." "Great" for depth ; for he rules even in the hearts of kings, of all men, overrules their thoughts, affections, nothing is hid from him. And "great" again for height ; being "a great King above all gods," ruling by his own absolute power and authority ; whereas all other kings have their sword from him, and rule by a delegated and vicarious power.—*William Nicholson.*

Verse 3.—"*His greatness is unsearchable.*" God is so great, that till Christ revealed the Father, Deity was lost in its own infinity to the perception of men. He who attempts to navigate an infinite ocean must come back to his starting point, never being able to cross. So the ancient philosophers, disputing as to the Divine Nature, were baffled by their own ingenuity, they had to confess that they comprehended nothing of God except that he was incomprehensible. Without Christ, men can only find out about God that they can never find him.—*Thomas Le Blanc.*

Verse 3 (last clause).—The Vulgate renders thus, "Of his greatness no *end.*" The Hebrew is, "Of his greatness no investigation." As the classic Greeks would say, ἀνεξιχνίαστος, *not to be traced out.*—*Simon de Muis,* 1587—1644.

Verse 3.—God had searched David through and through (Ps. cxxxix. 1), but David proved he could not search God's greatness.—*Martin Geier.*

Verses 3—6.—Verses 3 and 4 contain the material of praise, and verses 5 and 6 the praise itself. Verse 3 states a proposition, and verse 4 gives the amplification.—*Hermann Venema.*

Verse 4.—"*One generation shall praise thy works to another,*" etc. Deut. iv. 9, and vi. 7. Fathers teaching their sons the goodness and glory of God. This was a legal ordinance. The church and its worshippers are *collecting praises* of successive generations for the final Hallelujah celebration.—*Martin Geier.*

Verse 4.—"*One generation shall praise thy works to another.*" Singular is exchanged for plural in the Hebrew, "One generation shall praise (sing) thy works to another, and shall declare (plural) thy mighty acts." Here is melody first, the antiphony of the choirs responding to each other ; then harmony ; all generations will burst into chorus together.—*Hermann Venema.*

Verse 4.—"*One generation to another.*" The *tradition* of praise ! Each generation catches the strains from the last, echoes it, and passes it along to the next. One generation declares what it has seen, and passes on the praise to the generation which has not seen as yet the wonders celebrated.—*Simon De Muis.*

Verse 4.—"*One generation shall praise thy works to another,*" etc. Thus God provides for his Church. When Elijah is carried into heaven, Elisha must follow in the power and spirit of Elias. When one stream is slid and shed into the ocean, another circulates from the same ocean through the bowels of the earth into the springs under the mountains, and refreshes the scorched plains. When one star sets, another rises to guide the wandering traveller, and at length the bright morning lamp glitters in the east, and then the glorious Sun of Righteousness. While the Church sits fainting under a juniper-tree in the wilderness, there shall fly prophets to feed her till the blessed resurrection of the witnesses. It's our high duty to study present work, and prize present help, and greatly rejoice when the Lord sends forth, as once he did, both Boanerges and Barnabas together. Pray for the mantle, girdle, and blessing of Elijah, for the love of John, and the zeal of Paul, to twine hands together to draw souls to heaven ; till the Beloved comes like a roe or a young hart upon the mountains of spices ; till the shadows flee away ; till the day dawn, and the Day-star arise in your hearts.— *Samuel Lee, in his Preface to Row's "Emmanuel,"* 1679.

Verse 4.—"*One generation shall praise thy works to another.*" There is no phenomenon of human life more solemn than its succession of generations. "One generation passeth away, another generation cometh." And, as if to put this in a light as affecting and indelible as possible, the psalmist immediately adds, "but the earth abideth for ever." A thought that gleams like a lightning flash across this panorama of life, burning it into the beholder's brain for ever. Even the rude, gross, material earth, which we were created to subdue, and upon which we so proudly tread, is represented as having to the palpable sense this advantage over us. The abiding earth constitutes a little eternity, compared with the duration of its changing inhabitants. We come into it, and pass over it, obliterating, perhaps, some footprints in its dust by the impress of our own, to be in their turn effaced, and then leave it with amazing rapidity, as a hireling man accomplishes his days.—*Henry Allon,* 1852.

Verse 5.—"*I will speak of the glorious honour,*" etc. The word which we here translate "*speak,*" is considered by Hebrew critics to include also the idea of "expatiating," "speaking at large" ; not merely "alluding to incidentally," but "entering into particulars" ; as though one took delight in speaking upon the matter in hand. Now there is something very satisfactory in entering into particulars ; we can often gather light upon a great truth by having had set before us some of the particulars connected with it ; we can often understand what is too high for us, *in* itself and *by* itself, by some examples which bring it within reach of our dull understandings. We are like men who want to attain a height, who have not wings to fly up to it, but who can reach it by going up a ladder step by step. Particulars are often like the rounds of a ladder, little, it may be, in themselves, but very helpful to us ; and to dwell upon particulars is often of use to ourselves ; it certainly is to many with whom we converse.

Let us remember, that circumstanced as we are in our present state, we have no faculties for grasping in its simple grandeur the glorious honour of the majesty of God. We know most of God from what we know of his doings amongst the children of men. Hereafter, the Lord's people shall, no doubt, have much revealed to them of the glorious honour of the majesty of God, which they could now neither bear nor understand ; meanwhile they have to know him chiefly by what he has said and done ; and if only our eyes be open, we shall be at no loss to recognise in these the glorious honour of his majesty.—*Philip Bennett Power.*

Verse 5.—"*I will speak,*" etc. "I will *muse*" is better than "speak," as being the primary and more usual sense of the Hebrew word.   It suggests that these glorious qualities of God's character and deeds should be not merely talked about and extolled in song, but be deeply pondered, laid close upon our very heart, so that the legitimate impression may be wrought into our very soul, and may mould our whole spirit and character into God's own moral image.—*Henry Cowles.*

Verse 5.—With what a cumulus of glowing terms does Holy Writ seek to display the excellence of Deity !   By these descriptions, those attributes which are feebly imitated or reflected in what we call *good* among created things are declared to exist in God, infinitely, immutably, ineffably.—*Martin Geier.*

Verse 5.— "*Thy wonderful works.*"   Heb. : " *the words of thy wonderful works.*" Thus the Psalmist declares that the records left of God's olden doings in the history of Israel are very precious.   He has heard them.   Moses and Aaron and others spoke them.   He delights in them ; he will sing them again on his own harp.—*Hermann Venema.*

Verses 5 *and* 6.—Verse 5 speaks of God's *opera mirabilia ;* verse 6 of his *opera terribilia.*   The former delight his saints ; the latter terrify the wicked.—*John Lorinus.*

Verse 6.—"*And men shall speak of the might of thy terrible acts.*"   When men do not mark his works of mercy and bounty, the Lord will show unto them works of justice, that is, terrible works, and give them matter of talking upon this account.—*David Dickson.*

Verse 6 (*last clause*).—To " *declare*" here means either in speech or song ; not merely to *predicate* as a fact, but to *proclaim* in praise.   The Hebrew word has this width of meaning ; not merely to declare in cold utterance, concerning mere history.—*Hermann Venema.*

Verse 6.—"*Thy greatness.*"   All men are enamoured of greatness.   Then they must seek it *in* God, and get it *from* God.   David did both.   All history shows the creature aspiring after this glory.   Ahasuerus, Astyages, Cyrus, Cambyses, Nebuchadnezzar, were all called *the great.*   Alexander the Great, when he came to the Ganges, ordered his statue to be made of more than life size, that posterity might believe him to have been of nobler stature.   In Christ alone does man attain the greatness his heart yearns for—the glory of perfect goodness.—*Thomas Le Blanc.*

Verse 6.—"*Thy greatness.*"   Or, according to the written text, *greatnesses.*   So Aquila and Jerome.   The parallelism is decidedly in favour of the plural.—*A. S. Aglen.*

Verse 7.—There is an extensive and an intensive greatness, and both must be found in our praises of God.   First, an extensive greatness in regard of their number ; we must be frequent and plentiful in the duty : we must "*Abundantly utter the memory of God's great goodness.*"   Secondly, there must be an intensive greatness in our praises, in regard of the degree, fervour and heat of them.   They must be high, and vehement, fervent, flaming, zealous and affectionate, full of life and vigour ; our spirits must be raised, our hearts and tongues enlarged in the performance of this duty.   God's glorious name, as it is in Nehem. ix. 5, " is exalted above all blessing and praise," above our devoutest and most zealous praises ; and therefore surely faint, heartless, and lifeless praises are so far from reaching him, as that they may seem to be meant of another, and a lower object. God then is not praised at all if he be not greatly praised.   Weak and dull praises are dispraises ; for a person or thing is not honoured or praised, unless there be some proportion between the honour and praise and the worthiness of the person or thing honoured and praised.—*Henry Jeanes, in* "*The Works of Heaven upon Earth,*" 1649.

Verse 7.—"*Abundantly utter.*"   The word contains the idea of boiling or bubbling-up like a fountain.   It signifies, a holy fluency about the mercy of God. We have quite enough fluent people about, but they are many of them idlers for whom Satan finds abundant work to do.   The Lord deliver us from the noise of fluent women ; but it matters not how fluent men and women are if they will be fluent on the topic now before us. Open your mouths ; let the praise pour forth ; let it come, rivers of it. Stream away ! Gush away, all that you possibly can. *"They shall abundantly utter the memory of thy great goodness."* Do not stop the joyful speakers, let them go on for ever. They do not exaggerate, they cannot. You say they are enthusiastic, but they are not half up to the pitch yet ; bid them become more excited and speak yet more fervently. Go on, brother, go on ; pile it up ; say something greater, grander, and more fiery still ! You cannot exceed the truth. You have come to a theme where your most fluent powers will fail in utterance. The text calls for a sacred fluency, and I would exhort you liberally to exercise it when you are speaking on the goodness of God.—*C. H. S.*

Verse 7.—Too many witnesses of God's goodness are silent witnesses. Men do not enough speak out the testimonies that they might bear in this matter. The reason that I love the Methodists—good ones—is, that they have a tongue to their piety. They fulfil the command of God,—to be fervent in spirit.—*Henry Ward Beecher.*

Verse 7.—

> The thought of our past years in me doth breed
> Perpetual benedictions.
>
> —*William Wordsworth*, 1770—1805.

Verse 7. —*" They shall sing of thy righteousness,"* or *justice.* To sing of goodness, mercy, forgiveness, is natural ; but a *song of justice* is singular. Here is the beauty of David's praise, that he sees subject of delight as much in the righteousness of God as in his mercy.—*John Lorinus.*

Verse 7.—*" They shall sing of thy righteousness."* The righteousness of God, whereby he justifieth sinners, and sanctifieth the justified, and executeth judgment for his reconciled people, is the sweetest object of the church's joy.—*David Dickson.*

Verse 7.—*" Thy righteousness"* (read in connection with next verse). It is an easy thing to conceive the glory of the Creator, manifested in the good of an innocent creature ; but the glory of the righteous Judge, manifested in the good of the guilty criminal, is the peculiar, mysterious wisdom of the Cross. It is easy to perceive God's righteousness declared in the punishment of sins ; the Cross alone declares " His righteousness for the remission of sins." It magnifies justice in the way of pardoning sin, and mercy in the way of punishing it.—*John M'Laurin* 1693—1754.

Verse 8.—*" The Lord is gracious,"* etc. The proclamation of the Lord to Moses (Exod. xxxiv. 6) is the fountain-head of these epithets.—*James G. Murphy.*

Verse 8.—In God there is no passion, only compassion.—*Richard Rothe*, 1799—1867.

" Verse 8.—*Of great mercy."* Mercy hath misery for its object, and is that attribute towards which the eyes of a fallen world must necessarily be turned. The Psalmist hath, accordingly, introduced her last with great pomp and splendour, seated in her triumphal chariot, and invested with a supremacy over all the works of God. She is above the heavens, and over all the earth, so that the whole creation findeth that refuge under the shadow of her wings of which, by reason of man's transgression, it standeth in need.—*Samuel Burder.*

Verse 9.—*" The Lord is good to all,"* etc. According to the doctrine of Christianity, we are not the creatures of a God who takes no care of his beings, and leaves them to themselves ; not the offspring of a father who disowns his children, who does not concern himself about them, and is indifferent to their happiness and their misery. No ; never has God, according to that comfortable doctrine, left himself unwitnessed to man ; never withdrawn from him his fatherly providence and love ; never abandoned the fortunes of his feeble, helpless, untutored children, to blind chance or to their own ignorance. No ; from their first progenitor, to his latest posterity, he has himself provided for their support, their instruction, their guidance, their progress to higher attainments. He has constantly revealed himself to them in various ways ; constantly shed innumerable benefits on them ; sometimes lovingly correcting, and sometimes bountifully blessing them ; has constantly been nigh to them, and has left them in want of no means for becoming wiser and better.—*George Joachim Zollikofer*, 1730—1788.

Verse 9.—"*The Lord is good to all,*" etc. God's pity is not as some sweet cordial, poured in dainty drops from a golden phial. It is not like the musical water-drops of some slender rill, murmuring down the dark side of Mount Sinai. It is wide as the whole scope of heaven. It is abundant as all the air. If one had art to gather up all the golden sunlight that to-day falls wide over all the continent, falling through every silent hour; and all that is dispersed over the whole ocean, floating from every wave ; and all that is poured refulgent over the northern wastes of ice, and along the whole continent of Europe, and the vast outlying Asia and torrid Africa—if we could in any wise gather up this immense and incalculable outflow and treasure that falls down through the bright hours, and runs in liquid ether about the mountains, and fills all the plains, and sends innumerable rays through every secret place, pouring over and filling every flower, shining down the sides of every blade of grass, resting in glorious humility upon the humblest things—on sticks, and stones, and pebbles—on the spider's web, the sparrow's nest, the threshold of the young foxes' hole, where they play and warm themselves—that rests on the prisoner's window, that strikes radiant beams through the slave's tear, and puts gold upon the widow's weeds, that plates and roofs the city with burnished gold, and goes on in its wild abundance up and down the earth, shining everywhere and always, since the day of primal creation, without faltering, without stint, without waste or diminution ; as full, as fresh, as overflowing to-day as if it were the very first day of its outlay—if one might gather up this boundless, endless, infinite treasure, to measure it, then might he tell the height, and depth, and unending glory of the pity of God ! That light, and the sun, its source, are God's own figure of the immensity and copiousness of his mercy and compassion.—*Henry Ward Beecher*, 1873.

Verse 9.—Even the worst taste of God's mercy ; such as fight against God's mercy taste of it ; the wicked have some crumbs from mercy's table. "*The Lord is good to all.*" Sweet dewdrops are on the thistle as well as on the rose. The diocese where mercy visits is very large. Pharaoh's head was crowned though his heart was hardened.—*Thomas Watson.*

Verse 9.—"*His tender mercies are over all his works.*" When the sensible sinner is seeking faith of God, he may plead the *largeness* of mercy. God's mercy is like the firmament spread over all this lower world ; and every infirm creature partakes more or less of its influence, according to its exigence and capacity. True, may he say, I have made myself, by sin, the vilest of all creatures ; I am become worse than the beasts that perish ; as vile as a worm, as loathsome as a toad, by reason of the venomous corruption that is in my heart, and my woeful contrariety to the nature of a holy God. But there is " *mercy over all,*" even over such vile and loathsome creatures as these ; there may be some over me, though wrath do now abide on me. Oh, let that mercy, whose glory it is to stretch itself over all, reach my soul also ! Oh, that the blessed and powerful influence thereof would beget faith in my heart !—*David Clarkson.*

Verse 9.—"*His tender mercies.*" The nature and force of the word רחמים, is properly the *bowels ;* that is, there are *tender mercies in God* (so we term it in the *Benedictus*). Not of the ordinary sort, slight, and such as pierce not deep, come not far ; but such as come *de profundis*, from the very *bowels* themselves, that affect that part, make the *bowels* relent. And what *bowels ?* Not the *bowels* of the common man (for then מעים had been the right word), but רחמם are the *bowels* of a *parent* (so, we said, the word signifies), and this adds much ; adds to *mercy* στοςγὴ, *natural love ;* to one strong affection another as strong or stronger than it. And what *parent?* the more pitiful of the twain, the *mother*. For רחם (the singular of this word) is Hebrew for the *womb*. So as this, to the two former addeth the sex ; the sex holden to be the more compassionate. Of all mercies, those of the *bowels ;* and of all bowels, the bowels of a *parent ;* and of the two parents, those of the *mother :* such pity as the mother takes of the children of her womb. *Mercies* are in God ; *such mercies* are in God.

"*Over all.*" It is good news for us that these mercies are in God ; but, better yet, that they are in him with a *super*—"over." But, best of all, that that *super* is a *super omnia*—"over all." Much is said in few words to mercy's praise when 'tis said, *super omnia. Nihil supra* were much, none above it : but it is written *super omnia, above all.* He that saith this, leaves no more to say ; there is no higher degree ; *super omnia* is the superlative.

All that are *above* are not *over.* It is not *above* only, as an obelisk or Maypole, higher than all about them, but have neither shadow nor shelter ; no good they do ! Mercy hath a broad top, spreading itself *over* all. It is so *above* all, as it is *over* them, too. As the vault of this chapel is *over* us, and the great vault of the firmament *over* that ; the *super* of latitude and expansion, no less than of altitude and elevation. And this to the end that all may retire to it, and take covert ; it *over* them, and they *under* it. Under it, under the *shadow* of it, as of Esay's "great rock in the wilderness," from the *heat :* under it, under the *shelter* of it as of Daniel's "great tree," from the tempest. (Isai. xxxii. 2 ; Dan. iv. 11, 12).— *Lancelot Andrewes.*

Verse 10.—"*All thy works shall praise thee, O* Lord." It is a poor philosophy and a narrow religion which does not recognise God as all in all. Every moment of our lives, we breathe, stand, or move in the temple of the Most High ; for the whole universe is that temple. Wherever we go, the testimony to his power, the impress of his hand, are there. Ask of the bright worlds around us, as they roll in the everlasting harmony of their circles, and they shall tell you of him whose power launched them on their courses ; ask of the mountains, that lift their heads among and above the clouds, and the bleak summit of one shall seem to call aloud to the snow-clad top of another, in proclaiming their testimony to the Agency which has laid their deep foundations. Ask of ocean's waters ; and the roar of their boundless waves shall chant from shore to shore a hymn of ascription to that Being, who hath said, "Hitherto shall ye come and no further." Ask of the rivers ; and, as they roll onward to the sea, do they not bear along their ceaseless tribute to the ever-working Energy, which struck open their fountains and poured them down through the valleys ? Ask of every region of the earth, from the burning equator to the icy pole, from the rock-bound coast to the plain covered with its luxuriant vegetation ; and will you not find on them all the record of the Creator's presence ? Ask of the countless tribes of plants and animals ; and shall they not testify to the action of the great Source of Life ? Yes, from every portion, from every department of nature, comes the same voice ; everywhere we hear thy name, O God ! everywhere we see thy love ! Creation, in all its length and breadth, in all its depth and height, is the manifestation of thy Spirit, and without thee the world were dark and dead. The universe is to us as the burning bush which the Hebrew leader saw : God is ever present in it, for it burns with his glory, and the ground on which we stand is always holy.— "*Francis*" (*Viscount Dillon*).

Verse 10.—Marvellous is it that man is not always praising, since everything amidst which he dwells is continually inviting praise.—*Gregory the Great.*

Verse 10.—"*All thy works shall praise thee, O* Lord," etc. "*All*" God's "*works*" do "*praise*" him, as the beautiful building praiseth the builder, or the well-drawn picture praiseth the painter : but his "*saints bless*" him, as the children of prudent and tender parents rise up and call them blessed. Of all God's works, his saints, the workmanship of his grace, the first-fruits of his creatures, have most reason to bless him.—*Matthew Henry.*

Verse 10.—"*All thy works shall praise thee, O* Lord," etc. There are two words by which our thankfulness to God is expressed, *praising* and *blessing.* What is the difference ? Praise respecteth God's excellences, and blessing respecteth God's benefits. We may praise a man that never hath done us good, if he be excellent and praiseworthy ; but blessing respecteth God's bounty and benefits ; yet they are often used promiscuously.—*Thomas Manton.*

Verse 10.—"*And thy saints shall bless thee.*" The lily lifts itself upon its slender stem, and displays its golden petals and its glittering ivory leaves ; and by its very existence it praises God. Yonder deep and booming sea rolls up in storm and tempest, sweeping everything before it ; and every dash of its waves praises God. The birds in the morning, and some of them all through the night, can never cease from praising ; uniting with the ten thousand other voices which make ceaseless concert before the throne. But observe, neither the flower, nor the sea, nor the bird, praises with intent to praise. To them it is no exercise of intellect, for they do not know God, and cannot understand his worthiness ; nor do they even know that they are praising him. They exhibit his skill, and his goodness, and so forth, and in so doing they do much ; but we must learn to do more. When you and I praise God, there is the element of will, of intelligence, of desire, of intent ; and in the saints of God there is another element, namely, that of love to him, of reverent gratitude towards him, and this turns the praise into blessing. A man is an eminent painter, and you exclaim, " His pencil is instinct with life." Still, the man is no friend of yours, you pronounce no blessings on his name. It may be that your feeling towards him is that of deep regret that such abilities should be united with so ill a character. A certain person is exceedingly skilful in his profession, but he treats you unjustly, and, therefore, though you often praise him for his extraordinary performances, you cannot bless him, for you have no cause to do so. I am afraid that there might be such a feeling as that of admiration of God for his great skill, his wonderful power, his extraordinary justness, and yet no warmth of love in the heart towards him ; but in the saints the praise is sweetened with love, and is full of blessing.—*C. H. S.*

Verses 10, 11.—If not only irrational, but inanimate creatures praise God by giving occasion for his praise ; then how much more should men set forth his praise, who are not only living, but reasonable creatures ! And if creatures without life and reason should provoke mankind in general, as having life and reason, to praise God ; how much more should godly men be provoked by them to sing his praise, they having not only life, which stars have not ; and reason, which birds and beasts have not ; but grace, which the most of men have not ! Among visible creatures, men have most reason (because they have reason) to praise God ; and among men gracious men have most reason to praise God, because they have grace. And therefore as soon as ever David had said, "*All thy works shall praise thee, O* LORD," he adds in the next words, " *and thy saints shall bless thee. They shall speak of the glory of thy kingdom, and talk of thy power.*" As if he had said, As all thy works, O Lord, praise thee, so saints (who are the choicest pieces of thy workmanship) have cause to do it above all : they cannot but be speaking and talking of thy kingdom and power, which are very glorious. —*Joseph Caryl.*

Verse 11.—"*They shall speak of the glory of thy kingdom,*" etc. The glory of a kingdom is synonymous with its power. The power of a kingdom consists in the number of its subjects, and the sufficiency of its revenues to maintain them. Now, the glory, or the power of God's kingdom, may be inferred from the difference between it and that of man. There are four points of difference. First, the kings of this world have but *few subjects,* with but little wealth,—not more than the population and riches of one kingdom, or one province, while God reigns over all angels, all men, all demons ; and all wealth on land, in the sea, or in the air, belongs to him. There is another difference, that while the kings of this world rule their subjects, they are still ruled by them, they are *dependent on them,* could do nothing without them ; and, however abundant their revenues may be, they are generally in want, nay, even in debt, and, consequently, always calling for fresh tributes and taxes ; but God, while he governs all, is subject to none, because he needs nobody's help or assistance. Instead of being in want, he abounds in everything, because he could, in one moment, bring from nothing much more than he now beholds or enjoys. The third difference is a consequence of the second, while the kings of this world seem so to enjoy their honours and dignities, they are, at the same time, *suffering acutely from interior fears*, doubts, and cares, which have sometimes been so burdensome, as to cause them to abdicate altogether. God never suffers such pressure, is subject to no fear, no misgivings, but reigns absolutely in perfect tranquillity. The fourth difference, an essential one, is, that the kings of the world *reign but for a time;* but God reigneth for ever.—*Robert Bellarmine.*

Verse 11.—"*They shall speak . . . and talk.*" Joy and sorrow are hard to conceal; as from the countenance, so from the tongue. There is so much correspondence betwixt the heart and tongue that they will move at once: every man therefore speaks of his own pleasure and care; the hunter and falconer of his game; the ploughman of his team; the soldier of his march and colours. If the heart were as full of God, the tongue could not refrain from talking of him: the rareness of Christian communication argues the common poverty of grace. If Christ be not in our hearts, we are godless; if he be there without our joy, we are senseless; if we rejoice in him and speak not of him, we are shamefully unthankful. Every man taketh, yea, raiseth occasion, to bring in speech of what he liketh. As I will think of thee always, O Lord, so it shall be my joy to speak of thee often; and if I find not opportunity, I will make it.—*Joseph Hall.*

Verse 13.—The Kingdom of God is his government of the world. The glory of it becomes especially conspicuous in this, that he raises the dominion of his anointed over all the kingdoms of the world: comp. Ps. lxxxix. 27. "*Thy kingdom is a kingdom of all eternities*" (verse 13), and so must also the kingdom of thine anointed be an eternal one, and will survive all the transitory kingdoms of this world, however highly they may puff themselves up.—*D. W. Hengstenberg.*

Verse 13.—On the door of the old mosque in Damascus, which was once a Christian church, but for twelve centuries has ranked among the holiest of the Mahomedan sanctuaries, are inscribed these memorable words: "Thy kingdom, O Christ, is an everlasting kingdom, and thy dominion endureth throughout all generations." Though the name of Christ has been regularly blasphemed, and the disciples of Christ regularly cursed for twelve hundred years within it, the inscription has, nevertheless, remained unimpaired by time, and undisturbed by man. It was unknown during the long reign of Mahomedan intolerance and oppression; but when religious liberty was partially restored, and the missionaries were enabled to establish a Christian church in that city, it was again brought to light, encouraging them in their work of faith and labour of love.—*From John Bate's "Cyclopædia of Illustrations,"* 1865.

Verses 13, 14.—What we admire in these verses, is their combining the magnificence of unlimited power with the assiduity of unlimited tenderness. It is this combination which men are apt to regard as well-nigh incredible, supposing that a Being so great as God can never concern himself with beings so inconsiderable as themselves. Tell them that God lifteth up those that be bowed down, and they cannot imagine that his kingdom and dominion are unbounded; or tell them, on the other hand, of the greatness of his empire, and they think it impossible that he should uphold all that fall.—*Henry Melvill.*

Verse 14.—"*The* LORD *upholdeth all that fall,*" etc. It is noteworthy how the psalmist proceeds to exhibit the mightiness of God's kingdom, not by its power "to break in pieces and bruise," like the iron legs of the statue in Nebuchadnezzar's vision (Dan. ii. 40), but by the King's readiness to aid the weak. Even a heathen could see that this was the noblest use of power.

Regia (crede mihi) res est succurrere lapsis.

Ovid., Ep. de Panto, ii. 9, 11.

It is a kingly thing to help the fallen.

—*Neale and Littledale.*

Verse 14.—"*The* LORD *upholdeth all that fall,*" etc. נֹפְלִים, *nophelim*, the *falling,* or those who are not able to keep their feet ; the weak. He *shores* them up ; he is their *prop*. No man falls through his own weakness merely ; if he rely on God, the strongest foe cannot shake him.—*Adam Clarke.*

Verse 14.—"*And raiseth up all those that be bowed down,*" *incurvatos.* Many who do not actually fall are reduced to distress that may be even more painful ; for the struggling are greater sufferers than the actually passive. Men are *bowed down* physically by infirmity ; mentally, by care ; spiritually, by remorse ; some are even crushed by all three burdens. For all such there is help in a Mighty One. But none can help themselves alone : none are raised but by supernatural interposition—*non nisi opitulante Domino.—Martin Geier.*

Verse 14.—"*The* Lord *upholdeth all that fall.*" The word here used is a participle, literally, "*The Lord sustaining*"; that is, the Lord *is* a Sustainer or Upholder of all that fall.—*Albert Barnes.*

Verse 14.—"*And raiseth up all those that be bowed down.*" Alphonsus, King of Arragon, is famous for helping with his own hand one of his subjects out of a ditch. Of Queen Elizabeth it is recorded, to her eternal praise, that she hated (no less than did Mithridates) such as sought to crush virtue forsaken of fortune. Christ bruiseth not the broken reed, but upholdeth it, he quencheth not the smoking wick, but cherisheth it.—*John Trapp.*

Verses 14—19.—The Psalmist sets up a splendid argument. Having praised the kingdom, he goes on to display *seven glories* peculiar to kings, and shows that in Jehovah these shine supremely. Verses 14 to 19 contain each a royal virtue.—*John Lorinus.*

Verse 15.—"*The eyes of all wait upon thee.*" God cannot be overmastered by what is great and enormous, so neither can he overlook what is small and insignificant. God is that being to whom the only great thing is himself ; and, therefore, when " the eyes of all wait upon him," the seraph gains not attention by his gaze of fire, and the insect loses it not through the feebleness of vision. Archangels, and angels, and men, and beasts of the field, and fowls of the air, and fish of the sea, draw equally the regard of him, who, counting nothing great but himself, the Creator, can pass over as small no fraction of the creature.—*Henry Melvill.*

Verse 15.—Doth not nature teach you to pray ? Ask the brutes, the ravens, lions, etc. (Job xxxviii. 41 ; Ps. cxlvii. 9 ; civ. 27 ; cxlv. 15) ; not as if these unreasonable creatures could know and worship God, but because nature hath taught them so much of this duty as they are capable of and can bear ; they have some sense of their burdens and wants, they groan and cry, and desire to be eased ; and the Lord hearkeneth to this voice and saith, " Now the poor creature is crying to me, and I will pity it." Ah ! shall the beasts in their own way cry to God, and wilt thou be silent ? Hath the Lord elevated thee so far above these inferior creatures, and fitted thee for the immediate acts of his worship, and for a higher communion with himself, and wilt thou not serve him accordingly ? Hath he given thee a heart and a spiritual soul, as he hath given the brutes a sensitive appetite and natural desires, and shall they cry to God with the one, and not thou with the other ?—*Alexander Pitcairne,* 1664.

Verse 15.—"*Eyes . . . wait upon thee.*" Many dumb beggars have been relieved at Christ's gate by making signs.—*William Secker.*

Verse 15.—In agony nature is no atheist, the mind which knows not where to fly, flies to God.—*Hannah More,* 1745—1833.

Verse 15.—The creatures are his, and therefore to be received with thanksgiving ; this our Saviour performed with great vigour and zeal ; thus teaching us, when " looking up to heaven," that " *the eyes of all* " ought, in the most literal sense, " *to wait* " upon that Lord " *who gives them their meat in due season.*" . . . A secret sense of God's goodness is by no means enough. Men should make solemn and outward expressions of it, when they receive his creatures for their support ; a service and homage not only due to him, but profitable to themselves.— *George Stanhope,* 1660—1728.

Verse 15.—While atheism, in its strict signification, namely, that of total denial of God's existence, is scarcely, if at all, to be found on earth ; atheism, as regards the denial of God's providence, is the espoused creed of hundreds amongst us. . . . Providence, which is confessed in great things, is rejected in small things ; and even if you can work up men to an easy confession that God presideth over national concerns, you will find them withdrawing individuals from his scrutiny. We bring against this paring down of God's providence a distinct charge of atheism. If we confess the existence of a God at all, we read it in the workmanship of the tiniest leaf, as well as in the magnificent pinnacles of Andes and Alps : if we believe in the providence of God at all, we must confess that he numbers the hairs of our heads, as well as marshals the stars of the firmament ; and that providence is not universal, and therefore cannot be godlike, if a sparrow, any more than a seraph, flit away unregarded.

Now, the words before us set themselves most strenuously against this popular atheism. The whole creation is represented as fastening its gaze on the universal Parent, and as drawing from his fulness the supply of every necessity. *"The eyes of all wait upon thee ; and thou givest them their meat in due season."* There is made, you observe, no exception whatever ; the exhibition is simply that of every rank and order of beings looking to the Almighty, confessing dependence upon him, and standing environed by his guardianship. So that, in place of anything which approximates to the abandonment of our creation, the Psalmist asserts a ceaseless attention to its wants, the suspension of which for an instant would cause chill and darkness throughout the whole universe.—*Henry Melvill.*

Verse 15.—*"Thou givest them their meat in due season."* The meat which endures to everlasting life ; the flesh of Christ, which is meat indeed ; the doctrines of the gospel, which, as some of them are milk for babes, others are meat for strong men, or strong meat for experienced believers ; and these are given forth under Christ's direction, by his ministering servants, who are his wise and faithful stewards, that give to every one of the family their portion of meat in due season, which is the word fitly spoken ; and, when it is so, how good it is ! Luke xii. 42 ; Prov. xv. 23. This is food convenient for them, given out *in his time,* as in the original ; either in the Lord's time, when he sees best, or in *their* time, as the Syriac version, when they most need it, and it will do them most good.—*John Gill.*

Verse 15 (*second clause*).—It is said that God gives them *"their food,"* and *"in its season,"* for the very variety of it serves more to illustrate the providence of God. Each has its own way of feeding, and the different kinds of aliment are designed and adapted for different uses. David therefore speaks of the food which is particular to them. The pronoun is not in the plural, and we are not to read *in their* season, as if it applied to the animals. The food he notices as given in its season ; for here also we are to notice the admirable arrangements of divine providence, that there is a certain time appointed for harvest, vintage, and hay crop, and that the year is so divided into intervals, that the cattle are fed at one time on grass, at another on hay, or straw, or acorns, or other products of the earth. Were the whole supply poured forth at one and the same moment, it could not be gathered together so conveniently ; and we have no small reason to admire the seasonableness with which the different kinds of fruit and aliment are yearly produced.—*John Calvin.*

Verse 15.—Mr. Robertson told of a poor child who was accustomed to see unexpected provision for his mother's wants arrive in answer to prayer. The meal-barrel in Scotland is everything to a hungry boy : so he said, " Mither, I think God aye hears when we're scraping the bottom o' the barrel."—*"The Christian."*

Verses 15—17.—Who can fear that, because God's ways are unsearchable, they may not be all tending to the final good of his creatures, when he knows that with the tenderness of a most affectionate parent this Creator and Governor ministers to the meanest living thing ? Who can be disquieted by the mysteriousness of the Divine dealings when he remembers that they are those of one who never ceases for a solitary moment to consult the happiness of whatsoever he hath formed? Who, in short, can distrust God because clouds and darkness are round about him, when there is light enough to show that he is the vigilant guardian of every tenant of this earth, that his hand upholds, and his breath animates. and his bounty nourishes, the teeming hordes of the city, and the desert, and the ocean? It seems that there is thus a beautiful, though tacit process of reasoning in our text, and that the seventeenth verse is set in its proper connection. It is as though David had said, "Come, let us muse on the righteousness of God. He would not be God if he were not righteous in all his ways and holy in all his works; and therefore we may be sure that whatsoever he does is the best that could be done, whether or not we can discover its excellence."

Yes, this may be true, but when we look on the divine dealings what an abyss of dark waters there is! How unsearchable, how unfathomable are God's judgments! We admit it; but being previously convinced of God's righteousness, we ought not to be staggered by what is dark in his dispensations.

"True," you reply, "but the mind does not seem satisfied by this reasoning; it may be convincing to the intellect, but it does not address itself to the feelings." Well, then, pass from what is dark in God's dealing to what is clear. He is about your path and about your bed; he "preserveth man and beast"; "his tender mercies are over all his works." Is this a God of whom to be suspicious? Is this a God to mistrust? Oh! surely if you will fortify yourselves by such facts as these—"Thou, O Lord, satisfiest the desire of every living thing," "*The eyes of all wait upon thee; and thou givest them their meat in due season*"—if, I say, you will fortify your minds by such facts as these, you will be able at all times and in all circumstances to join heartily in the acknowledgment of the psalmist—"*The Lord is righteous in all his ways and holy in all his works.*"—*Henry Melvill.*

Verse 16.—

> Thou openest thy hand of grace
> And thou dost satisfy
> The wants of all in every place
> Who for thy presence cry.
> —*Thomas MacKellar*, 1883.

Verse 16.—"*Thou openest thy hand.*" This seems as if depicted from a housekeeper's habit of feeding a brood of chickens and other creatures. She flings abroad with full and open hand a large supply, not measuring to a grain just what might be enough.—*Martin Geier.*

Verse 16.—"*Thou openest thy hand.*" What an idea does this convey of the *paternal goodness* of the great Father of his creation! How opposite to the conduct of many of his creatures one to another, whose hands and hearts are *shut!* What an idea also does it convey of the *ease* with which the wants of the whole creation are supplied! Let me pause a moment and think of their wants. What a quantity of vegetable and animal food is daily consumed in one town: what a quantity in a large city like London: what a quantity in a nation: in the whole world! But *men* do not compose a hundredth part of "every living thing"! What innumerable wants throughout all animate nature; in the earth, in the air, in the waters! Whence comes their supply? "Thou openest thy hand," and all are satisfied. And can all these wants be supplied by only *the opening of his hand?* What then must sin be, and salvation from it? That is a work of wonderful expense. God openeth his hand and satisfieth all creation, but he must purchase the Church *with his blood.* . . . In what a *variety of ways* are our wants supplied. The earth is fruitful, the air is full of life, the clouds empty themselves upon the earth, the sun pours forth its genial rays; but the operation of all these second causes is only *the opening of his hand!* Nay further: look we to *instruments* as well as means? Parents feed us in our childhood, and supply our youthful wants; ways are opened for our future subsistence; connexions are formed, which prove sources of comfort; friends are kind in seasons of extremity; supplies are presented from quarters that we never expected. What are all these but *the opening of his hand?* If his hand were shut, what a world would this be ! The heavens brass, the earth iron ; famine, pestilence, and death must follow. See Ps. civ. 27—29.

Consider next the term " *hand*." There is a difference between the *hand* and the *heart*. God opens his hand, in the way of providence, towards his worst enemies. He gave Nebuchadnezzar all the kingdoms of the earth. But he opens his *heart* in the gospel of his Son. This is the better portion of the two. While we are thankful for the one, let us not rest satisfied in it : it is merely a *hand* portion. Rather let us pray with Jabez to be blessed *indeed ;* and that we might have a Joseph's portion ; not only the precious things of the earth and the fulness thereof, but " the good will of him that dwelt in the bush !"

"*Thou satisfiest the desire,*" etc. God does not give grudgingly. It seems to be a characteristic of the divine nature, both in the natural and moral world, to raise desires, not with a view to disappoint, but to satisfy them. O what a consoling thought is this ! If there be any desires in us which are not satisfied, it is through their being self-created ones, which is our own fault ; or through artificial scarcity from men's luxury, which is the fault of our species. God raises no desires as our Creator, but he gives enough to satisfy them ; and none as our Redeemer and Sanctifier but what shall be actually satisfied. O the wonderful munificence of God ! " How great is his goodness, and how great is his beauty !" —*Andrew Fuller.*

Verse 16 (second clause).—The word רצון, *ratson,* some render " *desire,*" as though he meant that God supplies each kind of animal with food according to its wish. And a little afterwards we do indeed find it used in that sense. Others, however, refer it rather to God's feeding them of his mere good pleasure and kindness ; it is not enough to say that our food is given us by God, unless we add, as in the second clause of the verse, that his kindness is gratuitous, and that there is no extrinsic cause whatever moving him to provide so liberally for every living creature. In that case the cause is put for the effect ; the various kinds of provision being effects of his good pleasure—χαρισματα της χαριτος.—*John Calvin.*

Verse 17.—"*The* LORD *is righteous in all his ways,*" etc. The ground upon which praise is here ascribed to God may seem a common one, being in every one's mouth ; but in nothing is wisdom shown more than in holding fast the truth, that God is just in all his ways, so as to retain in our hearts an unabated sense of it amidst all troubles and confusions. Though all acknowledge God to be just, most men are no sooner overtaken by affliction than they quarrel with his severity : unless their wishes are immediately complied with, they are impatient, and nothing is more common than to hear his justice impeached. As it is everywhere abused by the wicked imputations men cast upon it, here it is very properly vindicated from such ungrateful treatment, and asserted to be constant and unfailing, however loudly the world may disparage it. It is expressly added, " *in all his ways and works* " *;* for we fail to give God due honour unless we recognise a constant tenor of righteousness in the whole progress of his operation. Nothing is more difficult in the time of trouble, when God has apparently forsaken us, or afflicts us without cause, than to restrain our corrupt feelings from breaking out against his judgments ; as we are told of the Emperor Mauricius in a memorable passage of history, that seeing his sons murdered by the wicked and perfidious traitor Phocas, and being about to be carried out himself to death, he cried out —" Thou art righteous, O God, and just are thy judgments."—*John Calvin.*

Verse 17.—"*Holy in all his works.*" God is good, the absolute and perfect ; and from good nothing can come but good : and therefore all which God has made is good, as he is ; and therefore if anything in the world seems to be bad, one of two things must be true of it.

Either it is *not* bad, though it seems so to us ; and God will bring good out of it in his good time, and justify himself to men, and show us that he is holy in all his works, and righteous in all his ways. Or else—

If the thing be really bad, then God did not make it. It must be a disease, a mistake, a failure, of man's making, or some person's making, but not of God's

making. For all that he has made he sees eternally ; and behold, it is very good.
—*Charles Kingsley, in "The Good News of God,"* 1878.

Verse 18.—*"The Lord is nigh."* The nearness or remoteness of a friend is very
material and considerable in our troubles, distresses, wants, dangers. etc. I have
such a friend and he would help me, but he lives so far off ; and I have another
friend that has a great love for me, that is able to counsel me, and to speak a
word in season to me, and that in my distress would stand close to me, but he is
so remote. I have a special friend, that did he know how things stand with me
would make my burdens his, and my wants his, and my sorrows his ; but he is in
a far country, he is at the Indies, and I may be undone before I can hear from
him. But it is not thus with you, O Christians ! who have a God so nigh unto
you, who have the signal presence of God in the midst of you, yea, who have a
God always standing by you, "The Lord stood by me," etc. 2 Tim. iv. 17.—
Thomas Brooks.
    Verse 18.—*"Them that call upon him."* To call upon the name of the Lord im-
plies *right faith*, to call upon him as he *is ; right trust* in him, leaning upon him,
right devotion, calling upon him as he has appointed ; *right life*, ourselves who call
upon him being, or becoming by his grace, what he wills. They *" call "* not
" upon the Lord," but upon some idol of their own imagining, who call upon him
as other than he has revealed himself, or remaining themselves other than those
whom he has declared that he will hear. For such *deny* the very primary attribute of God, his truth. *Their* God is not a God of truth.—*Edward Bouverie
Pusey,* 1800—1882.
    Verse 18.—*"To all that call upon him in truth."* Because there is a counter-
feit and false sort of worshipping, and calling upon God, which is debarred from
the benefit of this promise, to wit, when the party suppliant is not reconciled, nor
seeking reconciliation through Christ the Mediator, or is seeking something not
promised, or something for a carnal end, that he may bestow it on his lusts ;
therefore he who hath right unto this promise must be a worshipper of God in
faith, and sincere intention ; and to such the Lord will show himself *" nigh."*—
David Dickson.
    Verse 18.—To call upon God in truth is, first, to repose an implicit confidence
in the faithfulness of his promise, and to look for unlimited answers to prayer
from the riches of his grace in Christ Jesus. But it is also, in the next place, to
feel our own urgent need of the things for which we supplicate, and to realize an
earnest and unfeigned concern to obtain them. "What things ye desire when ye
pray," said the Lord, "believe that ye receive them, and ye shall have them ";
and hence we gather, that the hearty desire, arising out of the consciousness of
need, is an integral and inseparable part of genuine and effectual prayer.—*Thomas
Dale,* 1853.
    Verses 18, 19.—God's people are a praying people, a generation of seekers, and
such commonly are speeders. God never said to the seed of Jacob, Seek ye my
face in vain. They seek his face, righteousness and strength, and he is found of
them. . . . The saints alone betake themselves to God and his help, run to him
as their sanctuary ; others fly from God's presence, run to the rocks, and the tops
of the ragged rocks, call to the hills and the mountains ; but a child of God goes
only and tells his Father, and before him lays open his cause ; as good Hezekiah
did, when Rabshakeh came out against him ; "O Lord, I am oppressed, undertake
for me "; or the Church (Isai. xxxiii. 2), "Be thou our arm every morning, and
our salvation in time of trouble." They only sensibly need, and so alone crave
and implore divine succour ; and God will not suffer his people to lose the precious treasure of their prayers. *"The Lord is nigh unto all them that call upon him ;
he will fulfil their desire, he will hear their cry,"* etc. That God who prepares his
people's heart to pray, prepares also his own ear to hear ; and he that promiseth
to hear before we call, will never deny to hearken when we cry unto him. As
Calvin saith : "Oppressions and afflictions make man cry, and cries and supplications make God hear."—*F. E., in "The Saint's Ebenezer,"* 1667.

Verse 19.—*"He will fulfil the desire of them that fear him."* This is for comfort for all poor broken hearts in whom God hath engendered the true desire of grace. Let such know that the first step to grace is to see they have no grace ; and the first degree of grace is the *desire* of grace. It is not with the body as with the soul, if you will be healed you shall be healed. A man may desire to be healed corporally, and yet his disease continue upon him ; but it is not so with the soul : if thou wilt say, " Christ heal me," thou shalt be made whole. If a man have but the true desire of grace it shall be given him : " Lord, thou hast heard the desire of the humble " (Ps. x. 17) : when the poor soul is humbled before God in the sense of the want of grace, and breathes and desires after it, the Lord will grant such desires : *"He will fulfil the desire of them that fear him : he also will hear their cry, and will save them."* One said, " the greatest part of Christianity is to desire to be a Christian." And another said, " The total sum of a man's religion in this life consists in the true desires of saving grace." This was the perfection Saint Paul attained unto (Rom. vii. 18) : " To will is present with me ; but how to perform that which is good I find not." Saint Paul we know was the child of God, and one dearly beloved of God ; yet that was the pitch of his godliness ; it consisted more in desire than accomplishment. Canst thou approve by evident and sound arguments that thou hast the true desires of grace ? Then know for thy comfort that the Lord's spirit of grace hath been moving and stirring in thee : " It is God that worketh in you both the will and the deed " (Phil. ii. 13), and that of his good pleasure, not only of his bounty, from whence he hath bestowed many graces, even upon such as he will damn afterwards for their accursed abuse of them, with the neglect of the power thereof. But if God hath set thy will, and the stream of thy affections and desires, to himself and to grace, it is an evidence of God's good pleasure from which he did at first elect thee, and gave his Son to redeem thee.—*William Fenner* (1560—1640), *in "The Riches of Grace."*

Verse 19.—*"He will fulfil the desire of them that fear him."* God will not grant us every desire, that is our mercy ; for, 1. Some of them are *sinful.* David desired to be revenged on Nabal and his innocent family. Jonah desired Nineveh's ruin. 2. Others would *not be for our good.* David desired the life of the child he had by Bathsheba ; David also desired the life of Jonathan ; neither of which would have been for his good. Nay, not every *righteous* desire. It is a righteous desire for a minister to desire the salvation of those that hear him. So Paul declared, " I would to God that all that are here present were altogether such as I am" : Acts xxvi. 29. So again, " I could wish that myself were accursed from Christ for my brethren, my kinsmen according to the flesh" : Rom. ix. 1. David *desired* to build a house for God, and it was a righteous desire, for God took it well at his hands ; yet he did not grant it. Kings and prophets desired to see the Lord Messiah, and yet did not see him. How then are we to understand it ? Answer. The sum or substance of their desires shall be fulfilled. What is the main desire of a seaman ? that he may arrive at the haven. So saints will be brought to their desired haven. What of a pilgrim ? See Heb. xi. 16. So all the desires of a Christian are summed up in this, *That he may eternally enjoy God and be like him.* Doubtless there is great mystery in these things. However, I think it is certain that, when God raises a spiritual desire in a person, it is *often,* though not *always,* with an intention to bestow the object desired.—*Andrew Fuller.*

Verse 19 (*first clause*).—God will fulfil the will of those who fear to disobey *his* will.—*Simon de Muis.*

Verse 19.—*"Desire"* is the largest and most comprehensive word that can be used ; it contains all things in it . . . Nothing good, nothing necessary, nothing profitable, but comes under this word *" desire."* When God promises to *"fulfil the desires of them that fear him,"* he doth promise all good things ; desire comprehends all that can be desired.—*Ralph Robinson.*

Verse 19.—*"He will hear their cry,"* etc. A mark of a great king—he gives willing audience to suppliants.—*Johannes Paulus Palanterius.*

Verse 19.—*"He will hear and save."* How true a description of Christ in his constant office. He heard Mary Magdalene and saved her. He heard the Canaanitish woman, and saved her daughter. He heard the cry of the two blind men and enlightened them. He heard the lepers and cleansed them. He heard the cry of the dying thief and promised him Paradise. Never has one yet cried to King Jesus who has not been heard and delivered.—*Thomas Le Blanc.*

Verse 20.—*"The Lord preserveth,"* etc. God's mercy and God's justice ; he preserves and he destroys. Philip IV. of France, surnamed the Beautiful, on his escutcheon emblazoned a sword and an olive branch, with the motto, *Utrumque,* i. e. " one or the other." A truly great king is master of either art—war and peace.—*Thomas Le Blanc.*

Verse 20.—Those who were called " them that *fear* him" are now denominated " them that *love* him."—*Simon de Muis.*

Verse 20.—*"All the wicked will he destroy."* God has so many different, unsearchable ways of taking wicked men out of the world, and sending them to hell, that there is nothing to make it appear that God had need to be at the expense of a miracle, or go out of the ordinary course of his providence, to destroy any wicked man at any moment.—*Jonathan Edwards.*

Verse 20.—*"All the wicked will he destroy."* It must not be overlooked that this declaration occurs in a song of praise. The whole of the context is utterly inconsistent with the expression of emotions of anger or revenge.—*Speaker's Commentary.*

Verse 20.—*"All the wicked will he destroy."* [Prayer-Book Version, " *scattereth abroad.*"] Like the ruins of a demolished building ; or rather, like an army, which the enemy has completely routed.—*William Keatinge Clay.*

Verse 20.—*"Preserveth"* . . . *" destroy."* Notice this recurrent thought, that the guardianship of the good implies the destruction of the wicked.—*A. S. Aglen.*

HINTS TO THE VILLAGE PREACHER.

Verses 1, 2.—Praise. 1. Personal praise. 2. Daily praise. 3. Enthusiastic praise. 4. Perpetual praise. Or : I. The attractive theme of the song. II. The increasing fulness of the song. III. The unending life of the singer.—*C. A. D.*

Verses 1 & 2.—The four " I wills" of praise. Praise to the King ; praise to the divine character ; praise for all time ; praise for all eternity.

Verse 2.—*Every day ; for ever.* I. Day by day for ever God and I will endure. II. Day by day for ever our present relations will continue. He the God, I the creature ; he the Father, I the child ; he the blessing, I the blest. III. Day by day for ever he shall have my homage.—*W. B. H.*

Verse 3.—I. The dignity of man is here implied in his capacity for praising God greatly. II. His immortality in his capacity for praising his unsearchable greatness.—*G. R.*

Verse 3 (*last clause*).—The unsearchable greatness of God. Consider it, I. As a fact amply demonstrated. II. As a rebuke to despondency : see Isaiah xl. 28. III. As the stay of a soul oppressed by mysteries. IV. As indicating a subject for our everlasting study.—*J. F.*

Verse 4.—I. Our obligation to past generations. II. Our duty to generations to come.—*G. R.*

Verses 5—7.—The Antiphon. I. To praise God is a personal duty : " I will." II. Its right performance will excite others to engage in it : " And men shall." III. The accompaniment of others in praise will re-act upon ourselves. " And I will " ; " And they shall abundantly," etc. IV. Such praise widens and expands as it rolls along. Beginning with God's majesty and works, it extends to his acts, greatness, goodness, and righteousness.—*C. A. D.*

Verses 5—7.—I. Subjects for praise. 1. Divine majesty. 2. Divine works.
3. Divine judgments. 4. Divine greatness. 5. Divine goodness. 6. Divine
righteousness. II. Of whom is it required. 1. Personal; "I will speak." 2.
Universal; "men shall speak."—*G. R.*

Verses 6, 7.—I. *The awe-struck talk.* Silent as to mercies and promises, men
must speak when God's terrible acts are among them. II. *The bold avowal.* One
individual declares God's greatness in power, wisdom, truth and grace. This
leads others to the same conclusion, and hence—III. *The grateful outpouring.*
Many bless the Lord's great goodness in a song fresh, free, constant, joyous, refreshing, abundant, like the gush of a spring. IV. *The select song.* They *utter*
goodness but *sing* of righteousness. This is a noteworthy topic for a discourse.

Verse 7.—See "Spurgeon's Sermons," No. 1468: "The Philosophy and Propriety of Abundant Praise."

Verse 8.—I. Grace to the unworthy. II. Compassion to the afflicted. III.
Forbearance to the guilty. IV. Mercy to the penitent.—*G. R.*

Verse 9.—The universal goodness of God in no degree a contradiction to the
special election of grace.

Verse 10.—See "Spurgeon's Sermons," No. 1796: "Concerning Saints."

Verse 11.—The glory of Christ's kingdom. The glory of this kingdom is mani-
fested,—I. In its origin. II. In the manner and spirit of its administration. III.
In the character of its subjects. IV. In the privileges that are attached to it.—
Robert Hall.

Verses 11, 12.—Talk transfigured. I. The faculty of talk is extensively possessed. II. Is commonly misused. III. May be nobly employed. IV. Will
then be gloriously useful.—*C. A. D.*

Verses 11—13.—To show the greatness of God's kingdom, David observes, 1.
The pomp of it. Would we by faith look within the veil, we should "speak of
the glory of his kingdom" (verse 11); "and the glorious majesty of it" (verse 12).
2. *The power of it.* When "they speak of the glory of God's kingdom," they
must "talk of his power," the extent of it, the efficacy of it. 3. *The perpetuity
of it* (verse 13). The thrones of earthly princes totter, and the flowers of their
crowns wither, monarchs come to an end; but, Lord, "thy kingdom is an everlasting kingdom."—*Matthew Henry.*

Verse 14.—The grace of God in his kindness to the undeserving and the miserable, who look to him for help. I. He "upholdeth all that fall." 1. A description, embracing (1) Sinners who have fallen lowest: (2) Backsliders who have
tripped most foully. 2. An act implying (1) Pity which draws nigh; (2) Power
which places the fallen upon their feet; (3) Preservation which keeps them
standing. II. He "raiseth up all those that are bowed down." Consolation for
those who are—1. Bowed down with shame and penitence. · 2. Oppressed with
perplexities and cares. 3. Weighted with a sense of weakness in the presence of
onerous duties. 4. Depressed because of prevailing error and sin around them.
—*J. F.*

Verse 14.—Help for the fallible. I. Whatever our present position we are
liable to fall. Sickness. Loss. Friendlessness. Sin. II. However low we fall
we are not below the reach of God's hand. III. Within the reach of God's hand
we shall experience the action of God's love. "Upholdeth." "Raiseth up."—
C. A. D.

Verses 15, 16.—Universal dependence and divine support. The Psalmist here
teaches—I. The Universality of Dependence amongst creatures: "The eyes of all
wait upon thee." We depend upon God for "life, and breath, and all things."
Entire dependence should beget deep humility. II. The Infinitude of the Divine
Resources: "And thou givest them their meat." His resources must be, 1, Infinitely vast. 2. Infinitely various. Both sufficient and adapted for all. III.
The Timeliness of the Divine Communications: "In due season." A reason for
patience if his gifts seem delayed. IV. The Sublime Ease of the Divine Communications: "Thou openest thine hand," and the countless needs of the universe
are satisfied. An encouragement to believing prayer. V. The Sufficiency of the

Divine Communications : " And satisfiest the desire of every living thing."
" God giveth to all liberally." Our subject urges all men to, 1. Gratitude. Constant provision should lead to constant thankfulness and consecration. 2. Trust.
(1) For temporal supplies. (2) For spiritual supplies. " Grace to help in time of
need" will surely be given to all who look to him.— *William Jones, in " The Homiletic Quarterly,"* 1878.

Verse 17.—I. What God declares himself to be. II. What his people find him
to be. III. What all creatures will ultimately acknowledge him to be.—*G. R.*

Verses 18—20.—Gather from these verses the character of God's people. I.
They call upon God. II. They fear God. III. They have desires towards God.
IV. They have answers from God. V. They love God.

Verse 18 (last clause).—True prayer, in what it differs essentially from mere
formalism.

· *Verse* 18.—At the palace gates. I. Directions to callers. 1. " Call upon
him "; let the repetition suggest pertinacity. 2. Call " in truth" ; sincerely,
with promises, in appointed way. II. Encouragement for callers. Jehovah is
nigh, with his ready ear, sympathizing heart, and helpful hand.—*W. B. H.*

Verses 18, 19.—The blessedness of prayer. I. Definition of prayer : " calling
upon God." II. Variety in prayer : " call, desire, cry." III. Essential characteristic of prayer : " truth." IV. God's nearness in prayer. V. Assured success of prayer. " He will fulfil, hear, save."—*C. A. D.*

Verse 20.—Those who love God are preserved *from* excessive temptation, falling into sin, despair, apostasy, remorse, famishing ; preserved *in* trial, persecution, depression, death ; preserved *to* activity, holiness, victory, glory.

Verse 20.—Solemn Contrasts. 1. Between human characters. " Them that
love him." " The wicked." 2. Between human destinies. " Preserveth."
" Destroy."—*C. A. D.*

Verse 20.—How the love of God is the opposite of wickedness, and wickedness
inconsistent with the love of God.

Verse 21.—Individual praise suggests the desire for universal praise. We like
company in a good deed ; we perceive the inadequacy of our own song ; we desire others to be happy ; we long to see that done which is right and good.

PSALM CXLVI.

DIVISION, &c.—*We are now among the Hallelujahs. The rest of our journey lies through the Delectable Mountains. All is praise to the close of the book. The key is high-pitched: the music is upon the high-sounding cymbals. O for a heart full of joyful gratitude, that we may run, and leap, and glorify God, even as these Psalms do.*

Alexander thinks that this song may be regarded as composed of two equal parts; in the first we see the happiness of those who trust in God, and not in man (1—5), while the second gives the reason drawn from the Divine perfections (5—10). This might suffice for our purpose; but as there is really no break at all, we will keep it entire. It is " one pearl," a sacred censer of holy incense, pouring forth one sweet perfume.

EXPOSITION.

PRAISE ye the LORD. Praise the LORD, O my soul.

2 While I live will I praise the LORD : I will sing praises unto my God while I have any being.

3 Put not your trust in princes, *nor* in the son of man, in whom *there is* no help.

4 His breath goeth forth, he returneth to his earth ; in that very day his thoughts perish.

5 Happy *is he* that *hath* the God of Jacob for his help, whose hope *is* in the LORD his God :

6 Which made heaven, and earth, the sea, and all that therein *is :* which keepeth truth for ever :

7 Which executeth judgment for the oppressed : which giveth food to the hungry. The LORD looseth the prisoners :

8 The LORD openeth *the eyes of* the blind : the LORD raiseth them that are bowed down : the LORD loveth the righteous :

9 The LORD preserveth the strangers ; he relieveth the fatherless and widow : but the way of the wicked he turneth upside down.

10 The LORD shall reign for ever, *even* thy God, O Zion, unto all generations. Praise ye the LORD.

1. "*Praise ye the* LORD," or, Hallelujah. It is saddening to remember how this majestic word has been trailed in the mire of late. Its irreverent use is an aggravated instance of taking the name of Jehovah our God in vain. Let us hope that it has been done in ignorance by the ruder sort ; but great responsibility lies with leaders who countenance and even copy this blasphemy. With holy awe let us pronounce the word HALLELUJAH, and by it summon ourselves and all others to adore the God of the whole earth. Men need to be called to praise ; it is important that they should praise ; and there are many reasons why they should do it at once. Let all who hear the word *Hallelujah* unite immediately in holy praise.

"*Praise the* LORD, *O my soul.*" He would practise what he had preached. He would be the leader of the choir which he had summoned. It is a poor business if we solely exhort others, and do not stir up our own soul. It is an evil thing to say, " Praise ye," and never to add, " Praise, O my soul." When we praise God let us arouse our innermost self, our central life : we have but one soul, and if it be saved from eternal wrath, it is bound to praise its Saviour. Come heart. mind, thought ! Come my whole being, my soul, my all, be all on flame with joyful adoration ! Up, my brethren ! Lift up the song ! "Praise ye the Lord." But what am I at ? How dare I call upon others, and be negligent myself ? If ever man was under bonds to bless the Lord I am that man, wherefore let me put my soul into the centre of the choir, and then let my better nature excite my whole manhood to the utmost height of loving praise. "O for a well-tuned harp !" Nay, rather, O for a sanctified heart. Then if my voice should be of the poorer sort, and somewhat lacking in melody, yet my soul without my voice shall accomplish my resolve to magnify the Lord.

2. "*While I live will I praise the* LORD." I shall not live here for ever. This mortal life will find a finis in death ; but while it lasts I will laud the Lord my God. I cannot tell how long or short my life may be ; but every hour of it shall be given to the praises of my God. While I live I'll love ; and while I breathe I'll bless. It is but for a while, and I will not while that time away in idleness, but consecrate it to that same service which shall occupy eternity. As our life is the gift of God's mercy, it should be used for his glory. "*I will sing praises unto my God while I have any being.*" When I am no longer in being on earth, I hope to have a higher being in heaven, and there I will not only praise, but *sing* praises. Here I have to sigh and praise, but there I shall only sing and praise. This "while I have any being" will be a great while, but the whole of it shall be filled up with adoration ; for the glorious Jehovah is my God, my own God by covenant, and by blood relationship in Christ Jesus. I have no being apart from my God, therefore, I will not attempt to enjoy my being otherwise than by singing to his honour. Twice the Psalmist says "I will" ; here first thoughts and second thoughts are alike good. We cannot be too firm in the holy resolve to praise God, for it is the chief end of our living and being that we should glorify God and enjoy him for ever.

3. "*Put not your trust in princes.*" If David be the author this warning comes from a prince. In any case it comes from the Spirit of the living God. Men are always far too apt to depend upon the great ones of earth, and forget the Great One above ; and this habit is the fruitful source of disappointment. Princes are only men, and men with greater needs than others ; why, then, should we look to them for aid ? They are in greater danger, are burdened with greater cares, and are more likely to be misled than other men ; therefore, it is folly to select them for our confidence. Probably no order of men have been so false to their promises and treaties as men of royal blood. So live as to deserve *their* trust, but do not burden them with your trust. "*Nor in the son of man, in whom there is no help.*" Though you should select one son of man out of the many, and should imagine that he differs from the rest and may be safely depended on, you will be mistaken. There is none to be trusted, no, not one. Adam fell ; therefore lean not on his sons. Man is a helpless creature without God ; therefore, look not for help in that direction. All men are like the few men who are made into princes, they are more in appearance than in reality, more in promising than in performing, more apt to help themselves than to help others. How many have turned away heart-sick from men on whom they once relied ! Never was this the case with a believer in the Lord. He is a very present help in time of trouble. In man there is no help in times of mental depression, in the day of sore bereavement, in the night of conviction of sin, or in the hour of death. What a horror when most in need of help to read those black words, NO HELP !

4. "*His breath goeth forth, he returneth to his earth.*" His breath goes from his body, and his body goes to the grave. His spirit goes one way, and his body another. High as he stood, the want of a little air brings him down to the ground, and lays him under it. Man who comes from the earth returns to the earth : it is the mother and sister of his body, and he must needs lie among his kindred as soon as the spirit which was his life has made its exit. There is a spirit in man, and when that goes the man goes. The spirit returns to God who gave it, and the flesh to the dust out of which it was fashioned. This is a poor

creature to trust in : a dying creature, a corrupting creature. Those hopes will surely fall to the ground which are built upon men who so soon lie under ground. *"In that very day his thoughts perish."* Whatever he may have proposed to do, the proposal ends in smoke. He cannot think, and what he had thought of cannot effect itself, and therefore it dies. Now that he is gone, men are ready enough to let his thoughts go with him into oblivion ; another thinker comes, and turns the thoughts of his predecessor to ridicule. It is a pitiful thing to be waiting upon princes or upon any other men, in the hope that they will think of us. In an hour they are gone, and where are their schemes for our promotion ? A day has ended their thoughts by ending *them ;* and our trusts have perished, for their thoughts have perished. Men's ambitions, expectations, declarations, and boastings all vanish into thin air when the breath of life vanishes from their bodies. This is the narrow estate of man : his breath, his earth, and his thoughts ; and this is his threefold climax therein,—his breath goeth forth, to his earth he returns, and his thoughts perish. Is this a being to be relied upon ? Vanity of vanities, all is vanity. To trust it would be a still greater vanity.

5. *"Happy is he that hath the God of Jacob for his help."* Heaped up is his happiness. He has happiness indeed : the true and the real delight is with him. The God of Jacob is the God of the covenant, the God of wrestling prayer, the God of the tried believer ; he is the only living and true God. The God of Jacob is Jehovah, who appeared unto Moses, and led the tribes of Jacob out of Egypt, and through the wilderness. Those are happy who trust him, for they shall never be ashamed or confounded. The Lord never dies, neither do his thoughts perish : his purpose of mercy, like himself, endures throughout all generations. Hallelujah ! *"Whose hope is in the* LORD *his God."* He is happy in help for the present and in hope for the future, who has placed all his confidence in Jehovah, who is his God by a covenant of salt. Happy is he when others are despairing ! Happiest shall he be in that very hour when others are discovering the depths of agony. We have here a statement which we have personally tried and proved : resting in the Lord, we know a happiness which is beyond description, beyond comparison, beyond conception. O how blessed a thing it is to know that God is our present help, and our eternal hope. Full assurance is more than heaven in the bud, the flower has begun to open. We would not exchange with Cæsar ; his sceptre is a bauble, but our bliss is true treasure.

In each of the two titles here given, namely, " the God of Jacob," and " Jehovah his God," there is a peculiar sweetness. Either one of them has a fountain of joy in it ; but the first will not cheer us without the second. Unless Jehovah be his God no man can find confidence in the fact that he was Jacob's God. But when by faith we know the Lord to be ours, then we are " rich to all the intents of bliss."

6. *" Which made heaven, and earth, the sea, and all that therein is."* Wisely may we trust our Creator : justly may we expect to be happy in so doing. He who made heaven can make a heaven for us, and make us fit for heaven. He who made the earth can preserve us while we are on earth, and help us to make good use of it while we sojourn upon it. He who made the sea and all its mysteries can steer us across the pathless deeps of a troubled life, and make it a way for his redeemed to pass over. This God who still makes the world by keeping it in existence is assuredly able to keep us to his eternal kingdom and glory. The making of the worlds is the standing proof of the power and wisdom of that great God in whom we trust. It is our joy that he not only made heaven, but the sea ; not only things which are bright and blessed, but things which are deep and dark. Concerning all our circumstances, we may say the Lord is there. In storms and hurricanes the Lord reigneth as truly as in that great calm which rules the firmament above. *" Which keepeth truth for ever."* This is a second and most forcible justification of our trust : the Lord will never permit his promise to fail. He is true to his own nature, true to the relationships which he has assumed, true to his covenant, true to his Word, true to his Son. He keeps true, and is the

keeper of all that is true. Immutable fidelity is the character of Jehovah's procedure. None can charge him with falsehood or vacillation.

7. "*Which executeth judgment for the oppressed.*" He is a swift and impartial administrator of justice. Our King surpasses all earthly princes because he pays no deference to rank or wealth, and is never the respecter of persons. He is the friend of the down-trodden, the avenger of the persecuted, the champion of the helpless. Safely may we trust our cause with such a Judge if it be a just one : happy are we to be under such a Ruler. Are we " evil entreated " ? Are our rights denied us ? Are we slandered ? Let this console us, that he who occupies the throne will not only think upon our case, but bestir himself to execute judgment on our behalf. "*Which giveth food to the hungry.*" Glorious King art thou, O Jehovah ! Thou dost not only mete out justice but thou dost dispense bounty ! All food comes from God ; but when we are reduced to hunger, and providence supplies our necessity, we are peculiarly struck with the fact. Let every hungry man lay hold on this statement, and plead it before the mercy-seat, whether he suffer bodily-hunger, or heart-hunger. See how our God finds his special clients among the lowest of mankind : the oppressed and the starving find help in the God of Jacob. "*The* LORD *looseth the prisoners.*" Thus he completes the triple blessing : justice, bread, and liberty. Jehovah loves not to see men pining in dungeons, or fretting in fetters : he brought up Joseph from the round-house, and Israel from the house of bondage. Jesus is the Emancipator, spiritually, providentially, and nationally. Thy chains, O Africa ! were broken by his hand. As faith in Jehovah shall become common among men freedom will advance in every form, especially will mental, moral, and spiritual bonds be loosed, and the slaves of error, sin, and death shall be set free. Well might the Psalmist praise Jehovah, who is so kind to men in bonds ! Well may the loosened ones be loudest in the song !

8. "*The* LORD *openeth the eyes of the blind.*" Jesus did this very frequently, and hereby proved himself to be Jehovah. He who made the eye can open it, and when he does so it is to his glory. How often is the mental eye closed in moral night ! And who can remove this dreary effect of the fall but the Almighty God ? This miracle of grace he has performed in myriads of cases, and it is in each case a theme for loftiest praise. "*The* LORD *raiseth them that are bowed down.*" This also Jesus did literally, thus doing the work peculiar to God. Jehovah consoles the bereaved, cheers the defeated, solaces the despondent, comforts the despairing. Let those who are bowed to the ground appeal to him, and he will speedily upraise them. "*The* LORD *loveth the righteous.*" He gives to them the love of complacency, communion, and reward. Bad kings affect the licentious, but Jehovah makes the upright to be his favoured ones. This is greatly to his glory. Let those who enjoy the inestimable privilege of his love magnify his name with enthusiastic delight. Loved ones, you must never be absent from the choir ! You must never pause from his praise whose infinite love has made you what you are.

9. "*The* LORD *preserveth the strangers.*" Many monarchs hunted aliens down, or transported them from place to place, or left them as outlaws unworthy of the rights of man ; but Jehovah made special laws for their shelter within his domain. In this country the stranger was, a little while ago, looked upon as a vagabond,— a kind of wild beast to be avoided if not to be assaulted ; and even to this day there are prejudices against foreigners which are contrary to our holy religion. Our God and King is never strange to any of his creatures, and if any are left in a solitary and forlorn condition he has a special eye to their preservation. "*He relieveth the fatherless and widow.*" These excite his compassion, and he shows it in a practical way by upraising them from their forlorn condition. The Mosaic law made provision for these destitute persons. When the secondary fatherhood is gone the child falls back upon the primary fatherhood of the Creator ; when the husband of earth is removed the godly widow casts herself upon the care of her Maker. "*But the way of the wicked he turneth upside down.*" He fills it with crooked places ; he reverses it, sets it down, or upsets it. That which the man

aimed at he misses, and he secures that for himself which he would gladly have avoided. The wicked man's way is in itself a turning of things upside down morally, and the Lord makes it so to him providentially : everything goes wrong with him who goes wrong.

10. "*The* Lord *shall reign for ever.*" Jehovah is King, and his kingdom can never come to an end. Neither does he die, nor abdicate, nor lose his crown by force. Glory be to his name, his throne is never in jeopardy. As the Lord ever liveth, so he ever reigneth. "*Even thy God, O Zion, unto all generations.*" Zion's God, the God of his worshipping people, is he who in every age shall reign. There will always be a Zion ; Zion will always have Jehovah for her King ; for her he will always prove himself to be reigning in great power. What should we do in the presence of so great a King, but enter into his courts with praise, and pay to him our joyful homage ? "*Praise ye the* Lord." Again they said Hallelujah. Again the sweet perfume arose from the golden vials full of sweet odours. Are we not prepared for an outburst of holy song ? Do not we also say—Hallelujah ? Here endeth this gladsome psalm. Here endeth *not* the praise of the Lord, which shall ascend for ever and ever. Amen.

EXPLANATORY NOTES.

Psalms cxlvi.—cxlviii.—At the dedication of the second Temple, in the beginning of the seventh year of Darius, Psalms cxlvi., cxlvii. and cxlviii., seem to have been sung ; for in the Septuagint Version they are styled the Psalms of Haggai and Zechariah, as if they had been composed by them for this occasion. This, no doubt, was from some ancient tradition ; but in the original Hebrew these psalms have no such title prefixed to them, neither have they any other to contradict it.—*Humphrey Prideaux.*

Psalms cxlvi.—cl.—We do not know who put together these different sacred compositions, or whether they were arranged on any particular principle. This, however, is obvious,—that the last series, those that close the whole, are full of praise. Though we meet frequently with grief and shame and tears in the former part, a great deal that presses upon the spirit,—and in the centre a great many references to the various vicissitudes and fortunes through which the church or the individual has passed,—yet, as we get towards the end, and as the book closes, it is *Hallelujah—praise.* As the ancient church ceases to speak to us, as she lays down her lyre, and ceases to touch it, the last tones are tones of heaven ; as if the warfare were done, the conflict accomplished, and she were anticipating either the revelations which are to make her glorious here, the " new thing" which God is about to " create" when he places her under another dispensation, or as you and I (I trust) shall do when we come to die, anticipating the praise and occupation of that eternity and rest for which we hope in the bosom of God.—*Thomas Binney,* 1798—1874.

Whole Psalm.—This Psalm gives in brief the Gospel of Confidence. It inculcates the elements of Faith, Hope, and Thanksgiving.—*Martin Geier.*

Verse 1.—"*Praise ye the Lord.*" The word here used is *Alleluia,* and this is very proper to be constantly used by us who are dependent creatures, and under such great obligations to the Father of mercies. We have often heard of prayer doing great wonders ; but instances also are not wanting of praise being accompanied with signal events. The ancient Britons, in the year 420, obtained a victory over the army of the Picts and Saxons, near Mold, in Flintshire. The Britons, unarmed, having Germanicus and Lupus at their head, when the Picts and Saxons came to the attack, the two commanders, Gideon-like, ordered their little army to shout *Alleluia* three times over, at the sound of which the enemy, being suddenly struck with terror, ran away in the greatest confusion, and left the Britons masters of the field. A stone monument to perpetuate the remembrance of this Alleluia victory, I believe, remains to this day, in a field near Mold.— *Charles Buck*, 1771—1815.

Verse 1.—*"Praise the* LORD, *O my soul."* The Psalmist calls upon the noblest element of his being to exercise its noblest function.—*Hermann Venema.*

Verse 2.—*"While I live will I praise the* LORD." Mr. John Janeway on his death-bed cried out thus,—" Come, help me with praises, yet all is too little. Come, help me, all ye mighty and glorious angels, who are so well skilled in the heavenly work of praise ! Praise him, all ye creatures upon earth ; let everything that hath being help me to praise God. Hallelujah ! Hallelujah ! Hallelujah ! Praise is now my work, and I shall be engaged in this sweet work now and for ever. Bring the Bible ; turn to David's Psalms, and let us sing a psalm of praise. Come, let us lift up our voices in the praises of the Most High. I will sing with you as long as my breath doth last, and when I have none, I shall do it better."

Verse 2.—*" While I live will I praise the* LORD." George Carpenter, the Bavarian martyr, being desired by some godly brethren, that when he was burning in the fire he would give them some sign of his constancy, answered, " Let this be a sure sign unto you of my faith and perseverance in the truth, that so long as I am able to hold open my mouth, or to whisper, I will never cease to praise God, and to profess his truth" ; the which also he did, saith mine author ; and so did many other martyrs besides.—*John Trapp.*

Verse 2.—*"I will sing praises unto my God while I have any being."* He had consecrated his entire earthly existence to the exercise of praise. And not only so, but he adds, *"I will sing praises unto my God while I have any being."* In which expression we may fairly conclude that the Psalmist stretches his thoughts beyond the limits of time, and contemplates that scene of eternal praise which shall succeed the less perfect songs of the church below.—*John Morison.*

Verse 2.—*" Unto my God."* Then praise is most pleasant, when in praising God we have an eye to him as ours, whom we have an interest in, and stand in relation to.—*Matthew Henry.*

Verse 2.—*" While I have any being."* Praise God for deliverances constantly. Some will be thankful while the memory of a deliverance is fresh, and then leave off. The Carthaginians used, at first, to send the tenth of their yearly revenue to Hercules ; and then by degrees they grew weary, and left off sending ; but we must be constant in our eucharistic sacrifice, or thank-offering. The motion of our praise must be like the motion of our pulse, which beats as long as life lasts. —*Thomas Watson.*

Verse 3.—*"Put not your trust in princes,"* etc. Through some kind of weakness, the soul of man, whensoever it is in tribulation here, despaireth of God, and chooseth to rely on man. Let it be said to one when set in some affliction, " There is a great man by whom thou mayest be set free "; he smileth, he rejoiceth, he is lifted up. But if it is said to him, " God freeth thee," he is chilled, so to speak, by despair. The aid of a mortal is promised, and thou rejoicest ; the aid of the Immortal is promised, and art thou sad ? It is promised thee that thou shalt be freed by one who needeth to be freed with thee, and thou exultest as at some great aid : thou art promised that great Liberator, who needeth none to free him, and thou despairest, as though it were but a fable. Woe to such thoughts : they wander far ; truly there is sad and great death in them.—*Augustine.*

Verse 3.—" Put not your trust in princes." The word rendered " princes" signifieth liberal, bountiful ones, ἐνεργέται, so princes would be accounted ; but there's no trusting to them without God, or against him.—*John Trapp.*

Verse 3.—" Put not your trust in princes." King Charles had given the Earl of Strafford a solemn pledge, on the word of a king, that he should not suffer in "life, honor, or fortune," yet with singular baseness and ingratitude, as well as short-sighted policy, gave his assent to the bill of attainder. On learning that this had been done, Strafford, laying his hand on his heart, and raising his eyes to heaven, uttered the memorable words, "Put not your trust in princes, nor in the sons of men, for in them there is no salvation."—*James Taylor, in the "Imperial Dictionary of Universal Biography,"* 1868.

Verse 3.—"*Put not your trust in princes.*" Shakespeare puts this sentiment into Wolsey's mouth :—

> " O how wretched
> Is that poor man that hangs on princes' favour !
> There is, betwixt that smile we would aspire to,
> That sweet aspect of princes, and their ruin,
> More pangs and fears than wars and women have :
> And when he falls, he falls like Lucifer,
> Never to hope again."

Verse 3.—"*Put not your trust in princes,*" etc. True, may some say, it were a folly to trust in weak princes, to trust in them for help who have no power to help ; but we will apply to mighty princes ; we hope there is help in them. No ; those words, " *in whom there is no help,*" are not a distinction of weak princes from strong, but a conclusion that there is no help in the strongest. That's strange. What ? No help in strong princes ! If he had said, no help in mean men, carnal reason would have consented ; but when he saith, " *Trust not in princes, nor in any son of man,*" one or other, who can believe this ? Yet this is divine truth ; we may write *insufficiency, insufficiency,* and a third time, *insufficiency,* upon them all ; the close of this verse may be their motto, " *There is no help in them.*"—*Joseph Caryl.*

Verse 3.—"*Princes.*" Earthly princes offer baubles to allure the soul from the pursuit of an eternal prize. Princes themselves have pronounced their principality to be their own greatest peril. Pope Pius V. said, " When I was a monk I had hope of my salvation ; when I became Cardinal I began to fear ; when I was made Pope I all but despaired of eternity."—*Thomas Le Blanc.*

Verse 3.—"*Nor in the son of man.*" All sons of man are like the man they are sprung of, who, being in honor, did not abide.—*Matthew Henry.*

Verse 3.—For one man to put confidence in another, is as if one beggar should ask an alms of another, or one cripple should carry another, or the blind lead the blind.—*Anthony Farindon.*

Verses 3, 4.—You see the first and the last, highest and lowest, of all the sons of Adam, they may be made honorable " *princes,*" but they are born sinful, " *the sons of men* " *;* born weak, ' *there is no help in them* " *;* born mortal, " *their breath departeth* " *;* born corruptible, " *they return to their earth* " *;* and lastly, the mortality and corruption is not only in their flesh, but in some part or remnant of their spirits, for " *their thoughts perish.*" The prophet (if you mark it) climbeth up by degrees to the disabling of the best men amongst us, and in them of all the rest. For if princes deserve not confidence, the argument must needs hold by comparison, much less do meaner men deserve it. The order of the words is so set that the members following are evermore either the reason or some confirmation to that which went before. " *Trust not in princes.*" Why ? Because they are " *the sons of men.*" Why not in " *the sons of men* " *?* Because there is *no help in them.* Why is there no help in them ? Because when " *their breath goeth forth, they turn again to their earth.*" What if their flesh be corrupted ? Nay, " *their thoughts* " also " *come to nothing.*"

For, first, this first order and rank which the prophet hath here placed, the princes and gods of the earth, are by birth *men ;* secondly, *weak* men, and such in whom *no help is ;* thirdly, not only weak, but *dying,* their breath goeth out ; fourthly, not only dying, but subject to dissolution, *they turn to the earth ;* fifthly, if their bodies only were dissolved, and their intentions and actions might stand, there were less cause to distrust them ; but their *thoughts* are as transitory as their bodies.—*John King* (1559 ?—1621), *in a Funeral Sermon.*

Verses 3, 4.—The Psalmist inscribes an antithesis. Princes, though masters of armies, possessors of riches, loaded with honors, revelling in pleasures, are at the mercy of a ruthless Black Prince. Death is tyrant over prince and peasant alike. The very pleasures which are envied are often ministers of death to voluptuous princes.—*Thomas Le Blanc.*

Verse 4.—" *He returneth to his earth.*" The earth—the dust—*is* " *his.*" 1. It is " *his* " as that from which he was made : he turns back to what he was, Genesis iii. 19. "Dust thou art, and unto dust shalt thou return." 2. The earth—the dust—the grave is " *his,*" and it is his home—the place where he will abide. 3. It is " *his* " as it is the only property which he has in reversion. All that a man—a prince, a nobleman, a monarch, a millionaire—will soon have will be his grave, his few feet of earth. *That* will be his by right of possession, by the fact that for the time being he will occupy it, and not another man ! But that, too, may soon become another man's grave, so that even there he is a tenant only for a time ; he has no permanent possession *even of a grave.*—*Albert Barnes.*

Verse 4.—" *His breath goeth forth.*" There is the death's-head, the mortality of man indeed, that a breath is as much as his being is worth. Our soul, that *spiraculum vitarum* (breath of lives), the Lord inspired it, not into Adam's eye, or ear, or mouth, but into his nostrils, which may show to man his imbecility, *cujus anima in naribus,* whose soul is in his nostrils, and dependeth upon a breath, as it were ; for the very soul must away if but breath expires ; soul and breath go forth together.

Now hear this, all ye people, ponder it high and low ; your castle is built upon the very air, the subsistence is in your nostrils, in a breath that is gone in the twinkling of an eye. Wherefore David maketh a question, saying, "Lord, what is man ?" He answereth himself also : " Man is a vanishing shadow " (Ps. cxliv. 3, 4), a shadow of smoke, or the dream of a shadow rather, as the poet speaketh. Blessed therefore are the poor in spirit ; this advantage have all afflicted ones, that they have checks enough to call them home, and make them see they be but men. The curtain of honour, profit, or pleasure, hard it is and rare to draw aside when it is spread over us : " man in honour understandeth not " (Ps. xlix. 20). To great ones therefore be it spoken ; the psalm intendeth it of very princes : " *His breath goeth forth.*"

See we now the continuedness, *exit,* " *it goeth* " ; as if it were now presently in its passage : showing this, that *Homo vivens continuè moritur,* that life is a continued death ; our candle lightens, consumes, and dies : as in the passing of an hour-glass, every minute some sand falleth, and the glass once turned, no creature can intreat the sands to stay, but they continue to fall till all are gone : so is our life, it shortens and dies every minute, and we cannot beg a minute of time back, and that which we call death is but the termination, or consummation of it.—*Thomas Williamson ; in a Sermon, entitled, " A Comfortable Meditation of Humane Frailtie and Divine Mercie,*" 1630.

Verse 4.—The primary idea of *breath* and the secondary one of *spirit* run into each other in the usage of the Hebrew word רוח, so that either may be expressed in the translation without entirely excluding the other.—*Joseph Addison Alexander.*

Verse 4.—" *His breath* (or spirit) *goeth forth.*" Now I come to the liberty of the spirit, that it recedes inviolate ; 1. In Act ; " *it goeth* ": 2. In Essence ; " *it goeth forth.*"

1. Our spirit is *free in the act ;* it is not snatched, as it were ; " *it goeth.*" A soul in life sealed to eternity by the first fruits of the Spirit hath its good issue, its free passing, its hopes even in death ; for let this breath fade, *fidelis Deus,* God who cannot lie, will stand nigh us in that exigency, and begin to help where man leaveth. The Holy Spirit, whose name is the Comforter, will not omit and leave off his own act or office in the great needs of death. Hence good Hilarion, having served the Lord Christ seventy years, checks his soul that it was so loth at the last to go forth, saying, *Egredere, O anima mea, egredere,* " Go forth, my soul, go forth." Devout Simeon sueth for a manumission : " Lord, now lettest thou thy servant depart in peace, according to thy word." The spirit goeth

forth ; it passes freely ; because it taketh up or embraceth the cross of Christ, as he commandeth us to do. But is the act at our will and liberty ? Not simply. We may not *projicere animam*, thrust or cast forth our breath or spirit ; *spiritus exit*, it goeth forth. Strive, we must, to cast the world out of us ; we may not cast ourselves out of the world. Saint Paul dareth not dissolve himself, though he could wish to be dissolved : God must part that which he joins ; God giveth, and God taketh away ; and if God say, as he doth to Lazarus, *Exi foras*, Come forth ; with faithful Stephen we must resign our spirit and all into his hands. When God biddeth us yoke, he is the wisest man that yieldeth his neck most willingly. When our great Captain recalls us, we must take the retreat in good part. But it is heathenish to force out the soul ; for when the misdeeming flesh, amidst our disasters, will not listen with patience for God's call, but rather shake off the thought of divine providence quite, then are we ready to curse God and die, and that is probably to leap *e fumo in flammam*, out of the sin of self-murder into hell. No, but God will have our spirits to pass forth upon good terms. *Spiritus exit*, " *the spirit goeth forth.*"

2. Secondly, the spirit goeth *free or inviolate in essence ;* death is not the end, but the outgoing of the soul, a transmigration or journey from one place to another. " *It goeth forth*" ; so the character of our weakness we see in the issue ; it is an argument of our eternity ; for man indeed is perishing, but so is not his spirit. The phœnix goes forth or out of his ashes, " the spirit returneth to God who gave it " (Eccl. xii. 7) ; that is, it abides still ; and as in the body it pleased God to inclose the soul for a season, so it may as well exist elsewhere without it, if God will ; for it hath no rise at all from the clay, yea, it bears in it immortality, an image of that breast whence it is breathed. The separate and very abstract acts of the spirit, even while it is in the body, the wondrous visions of the Lord to his prophets, usually when their bodies were bound up in sleep ; Saint Paul's rapture when he knew not whether he was in the body or out of it ; the admirable inventions and arts of men, manifest the soul's self-consisting. Not Socrates, and Cato, and the civilised heathen only, but the very savages believe this, and so entertain death, *ut exitum, non ut exitium*, as a dissolution, not as a destruction : *spiritus exit*, " *his spirit goeth forth.*"—*Thomas Williamson.*

Verse 4.—" *His breath goeth forth*," etc. The Hebrew gives the idea not that the *spirit*, but the mortal part of man will return to the dust. " His *soul* (fem. רוה) goeth forth," *i. e.*, returneth to God ; " returneth *he* (masc. שב) to his earth." As in Ecc. xii. 7 : " *He* " is the mortal man of clay, but " his *breath* " (*soul*) is the real immortal man.—*Simon de Muis.*

Verse 4.—" *He returneth to his earth.*" Returning, in its proper notion, is a-going back to that place from whence we came, so that in this clause here is a threefold truth, implied, expressed, inferred.

1. That which is *implied* in this phrase of returning is, that man in respect of his body came from the earth ; and as it is here implied, so it is expressed concerning the first man by Moses (Gen. ii. 7). " The Lord God formed man " (that is, the *body* of man) " of the dust " ; or according to the Hebrew " dust of the ground " ; and by St. Paul (1 Cor. xv. 47), where he saith, " The first man is of the earth, earthy." True it is, we are formed in our mother's womb ; but yet inasmuch as we all came from the first man, we are truly said to come from *the earth ;* only with this difference, that he immediately, we mediately are framed out of the earth. This truth was engraven in full characters upon the name of the first man, who is called *Adam*, from a word that signifieth *red earth*, and that very word is here used, perhaps to mind us of that earth whereof man was first made ; yea, according to the usual etymology, the name *homo*, which in the Latin is a common name to both sexes, is derived *ab humo*, from *the ground*. For this reason it is that the earth is called by the poet *magna parens*, the great parent of all mankind, and in the answer of the Oracle, *our mother ;* and in this respect we are said by Eliphaz " to dwell in houses of clay, whose foundation is in the dust," Job iv. 19.

2. That which is *expressed* is, that man (when he dieth) returneth to the earth,

πάντες λυόμενοι κόνις ἐσμέν, saith the poet, "We are all dust when dissolved." As the white snow when melted is black water ; so flesh and blood when bereaved of the soul become dust and ashes : in which respect St. Paul giveth this epithet of "vile" to our bodies. Phil. iii. 21. Indeed, man's original being from the earth, he had a natural propensity to earth ; according to the maxim, *Omne principiatum sequitur naturam principiorum*, "Everything hath an aptitude of returning to the principle whence it cometh" ; but yet had he not *turned away* from God he had never actually *returned* thither. It is sin which hath brought upon man a necessity of dying, and that dying brings a necessity of returning to the earth : in which respect it is observable, that the threat, "thou shalt die the death" (Gen. ii. 17), which was denounced against man before his fall, being afterwards renewed (iii. 19), is explained (as to temporal death) by these words, "to dust thou shalt return" ; so that now the motion of the little world man is like that of the great, *Circulare ab eodem puncto ad idem*, from the same to the same ; and that as in his *soul* from God to God, so in his *body* from the earth to the earth. The rivers come from the sea, and they return thither. The sun ariseth out of the east, and thither it returneth. Man is formed of the earth, and into earth he is again transformed : with which agreeth that of the poet Lucretius :

Cedit item retro de terra quod fuit ante.

3. That which is *inferred* in the emphatical pronoun "*his*," which is annexed to the noun "*earth*," is that the earth to which man returneth is *his ;* this being that which ariseth out of both the former conclusions ; since it is therefore *his earth* because he cometh from and returneth to it. Earth is man's Genesis and Analysis, his composition and resolution, his Alpha and Omega, his first and last ; *Ortus pulvis, finis cinis ;* earth is his both originally and finally. So that our bodies can challenge no alliance with, or property in anything so much as earth. For if we call those things *ours* which had only an external relation to us, as our friends, our horses, our goods, our lands ; much more may we call that *our earth* whereof we are made and into which we shall moulder ; no wonder it is here said to be "*his*" ; so elsewhere he is said to *be earth*, as being called by that name.— *Nathanael Hardy, in a Funeral Sermon entitled,* "*Man's Last Journey to His Long Home,*" 1659.

Verse 4.—"*In that very day his thoughts perish.*" The thoughts which the Psalmist here, no doubt, especially intends are those *purposes* which are in the minds of great men of doing good to those who are under, and depend upon them. The Hebrew word here used is derived from a verb that signifieth *to be bright : cogitationes serenœ*, those candid, serene, benign, benevolent thoughts which they have of advancing their allies, friends and followers. These thoughts are said to "*perish*" in "*that day*" wherein they are conceived ; so Tremellius glosseth. In which sense the instability of great men's favour is asserted, whose smiles are quickly changed into frowns, love into hatred, and so in a moment their mind being changed, their well-wishing thoughts vanish. But more rationally, "their thoughts perish in that day" wherein their *persons die*, because there is no opportunity of putting their purposes into execution. They perish like the child which comes to the birth, and there is no strength to bring forth ; or like the fruit which is plucked off before it be ripe. Whilst they live we may be deceived in our expectations by the alteration of their minds ; but, however, their condition is mortal, and when that great change by death comes, their designs (how wellsoever meant) must want success.

From hence it followeth, which is by some looked upon as a part of the meaning of the words, that the "*thoughts*" or *hopes of them who trust in them perish.* It is a true apothegm, *Major pars hominum expectando moritur ;* the greatest part of men perish by expectation. And good reason, inasmuch as their expectation, being misplaced, perisheth. How strongly this argument serveth to press the Psalmist's caution against confidence in man, though never so great, is obvious. It is true, princes and nobles being invested with honour, wealth and authority, have power in their hands, and perhaps they may have thoughts in their hearts to do thee good ; but, alas, how uncertain is the execution of those intentions, and therefore how foolish is it to depend upon them. " Trust in the Lord Jehovah " (saith the prophet), " for with him is everlasting strength." Ay, and with him is unchangeable goodness. It is safe building upon the rock, trusting upon God, whose thoughts of mercy are (like himself) from everlasting to everlasting ; but nothing is more foolish than to build on the sand, trust to men, whose persons, together with their thoughts, perish in a moment. Therefore let our resolution be that of David : " It is better to trust in the Lord than to put confidence in man ; it is better to trust in the Lord than to put confidence in princes," Psalm cxviii. 8, 9.—*Nathanael Hardy.*

Verse 4.—" In that very day his thoughts perish." At death a man sees all those thoughts which were not spent upon God to be fruitless. All worldly, vain thoughts, in the day of death perish and come to nothing. What good will the whole globe of the world do at such a time ? Those who have revelled out their thoughts in impertinences will but be the more disquieted ; it will cut them to the heart to think how they have spun a fool's thread. A Scythian captain having, for a draught of water, yielded up a city, cried out : " What have I lost ? What have I betrayed ?" So will it be with that man when he comes to die, who hath spent all his meditations upon the world ; he will say, What have I lost ? What have I betrayed ? I have lost heaven, I have betrayed my soul. Should not the consideration of this fix our minds upon the thoughts of God and glory ? All other meditations are fruitless ; like a piece of ground which hath much cost laid out upon it, but it yields no crop.—*Thomas Watson.*

Verse 4.—I would have you take this passage and illustrate it as applying to purposes, projects, and intentions. That, I think now, is precisely the idea intended to be conveyed. " *In that very day his thoughts perish* " ; his purposes, his projects—what he intended to do. These cherished thoughts are gone. My dear brethren, there is something here for us. You find many beautiful passages and instances in Scripture in which this idea is embodied and realised, sometimes with great beauty and poetic effect, in relation to the enemies of the church. " The enemy said, I will pursue, I will overtake, I will divide the spoil, my hand shall destroy them ; thou didst blow with thy wind, the sea covered them, they sank as lead in the mighty waters." In that very day their thoughts perished. " Have they not sped ? have they not divided the prey ? to every man a damsel or two ? to Sisera a prey of divers colours of needlework ? So let all thine enemies perish, O Lord." The sacred poet does not even suggest that they had perished ; but feeling that it was a fact, only lifts up her heart to God. " So let all thine enemies perish, O Lord." And so you will find in many parts of Scripture beautiful ideas like this concerning the purposes and intentions that were in men's hearts utterly " perishing " by God's just laying his hand upon them—the purposes that were in their hearts against the church.—*Thomas Binney.*

Verse 4.—" In that very day his thoughts perish." In the case of the rich fool (Luke xii. 16, 20) his " thoughts " of building larger barns, and of many years of ease and prosperity,—all his selfish and worldly schemes,—" perished " in that self-same night.—*John W. Haley, in " An Examination of the Alleged Discrepancies of the Bible,"* 1875.

Verse 4.—" His thoughts perish." The science, the philosophy, the statesmanship of one age is exploded in the next. The men who are the masters of the world's intellect to-day are discrowned to-morrow. In this age of restless and rapid change they may survive their own thoughts ; their thoughts do not survive them.—*J. J. Stewart Perowne.*

Verse 4.—" His thoughts perish." As the purposes of all about worldly things perish in the approaches of death, so do the purposes of some about spiritual and heavenly things. How many have had purposes to repent, to amend their lives and turn to God, which have been prevented and totally broken off by the extremity of pain and sickness, but chiefly by the stroke of death when they have (as they thought) " been about to repent," and (as we say) " turn over a new

leaf " in their lives ; they have been turned into the grave by death, and into
hell by the just wrath of God.—*Joseph Caryl.*

Verse 4.—" *His thoughts.*" Rather, " his false deceitful show " ; literally,
" his glitterings."—*Samuel Horsley,* 1733—1806.

Verse 4.—To trust man is to lean not on a pillar but on a little heap of dust.
The proudest element in man is his thought. In the thoughts of his heart he is
lifted up if nowhere else ; but, behold, even his proudest thoughts, says the Psalmist, will be degraded and perish in that dust to which he will return. Poor,
perishing pride ! Who should trust it ?—*Johannes Paulus Palanterius.*

Verse 5.—" *Happy is he.*" This is the last of the twenty-five places (or twenty-
six, if Psalm cxxviii. 2 be included) in which the word *ashre,* with which the
psalter begins, is found.—*Speaker's Commentary.*

. *Verse* 5.—Alas, how often do we trust when we should be afraid, and become
afraid when we should trust !—*Lange's Commentary.*

Verse 5.—" *The God of Jacob.*" A famous and significant description of God ;
and that, First, *in respect of his nature,* or the verity and reality of his being and
excellence. He is styled here by way of elegancy or emphasis, " *The God of
Jacob,*" saith Mollerus, to discern and distinguish the true God of Israel from all
Heathenish deities, and to explode all fictitious gods and all worships thereof.
As the true God is the God of Jacob, so the God of Jacob is the true God. He
is God alone, and there is no other besides him. . . . Secondly. This title or
appellation serves also to describe him *in his special relation to his people.* We find
him called by our Psalmist, " The mighty God of Jacob " : Ps. cxxxii. 5. He is
indeed the God of the whole earth, but in a peculiar manner " the God of *Israel* " :
Matt. xv. 31. . . . It is observable in Scripture that he styles not himself so frequently, in his revelations of himself to them, " the God of heaven and earth "
(though that also is a title full of encouragement), but " the God of Abraham,
Isaac, and Jacob " ; as if he had borne such choice goodwill, and had such a
peculiar care for these three men, as to overlook all the world besides them. So
near and intimate relation have God's people to him, that their interests are
mutually involved, and twisted in a reciprocal and covenant bond. They are his,
he is their portion ; their Beloved is theirs and they are his : they are called by his
name, the saints are styled his " holy ones," and the Church is termed expressly
" Christ." Yea, he condescends to be called by their name ; he assumes the
name of *Jacob,* Ps. xxiv. 6 : " This is the generation of them that seek him, that
seek thy face, O *Jacob.*"—*From " The Saints' Ebenezer," by F. E.,* 1667.

Verse 5.—" *The God of Jacob.*" This verse aptly warrants us to apply to all believers all the illustrations of *help* and *hope* furnished by Jacob in his exile when
none but God could help him.—*Simon de Muis.*

Verses 5, 6.—" *The God of Jacob . . . which made heaven and earth, the sea,
and all that therein is.*" It is a characteristic of these Psalms, to proclaim to all
nations which worshipped idols, that " the God of Jacob," " the God of Zion,"
is the Creator and Governor of all things ; and to make an appeal to all nations
to turn to him. All these Psalms have a *missionary character* and an *evangelical
function.* We may compare here the apostolic prayer at Jerusalem, after the
descent of the Holy Ghost at Pentecost : " They lifted up their voices to God
with one accord, and said, Lord, thou art God, *that made heaven and earth, and
the sea, and all that in them is* " (where the words are the same as in the Septuagint
in this place) : " Who by the mouth of thy servant David hast said, Why do the
heathen rage ?" Acts iv. 24, 25. The office of these Psalms is to declare to the
universe, that Jehovah, and he alone, is *Elohim ;* and to invite all to worship him
as such, by their oft repeated *Hallelujah.*—*Christopher Wordsworth.*

Verse 6.—" *Which keepeth truth for ever.*" Stored in his inexhaustible treasury
as the most costly jewel ever there. And that because the *truth* which he so
keeps, and which is the sustaining power which preserves the fabric of creation,

is the Eternal Word, his only begotten Son, Jesus Christ.—*Dionysius the Carthu-sian, and Ayguan, in Neale and Littledale.*

Verse 6.—" *Which keepeth truth for ever.*" God does indeed keep the truth from age to age—how else would the Book of God have lived ?—*John Lorinus.*

Verses 6-9.—The LORD, is an *Almighty* God, as the Creator of the universe ; next, he is a *faithful* God " who keepeth truth forever " ; further, he is a *right-eous* God (verse 7) a *bountiful* God (*ib.*) a *gracious* God (verses 7—9).—*J. J. Stewart Perowne.*

Verse 7.—" *Giveth food to the hungry.*" We learn from this that he is not al-ways so indulgent to his own as to load them with abundance, but occasionally withdraws his blessing, that he may succour them when reduced to hunger. Had the Psalmist said that God fed his people with abundance and pampered them, would not any of those under want, or in famine have immediately desponded ? The goodness of God is therefore properly extended farther to the feeding of the hungry.—*John Calvin.*

Verse 7.—" *Giveth food to the hungry.*" Now, that Jesus was that Lord of whom the Psalmist in this place, and in Ps. cxlv. 16, speaketh, was fully testified by the miracles which he wrought, in feeding many thousands with some few loaves and two small fishes, and in filling so many baskets with the fragments or relics of that small provision wherewith he had filled thousands. From these miracles, the people which had seen him do them, and tasted of his bounty, did rightly infer that he was the prophet which was to come into the world, as you may read, John vi. 14 ; and being supposed to be the prophet, they consequently presumed that he was likewise to be the King of Israel ; and out of this concert or presumption they would have enforced him to be their king, verse 15.—*Thomas Jackson, 1579—1640.*

Verse 7.—" *The Lord looseth the prisoners.*" As in that place of Isaiah (lxi. 1) the phrase of " opening the prison to them that are bound," is by the learned thought to be a prophetic elegance, to signify the cure of those that are deaf and dumb, whose souls consequently were shut up from being able to express them-selves, as language enables others to do ; so here also it may be used poetically, and then it will be directly parallel to that part of Christ's answer, " the deaf hear " (Matt. xi. 5). At the curing of such, Christ's form of speech was, Ephphatha, " be opened," as to the door of a prison, when those which were under restraint therein were to be let loose out of it, their fetters being shaken off from them. But then, 'tis further manifest, that those that were under any sore disease or lameness, etc., are said to be " bound by Satan " (Luke xiii. 16), and be " loosed " by Christ, when they were cured by him. So saith Christ (verse 12), " Woman, thou art loosed from thine infirmity : and immediately she was made straight." Her being " made straight " was her being loosed out of her restraint, or bonds, or prison. And in this latitude of the poetic or prophetic expression, the Lord's *loosing the prisoners* here will comprehend the walking of the lame, the lepers being cleansed, the hearing of the deaf, yea, and the raising up of the dead ; for those of all others are fastest bound, and so when they were raised, the style is as proper as to Lazarus in respect of the graveclothes, " loose them, and let him go."—*Henry Hammond.*

Verses 7, 8.—It ought not to pass without remark that the name Jehovah is re-peated here five times in five lines, to intimate that it is an almighty power, that of Jehovah, that is engaged and exerted for the relief of the oppressed ; and that it is as much to the glory of God to succour them that are in misery, as it is to ride on the heavens by his name JAH, Ps. lxviii. 4.—*Matthew Henry.*

Verse 8.—" *Openeth the eyes of the blind.*" Literally, " *openeth the blind* "—*i. e.*, maketh them to see. The expression may be used figuratively, as a remedy ap-plied either to physical helplessness, as Deut. xxviii. 29 ; Isa. lix. 9, 10 ; Job xii. 25 ; or to spiritual want of discernment, as Isa. xxix. 18 ; xlii. 7, 18 ; xliii. 8. Here the context favours the former.—*J. J. Stewart Perowne.*

Verse 8.—" *The* LORD *openeth the eyes of the blind.*" The Hebrew does not mention *the eyes* of the blind. Hilary renders it *sapientificat.* The Arabic version follows the same. Jehovah by his *wisdom illumines dark minds.* It is *mental* blindness which is the common affliction of men.—*John Lorinus.*

Verse 8.—" *The blind.*" The large number of blind persons to be seen feeling their way along the streets in Cairo and Alexandria has been noticed by Volney. " Walking in the streets of Cairo," he says, " out of a hundred persons whom I met, there were often twenty blind, eighteen one-eyed, and twenty others with eyes red, purulent, or spotted. Almost every one wears bandages, indicating that they either have or are recovering from ophthalmia." Ophthalmia is, in fact, one of the scourges of Egypt, as all physicians know. Its prevalence must be attributed in a great degree to the sand which the wind blows into the eyes ; but one can understand how in Oriental countries in general the excessive heat of the sun must make blindness much commoner than it is with us.

It is not therefore surprising to any one who knows the East to find the blind so often mentioned in the gospel history, and to meet in Scripture with so many allusions to this infirmity. Of the twelve maledictions of the Levites there is one against him " who maketh the blind to go out of the way " : Deut. xxvii. 18. " The spirit of God hath anointed me," said Jesus, quoting from Isaiah, " to preach the gospel to the poor, and recovery of sight to the blind " : Luke iv. 19. " The Lord," says David, " setteth at liberty them that are bound ; the Lord giveth sight to- the blind."—*Felix Bovet* (1824—), *in " Egypt, Palestine, and Phœnicia,"* 1882.

Verse 9.—" *The* LORD *preserveth the strangers.*" God has peculiar love for wanderers and pilgrims (Deut. x. 18), and Jacob was a stranger in a strange land when God showed himself to be the God of Jacob as his elect servant.—*Thomas Le Blanc.*

Verse 9.—" *The Lord preserveth the strangers.*" They who do not belong to Babylon, nor to this world, but the true pilgrims in a strange land.—*Robert Bellarmine.*

Verse 9.—" *He relieveth the fatherless and the widow.*" The olive-tree is not to be twice shaken, the vineyard is not to be twice gathered, nor are the sheaves of corn left in the fields to be gleaned ; all that belongs to the poor, to the widow and the orphan. It was allowable to pluck with the hand the ears of corn while passing through a neighbour's field (Deut. xxiii. 25), though a sickle might not be used. The law cares most anxiously for widows and orphans, for " God is a father of the fatherless and a judge of the widows " (Ps. lxviii. 5). A widow's raiment might not be taken in pledge, and both widows and orphans were to be invited to their feasts. An institution specially designed for the protection and relief of the poor was the second tithe, the so-called poor's-tithe. The first tithe belonged to the Levites. What remained over was again tithed, and the produce of this second tithe, devoted in the first two years to a feast in the sanctuary at the offering of first-fruits, was devoted in the third year to a feast in the dwelling-house, to which the Levites and the strangers, the widows and the orphans, were invited (Deut. xiv. 28, 29 ; xxvi. 12, 13).—*G. Uhlhorn, in " Christian Charity in the Ancient Church,"* 1883.

Verse 9.—" *The way of the wicked he turneth upside down.*" He overturns their plans, defeats their schemes ; makes their purposes accomplish what they did not intend they should accomplish. The Hebrew word here means to bend, to curve, to make crooked, to distort ; then, to overturn, to turn upside down. The same word is applied to the conduct of the wicked, in Ps. cxix. 78 : " They dealt perversely with me." The idea here is that the path is not a straight path ; that God makes it a crooked way ; that they are diverted from their design ; that through them he accomplishes purposes which they did not intend ; that he prevents their accomplishing their own designs ; and that he will make their plans subservient to a higher and better purpose than their own. This is the eleventh reason why those who put their trust in God are happy. It is that God is worthy of confidence and love, because he has all the plans of wicked men entirely under his control.—*Albert Barnes.*

Verse 9.—" *The way of the wicked he turneth upside down.*" As the potter's clay, when the potter hath spent some time and pains in tempering and forming it upon the wheel, and now the vessel is even almost brought to its shape, a man that stands by may, with the least push, put it clean out of shape, and mar all on a sudden that he hath been so long a-making : so is it that all the plots and contrivances of wicked men, all their turning of things upside down shall be but as the potter's clay ; for when they think they have brought all to maturity, ripeness, and perfection, when they look upon their business as good as done, all on a sudden all their labour is lost ; for God, who stands by all the while and looks on, will, with one small touch, with the least breath of his wrath, blast and break all in pieces.—*Edlin,* 1656.

Verse 9.—" *The way of the wicked he turneth upside down.*" All the ten clauses preceding lift up the poor saint step by step, higher and higher. At one word suddenly, like Satan falling as lightning from heaven, the wicked are shown dashed down the whole way from the summit of pride to the depths of hell.— *Johannes Paulus Palanterius.*

Verse 9.—" *The way of the wicked he turneth upside down.*" A striking illustration of the folly of counting God out of one's plans for life is given in the course of William M. Tweed, whose death is recently announced. Here was a man who sought wealth and power, and who for a time seemed successful in their pursuit. Apparently he did not propose to obey God or to live for a life to come. What he wanted was worldly prosperity. He thought he had it. He went to Congress. He gathered his millions. He controlled the material interests of the metropolis of his country. He openly defied public sentiment and courts of justice in the prosecution of his plans. He was a brilliant and therefore a dangerous example of successful villainy. But the promise of prosperity for the life which now is, is only to the godly. As William M. Tweed lay dying in a prison-house in the city he once ruled, his confession of bitter disappointment was, " My life has been a failure in everything. There is nothing I am proud of." If any young man wants to come to an end like this, the way to it is simple and plain. " The great God that formed all things both rewardeth the fool, and rewardeth transgressors." " *The way of the wicked he turneth upside down.*"—*American Sunday School Times,* 1878.

HINTS TO THE VILLAGE PREACHER.

Verse 1.—I. An exhortation : it is addressed to ourselves : " Praise ye the Lord." II. An example : the Psalmist cries to himself, " Praise the Lord." III. An echo : " Praise the Lord, O my soul." Let us say this to our own souls.

Verse 1.—Whom should I praise ? And why ? And when ? And how ?

Verse 1.—Public worship. I. Should be with a sense of fellowship : " Praise ye " : pleasures of communion in praise. II. Should never lose its individuality : " O my soul." God is only praised by individual hearts. Temptations to wandering in public services. III. Should be full of Jehovah's felt presence : each and all should worship *him* alone.— *W. B. H.*

Verse 2.—Work for here and hereafter. I. " While I live " ; or a period of uncertainty and mystery. II. " I will praise the Lord " ; or a service definite, determined, due, and delightful. Certainty amid uncertainty. III. " While I have any being " ; or an enthusiastic pre-engagement of eternity.— *W. B. H.*

Verse 3.—I. It dishonours God. II. It degrades you. III. It disappoints in every case.

Verse 4.—Decease, Decay, Defeat.

Verse 4 (second clause). The failure of man's projects, the disappearance of his philosophies, the disproving of his boastings.

Verse 5.—The secret of true happiness. I. *What it is not.* The man here mentioned has his work and warfare, for he needs help ; and he has not all he desires, for he is a man of hope. II. *What it is.* It lies in the *hath*, the *help*, and the *hope*, and these are all in God.

Verses 6, 7.—The God of our hope is, I. Creator. II. Truth-keeper. III. Vindicator. IV. Provider. V. Deliverer.

Verse 7 (*last clause*).—See " Spurgeon's Sermons," No. 484 : " The Lord—the Liberator."

Verse 7. The People's Rights. I. Three rights of humanity. Justice, Bread, Freedom. II. God's interventions in their behalf. Revolutions, Reforms, Re-generations. Christ's war with Satan. III. The magnificent supply of the three blessings in Christ's kingdom. IV. The men who are fashioned and trained under this *régime.*—*W. B. H.*

Verse 8 (*first clause*).—Spiritual blindness, its curse, cause, and cure.

Verse 8 (*second clause*).—Who are the people ? Who raises them ? How he does it. And what then ?

Verse 8 (*third clause*).—God's love to the righteous. I. He made them right-eous. II. They are like him. III. They love him. IV. Their purposes are one with his own.

Verse 9.—Observe the provision made in the Jewish law for the stranger. The way in which strangers were received by God. The truth that his chosen are strangers in the world. His design to gather in strangers in the latter days.

Verse 9 (*centre clause*).—The claims of orphans and widows upon the people of God.

Verse 9 (*last clause*).—Illustrated by Joseph's brethren, Haman, and others.

Verse 10.—I. A cause for praise—" The Lord shall reign for ever." II. A centre of praise : " O Zion." III. A cycle of praise : " all generations." IV. A call to praise : " Praise ye the Lord."

PSALM CXLVII.

SUBJECT.—*This is a specially remarkable song. In it the greatness and the condescending goodness of the Lord are celebrated. The God of Israel is set forth in his peculiarity of glory as caring for the sorrowing, the insignificant, and forgotten. The poet finds a singular joy in extolling one who is so singularly gracious. It is a Psalm of the city and of the field, of the first and the second creations, of the commonwealth and of the church. It is good and pleasant throughout.*

DIVISION.—*The song appears to divide itself into three portions. From 1 to 6, Jehovah is extolled for building up Zion, and blessing his mourners; from 7 to 11, the like praise is given because of his provision for the lowly, and his pleasure in them; and then, from 12 to 20, he is magnified for his work on behalf of his people, and the power of his word in nature and in grace. Let it be studied with joyful gratitude.*

EXPOSITION.

PRAISE ye the LORD : for *it is* good to sing praises unto our God ; for *it is* pleasant ; *and* praise is comely.

2 The LORD doth build up Jerusalem : he gathereth together the outcasts of Israel.

3 He healeth the broken in heart, and bindeth up their wounds.

4 He telleth the number of the stars ; he calleth them all by *their* names.

5 Great *is* our LORD, and of great power : his understanding *is* infinite.

6 The LORD lifteth up the meek : he casteth the wicked down to the ground.

1. "*Praise ye the* LORD," or Hallelujah. The flow of the broad river of the Book of Psalms ends in a cataract of praise. The present psalm begins and ends with Hallelujah. Jehovah and happy praise should ever be associated in the mind of a believer. Jove was dreaded, but Jehovah is beloved. To one and all of the true seed of Israel the Psalmist acts as choir-master, and cries, " Praise *ye* the Lord." Such an exhortation may fitly be addressed to all those who owe anything to the favour of God ; and which of us does not ? Pay him we cannot, but praise him we will, not only now, but for ever. " *For it is good to sing praises unto our God.*" It is good because it is right ; good because it is acceptable with God, beneficial to ourselves, and stimulating to our fellows. The goodness of an exercise is good argument with good men for its continual practice. Singing the divine praises is the best possible use of speech : it speaks of God, for God, and to God, and it does this in a joyful and reverent manner. Singing in the heart is good, but singing with heart and voice is better, for it allows others to join with us. Jehovah is *our* God, our covenant God, therefore let him have the homage of our praise ; and he is so gracious and happy a God that our praise may best be expressed in joyful song.

"*For it is pleasant ; and praise is comely.*" It is pleasant and proper, sweet and suitable to laud the Lord Most High. It is refreshing to the taste of the truly refined mind, and it is agreeable to the eye of the pure in heart : it is delightful both to hear and to see a whole assembly praising the Lord. These are arguments for song-service which men who love true piety, real pleasure, and strict propriety will not despise. Please to praise, for praise is pleasant : praise the Lord in the beauty of holiness, for praise is comely. Where duty and delight, benefit and beauty unite, we ought not to be backward. Let each reader feel that he and his family ought to constitute a choir for the daily celebration of the praises of the Lord.

2. "*The* LORD *doth build up Jerusalem.*" God appears both in the material and spiritual world as a Builder and Maker, and therein he is to be praised. His grace, wisdom, and power are all seen in the formation and establishment of the chosen seat of his worship ; once a city with material walls, but now a church composed of spiritual stones. The Jews rejoiced in the uprising of their capital from its ruins, and we triumph in the growth of the church from among a godless world. "*He gathereth together the outcasts of Israel*" ; and thus he repairs the waste places, and causes the former desolations to be inhabited. This sentence may relate to Nehemiah and those who returned with him ; but there is no reason why it should not with equal fitness be referred to David, who, with his friends, was once an outcast, but ere long became the means of building up Jerusalem. In any case, the Psalmist ascribes to Jehovah all the blessings enjoyed ; the restoration of the city and the restoration of the banished he equally traces to the divine hand. How clearly these ancient believers saw the Lord present, working among them and for them ! Spiritually we see the hand of God in the edification of the church, and in the ingathering of sinners. What are men under conviction of sin but outcasts from God, from holiness, from heaven, and even from hope ? Who could gather them from their dispersions, and make citizens of them in Christ Jesus save the Lord our God ? This deed of love and power he is constantly performing. Therefore let the song begin at Jerusalem our home, and let every living stone in the spiritual city echo the strain ; for it is the Lord who has brought again his banished ones, and builded them together in Zion.

3. "*He healeth the broken in heart, and bindeth up their wounds.*" This the Holy Spirit mentions as a part of the glory of God, and a reason for our declaring his praise : the Lord is not only a Builder, but a Healer ; he restores broken hearts as well as broken walls. The kings of the earth think to be great through their loftiness ; but Jehovah becomes really so by his condescension. Behold, the Most High has to do with the sick and the sorry, with the wretched and the wounded ! He walks the hospitals as the good Physician ! His deep sympathy with mourners is a special mark of his goodness. Few will associate with the despondent, but Jehovah chooses their company, and abides with them till he has healed them by his comforts. He deigns to handle and heal broken hearts : he himself lays on the ointment of grace, and the soft bandages of love, and thus binds up the bleeding wounds of those convinced of sin. This is compassion like a God. Well may those praise him to whom he has acted so gracious a part. The Lord is always healing and binding : this is no new work to him, he has done it of old ; and it is not a thing of the past of which he is now weary, for he is still healing and still binding, as the original hath it. Come, broken hearts, come to the Physician who never fails to heal : uncover your wounds to him who so tenderly binds them up !

4. "*He telleth the number of the stars.*" None but he can count the mighty host, but as he made them and sustains them he can number them. To Jehovah stars are as mere coins, which the merchant tells as he puts them into his bag. "*He calleth them all by their names.*" He has an intimate acquaintance with each separate orb, so as to know its name or character. Indeed, he gives to each its appropriate title, because he knows its constitution and nature. Vast as these stars are, they are perfectly obedient to his bidding ; even as soldiers to a captain who calls their names, and allots them their stations. Do they not rise, and set, and move, or stand, precisely according to his order ? What a change is here from the preceding verse ! Read the two without a break, and feel the full force of the contrast. From stars to sighs is a deep descent ! From worlds to wounds is a distance which only infinite compassion can bridge. Yet he who acts a surgeon's part with wounded hearts, marshals the heavenly host, and reads the muster-roll of suns and their majestic systems. O Lord, it is good to praise thee as ruling the stars, but it is pleasant to adore thee as healing the broken in heart !

5. " *Great is our Lord.*" Our Lord and King is great—magnanimous, infinite, inconceivably glorious. None can describe his majesty, or reckon up the number of his excellencies. " *And of great power.*" Doing as he wills, and willing to do mighty deeds. His acts reveal something of his might, but the mass of his power is hidden, for all things are possible with God, even the things impossible with men. " *His understanding is infinite.*" There is no fathoming his wisdom, or measuring his knowledge. He is infinite in existence, in power, and in knowledge; as these three phrases plainly teach us. The gods of the heathen are nothing, but our God filleth all things. And yet how condescending ! For this is he who so tenderly nurses sick souls, and waist to be gracious to sinful men. He brings his boundless power and infinite understanding to bear upon human distress for its assuagement and sanctification. For all these reasons let his praise be great : even could it be infinite, it would not exceed his due. In the building of his church and the salvation of souls, his greatness, power, and wisdom are all displayed : let him be extolled because of each of these attributes.

6. " *The* LORD *lifteth up the meek : he casteth the wicked down to the ground.*" He reverses the evil order of things. The meek are down, and he lifts them up ; the wicked are exalted, and he hurls them down to the dust. The Lord loves those who are reverent to himself, humble in their own eyes, and gentle to their fellow-men : these he lifts up to hope, to peace, to power, to eternal honour. When God lifts a man, it is a lift indeed. Proud men are, in their own esteem, high enough already ; only those who are low will care to be lifted up, and only such will Jehovah upraise. As for the wicked, they must come down from their seats of vain glory. God is accustomed to overthrow such ; it is his way and habit. None of the wicked shall in the end escape. To the earth they must go ; for from the earth they came, and for the earth they live. It is one of the glories of our God for which his saints praise him, that he hath put down the mighty from their seats, and hath exalted them of low degree. Well may the righteous be lifted up in spirit and the wicked be downcast as they think of the judgments of the Lord God.

In this verse we see the practical outcome of that character of Jehovah, which leads him to count and call the stars as if they were little things, while he deals tenderly with sorrowful men, as if they were precious in his esteem. He is so great that nothing is great to him, and he is so condescending that nothing is little to him : his infinite majesty thus naturally brings low the lofty and exalts the lowly.

7 Sing unto the LORD with thanksgiving ; sing praise upon the harp unto our God :

8 Who covereth the heaven with clouds, who prepareth rain for the earth, who maketh grass to grow upon the mountains.

9 He giveth to the beast his food, *and* to the young ravens which cry.

10 He delighteth not in the strength of the horse : he taketh not pleasure in the legs of a man.

11 The LORD taketh pleasure in them that fear him, in those that hope in his mercy.

7. In this paragraph the contrast announced in the former section is enlarged upon from another point of view, namely, as it is seen in nature and in providence.

" *Sing unto the* LORD *with thanksgiving*"; or rather, " respond to Jehovah." He speaks to us in his works, let us answer him with our thanks. All that he does is gracious, every movement of his hand is goodness ; therefore let our hearts reply with gratitude, and our lips with song. Our lives should be responses to divine love. Jehovah is ever engaged in giving, let us respond with thanksgiving.

" *Sing praise upon the harp unto our God.*" Blend music with song. Under a dispensation of ritual the use of music was most commendable, and suitable in the great corgregation : those of us who judge it to be less desirable for public worship, under a spiritual economy, because it has led to so many abuses, nevertheless rejoice in it in our privacy, and are by no means insensible to its charms. It seems a profanation that choice minstrelsy should so often be devoted to unworthy themes : the sweetest harmonies should be consecrated to the honour of the Lord. He is *our* God, and this fact is one choice joy of the sing. We have chosen him because he has chosen us ; and we see in him peculiarities which distinguish him from all the pretended deities of those among whom we dwell. He is *our* God in covenant relationship for ever and ever, and to him be praise in every possible form.

8. " *Who covereth the heaven with clouds.*" He works in all things, above as well as below. Clouds are not caused by accident, but produced by God himself, and made to assume degrees of density by which the blue firmament is hidden. A sky-scape might seem to be a mere fortuitous concourse of vapours, but it is not so : the Great Artist's hand thus covers the canvas of the heavens. " *Who prepareth rain for the earth.*" The Lord prepares clouds with a view to rain, and rain with an eye to the fields below. By many concurrent circumstances all things are made ready for the production of a shower ; there is more of art in the formation of a rain-cloud and in the fashioning of a rain-drop, than appears to superficial observers. God is in the vapour, and in the pearly drop which is born of it. " *Who maketh grass to grow upon the mountains.*" By the far-reaching shower he produces vegetation where the hand of man is all unknown. He cares not only for Goshen's fertile plains, but for Carmel's steep ascents. God makes the heavens the servants of the earth, and the clouds the irrigators of the mountain meadows. This is a kind of evolution about which there can be no dispute. Nor does the Lord forget the waste and desolate places, but causes the lone hills to be the first partakers of his refreshing visitations. This is after the manner of our God. He not only causes rain to descend from the heavens to water the grass, and thus unites the skies and the herbs by a ministry of mercy ; but he also thinks of the rocky ledges among the hills, and forgets not the pastures of the wilderness. What a God is this !

> " Passing by the rich and great,
> For the poor and desolate."

9. " *He giveth to the beast his food.*" By causing the grass to grow on the hills the Lord feeds the cattle. God careth for the brute creation. Men tread grass under foot as though it were nothing, but God causeth it to grow : too often men treat their cattle with cruelty, but the Lord himself feedeth them. The great God is too good, and, indeed, too great to overlook things that are despised. Say not, " Doth God care for oxen ?" Indeed he does, and he permits himself to be here described as giving them their food as husbandmen are wont to do. " *And to the young ravens which cry.*" These wild creatures, which seem to be of no use to man ; are they therefore worthless ? By no means ; they fill their place in the economy of nature. When they are mere fledgelings, and can only clamour to the parent birds for food, the Lord does not suffer them to starve, but supplies their needs. Is it not wonderful how such numbers of little birds are fed ! A bird in a cage under human care is in more danger of lacking seed and water than any one of the myriads that fly in the open heavens, with no owner but their Creator, and no provider but the Lord. Greatness occupied with little things makes up a chief feature of this psalm. Ought we not all to feel special joy in praising One who is so specially remarkable for his care of the needy and the forgotten ? Ought we not also to trust in the Lord ? for he who feeds the sons of the raven will surely nourish the sons of God ! Hallelujah to him who both feeds the ravens and rules the stars ! What a God art thou, O Jehovah !

10. " *He delighteth not in the strength of the horse.*" Not to great and strong animals doth the Creator in any measure direct his special thought ; but in lesser

living things he has equal pleasure. If man could act the Creator's part, he would take peculiar delight in producing noble quadrupeds like horses, whose strength and speed would reflect honour upon their maker ; but Jehovah has no such feeling ; he cares as much for helpless birds in the nest as for the war-horse in the pride of its power. *" He taketh not pleasure in the legs of a man."* These are the athlete's glory, but God hath no pleasure in them. Not the capacities of the creature, but rather its weakness and necessity, win the regard of our God. Monarchs trust in their cavalry and infantry ; but the King of kings exults not in the hosts of his creatures as though they could lend power to him. Physical or material greatness and power are of no account with Jehovah ; he has respect to other and more precious qualities. Men who boast in fight the valour of gigantic might, will not find themselves the favourites of God : though earthly princes may feast their eyes upon their Joabs and their Abners, their Abishais and Asahels, the Lord of hosts has no pleasure in mere bone and muscle. Sinews and thews are of small account, either in horses or in men, with Him who is a spirit, and delights most in spiritual things. The expression of the text may be viewed as including all creature power, even of a mental or moral kind. God does not take pleasure in us because of our attainments, or potentialities : he respects character rather than capacity.

11. *" The* LORD *taketh pleasure in them that fear him, in those that hope in his mercy."* While the bodily powers give no content to God, spiritual qualities are his delight. He cares most for those emotions which centre in himself : the fear which he approves is fear *of him*, and the hope which he accepts is hope *in his mercy*. It is a striking thought that God should not only be at peace with some kinds of men, but even find a solace and a joy in their company. Oh ! the matchless condescension of the Lord, that his greatness should take pleasure in the insignificant creatures of his hand. Who are these favoured men in whom Jehovah takes pleasure ? Some of them are the least in his family, who have never risen beyond hoping and fearing. Others of them are more fully developed, but still they exhibit a blended character composed of fear and hope : they fear God with holy awe and filial reverence, and they also hope for forgiveness and blessedness because of the divine mercy. As a father takes pleasure in his own children, so doth the Lord solace himself in his own beloved ones, whose marks of new birth are fear and hope. They fear, for they are sinners ; they hope, for God is merciful. They fear him, for he is great ; they hope in him, for he is good. Their fear sobers their hope ; their hope brightens their fear : God takes pleasure in them both in their trembling and in their rejoicing.

Is there not rich cause for praise in this special feature of the divine character ? After all, it is a poor nature which is delighted with brute force ; it is a diviner thing to take pleasure in the holy character of those around us. As men may be known by the nature of the things which give them pleasure, so is the Lord known by the blessed fact that he taketh pleasure in the righteous, even though that righteousness is as yet in its initial stage of fear and hope.

12 Praise the LORD, O Jerusalem ; praise thy God, O Zion.

13 For he hath strengthened the bars of thy gates ; he hath blessed thy children within thee.

14 He maketh peace *in* thy borders, *and* filleth thee with the finest of the wheat.

15 He sendeth forth his commandment *upon* earth : his word runneth very swiftly.

16 He giveth snow like wool : he scattereth the hoarfrost like ashes.

17 He casteth forth his ice like morsels ; who can stand before his cold ?

18 He sendeth out his word, and melteth them : he causeth his wind to blow, *and* the waters flow.

19 He sheweth his word unto Jacob, his statutes and his judgments unto Israel.

20 He hath not dealt so with any nation : and *as for his* judgments, they have not known them.   Praise ye the LORD.

12. "*Praise the Lord, O Jerusalem ; praise thy God, O Zion.*"   How the poet insists upon praise : he cries *praise, praise*, as if it were the most important of all duties.   A peculiar people should render peculiar praise.   The city of peace should be the city of praise ; and the temple of the covenant God should resound with his glories.   If nowhere else, yet certainly in Zion there should be joyful adoration of Zion's God.   Note, that we are to praise the Lord in our own houses in Jerusalem as well as in his own house in Zion.   The holy city surrounds the holy hill, and both are dedicated to the holy God, therefore both should ring with hallelujahs.

13. "*For he hath strengthened the bars of thy gates.*"   Her fortifications were finished, even to the fastenings of the gates, and God had made all sound and strong, even to her bolts and bars : thus her security against invading foes was guaranteed.   This is no small mercy.   Oh, that our churches were thus preserved from all false doctrine and unholy living !   This must be the Lord's doing ; and where he has wrought it his name is greatly to be praised.   Modern libertines would tear down all gates and abolish all bars ; but so do not we, because of the fear of the Lord.   "*He hath blessed thy children within thee.*"   Internal happiness is as truly the Lord's gift as external security.   When the Lord blesses "thy sons in the midst of thee," thou art, O Zion, filled with a happy, united, zealous, prosperous, holy people, who dwell in communion with God, and enter into the joy of their Lord.   When God makes thy walls salvation thy gates must be praise.   It would little avail to fortify a wretched, starving city ; but when the walls are strengthened, it is a still greater joy to see that the inhabitants are blessed with all good gifts.   How much our churches need a present and abiding benediction.

14. "*He maketh peace in thy borders.*"   Even to the boundaries quiet extends ; no enemies are wrangling with the borderers.   If there is peace there, we may be sure that peace is everywhere.   "When a man's ways please the Lord he maketh even his enemies to be at peace with him."   Peace is from the God of peace.   Considering the differing constitutions, conditions, tastes, and opinions of men, it is a work of God when in large churches unbroken peace is found year after year ; and it is an equal wonder if worldlings, instead of persecuting the godly, treat them with marked respect.   He who builds Zion is also her Peace-maker, the Lord and Giver of peace.   "*And filleth thee with the finest of the wheat.*"   Peace is attended with plenty,—plenty of the best food, and of the best sort of that food.   It is a great reason for thanksgiving when men's wants are so supplied that they are filled : it takes much to fill some men : perhaps none ever are filled but the inhabitants of Zion ; and they are only to be filled by the Lord himself.   Gospel truth is the finest of the wheat, and those are indeed blessed who are content to be filled therewith, and are not hungering after the husks of the world.   Let those who are filled with heavenly food fill their mouths with heavenly praise.

15. "*He sendeth forth his commandment upon earth.*"   His messages fly throughout his dominions : upon earth his warrants are executed as well as in heaven.   From his church his word goes forth ; from Zion he missions the nations with the word of life.   "*His word runneth very swiftly*" : his purposes of love are speedily accomplished.   Oriental monarchs laboured hard to establish rapid postal communication ; the desire, will, and command of the Lord flash in an instant from pole to pole, yea, from heaven to earth.   We who dwell in the centre of the Lord's dominions may exceedingly rejoice that to the utmost extremity of the realm the divine commandment speeds with sure result, and is not hindered by

distance or time. The Lord can deliver his people right speedily, or send them supplies immediately from his courts above. God's commands in nature and providence are fiats against which no opposition is ever raised ; say, rather, to effect which all things rush onward with alacrity. The expressions in the text are so distinctly in the present that they are meant to teach us the present mission and efficiency of the word of the Lord, and thus to prompt us to present praise.

16. Here follow instances of the power of God upon the elements. "*He giveth snow like wool.*" As a gift he scatters the snow, which falls in flakes like fleecy wool. Snow falls softly, covers universally, and clothes warmly, even as wool covers the sheep. The most evident resemblance lies in the whiteness of the two substances ; but many other likenesses are to be seen by the observant eye. It is wise to see God in winter and in distress as well as in summer and prosperity. He who one day feeds us with the finest of the wheat, at another time robes us in snow : he is the same God in each case, and each form of his operation bestows a gift on men. "*He scattereth the hoarfrost like ashes.*" Here again the Psalmist sees God directly and personally at work. As ashes powder the earth when men are burning up the rank herbage ; and as when men cast ashes into the air they cause a singular sort of whiteness in the places where they fall, so also does the frost. The country people talk of a black frost and a white frost, and the same thing may be said of ashes, for they are both black and white. Moreover, excessive cold burns as effectually as great heat, and hence there is an inner as well as an outer likeness between hoar-frost and ashes. Let us praise the Lord who condescends to wing each flake of snow and scatter each particle of rime. Ours is no absent or inactive deity : he worketh all things, and is everywhere at home.

17. "*He casteth forth his ice like morsels.*" Such are the crumbs of hail which he casts forth, or the crusts of ice which he creates upon the waters. These morsels are *his* ice, and *he* casts them abroad. The two expressions indicate a very real presence of God in the phenomena of nature. "*Who can stand before his cold?*" None can resist the utmost rigours of cold any more than they can bear the vehemence of heat. God's withdrawals of light are a darkness that may be felt, and his withdrawals of heat are a cold which is absolutely omnipotent. If the Lord, instead of revealing himself as a fire, should adopt the opposite manifestation of cold, he would, in either case, consume us should he put forth all his power. It is ours to submit to deprivations with patience, seeing the cold is *his* cold. That which God sends, whether it be heat or cold, no man can defy with impunity, but he is happy who bows before it with childlike submission. When we cannot stand before God we will gladly lie at his feet, or nestle under his wings.

18. "*He sendeth out his word, and melteth them.*" When the frost is sharpest, and the ice is hardest, the Lord intervenes ; and though he doth no more than send his word, yet the rocks of ice are dissolved at once, and the huge bergs begin to float into the southern seas. The phenomena of winter are not so abundant in Palestine as with us, yet they are witnessed sufficiently to cause the devout to bless God for the return of spring. At the will of God snow, hoar-frost, and ice disappear, and the time of the opening bud and the singing of birds has come. For this let us praise the Lord as we sun ourselves amid the spring flowers. "*He causeth his wind to blow, and the waters flow.*" The Lord is the great first cause of everything ; even the fickle, wandering winds are caused by him. Natural laws are in themselves mere inoperative rules, but the power emanates directly from the Ever-present and Ever-potent One. The soft gales from the south, which bring a general thaw, are from the Lord, as were those wintry blasts which bound the streams in icy bonds. Simple but effectual are the methods of Jehovah in the natural world ; equally so are those which he employs in the spiritual kingdom ; for the breath of his Holy Spirit breathes upon frozen hearts, and streams of penitence and love gush forth at once.

Observe how in these two sentences the word and the wind go together in nature. They attend each other in grace ; the gospel and the Holy Spirit cooperate in salvation. The truth which the Spirit breathed into prophets and apostles he breathes into dead souls, and they are quickened into spiritual life.

19. "*He sheweth his word unto Jacob, his statutes and his judgments unto Israel.*" He who is the Creator is also the Revealer. We are to praise the Lord above all things for his manifesting himself to us as he does not unto the world. Whatever part of his mind he discloses to us, whether it be a word of instruction, a statute of direction, or a judgment of government, we are bound to bless the Lord for it. He who causes summer to come in the place of winter has also removed the coldness and death from our hearts by the power of his word, and this is abundant cause for singing unto his name. As Jacob's seed of old were made to know the Lord, even so are we in these latter days; wherefore, let his name be magnified among us. By that knowledge Jacob is ennobled into Israel, and therefore let him who is made a prevailing prince in prayer be also a chief musician in praise. The elect people were bound to sing hallelujahs to their own God. Why were they so specially favoured if they did not, above all others, tell forth the glory of their God?

20. "*He hath not dealt so with any nation.*" Israel had clear and exclusive knowledge of God, while others were left in ignorance. Election is the loudest call for grateful adoration. "*And as for his judgments, they have not known them*"; or, "*and judgments they had not known them,*" as if not knowing the laws of God, they might be looked upon as having no laws at all worth mentioning. The nations were covered with darkness, and only Israel sat in the light. This was sovereign grace in its fullest noontide of power. "*Praise ye the Lord.*" When we have mentioned electing, distinguishing love, our praise can rise no higher, and therefore we close with one more hallelujah.

EXPLANATORY NOTES.

Whole Psalm.—The whole psalm is an invitation unto praising of God. Arguments therein are drawn, First, from God's *general goodness* to the world (verses 4, 8, 9, 16—18): Secondly, from his *special mercy to his Church.* 1. In *restoring* it out of a sad and broken condition (verses 2, 3). 2. In *confirming* it in a happy and prosperous estate, both temporal, in regard of strength, peace, and plenty (verses 12—14); and spiritual, in regard of his word, statutes, and judgments, made known unto them (verses 19, 20). Lastly, these mercies are all commended by the *manner* of bestowing them—*powerfully* and *swiftly.* He doth it by a word of command, and by a word of speed: "He sendeth forth his commandment upon earth: his word runneth very swiftly" (verse 15).

The temporal part of this happy estate, together with the manner of bestowing it, is herein described, but we must by no means exclude the spiritual meaning. And what can be wanting to a nation which is " strengthened " with walls, " blessed " with multitudes, hath " peace " in the border, " plenty " in the field, and, what is all in all, God in the sanctuary: God the bar of the " gate," the Father of the children, the crown of the " peace," the staff of the " plenty " ? They have a " gate " restored, a " city " blessed, a " border " quieted, a " field " crowned, a " sanctuary " beautified with the oracles of God. What can be wanting to such a people, but a mouth filled, a heart enlarged, a spirit exalted in the praises of the Lord ? " Praise the Lord, O Jerusalem; praise thy God, O Zion," etc. (verse 12).—*Edward Reynolds in a Sermon entitled " Sion's Praises,"* 1657.

Whole Psalm.—The God of Israel, what he has done, what he does, what he can do—this is the " *Hallelujah* " note of his song. So gladsome is the theme, that in verse 1 we find a contribution for it levied on Ps. xxxiii. 1, xcii. 1, and cxxxv. 3; each must furnish its quota of testimony to the desirableness of giving praise to such a God.—*Andrew A. Bonar.*

Verse 1.—" *Praise ye the Lord.*" *Alleluia.* An expression in sound very similar to this seems to have been used by many nations, who can hardly be supposed to have borrowed it from the Jews. Is it impossible that this is one of the most ancient expressions of devotion? From the Greeks using ἐλελεῦ ἰῇ, as a solemn beginning and ending of their hymns to Apollo, it should seem that they knew it; it is said also to have been heard among the Indians in America, and *Alla, Alla,* as the name of God, is used in great part of the East : also in composition. What might be the primitive stock which has furnished such spreading branches? —*Augustin Calmet,* 1672—1757.

Verse 1.— " *It is good to sing praises unto our God.*" Singing is necessarily included and recognised in the praise of psalms. That the joyful should sing is as natural as that the afflicted should pray—rather more natural. Song as the expression of cheerfulness is something universal in human nature; there were always, both in Israel and among all other nations, songs of joy. Hence it is constantly mentioned in the prophets, by whom joyous singing is used as a frequent figure, even as they threaten that God will take away the song of the bridegroom and the bride, and so forth. The *singing* of men is in itself good and noble. The same God who furnished the birds of heaven with the notes wherein they unconsciously praise their Creator, gave to man the power to sing. We all know how highly Luther, for example, estimated the gift and the art of song. Let him to whom it is granted rejoice therein; let him who lacks it seek, if possible, to excite it; for it is a good gift of the Creator. Let our children learn to sing in the schools, even as they learn to read. Our fathers sang more in all the affairs of life than we do; our tunes are in this respect less fresh, and artless, and joyous. There are many among us who never sing, except when adding their voices to the voice of the church,—and therefore they sing so badly there. Not that a harsh song from a good heart is unacceptable to God; but he should have our best. As David in his day took care that there should be practised singers for the sanctuary, we also should make provision for the church's service of song, that God may have in all respects a perfect offering. How gracious and lovely is the congregation singing with the heart acceptable songs!—*Rudolf Stier, in " The Epistle of James Expounded,"* 1859.

Verse 1.—The translation here is doubtful. It may either be rendered, " Praise the Lord for *he* is good," or, " for *it (praise)* is good." Why is it declared to be "*pleasant* " and " *comely* " to praise the Deity? Not only because if we glorify him he will also glorify us, but because he is so infinitely glorious that we are infinitely honoured simply in being reckoned worthy to worship One so great. —*John Lorinus.*

Verse 1.— " *It is good to sing praises unto our God ; for it is pleasant ; and praise is comely.*" These points are worthy of careful consideration.

I. To praise God is " *good* " for divers reasons. 1. That is good which God commands (Mic. vi. 8). So that thanksgiving is no indifferent action, no willworship, but it is *cultus institutus,* not to be neglected. 2. It raiseth the heart from earth to heaven; and being the work of angels and saints in heaven, joins us with that choir above. 3. It is good, again, because by it we pay, or at least acknowledge, a debt, and this is common justice. 4. Good, because for it we are like to receive a good and a great reward; for if he that prays to God is like to be rewarded (Matt. vi. 6), much more that man who sings praises to him; for in prayer we consult with our own necessities, in our praises we honour God, and bless him for his gifts.

II. To praise God is " *pleasant.*" 1. Because it proceeds out of love; for nothing is more pleasant to him that loves, than to make sonnets in the praise of that party he loves. 2. Because it must needs please a man to perform that duty for which he was created; for to that end God created men and angels, that they should praise him. 3. Because God is delighted with it, as the sweetest sacrifice (Ps. l. 23). 4. It is pleasant to God, because he is delighted with those virtues which are in us,—faith, hope, charity, religion, devotion, humility, etc., of all which our praises are a manifestation and exercise.

III. To praise God is " *comely* "; for there is no greater stain than ingratitude; it is made up of a lie and injustice. There is, then, all the decency in the world in praise, and it is comely that a man be thankful to his God, who freely gives him all things.— *William Nicholson.*

Verse 1.—David, to persuade all men to thankfulness, saith, " *It is a good and pleasant thing* " to be thankful. If he had said no more but " *good*," all which love goodness are bound to be thankful ; but when he saith not only " *good*," but " *pleasant* " too, all which love pleasure are bound to be thankful ; and therefore, as Peter's mother-in-law, so soon as Christ healed her of a fever, rose up immediately to minister unto him (Matt. viii. 15), so we, so soon as Christ hath done anything for us, should rise up immediately to serve him.—*Henry Smith.*

Verse 1.—There is no heaven, either in this world, or the world to come, for people who do not praise God. If you do not enter into the spirit and worship of heaven, how should the spirit and joy of heaven enter into you ? Selfishness makes long prayers, but love makes short prayers, that it may continue longer in praise.—*John Pulsford,* 1857.

Verse 1.—" *Praise.*" There is one other thing which is a serious embarrassment to praising through the song-service of the Church, and that is, that we have so few hymns of praise. You will be surprised to hear me say so ; but you will be more surprised if you take a real specimen of praising and search for hymns of praise. You shall find any number of hymns that talk about praise, and exhort you to praise. There is no lack of hymns that say that God ought to be praised. But of hymns that praise, and say nothing about it, there are very few indeed. And for what there are we are almost wholly indebted to the old churches. Most of them came down to us from the Latin and Greek Churches . . . There is no place in human literature where you can find such praise as there is in the Psalms of David.—*Henry Ward Beecher.*

Verse 2.—" *The Lord doth build up Jerusalem,*" etc. If this psalm were written on occasion of the return from Babylon, and the rebuilding of the earthly city, the ideas are to be transferred, as in other psalms of the same kind, to a more important restoration from a much worse captivity, and to the building up of the church under the gospel, when Christ " gathered together in one the children of God that were scattered abroad " (John xi. 52) ; that is, in the words of our psalm, he " *gathered together the outcasts of Israel.*" So shall he again, at the resurrection, " gather together his elect from the four winds " (Matt. xxiv. 31), and " build up a Jerusalem," in which they shall serve and praise him for ever.—*George Horne.*

Verse 2.—" *The Lord doth build up Jerusalem,*" etc.

> Jerusalem ! Jerusalem ! the blessing lingers yet
> On the city of the chosen, where the Sabbath seal was set ;
> And though her sons are scattered, and her daughters weep apart,
> While desolation, like a pall, weighs down each faithful heart ;
> As the plain beside the waters, as the cedar on the hills,
> She shall rise in strength and beauty when the Lord Jehovah wills :
> He has promised her protection, and the holy pledge is good,
> 'Tis whispered through the olive groves, and murmured by the flood,
> As in the Sabbath stillness the Jordan's flow is heard,
> And by the Sabbath breezes the hoary trees are stirred.
>
> —*Mrs. Hale, in " The Rhyme of Life."*

Verse 2—" *He gathereth together the outcasts of Israel.*" Wonder not that God calls together " *the outcasts,*" and singles them out from every corner for a return ; why can he not do this, as well as " tell the number of the stars, and call them all by their names " ? There are none of his people so despicable in the eye of man, but they are known and regarded by God. Though they are clouded in the world, yet they are the stars of the world ; and shall God number the inanimate stars in the heavens, and make no account of his living stars on the earth ? No ; wherever they are dispersed, he will not forget them : however they are afflicted, he will not despise them. The stars are so numerous that they are innumerable by man ; some are visible and known by men, others lie more hid and undiscovered in a confused light, as those in the milky way ; a man cannot see one of them distinctly. God knows all his people. As he can do what is above the power of man to perform, so he understands what is above the skill of man to discover.—*Stephen Charnock.*

Verse 2.—" *He gathereth together the outcasts of Israel.*" David might well have written feelingly about the " *outcasts,*" for he had himself been one ; and even from Jerusalem, in his age, when driven forth from thence by his unnatural son, he went up by the ascent of Olivet, weeping and barefooted, and other " *outcasts* " with him, weeping also as they went.—*Barton Bouchier.*

Verse 3.—" *He healeth the broken in heart,*" etc. Here are two things contained in this text ; the *patients* and the *physician.* The patients are the broken in heart. The physician is Christ ; it is he who bindeth up their wounds.

The patients here are felt and discerned to have two wounds or maladies ; brokenness of heart, and woundedness : he binds up such. Brokenness of heart presupposeth a former wholeness of heart. Wholeness of heart is twofold ; either wholeness of heart *in sin,* or wholeness of heart *from sin.* First, wholeness of heart *from sin* is when the heart is *without sin ;* and so the blessed angels have whole hearts, and so Adam and Eve, and we in them, before the fall, had whole hearts. Secondly, wholeness of heart *in sin ;* so the devils have whole hearts, and all men since the fall, from their conception till their conversion, have whole hearts ; and these are they that our Saviour intends,—" The whole need not the physician, but they that are sick.

Brokenness of heart may be considered two ways ; first, *in relation to wholeness of heart in sin :* so brokenness of heart is not a malady, but the commencement of the cure of a desperate disease. Secondly, *in relation to wholeness of heart from sin ;* and so it is a malady or sickness, and yet peculiar to one blood alone, namely, God's elect ; for though the heart be made whole in its desire towards God, yet it is broken for its sins. As a man that hath a barbed arrow shot into his side, and the arrow is plucked out of the flesh, yet the wound is not presently healed ; so sin may be plucked out of the heart, but the scar that was made with plucking it out is not yet cured. The wounds that are yet under cure are the plagues and troubles of conscience, the sighs and groans of a hungering soul after grace, the stinging poison that the serpent's fang hath left behind it ; these are the wounds.

Now the heart is broken three ways. First, *by the law ;* as it breaks the heart of a thief to hear the sentence of the law, that he must be hanged for his robbery ; so it breaks the heart of the soul, sensibly to understand the sentence of the law,—Thou shalt not sin ; if thou do, thou shalt be damned. If ever the heart come to be sensible of this sentence,—" Thou art a damned man," it is impossible to stand out under it, but it must break. " Is not my word like a hammer, that breaketh the rock in pieces ?" (Jer. xxiii. 29). Can any rock-heart hold out and not be broken with the blows of it ? Indeed, thus far a man may be broken, and yet be a reprobate ; for they shall all be thus broken in hell, and therefore this breaking is not enough.

Secondly, *by the Gospel ;* for if ever the heart come to be sensible of the love of the Gospel, it will break all to shatters. " Rend your heart ; for the Lord is gracious," etc. : Joel ii. 13. When all the shakes of God's mercy come, they all cry " Rend." Indeed, the heart cannot stand out against them, if it once feel them. Beat thy soul upon the gospel : if any way under heaven can break it, this is the way.

Thirdly, the heart is broken *by the skill of the minister* in the handling of these two, the law and the gospel : God furnisheth him with skill to press the law home, and gives him understanding how to put the gospel, and by this means doth God break the heart : for, alas, though the law be never so good a hammer, and although the gospel be never so fit an anvil, yet if the minister lay not the soul upon it the heart will not break : he must fetch a full stroke with the law, and he must set the full power of the gospel at the back of the soul, or else the heart will not break.

"*He healeth the broken in heart.*" Hence observe, that *Christ justifies and sanctifies;* for that is the meaning.

1. First, because *God hath given Christ grace to practise for the sake of the broken in heart;* and therefore if this be his grace, to heal the broken-hearted, certainly he will heal them. "The Spirit of the Lord is upon me," etc. He hath sent me to heal the broken-hearted," etc. : Luke iv. 18. If he be *created* master of this art, even for this purpose. to heal the broken in heart, he will verily heal them, and none but them. He is not like Hosander and Hippocrates, whose father appointed them both to be physicians ; he appointed his son Hippocrates to be a physician of horses, yet he proved a physician for men ; he appointed Hosander to be a physician for men, and he proved a physician for horses. Jesus is not like these ; no, no ; he will heal those whom he was appointed to heal.

2. Because *Christ hath undertaken to do it.* When a skilful physician hath undertaken a cure, he will surely do it : indeed, sometimes a good physician may fail, as Trajan's physician did, for he died under his hands ; on whose tomb this was written, "Here lies Trajan the emperor, that may thank his physician that he died." But if Christ undertake it, thou mayest be sure of it ; for he tells thee that art broken in heart that he hath undertaken it, he hath felt thy pulse already. Is. lvii. 15. He doth not only undertake it, but he saith he will go *visit* his sick patient, he will come to thy bedside, yea, he will come and dwell with thee all the time of thy sickness ; thou shalt never want anything, but he will be ready to help thee : thou needest not complain and say, "Oh, the physician is too far off, he will not come at me." I dwell in the high places indeed, saith God, but yet I will come and dwell with thee that art of an humble spirit. Thou needest not fear, saying, "Will a man cure his enemies ? I have been an enemy to God's glory, and will he yet cure me ?" Yea, saith Christ, if thou be *broken in heart* I will bind thee up.

3. Thirdly, because *this is Christ's charge,* and he will look to his own calling : "The Lord hath sent me to bind up the broken-hearted" (Isai. lxi. 1). . . . Neither needest thou fear thine own poverty, because thou hast not a fee to give him ; for thou mayest come to him by way of begging ; he will look to thee for nothing ; for, "To him will I look that is poor," etc. : Isai. lxvi. 2.

4. Fourthly, *none but the broken in heart will take physic of Christ.* Now this is a physician's desire, that his patient would cast himself upon him ; if he will not, the physician hath no desire to meddle with him. Now none but the broken in heart will take such physic as Christ gives, and therefore he saith, "To him will I look that is of a broken heart, and trembles at any words" : Isai. lvi. 2. When I bid him take such a purge, saith God, he trembles, and he takes it.—*William Fenner, in a Sermon entitled,* "*The Sovereign Virtue of the Gospel,*" 1647.

Verse 3.—

> O Thou who dry'st the mourner's tear,
>   How dark this world would be,
> If, when deceived and wounded here,
>   We could not fly to Thee !
> The friends, who in our sunshine live,
>   When winter comes are flown ;
> And he who has but tears to give
>   Must weep those tears alone.
> But Thou wilt heal that broken heart,
>   Which, like the plants that throw
> Their fragrance from the wounded part,
>   Breathes sweetness out of woe.
>
> When joy no longer soothes or cheers,
>   And e'en the hope that threw
> A moment's sparkle o'er our tears
>   Is dimmed and vanished too ;
> Oh ! who would bear life's stormy doom,
>   Did not Thy wing of love
> Come, brightly wafting through the gloom
>   Our peace-branch from above ?

Then sorrow, touched by Thee, grows bright
　　With more than rapture's ray;
As darkness shows us worlds of light
　　We never saw by day!

—Thomas Moore, 1779—1852.

Verse 3.—" He healeth the broken in heart." The broken in heart is one whose heart is affected with the evil of sin, and weeps bitter tears on account of it; one who feels sorrow, shame, and anguish, on the review of his past sinful life, and his base rebellion against a righteous God. Such a one has a broken heart. His heart is broken at the sight of his own ingratitude—the despite done by him to the strivings of the Holy Spirit. His heart is broken when he considers the numberless invitations made to him in the Scriptures, all of which he has wickedly slighted and despised. His heart is broken at the recollection of a thousand kind providences to him and to his family, by day and by night, all sent by God, and intended for his moral, spiritual, and eternal benefit, but by him basely and wantonly abused. His heart is broken at the consideration of the love and compassion of the adorable Redeemer; the humiliation of his birth; the devotedness of his life; the reproach, the indignity of his sufferings; the ignominy and anguish of his death. His heart is broken when his conscience assures him that all this humiliation, this suffering, this death, was for him, who had so deliberately and repeatedly refused the grace which the blood and righteousness of Christ has purchased. It is the sight of Calvary that fills him with anguish of spirit, that overwhelms him with confusion and self-abasement. While he contemplates the amazing scene, he stands, he weeps, he prays, he smites upon his breast, he exclaims, " God be merciful to me a sinner !" And adds, " O wretched man that I am, who shall deliver me from the body of this death ?"

The broken in heart must further be understood as one who seeks help from God alone, and will not be comforted till he speaks peace to his soul.

The act of God, in the scripture before us, is the moral and spiritual health of man—of man, who had brought disease on himself—of man, by his own rebellion against his Creator—of man, who had, in ten thousand ways, provoked the justice of heaven, and deserved only indignation and eternal wrath—the health of man, whom, in an instant, he could hurl to utter destruction. The saving health here proposed is the removal of all guilt, however contracted, and of all pollution, however rooted. It is the communication of God's favour, the riches of his grace, the implantation of his righteousness.

To effect the healing of the broken heart, God has, moreover, appointed a Physician, whose skill is infallible, whose goodness and care are equal to his skill. That Physician is none other than the Son of God. In that character has he been made known to us. " They that be whole need not a physician, but they that be sick." The prophet Isaiah introduces his advent in the most sublime language: " He hath sent me to bind up the broken-hearted, to proclaim liberty to the captives, and the opening of the prison to them that are bound."

The health, the moral and spiritual soundness of the soul, my brethren, is derived from the atoning sacrifice of Christ. The grace of God flows to the broken in heart through his manhood, his godhead, his righteousness, his truth; through his patience, his humility, his death and passion; through his victory over sin, his resurrection, and ascension into heaven. Here, thou broken in heart, thou sorrowing, watching penitent; here is the medicine, here the Physician, here the cure, here the health thou art seeking.

The healing of the broken in heart must be further understood as effected through the agency of the Holy Spirit. It is done by the Spirit of God, that it may be done, and that it may be well done; and that all the praise, the glory of that which is done, may be ascribed to the plenitude, the freeness, the sovereignty of his grace. The Spirit of God, however, uses means. The means of grace are appointed expressly for this purpose; the blessing of health is there applied. There, under the sound of the everlasting gospel, while looking by faith to Christ, and appropriating his merits, he healeth the broken in heart. There, while commemorating the dying love of Christ, and applying its benefits by faith to the soul, he healeth the broken in heart. There, while the soul, sensible of his goodness, is offering up the song of praise, and trusting alone in his mercy, he healeth the broken in heart. There, while prostrate at his footstool, supplicating his grace, resting on his finished redemption, he healeth the broken in heart. In the private acts of devotion the Spirit of God also is near to bless and save. There, while reading and believing his holy Word, while meditating on its meaning; there, while in secret, solemn prayer, the soul takes hold on God in Christ Jesus; he healeth the broken in heart.—*Condensed from a Sermon by Thomas Blackley,* 1826.

Verse 3.—"*He healeth the broken in heart.*" I do indeed most sincerely sympathise with you in this fresh sorrow. "Thy breaking waves pass over me." The trial, so much the heavier that it is not the first breaking in, but the waters continuing still, and continuing to rise, until deep calleth unto deep at the noise of God's water-spouts, "Yea, and thy billows all." In such circumstances, we are greatly tempted to wonder if it be true, of the Holy One in the midst of us, that a bruised reed he will not break, that the smoking flax he will not quench. We may not, however, doubt it, nor even in the day of our grief and our desperate sorrow, are we at liberty to call it in question. Our God is the God of the broken heart. The deeper such a heart is smitten, and the more it bleeds, the more precious it is in his sight, the nearer he draws to it, the longer he stays there. " I dwell with him who is of a contrite heart." The more abundantly will he manifest the kindness and the glory of his power, in tenderly carrying it in his bosom, and at last binding up its painful wounds. " He healeth the broken in heart." " O, thou afflicted, tossed with tempest, and not comforted, behold, I will lay thy stones with fair colours, and lay thy foundations with sapphires." Weeping Naomi said, " Call me Marah, for the Lord hath dealt very bitterly with me." Afterwards, happy Naomi took the child of her own Ruth, and laid it in her bosom, and sweetly found that the days of her mourning were ended.

My dear friend, this new gash of deep sorrow was prepared for you by the Ancient of Days. His Son—and that Son is love—watched over the counsels of old, to keep and to perform them to the minutest circumstance.—*John Jameson,* 1838.

Verse 4.—" *He telleth the number of the stars,*" etc. In which similitude he showeth, that albeit Abraham could not comprehend the multitude of the children, either of his faith or of his flesh, more than he could count the number of the stars; yet the Lord knoweth every believer by name, as he knoweth every star and can call every one by its name.—*David Dickson.*

Verse 4.—" *He telleth the number of the stars,*" etc. Among the heathen every constellation represented some god. But the Scriptures show Jehovah, not as one of many starry gods, but as the one God of all the stars. He is, too, as he taught his people by Abraham, the God of a firmament of nobler stars. His people are scattered and trodden as the sands of the sea-shore. But he turns dust and dirt to stars of glory. He will make of every saint a star, and Heaven is his people's sky, where broken-hearted sufferers of earth are glorified into glittering galaxies.—*Hermann Venema.*

Verse 4.—" *He calleth them all by their names.*" Literally, " calleth names to all of them," an expression marking not only God's power in marshalling them all as a host (Is. xl. 26), but also the most intimate knowledge and watchful care, as that of a shepherd for his flock. John x. 3.—*J. J. Stewart Perowne.*

Verse 4.—" *He calleth them all by their names.*" They render a due obedience to him, as servants to their master. When he singles them out and calls them by name to do some official service, he calls them out to their several offices, as the general of an army appoints the station of every regiment in a battalion; or, " *he calls them by name,*" *i. e.* he imposeth names upon them, a sign of dominion, the giving names to the inferior creatures being the first act of Adam's derivative dominion over them. These are under the sovereignty of God. The stars by their influences fight against Sisera (Jud. v. 20) ; and the sun holds in its reins, and stands stone-still to light Joshua to a complete victory : Josh. x. 12. They are all marshalled in their ranks to receive his word of command, and fight in close order, as being desirous to have a share in the ruin of the enemies of their sovereign.—*Stephen Charnock.*

Verse 4.—The immense distance at which the nearest stars are known to be placed, proves that they are bodies of a prodigious size, not inferior to our own sun, and that they shine, not by reflected rays, but by their own native light. But bodies encircled with such refulgent splendour, would be of little use in Jehovah's empire, unless surrounding worlds were cheered by their benign influence, and enlightened by their beams. Every star is therefore concluded to be a sun surrounded by planetary globes. Nearly a thousand of these luminaries may be seen in a clear winter's night by the naked eye. But these do not form the eighty-thousandth part of what may be descried by the help of telescopes. While Dr. Herschel was exploring the most crowded part of the milky way, in one quarter of an hour's time no less than 116,000 stars passed through the field of view of his telescope. It has been computed, that nearly one hundred millions of stars might be perceived by our most perfect instruments, if all the regions of the sky were thoroughly explored. But immeasurable regions of space lie beyond the utmost boundaries of human vision, even thus assisted, into which imagination itself can scarcely penetrate, but which are doubtless filled with operations of divine wisdom and divine omnipotence.—*Thomas Dick, in " The Christian Philosopher."*

Verse 5.—" *His understanding is infinite.*" Hebrew : " *Of his understanding there is no number.*" God is incomprehensible. In *place ;* in *time ;* in *understanding ;* in *love.* First, in *place ;* because no place, no space, can be imagined so great, but God exceeds it, and may be found beyond it. Secondly, in *time ;* because he exceeds all time : for he was before all time that can be conceived, and shall be after all time. Time is a created thing, to attend upon the creation and continuance of all things created and continued by God. Thirdly, in *understanding ;* because no created understanding can comprehend him so that nothing of God may be hid from it. Fourthly, in *love* because God doth exceed all love : no creature can love God according to his worth. All these ways of incomprehensibleness follow upon his infiniteness.—*Thomas Larkham, in " The Attributes of God Unfolded, and Applied,"* 1656.

Verse 5.—" *His understanding is infinite.*" The Divine wisdom is said to be " *without number* " ; that is, the objects of which this wisdom of God can take cognisance are innumerable.—*Simon de Muis.*

Verse 5.—In this verse we have three of God's attributes, his greatness, his power, and his knowledge ; and though only the last of these be expressly said to be *infinite,* yet is the same implied also of the two former ; for all the perfections of God being essential to him, must need be infinite as he himself is ; and therefore what is affirmed of one must, by a parity of reason, be extended to the rest.—*John Conant,* 1608—1693.

Verse 6.—" *The Lord lifteth up the meek,*" etc. The meek need not envy the lofty who sweep the earth with their gay robes, any more than real royalty is jealous of the kingly hero who struts his hour upon the stage. They shall be princes and rulers long after these actors have laid aside their tinselled crowns.

How wonderful shall be the reversal when God shall place the last first and the first last ! Moralists have often pointed us to the ruler of a hundred broad kingdoms lying down at last in six feet of imprisoning clay ; but God shall show us the wayside cottager lifted into the inheritance of the universe.—*Evangelical Magazine.*

Verses 7—9. God creates, and then fails not to supply. Analogically, the Lord buildeth Jerusalem, and provides for the wants of the inhabitants ; by spiritual inference, the saints argue that Christ establishes his church and gives all the gracious gifts which are needed in that institution.— *John Lorinus.*

Verses 8, 9.—"*Mountains . . . ravens.*" Wonderful Providence which takes cognisance of the mountainous and the minute alike. The All-Provider descends from august and sublime heights to save the meanest creature from starvation—extending constant care to the wants of even those abject little objects, the young ravens, Heb. "the sons of the raven."—*Martin Geier.*

Verse 8.—"*Clouds. . . . rain. . . . grass.*" There is a mutual dependence and subordination between all second causes. The creatures are serviceable to one another by mutual ministries and supplies ; the earth is cherished by the heat of the heavens, moistened by the water, and by the temperament of both made fruitful ; and so sendeth forth innumerable plants for the comfort and use of living creatures, and living creatures are for the supply of man. It is wonderful to consider the subordination of all causes, and the proportion they bear to one another. The heavens work upon the elements, the elements upon the earth, and the earth yieldeth fruits for the use of man. The prophet taketh notice of this admirable gradation : "I will hear the heavens, and the heavens shall hear the earth ; and the earth shall hear the corn, and the wine, and the oil ; and the corn, and the wine, and the oil, shall hear Jezreel" (Hosea ii. 21, 22). We look to the fields for the supplies of corn, wine, and oil ; but they can do nothing without clouds, and the clouds can do nothing without God. The creatures are beholden to one another, and all to God. In the order of the world there is an excellent chain of causes, by which all things hang together, that so they may lead up the soul to the Lord.— *Thomas Manton.*

Verse 8.—"*Who prepareth rain ?*" The rain-cloud parts with its contents only when God commands it, and *as* he commands, whether in the soft gentle shower or in the drenching downpour that floods the fields and obstructs the labours of the husbandman.— *Thomas Robinson, in "Homiletical Commentary on the Book of Job,"* 1876.

Verse 8.—"*Who maketh grass to grow upon the mountains.*" The wild grasses are taken, as it were, under the special providence of God. In the perennial verdure in regions above the zone of man's cultivation, we have a perpetual proof of God's care of the lower animals that neither sow nor reap. The mountain grasses grow spontaneously ; they require no culture but such as the rain and the sunshine of heaven supply. They obtain their nourishment directly from the inorganic soil, and are independent of organic materials. Nowhere is the grass so green and vigorous as on the beautiful slopes of lawn-like pasture high up in the Alps, radiant with the glory of wild flowers, and ever musical with the hum of grasshoppers, and the tinkling of cattle-bells. Innumerable cows and goats browse upon them ; the peasants spend their summer months in making cheese and hay from them for winter consumption in the valleys. This exhausting system of husbandry has been carried on during untold centuries ; no one thinks of manuring the Alpine pastures ; and yet no deficiency has been observed in their fertility, though the soil is but a thin covering spread over the naked rocks. It may be regarded as a part of the same wise and gracious arrangement of Providence, that the insects which devour the grasses on the *Kuh* and *Schaf Alpen,* the pasturages of the cows and sheep, are kept in check by a predominance of carnivorous insects. In all the mountain meadows it has been ascertained that the species of carnivorous are at least four times as numerous as the species of herb-eating insects. Thus, in the absence of birds, which are rare in Switzerland, the pastures are preserved from a terrible scourge. To one not aware of this check, it may seem surprising how the verdure of the Alpine pastures should be so rich and luxuriant considering the immense development of insect life. The grass, whenever the sun shines, is literally covered with them—butterflies of gayest hues, and beetles of brightest iridescence ; and the air is filled with their loud murmurs. I remember well the vivid feeling of God's gracious providence, which possessed me when passing over the beautiful Wengern Alp at the foot of the Jungfrau, and seeing, wherever I rested on the green turf, alive with its tiny inhabitants, the balance of nature so wonderfully preserved between the herb which is for man's food and the moth before which he is crushed. Were the herbivorous insects allowed to multiply to their full extent, in such favourable circumstances as the warmth of the air and the verdure of the earth in Switzerland produce, the rich pastures which now yield abundant food for upwards of a million and a half of cattle would speedily become bare and leafless deserts. Not only in their power of growing without cultivation, but also in the peculiarities of their structure, the mountain grasses proclaim the hand of God. Many of them are viviparous. Instead of producing flowers and seed, as the grasses in the tranquil valleys do, the young plants spring from them perfectly formed. They cling round the stem and form a kind of blossom. In this state they remain until the parent stalk withers and falls prostrate on the ground, when they immediately strike root and form independent grasses. This is a remarkable adaptation to circumstances ; for it is manifest that were seeds instead of living plants developed in the ears of the mountain grasses, they would be useless in the stormy regions where they grow. They would be blown away far from the places they were intended to clothe, to spots foreign to their nature and habits, and thus the species would speedily perish.

The more we think of it, the more we are struck with the wise foresight which suggested the creative fiat, " Let the earth bring forth grass." It is the most abundant and the most generally diffuse of all vegetation. It suits almost every soil and climate.—*Hugh Macmillan, in " Bible Teachings in Nature,"* 1868.

Verses 8, 9.—The Hebrews had no notion of what we denominate " secondary laws," but believed that God acted directly upon matter, and was the immediate, efficient cause of the solemn order, and the varied and wonderful phenomena of nature. Dispensing thus with the whole machinery of cause and effect, as we employ those terms in philosophical language, their minds were brought into immediate contact with God in his manifold works, and this gave, both to devotion and the spirit of poetry, the liveliest inspiration and the freest scope of action. Heaven and earth were governed by his commands ; the thunder was his " voice," the lightning his " arrows." It is he who " causeth the vapour to ascend from the ends of the earth." When the famished city should call upon the corn, the wine, and the oil, and those should call upon the earth for nourishment, and the parched earth should call upon the heavens for moisture, and the heavens should call upon the Lord for permission to refresh the earth, then Jehovah would hear and supply. He gave the rain, and he sent the drought and famine. The clouds were not looked upon merely as sustained by a law of specific gravity, but God spread them out in the sky ; these clouds were God's chariot, the curtains of his pavilion, the dust of his feet. Snow and hail were fearful manifestations of God, often sent as the messengers of his wrath.—*F. G. Hubbard, in " Bate's Encyclopædia,"* 1865.

Verses 8, 9.—God by his special providence prepares *"food"* for those who have no other care taken for them. *" Beasts "* that live among men are by men taken care of ; they enrich the ground with manure, and till the ground ; and that brings forth corn for the use of these cattle as well as men. But the *wild beasts* that live upon the *mountains,* and in the woods and desert places, are fed only from the heavens : the *" rain "* that from thence distils enricheth those dry hills and *" maketh grass to grow "* there, which else would not, and so God giveth to these *wild beasts* their food after the same manner of Divine Providence as in the end of the verse he is said to provide for the *" young ravens."*—*Henry Hammond.*

Verse 9.—*" The young ravens cry."* The strange stories told by Jewish and Arabian writers, on the raven's cruelty to its young, in driving them out of their nests before they are quite able to provide for themselves, are entirely without foundation, as no bird is more careful of its young ones than the raven. To its habit of flying restlessly about in search of food to satisfy its own appetite and that of its young ones, may perhaps be traced the reason of its being selected by the sacred writers as an especial object of God's protecting care.—*W. Houghton, in "The Bible Educator."*

Verse 9.—"*The young ravens cry.*" While still unfledged the young ravens have a strange habit of falling out of their nests, and flapping their wings heavily to the ground. Next morning they are found by the shepherds sitting croaking on the ground beneath their former homes, and are then captured and taken away with comparative ease.—*J. G. Wood, in "The Illustrated Natural History,"* 1869.

Verse 9.—"*The young ravens cry.*" The evening proceedings and manœuvres of the rooks are curious and amusing in the autumn. Just before dusk they return in long strings from the foraging of the day, and rendezvous by thousands over Selbourne-down, where they wheel round in the air, and sport and dive in a playful manner, all the while exerting their voices, and making a loud cawing, which, being blended and softened by the distance that we at the village are below them, becomes a confused noise or chiding ; or rather a pleasing murmur, very engaging to the imagination, and not unlike the cry of a pack of hounds in hollow, echoing woods, or the rushing of the wind in tall trees, or the tumbling of the tide upon a pebbly shore. When this ceremony is over, with the last gleam of day, they retire for the night to the deep beechen woods of Tisted and Ropley. We remember a little girl, who, as she was going to bed, use to remark on such an occurrence, in the true spirit of physico-theology, that the rooks were saying their prayers, and yet this child was much too young to be aware that the Scriptures had said of the Deity that " He feedeth the ravens that call upon him." —*Gilbert White* (1720—1793), *in " The Natural History of Selborne.*

Verse 9.—

> Behold, and look away your low despair ;
> See the light tenants of the barren air :
> To them, nor stores, nor granaries belong,
> Nought but the woodlands and the pleasing song ;
> Yet, your kind heavenly Father bends his eye
> On the least wing that flits along the sky.
> To him they sing when Spring renews the plain ;
> To him they cry in Winter's pinching reign ;
> Nor is the music, nor their plaint, in vain.
> He hears the gay, and the distressful call,
> And with unsparing bounty fills them all.
> Will he not care for you, ye faithless, say ?
> Is he unwise ? Or, are ye less than they ?

—James Thomson, 1700—1748.

Verse 9.—It is related of Edward Taylor, the sailor-preacher of Boston, that on the Sunday before he was to sail for Europe, he was entreating the Lord to care well for his church during his absence. All at once he stopped, and ejaculated, " What have I done ? Distrust the Providence of heaven ! A God that gives a whale a ton of herrings for a breakfast, will he not care for my children ?" and then went on, closing his prayer in a more confiding manner.—*From " Eccentric Preachers," by C. H. S.*

Verse 10.—The two clauses of this verse are probably intended to describe *cavalry* and *infantry*, as forming the military strength of nations. It is not to those who trust in such resources that Jehovah shows favour, but to those who rely on his protection (verse 11).—*Annotated Paragraph Bible.*

Verses 10, 11.—When a sinner is brought upon his knees, and becomes a suppliant, when as he is laid low by affliction, so he lieth low in prayer and supplication, then the Lord will be favourable to him, and show his delight in him. " *The Lord delighteth not in the strength of the horse : he taketh not pleasure in the legs of a man.*" No man is favoured by God because of his outward favour, because he hath a beautiful face, or strong, clean limbs ; yea, not only hath the Lord no pleasure in any man's legs, but not in any man's brains, how reaching soever, nor in any man's wit how quick soever, nor in any man's judgment how deep soever, nor in any man's tongue how eloquent or well spoken soever ; but " *The Lord taketh pleasure in them that fear him, in those that hope in his mercy,*" in those that walk humbly with him, and call upon him. . . . All the beauties and rarities both of persons and things are dull and flat, yea, wearisome and loathsome to God, in comparison of a gracious, honest, humble soul. Princes have their favourites (Job xxxiii. 26) ; they are favourable to some above many, either because they are beautiful and goodly persons, or because they are men of excellent speech, prudence and deportment. All godly men are God's favourites ; he is favourable to them not only above many men in the world, but above all the men of this world, who have their portion in this life ; and he therefore favours them, because they are the purchase of his Son and the workmanship of his Spirit, convincing them of, and humbling them for, their sins, as also creating them after God in righteousness and true holiness. Such shall be his favourites.—*Joseph Caryl.*

Verse 11.—" *Them that fear him, those that hope in his mercy.*" Patience and fear are the fences of hope. There is a beautiful relation between hope and fear. The two are linked in this verse. They are like the cork in a fisherman's net, which keeps it from sinking, and the lead, which prevents it from floating. Hope without fear is in danger of being too sanguine ; fear without hope would soon become desponding.—*George Seaton Bowes, in " In Prospect of Sunday;*" 1880.

Verse 11.—" *Them that fear him, those that hope in his mercy.*" A sincere Christian is known by both these ; a fear of God, or a constant obedience to his commands, and an affiance, trust, and dependence upon his mercies. Oh, how sweetly are both these coupled, a uniform sincere obedience to him, and an unshaken constant reliance on his mercy and goodness ! The whole perfection of the Christian life is comprised in these two—believing God and fearing him, trusting in his mercy and fearing his name ; the one maketh us careful in avoiding sin, the other diligent to follow after righteousness ; the one is a bridle from sin and temptations, the other a spur to our duties. Fear is our curb, and hope our motive and encouragement ; the one respects our duty, and the other our comfort ; the one allayeth the other. God is so to be feared, as also to be trusted ; so to be trusted, as also to be feared ; and as we must not suffer our fear to degenerate into legal bondage, but hope in his mercy, so our trust must not degenerate into carnal sloth and wantonness, but so hope in his word as to fear his name. Well, then, such as both believe in God and fear to offend him are the only men who are acceptable to God and his people. God will take pleasure in them, and they take pleasure in one another.—*Thomas Manton.*

Verse 11.—" *Fear* " and " *Hope* " are the great *vincula* of Old Testament theology, bracketing and including in their meaning all its ideas.—*Thomas Le Blanc.*

Verse 11.—*Fear* and *hope* are passions of the mind so contrary the one to the other, that with regard to the same object, it is strange they should meet in the same laudable character ; yet here we see they do so, and it is the praise of the same persons, that they both fear God, and hope in him. Whence we may gather this doctrine : That in every concern that lies upon our hearts, we should still endeavour to keep the balance even between hope and fear.

We know how much the health of the body depends upon a due temperament of the humours, such as preserves any one from being predominant above the rest ; and how much the safety and peace of the nations result from a due balance of trade and power, that no one grow too great for its neighbours ; and so necessary is it to the health and welfare of our souls, that there be a due proportion maintained between their powers and passions, and that the one may always be a check upon the other, to keep it from running into extremes ; as in these affections mentioned in the text. A holy fear of God must be a check upon our hope, to keep that from swelling into presumption ; and a pious hope in God must be a check upon our fear, to keep that from sinking into despondency. This balance must, I say, by a wise and steady hand, be kept even in every concern that lies upon our hearts, and that we have thoughts about. I shall enumerate those that are of the greatest importance. We must keep up both hope and fear. 1. As to the concerns of our souls, and our spiritual and eternal state. 2. As to our outward concerns, relating to the body and the life that now is. 3. As to the public concerns of the church of God, and our own land and nation.

In reference to each of these, we must always study and strive to support that affection, whether it be hope or fear, which the present temper of our minds and circumstances of our case make necessary to preserve us from an extreme.—*Matthew Henry.*

Verse 12.—That all Creation must involuntarily praise the Lord, and that the primary duty of conscious intelligence is the willing praise of the same Deity, are the two *axioms* of the Psalmist's theology. He has in the first part of this psalm been stating the first, and now he is about to announce the second.—*Martin Geier.*

Verse 13.—" *He hath strengthened the bars of thy gates.*"—Blessed is the city whose gates God barreth up with his power, and openeth again with his mercy. There is nothing can defend where his justice will strike ; and there is nothing can offend where his goodness will preserve.—*Thomas Adams.*

Verses 13, 14.—The psalmist recites four arguments from which he would have Zion sing praises. 1. Security and defence. 2. Benediction. 3. Peace. 4. Sustenance or provision.

1. *Security.* Jerusalem is a city secure, being defended by God : " *For he hath strengthened the bars of thy gates.*" Gates and bars do well to a city, but then only is the city secure when God makes them strong. The true munition of a city is God's defence of it. Arms, laws, wealth, etc., are the bars, but God must put strength into them.

2. *Benediction.* Jerusalem is a happy city, for "*he hath blessed thy children within thee,*" thy kings, princes, magistrates, &c., with wisdom, piety, &c.

3. *Peace.* Jerusalem is a peaceable city. " *He maketh peace in thy borders,*" the very name intimates so much ; for Jerusalem interpreted is *visio pacis*—Vision of peace.

4. *Abundance.* Jerusalem is a city provided by God with necessary food and provision ; for " *He filleth thee with the finest of the wheat.*"— *William Nicholson.*

Verse 14.—" *He maketh peace in thy borders,*" etc. There is a political peace—peace in city and country ; this is the fairest flower of a Prince's crown ; peace is the best blessing of a nation. It is well with bees when there is a noise ; but it is best with Christians when, as in the building of the Temple, there is no noise of hammer heard. Peace brings plenty along with it ; how many miles would some go on pilgrimage to purchase this peace ! Therefore the Greeks made Peace to be the nurse of Pluto, the God of wealth. Political plants thrive best in the sunshine of peace. " *He maketh peace in thy borders, and filleth thee with the finest of the wheat.*" The ancients made the harp the emblem of peace : how sweet would the sounding of this harp be after the roaring of the cannon ! All should study to promote this political peace. The godly man, when he dies, " enters into peace " (Isai. lvii. 2) ; but while he lives, peace must enter into him.—*Thomas Watson.*

Verse 14.—" *He maketh peace.*" The Hebrews observe that all the letters in the name of God are *literæ quiescentes,* letters of rest. God only is the centre where the soul may find rest : God only can speak peace to the conscience.—*John Stoughton.*—1639.

Verse 14.—" *Finest of the wheat.*" If men give much it is in cheap and coarse commodity. Quantity and quality are only possible with human production *in in verse ratio ;* but the Lord gives the *most* and *best* of all supplies to his pensioners. How truly the believer under the gospel knows the inner spirit of the meaning here ! The Lord Jesus Christ says, " My peace I give unto you." And when he sets us at rest and all is reconciliation and peace, then he feeds us with *himself*—his body, the finest wheat, and his blood, the richest wine.—*Johannes Paulus Palanterius.*

Verse 15.—" *His word runneth very swiftly.*" There is not a moment between the shooting out of the arrow and the fastening of it in the mark ; both are done in the very same atom and point of time. Therefore we read in the Scripture of the immediate effects of the word of Christ. Saith he to the leprous man, " Be thou clean. And immediately his leprosy was cleansed " : Matt. viii. 3. And to the blind man, " Go thy way ; thy faith hath made thee whole. And immediately he received his sight " ; Mark x. 52. No arrow makes so immediate an impression in the mark aimed at as the arrow of Christ's word. No sooner doth Christ say to the soul, Be enlightened, be quickened, be comforted, but the work is done. —*Ralph Robinson.*

Verse 16.—" *He giveth snow like wool.*" There are three things considerable in snow, for which it is compared to wool. First, for the *whiteness* of it. Snow is white as wool ; snow is so exceeding white that the whiteness of a soul cleansed by pardoning grace, in the blood of Christ, is likened unto it (Isai. i. 18) ; and the latter part of the same verse intimates that the whiteness of snow bears resemblance to that of wool. The whiteness of snow is caused by the abundance of air and spirits that are in that pellucid body, as the naturalists speak. Any thing that is of a watery substance, being frozen or much wrought upon by cold, appears more white ; and hence it is that all persons inhabiting cold climates or countries, are of a whiter complexion than they who inhabit hot. Secondly, snow is like wool for *softness*, 'tis pliable to the hand as a lock or fleece of wool. Thirdly, snow is like wool (which may seem strange) with respect to the *warmness* of it. Though snow be cold in itself, yet it is to the earth as wool, or as a woollen cloth or blanket that keeps the body warm. Snow is not warm formally, yet it is warm effectively and virtually ; and therefore is it compared to wool.—*Joseph Caryl.*

Verse 16.—" *Like wool.*" Namely, curled and tufted, and as white as the snow in those countries. Isai. i. 18 ; Rev. i. 14.—*John Diodati.*

Verse 16.—" *Snow like wool.*" The ancients used to call *snow εριωδες υδωρ, woolly water* (Eustathius, in Dionys. Perieget. p. 91). Martial gives it the name of *densum vellus aquarum, a thick fleece of waters* (Epigram. l. iv. Ep. 3). Aristophanes calls clouds, *flying fleeces of wool* " (Nubes, p. 146). Pliny calls it *the froth of the celestial waters* (Nat. His. lib. xvii. cap. 2).—*Samuel Burder.*

Verse 16.—" *He giveth snow like wool.*" In Palestine snow is not the characteristic feature of winter as it is in northern latitudes. It is merely an occasional phenomenon. Showers of it fall now and then in severer seasons on the loftier parts of the land, and whiten for a day or two the vineyards and cornfields : but it melts from the green earth as rapidly as its sister vapours vanish from the blue sky. . . . But the Psalmist seized the occasional snow, as he seized the fleeting vapour, and made it a text of his spiritual meditations. Let us follow his example.

" *He giveth snow like wool,*" says the Psalmist. This comparison expressly indicates one of the most important purposes which the snow serves in the economy of nature. It covers the earth like a blanket during that period of winter sleep which is necessary to recruit its exhausted energies, and prepare it for fresh efforts in the spring ; and being, like wool, a bad conductor, it conserves the latent heat of the soil, and protects the dormant life of plant and animal hid under it from the frosty rigour of the outside air. Winter-sown wheat, when defended by this covering, whose under surface seldom falls much below 32 Fahr., can thrive even though the temperature of the air above may be many degrees below the freezing-point. Our country, enjoying an equable climate, seldom requires this protection ; but in northern climates, where the winter is severe and prolonged, its beneficial effects are most marked. The scanty vegetation which blooms with such sudden and marvellous loveliness in the height of summer, in the Arctic regions and on mountain summits, would perish utterly were it not for the protection of the snow that lies on it for three quarters of a year.

But it is not only to Alpine plants and hybernating animals that God gives snow like wool. The esquimaux take advantage of its curious protective property, and ingeniously build their winter huts of blocks of hardened snow ; thus, strangely enough, by a homœopathic law, protecting themselves against cold by the effects of cold. The Arctic navigator has been often indebted to walls of snow banked up around his ship for the comparative comfort of his winter quarters, when the temperature without has fallen so low that even chloric ether became solid. And many a precious life has been saved by the timely shelter which the snow-storm itself has provided against its own violence. But while snow thus warms in cold regions, it also cools in warm regions. It sends down from the white summits of equatorial mountains its cool breath to revive and brace the drooping life of lands sweltering under a tropic sun ; and from its lofty inexhaustible reservoirs it feeds perennial rivers that water the plains when all the wells and streams are white and silent in the baking heat. Without the perpetual snow of mountain regions the earth would be reduced to a lifeless desert.

And not only does the Alpine snow thus keep always full rivers that water the plains, but, by its grinding force as it presses down the mountains, it removes particles from the rocks, which are carried off by the rivers and spread over the plains. Such is the origin of a large part of the level land of Europe. It has been formed out of the ruins of the mountains by the action of snow. It was by the snow of far-off ages that our valleys and lake-basins were scooped out, the form of our landscapes sculptured and rounded, and the soil formed in which we grow our harvests. Who would think of such a connection ? And yet it is true ! Just as each season we owe the bloom and brightness of our summer fields to the gloom and blight of winter, so do we owe the present summer beauty of the world to the great secular winter of the glacial period. And does not God bring about results as striking by agencies apparently as contradictory in the human world ? He who warms the tender latent life of the flowers by the snow, and moulds the quiet beauty of the summer landscape by the desolating glacier, makes the cold of adversity to cherish the life of the soul, and to round into spiritual loveliness the harshness and roughness of a carnal, selfish nature. Many a profitable Christian life owes its fairness and fruitfulness to causes which wrecked and wasted it for a time. God giveth snow like wool ; and chill and blighting as is the touch of sorrow, it has a protective influence which guards against greater evils ; it sculptures the spiritual landscape within into forms of beauty and grace, and deepens and fertilizes the soil of the heart, so that in it may grow from God's own planting the peaceable fruits of righteousness.

And now let us look at the Giver of the snow. " He giveth snow like wool." " The snow-flake," as Professor Tyndall strikingly says, " leads back to the sun " —so intimately related are all things to each other in this wonderful universe. It leads further and higher still—even to him who is our sun and shield, the light and heat of all creation. The whole vast realm of winter, with its strange phenomena, is but the breath of God—the Creative Word—as it were, congealed against the blue transparency of space, like the marvellous frost-work on a window-pane. The Psalmist had not the shadow of a doubt that God formed and sent the annual miracle of snow, as he had formed and sent the daily miracle of manna in the desert. It was a common-place thing ; it was a natural, ordinary occurrence ; but it had the Divine sign upon it, and it showed forth the glory and goodness of God as strikingly as the most wonderful supernatural event in his nation's history. When God would impress Job with a sense of his power, it was not to some of his miraculous, but to some of his ordinary works that he appealed. And when the Psalmist would praise God for the preservation of Israel and the restoration of Jerusalem—as he does in the psalm from which my subject is taken —it is not to the wonderful miraculous events with which the history of Israel abounded that he directs attention, but to the common events of Providence and the ordinary appearances and processes of nature. He cannot think enough of the Omnipotent Creator and Ruler of the Universe entering into familiar relations with his people, and condescending to their humblest wants. It is the same God that " giveth snow like wool," who " shows his word unto Jacob, and his statutes and commandments unto Israel." And the wonder of the peculiarity is enhanced by thoughts borrowed from the wonders of nature. We know a thousand times more of the nature, formation, and purpose of the snow than the Psalmist did. But that knowledge is dearly earned if our science destroys our faith. What amount of precision of scientific knowledge can compensate us for the loss of the spiritual sensibility, which in all the wonders and beauties of the Creation brings us into personal contact with an infinitely wise mind and an infinitely loving heart?—*Hugh Macmillan, in " Two Worlds are Ours,"* 1880.

Verse 16.—*" Snow."* It is worth pausing to think what wonderful work is going on in the atmosphere during the formation and descent of every snow shower ; what building power is brought into play ; and how imperfect seem the productions of human minds and hands when compared with those formed by the blind forces of nature. But who ventures to call the forces of nature blind ? In reality, when we speak thus, we are describing our own condition. The blindness is ours ; and what we really ought to say, and to confess, is that our powers are absolutely unable to comprehend either the origin or the end of the operations of nature.—*John Tyndall, in " The Forms of Water,"* 1872.

Verses 16, 17.—The Lord takes the ice and frost and cold to be his ; it is not only *his sun*, but *his ice*, and *his frost :* ' he scattereth *his hoar frost* like ashes." The frost is compared to ashes in a threefold respect. First, because the hoar frost gives a little interruption to the sight. If you scatter ashes into the air, it darkens the light, so doth the hoar frost. Secondly, the hoary frost is like ashes because near in colour to ashes. Thirdly, 'tis like, because there is a kind of burning in it : frost burns the tender buds and blossoms, it nips them and dries them up. The hoar frost hath its denomination in the Latin tongue from *burning*, and it differs but very little from that word which is commonly used in Latin for a coal of fire. The cold frost hath a kind of scorching in it, as well as the hot sun. Unseasonable frosts in the spring scorch the tender fruits, which bad effect of frost is usually expressed by *carbunculation* or blasting.—*Joseph Caryl.*

Verse 17.—*" He casteth forth his ice like morsels."* Or, *shivers of bread.* It is a worthy saying of one from this text,—The ice is bread, the rain is drink, the snow is wool, the frost a fire to the earth, causing it inwardly to glow with heat ; teaching us what to do for God's poor.—*John Trapp.*

Verse 17.—*" He casteth forth his ice like morsels."* The word here translated *" morsels,"* means, in most of the places where it occurs in the Bible, *pieces of bread*, exactly the LXX. ψωμούς ; for this very ice, this wintry cold, is profitable to the earth, to fit it for bearing future harvests, and thus it matures the *morsels of bread* which man will yet win from the soil in due season.—*Genebrardus, in Neale and Littledale.*

Verse 17.—*" Morsels."* Or, *crumbs.* Gen. xviii. 5 ; Judges xix. 5. Doubtless the allusion is to hail.—*A. S. Aglen.*

Verse 17.—*" It is extremely severe,"* said his sister to Archbishop Leighton one day, speaking of the season. The good man only said in reply, " But thou, O God, hast made summer and winter."—*From J. N. Pearson's Life of Archbishop Leighton,* 1830.

Verse 18.—*" He sendeth out his word, and melteth them."* Israel in the captivity had been ice-bound, like ships of Arctic voyagers in the Polar Sea ; but God sent forth the vernal breeze of his love, and the water flowed, the ice melted, and they were released. God turned their captivity, and, their icy chains being melted by the solar beams of God's mercy, they flowed in fresh and buoyant streams, like " rivers of the south," shining in the sun. See Ps. cxxvi. 4. So it was on the day of Pentecost. The winter of spiritual captivity was thawed and dissolved by the soft breath of the Holy Ghost, and the earth laughed and bloomed with spring-tide flowers of faith, love, and joy.—*Christopher Wordsworth.*

Verse 19.—Here we see God in compassion bending down, in order to communicate to the deeply fallen son of man something of a blessed secret, of which, without his special enlightenment, the eye would never have seen anything, nor the ear ever have heard.—*J. J. Van Oosterzee, on " The Image of Christ."*

Verses 19, 20.—If the publication of the law by the ministry of angels to the Israelites were such a privilege that it is reckoned their peculiar treasure—" *He hath shewed his statutes unto Israel ; he hath not dealt so with any nation* "—what is the revelation of the gospel by the Son of God himself ? For although the law is obscured and defaced since the fall, yet there are some ingrafted notions of it in human nature ; but there is not the least suspicion of the gospel. The law discovers our misery, but the gospel alone shows the way to be delivered from it. If an advantage so great and so precious doth not touch our hearts ; and, in possessing it with joy, if we are not sensible of the engagements the Father of mercies hath laid upon us ; we shall be the ungratefulest wretches in the world.—*William Bates.*

Verses 19, 20.—That some should have more means of knowing the Creator, others less, it is all from the mercy and will of God. His church hath a privilege and an advantage above other nations in the world ; the Jews had this favour above the heathens, and Christians above the Jews ; and no other reason can be assigned but his eternal love.—*Thomas Manton.*

Verse 20.—" *He hath not dealt so with any nation . . . Praise ye the Lord.*" The sweet psalmist of Israel, a man skilful in praises, doth begin and end this psalm with *Hallelujah.* In the body of the psalm he doth set forth the mercy of God, both towards all *creatures* in general in his common providence, and towards his *church* in particular. So in this close of the psalm : " He sheweth his word unto Jacob, and his statutes to Israel. He hath not dealt so with any nation." In the original 'tis, " He hath not dealt so with *every nation* ": that is, with *any* nation. In the text you may observe *a position* and *a conclusion. A position ;* and that is, that God deals in a singular way of mercy with his people above all other people. And then the *conclusion : "·Praise ye the Lord.*" Doctrine. That God deals in a singular way of mercy with his people, and therefore expects singular praises from his people.—*Joseph Alleine* (1633—1668), *in " A Thanksgiving Sermon."*

Verse 20.—See the wonderful goodness of God, who besides the light of nature, has committed to us the sacred Scriptures. The heathen are enveloped in ignorance. " *As for his judgments, they have not known them.*" They have the oracles of the Sybils, but not the writings of Moses and the apostles. How many live in the region of death, where the bright star of Scripture has never appeared ! We have the blessed Book of God to resolve all our doubts, and to point out a way of life to us. " Lord, how is it thou wilt manifest thyself unto us, and not unto the world ?"—John xiv. 22.—*Thomas Watson.*

HINTS TO THE VILLAGE PREACHER.

Verse 1.—Praise. Its profit, pleasure, and propriety.—*J. F.*

Verse 1.—The Reasonable Service. I. The methods of praise : by word, song, life ; individually, socially. II. The offerers of praise : " ye." III. The objects of praise : " the Lord, our God." IV. The reasons for praise : it is " good," " pleasant," " becoming."—*C. A. D.*

Verses 1—3.—I. The Privilege of Praising God. 1. It is good. 2. Pleasant. 3. Becoming. II. The Duty of Praising God. 1. For gathering a church for himself among men : " The Lord doth build up Jerusalem." 2. For the materials of which it is composed : " The outcasts," etc. 3. For the preparation of those materials for his purpose : " He healeth," etc. verse 3.—*G. R.*

Verse 2.—The Lord is Architect, Builder, Sustainer, Restorer, and Owner of the Church. In each relation let him be praised.

Verse 2.—The Great Gatherer. I. Strange persons sought for. II. Special search and means made use of. III. Selected centre to which he brings them. IV. Singular exhibition of them for ever and ever in heaven.

Verse 2.—First the church built and then the sinners gathered into it. A prosperous state of the church within necessary to her increase from without.

Verse 2.—See "Spurgeon's Sermons," No. 1302: "Good Cheer for Outcasts."

Verse 2.—Upbuilding and Ingathering. I. The church may be in a fallen condition. II. Its upbuilding is the Lord's work. III. He accomplishes it by gathering together its outcast citizens.—*C. A. D.*

Verse 3.—See "Spurgeon's Sermons," No. 53: "Healing for the Wounded."

Verse 3.—God a true physician, and a tender nurse.—*J. F.*

Verses 3, 4.—Heaven's Brilliants, and Earth's Broken Hearts. I. The Proprietor of the Stars with the Wounded. The stars left kingless for broken hearts. Jehovah! with lint and liniment and a woman's hand. Who binds together the stars, shall bind firmly grieved hearts. II. The Gentle Heart-healer with the Stars. Be all power intrusted to such tenderness. Its comely splendour. God guides the stars with an eye on wounded hearts. The hopefulness of prayer. III. Hearts, Stars, and Eternity. Some hearts shall " shine as the stars." Some stars shall expire in " blackness of darkness." God's hand and eye are everywhere making justice certain. Trust and sing.—*W. B. H.*

Verses 3, 4.—God's Compassion and Power. I. Striking diversity of God's cares: " hearts " and " stars." II. Wonderful variety of God's operations. Gently caring for human hearts. Preserving the order, regularity, and stability of creation. III. Blessed results of God's work. Broken hearts healed ; wounds bound up. Light, harmony, and beauty in the heavens. IV. Mighty encouragement to trust in God. God takes care of the universe ; may I not entrust my life, my soul, to him ? Where he rules unquestioned there is light and harmony ; let me not resist his will in my life.—*C. A. D.*

Verse 5.—A contemplation of God's greatness. I. Great in his essential nature. II. Great in Power. III. Great in wisdom. Let us draw inferences concerning the insignificance of man, &c.

Verse 6.—Reversal. I. In the estimate of the world the meek are cast down and the wicked lifted up. II. In the judgment of heaven the meek are lifted up and the wicked cast down. III. The judgment of heaven will, in the end, be found the true one.—*C. A. D.*

Verse 7.—The use and benefit of singing.

Verse 8.—God in all. The unity of his plan ; the co-operation of divine forces ; the condescending mercy of the result.

Verse 9.—See " Spurgeon's Sermons," No. 672 : " The Ravens' Cry."

Verse 11.—The singularity of our God, and of his favour. For which he is to be praised. I. *The objects of that favour distinguished.* 1. From physical strength. 2. From mental vigor. 3. From self-reliance. 4. From mere capacity for service. II. *The objects of that favour described.* 1. By emotions relating to God. 2. By the weakest forms of spiritual life. 3. By the highest degrees of it ; for the maturest saint fears and hopes. 4. By the sacred blend of it. Fear of our guilt, hope of his mercy. Fear of self, confidence in God. Hope of perseverance, fear of sinning. Hope of heaven, fear of coming short. Hope of perfection, mourning defects. III. *The blessing of that favour implied.* 1. God loves to think of them. 2. To be with them. 3. To minister to them. 4. To meet them in their fears and their hopes. 5. To reward them for ever.

Verse 11.—He takes pleasure in their persons, emotions, desires, devotions, hopes, and characters.—*W. W.*

Verse 12.—I. The Lord whom we praise. II. His praise in our houses—Jerusalem. III. Our praise in his house—Zion.

Verse 13.—A Strong Church. I. The utility and value of a strong church. II. The marks which distinguish it. 1. Gates well kept. 2. Increase of membership. 3. The converts blessed to others. III. The important care of a strong church : to trace all blessing to Zion's God.—*W. B. H.*

Verses 14, 15.—See " Spurgeon's Sermons," No. 425 : " Peace at Home, and Prosperity Abroad."

Verses 14, 15.—Church blessings. I. Peace. II. Food. III. Missionary energy. IV. The presence of God : the source of all blessing.

Verse 15 (*second clause*).—See "Spurgeon's Sermons," No. 1607 : "The Swiftly Running Word."

Verse 16.—The unexpected results of adversity : snow acting as wool.

Verses 16–18.—See "Spurgeon's Sermons," No. 670 : "Frost and Thaw."

Verse 19.—I. God's people. II. God's Word. III. God's revelation to the soul. IV. God's praise for this special revelation.

Verse 20.—Electing Grace inspires the Heart with Praise. I. God's love has chosen us. Hallelujah. II. God has intrusted us with his truth. Hallelujah. III. God has made us almoners of his bounty. Hallelujah. IV. God through us is to save the world. Hallelujah.— *W. B. H.*

PSALM CXLVIII.

The song is one and indivisible. It seems almost impossible to expound it in detail, for a living poem is not to be dissected verse by verse. It is a song of nature and of grace. As a flash of lightning flames through space, and enwraps both heaven and earth in one vestment of glory, so doth the adoration of the Lord in this psalm light up all the universe, and cause it to glow with a radiance of praise. The song begins in the heavens, sweeps downward to dragons and all deeps, and then ascends again, till the people near unto Jehovah take up the strain. For its exposition the chief requisite is a heart on fire with reverent love to the Lord over all, who is to be blessed for ever.

EXPOSITION.

PRAISE ye the LORD. Praise ye the LORD from the heavens : praise him in the heights.

2 Praise ye him, all his angels : praise ye him, all his hosts.

3 Praise ye him, sun and moon : praise him, all ye stars of light.

4 Praise him, ye heavens of heavens, and ye waters that *be* above the heavens.

5 Let them praise the name of the LORD : for he commanded, and they were created.

6 He hath also stablished them for ever and ever : he hath made a decree which shall not pass.

7 Praise the LORD from the earth, ye dragons, and all deeps :

8 Fire, and hail ; snow, and vapours ; stormy wind fulfilling his word :

9 Mountains, and all hills ; fruitful trees, and all cedars :

10 Beasts, and all cattle ; creeping things, and flying fowl :

11 Kings of the earth, and all people ; princes, and all judges of the earth :

12 Both young men, and maidens ; old men, and children :

13 Let them praise the name of the LORD : for his name alone is excellent ; his glory *is* above the earth and heaven.

14 He also exalteth the horn of his people, the praise of all his saints ; *even* of the children of Israel, a people near unto him. Praise ye the LORD.

1. "*Praise ye the* LORD." Whoever ye may be that hear this word, ye are invited, entreated, commanded, to magnify Jehovah. Assuredly he has made you, and, if for nothing else, ye are bound, upon the ground of creatureship, to adore your Maker. This exhortation can never be out of place, speak it where we may ; and never out of time, speak it when we may. "*Praise ye the* LORD *from the heavens.*" Since ye are nearest to the High and Lofty One, be ye sure to lead the song. Ye angels, ye cherubim and seraphim, and all others who dwell in the precincts of his courts, praise ye Jehovah. Do this as from a starting-point from which the praise is to pass on to other realms. Keep not your worship to yourselves, but let it fall like a golden shower from the heavens on men beneath. "*Praise him in the heights.*" This is no vain repetition ; but after the manner of

attractive poesy the truth is emphasized by reiteration in other words. Moreover, God is not only to be praised *from* the heights, but *in* them : the adoration is to be perfected in the heavens from which it takes its rise. No place is too high for the praises of the most High. On the summit of creation the glory of the Lord is to be revealed, even as the tops of the highest Alps are tipped with the golden light of the same sun which glads the valleys. Heavens and heights become the higher and the more heavenly as they are made to resound with the praises of Jehovah. See how the Psalmist trumpets out the word "PRAISE." It sounds forth some nine times in the first five verses of this song. Like minute-guns, exultant exhortations are sounded forth in tremendous force—*Praise ! Praise ! Praise !* The drum of the great King beats round the world with this one note—*Praise ! Praise ! Praise !* "Again they said, Hallelujah." All this praise is distinctly and personally for Jehovah. Praise not his servants nor his works ; but praise HIM. Is he not worthy of all possible praise ? Pour it forth before HIM in full volume ; pour it only there !

2. " *Praise ye him, all his angels.*" Living intelligences, perfect in character and in bliss, lift up your loudest music to your Lord, each one of you. Not one bright spirit is exempted from this consecrated service. However many ye be, O angels, ye are all *his* angels, and therefore ye are bound, all of you, to render service to your Lord. Ye have all seen enough of him to be able to praise him, and ye have all abundant reasons for so doing. Whether ye be named Gabriel, or Michael, or by whatever other titles ye are known, praise ye the Lord. Whether ye bow before him, or fly on his errands, or desire to look into his covenant, or behold his Son, cease not, ye messengers of Jehovah, to sound forth his praise while ye move at his bidding. " *Praise ye him, all his hosts.*" This includes angelic armies, but groups with them all the heavenly bodies. Though they be inanimate the stars, the clouds, the lightnings, have their ways of praising Jehovah. Let each one of the countless legions of the Lord of hosts show forth his glory ; for the countless armies are all *his*, his by creation, and preservation, and consequent obligation. Both these sentences claim unanimity of praise from those in the upper regions who are called upon to commence the strain—" *all* his angels, all his hosts." That same hearty oneness must pervade the whole orchestra of praising ones ; hence, further on, we read of all stars of light, all deeps, all hills, all cedars, and all people. How well the concert begins when all angels, and all the heavenly host, strike the first joyful notes ! In that concert our souls would at once take their part.

3. " *Praise ye him, sun and moon : praise him, all ye stars of light.*" The Psalmist enters into detail as to the heavenly hosts. As all, so each, must praise the God of each and all. The sun and moon, as joint rulers of day and night, are paired in praise : the one is the complement of the other, and so they are closely associated in the summons to worship. The sun has his peculiar mode of glorifying the Great Father of lights, and the moon has her own special method of reflecting his brightness. There is a perpetual adoration of the Lord in the skies : it varies with night and day, but it ever continues while sun and moon endure. There is ever a lamp burning before the high altar of the Lord. Nor are the greater luminaries allowed to drown with their floods of light the glory of the lesser brilliants, for all the stars are bidden to the banquet of praise. Stars are many, so many that no one can count the host included under the words, " all ye stars " ; yet no one of them refuses to praise its Maker. From their extreme brilliance they are fitly named " stars of light " ; and this light is praise in a visible form twinkling to true music. Light is song glittering before the eye instead of resounding in the ear. Stars without light would render no praise, and Christians without light rob the Lord of his glory. However small our beam, we must not hide it : if we cannot be sun or moon we must aim to be one of the " stars of light," and our every twinkling must be to the honour of our Lord.

4. " *Praise him, ye heavens of heavens.*" By these are meant those regions which are heavens to those who dwell in our heavens ; or those most heavenly of abodes where the most choice of spirits dwell. As the highest of the highest, so the

best of the best are to praise the Lord. If we could climb as much above the heavens as the heavens are above the earth, we could still cry out to all around us, " Praise ye the Lord." There can be none so great and high as to be above praising Jehovah. " *And ye waters that be above the heavens.*" Let the clouds roll up volumes of adoration. Let the sea above roar, and the fulness thereof, at the presence of Jehovah, the God of Israel. There is something of mystery about these supposed reservoirs of water ; but let them be what they may, and as they may, they shall give glory to the Lord our God. Let the most unknown and perplexing phenomena take up their parts in the universal praise.

5. " *Let them praise the name of the* LORD ; *for he commanded, and they were created.*" Here is good argument : The Maker should have honour from his works, they should tell forth *his* character by *their* praise ; and thus they should praise his *name*—by which his character is intended. The name of JEHOVAH is written legibly upon his works, so that his power. wisdom, goodness, and other attributes are therein made manifest to thoughtful men, and thus his name is praised. The highest praise of God is to declare what he is. We can invent nothing which would magnify the Lord : we can never extol him better than by repeating his name, or describing his character. The Lord is to be extolled as creating all things that exist, and as doing so by the simple agency of his word. He created by a command ; what a power is this ! Well may he expect those to praise him who owe their being to him. Evolution may be atheistic ; but the doctrine of creation logically demands worship ; and hence, as the tree is known by its fruit, it proves itself to be true. Those who were created by command are under command to adore their Creator. The voice which said " Let them be," now saith " Let them praise."

6. " *He hath also stablished them for ever and ever.*" The continued existence of celestial beings is due to the supporting might of Jehovah, and to that alone. They do not fail because the Lord does not fail them. Without his will these things cannot alter ; he has impressed upon them laws which only he himself can change. Eternally his ordinances are binding upon them. Therefore ought the Lord to be praised because he is Preserver as well as Creator, Ruler as well as Maker. " *He hath made a decree which shall not pass.*" The heavenly bodies are ruled by Jehovah's decree : they cannot pass his limit, or trespass against his law. His rule and ordination can never be changed except by himself, and in this sense his decree " shall not pass " : moreover, the highest and most wonderful of creatures are perfectly obedient to the statutes of the Great King, and thus his decree is not passed over. This submission to law is praise. Obedience is homage ; order is harmony. In this respect the praise rendered to Jehovah from the " bodies celestial " is absolutely perfect. His almighty power upholds all things in their spheres, securing the march of stars and the flight of seraphs ; and thus the music of the upper regions is never marred by discord, nor interrupted by destruction. The eternal hymn is for ever chanted ; even the solemn silence of the spheres is a perpetual psalm.

7. " *Praise the* LORD *from the earth.*" The song descends to our abode, and so comes nearer home to us. We who are " bodies terrestrial," are to pour out our portion of praise from the golden globe of this favoured planet. Jehovah is to be praised not only *in* the earth but *from* the earth, as if the adoration ran over from this planet into the general accumulation of worship. In the first verse the song was " from the heavens " ; here it is " from the earth " : songs coming down from heaven are to blend with those going up from earth. The " earth " here meant is our entire globe of land and water : it is to be made vocal everywhere with praise. " *Ye dragons, and all deeps.*" It would be idle to inquire what special sea-monsters are here meant ; but we believe all of them are intended, and the places where they abide are indicated by " all deeps." Terrible beasts or fishes, whether they roam the earth or swim the seas, are bidden to the feast of praise. Whether they float amid the teeming waves of the tropics, or wend their way among the floes and bergs of polar waters, they are commanded by our sacred poet to yield their tribute to the creating Jehovah. They pay no service to man ;

let them the more heartily confess their allegiance to the Lord. About " dragons " and " deeps " there is somewhat of dread, but this may the more fitly become the bass of the music of the psalm. If there be aught grim in mythology, or fantastic in heraldry, let it piaise the incomprehensible Lord.

8. " *Fire and hail.*" Lightning and hailstones go together. In the plagues of Egypt they co-operated in making Jehovah known in all the terrors of his power. Fire and ice-morsels are a contrast in nature, but they are combined in magnifying the Lord. " *Snow and vapours.*" Offsprings of cold, or creations of heat, be ye equally consecrated to his praise. Congealed or expanded vapours, falling flakes or rising clouds, should, rising or falling, still reveal the praises of the Lord. " *Stormy wind fulfilling his word.*" Though rushing with incalculable fury, the storm-wind is still under law, and moves in order due, to carry out the designs of God. It is a grand orchestra which contains such wind-instruments as these! He is a great leader who can keep all these musicians in concert, and direct both time and tune.

9. " *Mountains, and all hills.*" Towering steeps and swelling knolls alike declare their Creator. " All hills " are to be consecrated ; we have no longer Ebal and Gerizim, the hill of the curse and the hill of the blessing, but all our Ebals are turned to Gerizims. Tabor and Hermon, Lebanon and Carmel, rejoice in the name of the Lord. The greater and the lesser mounts are one in their adoration. Not only the Alps and the mountains of the Jura thunder out his praise; but our own Cotswolds and Grampians are vocal with songs in his honour. " *Fruitful trees, and all cedars.*" Fruit trees and forest trees, trees deciduous or evergreen, are equally full of benevolent design, and alike subserve some purpose of love ; therefore for all and by all let the great Designer be praised. There are many species of cedar, but they all reveal the wisdom of their Maker. When kings fell them, that they may make beams for their palaces, they do but confess their obligation to the King of trees, and to the King of kings, whose trees they are. Varieties in the landscape are produced by the rising and falling of the soil, and by the many kinds of trees which adorn the land : let all, and all alike, glorify their one Lord. When the trees clap their hands in the wind, or their leaves rustle in the gentle breath of Zephyr, they do to their best ability sing out unto the Lord.

10. " *Beasts, and all cattle.*" Animals fierce or tame ; wild beasts and domestic cattle ; let all these show forth the praises of Jehovah. Those are worse than beasts who do not praise our God. More than brutish are those who are wilfully dumb concerning their Maker. " *Creeping things, and flying fowl.*" The multitudes that throng the earth and the air ; insects of every form and birds of every wing are called upon to join the universal worship. No one can become familiar with insect and bird life without feeling that they constitute a wonderful chapter in the history of divine wisdom. The minute insect marvellously proclaims the Lord's handiwork : when placed under the microscope it tells a wondrous tale. So, too, the bird which soars aloft displays in its adaptation for an aerial life an amount of skill which our balloonists have in vain attempted to emulate. True devotion not only hears the praises of God in the sweet song of feathered minstrels, but even discovers it in the croaking from the marsh, or in the buzz of " the blue fly which singeth in the window-pane." More base than reptiles, more insignificant than insects, are songless men.

11. " *Kings of the earth, and all people : princes, and all judges of the earth.*" Now the poet has reached our own race, and very justly he would have rulers and subjects, chieftains and magistrates, unite in worshipping the sovereign Lord of all. Monarchs must not disdain to sing, nor must their people refrain from uniting with them. Those who lead in battle and those who decide in courts must neither of them allow their vocations to keep them from reverently adoring the Chief and Judge of all. All people, and all judges, must praise the Lord of all. What a happy day it will be when it is universally acknowledged that through our Lord Jesus, the incarnate Wisdom, " kings reign and princes decree justice " ! Alas, it is not so as yet ! kings have been patrons of vice, and princes ringleaders in folly. Let us pray that the song of the Psalmist may be realized in fact.

12. "*Both young men, and maidens; old men, and children.*" Both sexes and all ages are summoned to the blessed service of song. Those who usually make merry together are to be devoutly joyful together : those who make up the ends of families, that is to say, the elders and the juveniles, should make the Lord their one and only end. Old men should by their experience teach children to praise ; and children by their cheerfulness should excite old men to song. There is room for every voice at this concert : fruitful trees and maidens, cedars and young men, angels and children, old men and judges—all may unite in this oratorio. None, indeed, can be dispensed with : for perfect psalmody we must have the whole universe aroused to worship, and all parts of creation must take their parts in devotion.

13. "*Let them praise the name of the* LORD." All that is contained in the name or character of Jehovah is worthy of praise, and all the objects of his creating care will be too few to set it forth in its completeness. "*For his name alone is excellent.*" It alone deserves to be exalted in praise, for alone it is exalted in worth. There is none like unto the Lord, none that for a moment can be compared unto him. His unique name should have a monopoly of praise. "*His glory is above the earth and heaven*": it is therefore alone because it surpasses all others. His royal splendour exceeds all that earth and heaven can express. He is himself the crown of all things, the excellency of the creation. There is more glory in him personally than in all his works united. It is not possible for us to exceed and become extravagant in the Lord's praise : his own natural glory is infinitely greater than any glory which we can render to him.

14. "*He also exalteth the horn of his people.*" He hath made them strong, famous, and victorious. His goodness to all his creatures does not prevent his having a special favour to his chosen nation : he is good to all, but he is God to his people. He lifts up the down-trodden, but he in a peculiar manner lifts up his people. When they are brought low he raises up a horn for them by sending them a deliverer ; when they are in conflict he gives them courage and strength, so that they lift up their horn amid the fray ; and when all is peaceful around them, he fills their horn with plenty, and they lift it up with delight. "*The praise of all his saints.*" He is their glory: to him they render praise ; and he by his mercy to them evermore gives them further reasons for praise, and higher motives for adoration. He lifts up their horn, and they lift up his praise. He exalts them, and they exalt him. The Holy One is praised by holy ones. He is their God, and they are his saints ; he makes them blessed, and they bless him in return. "*Even of the children of Israel.*" The Lord knoweth them that are his. He knows the name of him with whom he made a covenant, and how he came by that name, and who his children are, and where they are. All nations are bidden in verse 11 to praise the Lord ; but here the call is specially addressed to his elect people, who know him beyond all others. Those who are children of privilege should be children of praise. "*A people near unto him,*" near by kin, and near by care ; near as to manifestation and near as to affection. This is a highly honourable description of the beloved race ; and it is true even more emphatically of the spiritual Israel, the believing seed. This nearness should prompt us to perpetual adoration. The Lord's elect are the children of his love, the courtiers of his palace, the priests of his temple, and therefore they are bound beyond all others to be filled with reverence for him, and delight in him. "*Praise ye the* LORD," or, *Hallelujah.* This should be the Alpha and Omega of a good man's life. Let us praise God to the end, world without end. The field of praise which lies before us in this psalm is bounded at beginning and end by landmarks in the form of Hallelujahs, and all that lieth between them is every word of it to the Lord's honour. Amen.

EXPLANATORY NOTES.

*Psalms cxlviii.—cl.—*The last three psalms are *a triad of wondrous praise,* ascending from praise to higher praise, until it becomes " joy unspeakable and full of glory "—exultation which knows no bounds. The joy overflows the soul, and spreads throughout the universe ; every creature is magnetized by it, and drawn into the chorus. Heaven is full of praise, the earth is full of praise, praises rise from under the earth, " everything that hath breath " joins in the rapture. God is encompassed by a loving, praising creation. Man, the last in creation, but the first in song, knows not how to contain himself. He dances, he sings, he commands all the heavens, with all their angels, to help him, " beasts and all cattle, creeping things and flying fowl " must do likewise, even " dragons " must not be silent, and " all deeps " must yield contributions. He presses even dead things into his service, timbrels, trumpets, harps, organs, cymbals, high-sounding cymbals, if by any means, and by all means, he may give utterance to his love and joy.—*John Pulsford.*

*Whole Psalm.—*In this splendid anthem the Psalmist calls upon the whole creation, in its two great divisions (according to the Hebrew conception) of heaven and earth, to praise Jehovah : things with and things without life, beings rational and irrational, are summoned to join the mighty chorus. This psalm is the expression of the loftiest devotion, and it embraces at the same time the most comprehensive view of the relation of the creature to the Creator. Whether it is exclusively the utterance of a heart filled to the full with the thought of the infinite majesty of God, or whether it is also an anticipation, a prophetic forecast, of the final glory of creation, when at the manifestation of the sons of God, the creation itself also shall be redeemed from the bondage of corruption (Rom. viii. 18—23), and the homage of praise shall indeed be rendered by all things that are in heaven and earth and under the earth, is a question into which we need not enter.—*J. J. Stewart Perowne.*

*Whole Psalm.—*Milton, in his Paradise Lost (Book V., line 153. &c.), has elegantly imitated this psalm, and put it into the mouth of Adam and Eve as their morning hymn in a state of innocency.—*James Anderson.*

*Whole Psalm.—*Is this universal praise never to be realized ? is it only the longing, intense desire of the Psalmist's heart, which will never be heard on earth, and can only be perfected in heaven ? Is there to be no jubilee in which the mountains and the hills shall break forth into singing, and all the trees of the field shall clap their hands ? If there is to be no such day, then is the word of God of none effect ; if no such universal anthem is to swell the chorus of heaven and to be re-echoed by all that is on earth, then is God's promise void. It is true, in this psalm our translation presents it to us as a call or summons for every thing that hath or hath not breath to praise the Lord—or as a petition that they may praise ; but it is in reality a prediction that they *shall* praise. . . . This psalm is neither more nor less than a glorious prophecy of that coming day, whne not only shall the knowledge of the Lord be spread over the whole earth, as the waters cover the sea, but from every created object in heaven and in earth, animate and inanimate, from the highest archangel through every grade and phase of being, down to the tiniest atom—young men and maidens, old men and children, and all kings and princes, and judges of the earth shall unite in this millennial, anthem to the Redeemer's praise.—*Barton Bouchier.*

Verse 1.—"Praise ye the LORD," etc. All things praise, and yet he says, *"Praise ye."* Wherefore doth he say, *"Praise ye,"* when they are praising ? Because he delighteth in their praising, and therefore it pleaseth him to add, as it were, his own encouragement. Just as, when you come to men who are doing any good work with pleasure in their vineyard or in their harvest-field, or in some other matter of husbandry, you are pleased at what they are doing, and say, " Work on," " Go on" ; not that they may begin to work, when you say this, but, because you are pleased at finding them working, you add your approbation and encouragement. For by saying, " Work on," and encouraging those who are working, you, so to speak, work with them in wish. In this sort of encouragement, then, the Psalmist, filled with the Holy Ghost, saith this.—*Augustine.*

Verse 1.—The thrice-repeated exhortation, *"Praise . . Praise . . Praise,"* in this first verse is not merely imperative, nor only hortative, but it is an exultant hallelujah.—*Martin Geier.*

Verse 1.—*"From the heavens : praise him in the heights."* Or, high places. As God in framing the world begun above, and wrought downward, so doth the Psalmist proceed in this his exhortation to all creatures to praise the Lord.—*John Trapp.*

Verse 1.—*"Praise him in the heights."* The principle applied in this verse is this, that those who have been exalted to the highest honours of the created universe, should proportionately excel in their tribute of honour to him who has exalted them.—*Hermann Venema.*

Verse 1.—Bernard, in his sermon on the death of his brother Gerard, relates that in the middle of his last night on earth his brother, to the astonishment of all present, with a voice and countenance of exultation, broke forth in the words of the Psalmist—*"Praise the Lord of heaven, praise him in the heights !"*

Verse 2.—*"Praise ye him, all his angels."* Angels are first invoked, because they can praise God with humility, reverence, and purity. The highest are the humblest, the leaders of all created hosts are the most ready themselves to obey. —*Thomas Le Blanc.*

Verse 2.—*"Praise ye him, all his angels."* The angels of God were his first creatures ; it has even been thought that they existed prior to the inanimate universe. They were already praising their Maker before the light of day, and they have never ceased their holy song. Angels praise God best in their holy service. They praised Christ as God when they sang their *Gloria in Excelsis* at the Incarnation, and they praised him as man when they ministered to him after his temptation and before his crucifixion. So also now angels praise the Lord by their alacrity in ministering to his saints.—*John Lorinus.*

Verse 2.—*"Praise ye him, all his hosts."* That is, his creatures (those above especially which are as his *cavalry*) called his " hosts," for, 1. Their number ; 2, their order ; 3, their obedience.—*John Trapp.*

Verse 3.—*"Praise ye him, sun and moon,"* etc. How does the *sun* specially praise Jehovah ? 1. By its beauty. Jesus son of Sirach calls it the " globe of beauty." 2. By its fulness. Dion calls it " the image of the Divine capacity." 3. By its exaltation. Pliny calls it *cœli rector,* " the ruler of heaven." 4. By its perfect brightness. Pliny adds that it is " the mind and soul of the whole universe." 5. By its velocity and constancy of motion. Martian calls it " the Guide of Nature."

God the Supreme was depicted by the ancients holding in his hand a wreath of stars, to show the double conception, that they both obey and adorn him.— *Thomas Le Blanc.*

Verses 3, 4.—Let the sun, the fount of light, and warmth, and gladness, the greater light which rules the day, the visible emblem of the Uncreated Wisdom, the Light which lighteth every man, the centre round whom all our hopes and fears, our wants and prayers, our faith and love, are ever moving,—let the moon, the lesser light which rules the night, the type of the Church, which giveth to the world the light she gains from the Sun of Righteousness,—let the stars, so vast in their number, so lovely in their arrangement and their brightness, which God hath appointed in the heavens, even as he hath appointed his elect to shine for ever and ever,—let all the heavens with all their wonders and their worlds, the depths of space above, and the waters which are above the firmament, the images of God's Holy Scripture and of the glories and the mysteries contained

therein,—let these ever praise him who made and blessed them in the beginning
of the creation.—*J. W. Burgon.*

Verses 3, 4.—

> Praise him, thou golden-tressèd sun :
> Praise him thou fair and silver moon,
>   And ye bright orbs of streaming light ;
> Ye floods that float above the skies,
> Ye heav'ns, that vault o'er vault arise,
>   Praise him, who sits above all height.
>
> —*Richard Mant.*

Verse 4.—"*Praise him, ye heavens of heavens,*" etc. From the heavenly inhabitants the poetic strain passes in transition to the *heavens* themselves. There are
orders of heavens, ranks and heights supreme, and stages and degrees of lower
altitude. This verse sublimely traverses the immensities which are the home of
the most exalted dignities who wait on Deity, and then it descends to the firmament where the meteors flash forth, and where the heavens stoop to lift the clouds
that aspire from earth. And the idea sustained is that all these vast realms,
higher and lower, are one temple of unceasing praise.—*Hermann Venema.*

Verse 4.—The ancients thought there was an ethereal and lofty ocean in which
the worlds floated like ships in a sea.—*Thomas Le Blanc.*

Verses 5, 6.—This is the account of creation in a word—He spake ; it was done.
When Jesus came, he went everywhere showing his Divinity by this evidence,
that his word was omnipotent. These verses declare two miracles of God's Will
and Word, viz., the creation and consolidation of the earth. Jehovah first produced matter, then he ordered and established it.—*John Lorinus.*

Verse 6.—"*He hath also stablished them for ever and ever,*" etc. Here two things
are set before us, the permanence and the cosmic order of creation. Each created
thing is not only formed to endure, in the type or the development, if not in the
individual, but has its place in the universe fixed by God's decree, that it may
fulfil its appointed share of working out his will. They raise a question as to the
words "*for ever and ever,*" how they can be reconciled with the prophecy, Isaiah
lxv. 17 : " Behold, I create new heavens and a new earth : and the former shall
not be remembered, nor come into mind " ; a prophecy confirmed by the Lord
himself, saying, " Heaven and earth shall pass away," and seen fulfilled in vision
by the beloved disciple. Matt. v. 18 ; Rev. xxi. 1. And they answer that just
as man dies and rises again to incorruption, having the same personality in a
glorified body, so will it be with heaven and earth. Their qualities will be
changed, not their identity, in that new birth of all things.—*Neale and Littledale.*

Verse 6.—"*For ever and ever.*"

> My heart is awed within me, when I think
> Of the great miracle which still goes on,
> In silence, round me—the perpetual work
> Of thy creation, finished, yet renewed
> For ever.
>
> —*William Cullen Bryant,* 1794—1878.

Verse 6.—"*He hath made a decree,*" etc. Rather, *He hath made an ordinance, and
will not transgress it.* This is more obvious and natural than to supply a new subject to the second verb, " and none of them transgress it." This anticipates, but
only in form, the modern scientific doctrine of the inviolability of natural order.
It is the imperishable faithfulness of God that renders the law invariable.—*A. S.
Aglen.*

Verse 7.—"*Dragons.*" The word *tanninim,* rendered " *dragons,*" is a word
which may denote whales, sharks, serpents, or sea-monsters of any kind (Job vii.
1 ; Ezek. xxix. 3).—*John Morison.* .

Verse 7.—"*Sea-monsters,*" in Revised Version. Fishes constrain our admiration, as a created wonder, by the perfection of their form, their magnitude, their adaptation to the element they inhabit, and their multitude. Thus their very nature praises the Creator.—*Thomas Le Blanc.*

Verses 7, 8.—He calls to the *deeps, fire, hail, snow, mountains, and hills,* to bear a part in this work of praise. Not that they are able to do it actively, but to show that man is to call in the whole creation to assist him passively, and should have so much charity to all creatures as to receive what they offer, and so much affection to God as to present to him what he receives from him. *Snow* and *hail* cannot bless and praise God, but man ought to bless God for those things, wherein there is a mixture of trouble and inconvenience, something to molest our sense, as well as something that improves the earth for fruit.—*Stephen Charnock.*

Verses 7—10.—Here be many things easy to be understood, they are clear to every eye ; as when David doth exhort " kings " and " princes," " old men " and " babes " to praise God ; that is easy to be done, and we know the meaning as soon as we look on it ; but here are some things again that are hard to be understood, dark and obscure, and they are two :—

First, in that David doth exhort *dumb, unreasonable, and senseless creatures* to praise God, such as cannot hear, at least cannot understand. Doth the Holy Ghost in the gospel bid us avoid impertinent speeches, and vain repetitions, and shall we think he will use them himself ? No, no. But,

Secondly, not only doth he call upon these creatures, but also he calls upon the " deeps " and the " seas " to praise God ; these two things are hard to be conceived. But to give you some reasons.

The first reason may be this, why David calls upon the unreasonable creatures to perform this duty,—*He doth his duty like a faithful preacher,* whether they will hear or no that he preaches to, yet he will discharge his soul : a true preacher, he speaks forth the truth, and calls upon them to hear, though his auditors sleep, are careless, and regard it not. So likewise doth David, in this sense, with these creatures ; he doth his duty, and calls upon them to do it, though they understand not, though they comprehend it not. And likewise he doth it to show his vehement desire for all creatures to praise God.

The second reason may be this : *he doth it craftily,* by way of policy, to incite others to perform this duty, that if such creatures as they ought to do this, then those that are above them in degree have more cause, and may be ashamed to neglect it ; as an ill-governed master, though he stay himself at home, yet he will send his servants to church : so David, being conscious of his own neglect, yet he calls upon others not to be slack and negligent : though he came infinitely short of that he should do, yet he shows his own desire for all creatures to perform this duty.

But if these reasons will not satisfy you, though they have done many others, a third reason may be this : *to set forth the sweet harmony that is among all God's creatures ;* to show how that all the creatures being God's family, do with one consent speak and preach aloud God's praise ; and therefore he calls upon some above him, some below him, on both sides, everywhere, to speak God's praise ; for every one in their place, degree, and calling, show forth, though it be in a dumb sense and way, their Creator's praise.

Or, fourthly and lastly, which I think to be a good reason : *zeal makes men speak and utter things impossible ;* the fire of zeal will so transport him that it will make him speak things unreasonable, impossible, as Moses in his zeal desired God, for the safety of Israel, " to blot his name out of his book " ; and Paul wished himself " anathema," accursed or separate from Christ, for his brethren's salvation, which was a thing impossible, it could not be.—*John Everard, in "Some Gospel Treasures,"* 1653.

Verses 7—10.—The ox and the ass acknowledge their master. The winds and the sea obey him. It should seem that as there is a religion above man, the religion of angels, so there may be a religion beneath man, the religion of dumb creatures. For wheresoever there is a service of God, in effect it is a religion. Thus according to the several degrees and difference of states—the state of nature, grace, and glory—religion may likewise admit of degrees.—*G. G., in a sermon entitled "The Creatures Praysing God,"* 1662.

Verse 8.—this verse arrays in striking order three elements that are ever full of movement and power—*ignea, aquea, aërea ;* fire (or caloric), water (or vapour), and air (or wind). The first includes meteors, lightnings and thunders ; the second, snow, hoar-frost, dew, mist and rain ; the third, breezes, tempests and hurricanes. —*Hermann Venema.*

Verse 8.—*"Fire and hail."* These are contrasted with one another. *"Snow and mist."* The mist is the vapour raised by the heat of the sun, and therefore suitably contrasted with the snow, which is the effect of cold. *"Stormy wind"* (Ps. cvii. 25), which accompanies the changes of temperature in the air.—*James G. Murphy.*

Verse 8.—*"Snow."* As sure as every falling flake of winter's snow has a part in the great economy of nature, so surely has every Word of God which falls within the sanctuary its end to accomplish in the moral sphere. I have stood on a winter day and seen the tiny flakes in little clouds lose themselves one by one in the rushing river. They seemed to die to no purpose—to be swallowed up by an enemy which ignored both their power and their existence. And so have I seen the Word of God fall upon human hearts. Sent of God, from day to day and from year to year, I have seen it dropping apparently all resultless into the fierce current of unbelief—into the fiercer gulf-stream of worldliness which was sweeping through the minds and the lives of the hearers. But as I stood upon the river's bank and looked upon what seemed to be the death of the little fluttering crystal, a second thought assured me that it was but death into life, and that every tiny flake which wept its live away in the rushing waters, became incorporate with the river's being. So when I have seen the Word of God fall apparently fruitless upon the restless, seething, rushing current of human life, a recovered faith in the immutable declaration of God has assured me that what I looked upon was not a chance or idle death, but rather the falling of the soldier, after that he had wrought his life-force into the destiny of a nation and into the history of a world. And so it must ever be. The Word of God ever reaches unto its end.—*S. S. Mitchell, in a Sermon entitled "The Coming of the Snow and the Coming of the Word,"* 1884.

Verse 8.—The *"stormy wind"* is the swift messenger of God, Ps. cxlvii. 15. The hurricane fulfils the divine command. See Matt. viii. 27. " Even the winds and the sea obey him." The *"wind"* is the minister of judgment. See Ezek. xiii. 13. The words of this verse have special use ; for men are exceedingly apt to ascribe the violence of tempests to blind chance.—*Martin Geier.*

Verse 8.—The half-learned man is apt to laugh at the simple faith of the clown or savage, who tells us that rain comes from God. The former, it seems, has discovered that it is the product of certain laws of air, water, and electricity. But truly the peasant is the more enlightened of the two, for he has discovered the main cause, and the real Actor, while the other has found only the second cause, and the mere instrument. It is as if a friend were to send us a gift of ingenious and beautiful workmanship, and just as our gratitude was beginning to rise to the donor, some bystanders were to endeavour to damp it all, by telling us that the gift is the product of certain machinery he had seen.—*James MacCosh,* 1811.

Verse 9.—*"Mountains and all hills,"* etc. The diversifying of the face of the earth with higher and lower parts, with mountains, hills, and valleys, and the adorning of the face thereof with trees of varied sorts, contributeth much to the praise of God.—*David Dickson.*

Verse 9.—*"Mountains and all hills."* What voices have the hills ! How solemn the sounds of the mountains from their sublime solitudes ! The mountains thunder, and the hills re-echo ; but they speak peace and send down plenty to the vales in running rivulets.—*Thomas Le Blanc.*

Verse 9.—"*Fruitful trees and all cedars.*" The praise of God is in the rustling voices of the trees. They fulfil his purpose in giving fruit to refresh, and shelter and shadow for a covert, and their murmur is the soft cadence that chants mercy and grace. In India, the ancients reported that the trees were worshipped as divine, and death was a penalty awarded to those who cut them down. In classic mythology the groves were the homes of gods. Jehovah decreed that an ark of safety for man, and also a temple for himself, should be constructed of wood. Thus more than any other created things, the trees of the wood have redounded to his glory.—*Le Blanc.*

Verse 9.—"*Fruitful trees.*" Rather *fruit trees;* the fruit-bearing tree being representative of one division of the vegetable world, planted and reared by man; the "cedars" of the other, which are (Ps. civ. 16) of God's own plantation. So in verse 10 we have *wild* animals and *domesticated* animals.—*A. S. Aglen.*

Verse 9.—"*Trees.*"

> All creatures of the eternal God but man,
> In several sorts do glorify his name;
> Each tree doth seem ten thousand tongues to have,
> With them to laud the Lord omnipotent;
> Each leaf that with wind's gentle breath doth wave,
> Seems as a tongue to speak to that intent,
> In language admirably excellent.
> The sundry sorts of fragrant flowers do seem
> Sundry discourses God to glorify,
> And sweetest volumes may we them esteem;
> For all these creatures in their several sort
> Praise God, and man unto the same exhort.
>
> —*Peter Pett*, 1599.

Verse 9.—"*All cedars.*" Beautiful indeed is the pine forest in all seasons: in the freshness of spring, when the gnarled boughs are penetrated and mollified by the soft wind and the warm sun, and, thrilled with new life, burst out into fringes and tassels of the richest green, and cones of the tenderest purple; beautiful in the sultry summer, when among its cool, dim shadows the cheated hours all day sing vespers, while the open landscape is palpitating in the scorching heat; beautiful in the sadness of autumn, when its unfading verdure stands out in striking relief amid changing scenes, that have no sympathy with anything earthly save sorrow and decay, and directs the thoughts to the imperishableness of the heavenly Paradise; beautiful exceedingly in the depth of winter, when the tiers of branches are covered with pure, unsullied wreaths of snow, sculptured by the wind into curves of exquisite grace. It is beautiful in calm, when the tree-tops scarce whisper to each other, and the twitter of the golden wren sounds loud in the expectant hush; it is more than beautiful in storm, when the wild fingers of the wind play the most mournful music on its great harp-strings, and its full diapason is sublime as the roar of the ocean on a rock-bound shore. I do not wonder that the northern imagination in heathen times should have invested it with awe and fear as the favourite haunt of Odin and Thor; or that, in after times, its long rows of trunks, vanishing in the dim perspective, should have furnished designs for the aisles of Christian temples, and the sunset, burning among its fretted branches, should have suggested the gorgeous painted window of the cathedral. It looks like a place made for worship, all its sentiments and associations seem of a sacred and solemn character. Nature, with folded hands, as Longfellow says, seems kneeling there in prayer. It certainly reminds us in various ways of the power, wisdom, and goodness of him who thus spake by the mouth of his prophet: " I will plant in the wilderness the cedar, the fir tree, and the pine, and the box tree together: that they may see, and know, and consider, and understand together, that the hand of the Lord hath done this, and the Holy One of Israel hath created it."—*Hugh Macmillan, in "Bible Teachings in Nature,"* 1867.

Verse 10.—"*Creeping things.*" In public worship all should join. The little strings go to make up a concert, as well as the great.—*Thomas Goodwin.*

Verse 10.—" *Flying fowl.*" Thus the air is vocal. It has a hallelujah of its own. The " *flying fowl* " praise him ; whether it be " the stork that knoweth her appointed time" (Jer. viii. 7), or " the sparrow alone upon the housetop" (Ps. cii. 7), or " the raven of the valley" (Prov. xxx. 17), or the eagle " stirring up her nest, and fluttering over her young" (Deut. xxxii. 11), or the turtle making its voice to be heard in the land (Song. ii. 12), or the dove winging its way to the wilderness (Ps. lv. 6). This is creation's harp (truer and sweeter than Memnon's) which each sunrise awakens, " turning all the air to music."—*Horatius Bonar, in* "*Earth's Morning ; or, Thoughts on Genesis,*" 1875.

Verse 11.—"*Kings of the earth, and all people ; princes.*" As kings and princes are blinded by the dazzling influence of their station, so as to think the world was made for them, and to despise God in the pride of their hearts, he particularly calls them to this duty ; and, by mentioning them first, he reproves their ingratitude in withholding their tribute of praise when they are under greater obligations than others. As all men originally stand upon a level as to condition, the higher persons have risen, and the nearer they have been brought to God, the more sacredly are they bound to proclaim his goodness. The more intolerable is the wickedness of kings and princes who claim exemption from the common rule, when they ought rather to inculcate it upon others, and lead the way. He could have addressed his exhortation at once summarily to all men, as indeed he mentions *people* in general terms ; but by thrice specifying *princes* he suggests that they are slow to discharge the duty, and need to be urged to it.—*John Calvin.*

Verse 11.—"*Kings of the earth*" ; " *judges of the earth*" ; these are not proud but humiliating titles ; for *earthly* kings and *earthly* judges will not be kings and judges long.

Verse 12.—"*Both young men, and maidens ; old men, and children.*" The parties are mentioned by couples, being tied two and two together. "*Young men and maidens ; old men and children.*" And here is a double *caveat ;* fiirst, against presumption ; and secondly, against despair. First, that the younger sort might desire to praise God, they are exhorted to address themselves to the service of God, to remember their Creator in the days of their youth. Secondly, for aged men, that they might not doubt of the acceptation of their service, our Prophet exhorts them also. For the first, you know, David calls upon the sun and the moon to praise God. Should the sun reply, I will not do it in the morning, or at noon time, but when I am about to set ? or the moon reply, I will not in the full, but in the wane ? or the tree, not in the spring time, or in the summer, but at the fall of the leaf ? So likewise, thou young man, defer not the time of praising God : take the swing of thy youth, and do not defer to apply thyself to the service of God till thy old age ; but remember that for all these things thou shalt come to judgment. He that styles himself by the title *I AM*, cares not for I will be, or I have been, but he that is at this present : take heed, therefore, thou strong and lusty young man : the Devil that holds thee now will every day tie a new cord about thee. Consider this, you that are yet young, whom the morning sun of light adorns with his glorious rays : everyone doth not live to be old. Let us not procrastinate in God's service ; for the longer we defer to serve God, the farther God's grace is distant from us, and the dominion of Satan is more strengthened in our hearts ; the more we delay, the more is our debt, the greater our sin, and the less our grace. I will commend this lesson unto all. He that doth not repent to-day hath a day more to repent of, and a day less to repent in. I shall conclude with a hearty exhortation for us all, of what sex, age, and degree soever ; I could wish that all our lives might end like this book of Psalms, in blessing and praising Almighty God.—*Thomas Cheshire, in* "*A Sermon preached, in Saint Paule's Church,*" 1641.

Verse 12.—"*Old men.*" Think not, ye who are now near the end of life, that your tongues may without blame be silent in the praises of the Lord, because you are come to those years in which men say, they " have no pleasure in them."

Were you not frequently praising God when you were children and young men? Have you less, or have you not greater, reason now to praise God than in those early days of life?

Old men ought to be better qualified than young persons to show forth the glory both of the perfections and works of God, because they have enjoyed more time, and more abundant opportunities than their juniors, for attaining the knowledge of God, and of those glorious perfections and works which furnish us with endless materials for praise. " Days should speak, and the multitude of years should teach wisdom."

The heavens are constantly declaring " the glory of God, and the firmament showeth forth his handy work. Day unto day uttereth speech, and night unto night showeth knowledge." Have you, then, lived twenty thousand days and twenty thousand nights? What deep impressions ought to be made upon your spirits, of those wonders which have been preached in your ears or eyes, ever since you could use your bodily senses as ministers to your intellectual powers! All the works of God praise him, by showing forth how wonderful in power, and goodness, and wisdom, the Creator is. Your tongues are indeed inexcusable, if they are silent in the praises of him whose glory is proclaimed by every object above or around them, and even by every member of their own bodies, and every faculty of their souls. But old men are doubly inexcusable, if they are inattentive to those precious instructions which are given them by all the works of God which they have seen, or of which they have been informed, every day since the powers of their rational natures began to operate.

But old men in this highly favoured land have been blessed with more excellent instructions than those which are given them by the mountains and fruitful valleys, by the dragons of the desert or the deep, or by the fowls of heaven, and the beasts of the earth, or by the sun and stars of heaven. For many more years than young men or maidens you have been learners, or you are very blamable if you have not been at the school of Christ. You were early taught to read the Word of God. In the course of fifty or sixty years, you have probably heard six thousand religious discourses from the ministers of Christ, not to mention other excellent means you have enjoyed for increasing in the knowledge of God. " For the time," says Paul to the Hebrew Christians, " ye might have been teachers." May I not say the same to all aged Christians, who have had the Bible in their possession, and have enjoyed opportunities of frequenting the holy assemblies from their earliest days? May it not be expected that your hearts and your mouths will be filled with the praises of God, not only as your Maker, but as your Redeemer?

But there are many things more especially relating to themselves, which should induce the aged to abound in this duty of praise to God.

Consider how long you have lived. Is not every day of life, and even every hour, and every moment, an undeserved mercy? You might have been cut off from the breast and the womb, for you were conceived in iniquity and born in sin. How many of your race have been cut off before they could distinguish between their right hand and their left, before they could do good or evil! Since you were moral agents, not a day has passed in which you were not chargeable with many sins. What riches of long-suffering is manifested in a life of sixty or seventy years! If you have lived in a state of sin all that time, have you not reason to be astonished, that you are not already in a condition which would for ever render it impossible for you to utter the voice of praise? Give glory, therefore, to that God who has still preserved you alive.

Consider with what mercies your days have been filled up. God's mercies have been new to you every morning, although every day you have sinned against him. Reflections on your own conduct through life will suggest to you many reasons for praise and thanksgiving. But on this part of the subject it is proper to put you in mind of the two great classes into which men are divided: saints and sinners. If you belong to the former class, who is it that has made you to differ from others? Give thanks to him who delivered you from the power of darkness and translated you into the kingdom of his dear Son. Have you been enabled to do some good works in the course of your lives? For every one of them bless God, who wrought "in you both to will and to do of his good pleasure." Have any of your endeavours been successful to bring about the reformation of any of your fellow-men, or to promote their spiritual welfare? What sufficient thanks can you render to God for making you the humble ministers of his grace?

But there are too many of the old who have no reason to think that they have yet passed from death to life. These, certainly, are very unfit to praise God, and will not be able to praise him with their hearts, unless that change pass upon them, without which no man shall ever enter into the kingdom of heaven. Yet, surely, they have great reason to praise the Lord; and they may see good reason for it, although they cannot carry their knowledge into practice. You have, indeed, greater reason to praise God that you are in the land of the living, than those who are in a better state; because, if you were deprived of your present life, nothing is left for you but the terrors of eternal death. Bless God, ye who have lived fifty or sixty years in sin, and have been all along spared in a world so full of mercy. You are still called by the gospel to receive that salvation which you have long treated with contempt.—*Condensed from a Sermon by George Lawson* (1749—1820), *entitled, "The Duty of the Old to praise God."*

Verse 12.—"*Old men and children.*" It is interesting always to see a friendship between the old and the young. It is striking to see the aged one retaining so much of freshness and simplicity as not to repel the sympathies of boyhood. It is surprising to see the younger one so advanced and thoughtful, as not to find dull the society of one who has outlived excitability and passion.—*Frederick William Robertson.*

Verses 12, 13.—The psalms are church songs, and all who belong to the church are to sing them. "*Both young men, and maidens; old men, and children; let them praise the name of the* LORD." The ripe believer who can triumph in the steadfast hope of God's glory, is to lend his voice to swell the song of the church when she cries to God out of the depths'; and the penitent, who is still sitting in darkness, is not to refrain his voice when the church pours out in song her sense of God's love. The whole church has fellowship in the psalms.—*William Binnie, in "The Psalms, their History, Teachings, and Use,"* 1870.

Verses 12, 13.—"*Old men . . Let them praise the name of the* LORD." It is a favourite speculation of mine that if spared to sixty we then enter on the seventh decade of human life, and that this, if possible, should be turned into the Sabbath of our earthly pilgrimage and spent sabbatically, as if on the shores of an eternal world, or in the outer courts, as it were, of the temple that is above, the tabernacle in heaven.—*Thomas Chalmers.*

Verse 13.—"*Let them praise.*" Exactly as at the close of the first great division of the anthem (verse 5), and, in the same way as there, the reason for the exhortation follows in the next clause. But it is a different reason. It is no longer because he has given them a decree, bound them as passive, unconscious creatures by a law which they cannot transgress. (It is the fearful mystery of the reasonable will that it can transgress the law.) It is because his name is exalted, so that the eyes of men can see, and the hearts and tongues of men confess it; it is because he has graciously revealed himself to, and mightily succoured, the people whom he loves, the nation who are near to him. If it be said that what was designed to be a Universal Anthem is thus narrowed at its close, it must be remembered that, however largely the glory of God was written on the visible creation, it was only to the Jew that any direct revelation of his character had been made.—*J. J. Stewart Perowne.*

Verse 13.—"*The name of Jehovah.*" Jehovah is a name of great power and efficacy, a name that hath in it five vowels, without which no language can be expressed; a name that hath in it also three syllables, to signify the Trinity of Persons, the eternity of God, One in Three, and Three in One; a name of such dread and reverence amongst the Jews, that they tremble to name it, and therefore they use the name *Adonai* (Lord) in all their devotions. And thus ought every one to stand in awe, and sin not by taking the name of God in vain ; but to sing praises, to honour, to remember, to declare, to exalt, and bless it ; for holy and reverend, only worthy and excellent is his name.—*Rayment, 1630.*

Verse 14.—"*His people, the praise of all his saints.*" But among all, one class in particular is called on to praise him, for they have an additional motive for so doing, namely, " *his people,*" and " *his saints.*" As man above all the creatures, so among men his elect or chosen, who are the objects of his special grace, and, above all, of his redeeming love. "*He also exalteth the horn of his people*"— exalts them, one and all, from the death of sin to the life of righteousness, and consequent on this, from the dust of earth to the glory of heaven. "*The praise of all his saints*" ; and, yet again, among them, of one people in particular— "*even of the children of Israel, a people near unto him.*" "*Near to him*" of old, and yet again to be—yea, nearest of all the peoples of the earth—when he recalls them from their dispersion, and again places his name and his throne among them. HALLELUJAH—PRAISE YE THE LORD.— *William De Burgh.*

Verse 14.—"*A people near unto him.*" Jesus took our nature, and became one with us ; thus he is " *near* " unto us ; he gives us his Holy Spirit, brings us into union with himself, and thus we are near to him. This is our highest honour, an unfailing source of happiness and peace. We are near to him in point of *relation*, being his children ; near to him in point of *affection*, being loved with an ever-lasting love ; we are near to him in point of *union*, being members of his body, of his flesh, and of his bones ; we are near to him in point of *fellowship*, walking with him as a man walketh with his friend ; we are near to him in point of *attention*, being the objects of his daily, hourly, tender care ; we shall soon be near to him in point of *locality*, when our mansion is prepared, for we shall depart to be with Christ, which is far better. We are near to him when poor, and when deeply tried ; and if ever nearer at one time than another, we shall be nearest to' him in death. If we are near unto him, he will sympathize with us in all our sorrows, assist us in all our trials, protect us in all our dangers, hold intercourse with us in all our lonely hours, provide for us in all seasons of necessity, and honourably introduce us to glory. Let us realize this fact daily—we are near and dear to our God.—*James Smith.*

HINTS TO THE VILLAGE PREACHER.

Whole Psalm.—I. What is implied in the invitation to the natural creation to praise God. 1. That praise is due to God on its account. 2. That it is due from those for whose benefit it was created. 3. That it is a reproof to those who do not praise God who are actually capable of it. " If these should hold their peace, the stones would immediately cry out." II. What is implied in the invitation to innocent beings to praise God. " Praise ye the Lord from the heavens. Praise ye him all his angels, praise ye him all his hosts" : verses 1, 2.—1. That they owe their creation in innocence to God. 2. That they owe their preservation in innocence to him. 3. That they owe the reward of their innocence to him. III. What is implied in the invitation to fallen beings to praise God : " Kings of the earth and all people," &c. : verses 11—13.—1. That God is merciful and ready to forgive. " Not willing that any should perish," etc. They would not be called upon to praise God if they were irrecoverably lost. Our Lord would not when on earth accept praise from an evil spirit. 2. That means of restoration from the fall are provided by God for men. Without this they would have no hope, and could offer no praise. IV. What is implied in the invitation to the redeemed to praise God : verse 14.—1. That God is their God. 2. That all his perfections are engaged for their present and eternal welfare. —*G. R.*

Verse 1.—"*Praise ye the Lord.*" I. The Voice—of Scripture, of nature, of grace, of duty. II. The Ear on which it rightly falls—of saints and sinners, old and young, healthy and sick. It falls on our ear. III. The Time when it is heard. Now, ever, yet also at special times. IV. The Response which we will give. Let us now praise with heart, life, lip.

Verse 1 (*second and third clauses*).—I. The character of the praises of heaven. II. How far they influence us who are here below. III. The hope which we have of uniting in them.

Verse 2.—I. The angels as praiseful servants. II. The other hosts of God, and how they praise him. III. The rule without exception : " *all—all.*" Imagine one heavenly being living without praising the Lord !

Verse 3.—I. God's praise continual both day and night. II. Light the leading fountain of this praise. III. Life behind all, calling for the praise.

Verses 5, 6.—Creation and conservation, two chief reasons for praise.

Verse 7.—God's praise from dark, deep, and mysterious things.

Verse 8.—Canon Liddon preached in St. Paul's on Sunday afternoon, December 23, 1883, and took for his text Ps. cxlviii. 8, "*Wind and storm fulfilling his word.*" He spoke of the divine use of destructive forces. I. In the physical world we see wind and storm fulfilling God's word. 1. The Bible occasionally lifts the veil, and shows us how destructive forces of Nature have been the servants of God. 2. Modern history illustrates this vividly. II. In the human, spiritual, and moral world, we find new and rich application of the words of the text. 1. In the State we see the storm of invasion and the storm of revolution fulfilling God's word. 2. In the Church we see the storm of persecution and the storm of controversy fulfilling God's word. 3. In the experience of individual life we see outward troubles, and inward storms of religious doubts fulfilling God's word.—*The Contemporary Pulpit*, 1884.

Verse 9.—"*Trees.*" The glory of God as seen in trees.

Verse 10.—The wildest, the quietest, the most depressed, and the most aspiring should each have its song.

Verses 11—13.—I. The universal King. Alone in excelling. Supreme in glory. II. The universal summons. Of all nations, ranks, classes and ages. Foreshadowing the Judgment. III. The universal duty : praise,—constant, emphatic, growing.— *W. B. H.*

Verse 12.—God to be served by strength and beauty, experience and expectation.

Verse 12.—"*And children.*" A Children's Address. I. Where the children are found (verses 11 and 12). In royal and distinguished society : yet not lost or overlooked. II. What they are called to. "Praise the Lord." Even they have abundant reason. III. What are the lessons of the subject ? 1. Children should come up with their parents on the Sabbath. 2. Children should unite in heart and voice in God's praises. 3. Children should seek fitness for this praise by believing in Christ.— *W. B. H.*

Verse 14.—The Favoured People and their God. I. What he does for them. II. What he makes them : "Saints." III. Who they are : "Children of Israel." IV. Where they are : "Near unto him." V. What they do for him : "Praise ye the Lord."

PSALM CXLIX.

We are almost at the last Psalm, and still among the Hallelujahs. This is "a new song," evidently intended for the new creation, and the men who are of new heart. It is such a song as may be sung at the coming of the Lord, when the new dispensation shall bring overthrow to the wicked and honour to all the saints. The tone is exceedingly jubilant and exultant. All through one hears the beat of the feet of dancing maidens, keeping time to the timbrel and harp.

EXPOSITION.

PRAISE ye the LORD. Sing unto the LORD a new song, *and* his praise in the congregation of saints.

2 Let Israel rejoice in him that made him : let the children of Zion be joyful in their King.

3 Let them praise his name in the dance : let them sing praises unto him with the timbrel and harp.

4 For the LORD taketh pleasure in his people : he will beautify the meek with salvation.

5 Let the saints be joyful in glory : let them sing aloud upon their beds.

6 *Let* the high *praises* of God *be* in their mouth, and a two-edged sword in their hand ;

7 To execute vengeance upon the heathen, *and* punishments upon the people ;

8 To bind their kings with chains, and their nobles with fetters of iron ;

9 To execute upon them the judgment written : this honour have all his saints. Praise ye the LORD.

1. "*Praise ye the* LORD." Specially you, ye chosen people, whom he has made to be his saints. You have praised him aforetime, praise him yet again ; yea, for ever praise him. With renewed zeal and fresh delight lift up your song unto Jehovah. "*Sing unto the* LORD *a new song.*" Sing, for it is the fittest method for expressing reverent praise. Sing a hymn newly composed, for you have now a new knowledge of God. He is ever new in his manifestations ; his mercies are new every morning ; his deliverances are new in every night of sorrow ; let your gratitude and thanksgivings be new also. It is well to repeat the old ; it is more useful to invent the new. Novelty goes well with heartiness. Our singing should be " unto the Lord " ; the songs we sing should be of him and to him, " for of him, and to him, and through him are all things." Among our novelties there should be new songs : alas ! men are fonder of making new complaints than new psalms. Our new songs should be devised in Jehovah's honour ; indeed all our newest thoughts should run towards him. Never can we find a nobler subject for a song than the Lord, nor one more full of fresh matter for a new song, nor one which we are personally so much bound to sing as a new song " unto the Lord." "*And his praise in the congregation of saints.*" Saints are precious, and a congregation of saints is a treasure house of jewels. God is in the midst of saints, and because of this we may well long to be among them. They are so full of his praise that we feel at home among them when we are ourselves full of praise. The sanctuary is the house of praise as well as the house of prayer. All

saints praise God : they would not be saints if they did not. Their praise is sincere, suitable, seasonable, and acceptable. Personal praise is sweet unto God, but congregated praise has a multiplicity of sweetnesses in it. When holy ones meet, they adore The Holy One. Saints do not gather to amuse themselves with music, nor to extol one another, but to sing his praise whose saints they are. A congregation of saints is heaven upon earth : should not Jehovah, the Lord of saints, have all the praise that can come from such an assembly ? Yet at times even saintly conclaves need to be stirred up to thanksgiving ; for saints may be sad and apprehensive, and then their spirits require to be raised to a higher key, and stimulated to happier worship.

2. "*Let Israel rejoice in him that made him.*" Here is that new creation which calls for the new song. It was Jehovah who made Israel to be Israel, and the tribes to become a great nation : therefore let the Founder of the nation be had in perpetual honour. Joy and rejoicing are evidently to be the special characteristics of the new song. The religion of the dead in sin is more apt to chant dirges than to sing hallelujahs ; but when we are made new in the spirit of our minds we joy and rejoice in him that made us. Our joy is in our God and King : we choose no lower delight. "*Let the children of Zion be joyful in their King.*" Those who had seen the tribes formed into a settled kingdom as well as into a united nation should rejoice. Israel is the nation, Zion is the capital of the kingdom : Israel rejoices in her Maker, Zion in her King. In the case of our God we who believe in him are as glad of his Government as we are of his Creation : his reign is as truly the making of us as was his divine power. The children of Israel are happy to be made a people ; the children of Zion are equally happy to be ruled as a people. In every character our God is the source of joy to us : this verse issues a permit to our joy, yea it lays an injunction upon us to be glad in the Lord.

3. "*Let them praise his name in the dance: let them sing praises unto him with the timbrel and harp.*" Thus let them repeat the triumph of the Red Sea, which was ever the typical glory of Israel. Miriam led the daughters of Israel in the dance when the Lord had triumphed gloriously ; was it not most fit that she should ? The sacred dance of devout joy is no example, nor even excuse, for frivolous dances, much less for lewd ones. Who could help dancing when Egypt was vanquished, and the tribes were free ? Every mode of expressing delight was bound to be employed on so memorable an occasion. Dancing, singing, and playing on instruments were all called into requisition, and most fitly so. There are unusual seasons which call for unusual expressions of joy. When the Lord saves a soul its holy joy overflows, and it cannot find channels enough for its exceeding gratitude : if the man does not leap, or play, or sing, at any rate he praises God, and wishes for a thousand tongues with which to magnify his Saviour. Who would wish it to be otherwise ? Young converts are not to be restrained in their joy. Let them sing and dance while they can. How can they mourn now that their Bridegroom is with them ? ` Let us give the utmost liberty to joy. Let us never attempt its suppression, but issue in the terms of this verse a double license for exultation. If any ought to be glad it is the children of Zion ; rejoicing is more fit for Israel than for any other people : it is their own folly and fault that they are not oftener brimming with joy in God, for the very thought of him is delight.

4. "*For the* LORD *taketh pleasure in his people*" *;* and therefore they should take pleasure in him. If our joy be pleasing to him let us make it full. What condescension is this on Jehovah's part, to notice, to love, and to delight in his chosen ! Surely there is nothing in our persons, or our actions, which could cause pleasure to the Ever-blessed One, were it not that he condescends to men of low estate. The thought of the Lord's taking pleasure in us is a mine of joy never to be exhausted. "*He will beautify the meek with salvation.*" They are humble, and feel their need of salvation ; he is gracious, and bestows it upon them. They lament their deformity, and he puts a beauty upon them of the choicest sort. He saves them by sanctifying them, and thus they wear the beauty of holiness, and the beauty of a joy which springs out of full salvation. He

makes his people meek, and then makes the meek beautiful. Herein is grand argument for worshipping the Lord with the utmost exultation : he who takes such a pleasure in us must be approached with every token of exceeding joy.

God taketh pleasure in all his children as Jacob loved all his sons ; but the meek are his Josephs, and upon these he puts the coat of many colours, beautifying them with peace, content, joy, holiness, and influence. A meek and quiet spirit is called "an ornament," and certainly it is "the beauty of holiness." When God himself beautifies a man, he becomes beautiful indeed and beautiful for ever.

The verse may be read, "He shall beautify the meek with salvation," or "He shall beautify the afflicted with deliverance," or, "He shall beautify the meek with victory" ; and each of these readings gives a new shade of meaning, well worthy of quiet consideration. Each reading also suggests new cause for joyful adoration. "O come, let us sing unto the Lord."

5. "*Let the saints be joyful in glory.*" God has honoured them, and put a rare glory upon them ; therefore let them exult therein. Shall those to whom God is their glory be cast down and troubled ? Nay, let their joy proclaim their honourable estate. "*Let them sing aloud upon their beds.*" Their exultation should express itself in shouts and songs, for it is not a feeling of which they have any need to be ashamed. That which is so fully justified by fact, may well be loudly proclaimed. Even in their quietest retreats let them burst into song ; when no one hears them, let them sing aloud unto God. If confined by sickness let them joy in God. In the night watches let them not lie awake and weep, but like nightingales let them charm the midnight hours. Their shouts are not now for the battlefield, but for the places of their rest : they can peacefully lie down and yet enjoy the victory with which the Lord has beautified them. Without fighting, faith wins and sings the victory. What a blessing to have our beds made into thrones, and our retirements turned into triumphs !

6. "*Let the high praises of God be in their mouth, and a two-edged sword in their hand.*" It seems they are not always on their beds, but are ready for deeds of prowess. When called to fight, the meek are very hard to overcome ; they are just as steady in conflict as they are steadfast in patience. Besides, their way of fighting is of an extraordinary sort, for they sing to God but keep their swords in their hands. They can do two things at a time : if they do not wield the trowel and the sword, at least they sing and strike. In this Israel was not an example, but a type : we will not copy the chosen people in making literal war, but we will fulfil the emblem by carrying on spiritual war. We praise God and contend with our corruptions ; we sing joyfully and war earnestly with evil of every kind. Our weapons are not carnal, but they are mighty, and wound with both back and edge. The word of God is all edge ; whichever way we turn it, it strikes deadly blows at falsehood and wickedness. If we do not praise we shall grow sad in our conflict ; and if we do not fight we shall become presumptuous in our song. The verse indicates a happy blending of the chorister and the crusader.

Note how each thing in the believer is emphatic : if he sings, it is high praises, and praises deep down in his throat, as the original hath it ; and if he fights, it is with the sword, and the sword is two-edged. The living God imparts vigorous life to those who trust him. They are not of a neutral tint : men both hear them and feel them. Quiet is their spirit, but in that very quietude abides the thunder of an irresistible force. When godly men give battle to the powers of evil each conflict is high praise unto the God of goodness. Even the tumult of our holy war is a part of the music of our lives.

7. "*To execute vengeance upon the heathen, and punishments upon the people.*" This was once literally the duty of Israel : when they came into Canaan they fulfilled the righteous sentence of the Lord upon guilty nations. At this hour, under the gentler dispensation of grace, we wrestle not with flesh and blood ; yet is our warfare none the less stern, and our victory none the less sure. All evil shall eventually be overthrown : the Lord shall display his justice against evildoers, and in that warfare his servants shall play their parts. The saints shall

judge the world. Both the conflict and the victory at the end of it shall cause glory to God, and honour to his holy ones.

8. "*To bind their kings with chains, and their nobles with fetters of iron.*" Thus are the greatest enemies of Jehovah and his people reduced to shame, rendered helpless, and themselves punished. This was Israel's boast in actual fact, it is ours spiritually. The chief powers of evil shall be restrained and ultimately destroyed. Those who made captives of the godly shall themselves be made captive. The powers of evil cannot bind *our* King, but by his power *their* king shall be bound with a great chain, and shut up in the bottomless pit, that he may at length be trodden under the feet of saints.

9. "*To execute upon them the judgment written.*" Israel as a nation had this to do, and did it, and then they rejoiced in the God who gave success to their arms. *We* praise our God after another fashion ; we are not executioners of justice, but heralds of mercy. It would be a sad thing for any one to misuse this text : lest any warlike believer should be led to do so, we would remind him that the execution must not go beyond the sentence and warrant ; and we have received no warrant of execution against our fellow men. Christians have no commission of vengeance ; it is theirs to execute the command of mercy, and that alone. "*This honor have all his saints.*" All the godly shared in the triumphs of the Lord when he smote Israel's foes. *We* have like honour, but it is shown in victories of another sort. All the holy ones are sent upon errands by their holy Lord. The honours described in this psalm are common to all the family of grace ; and such service as the Lord appoints is to be undertaken by every one of them, without exception. The Lord honours all his chosen here, and he will glorify them all hereafter : this rule is without exception. Surely in this we have the best argument for glorifying the Lord, wherefore we close our new song with another Hallelujah, "*Praise ye the Lord.*"

EXPLANATORY NOTES.

Whole Psalm.—The foregoing psalm was a hymn of praise to the Creator ; this is a hymn to the Redeemer.—*Matthew Henry.*

Whole Psalm.—The New Testament spiritual church cannot pray as the Old Testament national church here prays. Under the illusion that it must be used as a prayer without any spiritual transmutation, Psalm cxlix. has become the watchword of the most horrible errors. It was by means of this psalm that Caspar Scloppius, in his *Classicum Belli Sacri*, which, as Bakius says, is written, not with ink, but with blood, inflamed the Roman Catholic princes to the Thirty Years' Religious War. And in the Protestant church Thomas Müntzer stirred up the War of the Peasants by means of this psalm. We see that the Christian cannot make such a psalm directly his own, without disavowing the apostolic warning, " The weapons of our warfare are not carnal " (2 Cor. x. 4). The praying Christian must therefore transpose the letter of this psalm into the spirit of the New Covenant.—*Franz Delitzsch.*

Verse 1.—"*A new song*" ; for this psalm is a song of renovation. If Israel when restored and renewed had new cause for rejoicing, much more should the New Covenant Israel feel constrained to strike the new note of triumph. Infidels blaspheme, the ungrateful murmur, the thoughtless are silent, the mournful weep, all acting according to their old nature ; but new men take up a new mode, which is the divinely-inspired song of peace, charity, and joy in the Lord.— *Johannes Paulus Palanterius.*

Verse 1.—"*A new song.*" The old man hath an old song, the new man a new song. The Old Testament is an old song, the New Testament is a new song. . . . Whoso loveth earthly things singeth an old song : let him that desireth to sing a new song love the things of eternity. Love itself is new and eternal ; therefore is it ever new, because it never groweth old.—*Augustine.*

Verse 1.—*"Saints."*—A title not to be restricted to the godly of the first times, but common to all that are saved in all after-times also, as Eph. iv. 12.   This name putteth mere morality and formal profession out of countenance, as the sun doth a glow-worm.   Saintship is a matter of Divine workmanship, and therefore it is far more remarkable than human excellence.   We should keep up the name of " saints," that the reality of the true religion be not lowered by avoiding this title ; for in these times it is to be feared that the name is out of use, because holiness itself is out of fashion.—*Thomas Goodwin.*

Verse 2.—*"Let Israel rejoice,"* etc.   Give us, oh, give us the man who sings at his work !   Be his occupation what it may, he is equal to any of those who follow the same pursuit in silent sullenness.   He will do more in the same time—he will do it better—he will persevere longer.   One is scarcely sensible of fatigue whilst he marches to music.   The very stars are said to make harmony as they revolve in their spheres.   Wondrous is the strength of cheerfulness, altogether past calculation its powers of endurance.   Efforts to be permanently useful must be uniformly joyous—a spiritual sunshine—graceful from very gladness—beautiful because bright.—*Thomas Carlyle.*

Verse 2.—*"Rejoice in him that made him ; let the children of Zion be joyful."* You are never right until you can be heartily merry in the Lord, nor until you can enjoy mirth in connection with holiness.— *Walter Marshall.*

Verse 2.—*"Him that made him."*   Jehovah is called *Maker*, as one who formed Israel as a nation, and constituted the people a kingdom, though they had been a race of slaves.   This is more than a general creation of men.—*Hermann Venema.*

Verse 2.—Literally the Hebrew here brings forward the mystic doctrine of the Trinity, for it reads, " Let Israel rejoice in God *his Makers,"*—*Simon de Muis.*

Verse 2.—*"Joyful in their King."*   I beg the reader to remark with me, here is nothing said of Israel being joyful in what their king had done for them. These things, in their proper place, became sweet subjects of praise.   But the subject of praise in which Israel is now to be engaged is Jesus himself.   Reader, pause over this apparently small, but most important, distinction.   The Lord is gracious in his gifts, gracious in his love, gracious in his salvation.   Every thing he gives, it is from his mercy, and ever to be so acknowledged.   But Jesus' gifts are not himself : I cannot be satisfied with his gifts, while I know that to others he gives his *Person.*   It is Jesus himself I want.   Though he give me all things that I need, yet if he be to me himself all things that I need, in him I have all things. Hence, therefore, let us see that Jesus not only gives us all, but that he is our all. —*Robert Hawker.*

Verse 3.—*" The dance "* was in early times one of the modes of expressing religious joy (Ex. xv. 20 ; 2 Sam. vi. 16).   When from any cause men's ideas shall undergo such a revolution as to lead them to do the same thing for the same purpose, it will be time enough to discuss that matter.   In our time, dancing has no such use, and cannot, therefore, in any wise be justified by pleading the practice of pious Jews of old.—*William Swan Plumer.*

Verse 3.—*"Let them sing praises unto him with the timbrel and harp."*   They who from hence urge the use of music in religious worship, must, by the same rule, introduce dancing, for they went together, as in David's dancing before the ark (Judges xxi. 21).   But whereas many Scriptures in the New Testament keep up singing as a gospel ordinance, none provide for the keeping up of music and dancing ; the gospel canon for psalmody is to " sing with the spirit and with the understanding."—*Matthew Henry.*

Verse 3.—*" Timbrel."*   The *toph* was employed by David in all the festivities of religion (2 Sam. vi. 5).   The occasions on which it was used were mostly joyful, and those who played upon it were generally females (Psalm lxviii. 25), as was the case among most ancient nations, and is so at the present day in the East. The usages of the modern East might adequately illustrate all the scriptural allusions to this instrument, but happily we have more ancient and very valuable illustration from the monuments of Egypt. In these we find that the tambourine was a favourite instrument, both on sacred and festive occasions. There were three kinds, differing, no doubt, in sound as well as in form ; one was circular, another square or oblong, and the third consisted of two squares separated by a bar. They were all beaten by the hand, and often used as an accompaniment to the harp and other instruments. The tambourine was usually played by females, who are represented as dancing to its sound without the accompaniment of any other instrument.—*John Kitto.*

Verse 3.—*"Harp."* Of the *kinnor* the Scripture affords little further information than that it was composed of the sounding parts of good wood, and furnished with strings. Josephus asserts that it was furnished with ten strings, and played with a *plectrum ;* which, however, is not understood to imply that it never had any other number of strings, or was always played with the *plectrum.* David certainly played it with the hand (1 Sam. xvi. 23 ; xviii. 10 ; xix. 9) ; and it was probably used in both ways, according to its size. That this instrument was really a *harp* is now very generally denied (*Kitto*). The reader will, by this time, have balanced the probabilities as to the nature and construction of the *kinnor ;* and most likely he will be led to think that it was either a *guitar* or *lyre,* a belief which seems to be gaining ground, on account of the aptitude of such instruments for the uses to which the *kinnor* was devoted.—*J. Stainer.*

Verse 4.—*"For the Lord taketh pleasure in his people."* In the text there are two causes assigned why the saints should be excited to praise the Lord, and to be joyful in their King.

I.—THE DELIGHT WHICH THE LORD HAS IN THE SAINTS. "He taketh pleasure in his people." In this statement there are three subjects for inquiry, namely : 1. *Who* are the Lord's people ? 2. *Why* he takes pleasure in them ? 3. *In what respects* he takes pleasure in them ?

1. *Who are the Lord's people ?* Many are the names and titles given to them in Scripture. We find one in the second clause of the text ; but it equally belongs to the first. "He will beautify *the meek.*" The scriptural term "*meekness*" is one which singularly characterizes and distinguishes the true Christian. It, in fact, contains in itself a combination of graces, which are most evidently the fruit of the Spirit, and can grow on no other tree than on the Christian vine. *Meekness,* as a Christian grace, may be considered as it respects both God and man. As it respects God, it implies poverty of spirit ; humiliation of heart arising from a sense of guilt and a feeling of corruption ; submission to God's will ; silence and patience under his rod ; acquiescence with his dispensations ; and a surrender of our own natural desires and inclinations to his overruling appointments. As it respects man, meekness comprehends lowliness of mind, and a readiness to prefer others before ourselves ; gentleness of disposition and behaviour ; forbearance under provocations ; forgiveness of injuries ; quietness of spirit, and moderation in pushing forward our own interest and benefit. These are the qualities which distinguish "*the meek.*" Are not these, my brethren, the graces and tempers and dispositions which characterize and adorn true Christians ? *They* are, in an especial manner, "*the meek* upon earth." In fact, there are, and can be, no others to whom this title really belongs. No man in his natural state can be *meek,* in the Scriptural sense of the word.

2. But *why* does the Lord "take pleasure" in them ? Is there anything in them of *their own,* which he can regard with complacency and delight ? No : they know and feel that they have no pretensions of this kind. It is not for their sake, but for his own sake ; for his name's, his truth's, and his mercy's sake, that he has now a favour unto them. The Lord "taketh pleasure in his people," because they are his people ; those whom he has purchased by his blood, renewed by his Spirit, and redeemed by his power. He "taketh pleasure in them," because in them he is himself honoured and glorified ; because he sees in them the travail of his soul, the fruit of his suffering and mediation ; because of the work which he has already begun in them ; because they already exhibit some traces of

his own image, some transcript of that mind which was in him, who was " meek and lowly in heart."

3. *In what respects* the Lord takes pleasure in his people. First : the Lord takes pleasure in them, inasmuch as he delights in *the exercise of their graces towards him.* They all believe in him, and have faith in his word and promises ; they rely on his truth and power ; they hope in his mercy ; they fear his displeasure ; they love his person and name. Secondly : the Lord hath pleasure in *the services* of his people. It is true, that they can do but little for him, and that little is nothing worth. At the best they can but render to him of his own again. But he regards their services, not with an eye to their intrinsic value in themselves, but for the sake of the willing mind from which they flow. He takes pleasure in their poor attempts to please him, because they are attempts. He weighs not the worth or merit of the action, but the principle and motive from which it springs. Thirdly : the Lord hath pleasure in the *prosperity* of his people. His name is love ; his nature is goodness ; and can we doubt but that he loves to see his people happy ? Nay, we are expressly told that " he rejoiceth over them with joy" ; that " he rejoiceth over them to do them good." Even in those dispensations which in themselves are grievous and painful he is seeking their good, and in the end promoting their happiness. What consolations do these reflections furnish to the *meek* and suffering servants of the Lord !

II.—Let us now consider THE LORD'S GRACIOUS DESIGNS concerning his people : "*He will beautify them with salvation.*" He designs not only to save, but to adorn and honour his people. Those " whom he justifies, them he also glorifies." He " will *beautify* them with salvation" ; a promise relating both to the present life and to the future one.

1. *To the present life.* It is the purpose of God to beautify his people with salvation in this world. There are many passages in the Scripture which intimate this purpose, and lead us to this view of the happy effects of religion, even in the present life. When the prodigal returned home to his father's house, contrite, penitent, and reformed, he was not only received with kindness, assured of forgiveness, and welcomed as a son, but he was *adorned* and *beautified* (Luke xv. 22). So in the forty-fifth Psalm, the church, the bride of Christ, is thus described : " The king's daughter is all glorious within : her clothing is of wrought gold. She shall be brought unto the king in raiment of needlework." " So shall he greatly desire thy *beauty.*" See also Eph. v. 25—27.

But what is the glory, the beauty, which is here meant in these passages, with which Christ will adorn and beautify his people ? It is " the beauty of holiness." We have already seen that the meek and quiet spirit by which the Christian is distinguished is an " ornament" to him ; and we read in another place that he is " adorned " with good works. It is the great object of the gospel to sanctify all who embrace it, to restore them to the image of God which they have lost through sin.

2. We may now consider this promise as it relates *to the future world.* Lovely and glorious as are the saints on earth, their beauty falls far short of the perfection to which it will attain hereafter. They are " predestinated to be conformed to the image of the Son" ; and when they awake up in another world, it will be after his likeness, without any remaining blemish, defect, or spot. Carry forward your thoughts to the morning of the resurrection, when this corruption shall have put on incorruption, this mortal immortality ; when the body, raised in honour and glory, shall be clothed in its beauteous apparel, and being made like unto Christ's glorious body, shall shine as the sun in the firmament ; when now, once more united to its kindred and sanctified spirit, it shall no longer be a weight, and a clog, and a hindrance, but become a furtherer of its joy, and a sharer and a helper in its spiritual happiness. This is the meaning of the text, this is the *beauty* which he has designed for his people, and for which he is now preparing them. In the contemplation of these, with reason may it be said to them, " Praise ye the Lord."—*Condensed from a Sermon by Edward Cooper*, 1826.

Verse 4.—Here is *ratio propositionis,* the important reason of the proposed praising of the Lord. Those who know that they are objects of Divine complacency are likely to act on the principle of reciprocity. God takes pleasure in sanctifying, justifying and glorifying them ; they must surely take pleasure in extolling him as Friend, Protector, Law-giver, Leader, King, God !—*Simon de Muis.*

Verse 4.—*"He will beautify the meek with salvation."* Meekness not only gives great peace of mind, but often adds a lustre to the countenance. We only read of three in Scripture whose faces shone remarkably—viz., Christ, Moses, and Stephen—and they were eminent for meekness.—*Matthew Henry.*

Verse 4.—*"The meek."* In the Hebrew עֲנָוִים, *anavim,* means *poor and afflicted ones ;* but the term came afterwards to be applied to *merciful persons,* as bodily afflictions have a tendency to subdue pride, while abundance begets cruelty.—*John Calvin.*

Verse 5.—*"Let the saints be joyful,"* etc. Here begins a beautiful exegesis of the former passage. A protected people may rejoice with confidence. An anxious and fearful people could not sing aloud on their couches of repose.—*Simon de Muis.*

Verse 5.—*"Let the saints be joyful in glory : let them sing aloud upon their beds."* At what time soever God is pleased to inspire his grace and comfort into us, we ought to rejoice therein, and by night on the bed to seek him whom our soul loveth ; abridging that time of rest and ease, that it may become as beneficial unto us as the day itself. David was not satisfied by offering the sacrifice of thanksgiving in the courts of the Lord's house, and paying his vows in the presence of all the people ; but in the night also he would continue his song of God's mercy. Like that excellent bird, the nightingale, which is never weary nor spent by continuing her delightful notes, so this sweet singer of Israel was incessant in praising the Lord ; not giving sleep to his eyes until he had blessed his holy name. In time of affliction he made his bed to swim, praying unto the Lord to return and deliver his soul. Now in prosperity he gives thanks for the blessings he doth receive. When our bones are vexed, and our sleep departeth from us, we pray unto God to deal mercifully with us ; but when our diseases are healed, we do not return to give thanks, being soon overtaken with heaviness and security. And yet David did endeavour to watch in the night, that he might sing praise unto the Lord. He did not then only meditate in the law of God, when he could not take any rest (as Ahasuerus had the book of the records of the Chronicles read before him, when he could not sleep) ; for now he might lie down in peace, and sleep, when God made him to dwell in safety. Much less did he intend to procure sleep by a sinister performance of any good duty, like those who, by singing, or reading, or hearing, or meditating, will have an unworthy aim to bring themselves asleep. David saith, *"Let the saints sing aloud upon their beds"* : thereby to testify their cheerful devotion, and also to chase away the spirit of slumber.—*William Bloys, in "Meditations upon the xlii. Psalm,"* 1632.

Verse 5.—*"The saints in glory"* shall rest from their labours, but not from their praises.—*Robert Bellarmine.*

Verse 5.—*"Upon their beds,"* where before in the loneliness of night they consumed themselves with grief for their shame. Comp. Hosea vii. 14.—*E. W. Hengstenberg.*

Verse 5.—The saints of God know most of domestic joy and peace. As the word of Jesus in John xiv. records, they have sorrows in plenty, but the more of these, the greater will be their joy, because their sorrows are to be transmuted into joys. They are to sing aloud *" on their beds,"* or rather couches, for on these the Orientals not only sleep, but also dine, and feast. So this verse calls on the saints to hold a banquet, a feast of fat things. They are, as David sings in Ps. xxiii., to sit at the table prepared by the Lord in the presence of their enemies.—*Johannes Paulus Palanterius.*

Verse 5.—This verse has been fulfilled in solemn crises of saintly life. On beds of death, and at the scaffold and the stake, joy and glory have been kindled in the hearts of Christ's faithful witnesses.—*Thomas Le Blanc.*

Verse 5.—How I long for my bed ! Not that I may sleep—I lie awake often and long ! but to hold sweet communion with my God. What shall I render unto him for all his revelations and gifts to me ? Were there no historical evidence of the truth of Christianity, were there no well-established miracles, still I should believe that the religion propagated by the fishermen of Galilee is divine. The holy joy it brings to me must be from heaven. Do I write this boastingly, brother ? Nay, it is with tears of humble gratitude that I tell of the goodness of the Lord. —*From a private letter from Bapa Padmanji, in "Feathers for Arrows,"* 1870.

Verse 6.—*"Let the high praises of God be in their mouth and a two-edged sword in their hand."* Praise and power go ever hand in hand. The two things act and react upon each other. An era of spiritual force in the Church is always one of praise ; and when there comes some grand outburst of sacred song, we may expect that the people of God are entering upon some new crusade for Christ. Cromwell's Ironsides were sneeringly called psalm-singers ; but God's psalm-singers are always Ironsides. He who has a " new song in his mouth" is ever stronger, both to suffer and to labour, than the man who has a dumb spirit and a hymnless heart. When he sings at his work, he will both do more and do it better than he would without his song. Hence, we need not be surprised that all through its history the Church of God has travelled " along the line of music." —*William Taylor, in "The Study,"* 1873.

Verse 6.—*"The high praises of God."* This expression needs a little explication, because so variously rendered by most interpreters ; some rendering it only, exaltations of God ; others, praisings exalting God ; others, sublime praises of God ; others, praises highly uttered unto God : the reason whereof is, because the word *romemoth* in the text signifies sometimes actively, and then it notes the height, exaltation, and lifting up of anything to the observation of others ; and sometimes passively, and then it notes the height, worth, excellency of the thing that is exalted, or lifted up, in itself. But the scope and nature of the duty prescribed in the text necessarily comprehends both—as well the high acts for which God is to be praised, as the high praises to be given unto God for those high acts ; but especially the latter, namely, the height and excellency of the duty of praise to be performed for those high acts of God. This appears from the whole argument of the psalm, which is entirely laudatory, as also from the instrument wherewith these high praises are to be performed, namely, the " mouth," " *the high praises of God in their mouth*" *;* showing that the height herein mentioned is a property of man's work in praising God, and not only of the work of God, for which he is to be praised. In my observations I shall comprehend both, and all the particulars in the duty prescribed besides, which is this—

The duty of praising God is a high duty, which must exalt and lift up the high God in it.

This truth I shall labour to demonstrate, 1. From the Object. 2. The Effect. 3. Their Price. 4. Their Performance ; or, to use the School terms, they are " *high* " : 1. Objectivè. 2. Effectivè. 3. Appreciativè. 4. Perfectivè.

1. The praises of God are " *high* " in relation to their *Object*, which is none other but the Most High God, and that in the consideration of his transcendent height and sublimity over and above all other things or persons : so the Psalmist's resolution intimates (Ps. vii. 17), " I will praise the LORD according to his righteousness," which he expresseth in the following words, " To sing praise to the name of the Lord most high" ; and Ps. xcii. 1 : " It is a good thing to give thanks unto the LORD, and to sing praises unto thy name, O most High." In which places, and very many more in the Scriptures, it is evident that the Lord, considered in his highest sublimity, is the object of high praise, and that by most special and peculiar appropriation of it unto himself, and none other (Isai. xlii. 8).

2. In the second place, the praises of God will appear to be of a high, sublime nature, from the high *effect*, the genuine and proper fruit they produce, viz., that although their object, to whom they are peculiarly appropriate (I mean the Lord himself) be in his own nature, and of himself, most infinitely high and transcend-

ent, yet by the attribution and performance of praise unto him, doth he account his name, his power, his wisdom, and justice, and himself to be exalted thereby. What else do those expressions in Scripture imply wherein it is asserted, that by this high duty of praise the high Jehovah is exalted (Ps. cviii. 32) ; His sublime perfections are extolled and lifted up (Ps. lxviii. 4) ; His great Name is magnified (Luke i. 64) ; His infinite majesty is glorified (Ps. l. 23) ? Oh how high must be that duty, that adds height to the high God, that magnifies the great God, and glorifies the God of glory, and makes him higher, greater, and more glorious than he was before !

3. Thirdly, the praises of God are of a high nature, *appreciativè*, in respect of *the high estimation the Lord himself hath of them*, which appears two ways : (1.) By the high price wherewith he purchaseth them ; (2.) By the high delight he takes in them, after he hath procured them.

First. The *price* wherewith God is willing to purchase them is very high, for not only the expense of all his wisdom, power, and goodness, put forth in creation, not only the layings out of all his counsel, care, love, and faithfulness in providence and preservation ; but also the rich treasure of his promises, covenant, grace, yea, the precious blood of his own Son, in our redemption, is given freely, absolutely, intentionally, and ultimately, for no other thing but the purchase of high praises to God (Eph. i. 5, 6). All that God doth and giveth ; all that Christ doth and suffereth, is for the praise of the glory of his grace. I confess, consider men's highest praises of God, as they are man's performance, they are poor and inconsiderable things ; but consider them as they are the testimonies and expressions of a believing heart, declaring and making known the unspeakable wisdom, faithfulness, bounty, and excellencies of God, exercised in his works ; in this notion the Scripture declares the heart of God to be so taken with the desire of them, that he is willing to give heaven, earth, Himself, and Son to poor men for the praises of their hearts, hands, and tongues ; and accounts himself abundantly satisfied. Therefore, when his people will speak good of his name, they speak of him in the dialect of angels' notes, " *the high praises of God.*"

Secondly. The high value that God hath of " high praises" will be evident by the *high delight and pleasure* God takes in them thus purchased ; for skilful artists, and high-principled, elevated understandings, never take pleasure or delight in any thing or work which is not answerable to their highest principles, and proportionable to their uttermost skill and desire. Now the Lord, who is of the most perfect understanding, and deepest skill and knowledge, declares himself to take infinite delight in his people's praises. It is his solace and pleasure to be attended with them, either in earth or in heaven, by men or angels ; and his soul is ravished with the thoughts and contemplation of them.

4. In the fourth place, the praises of God are high, and of a high nature *per-fectivè*, that is, in respect of the high measure of grace they are to be attended withal in *their performance :* the Lord requiring the duty of high praise to be performed with a great measure of Scripture-light, with a high degree of effectual faith, and with a more ample proportion of practical holiness than any other of the most solemn exercises of his public worship.—*Condensed from a Sermon by Samuel Fairclough, entitled "The Prisoner's Praise,"* 1650.

Verse 8.—" *To bind their kings with chains,*" etc. Agrippa was captive to Paul. The word had him in bands like a prisoner, and made him confess against himself before Festus that he was " almost persuaded to be a Christian." Then it was verified which before was prophesied, " *They shall bind kings in chains, and nobles in fetters of iron.*" Oh, the majesty and force of the word !—*Henry Smith.*

Verse 8.—It was once the saying of Pompey, that with one stamp of his foot he could raise all Italy up in arms ; and the mighty men of the world may have nations, kingdoms, and commonwealths at their command, but yet God is more powerful than they all. If he do but arise, they shall all of them fly before him. If he once fall to fettering of princes, it shall be done so sure, that no flesh shall be able to knock off their bolts again.—*Stephen Gosson,* 1554—1623.

Verse 9.—"*This honour have all his saints.*" All other glories and honours are but feminine, weak, poor things to it. God is their glory; honoured they are with his blessed presence, honoured with his sight, with his embraces; they see him and enjoy him. This is the very glory of their honour, the height and pitch of all, for " in thy presence is joy, and at thy right hand there is pleasure for evermore," honour advanced into eternal gl_ y; and " *this honour* " also " *have all his saints* "; some *in spe,* and some *in re,* some *in hope,* and some *in deed ;* all either in promise or in possession.—*Mark Frank.*

Verse 9.—"*This honour have all his saints.*" "*His* saints" emphatically ; Divine providence foreseeing that in after ages some would usurp the title of saintship to whom it did not belong. " His saints" exclusively ; casting out saint traitors, as Beckett and Garnet ; saint hypocrites, and many others ; who, in the same sense as *auri sacra fames,* may be termed *sacri,* or *sancti,* sain.ts. But, what honour have all his saints? Mark what went before—" as it is written"; but by whom, and where ? Though chapters and verses be of later date, the Holy Spirit might have cited the book. O no ! He, to quicken our industry, refers us to the Word at large. However, " search the Scriptures," and therein we shall meet with many honours afforded to the saints ; both whilst they were living, and when they were dead.

Honour to their memories is sometimes paid them very abundantly, even by those who formerly were so niggardly and covetous as not to afford them a good word in their lifetime.

Many are made converts by the godly ends of good men ; as the centurion himself, who attended and ordered the crucifying of Christ, after his expiring broke forth into that testimony of him,—" Verily, this was the Son of God." So, such as rail at, revile, curse, condemn, persecute, execute pious people, speak other language of them when such men have passed the purgation of death, and confess them faithful and sincere servants of God.

The last " *honour* " is imitation of their virtuous examples. The Papists brag that Stapleton, their great controversial divine, was born on that very day whereon Sir Thomas More was put to death ; but Providence so ordereth it that out of the ashes of dead saints many living ones do spring and sprout, by following the pious precedents of such godly persons deceased.—*Thomas Fuller,* in "*Abel Redivivus.*"

HINTS TO THE VILLAGE PREACHER.

Verse 1.—"*Praise ye the Lord.*" I. The one work of a life. II. The work of the truly living of all degrees. III. Their work in many and various forms. IV. A work for which there is abundant cause, reason, and argument.

Verse 1.—I. A wonderful gift—to be a saint. II. A wonderful people—who are saints. III. A wonderful assembly—a congregation of saints. IV. A wonderful God—the object of their song.

Verses 1, 2.—*The new song of the saints.* I. The saints are God's children by the new birth. II. The new birth has given them a new heart. III. The new heart utters itself in a new song.—*C. A. D.*

Verses 1, 5.—I. We must praise God in public, " in the congregation of the saints" : the more the better ; it is like to heaven. II. We must praise him in private. " Let the saints" be so transported with their joy in God as to " sing aloud upon their beds," when they awake in the night, as David ; Ps. cxix. 62.—*Matthew Henry.*

Verse 2.—The duty, reasonableness, and benefit of holy joy.

Verse 2.—A peculiar people, their peculiar God, and their peculiar joy in him.

Verse 2 (second clause).—Christ's people may well rejoice :—I. In the majesty of his person. II. In the righteousness of his rule. III. In the extent of his conquests. IV. In the protection they enjoy under him. V. In the glory to which he will raise them.—*From "The Homiletical Library," 1882.*

Verses 2, 4.—The cause given to God's Israel for Praise. Consider, I. God's doings for them. They have reason to rejoice in God, and employ themselves in his service ; for it is he that "made" them. II. God's dominion over them. This follows upon the former : if he made them he is their King. III. God's delight in them. He is a King that rules by love, and therefore to be praised. IV. God's designs concerning them. Besides the present complacency he hath in them, he hath prepared for their future glory. "He will beautify the meek," etc.—*Matthew Henry.*

Verse 4.—The text bears other renderings. Read as in Authorized Version. I. *The character to be aimed at*—"*the meek.*" 1. Submissive to God. To his truth. To his dealings. 2. Gentle towards men. Bearing with patience. Forgiving with heartiness. Loving with perseverance. 3. Lowly in ourselves. II. *The favour to be enjoyed*—"*beautify.*" 1. The beauty of gentleness. 2. The beauty of peace. 3. The beauty of content. 4. The beauty of joy. 5. The beauty of holiness. 6. The beauty of respect and influence. III. *The good results to be expected.* 1. God will be glorified and Christ manifested. 2. Men will be attracted. 3. Heaven will be anticipated.

Verse 4 (*first clause*).—The Lord's taking pleasure in his people is, I. A wonderful evidence of his grace. II. The highest honour they can desire. III. Their security for time and eternity.—*J. F.*

Verse 5.—*Saintly joy.* I. The state to which God has lifted the saints : "glory," in contrast with sin, reproach, affliction. II. The emotion which accordingly befits the saints : "be joyful." III. The utterance of that emotion incumbent on the saints : "sing aloud."—*C. A. D.*

Verse 5 (*second clause*).—Let them praise God—I. Upon their beds of *rest,* upon their *nightly* couch. 1. Because of what God has done for them during the day. 2. Because sleep is the gift of God. 3. Because they have a bed to lie upon. 4. Because the Lord is their keeper (Psalm iv. 5, 8). II. Upon their beds of *sickness.* 1. Because it is God's will they should suffer. 2. Because affliction is often a proof of God's love. 3. Because, if sanctified, sickness is a great blessing. 4. Because praise offered upon a bed of sickness is a testimony to the power of religion. III. Upon their beds of *death.* 1. Because the sting of death is removed. 2. Because their Lord has passed through death. 3. Because Christ is with them while they suffer. 4. Because of what awaits them. 5. Because they have the glorious hope of resurrection.—*C. W. Townsend, of Inskip,* 1885.

Verse 6.—I. The Christian life a combination of adoration and conflict. II. In each case it should be at its best : "high praises," "two-edged sword." III. In each case holiness should be conspicuous : it is of saints that the text speaks.

Verse 8.—The restraining and subduing power of the gospel.

Verse 9.—The honour common to all saints.

PSALM CL.

We have now reached the last summit of the mountain chain of Psalms. It rises high into the clear azure, and its brow is bathed in the sunlight of the eternal world of worship. It is a rapture. The poet-prophet is full of inspiration and enthusiasm. He stays not to argue, to teach, to explain; but cries with burning words, " Praise him, Praise him, Praise ye the LORD."

EXPOSITION.

PRAISE ye the LORD. Praise God in his sanctuary : praise him in the firmament of his power.

2 Praise him for his mighty acts : praise him according to his excellent greatness.

3 Praise him with the sound of the trumpet ; praise him with the psaltery and harp.

4 Praise him with the timbrel and dance : praise him with stringed instruments and organs.

5 Praise him upon the loud cymbals : praise him upon the high sounding cymbals.

6 Let everything that hath breath praise the LORD. Praise ye the LORD.

1. *"Praise ye the LORD."* Hallelujah ! The exhortation is to all things in earth or in heaven. Should they not all declare the glory of him for whose glory they are, and were created ? Jehovah, the one God, should be the one object of adoration. To give the least particle of his honour to another is shameful treason ; to refuse to render it to him is heartless robbery. *"Praise God in his sanctuary."* Praise El, or the strong one, in his holy place. See how power is mentioned with holiness in this change of names. Praise begins at home. " In God's own house pronounce his praise." The holy place should be filled with praise, even as of old the high-priest filled the *sanctum sanctorum* with the smoke of sweet-smelling incense. In his church below and in his courts above hallelujahs should be continually presented. In the person of Jesus God finds a holy dwelling or sanctuary, and there he is greatly to be praised. He may also be said to dwell in holiness, for all his ways are right and good ; for this we ought to extol him with heart and with voice. Whenever we assemble for holy purposes our main work should be to present praises unto the Lord our God. *"Praise him in the firmament of his power."* It is a blessed thing that in our God holiness and power are united. Power without righteousness would be oppression, and righteousness without power would be too weak for usefulness ; but put the two together in an infinite degree and we have God. What an expanse we have in the boundless firmament of divine power ! Let it all be filled with praise. Let the heavens, so great and strong, echo with the praise of the thrice holy Jehovah, while the sanctuaries of earth magnify the Almighty One.

2. *"Praise him for his mighty acts."* Here is a reason for praise. In these deeds of power we see himself. These doings of his omnipotence are always on behalf of truth and righteousness. His works of creation, providence, and redemption, all call for praise ; they are his acts, and his acts of might, therefore let him be praised for them. *"Praise him according to his excellent greatness."* His being is unlimited, and his praise should correspond therewith. He possesses

a multitude or a plenitude of greatness, and therefore he should be greatly praised. There is nothing little about God, and there is nothing great apart from him. If we were always careful to make our worship fit and appropriate for our great Lord how much better should we sing ! How much more reverently should we adore ! Such excellent deeds should have excellent praise.

3. *"Praise him with the sound of the trumpet."* With the loudest, clearest note call the people together. Make all men to know that we are not ashamed to worship. Summon them with unmistakable sound to bow before their God. The sound of trumpet is associated with the grandest and most solemn events, such as the giving of the law, the proclamation of jubilee, the coronation of Jewish kings, and the raging of war. It is to be thought of in reference to the coming of our Lord in his second advent and the raising of the dead. If we cannot give voice to this martial instrument, at least let our praise be as decided and bold as if we could give a blast upon the horn. Let us never sound a trumpet before us to our own honour, but reserve all our trumpeting for God's glory. When the people have been gathered by blast of trumpet, then proceed to *"praise him with the psaltery and harp."* Stringed instruments are to be used as well as those which are rendered vocal by wind. Dulcet notes are to be consecrated as well as more startling sounds. The gospel meaning is that all powers and faculties should praise the Lord—all sorts of persons, under all circumstances, and with differing constitutions, should do honour unto the Lord of all. If there be any virtue, if there be any talent, if there be any influence, let all be consecrated to the service of the universal Benefactor. Harp and lyre—the choicest, the sweetest, must be all our Lord's.

4. *"Praise him with the timbrel and dance."* Associated with the deliverance at the Red Sea, this form of worship set forth the most jubilant and exultant of worship. The hands and the feet were both employed, and the entire body moved in sympathy with the members. Are there not periods of life when we feel so glad that we would fain dance for joy ? Let not such exhilaration be spent upon common themes, but let the name of God stir us to ecstasy. Let us exult as we cry,—

> "In the heavenly Lamb thrice happy I am,
> And my heart it doth dance at the sound of his name."

There is enough in our holy faith to create and to justify the utmost degree of rapturous delight. If men are dull in the worship of the Lord our God they are not acting consistently with the character of their religion. *"Praise him with stringed instruments and organs."* We have here the three kinds of musical instruments : timbrels, which are struck, and strings, and pipes : let all be educated to praise the Lord. Nothing is common and unclean : all may be sanctified to highest uses. Many men, many minds, and these as different as strings and pipes ; but there is only one God, and that one God all should worship. The word translated "organs" signifies pipe—a simpler form of wind instrument than the more modern and more elaborate organ. Doubtless many a pious shepherd has poured out gracious pastorals from a reed or oaten pipe, and so has magnified his God.

5. *"Praise him upon the loud cymbals: praise him upon the high sounding cymbals."* Let the clash of the loudest music be the Lord's : let the joyful clang of the loftiest notes be all for him. Praise has beaten the timbrel, swept the harp, and sounded the trumpet, and now for a last effort, awakening the most heavy of slumberers, and startling the most indifferent of onlookers, she dashes together the disks of brass, and with sounds both loud and high proclaims the glories of the Lord.

6. *"Let everything that hath breath praise the LORD."* "Let all breath praise him" : that is to say, all living beings. He gave them breath, let them breathe his praise. His name is in the Hebrew composed rather of breathings than of letters, to show that all breath comes from him : therefore let it be used for him. Join all ye living things in the eternal song. Be ye least or greatest, withhold not your praises. What a day will it be when all things in all places unite to

glorify the one only living and true God ! This will be the final triumph of the church of God.

"*Praise ye the* LORD." Once more, Hallelujah ! Thus is the psalm rounded with the note of praise ; and thus is the Book of Psalms ended by a glowing word of adoration. Reader, wilt not thou at this moment pause a while, and worship the Lord thy God ? Hallelujah !

EXPLANATORY NOTES.

Whole Psalm.—Each of the last five psalms begins and ends with *Hallelujah!*— "*Praise ye the Lord.*" And each Psalm increases in praise, love, and joy, unto the last, which is praise celebrating its ecstasy. The elect soul, the heir of God, becomes " eaten up" with the love of God. He begins every sentence with *Hallelujah;* and his sentences are very short, for he is in haste to utter his next *Hallelujah,* and his next, and his next. He is as one out of breath with enthusiasm, or as one on tiptoe, in the act of rising from earth to heaven. The greatest number of words between any two Hallelujahs is four, and that only once : in every other instance, between one Hallelujah and another there are but two words. It is as though the soul gave utterance to its whole life and feeling in the one word, *Hallelujah!* The words, " Praise ye the Lord !" or " Praise him !" " Praise him !" " Praise him !" are reiterated no fewer than twelve times in a short psalm of six short verses.—*John Pulsford, in "Quiet Hours,"* 1857.

Whole Psalm.—And now, in the last psalm of all, we see an echo to the first psalm. The first psalm began with " Blessed," and it ended with " Blessed,"— " Blessed are all they that meditate on God's law and do it." Such was the theme of the first psalm ; and now the fruit of that blessedness is shown in this psalm, which begins and ends with Hallelujah.—*Christopher Wordsworth.*

Whole Psalm.—In his *Cours de Littérature,* the celebrated Lamartine, probably regarding the last four psalms (the Hallelujah psalms) as one whole (as Hengstenberg also does) thus speaks :—" The last psalm ends with a chorus to the praise of God, in which the poet calls on all people, all instruments of sacred music, all the elements, and all the stars to join. Sublime finale of that opera of sixty years sung by the shepherd, the hero, the king, and the old man ! In this closing psalm we see the almost inarticulate enthusiasm of the lyric poet ; so rapidly do the words press to his lips, floating upwards towards God, their source, like the smoke of a great fire of the soul waited by the tempest ! Here we see David, or rather the human heart itself with all its God-given notes of grief, joy, tears, and adoration—poetry sanctified to its highest expression ; a vase of perfume broken on the step of the temple, and shedding abroad its odours from the heart of David to the heart of all humanity ! Hebrew, Christian, or even Mohammedan, every religion, every complaint, every prayer has taken from this vase, shed on the heights of Jerusalem, wherewith to give forth their accents. The little shepherd has become the master of the sacred choir of the Universe. There is not a worship on earth which prays not with his words, or sings not with his voice. A chord of his harp is to be found in all choirs, resounding everywhere and for ever in unison with the echoes of Horeb and Engedi ! David is the Psalmist of eternity ; what a destiny—what a power hath poetry when inspired by God ! As for myself, when my spirit is excited, or devotional, or sad, and seeks for an echo to its enthusiasm, its devotion, or its melancholy, I do not open Pindar or Horace, or Hafiz, those purely Academic poets : neither do I find within myself murmurings to express my emotion. I open the Book of Psalms, and there I find words which seem to issue from the soul of the ages, and which penetrate even to the heart of all generations. Happy the bard who has thus become the eternal hymn, the personified prayer and complaint of all humanity ! If we look back to that remote age when such songs resounded over the world ; if we consider that while the lyric poetry of all the most cultivated nations only sang of wine, love, blood, and the victories of coursers at the games of Elidus, we are seized with profound astonishment at the mystic accents of the shepherd prophet, who speaks to God the Creator as one friend to another, who understands and praises his great works, admires his justice, implores his mercy, and becomes, as it were, an anticipative echo of the evangelic poetry, speaking the soft words of Christ before his coming. Prophet or not, as he may be considered by Christian or sceptic, none can deny in the poet-kin an inspiration granted to no other man. Read Greek or Latin poetry after a psalm, and see how pale it looks."—*William Swan Plumer.*

Whole Psalm.—The first and last of the psalms have both the same number of verses, are both short and very memorable ; but the scope of them is very different ; the first psalm is an elaborate instruction in our duty, to prepare us for the comforts of our devotion ; this is all rapture and transport, and perhaps was penned on purpose to be the conclusion of those sacred songs, to show what is the design of them all, and that is, to assist us in praising God.—*Matthew Henry.*

Whole Psalm.—Thirteen hallelujahs, according to the number of the tribes (Levi, Ephraim and Manasseh making three), one for each.—*John Henry Michaëlis,* 1668—1738.

Whole Psalm.—Some say this psalm was sung by the Israelites, when they came with the first fruits into the sanctuary with the baskets on their shoulders. *Thirteen* times in this short psalm is the word *praise* used ; not on account of thirteen perfections or properties in God, as Kimchi thinks ; but it is so frequently, and in every clause used, to show the vehement desire of the Psalmist that the Lord might be praised ; and to express his sense of things, how worthy he is of praise ; and that all ways and means to praise him should be made use of, all being little enough to set forth his honour and glory.—*John Gill.*

Whole Psalm.—There is an interesting association connected with this psalm which deserves to be recorded : that in former times, when the casting of church bells was more of a religious ceremony, this psalm was chanted by the brethren of the guild as they stood ranged around the furnace, and while the molten metal was prepared to be let off into the mould ready to receive it. One may picture these swarthy sons of the furnace with the ruddy glow of the fire upon their faces as they stand around, while their deep voices rung forth this Hymn of Praise. —*Barton Bouchier.*

Verse 1.—*"Praise ye the Lord."* Praise God with a strong faith ; praise him with holy love and delight ; praise him with an entire confidence in Christ ; praise him with a believing triumph over the powers of darkness ; praise him with an earnest desire towards him, and a full satisfaction in him ; praise him by a universal respect to all his commands ; praise him by a cheerful submission to all his disposals ; praise him by rejoicing in his love, and solacing yourselves in his great goodness ; praise him by promoting the interests of the kingdom of his grace ; praise him by a lively hope and expectation of the kingdom of his glory. —*Matthew Henry.*

Verse 1.—*"In his sanctuary."* בְּקָדְשׁוֹ. Many have been the notions of the commentators as to the shade of meaning here ; for the word differs from the form in Ps. xx. 2. מִקֹּדֶשׁ (*from the sanctuary*). The Vulgate adopts the plural rendering, *in sanctis ejus,* "in his holy places." Campensis renders it, *ob insignem sanctitatem ipsius,* "because of his excellent holiness." Some see under the word an allusion to the holy tabernacle of Deity, the flesh of Christ. Luther, in 'his German version, translates thus : *in seinem Heiligthum,* "in his holiness." The same harmony of comparative thought appears in the two clauses of this verse as in such passages as 1 Kings viii. 13, 49 ; Is. lvii. 15. The place of worship where God specially hears prayer and accepts praise, and the firmament where angels fly at his command, and veil their faces in adoration, are each a sanctuary. The sanctuary is manifestly here looked at as the temple of grace, the firmament as the temple of power. So the verse proclaims both grace and glory.—*Martin Geier.*

Verse 1.—"*Praise God in his sanctuary.*" The Septuagint, Vulgate Latin, and the eastern versions, render it, "*in his holy ones*"; among his saints, in the assembly of them, where he is to be feared and praised: it may be translated, "*in his Holy One,*" and be understood of Christ, as it is by Cocceius. . . . Some render it, "*for*" or "*because of his holiness.*" The perfection of holiness in him; in which he is glorious and fearful in the praises of, and which appears in all his works of providence and grace.—*John Gill.*

Verse 1.—"*Praise God.*" In many places we have the compound word, חללו־יה, *halelujah*, praise ye Jehovah; but this is the first place in which we find הללו־אל, *halelu-el*, praise God, or the strong God. Praise him who is Jehovah, the infinite and self-existent Being; and praise him who is God, *El*, or *Elohim*, the great God in covenant with mankind, to bless and save them unto eternal life.—*Adam Clarke.*

Verse 1.—Psalm cl. gives the full praise to Jehovah in a double character, *the sanctuary and the firmament of his power*, for his ways which come from the firmament of his power were always according to the sanctuary in which he governed Israel, and made good the revelation of himself there.—*John Nelson Darby*, 1800—1882.

Verse 2.—"*Praise him for his mighty acts*," etc. The reasons of that praise which it becomes all intelligent creatures, and especially redeemed men, to render to Jehovah, are here assigned. We are to praise Jehovah "in his sanctuary," in the place where his glory dwells, where his holiness shines forth with ineffable splendour; we are to praise him in the wide expanse over which he has spread the tokens of his power, whether in the heaven above, or in the earth beneath; we are to praise him for those omnipotent acts whereby he hath shown himself to be above all gods; we are to praise him in a manner suited to the excellent majesty of a Being whom all the heavens adore, and who is wonderful in counsel and excellent in working. His holiness, the infinity of his operations, the miraculous power which he has displayed, the unspotted excellence of his administration, call for loudest songs of praise from all whose reason enables them to rise to the contemplation of the great Supreme.—*John Morison.*

Verse 2.—"*Praise him according to his excellent greatness.*" There is required special understanding and knowledge of the nature and worth of the mercy for which the duty of praise is undertaken; for God will not be praised confusedly, but distinctly and proportionably to his dispensation: "*Praise him according to his wondrous works*"; which is to be the prime and proper matter of their high praises, even his more proper and peculiar high acts, then to be remembered, as is largely expressed in Moses' praise for the particular mercy of coming safe through the Red Sea (Exod. xv.); and Deborah's high praise for deliverance from the host of Sisera (Judges v.); where the chiefest and highest part of the celebration and exaltation of God in his praise consists in the declaration and commemoration of the particulars of God's special goodness in their present deliverance. Thus, you see, the first thing that God looks for is proportionable praise, great praise for a great God, doing great things, and high praises for a high God, doing high things.—*Samuel Fairclough.*

Verse 2.—"*Praise him according to his excellent greatness,*" or, as the words may bear, "according to his *muchness of greatness*"; for when the Scripture saith, "God is great," this positive is to be taken as a superlative. "God is great," that is, he is greatest, he is greater than all; so great that all persons and all things are little, yea, nothing before him. Isaiah xl. 15: "Behold, the nations are (to him but) as a drop of a bucket, and are counted as the small dust of the balance: behold, he taketh up the isles as a very little thing. And Lebanon is not sufficient to burn, nor the beasts thereof sufficient for a burnt offering. All nations before him are as nothing; and they are counted to him less than nothing, and vanity." How great is God, in comparison of whom the greatest things are little things, yea, the greatest things are nothing!—*Joseph Caryl.*

Verse 3.— *Trumpets* and *horns* are the only instruments concerning which any directions are given in the law.—*James Anderson.*

Verse 3.—"*Trumpet.*" Of natural horns and of instruments in the shape of horns the antiquity and general use are evinced by every extensive collection of antiquities. . . . The Hebrew word *shophar*, rendered " trumpet," seems, first to denote horns of the straighter kind, including, probably, those of neat-cattle, and all the instruments which were eventually made in imitation of and in improvement upon such horns. The name *shophar* means *bright* or *clear*, and the instrument may be conceived to have been so called from its clear and shrill sound, just as we call an instrument a " clarion," and speak of a musical tone as " brilliant" or " clear." In the service of God this *shophar*, or *trumpet*, was only employed in making announcements, and for calling the people together in the time of the holy solemnities, of war, of rebellion, or of any other great occasion. The strong sound of the instrument would have confounded a choir of singers, rather than have elevated their music. (*John Kitto.*) The *shophar* is especially interesting to us as being the only Hebrew instrument whose use on certain solemn occasions seems to be retained to this day. Engel, with his usual trustworthy research, has traced out and examined some of those in modern synagogues. Of those shown in our engraving, one is from the synagogue of Spanish and Portuguese Jews, Bevis Marks, and is, he says, one foot in length ; the other is one used in the Great Synagogue, St. James's-place, Aldgate, twenty-one inches in length. Both are made of horn.—*James Stainer.*

Verse 3.—The "*psaltery*" was a ten-stringed instrument. It is constantly mentioned with the "*harp.*" The *psaltery* was struck with a plectrum, the *harp* more gently with the fingers. "*Psaltery and harp*" speak to us in figure of " law and gospel."—*Thomas Le Blanc.*

Verse 3.—On "*psaltery*" (*nebel*) see Note on Ps. cxliv. 9, and on "*harp*" see Note on Ps. cxlix. 3.

Verses 3, 4, 5.—As St. Augustine says here, " No kind of faculty is here omitted. All are enlisted in praising God." The breath is employed in blowing the trumpet ; the fingers are used in striking the strings of the psaltery and the harp ; the whole hand is exerted in beating the timbrel ; the feet move in the dance ; there are stringed instruments (literally *strings*) ; there is the organ (the '*ugab*, *syrinx*) composed of many pipes, implying *combination*, and the cymbals clang upon one another.— *C. Wordsworth.*

Verses 3, 4, 5.—The variety of musical instruments, some of them made use of in the camp, as trumpets ; some of them more suitable to a peaceable condition, as psalteries and harps ; some of them sounding by blowing wind in them ; some of them sounding by lighter touching of them, as stringed instruments ; some of them by beating on them more sharply, as tabrets, drums and cymbals : some of them sounding by touching and blowing also, as organs : all of them giving some certain sound, some more quiet, and some making more noise : some of them having a harmony by themselves ; some of them making a concert with other instruments, or with the motions of the body in dancings, some of them serving for one use, some of them serving for another, and all of them serving to set forth God's glory, and to shadow forth the duty of worshippers, and the privileges of the saints. The plurality and variety (I say) of these instruments were fit to represent divers conditions of the spiritual man, and of the greatness of his joy to be found in God, and to teach what stirring up should be of the affections and powers of our soul, and of one another, unto God's worship ; what harmony should be among the worshippers of God, what melody each should make in himself, singing to God with grace in his heart, and to show the excellency of God's praise, which no means nor instrument, nor any expression of the body joined thereunto, could sufficiently set forth in these exhortations to praise God with trumpet, psaltery, &c.—*David Dickson.*

Verses 3, 4, 5.—Patrick has an interesting note on the many instruments of music in Psalm cxlix., which we quote here : " The ancient inhabitants of Etruria used the trumpet ; the Arcadians, the whistle ; the Sicilians, the pectid ; the Cretians, the harp ; the Thracians, the cornet ; the Lacedemonians, the pipe ; the Egyptians, the drum ; the Arabians, the cymbal. (Clem. Pædag. ii. 4.) May we not say that in this Psalm's enumeration of musical instruments, there is a reference to the variety which exists among men in the mode of expressing joy, and exciting to feeling ?—*Andrew A. Bonar.*

Verse 4.—"*Stringed instruments.*" *Minnim* [which is derived from a root signifying " division," or " distribution," hence *strings*] occurs in Ps. xlv. 8, and cl. 4, and is supposed by some to denote a stringed instrument, but it seems merely a poetical allusion to the *strings* of any instrument. Thus, in Ps. xlv. 8, we would read, " Out of the ivory palaces *the strings* (*i.e.* concerts of music) have made thee glad " ; and so in Ps. cl. 4, " Praise him with *strings* (stringed instruments), and *'ugabs.*"—*John Kitto.*

Verse 4.—"*Organs.*" עֻגָּב, '*ugab* is the word rendered " *organ*" in our version. The Targum renders the word simply by אבובא, *a pipe ;* the Septuagint varies, it has κιθάρα in Genesis, ψάλμος in Job, and ὄργανον in the Psalms. The last is the sense which the Arabic, Syriac, Latin, English, and most other versions have adopted. The *organon* simply denotes a double or manifold pipe ; and hence, in particular, the Pandæan or shepherd's pipe, which is at this day called a " mouth organ," among ourselves. (*Kitto.*) A collection of tubes of different sizes, stopped at one end and blown at the other, forms the musical instrument known as Pan's pipes, in the Greek *syrinx,* σύρυγξ .... Was the '*ugab* a *syrinx* or an organ ? As the former seems to have been the more ancient of the two, and as '*ugab* is included in the very first allusion to musical instruments in the Bible, it wo'ld seem reasonable to say at once that it was a *syrinx,* especially as this instrument was, and is to this day, commonly met with in various parts of Asia. Yet it would, indeed, be strange if such an instrument were selected for use in divine worship ; and that the '*ugab* was so used is proved beyond a doubt by its mention in Ps. cl. : " Praise him with the *minnim* and '*ugab.* Its mention here in antithesis to a collective name for stringed instruments, surely points to the fact of its being a more important instrument than a few river-reeds fixed together with wax. Let us not forget that we have but one and the same name for the single row of about fifty pipes, placed, perhaps, in a little room, and the mighty instrument of five thousand pipes, occupying as much space as an ordinary dwelling-house. . . . Each is an organ. May it not have been the case that the '*ugab,* which in Gen. iv. 21 is mentioned as the simply-constructed *wind*-instrument, in contrast to the simple *stringed*-instrument, the *kinnor,* was a greatly inferior instrument to that which in Ps. cl. is thought worthy of mention by the side of a term for the whole string power ?—*J. Stainer.*

Verse 5.—" *Loud cymbals .... high-sounding cymbals.*" This important passage clearly points to two instruments under the same name, and leaves us to conclude that the Hebrews had both hand-cymbals and finger-cymbals (or castanets), although it may not in all cases be easy to say which of the two is intended in particular texts.—*John Kitto.*

Verse 5 (Prayer Book Version).—" *Praise him upon the well-tuned cymbals : praise him upon the loud cymbals.*" As I have heard these words read monthly in our churches, it has often come into my thoughts that when we intend to glorify God with our cymbals, it should not be our only care to have them loud enough, but our first care should be to have them well tuned, else the louder the worse. Zeal does very well—there is great, yea, necessary use for it in every part of God's service. The cymbal will be flat, it will have no life or spirit in it, it will not be loud enough without it. But if meekness, peaceableness, and moderation do not first put the cymbal into good tune, the loudness will but make it the more ungrateful in the player, the more ungrateful to the hearer.—*Robert Sanderson,* 1587 —1662.

Verse 6.—" Praise ye the Lord." As the life of the faithful, and the history of
the church, so also the Psalter, with all its cries from the depths, runs out into a
Hallelujah.—*E. W. Hengstenberg.*

Verse 6.—" Praise ye the Lord." When we have said all we are able to say for
God's praise, we are but to begin anew ; for this are we taught by the renewing
of the exhortation, in the close of sundry psalms, and here also at the end of all
the psalms : *" Praise ye the* Lord.*"—David Dickson.*

Verse 6.—" Let all breath praise Jah ! Hallelujah." The very ambiguity of
" all breath " gives extraordinary richness of meaning to this closing sentence.
From the simple idea of wind instruments, mentioned in the context, it leads us,
by a beautiful transition, to that of vocal, articulate, intelligent praise, uttered by
the breath of living men, as distinguished from mere lifeless instruments. Then,
lastly, by a natural association, we ascend to the idea expressed in the common
version, *" everything that hath breath,"* not merely all that lives, but all that has
a voice to praise God. There is nothing in the Psalter more majestic or more
beautiful than this brief but most significant *finale,* in which solemnity of tone
predominates, without however in the least disturbing the exhilaration which the
close of the Psalter seems intended to produce, as if in emblematical allusion to
the triumph which awaits the church and all its members, when through much
tribulation they shall enter into rest.—*Joseph Addison Alexander.*

HINTS TO THE VILLAGE PREACHER.

Verse 1.—" Praise God in his sanctuary." I. In his personal holiness. II. In
the person of his Son. III. In heaven. IV. In the assembly of saints. V. In
the silence of the heart.

*Verses 1—6.—*God should be praised. Where ? (*verse 1*). Wherefore ? (*verse 2*).
Wherewith ? (*verses 3—5*). By whom ? (*verse 6*).—*C. A. D.*

Verse 2.—" His excellent greatness." Wherein the greatness of God is specially
excellent, and where it is best seen.

Verse 2.—" Praise him for his mighty acts." I. For us. Election. Redemption. Inspiration. II. In us. The work of enlightenment in the understanding ; purification in the heart ; quickening in the conscience ; subjugation in the
will. III. By us. Thought through us ; felt through us ; spoke through us ;
worked through us. To him be all the glory !—*W. J.*

Verse 2.—" Praise him according to his excellent greatness." I. Reverently, according to the greatness of his being. II. Gratefully, according to the greatness of
his love. III. Retrospectively, according to the greatness of his gifts. IV. Pro-
spectively, according to the greatness of his promises.—*W. J.*

*Verse 2.—*What the exhortation requires. I. That men should study God's
works, and observe the glory of God in them. II. That they should meditate on
his greatness till they realize its excellence. III. That they should openly proclaim the honor due to him. IV. That they should not contradict in their life
the praise they speak.—*J. F.*

Verse 3.—" Praise him with the sound of the trumpet." I. When you fight.
II. When you conquer. III. When you assemble. IV. When you proclaim his
Word. V. When you welcome Jubilee.

*Verses 3—6.—*I. The variety of the ancient service of worship necessitating
serious expenditure ; consecration of high talent ; hard and constant toil. II.
The lessons of such service. 1. God should be worshipped royally. 2. The
efforts of the best genius are his rightful tribute. 3. All human ability cannot

place a worthy offering at his feet. III. The soul and essential of true worship. IV. God's requirements as to worship in these present times.— *W. B. H.*

Verse 6.—I. The august Giver of " life, and breath, and all things." II. The due and true use of the gifts of life. III. The resultant swathing of earth in consecrated atmosphere, and millennial hallelujahs.— *W. B. H.*

Verse 6.—A fitting close to the psalter, considered as a desire, a prayer, or an exhortation. I. As a desire, it realizes the glory due to God, the worship ennobling to man, the disposition of heart which would make all the world into a holy brotherhood. II. As a prayer, it seeks the downfall of every superstition, the universal spread of the truth, the conversion of every soul. III. As an exhortation, it is plain, pertinent, pure in its piety, perfect in its charity.—*J. F.*

HALLELUJAH!

INDEX.

Chiefly for Pastoral Use and Aid.

A.

Aaron, Anointing of, from God thro' Moses, vii. 129 ; house of, 160.

Abraham, in what sense a prophet, v. 70.

Absolution, Plenary, iv. 475.

Abstinence, Total, from evil desires, practices, etc., vii. 291.

Access to God desired, boldly accepted, v. 351.

Activity of evil and evil-doers, iii. 89.

Advent of the Lord, Longings for. i. 196; prayer for the second, iii. 255 ; accompaniments of, iv. 368.

Afflicted souls, A sermon for, i. 73 : consolation for, 467 ; comfort for, iii. 430; may pray, iv. 443 ; should and can pray, 443 ; sure of God's help, vii. 274.

Afflictions, Blessings of, ii. 154 ; sent by God, 260 ; removed by God, 260 ; design of, iii. 203 ; of God's people, iv. 152 ; mysterious, tho' just, 153 ; long continued, 153 ; God's hand to be recognized in, 196 ; trials of faith,'v. 112 ; chastisements severe but limited, 351 ; believer in times of, vi. 156 ; come to saints from wicked men, vii. 64 ; reason for, comfort under, 64.

Aged observer, ii. 219.

Alphabetical or acrostic Psalms, Ps. xxv., i. 44 ; Ps. xxxiv., ii. 135 ; Ps. cxi., v. 208 ; Ps. cxii., v. 224 ; Ps. cxix., vii. 1, 2 ; Ps. cxlv., vii. 351.

Amen, and Amen, iv. 170, 196 ; v. 112.

Ancestors, How we may partake of sins of, v. 110.

"Angel of the Lord," ii. 153.

Angels, Ministry of, ii. 153 ; iii. 60 ; iv. 26 ; v. 38 ; nature of, v. 38 ; the Lord of, 38 ; angel by the throne, vii. 84.

Anger, Divine, when hope of the righteous, i. 87 ; cease from, etc., ii. 218 ; of God, iii. 410 ; force of when kindled, iv. 335.

Anointing, priestly, Fragrance of, vii. 128, 129.

Answer to prayer, iv. 98 ; answer of peace, 98.

Antiphon, the " I will " and " men shall," vii. 376.

Apostolic succession, The true, iv. 445.

Appeal to God, iii. 314 ; to divine goodness, iv. 196 ; and wisdom, 196.

" Appointed to die," deep, spiritual distress, iv. 12.

Arrows of God, what they are, whom they strike, etc., ii. 377 ; why children called arrows, vii. 40, 41.

Asaph, Twelve of the Psalms attributed to, iii. 338.

Ascension of Christ, Teachings of the, i. 439 ; ii. 401 ; iii. 256.

Assurance, Enjoyed, i. 466 ; full, in the Lord, ii. 173 ; language of, vii. 273.

Astonishment, Wine of, iii. 103.

Atheism, Folly of, i. 196 ; iii. 8 ; source, creed, fruits, i. 196 ; seal of in the heart, iii. 8 ; prosperity helps to create, 35 ; open question of the atheist, 365 ; practical atheists, iv. 315.

Awake. *See* Waking.

Awe, the soul of worship, ii. 134 ; holy, caused by what, v. 262.

Awe-struck talk, bold avowal, etc., vii. 377.

B.

Babylon, Weeping by the waters of, vii. 201.

Baca, Valley of, application of, iv. 81, 82.

Bad company, Evil results of, i. 483 ; words. ii. 187 ; lodgings, vi. 413.

Bane and antidote, ii. 154.

Banner of the Gospel, To fight under, iii. 103.

Believer, Joys of, i. 48 ; how to win the ungodly, 48 ; vesper song for, 48 ; greatest dread of, 73 ; trust in God, 87 ; snares in the way of, 144 ; seeking for the true gold, 240 ; goodly heritage of, 241 ; live because the Lord lives, 241 ; heart of proved, 264 ; goings of in God's paths, 264 ; exploits of, recoun - ed, 302 ; calling of as to God's works, 481 ; challenge of, ii. 21 ; position, support, etc., 21 ; trouble transient, joy permanent, 61 ; raiment of, 61 ; requiem of, 87 ; gladness of, 113 ; real safety in perils, 154 ; portrayed, 217 ; delight and desire of, 218 ; character, position, etc.,